Engineering Reliable Service Oriented Architecture:

Managing Complexity and Service Level Agreements

Nikola Milanovic
Model Labs - Berlin, Germany

Senior Editorial Director:	Kristin Klinger
Director of Book Publications:	Julia Mosemann
Editorial Director:	Lindsay Johnston
Acquisitions Editor:	Erika Carter
Development Editor:	Joel Gamon
Production Coordinator:	Jamie Snavely
Typesetters:	Keith Glazewski & Natalie Pronio
Cover Design:	Nick Newcomer

Published in the United States of America by
Information Science Reference (an imprint of IGI Global)
701 E. Chocolate Avenue
Hershey PA 17033
Tel: 717-533-8845
Fax: 717-533-8661
E-mail: cust@igi-global.com
Web site: http://www.igi-global.com

Library of Congress Cataloging-in-Publication Data

Engineering reliable service oriented architecture : managing complexity and service level agreements / Nikola Milanovic, editor.
p. cm.
Includes bibliographical references and index.
Summary: "This book presents a guide to engineering reliable SOA systems and enhances current understanding of service reliability"--Provided by publisher.
ISBN 978-1-60960-493-6 (hardcover) -- ISBN 9781609604943(ebook) 1. Service-oriented architecture (Computer science) 2. Computer networks--Reliability. I. Milanovic, Nikola.
TK5105.5828.E54 2011
004.6--dc22
2010033596

British Cataloguing in Publication Data
A Cataloguing in Publication record for this book is available from the British Library.

All work contributed to this book is new, previously-unpublished material. The views expressed in this book are those of the authors, but not necessarily of the publisher.

Table of Contents

Foreword xiii

Preface xv

Section 1
Service Level Agreements

Chapter 1
Design of Quality Aspects in Service Oriented Architecture through Service Level Agreements: The Streaming Case Study 1
Marco Massarelli, Universitá degli Studi di Milano-Bicocca, Italy
Claudia Raibulet, Universitá degli Studi di Milano-Bicocca, Italy
Daniele Cammareri, Universitá degli Studi di Milano-Bicocca, Italy
Nicolò Perino, University of Lugano, Switzerland

Chapter 2
Flexible and Dynamic SLAs Management in Service Oriented Architectures 22
Giuseppe Di Modica, Università di Catania, Italy
Orazio Tomarchio, Università di Catania, Italy

Chapter 3
Quality of Service Monitoring, Diagnosis, and Adaptation for Service Level Management 41
Guijun Wang, Boeing Research & Technology, USA
Changzhou Wang, Boeing Research & Technology, USA
Haiqin Wang, Boeing Research & Technology, USA
Rodolfo A. Santiago, Boeing Research & Technology, USA
Jingwen Jin, Boeing Research & Technology, USA
David Shaw, Boeing Research & Technology, USA

Chapter 4
Supporting Service Level Agreement with Service Discovery 59
Andrea Zisman, City University, UK

Section 2
Service Composition

Section 3
Reliability and Fault Tolerance

Detailed Table of Contents

Section 1
Service Level Agreements

Proper specification of service level agreement (SLA) is the main pre-condition for successful implementation of non-functional properties, such as availability. In this section, several approaches and case studies for treating SLA are presented.

Massarelli et al. discuss the value of Service Level Agreements (SLA) used as contract on both the provider and requester side. They argue that, although helpful, SLAs do not necessarily guarantee smooth interaction in an SOA environment, as unexpected runtime errors may corrupt service execution. They thus propose adaptive method for SLA runtime management that can monitor and perform changes during service execution phase. They validate this approach using a case study from the multimedia application domain.

Di Modica and Tomarchio report that, although Service Level Agreements (SLAs) are the most common mechanism used to establish agreements on the quality of service, they have not been taken up by business stakeholders yet due to the low flexibility and usability, together with the lack of interoperability. Therefore, SLA frameworks must improve support for SLA modeling, representation, publication, discovery, negotiation, monitoring, and enforcement. The authors then propose an SLA management framework addressing these issues.

Wang et al. present a service level management framework offering two benefits: incorporating monitoring and diagnosis services as an integral part of the QoS management. Using the data obtained from the monitoring service, diagnosis service detects system condition changes and reasons for the causes of QoS level degradation. The framework can then proactively adapt to optimize QoS provisioning. Thus, real-time automated resource optimization is used to satisfy client requirements.

Zisman argues that creation, maintenance, and evolution of Service Level Agreements (SLAs) represent the main challenges in order to establish an effective evaluation and enforcement of quality of services and their providers. The author then presents an approach for SLA creation that is based on an iterative service discovery process. Services that can provide the functionalities and satisfy properties and constraints of service-based systems during their design phase are identified and used to (re-) formulate service level agreements between services participating in the system, as well as the design models of these systems. Service requests, describing structural, behavioral, and quality properties are matched against service specifications. Thus, service level agreement between two entities is automatically generated.

Hofer et al. present the work on configurability of non-functional properties in embedded systems. The authors propose a framework for making non-functional properties such as reliability, performance, or memory usage indirectly configurable and maintainable. They introduce configurable architectural properties which have no functional influence on the target system, but impact its non-functional properties. Additionally, a feedback is proposed that gains information about non-functional properties of an already configured system and assists in further configuration tasks.

Giallonardo and Zimeo identify quality of service and semantics as the key pre-conditions to fulfill the real promise of autonomous and dynamic business to business interactions. The authors explore the role that ontologies have on specifying service requirements, discovery, and composition. They propose onQoS ontology and onQoS-QL query language.

Section 2
Service Composition

Service composition is the most straightforward method of managing complexity in SOA. However, service composition with respect to non-functional properties presents a new set of problems and challenges, some of which are treated in this section.

Harney and Doshi explore Web Service composition in volatile environments, where parameters and properties of component services may change during execution. The authors propose a hierarchical Web Service composition mechanism as a solution. They show how hierarchical compositions may be specified and how adaptation to changes in the environment is performed. Experimental data confirm the efficiency of this approach to complex hierarchical composition problem.

Blanco, Cardinale, and Vidal discuss the problem of identifying a service composition that best meets functional and non-functional user requirements. The complexity of this problem depends on the number of available services; thus, the definition of techniques that efficiently identify optimal service compositions is a challenging problem, particularly in large-scale environments. The authors propose a hybrid cost-based approach that receives and considers at the same time, a functional user request expressed by a pair of input and output attribute sets, and a non-functional condition represented by a set of QoS parameter permissible values.

Cheikh proposes a service composition model considering available services that have access control constraints. The constraints are defined using conditional communicating automata, where communication is performed via bounded ports. As the scalability of service composition frameworks is one of the most limiting factors, the author investigates complexity in detail.

Liu and Georgalas develop a novel approach for specifying non-functional properties of telecom operation support systems applications in the NGOSS framework. They introduce two categories of non-functional specification techniques: qualitative and quantitative. In addition, the authors explore a method for specification of trade-offs between non-functional requirements.

Ezenwoye and Sadjadi argue that there is a rising need to deliver reliable service compositions with precise Quality of Service attributes covering functional correctness, performance, and dependability, especially since the current BPEL standard provides limited constructs for specifying exceptional behavior and recovery actions. The authors propose a language-based approach for transparently adapting BPEL processes in order to improve reliability. This approach addresses reliability at the business process layer using a code generator, which weaves fault-tolerant code to the original code and an external proxy. Furthermore, software design patters for fault-tolerant adaptive service composition are presented.

Section 3
Reliability and Fault Tolerance

In the world where on-demand and trustworthy service delivery is one of the main preconditions for successful business, service and business process availability is of the paramount importance and cannot be compromised. For that reason, service availability is coming into central focus of the IT operations and management research and practice. This section presents approaches for estimating service reliability and designing fault-tolerant SOA systems.

Taweel and Tyson investigate predictability of non-functional properties such as capability, reliability, compatibility, performance, et cetera in complex service compositions. The authors explore various approaches to predicting quality attributes before actual composition can take place and propose a novel way to predicting reliability of service-based systems from its individual services.

Milanovic and Milic present a framework for modeling business process and service availability. The approach takes into account services, the underlying ICT-infrastructure, and people. Based on a fault model and the infrastructure graph, availability models are automatically generated and solved. It is thus possible to calculate steady-state, interval, and user perceived availability at all levels, from atomic services to complex business processes.

Sadi, Myers, and Sanchez investigate the failure analysis of SOA systems. They propose the metric for scanning a system model and flagging those components that are more likely to fail. Based on this analysis, design changes are suggested which should improve availability and eliminate risks.

Chapter 15
Design and Deployment of Service Oriented Applications with Non-Functional Requirements 315
László Gönczy, Budapest University of Technology and Economics, Hungary
Dániel Varró, Budapest University of Technology and Economics, Hungary

Gönczy and Varró propose a model-driven approach to efficiently design and deploy standards-compliant service configurations with non-functional parameters (with special focus on reliable messaging). They describe how to develop a structural diagram for service configuration with constraints, how to automatically generate service descriptors based on these models, and how to deploy such services. The process is supported by a toolchain.

Chapter 16
Dependability Assessment of Service-Oriented Architectures Using Fault Injection 340
Nik Looker, Durham University, UK
Malcolm Munro, Durham University, UK

Looker and Munro argue that dependability assessment is an important aspect of any software system which shows the degree of trust and quality of service that is delivered by a system. They discuss service dependability and present different techniques that may be used in dependability assessment of SOA systems. A number of cases studies are used to show the practicality of the techniques used.

Compilation of References 360

About the Contributors 389

Index 397

Foreword

In the world where systems complexity is permanently increasing and cost of maintenance plays a main role in the total cost of ownership, the quote by Leonardo da Vinci, "Simplicity is the ultimate sophistication," gains new significance. Especially, one way to introduce simplicity is to use the abstraction of services that is the major focus of this book. Nikola Milanovic and his colleagues introduce in this volume methodologies to engineer reliable Service Oriented Architectures (SOAs) which lead to managing complexity by treating applications as services, and devising Service Level Agreements which, in principle, simplify life of both system providers and customers. It goes without saying that the progress to service science and service engineering will simplify system design and implementation, and will deliver higher availability and performance, as well as cost transparency.

The world is moving towards the open system science, where, in addition to classical synthesis and analysis, the dimension of management has to be considered. And so it is with services where management plays a critical role. Managing resources, optimizing performance and dependability, as well as minimizing cost, are and will be ongoing challenges for SOA. This is due to open-ended systems, multiple degrees of freedom, growing complexity, frequent configurations and reconfigurations, upgrades, updates, cyber attacks, and new requirements, especially regarding the real time.

This volume addresses many of these problems and concerns by offering an entire spectrum of solutions ranging from managing via Service Level Agreements and Service Level Management contracts on the expectations side to real implementations and fault injection for estimating resilience from the engineering perspective. We also can gain an insight into both analysis and synthesis for the all important problem of service composition. Service compositions, if successful, will dramatically change the spectrum of service offering, but to get to this point we need to solve a number of problems, such as: feasibility of compositions, Quality of Service of composed services, overhead of a composition process, automation of composition, and cost of composed service. Many of them are addressed in this volume. Finally, the question of service availability and fault tolerance gains significance in the service environment where proliferation of computer applications to all walks of life and growing expectations by users with regard to reliance will force service providers to search for dependable, fault-tolerant SOAs. Several contributions in this volume offer interesting approaches to these challenges.

The trend in this decade is "zero-mania" by focusing on minimization of cost, power consumption, downtime, time-to-market, et cetera. This trend is relevant to the SOA community as the services are expected to be provided for a low cost, with minimal downtime and have to be developed quickly to meet ever more diversified market needs. The result is that the time for modelling, measurements, and assessment is limited, and once some hypotheses are verified in part, they frequently become obsolete due to new technologies, environments, and applications. Not surprisingly, the computer science community can boast a relatively small number of useful "laws" and principles, not only due to complexity and system dynamics, but also due to immense diversity of applications. The SOA approach has a real chance to change all this, and might be able to find rules for quantifying services by attaching to them aforementioned attributes. This, in turn, may lead to a development of some "laws" for trading the performance, cost, and Quality of Service quantifiable attributes such as service availability. One should not forget the qualitative attributes as they do play an important role, not only in our daily lives, but in the SOA world as well ("beauty is in the eyes of the beholder").

This volume is a significant contribution to pave the way for such "laws" where both formal and empirical methods are necessary to create a world with a plethora of services which are well understood by developers, providers, and customers and deliver highly-available, secure, trusted services in environments ranging from cyber-physical systems to cloud computing.

Miroslaw Malek
Humboldt University Berlin, Germany
September 1, 2010

***Miroslaw Malek** is professor and holder of Chair in Computer Architecture and Communication at the Department of Computer Science at Humboldt University in Berlin. His research interests focus on dependable, embedded and distributed systems including failure prediction, dependable architectures and service availability. He authored and co-authored over 200 publications including six books, has supervised 25 Ph.D. dissertations (ten of his students are professors) and founded, organized and co-organized numerous workshops and conferences. He serves on editorial boards of several journals and is consultant to government and companies on technical and strategic issues in information technology. Malek received his PhD in Computer Science from the Technical University of Wroclaw in Poland, spent 17 years as professor at the University of Texas at Austin and was also, among others, visiting professor at Stanford, Universita di Roma "La Sapienza", Keio University, Technical University in Vienna, New York University, Chinese University of Hong Kong, and guest researcher at Bell Laboratories and IBM T.J. Watson Research Center.*

Preface

Dynamic, trustworthy, and reliable service delivery in Service Oriented Architectures (SOA) is at present one of the main preconditions for successful and sustainable business operations. Service and business process reliability is, therefore, of paramount importance and cannot be compromised. Even today, services are simply expected to be delivered reliably and on demand, and this requirement will be even more important in the near future. Unreliable and incorrect services can corrupt business processes causing an impact ranging from lost opportunity or money to loss of lives. Our current understanding of service reliability properties is rather sketchy, limited, and mostly empirical. Regardless of this fact, services are already widely used as the new paradigm to build software architectures and enable complex business processes.

Several methodologies can be used to engineer reliable SOA systems: quantitative, qualitative, and analytical. Quantitative engineering is based on real-time measurement and monitoring. Whereas it has proven itself in several areas (e.g., hardware benchmarks and testing), it is difficult to apply to SOA because of the lack of adequate metrics and instrumentation. Qualitative engineering is performed informally (e.g., through questionnaires and interviews) and using best-practice frameworks (e.g., ITIL). Qualitative results are easy to misinterpret, difficult to compare, and depend heavily on the party that is performing the analysis. Analytical methods are used to model services and their behavior and calculate or simulate their reliability. Up to now, however, classical analytical methods have been applied to engineer service availability with mixed success and relatively low industry penetration due to scalability, complexity and evolution problems.

With the recent advance of cloud computing and software as a service paradigms, importance of the ability to model and assess service reliability has only increased. For example, with the technical (hardware and software) infrastructure growing much more complex in recent years, many SaaS providers have experienced an increasing number of outages, some of them also extremely long lasting. Consequently, fears were raised that inability to provide strictly defined service level agreement in terms of the maximum number of downtime hours per year may lead to rejection of the entire SaaS paradigm by the users. Many CTOs even speculated that they consider returning to locally hosted solutions, where SaaS products may be used as a backup application only. The increased usage of virtualization and server consolidation makes the problem even more acute, because virtual machine and/or application migration influence reliability and service level agreements of affected services, applications and processes.

Similar problems are evident in large scale SOA infrastructures (such as telecommunications sector or power grid communication). Recent blackouts and frequent failures of cellular communication services are just some of the numerous examples. Even worse, repair teams often depend on the same infrastructure, thus prolonging the failures.

These frequent problems vividly illustrate our inability to engineer complex and reliable SOA systems satisfactorily. They further indicate that reliable SOA systems must consider not only hardware and software properties, but also the underlying (network) infrastructure, configuration, and the people maintaining and using it.

This book attempts to address these issues and present a guide to the engineering of reliable SOA systems. It comprises three sections, treating service level agreements as the basic building block of reliable SOA systems, service composition as the mean of conquering complexity of SOA infrastructures with respect to reliability properties and finally several methods for design, and implementation of fault-tolerant and reliable SOA applications.

Proper specification of service level agreement (SLA) is the main pre-condition for successful implementation of non-functional properties, such as reliability. In Chapter 1, Massarelli et al. discuss the value of Service Level Agreements (SLA) used as contracts, and the authors propose an adaptive method for SLA runtime management that can monitor and perform changes during service execution phase. Di Modica and Tomarchio report in Chapter 2 that, although Service Level Agreements (SLAs) are the most common mechanism used to establish agreements on the quality of service, they have not been taken up by business stakeholders yet due to the low flexibility and usability, together with the lack of interoperability. The authors then propose an SLA management framework addressing these issues. In Chapter 3, Wang et al. present a service level management framework offering two benefits: incorporating monitoring and diagnosis services as an integral part of the QoS management. Zisman argues in Chapter 4 that creation, maintenance, and evolution of Service Level Agreements (SLAs) represent the main challenges in order to establish an effective evaluation and enforcement of quality of services and their providers. The author then presents an approach for SLA creation that is based on an iterative service discovery process. In Chapter 5, Hofer et al. present the work on configurability of non-functional properties in embedded systems. The authors propose a framework for making non-functional properties such as reliability, performance, or memory usage indirectly configurable and maintainable. Finally, Giallonardo and Zimeo explore in Chapter 6 the role that ontologies have on specifying service requirements, discovery and composition.

Service composition is the most straightforward method of managing complexity in SOA. However, service composition, with respect to non-functional properties, presents a new set of problems and challenges. In Chapter 7, Harney and Doshi explore Web Service composition in volatile environments, where parameters and properties of component services may change during execution. The authors propose a hierarchical Web Service composition mechanism as a solution. Blanco, Cardinale, and Vidal discuss in Chapter 8 the problem of identifying a service composition that best meets functional and non-functional user requirements. The authors propose a hybrid cost-based approach that receives and considers at the same time, a functional user request expressed by a pair of input and output attribute sets, and a non-functional condition represented by a set of QoS parameter permissible values. Cheikh proposes in Chapter 9 a service composition model considering available services that have access control constraints. As the scalability of service composition frameworks is one of the most limiting factors, the author investigates complexity in detail. In Chapter 10, Liu and Georgalas develop a novel approach for specifying non-functional properties of telecom operation support systems applications in the NGOSS framework. In Chapter 11, Ezenwoye and Sadjadi propose a language-based approach for transparently adapting BPEL processes in order to improve reliability. This approach addresses reliability at the business process layer using a code generator, which weaves fault-tolerant code to the original code and an external proxy.

In the world where on-demand and trustworthy service delivery is one of the main preconditions for successful business, service and business process availability is of the paramount importance and cannot be compromised. For that reason service availability is coming into central focus of the IT operations and management research and practice. Taweel investigates in Chapter 12 predictability of non-functional properties such as capability, reliability, compatibility, performance, et ceter. in complex service compositions. In Chapter 13, Milanovic and Milic present a framework for modeling business process and service availability. The approach takes into account services, the underlying ICT-infrastructure, and people. Sadi, Myers, and Sanchez investigate in Chapter 14 the failure analysis of SOA systems. They propose the metric for scanning a system model and flagging those components that are more likely to fail. In Chapter 15, Gönczy and Varró propose a model-driven approach to efficiently design and deploy standards-compliant service configurations with non-functional parameters, with special focus on reliable messaging. Looker and Munro argue in Chapter 16 that dependability assessment is an important aspect of any software system which shows the degree of trust and quality of service that is delivered by a system. They discuss service dependability and present different techniques that may be used in dependability assessment of SOA systems.

The book enhances our current understanding of service reliability and at the same time discovers new application possibilities, concepts, and challenges. Therefore, it can be read by both practitioners and researchers wishing to explore state-of-the art results from the field of reliable SOA application engineering.

Nikola Milanovic
Model Labs - Berlin, Germany

Section 1
Service Level Agreements

Proper specification of service level agreement (SLA) is the main pre-condition for successful implementation of non-functional properties, such as availability. In this section, several approaches and case studies for treating SLA are presented.

Chapter 1
Design of Quality Aspects in Service Oriented Architecture through Service Level Agreements:
The Streaming Case Study

Marco Massarelli
Universitá degli Studi di Milano-Bicocca, Italy

Claudia Raibulet
Universitá degli Studi di Milano-Bicocca, Italy

Daniele Cammareri
Universitá degli Studi di Milano-Bicocca, Italy

Nicolò Perino
University of Lugano, Switzerland

ABSTRACT

The development of Service Oriented Architectures is a challenging task to achieve because of both functional and non-functional aspects which should be addressed. Quality requirements concerning the requested and provided services play a determinant role in this context. A low quality level of services at runtime may be of critical importance in their execution flow, thus there are requested mechanisms to monitor and enforce the quality levels of services directly and dynamically.

The definition of Quality of Services should be performed explicitly and clearly in order to be used properly in any phase of the services negotiation and provision. Service Level Agreements offer an appropriate mechanism for the definition and negotiation of services in Service Oriented Architectures. They have the power of contracts through which requesters of services specify their expectations in functional and qualitative terms. The providers of services engage themselves to fulfill such requirements. Being avail-

DOI: 10.4018/978-1-60960-493-6.ch001

able both at the requester and provider sides, the Service Level Agreements represent the appropriate mechanism through which quality requirements may be monitored and evaluated at runtime.

However, only the specification of quality requirements does not ensure that the provisioning of services flows smoothly. Unexpected problems may occur at runtime. Therefore, further means to enforce the quality aspects are needed. In this context, runtime adaptivity is an enhanced solution to address and fulfill this goal. Adaptivity enables the architecture to monitor and perform changes during the execution of services (including the change of the service provider) in order to ensure the requested and expected qualities properties specified in the Service Level Agreements.

This chapter gives a solution to design Service Oriented Architectures which defines and manages Service Level Agreements to enforce Quality of Services and achieves adaptivity at runtime. The validation of this proposed approach is performed through an actual case study in the context of the multimedia application domain.

INTRODUCTION

Service-orientation is one of the buzzwords of the moment among many different business areas. In the software world, service-orientation (Michelson, 2005) means designing, building or migrating pieces of software so that they are independent from the context in which they can be exploited. Service Oriented Architectures (SOA) (MacKensie, Laskey, McCabe, Brown, Metz & Hamilton, 2006; Raibulet & Demartini, 2004) are built on the following concept: they make large usage of services, as if the last were software components ready to be exploited through a series of strategies which overcome issues and difficulties that arise from such a usage.

Given the ubiquitous diffusion of the Internet, a requester can take advantage of service providers virtually located in any place on the globe. Loose-coupling (Hagel & Brown, 2002; He, 2003) between services and their providers can be now fully achieved by exploiting those providers which best suit requests, choosing among many of them due to the connection ability granted by the Internet. Exploiting services offered by entities that are unknown at design time poses a great stress on the quality aspects of the service provisioning. A solution to these problems should have a way to request not only services identified by a name or a function, but also characterized by their qualities.

The Quality of Service (QoS) (Mani & Nagarajan, 2002) concept is becoming more popular as service-orientation spreads in the software community. If a system wants to be sure on the quality levels of a service, it should have a way to describe those needs and to exploit them explicitly at runtime. QoS enable this by modeling the user expectations or requirements as qualities with measurable properties and acceptable values or ranges. As an example in the multimedia context we might consider the "HD Video" as a quality request: this refers to the picture size of a media and it has some specific values associated to it, such as 1280x720 and 1920x1080 pixels. When evaluating the quality of a requested media, we might then refer to its picture size to establish different levels of quality: "Low" when it is different from the two values given above (because of potential up or down scaling resulting in quality issues), "Medium" or "Sufficient" when it equals 1280x720 pixels and "High" when it equals 1920x1080 pixels. If a user wants to watch a "HD Video", a QoS-enabled architecture would be able to deliver a content that will satisfy the user request by providing videos with "Medium" or "High" levels of quality related to their picture size.

Requesting a service from a provider becomes therefore more complex, as it contains more than just a function invocation along with data useful to its execution. The requester and the provider have to agree on quality properties and levels specific for a single service request. Booking of services may be of interest and this should be included in the negotiation with the provider. Service Level Agreements (SLA) (Jin, Machiraju, & Sahai, 2002) represent a valid mechanism to achieve the foretold goals, and even more. They hold the description of the requested service along with quality constraints, validity period of the request and other terms. SLA can be negotiated between two parties and when an agreement is reached, the SLA contain the assurance on the quality levels.

Even using SLA to ensure that the QoS guaranteed by the provider of a service are those expected by the requester, unforeseen problems may arise at provisioning time and hinder the execution workflow either with low levels of quality or even with an interruption of the provisioning of a service. Runtime adaptivity (Cheng, de Lemos, Giese, Inverardi & Magee, 2009; Raibulet, 2008) seems to be the solution to overcome these issues. Essentially, it means that a system is constantly aware of itself and of its execution environment (e.g., by monitoring the state of the provisioning and by having a list of different providers for a given service). Should a problem arise that could slow or stop the execution workflow, the adaptive mechanisms would have the ability to switch from the current provider to another one at runtime. SLA are especially appropriate for this task since they can also hold the information on the strategies adopted by the requester, in case the provider does not meet the agreed QoS.

In this chapter we propose a SOA model for enforcing quality aspects on service provisioning by exploiting SLA and adaptivity specific mechanisms. Our architectural model, or framework model, should be able to receive service requests coupled with desired QoS. After a request is received it should manage the execution workflow and contact service providers, as well as negotiate SLA for the specific service provision. Adaptation is performed dynamically whenever QoS are no longer guaranteed or a provider becomes unavailable. In previous work (Massarelli, Raibulet, Cammareri & Perino, 2009; Raibulet & Massarelli, 2008) we have introduced briefly several aspects of our framework model.

The rest of the chapter is organized as following. The Background Section introduces the main concepts used in this chapter. The Proposed Model Section describes in detail the architectural model of our solution. An application of our approach in an actual scenario is illustrated in the Architecture Exemplification through a Case Study Section. The Related Work Section discusses similar solutions by introducing their advantages and limitations. The lessons learned and future work are dealt within the last section of this chapter.

BACKGROUND

The background concerns the four main keywords of this chapter: Service Oriented Architecture, Quality of Service, Service Level Agreement and adaptivity.

Service Oriented Architecture

With the term Service Oriented Architecture (SOA) is denoted a software architecture based on the loose-coupling between a service and its providers (Erl, 2005).

Newcomer and Lomow (2005) describe the SOA concept as "a style of design that guides all aspects of creating and using business services throughout their lifecycle (from conceptions to retirement), as well as defining and provisioning the IT infrastructure that allows different applications to exchange data and participate in business processes regardless of the operating system or programming languages underlying those applications". Furthermore, they define a service as "an IT asset that corresponds to real-world business activities or recognizable business functions and that can be accessed according to the service policies that have been established for the services". These definitions emphasize the two central concepts of a SOA: (1) the services are used independently with respect to their current location, implementation paradigm or execution platform, and (2) the loose-coupling between the consumers and the providers of services. In addition, they outline that the provisioning of services may be based on different policies which are related to the non-functional (Franch, 1998; Jingjun, Furong, Yang & Liguo, 2007; Wada, Suzuki & Oba, 2006) aspects of services (e.g., authorization, availability, costs, reliability levels, security. performance).

Due to its architectural centric nature, a SOA enhances the efficiency, agility and productivity of enterprise information systems by considering services as the primary means through which solution logic is represented in support of the realization of strategic goals associated with service-oriented computing, as well as the most fundamental unit of the service-oriented solution logic (Erl, 2005). Platform and language independence, flexibility and encapsulation are several of the most important characteristics of SOA. They enable the reuse of legacy systems and the creation of new business processes by composing already available services. Moreover, they provide a solution to the current needs and trends of aggregating services into larger ones, and of using services as front-ends for other services.

SOA is an architectural style (Taylor, Medvidović & Dashofy, 2009) which can be implemented in various ways. However, delivering Web Services through a SOA is the most typical and wide-spread scenario. In this context, the standardization of the main concepts and mechanisms to develop, exploit and interact with SOA-based systems is of fundamental importance. Significant efforts have been concentrated on the specification of the Web Service Definition Language (WSDL) (W3C Web Service Definition Language, 2001) for the description of services, Simple Object Access Protocol (SOAP) (W3C Simple Object Access Protocol, 2007) for the exchange of messages, UDDI (Cover, 2008) for publishing services or WS-BPEL (Oasis Open, 2007) for the definition of business process.

A typical SOA system implemented through Web Services is shown Figure 1. A provider publishes a service through a registry. A client searches for services in a registry. After discovering the desired service, the client accesses it directly.

The role of the service registry is fundamental in the search phase which can be done either manually or automatically. The automatic discovery of services through their semantics is one of the most challenging open issues of SOA. This involves the automatic evaluation of both the

Figure 1. A generic example of a SOA

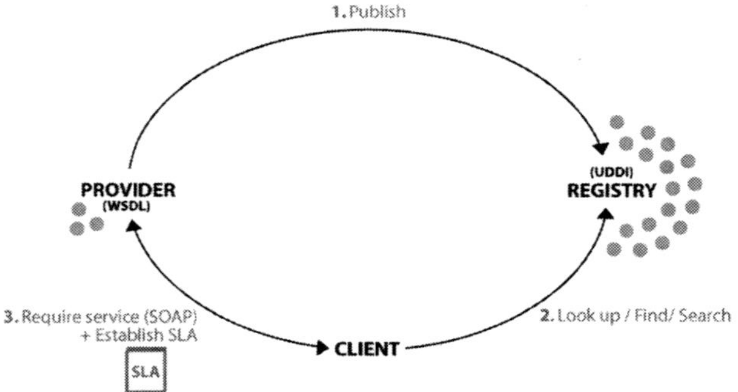

functional and non-functional features of a service, as well as the automatic generation and acceptance of contracts between clients and providers.

Quality of Services

The term Quality of Service (QoS) (Aagedal, 2001) may be exploited in resource reservation control mechanisms to guarantee a certain level of performance during the provision of services. The modeling and exploitation of QoS has gained the attention of the software engineering community in general and of the object-oriented area (OMG Adopted Specification, 2004) in particular due to the role they play in the development of nowadays information systems.

In the context of an open and distributed environment such as a SOA, the variety and the multitude of the providers offering similar or identical services have increased the importance of QoS. Clients consider not only what services do (their functional aspects), but also how well they do it (their non-functional aspects). In this scenario, QoS becomes fundamental information based on which clients may evaluate and decide which services to exploit. This is the user-oriented facet of the QoS.

QoS may be seen as a general term with several meanings (Contreras & Sourrouille, 2001). At lower level, a QoS is a quantitative description of a service. At higher level, QoS measures the expectations and the satisfaction of clients regarding a service or compositions of services and it may be expressed in terms of quantitative and qualitative values. Furthermore, QoS may be classified as subjective and objective. Subjective QoS concern the user perspective, while the objective one is measured and hence it is easier to estimate.

Liu, Ngu and Zeng (2004) assert that a model for specifying the QoS must be flexible and extensible because of domain-specific QoS. Hence, it is not practical to have a single QoS model which is used for the description of the non-functional aspects of services in every domain.

Evaluation of QoS is a critical task especially in the compositions of services. Standalone services should be evaluated in order to compute the optimal QoS of the composite ones because optimal QoS of standalone services may not lead to optimal QoS of a composite services (Arcelli, Raibulet & Tisato, 2004). A reliable specification of QoS should not be made only by vendors, but also by the clients or by automatic measurement (whenever it is possible), because of the natural tends of vendors to manipulate values or not to be neutral. QoS evaluation is not a trivial task. Moreover, it may lead to significant overheads (Liu, Ngu & Zeng, 2004). A solution to avoid vendors to publish not valid QoS and to assure clients to receive the services with the expected and requested QoS (which they pay for) is to establish Service Level Agreements.

Service Level Agreement

Service Level Agreements (SLA) (Erl, 2005; Jin, Machiraju, & Sahai, 2002) are contracts negotiated between the requester and the provider of a service. These contracts define the functional and non-functional requirements expressed by a client and agreed by a provider for a specific service or a set of services. A SLA is composed of different parts related to different aspects of the service provisioning: purpose, parties, validity period, scope, restrictions, service-level objectives, penalties, optional services, exclusions, administration. A SLA may describe through the service-level objectives the QoS negotiated between the user and the provider and hence, expected by the user during the service deliver.

Establishing SLA leads to at least two advantages: a SLA represents explicitly the expectations of the consumers, as well as the guarantees offered by the providers, and a SLA is signed by both parties and available to both parties, hence modifications can be required by either part. In a competitive business environment it is very important for vendors to provide services with a high standard of QoS. The definition of SLA between providers and customers assure that providers supply to customers the services that they have paid for. This constrains vendors to design and publish services after they understood their real capabilities because of legal and monetary implications of penalties. On the other hand, publishing lower QoS in order to avoid the risk of penalties leads to the provisioning of services which are not fully capitalized on their capabilities. Hence, it is very important for vendors to find an appropriate trade-off between the risks and the benefits of all the parties.

Adaptivity

Affirmations such as "adaptivity has become a common requirement" (Dantas & Borba, 2003) of today information systems or "all future systems will be adaptive and intelligent" (Sterling & Juan, 2005) occur frequently in the scientific literature testifying that adaptivity is a hot and challenging research topic nowadays.

Adaptivity enables software to modify its structure and behavior in response to changes occurred internally (inside a software system) or externally (in its execution environment) (Chen & Kotz, 2000; Cheng, de Lemos, Giese, Inverardi & Magee, 2009; Chorfi & Jemni, 2004; Raibulet, 2008). The most challenging issue in adaptive systems is to determine what are they adaptive to and to what extent (Garlan, Cheng, Huang, Schmerl & Steenkiste, 2004). Adaptivity is mostly exploited to address the ever growing complexity of today's information systems as well as to improve productivity and performance, and automate configuration, re-configuration, control and management tasks. Primarily, adaptivity has been used in the context of control systems. Nowadays, its advantages are exploited in various types of systems and in various domains among which there can be mentioned operating systems, networks, robotics, artificial intelligence, e-learning, multimedia, information retrieval and Web Services. This list of the application domains testifies that adaptivity is a complex task with different facets (Raibulet, 2008) which is challenging both to design and to evaluate (Raibulet & Masciadri, 2009).

In the context of a SOA, where services are loosely coupled with their consumers, the same service can be required in various contexts and with different characteristics. Adaptivity denotes the ability of the provider to offer a service in the most appropriate way for the current customer and its current context (Nagarajan, Verma, Sheth, Miller & Lathem, 2006). Usually, this may be achieved by defining various levels of quality for the same service and, based on the current service request, ensure the appropriate quality level.

In our approach, adaptivity offers to the system the ability to modify its own behavior as a response to its operating environment. By operating environment we mean anything observable by the software system at the provisioning time of a service.

The life-cycle of an adaptive system can be modeled as follows (Erl, 2005):

- Monitor and evaluate information: the system must have a way to get information on the key aspects of the service provisioning and furthermore, to have a set of rules to decide whether it must undergo adaptation or not.
- Plan changes: the system must have one or more strategies to deal with the need of changing its behavior. This may imply the modification of the requested qualities or the change of the service provider.
- Enact changes and collect information: after having decided what needs to be modified, the system must undergo adaptation. This might also imply changing the way it collects information: for example, when the change of a service provider has been performed, the means for quality moni-

toring might have been changed or just moved, thus forcing the system to update.

THE PROPOSED MODEL

The main goal of our solution is to design a service-oriented architecture able to manage services characterized not only by their functional but also by their non-functional qualities, which in our proposed model are granted and maintained by SLA exploitation and runtime adaptivity.

In SOA solutions, services are requested by indicating their name or functionality and eventually including parameters when needed. Furthermore, services are executed immediately or as soon as possible, after a request is received by the provider. Service requests handled by our framework may contain non-functional indications, specified by the application or user, indications which are parsed and then used internally during the negotiation of the service provisioning. These non-functional indications include high-level QoS along with service provision scheduling, since the user (or the application on his behalf) may be interested in postponing the execution of a requested service, thus booking it for future time.

SLA are used in our framework and stipulated between service consumers and providers. These contracts include the description of the requested service, both in terms of functionality and of desired quality and other non-functional aspects. Quality at this level is described by a monitorable property and a precise indication on the minimum level requested for that specific property. Considering a video playback service, for example, the user (or application) may request a video by indicating the required quality with a simple string such as "HD Video". When a SLA is established with a provider, it should contain this QoS request in a way that it is measurable and unambiguous, thus needing a lower-level interpretation of the input string. In this case it is pretty simple: the monitorable property is the video size (intended as pixel width and pixel height) and one acceptable value might be 1280x720 pixels, as this is the picture dimension for a standard "HD Ready" video.

SLA are organized in different parts which express the needs of the consumer and the warranties of the provider (Sturm, Morris & Jander, 2000). In the context of our solution we have used the following entries of a SLA: purpose and scope, Service-Level Objectives (SLO), Service-Level Indicators (SLI), and validity period. Purpose and scope hold a description of the requested service. SLO model the QoS which both parties agree on. SLI provide the means to monitor the actual performance of a service. Validity period expresses the time constraints of the service provisioning. Other parts such as restrictions and penalties can be used to model more complex warranties. SLA require that both parties place their signature on the document to make it valid; since we are dealing with an electronic version of the same document, a signature might just be a status flag, such as "accepted" or "pending", associated with a reference ID of both the requester and provider. Effective security measures should be considered when dealing with electronic signatures of documents: this is however an open issue and a ongoing research field, therefore we decided to demand it as a future development of our design.

SLA alone are not enough to ensure that the service provisioning flows smoothly, as unforeseen issues may arise at runtime and hinder the execution workflow. Therefore, our framework should be able to adapt itself to the changed operating environment by modifying the SLA to assure future quality levels or by changing a provider at runtime, when one or more non-functional aspects cannot be guaranteed by the current contractor. SLA really fit for this task since they can also describe penalties and adaptation strategies to overcome provisioning shortfalls.

Considering all the aforementioned issues along with further goals to reach, we designed an architectural model divided in four main components as shown in Figure 2: Application,

Figure 2. The architectural model of our approach

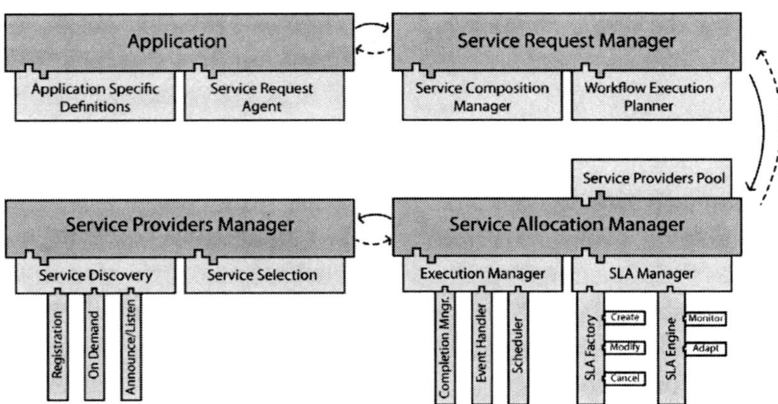

Service Request Manager, Service Allocation Manager, and Service Providers Manager. These components, as well as the modules inside them, provide well-defined interfaces and communicate using messages. This feature ensures modularity since modules or components may be customized or substituted with different ones, as long as they adhere to the required interface and message exchange model, thus showing no external differences from the architecture's point of view.

Application

Applications send their requests to the underlying architecture through their Service Request Agent (SRA). Basically, a SRA acts as a bridge between the application and the underlying architecture, by managing service requests coming from the user and answering to messages coming from the Service Request Manager (SRM). A service may be simply requested by providing its name or its description along with optional parameters, whenever they are needed.

Typically, an application does not know the details of the service it is requesting, leaving this burden to the architecture. Sometimes, however, it may need to request the provisioning of a custom or specific service which might be unknown to the architecture. For this reason, applications may have a library of custom service descriptions (called Application Specific Definitions) which they use with requests that depend on custom services (see Figure 2). These descriptions are attached to the request sent to the SRM and therefore, they must be compliant to the architectural model to be correctly parsed and used.

Requests are enriched by adding non-functional aspects such as desired QoS, which are expressed in generic and high-level terms, since they are then fine-tuned and mapped by the architecture itself. When a request for a custom service is created, QoS may be expressed in low-level terms, because the application already knows the details for that service provisioning. A further non-functional aspect which can be included in a request is its validity period. Applications may be interested in scheduling the service execution, thus effectively booking it, or they might want to have the service delivered before a specific deadline. The validity period holds the time range in which the provisioning for a specific service is needed.

A SRA performs also an additional task: it handles messages, notifications and errors coming from the underlying components. Messages may inform the application on the status of the service execution, providing details or information. Notifications may trigger application events, such as service provisioning completion, or request explicit user interaction if it is needed by the architecture. Error messages, typically indicating service execution failures, are sent to the application so that it can handle them appropriately.

Service Request Manager

The Service Request Manager (SRM) acts as the framework's input component, from the application's point of view, and it is in charge of handling requests coming from the SRA. Usually, an application does not know the details related to the service it is requesting, meaning that it addresses services by their name, function or description, leaving the job of parsing this information to the SRM.

Requested services may be categorized as atomic or simple, and composite. Requests coming from the SRA are not explicitly noted as atomic or composite, thus leaving the categorizing task to the Service Composition Manager (SCM). Atomic services are defined as services whose function is addressed completely by a single service provider, thus not requiring a complex planning. Composite services involve the execution of two or more atomic or composite services in order to obtain the requested result. For this last type of service it is very important to define a workflow which has to be followed to reach the requested goal. A workflow keeps track of the parameters needed to be sent to each service part of the requested one, the data sent and returned from services' executions and the non-functional requirements specific for each atomic service provisioning.

To be able to address all the aforementioned issues, our framework should to be able to parse the incoming request: this job is done by the SCM. This module holds a library of service definitions, compiled at design time by developers, which helps it decompose and understand the application's request. When a custom service is requested, the SCM uses the attached definition in order to correctly parse and understand the request; custom service definitions are recognized as they contain service definitions along with QoS parameters. When a request regards an atomic service, mapping is easy: the service description is directly retrieved and used to convert non-functional aspects to their corresponding low-level versions and parameters are assigned to the only service to execute. When the request concerns a composite service, the SCM has to retrieve the definitions of the required sub-services and associate the non-functional aspects and parameters to each of them. For this reason, composite service descriptions hold all the necessary mapping information and references to atomic services in order to let the SCM do its job.

When parsing is done, all this information is gathered in a document called Workflow Execution Plan, which is created by the Workflow Execution Planner (WEP) module. The service descriptions, their associated parameters, their non-functional aspects and their selection rules are all inserted in this document. All the data is stored in Case Packet Variables (Casati, Ilnicki, Jin & Shan, 2000), which are linked to Access Control Lists (ACL) (Casati, Ilnicki, Jin & Shan, 2000) defining read and write privileges related to each of them. This means that execution of different and dependant services can be obtained by storing results in a variable further used as a parameter for a consecutive service.

The Workflow Execution Plan owes its name to its most notable part: the workflow diagram which describes how execution of sub-services should be chained. This diagram is heavily based on the work done by Casati, Ilnicki, Jin and Shan (2000), thus being organized as a graph with nodes which represent service executions, flow controls or events, and errors. Each node is executed after the previous one has ended and in case a single one fails, it may be executed again for a given number of times. When this number is reached, an error is raised and the workflow execution halts or rollbacks to a previous node, resetting all the variables modified between that node and the current one. It should be noted that these rollbacks are client-side only, meaning that they involve actions performed locally by the application with no impact on service providers. Also, different procedures to be enacted on node failure may be inserted directly in the node description, thus customizing the architecture's failure handling behavior.

Service nodes are of two types: single and multiple. In the first case, the service execution is requested to a single provider, while in the other case execution is requested to a fixed number or to all the service providers known by the architecture. When there is a need for multiple executions of different types of services, split and join operations are used. Parallel executions in both solutions pose issues on completion detection and advance on the workflow diagram. To overcome these problems it is possible to define completion strategies such as wait for each service to end, wait for the first one to end or follow the custom rules defined by the user and stored in the workflow nodes description.

Each WEP is stored internally in the SCM, or attached to a custom service request, as a template associated to a composite service definition; this template can be automatically adapted to the specific parameters and services of the request and it is defined beforehand by developers at design time. Finally, when the WEP is completed, it is sent to the Service Allocation Manager which uses it to fulfill the application request.

Service Allocation Manager

The Service Allocation Manager (SAM) is in charge of handling service provisioning by following the directions and information contained in the WEP document. To achieve its goals, the SAM uses its three internal modules: Service Providers Pool, SLA Manager and Execution Manager.

Before starting its execution, the SAM needs a list of available providers for the current service: since a single service node should be executed by the provider which offers the most in terms of quality, the list should be ordered placing the best providers first, so that the SAM may just follow its order when contacting providers for the current service. The Service Providers Pool (SPP) is used to retrieve a provider from the list, which is nothing more than a Case Packet Variable (Casati, Ilnicki, Jin & Shan, 2000) and therefore, it may be filled in by previous service executions, by parameters given by the application or already stored in the template of the WEP. If the list is empty, the SPP contacts the Service Providers Manager (SPM) component to receive an ordered list of available providers for a given service. Each service has standard selection rules in their definition which are used by the SPM to order and filter candidate providers; it is also possible to define custom rules at design time and store them in specific Case Packet Variables in the WEP template. When the SAM needs to request a service providers list to the SPM, it checks for the existence of a custom selection rule associated to the current service and if it exists it is then attached to the request.

When a provider is returned by the SPP, the SAM uses the reference to negotiate the service execution via the SLA Manager. A SLA is created by the SLA Factory and it is negotiated with a given service provider by sending an initial request and then by exchanging the SLA document. The SLA Factory is also in charge of modifying this document and cancelling it whenever it is necessary by sending specific requests to the provider and eventually exchanging the updated document. In our architecture, SLA are modeled through the description given by Jin, Machiraju and Sahai (2002). It contains functional and non-functional requirements such as the requested service function, a validity period, QoS expressed at low-level as both a monitorable property and its requested value or value range, penalties for one or both parties and adaptation strategies. During its creation, a SLA is filled with all the data currently available to the architecture and stored in the service descriptions and in Case Packet Variables inside the WEP.

During the negotiation phase, a SLA is sent back and forth between the provider and the architecture and changes are made. Since the server has already been selected as one that is able to satisfy the minimum QoS values, negotiation is made as long as those requirements are granted. The client would state these values, or value ranges, and the server might then agree on them or offer higher provisioning quality for one or more of them. If the server does not agree on even one of the minimum levels, the contract is discarded and a new server is chosen. When both parties agree on the current contract and monitoring hooks are defined, the SLA is considered as definitive and the service execution may start as soon as it is intended.

During the service execution the architecture uses the SLA Engine to monitor the current status for the requested non-functional aspects, usually assuring that the requested QoS are granted. The monitoring hooks provide specific monitoring services related to each of the QoS, that enable the module to receive updates on the current QoS levels. As an example a monitoring hook might be related to an hypothetic QoS "video conversion bitrate" and provide regular updates on its value, that would be a number expressed in terms of "Kbps" or "Kilobit per second"; the architecture might then use this information to evaluate QoS and check if it is above the requested value or inside the requested value range. Adaptation strategies are enacted whenever this does not happen.

These strategies may involve different kinds of behavior: the shortcoming may be ignored and counted, so that, after a number of times, the provisioning is considered as insufficient from the quality point of view. Another strategy may involve a SLA re-negotiation, usually relaxing the QoS requests while keeping them sufficient for the user needs. When this strategy is adopted, the server accepts a temporarily change in the SLA in which the new values or value ranges for different QoS are lowered or changed; this new SLA has a limited validity after which the previous SLA becomes valid once again: this might help the provider to deal with exceptional issues as long as they impact the requested quality levels for just a short amount of time. In certain situations, actual QoS may be just too low to keep the current provider therefore, an adaptation strategy may involve SLA canceling. When this last strategy is adopted, a new SLA is created and negotiated with a different provider chosen by the SPP and if there are no other providers left, service execution stops raising an error or rolling back execution.

Penalties might be included in the SLA to justify some adaptation strategy behaviors, such as SLA canceling or QoS relaxation; a penalty might just state that under circumstances of severe QoS shortcomings, which would be described by using numeric limits specific of each type of QoS, the requester is entitled of receding the contract. QoS relaxation might be handled with penalties, by stating that after the resolution of the temporary SLA the original QoS should be granted otherwise giving the right to the client to switch on another provider. As a possibility, not covered by our study due to its complexity, even monetary penalties or some different sort of compensation might be specified in this part of the contract. It is also possible that in some cases the provider might not agree on some SLA modifications: in these cases penalties come in handy to describe precisely what it is not permitted and to give the right to both parties to act as described. Penalties in our study are used just to enable SLA canceling and QoS relaxation and providers are programmed to always accept modifications to SLAs after monitored provisioning shortcomings.

Event and notification nodes are treated by the Execution Manager. When an event node is reached, this module waits for an incoming notification that is compatible with the declaration contained in the event node. The Execution Manager has a known interface to be used by other agents in order to deliver notifications to the framework and each incoming notification is parsed by the Event Handler; the agents might be external, such as service providers, or internal, such as the scheduler or completion manager. Scheduling, for example, is done by placing in the workflow an event node that declares a time event with an associated timestamp; when the node is reached, the Execution Manager waits for an incoming event of the same type. The internal Scheduler module is activated by the Execution Manager upon detecting that a special type of event and then the Scheduler waits for the right time to send a notification using the Execution Manager interface.

The Execution Manager also handles service completion notifications coming from external services or by internal modules and let the workflow plan advance to the next node, by notifying the SAM. When it is needed, the notification is propagated back to the Service Request Manager and then to the Application. Generic and scheduled events completion is treated similarly and it is notified to the SAM, so that it may continue the execution by advancing to the next node or propagating them to the SRM and the Application as needed.

Service Providers Manager

The Service Providers Manager (SPM) is used whenever it is necessary to discover and select providers for a given service. The SAM sends a request to the SPM containing the service description, which holds one or more standard rules that can be used to calculate a synthetic score for the overall quality of each provider. These rules are based on the QoS needed for that specific service, but custom rules may be also included in the request to override the standard ones whenever it is needed. Let's consider a request for a service coming along with two QoS: video bitrate and audio bitrate. Video bitrate should be at least 720Kbps while audio bitrate 192Kbps. A standard rule may be as simple as the following: a score is calculated for each QoS, by dividing the value offered by the provider and the one requested by the user, then each score is multiplied by a weight, which is set as a standard to one divided by the number of requested QoS, and all scores are then summed together to obtain the final one. If a provider offers, for example, the video bitrate at 1024Kbps and audio bitrate at 192Kbps, it totals a score of 1.211, while a provider offering the video bitrate at 1024Kbps and audio bitrate at 384Kbps totals a score of 1.711, thus being considered better than the first one.

To apply one of these rules, the SPM must first compile a list of known and available service providers, each one associated to the QoS levels that they offer. This job is done by the Service Discovery module using one of three possible types of discovery: registration, on demand and announce/listen. The first type may be considered as static, since it requires providers to be registered on a list residing in the SPM, either manually by the user or automatically by the architecture at configuration time. The second type uses a dynamic approach: it queries a directory service for service providers, giving the name or description of the requested service and the required QoS, and then it uses the resulting set as a list. The last type of discovery uses an announce/listen model to obtain and store references to existing service providers: the SPM listens constantly for announces of their existence and when a new one is found a reference is stored locally. Each reference has a deadline after which it is removed from the stored list unless the provider announces itself again before that time. This list is then used as the current service providers list for selection policies.

When service discovery is done and a non-empty list of providers is ready, the Service Selection module selects the ones that offer at least the requested level for each QoS and then orders those providers based on the standard or custom rules. When the final and ordered list is ready, it is sent back to the SAM which uses it for the execution of services.

MODEL EXEMPLIFICATION THROUGH THE STREAMING CASE STUDY

Our architecture model has been validated through a case study focused on streaming services provisioning. The goal of this validation is to provide a meaningful example of a real scenario where our approach suits best, and to test it by designing a possible Workflow Execution Plan along with services needed for it.

The application example concerns the provisioning of streaming services which addresses the delivery of content large in size and long in duration. The provisioning quality plays a fundamental and determinant role for the satisfaction of the users' expectations. Furthermore, media may be incompatible with the user's playback capabilities, thus requiring the streaming service to transcode its contents in real-time.

In this context, customers have access to different Media Content Providers (MCP), each of them characterized by its media library, media format and streaming qualities, granted by a network of available streaming service providers. Additionally, a number of transcoding services are present and characterized by the input and output formats and streaming qualities. The streaming of media contents involves a time-critical approach to its provisioning: a customer has to receive enough data to play the media content in real-time. Thus, tuning the stream properties such as video resolution, audio fidelity or bit-rate, is essential to determine the quality of the service provisioning.

Since QoS are determinant and have to be assured, SLA come to address this task by describing exactly the user's needs and the provider's grants. When QoS levels fall below the agreed minimum values, the adaptive mechanisms (Raibulet, Ubezio & Gobbo, 2008; Raibulet, Arcelli & Mussino, 2006) have the ability to overcome the problem by adjusting those required levels and negotiating a modified SLA. In cases where adjusting QoS levels is not enough to assure a sufficient quality, switching from one provider to another at runtime is possible by effectively canceling the SLA and by negotiating a new one with a new provider.

A Look Inside the Media Streaming Service

In our case study we define a media-oriented streaming service as a composite type, since we require it to be able to provide more than just a stream for an already known content. We want it to be able to present Media Content Providers libraries and let us choose what to play based on required QoS. We expect the possibility to schedule service provisioning and we also want the ability to play content with formats not supported by our system.

A workflow diagram for the composite service is shown in Figure 3 and the description of each service node is the following:

- **Data Collection Service** – This service collects information concerning the user profile and playback environment. User profile information consists in stored accounts or authentication data for known Media Content Providers, billing information such as address or credit card number, service or application usage history, user preferences on this service or favorite contents. Playback environment information includes technical data on registered or available devices, such as screen or speakers. Data Collection Service is a composite service itself. It may use local services. It may be provided by the application itself and networked or online services (for example one that provides a media-device database).
- **Media Content Selection Service** – It is executed as a multiple service, thus contacting every Media Content Provider which is present in the Service Providers

Figure 3. The Media Streaming Service workflow diagram

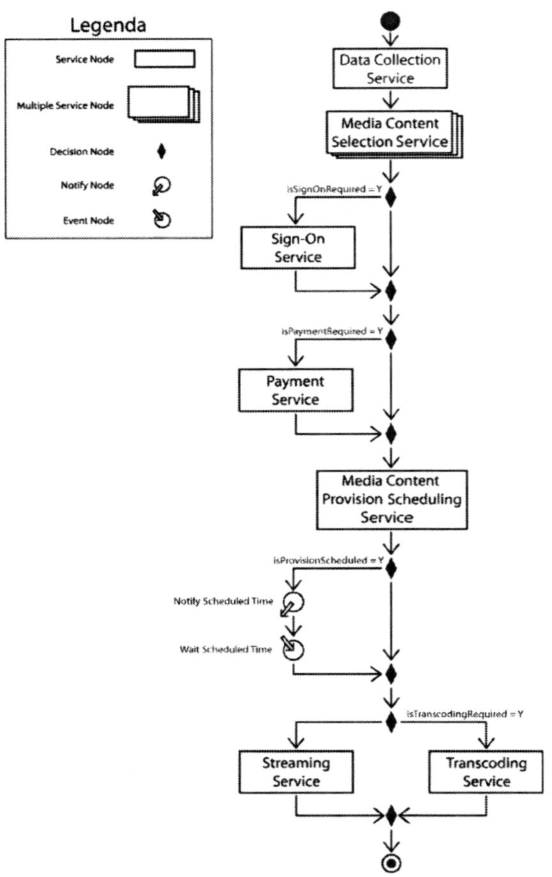

Pool. Each provider sends its media library and the user is prompted to select a content. When a media is selected, the owning provider sends detailed content information, such as description, reviews, price and discounts, possible streaming providers and, optionally, a short preview. The user has then the possibility to confirm its selection, thus storing in a Case Packet Variable all the data received on the content, including its identifier, and a reference to the Media Content Provider.

- **Sign-On Service** – When the selected content requires user authentication on the owning Media Content Provider, this service is contacted and the information needed is sent. If this information is not available in the Workflow Execution Plan variables, explicit user interaction is required: the notification is sent to the Application and the user is asked to insert the required data. The list of providers for this service may be already contained in a Case Packet Variable, previously filled by the Media Content Selection Service using data coming from the Media Content Provider that owns the selected content.
- **Payment Service** – The selected content may not be free of charge and may require a form of payment: this service is therefore used and data is sent, if present. Explicit interaction is required similarly to the Sign-On Service, prompting the user to insert the missing data. Since payment does not necessarily involve credit cards, but may be also done via services like Paypal or using a credit system, the list of providers for this service is given by the Media Content Selection Service and stored in a Case Packet Variable.
- **Media Content Provision Scheduling Service** – When content has been selected and required information is sent in case sign-on or payment were required, this service enables the architecture to negotiate a SLA for the content provisioning. In this context, the SLA is called Media Ticket, which, as the name implies, holds information on the media, such as content id and name, its Media Content Provider references, video and audio properties and media formats. Additionally the ticket includes a validity period for the stream provisioning, in cases where service booking is requested by the user, and other non-functional aspects, such as maximum

packet-loss or minimum data transfer rate. At the end of the negotiation the user has a complete SLA with all the information needed for stream provisioning, including available Streaming Service providers, given by the Media Content Provision Scheduling Service and stored in a Case Packet Variable.

- **Streaming Service** – This is the service which actually provides the requested content by streaming it to the user application. The list of providers should already be filled by the previous service and a Case Packet Variable should contain a valid Media Ticket. When requesting this service, the Media Ticket is sent as a parameter and acts as SLA during negotiation. Along with the ticket, the IP address and the port number are sent and used by the provider to stream the content to the user.
- **Transcoding Service** – Since the Media Ticket holds the details on both audio and video formats and Case Packet Variables contain playback system details, such as supported audio and video codec which were retrieved with the Data Collection Service, it is possible for the architecture to understand if the requested media will be played correctly on the user's system. If this is not possible, a Transcoding Service is used in place of the Streaming Service. The architecture looks for available providers using the Service Providers Pool and during negotiation it sends the Media Ticket and the playback system details, so that the provider may be able to find the most suitable format for both audio and video. Transcoding providers use the Media Ticket on behalf of the user and obtain the stream from the right Streaming Service. As soon as they receive the media they start transcoding it and they stream the result to the user in real-time.

Example of a Typical Application Scenario

The client uses the application on his laptop and requests the media streaming service execution. As he is interested in watching a movie after dinner he asks the application only to list the media coming from providers which allow scheduling. He is also interested in recent movies and therefore providers should only send lists containing media whose publishing date is not older than three months. The user selects his own Home Theater system as playback platform, thus requesting for contents suitable for a High Definition system. Video QoS are set to "HD Ready" and audio to "digital 5.1". He had used this service before and thus, he has a preference for previously contacted providers which granted the requested quality. An example of the application request code is shown in Figure 4.

The request is received by the framework and the SRM recognizes the composite service. It uses the SCM to parse and decompose that request and its non-functional aspects, and then the WEP creates the document used for execution and forwards it to the SAM. Figure 5 shows an example of how QoS appear at a lower level. Execution starts, information is collected and the user is prompted to select a media he prefers. When the selection is done the execution continues by authenticating the user with the data already contained in the document, as previously known providers were to be used, and payment is done using credits associated with the user account on the Media Content Provider.

The Media Ticket is finally created and negotiation starts with the Media Content Provision Scheduling Service, assuring that all the requested non-functional aspects will be granted. When this task is done the booking is accepted and the Media Ticket is updated with all the necessary information. The execution stops and the architecture waits for the booking time to advance, then it uses the playback system information and

Figure 4. An application request example

```
<ApplicationRequest>
    <name>MediaStreamingService</name>
    <paramList>
        <param>#StreamDestAddr</param>
        <param>#StreamDestPort</param>
    </paramList>
    <qosList>
        <qos>#VideoQuality</qos>
        <qos>#AudioQuality</qos>
        <qos>#Schedule</qos>
        <qos>#ContentAge</qos>
        <qos>#Favorites</qos>
    </qosList>
    <schedule>
        <date>2008-10-22 21:00 GMT+1</date>
    </schedule>
    <resourceList>
        <resource>
            <name>StreamDestAddress</name>
            <type>inputParameter</type>
            <value>151.168.49.190</value>
        </resource>
        <resource>
            <name>StreamDestPort</name>
            <type>inputParameter</type>
            <value>12165</value>
        </resource>
        <resource>
            <name>VideoQuality</name>
            <type>qos:video</type>
            <value>HD Ready</value>
        </resource>
        <resource>
            <name>AudioQuality</name>
            <type>qos:audio</type>
            <value>digital 5.1</value>
        </resource>
        <resource>
            <name>Schedule</name>
            <type>qos:schedule</type>
            <value>Yes</value>
        </resource>
        <resource>
            <name>ContentAge</name>
            <type>qos:age:media</type>
            <value>Recent</value>
        </resource>
        <resource>
            <name>Favorites</name>
            <type>qos:usage:favorites</type>
            <value>Media Content Providers</value>
        </resource>
    </resourceList>
<ApplicationRequest>
```

the Media Ticket to decide whether transcoding is necessary. Since the media is encoded with an unsupported codec, the execution proceeds to the Transcoding Service, sending the Media Ticket to it along with the system information.

The Transcoding Service uses the ticket and contacts one of the available Streaming Service providers, which were listed by the Media Content Provision Scheduling Service, and receives the stream. Then it starts transcoding and sends the result to the architecture, which keeps incoming video content in a buffer. We suppose that a problem occurs in service provisioning since the current provider does not send the minimum data per second, as agreed in the SLA. Our architecture parses the adaptation rules and chooses to cancel the SLA and change the provider for Transcoding Service. The Service Providers Pool is prompted to send a new provider and the SLA Manager negotiates a new contract. As soon as the process is finished and required data is sent, provisioning resumes without the user experiencing any interruption in the video playback, due to a buffer that held enough content to be played during the switch. Streaming goes on smoothly and service provisioning ends successfully.

Figure 5. A QoS mapping example

```
...
<resourceList>
    <resource>
        <name>VideoQuality</name>
        <type>qos:video</type>
        <value>HD Ready</value>
        <levelMapping>
            <level>
                <name>Other</name>
                <value>NOT [HD Ready] AND NOT [Full HD]</value>
                <metric>pixel:pictureSize</metric>
                <qualityCoefficient>0.5</qualityCoefficient>
            </level>
            <level>
                <name>HD Ready</name>
                <value>1280x720</value>
                <metric>pixel:pictureSize</metric>
                <qualityCoefficient>1.0</qualityCoefficient>
            </level>
            <level>
                <name>Full HD</name>
                <value>1920x1080</value>
                <metric>pixel:pictureSize</metric>
                <qualityCoefficient>1.5</qualityCoefficient>
            </level>
        </levelMapping>
    </resource>
    ...
</resourceList>
...
```

Related Work

Among the various approaches considering non-functional aspects in general and QoS in particular in service oriented architectures we have chosen the following.

A solution for QoS modeling, computation and policing in the context of Web Services in presented by Liu, Ngu and Zeng (2004). The goal of this work is to define an extensible model for QoS in order to provide a framework to select services and to create an open transparent QoS calculation method based on information published by vendors, active execution monitoring and clients' feedback. The proposed model takes into account both general-purpose QoS which are common for all types of services such as execution price, duration and reputation (a measure of trustworthiness calculated based on clients' feedback), and business related QoS specific to an application domain. This model allows the selection of a service from the available ones providing the same functionalities through the calculation of their QoS based on a normalized matrix of the values collected in a register. The consideration of clients' feedback is of relevant importance because it provides information on what they consider as determinant QoS for a selection of a service and, hence, vendors may improve those QoS of their services. Implicitly, the clients' feedback leads to more reliable values of QoS in registers. The main difference between this approach and the one presented in this chapter is that clients do not have any guarantee that during the execution of a service the QoS will be fulfilled. There is a higher probability that the promised QoS will be respected, however in the worst case the clients cannot claim any penalty. The main advantage of this approach is the usage of clients' feedback which helps in having objective QoS values when choosing a service.

A solution which aims to extend the UDDI registers capabilities in order to manage QoS and to efficiently select one of the services providing identical or similar functionalities is presented in Tian, Gramm, Ritter and Schiller (2004). This approach defines an extensible XML-based QoS model together with the mechanisms to automatically select the most suitable service considering the required QoS and to check the compliance of the service offers. The core element of this model is the service broker which is responsible to retrieve services and their functionalities from UDDI registers and QoS values from providers, as well as to receive requests from clients and to select the suited service. In addition of publishing their services, vendors must provide to the service broker both the description of services and of the QoS. Clients interact with the broker to retrieve a service. The service broker of this approach may be considered similar to the one presented in Liu, Ngu and Zeng (2004). The differences regard the fact that a register in Liu, Ngu and Zeng (2004) is defined for one type of service, while a service broker in Tian, Gramm, Ritter and Schiller (2004) is common to all service types and can be integrated with existing UDDI registers. Moreover, the approach of Liu, Ngu and Zeng (2004) considers costs as QoS, which can be weighted in order to meet clients' preferences, while a service broker selects the cheapest service which satisfies the QoS requested by clients. Finally, Tian, Gramm, Ritter and Schiller (2004) consider only values of QoS published by vendors and does not rely to a feedback system.

Liu, Ngu and Zeng (2004) and Tian, Gramm, Ritter and Schiller (2004) consider QoS only during the selection phase of a service, without addressing runtime problems related to the QoS during the delivery of services.

In Chen, Yu and Lin (2003) authors propose a solution to manage QoS in multimedia Web Services They introduce a new entity, called QoS Broker, which is responsible to collect QoS information, to select the most suitable service in response of a client request and to analyze and keep statistics of the QoS during and after service executions. Conceptually, the QoS broker is a separate entity which resides between the clients and providers. From the implementation point of view, it can be part of a client, of a UDDI register or even an independent service. The service selection considers not only service capabilities, but also the actual situation of servers, such as number and type of clients. The service selection is divided into two steps. The first step regards the discovery of services: the broker searches in its database services which can accomplish the client's request. The second step, called service confirmation, is a negotiation between the service provider and the broker in order to assure that QoS can be actually provided to the client. After the start of the service provisioning, if clients notice that QoS is far behind what promised, the broker can cancel the service execution and switch immediately to another provider which can accomplish the initial QoS requirements. Furthermore, clients collect QoS information about the service execution and send them to the QoS Broker, which keeps statistics over them.

This solution is the one closer to our approach also because of the multimedia application domain. However, it is the QoS broker which manages the QoS during the execution of services. If it fails to find another service provider, clients cannot claim any penalties, as in our approach. Moreover, the booking of services is not addressed in this work.

Casola, Fasolino, Mazzocca and Tramontana (2007) propose a meta-model to formalize the QoS and a decisional model to define a systematic approach for comparing different services. This is faced through a two-component framework. The first component consists of a SLA policy meta-model providing an approach to define and formalize QoS criteria by policies. The meta-model supports a hierarchical view of QoS which allows the decomposition of each quality characteristic into lower level measurable ones. The second component is a decision-making process which automates the selection of the best service based on providers' offers and customers' requests.

Casola, Fasolino, Mazzocca and Tramontana (2007) define SLA which capture and evaluate the QoS. The evaluation of QoS can be done only during the selection phase and not also during the execution of services. Moreover, as in the (Chen, Yu & Lin, 2003) approach the possibility to book services is not considered.

LESSONS LEARNED AND FUTURE WORK

Non-functional aspects such as Quality of Services may play a determinant role in a Service Oriented Architecture and software engineers should understand and address them when modeling a similar solution. This chapter has presented an architectural model that deals with both functional and non-functional issues through SLA management. One of the advantages of our approach is provided by the possibility to book services. Furthermore, we exploit runtime adaptivity to overcome quality and scheduling issues. We presented a case study to validate our model, trying to adapt it to a real world scenario. In the future we plan to consider new case studies belonging to domains different from the media streaming, thus further validating our architecture and discover new issues not yet considered.

One of the challenges to face in the service-oriented world is its heterogeneity: standards are not defined for every aspect and a number of custom solutions are present to address specific domain issues, as we have done with our model. A real, complete and solid solution to implement QoS management in service architectures has yet to be built. An appropriate way to achieve this goal would be adding semantic annotations to high-level QoS requested by the application because domain or service specific semantics enable efficient and reliable mapping of those QoS to their lower level counterparts. This might be a good improvement in our architecture and it is part of future efforts concerning this project.

A limitation of the current solution is the inability to compose services automatically. We use a fixed approach based on libraries of known and pre-made services to be able to plan their execution. Automatic service composition is the object of many current research projects, thus being not available in a well-established commercial platform. Semantics represent a promising way to solve this issue, since requests may be of new, instead of known services. The architecture would be able to understand these targets and build a workflow of services that ultimately lead to fulfill those objectives.

One of the other major issues of our solution is the definition of a valid business model. We just suppose that a number of content providers and transcoding services are present and willing to cooperate with each other. In the real world this is still unfeasible as different companies simply do not want to join a distributed and cooperative business model, because that means changing completely their way of working.

Ultimately, security aspects were intentionally not treated in the proposed solution, as our focus was centered on modeling an architecture able to manage QoS-based non-functional aspects of service provisioning in a service-oriented environment.

REFERENCES

W3C Simple Object Access Protocol. (2007). *SOAP information*. Retrieved from http://www.w3.org/TR/soap/

W3C Web Service Definition Language. (2001). *Homepage information*. http://www.w3.org/TR/wsdl

Aagedal, J. O. (2001). *Quality of Service support in development of distributed systems*. PhD Thesis, University of Oslo, Norway.

Adopted Specification, O. M. G. (2004). *UML profile for modeling Quality of Service and fault tolerance characteristics and mechanisms*. Retrieved from http://www. omg.org

Arcelli, F., Raibulet, C., & Tisato, F. (2004). Modeling QoS through architectural reflection. In *Proceedings of the 2005 International Conference on Software Engineering Research and Practice,* (pp. 347-363), Las Vegas, Nevada, USA.

Casati, F., Ilnicki, S., Jin, L.-J., & Shan, M.-C. (2000). An open, flexible, and configurable system for service composition. In *Proceedings of the 2nd International Workshop on Advanced Issues of E-Commerce and Web-Based Information Systems,* (pp. 125 – 132).

Casola, V., Fasolino, A. R., Mazzocca, N., & Tramontana, P. (2007). A policy-based evaluation framework for quality and security in Service Oriented Architectures. In *Proceedings of IEEE International Conference on Web Services,* (pp. 1181-1190).

Chen, G., & Kotz, D. (2000). *A survey of context-aware mobile computing research*. In (Technical Report TR2000-381), Darthmouth Computer Science. Hanover, USA.

Chen, H., Yu, T., & Lin, K. (2003). QCWS: An implementation of QoS-capable multimedia Web services. In *Proceedings of the Fifth International Symposium on Multimedia Software Engineering,* (pp. 38-45).

Cheng, B.H.C., de Lemos, R., Giese, H., Inverardi, P. & Magee, J. (2009). Software engineering for self-adaptive systems. (LNCS 5525).

Chorfi, H., & Jemni, M. (2004). PERSO: Towards an adaptive e-learning system. *Journal of Interactive Learning, 15*(4), 433–447.

Contreras, J. L., & Sourrouille, J. L. (2001). A framework for QoS management. In *Proceedings of the 39th International Conference and Exhibition on Technology of Object-Oriented Languages and Systems,* (pp. 183-193).

Cover, R. (2008). *Universal description, discovery, and integration*. Technical Report. Retrieved from http://xml.coverpages.org/uddi.html

Dantas, A., & Borba, P. (2003). Adaptability aspects: An architectural pattern for structuring adaptive applications with aspects. In *Proceedings of the 3rd Latin American Conference on Pattern languages of Programming,* (pp. 12-15).

Erl, T. (2005). *Service-Oriented Architecture: Concepts, technology and design*. USA: Prentice Hall PTR.

Franch, X. (1998). Systematic formulation of non-functional characteristics of software. In *Proceedings of the Third International Conference on Requirements Engineering,* (pp. 174-181).

Garlan, D., Cheng, S. W., Huang, A.-C., Schmerl, B., & Steenkiste, P. (2004). Rainbow: Architecture-based self-adaptation with reusable infrastructure. In *IEEE Computer, 37*(10), 46-54.

Hagel, J. III, & Brown, J. S. (2002). *Out of the box strategies for achieving profits today and growth tomorrow through Web Services*. Boston: Harvard Business School Press.

He, H. (2003). *What is Service-Oriented Architecture?* O'Reilly Press.

Jin, J., Machiraju, V., & Sahai, A. (2002). *Analysis on service level agreements of Web Services*. (Technical Report HPL-2002-180), HP Laboratories Palo Alto.

Jingjun, Z., Furong, L., Yang, Z., & Liguo, W. (2007). Non-functional attributes modeling in software architecture. In *Proceedings of the 8th ACIS International Conference on Software Engineering, Artificial Intelligence, Networking and Parallel/Distributed Computing,* (pp. 149-153).

Liu, Y., Ngu, A. H., & Zeng, L. S. (2004). QoS computation and policing in dynamic Web Service selection. In *Proceedings of the 13th International World Wide Web Conference,* (pp. 66-73). New York, USA.

MacKensie, C. M., Laskey, K., McCabe, F., Brown, P. F., Metz, R., & Hamilton, B. A. (2006). *Reference model for Service Oriented Architecture 1.0*. OASIS Committee Specification.

Mani, A., & Nagarajan, A. (2002). *Understanding Quality of Service for Web Services*. IBM Developer Works.

Massarelli, M., Raibulet, C., Cammareri, D., & Perino, N. (2009). Ensuring Quality of Services at runtime–a case study. In *Proceedings of the IEEE International Conference on Services Computing,* (pp. 540-543)

Michelson, B.M. (2005). *Service oriented world cheat sheet: A guide to key concepts, technology, and more*.

Nagarajan, M., Verma, K., Sheth, A. P., Miller, J. A., & Lathem, J. (2006). Semantic interoperability of Web Services–challenges and experiences. In *Proceedings of the 4th IEEE International Conference on Web Services,* (pp. 373-382).

Newcomer, E., & Lomow, G. (2005). *Understanding SOA with Web Services. (Independent Technology Guides)*. Addison-Wesley Professional.

Oasis Open. (2007). *OASIS Web Services business process execution language*. Retrieved from http://www.oasis-open.org/committees/tc_home.php?wg_abbrev=wsbpel

Raibulet, C. (2008). Facets of adaptivity. In *Proceedings of the 2nd European Conference on Software Architecture*, (LNCS 5292), (pp. 342-345).

Raibulet, C., Arcelli, F., & Mussino, S. (2006). Exploiting reflection to design and manage services for an adaptive resource management system. In *Proceedings of the IEEE International Conference on Service Systems and Service Management,* (pp. 1363-1368). Troyes, France.

Raibulet, C., & Demartini, C. (2004). Toward service oriented distributed architectures. In Y. Manolopoulos (Ed.), *Proceedings in Informatics 19, Distributed Data & Structures, 5,* 31-43. Canada: Carleton Scientific.

Raibulet, C., & Masciadri, L. (2009). Evaluation of dynamic adaptivity through metrics: An achievable target? In *Proceedings of the Joint IEEE/IFIP Conference on Software Architecture 2009 & European Conference on Software Architecture 2009,* (pp. 341-344).

Raibulet, C., & Massarelli, M. (2008). Managing non-functional aspects in SOA through SLA. In *Proceedings of the First IEEE International Workshop on Engineering Non-Functional INformation for Emerging Systems,* (pp. 701-705).

Raibulet, C., Ubezio, L., & Gobbo, W. (2008). Leveraging on strategies to achieve adaptivity in a distributed architecture. In *Proceedings of the 7th Workshop on Adaptive and Reflective Middleware,* (pp. 53-54). Leuven, Belgium.

Sterling, L., & Juan, T. (2005). The software engineering of agent-based intelligent adaptive systems. In *Proceedings of the International Conference on Software Engineering,* (pp. 704-705). St. Louis, Missouri.

Sturm, R., Morris, W., & Jander, M. (2000). *Foundations of service level management.* SAMS Publishing.

Taylor, R. N., Medvidović, N., & Dashofy, E. M. (2009). *Software architecture: Foundations, theory, and practice.* John Wiley & Sons, Inc.

Tian, M., Gramm, M., Ritter, H., & Schiller, J. (2004). Efficient selection and monitoring of QoS-aware Web Services with the WS-QoS framework. In *Proceedings of the IEEE/WIC/ACM International Conference on Web Intelligence,* (pp. 152-158). Washington, DC, USA.

Wada, H., Suzuki, J., & Oba, K. (2006). Modelling non-functional aspects in Service Oriented Architecture. In *Proceedings of the IEEE International Conference on Services Computing,* (pp. 222-229). Washington, DC, USA.

Chapter 2
Flexible and Dynamic SLAs Management in Service Oriented Architectures

Giuseppe Di Modica
Università di Catania, Italy

Orazio Tomarchio
Università di Catania, Italy

ABSTRACT

The increasing adoption of service oriented architectures across different administrative domains forces service providers to use effective mechanisms and strategies of resource management in order to guarantee the quality levels their customers demand during service provisioning. Service level agreements (SLA) are the most common mechanism used to establish agreements on the quality of a service (QoS) between a service provider and a service consumer. However, the proposed solutions have not been taken up by business stakeholders due to the low flexibility and usability together with the lack of interoperability. Any framework for SLA management should address several issues, such as SLA modeling and representation, SLA publication and discovery, protocols for establishing and negotiating SLAs, SLA monitoring and enforcement. This chapter addresses the issues related to the SLA management in service composition scenarios, which impose stronger requirements about flexibility of SLAs, and presents a framework for the management of dynamic SLAs.

INTRODUCTION

The extensive usage of information and communication technology in modern organizations affects B2B interactions too. While the interaction has traditionally mainly been based on manual processes, the use of digital means allows organizations to increase both the effectiveness and efficiency of their mutual interaction and consequently improves their business goals.

DOI: 10.4018/978-1-60960-493-6.ch002

Such interactions must be formalized to clearly define rights and obligations of all the involved parties. The formalization usually takes the form of a contract that defines the parties engaging in the collaboration, the goods, the services or funds exchanged, and details about the way this exchange takes place. The use of electronic contracts with automated support for their management allows an increase of effectiveness and efficiency in contract processing, opening new possibilities for interaction among the parties (Angelov & Grefen, 2001, 2004).

This issue becomes more important in Service Oriented Architecture (SOA) (Papazoglou, 2003; Papazoglou & van den Heuvel, 2007), which has imposed as the reference paradigm for automated business integration. The high level of interoperability offered by the SOA enables scenarios of world-wide and cross-domains service composition. In a service-oriented scenario a service may be the result of the composition of several services deployed in many administrative domains, each of which autonomously manages resources that are quantitatively and qualitatively different. The quality of the composite service delivered to the customer is strongly affected by all the services involved in the provision. In such a scenario, where the resource availability is highly dynamic, promising and guaranteeing specific QoS levels to the customer is a real challenge.

A service composition system that can leverage, aggregate and make use of individual services' QoS information to derive the optimal QoS of the composite service is still an ongoing research problem. This is partly due to the lack of an extensible QoS model and a reliable mechanism to compute and police QoS that is fair and transparent to both service customers and providers (Liu et al., 2004). Currently, most of the approaches dealing with QoS of web services only address some generic dimensions such as price, execution duration, availability and reliability. In some domains, such generic criteria might not be sufficient. A QoS model should also include domain specific criteria and be extensible. Most of the current approaches rely on service providers to advertise their *negotiable* QoS information and/or provide an interface to access the QoS values, which are subject to manipulation by the providers. Customers can then search among the service providers, negotiate for the QoS that best suits their needs and eventually sign an agreement for the service provision.

Service level agreements (SLAs) (Overton, 2002) are the most common mechanism used to establish agreements between two or more parties involved in the provision of a service. An SLA is a formal, negotiated agreement between a service provider and its customer (the service requester) involving parameters, both functional and not functional, related to the service to be provided.

The establishment of an SLA is just one of the tasks that should be fulfilled by an SLA management architecture. First, there is a need for a mechanism which enables, on the one hand, the Service Providers to advertise its capabilities under the form of SLA templates (*SLA publishing*) and, on the other one, the customers to discover them (*SLA discovering*). Before signing an SLA, the parties enter a negotiation step during which the parameters advertised in the SLA can still be modified according to the customer's needs and the provider's capabilities (*SLA negotiation*). After that, the SLA is signed by the parties and, from that moment on, is considered established (*SLA formation*). To verify that the SLA is actually honored the parties can monitor the quality level of the provided service against the one promised in the SLA (*SLA monitoring*). Finally, the SLA is either naturally terminated (its lifetime expires) or is voluntarily terminated by one of the parties (*SLA termination*).

This is a very rigid vision of the SLA: a contract is established, enforced and then terminated (either voluntarily or not). As we are going to show, this *static* vision does not meet the requirements of highly dynamic and unpredictable scenarios. Actually, while monitoring the provided QoS, the parties might want to re-negotiate (and therefore, modify) some terms of the SLA; if both had to agree with the modification, the SLA could be accordingly modified (*SLA re-negotiation and modification*). Giving the parties the chance to modify a running SLA would give it the proper level of flexibility needed to cope with more complex scenarios.

To the best of our knowledge, very few works in literature have addressed the need for a *dynamic* concept of SLA. In B2B scenarios, where service providers play both the roles of provider and customer, several one-to-one SLAs need to be signed. Because of the rigidity of the considered context, the overall QoS of the provided service can be strongly affected by any violation on each single SLA. If just one of the composing services violates its QoS guarantees at run-time, the final QoS delivered to the customer might get definitively compromised, to the detriment of the customer. In order to maximize both the profit of the service providers and the utility of the service consumers, the parties of an SLA must be allowed to re-negotiate at run-time the guarantees on the QoS whenever violations on such guarantees are expected to occur.

The chapter is organized as follows: Section 2 provides basic concepts and describe existing frameworks for SLA management, together with a review of the related works in this research area. Section 3 discusses motivation and requirements for more dynamic and flexible SLA schemes in the emerging service oriented architectures. Section 4 describes an architecture for the management of dynamic SLAs providing support for their re-negotiation. Finally Section 5 concludes the chapter.

BACKGROUND

A framework for the management of SLAs must address the following issues:

- *SLA publication and discovery*. There must exist a common mechanism for the service providers to publish the capabilities of their services and resources, and for the service customers to find the ones that match their needs;
- *Protocols for SLA formation*. The set of rules used by the parties involved in the provision of goods and services to negotiate and form SLAs;
- *SLA representation*. The specific document shared by the parties to represent the QoS terms, guarantees, payment and penalty terms within the SLA;
- *SLA monitoring and evaluation*. Once an SLA is formed, the provided resources must be monitored and their capabilities and/or performance constantly evaluated to ensure that they are meeting the QoS guarantees agreed in the SLA.

To represent an SLA, several specifications, often defined by XML based languages, have been recently proposed. Many of them are a complement to the service description implemented by WSDL (http://www.w3.org/TR/wsdl) and are used within a framework allowing the management of Web Services and their compositions. As for the protocols for the formation of SLAs, several proposals can be found in literature.

In the next section we describe two proposals of an SLA management framework, WSLA (Keller & Ludwig, 2003) and WS-Agreement (Andrieux et al., 2007). Both the proposals focus on the definition of a language and a protocol to represent and form SLAs. Both provide support for the SLA monitoring and evaluation, but lack of a support for the SLA publication/discovery. Since WSLA has been abandoned in favor of WS-Agreement (which represents its natural evolution) we will give a more detailed description of the latter. Then we will give a literature review of recent works in the area of SLA management.

Figure 1. WSLA life cycle

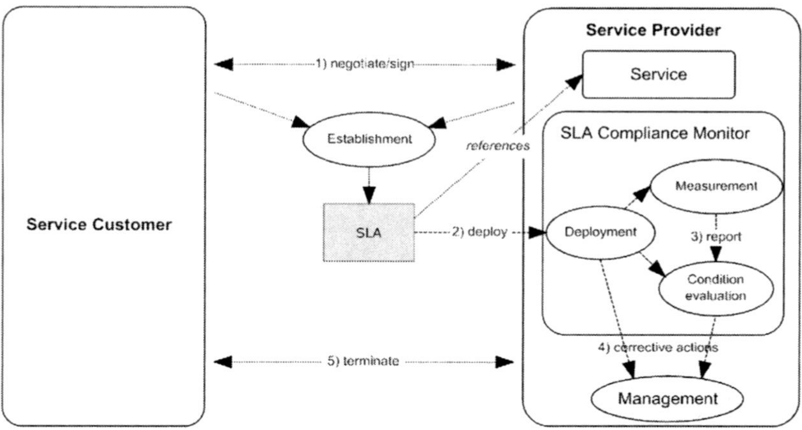

Language and Protocols for the Definition of SLA

WSLA

WSLA (Keller & Ludwig, 2003) is a framework proposed and developed by IBM for specifying and monitoring Service Level Agreements for Web Services. Although WSLA was designed for a Web Services environment, it is as well applicable to any inter-domain management scenario such as business process and service management or the management of networks, systems and applications in general. The WSLA framework consists of a flexible and extensible language based on XML Schema and a run-time architecture comprising several SLA monitoring services. WSLA enables service customers and providers to unambiguously define a wide variety of SLAs, specify the SLA parameters and the way how they are measured, and relate them to managed resource instrumentation.

WSLA defines four levels of abstraction of the SLA-related information in a distributed system:

- Resource metrics
- Composite metrics
- SLA parameters
- Business metrics

Being the four levels, from top to down, more specific for the customer and less specific for the provider. While a provider is primarily responsible for exposing a set of resources or composite metrics, a customer often needs to refine these according to his needs by specifying additional composite metrics. A customer is always involved, together with a provider, in the definition of SLA Parameters and needs to define his own business metrics to make sure the SLA data can be mapped to his business goals.

Figure 1 gives an overview of the SLA management life cycle, which consists of five distinct stages:

1. SLA Negotiation and Establishment
2. SLA Deployment
3. Service Level Measurement and Reporting
4. Corrective Management Actions
5. SLA Termination

The WSLA Language Specification defines a type system for the various SLA artifacts. It is based on XML Schema. WSLA is designed to accommodate the general structure of an SLA in three sections:

- The *Parties* section, that identifies all the contractual parties for the SLA;
- The *Service Descriptions* section, that specifies the characteristics of the service and its observable parameters;
- The *Obligations* section, that defines various guarantees and constraints that may be imposed on SLA parameters;

WS-Agreement

The WS-Agreement specification (Andrieux et al., 2007) was published as an Open Grid Forum (OGF) Proposed Recommendation. The objective of WS-Agreement is to define a language and protocol for:

- Establishing agreements between two parties
- Advertising the capabilities and requirements of service consumers and providers
- Creating agreements based on creation offers
- Monitoring the agreement compliance at run-time

This protocol uses an XML-based language to specify the nature of an agreement, and *agreement templates* to facilitate the discovery of compatible agreement parties. It is generally aimed to be a "one-shot" interaction, and is not directly intended to support negotiation. The agreement creation process is restricted to a simple request-response protocol: one party (the Agreement Initiator, generally acting on behalf of a Service Consumer) creates an agreement document, possibly based on an agreement template, and proposes it to the other party (the Agreement Responder, generally acting on behalf of a Service Provider). The responding party evaluates the agreement's offer and assesses its resources' utilization level before accepting or rejecting it.

An agreement between a Service Consumer and a Service Provider specifies one or more *Service Level Objectives* both as expressions of requirements of the Service Consumer and assurances from the Service Provider on the availability of resources and/or on service qualities. The specification provides a schema for defining the overall structure for an agreement document. The structure of an agreement is illustrated in Figure 2.

Figure 2. Structure of an agreement

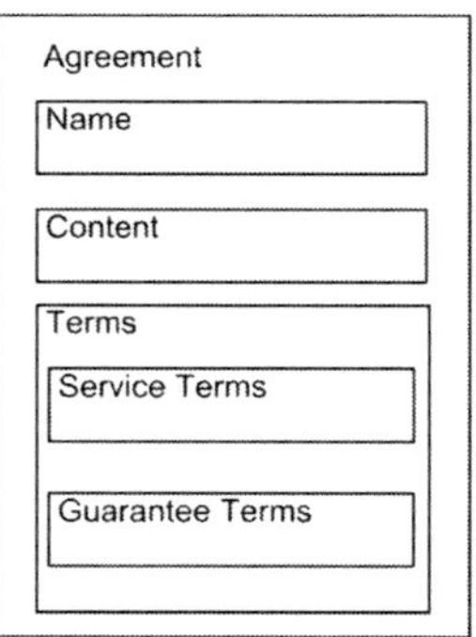

In this structure there are information on the agreement parties and a set of terms. The agreement terms represent contractual obligations and include a description of the service as well as the specific given guarantees. A *service description term* (element within the Service Term) can be a reference to an existing service, a domain specific description of a service or a set of observable properties of the service. A *guarantee term*, on the other hand, specifies non-functional characteristics in service level objectives as an expression over the properties of the service, an optional qualifying condition under which objectives are to be met, and an associated business value specifying the importance of meeting these objectives.

The conceptual model for the architecture of system interfaces based on WS-Agreement has two layers: the Agreement Layer and the Service Layer. The Agreement layer implements the communication protocol used to exchange information about SLAs between the Service Customer and the Service Provider (create, represent and monitor agreements), and it is responsible for ensuring

Figure 3. State model of the agreement

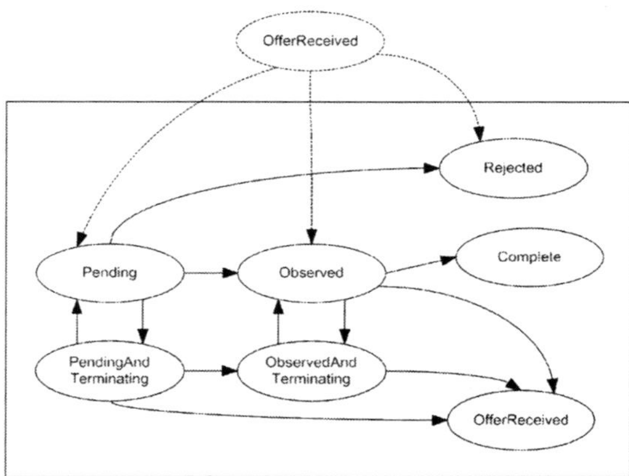

that the SLA guarantees are enforced by a suitable service provider. This layer handles well-formed requests to the service layer. The Service Layer represents the application-specific layer of the service being provided. The interfaces in this layer are domain-specific, and need not be altered when the Agreement layer is introduced.

The typical WS-Agreement life cycle has four stages:

1. *Exploration*: a Service Provider provides templates describing possible agreement parameters;
2. *Creation*: Consumer fills in parameters, and makes an offer;
3. *Operation*: Agreement state is available for monitoring as a *ResourceProperty*;
4. *Termination*: Agreement is destroyed explicitly or via soft state (termination time).

The Agreement States exposed to an Agreement Initiator observes the state model depicted in Figure 3.

The *Observed* state means that an Agreement offer has been proposed by the Agreement Initiator and has been accepted by the Agreement Responder; both parties are then obliged with respect to the service and guarantee terms of the agreement. When an Agreement offer has been made but still has not been accepted nor rejected, its state is said to be *Pending*. The *Rejected* state means that an Agreement offer has been made and rejected. The *Terminated* state means that an Agreement offer has been terminated by the Agreement Initiator and that the obligation no longer exists. Finally, the *Complete* state means that an Agreement offer has been received and accepted, and that all activities related to the Agreement are finished. For more details about the WS-Agreement specification the reader may refer to Andrieux et al. (2007).

Among the efforts for the implementation of a WS-Agreement compliant framework, two are worth citing. CREMONA (Creation and Monitoring of Agreements) is a WS-Agreement framework implemented by IBM (Ludwig et al., 2004). The CREMONA Java Library implements the WS-Agreement interfaces, provides management functionality for agreement templates and instances, and defines abstractions of service-providing systems that can be implemented in a domain-specific environment. WS-Agreement Framework (WSAG4J) (http://packcs-e0.scai.fraunhofer.de/wsag4j/) provides means to implement WS-Agreement services and the respective client-side access. It is middleware-agnostic, fully compliant with the WS-Agreement Specification version 1.0, and is implemented in Java.

Related Work

In GRID and SOA environments SLAs have been widely employed to establish agreements on the quality level of non-functional parameters that a service provider must grant whilst delivering a service to a customer. Many works in literature have embraced the SLA concept and have proposed frameworks for "SLA-based" resource management and scheduling. Within such frameworks SLAs have proved to be of great support for dealing with issues related to many services such as service discovery, advanced resource reservation, resource scheduling, service and resource monitoring.

In the VIOLA project (Waeldrich and Ziegler, 2006) a resource reservation mechanism based on WS-Agreement is responsible for the negotiation of resource allocation with the local scheduling systems. A Three-phase-commit-protocol (3PCP) is proposed to overcome the limitations of WS-Agreement. It is based on the creation of different types of agreements within a negotiation process, namely a Declaration of Intention Agreement, a Preparation Agreement, and a Commitment Agreement. All of these agreements are normal WS-Agreements, following a specific naming convention. This protocol basically aims at solving problems related to the creation of agreements on multiple sites.

The AssessGrid (Battre' et al., 2007) project focuses on risk management and assessment in Grid computing. The project's aim is to provide the service providers with risk assessment tools that will help them to make decisions on suitable SLA offers, by relating the risk of failure to penalty fees. Similarly, end-users get knowledge about the risk of an SLA violation by a resource provider that helps to make appropriate decisions regarding acceptable costs and penalty fees. A broker is the matchmaker between end-users and providers (i.e., the contractors). A negotiator module is responsible for negotiating SLAs with external contractors using the *WS-Agreement-Negotiation* protocol, which is an early version of the WS-Agreement protocol including little support for the negotiation.

GRIA (http://www.gria.org/) is a service-oriented infrastructure designed to support B2B collaborations through service provision across organizational boundaries. The framework includes a service manager with the ability to define the available resources (e.g. CPUs, applications, etc), assign portions of the resources to users by the way of service level agreements (SLAs) and bill for resource usage. Furthermore, a monitoring service is responsible for monitoring the activity of the services with respect to the agreed SLAs.

The BREIN consortium (http://www.eu-brein.com/) is working on a business framework prototype that will foster electronic business collaborations by taking the classical Grid approach. Among the others, the prototype's claimed capabilities are: Service Discovery with respect to SLA capabilities, SLA negotiation in a single-round phase, system monitoring and evaluation, SLA evaluation with respect to the agreed SLA. The WS-Agreement/WSLA specifications will be used to support the SLAs management. Dynamic SLAs are in the focus of the project.

In the context of the BEINGRID project (http://www.beingrid.com/) eighteen Business Experiments, designed to implement and deploy Grid solutions in industrial key sectors, have been conducted on top of a middleware of Grid services from across the Grid research domain. Almost half of the Experiments need a strong SLA support, thus justifying the need for an SLA management tool within a Business Grid. In the future a study on the composition of SLAs across business domains will be undertaken.

Akogrimo (http://www.mobilegrids.org/) uses SLAs both to define the service providers external relationships with their customers and also internally within the service provider to plan for anticipated resource usage. The Akogrimo service management system provides for four different stages: service advertisement, service negotiation (or service discovery), service reservation, service execution and monitoring. The WS-Agreement XML schema is used to represent SLAs in Akogrimo.

SLAs between service providers and customers are central to the conceptual model of NextGRID (http://www.nextgrid.org/). According to such model, a dynamic GRID infrastructure can only be realised through dynamically formed relationships defined though an SLA. NextGRID have used WS-Agreement and WSLA as inspiration for their own schema.

In Joita et al. (2005) the WS-Agreement specification is used as a basis on which negotiations between two parties may be conducted. An agent-based infrastructure takes care of the Agreement offer made by the requesting party; from this offer many one-to-one negotiations are started in order to find the service that best matches the offer.

The discussion about the opportunity of adopting dynamically modifiable SLAs is still open. We believe that, in order to satisfy the business requirements coming from GRID and, more generally, SOA environments this opportunity should be taken. The OGF (http://www.ogf.org/) as well as many of the above cited European grid projects are investigating on dynamic SLAs, but much work still has to be done in order to clearly identify the business requirements behind them.

In Frankova et al. (2006) the authors propose an extension of WS-Agreement allowing a run-time re-negotiation of the guarantees. Some modifications are proposed in the section wsag:GuaranteeTerm of the agreement schema, and a new section is added to define possible negotiations, to be agreed by the parties before the Agreement offer is submitted. In this work there is not an actual real-time re-negotiation because, after the agreement's acceptance, there is no interaction between the Service Provider and the Service Consumer.

In Sakellariou and Yarmolenko (2005) the authors specify the guarantee terms of an Agreement as functions rather than just values. The aim of the work was to minimize the number of re-negotiations necessary to reach some consensus on the values associated with the agreement terms. In Ziegler et al. (2008) the authors present a bilateral WS-Agreement based negotiation process used to dynamically negotiate SLA templates. They propose a simple extension of the WS-Agreement protocol in order to support a simple offer/counter-offer mode.

SLA@SOI (http://www.sla-at-soi.eu/) is a European project researching the systematic management of service-oriented infrastructures on the basis of formally specified SLAs. A specification for an SLA management framework will be produced. It will include SLA (re)negotiation, establishment, monitoring and enforcement.

DYNAMIC SLA

Generally speaking, a contract represents the formalization of the rights and the obligations between two or more parties. Usually, the penalties' section of a contract states the economic cost to be sustained by the party that violates the formal agreement. When a violation occurs, the service provision is interrupted, the related contract is terminated and a new contract must be negotiated and created. We argue that, besides the economic cost associated to the penalties, additional costs are associated to the just described termination/re-creation scenario.

In B2C contexts, often occurs that the provision of the service that the SLA applies to is brutally stopped because of the inability of a Service Provider to meet the SLA's Service Level Objectives, and the SLA is thus terminated. When a Service Provider decides to terminate an SLA, not only it incurs penalties, but has also wastes resources that might have been better scheduled. Furthermore the Service Provider has lost its credibility. As for the Service Consumer, if the objectives of an SLA are not met, he has wasted money for a service provision that eventually did not satisfy his expectations; even worse, when an SLA is terminated, he has to search for a different provider and re-negotiate for the service, with no assurance to obtain the same guarantees as he was given in the context of the just terminated SLA.

In a B2B context the probability that the provision of a service to the end Customer is not successfully carried out is much higher. The higher the number of services needed to serve the Customer's request, the higher the probability that the task is not accomplished.

Figure 4. Simple service-composition scenario: chain (a) and fork (b)

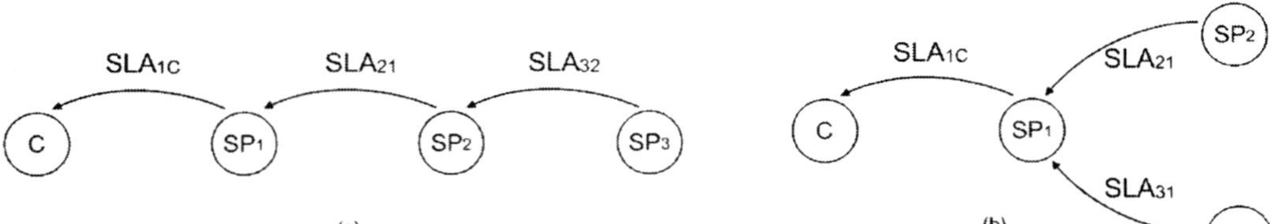

For instance, let us consider the case of a Customer C that wants to access a service offered by the Service Provider SP_1, which in its turn needs to access a service offered by the Service Provider SP_2 to satisfy the Customer's request. Again, let us assume that the service offered by SP_2 is built on top of another service offered by the Service Provider SP_3. For each service provision an SLA has to be signed. In the Figure 4(a) a graphic representation of this scenario is given.

The involved parties are represented by nodes, while the oriented edges represent the SLAs signed between pairs of parties and the respective roles that the parties play in the SLAs. For instance, the edge SLA_{21} oriented from SP_2 to SP_1 represents the SLA signed by the parties SP_1 and SP_2, being SP_2 the Service Provider and SP_1 the Service Consumer for that specific contract. The abnormal termination of a given SLA causes an interruption in the SLAs' chain, thus preventing the forwarding SLAs from being honored. For instance, if SP_2 for any reason did not attain the QoS target or, for any reason, stopped providing its service to SP_1, thus violating SLA_{21}, SP_1 would not be able to offer its service to C and then to honor SLA_{1C}. In this case, either it looks for another Service Provider offering the same service as offered by SP_2 or it has to terminate SLA_{1C}. Furthermore, in the latter case SP_2 might not need to access the service offered by SP_3 anymore (unless it has pending requests that might be satisfied with that service), and will likely decide to explicitly terminate SLA_{32}.

In the same scenario of service composition, let us now assume that C is not satisfied with the perceived quality of the service being offered by SP_1, and decides to negotiate with it for an improvement of the service's quality level. Though SP_1 has enough inbound resources to satisfy C's request, an increment of the capacity of the service offered by SP_2 is necessary to support the newly requested overall QoS. Thus SP_1 negotiates with SP_2 to obtain a better level of QoS. On its turn, SP_2 will not be able to provide the extra capacity unless SP_3 is willing to sustain a higher level of quality of the service it provides to SP_2. The original request of C can be satisfied only if the negotiations for the increment of service capacity offered by each provider are successful. In that case, the three SLAs can be modified and the quality of the services are adjusted to the new agreed levels.

Let us consider another scenario, in which a Service Provider needs to use two different services to offer its own service to the Customer, as depicted in the Figure 4(b).

In this case, if one of the services that SP_1 relies on was stopped or did not attain the QoS target, the provision of the final service to the Customer would be compromised. The violation of just one between SLA_{21} and SLA_{31} may cause the violation of SLA_{1C}.

Figure 5 depicts a more complex scenario, resulting from the composition of *chains* and *forks* as depicted in the previous two figures. In this case, several Service Providers are involved in the provision of a service for the Customer and

Figure 5. A complex service-composition scenario - forks and chains

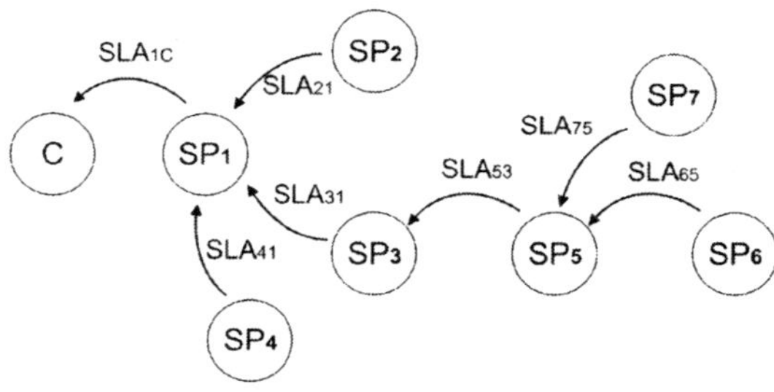

the probability of violation of the SLA regulating that service is very high. If, for instance, SP_6 for any reason was not able to honor SLA_{65}, such a violation might propagate through the chain of SLAs and might get to SP_1, thus affecting SLA_{1C}. The risk of violation is high not only for the SLAs in the chain that links SP_6 to C, but also for the rest of the SLAs.

We may conclude that in a service composition tree, the "breaking off" of an edge (SLA) linking any two nodes (service providers) may propagate throughout the tree affecting any other edge. As long as an SLA is a static and inflexible contract that regulates a transaction between two parties, the delivery of a service in service-composition scenarios involving multiple one-to-one SLAs among parties has a few chances to be successfully carried out. Furthermore, given the number of Service Providers and SLAs involved in the scenario, any single request of improvement of the quality of the service coming from the Customer has chances to be accommodated only if it is possible to modify on-the-run the SLAs signed by the involved parties. Summarizing, the main reason for a Service Provider to terminate an SLA is its inability to provide a service sustaining the QoS levels that are promised in the SLA. Therefore, there is a need for a flexible mechanism enabling the run-time re-negotiation of the guarantees on the QoS once violations on such guarantees are expected to occur. On the other hand, a mechanism that permits the re-negotiations of the guarantees on the QoS would also enable Service Providers and Service Customer to respectively offer and ask for upgrade or downgrade of the performance of the service provided at run-time. A new concept of SLA must be adopted: it should be a dynamic contract capable of reacting and adapting to changes in the context it works on. A high degree of flexibility is needed in order to reduce, during the provision of the service that the contract applies to, any possible risk of violation of the QoS guarantees agreed by the parties at the time of the contract sign.

We remark that in service composition scenarios there are several actors, in the dual role of provider and consumer of services, that stipulate one-to-one SLAs with each others. In devising a new dynamic concept of SLA, we must take into account a list of requirements, which follows from the considerations made earlier:

- both of the parties (Provider and Consumer) should be allowed to ask for the modification of the SLA they are taking part in. Both of the parties, for different reasons, can be interested in asking for an upgrade or a downgrade of the quality level of the service being provided;
- an SLA is worth being modified only if the modification cost does not exceed the cost for the termination of the SLA and the creation of a new one (the cost parameter including both penalties and inconveniences);
- the SLA expiration time should be re-negotiable within given time boundaries. In fact, most of times there is a strong need, for either the Service Provider or the Service Consumer, to modify just the lifetime of an SLA: usually, a Consumer might want to ask for an extension of the SLA lifetime for his particular convenience; conversely, a Provider might want to ask for a shortening of the SLA lifetime (e.g., because of

a temporary resource shortage he needs to reduce the SLA lifetime);

- it should be stated whether both functional and non-functional terms, or just the non-functional terms, can be modifiable (or re-negotiable) at run-time;
- each re-negotiable term should be accordingly tagged;
- each re-negotiable term should expose a "modification window", i.e., a time range within the SLA life time inside which modification proposals can be accepted. This restriction is necessary to avoid that any party might ask for a modification of a negotiable term right after the sign of the SLA or right before its expiration time;
- the modification proposal should have a time-to-live, i.e., the party receiving a modification proposal must respond within a useful time, otherwise the proposal shall be considered withdrawn. This is to avoid that any party requesting for a modification might wait indefinitely for a response;
- for each re-negotiable term, the parties should agree about the maximum time lapse needed to put in force the modification of a given term, i.e., the time between when a modification proposal is issued and when the actual modification should (at latest) be carried out;
- if the parties start re-negotiating for any service term, the current SLA is enforced until the modification does not actually take place. The modification proposal, therefore, should specify when exactly the desired modification should occur.
- the parties should agree on the maximum number of modifications that a re-negotiable term can undergo at run-time, and on how frequently a term's modification can be invoked;
- the party receiving and accepting the modification proposal should receive some kind of reward. The form and amount of the reward, again, might be agreed by the parties at negotiation time, and might include, e.g., adjusting the penalties clause or the cost for the service provision.

As already said in Section 2, the most relevant work addressing this research topic is being carried out by the Grid Resource Allocation Agreement Protocol Working Group (GRAAP-WG) within the OGF. The GRAAP-WG is trying to enhance the WS-Agreement specification in order to account for (re)negotiations of SLAs (https://forge.gridforum.org/projects/graap-wg/). Nevertheless, the WS-Agreement standard, in its latest version, is still far from fulfilling the requirements listed above.

An SLA compliant to the current WS-Agreement specification is a rigid contract whose terms can not be modified during its life cycle. The protocol for the creation of a WS-Agreement is based on a very simple Request-Response interaction between the parties. In theory there is no upper bound to the response time of a WS-Agreement creation offer, thus the proposal originator, once issued the offer, either waits indefinitely for a response or decide to withdraw it. When a WS-Agreement has been created it can not be modified and is effective until all the activities related to the Agreement are finished or until one of the signing party decides to terminate it.

WS-AGREEMENT EXTENSION FOR DYNAMIC SLAS MANAGEMENT

In this section, focusing on the requirements previously discussed, an approach aimed to enhance the flexibility of the WS-Agreement is presented. The key idea of the approach (based on Di Modica et al., 2009), consists of integrating new functionality to the protocol that enable the parties involved in a scenario of service composition to re-negotiate the levels of quality of the services, and to modify the guarantee terms of the WS-Agreements while the services are being provided. The proposed protocol does not support the process for the re-negotiation of the QoS levels, but provides the means to adjust the terms of a WS-Agreement accordingly to the outcome of an eventual negotiation process. The main modification being introduced to the current specification concerns some integrations to the XML schema of the WS-Agreement and an enhancement of the protocol with new interactions for the run-time modification of the WS-Agreement.

Modification to the Agreement Schema

We believe that the parts of an SLA that might be modified at run-time, while preserving at the same time the nature of the SLA itself, are those concerning the guarantees on the Service Terms. Specifically, in an WS-Agreement document the terms susceptible of modification are the *Service Level Objectives (SLOs)* in the *Guarantee Terms* section. In particular, we have introduced a new concept of SLO that can be modifiable according to some rules that limit both the time interval of modifiability of the SLO and the number of modifications that the SLO can undergo. Such parameters, once agreed by the parties at signing time, can not be further modified during the WS-Agreement's lifespan. Instead, what can be modified at run-time is the very objective to achieve.

Below is reported an excerpt of the new WS-Agreement's XML schema showing the modifications that have been introduced.

```
<xs:element name="ModifiableServiceLe
velObjective"
 type="wsag:ModifiableServiceLevelObj
ectiveType"/>

<xs:complexType
 name="ModifiableServiceLevelObjecti
veType">
 <xs:sequence>
 <xs:element
name="ModificationWindow"
 type="xs:TimeWindowType"/>
 <xs:element name="MinModificationsTr
iggerTime"
 type="xs:PercentageType"/>
 <xs:element name="Slo"
 type="xs:SloType"
 maxOccurs="unbounded"/>
 </xs:sequence>
</xs:complexType>

<xs:complexType name="SloType">
 <xs:sequence>
 <xs:element name="Objective"
 type="xs:anyType"/>
 <xs:element name="ScheduledTime"
 type="wsag:PercentageType"/>
 </xs:sequence>
</xs:complexType>
  <xs:complexType
name="TimeWindowType">
 <xs:sequence>
 <xs:element
name="NotEarlierThan"
type="PercentageType"/>
 <xs:element
name="NotLaterThan"
type="PercentageType"/>
 </xs:sequence>
</xs:complexType>

<xs:simpleType name="PercentageType"
 <xs:restriction base="xs:integer">
<xs:minInclusive value="0"/>
<xs:maxInclusive value="100"/>
 </xs:restriction>
</xs:simpleType>
```

First of all, it is worth noticing that a WS-Agreement's XML document conforming to the current specification's WS-Agreement XML schema is conform to the new schema too. The novelties introduced do not prevent Service

Providers and Service Customers to stipulate WS-Agreements based on the old concept of un-modifiable SLO. At protocol design time our purpose was, in fact, to maintain the backward compatibility with the original specification. The rest of the modifications that have been introduced do not alter the original protocol's functionality, but rather integrate a new one.

The modifiable SLO is composed of three elements: *ModificationWindow*, *MinModificationsTriggerTime* and *Slo*. In particular, *ModificationWindow* represents the time lapse during which carrying out the modification of the SLO is allowed. The upper bound and the lower bound of the interval are expressed as a percentage of the entire life cycle of the Agreement, which spans from the time that the Agreement proposal is accepted to the Agreement's expiration time (which is specified by the parameter *expirationTime* in the Agreement document). With the *MinModificationsTriggerTime* element the parties agree on the minimum time lapse between two subsequent modifications to be carried out on a given SLO. It has a percentage type, and is to be meant as a fraction of the *ModificationWindow* interval. This value, as will be shown later, fixes the maximum number of modifications that can be carried out on an SLO.

The *Slo* term represents the scheduling of a modification of the service level objective. It is composed of the *Objective* element, which contains the specification of the new service level objective, and of the *Scheduled* element, of percentage type, from which it is possible to come to the scheduling time of the modification. The *Slo* term's maximum occurrence is unbounded. The first occurrence of this element, actually, represents the service level objective that the parties agreed upon when the Agreement was signed. All the subsequent occurrences represent the scheduling of modification on the service level objective agreed, from time to time, by the parties. Obviously, there can be no more occurrences than the maximum number of allowed modifications.

Let then T_a be the Agreement's life time. The instants of time T_{ne} and T_{nl} defining the time interval within which modifications can be carried out are defined as follows:

$$T_{ne} = NotEarlierThan * T_a \quad (1)$$

$$T_{nl} = NotLaterThan * T_a \quad (2)$$

Through the *Scheduled* element it is possible to derive the modification scheduling time:

$$T_{mod} = T_{ne} + Scheduled * (T_{nl} - T_{ne}) \quad (3)$$

The minimum time lapse between two subsequent modifications on a given SLO can be calculated in the following way:

$$T_{slot} = MinModificationsTriggerTime * (T_{nl} - T_{ne}) \quad (4)$$

From T_{slot} we can derive the the maximum number of allowed modifications:

$$MaxCount = 1 + (T_{nl} - T_{ne}) / T_{slot} \quad (5)$$

Figure 6 shows the timing for the modification process within the entire Agreement's life span. In this specific case, we have depicted two modifications that have been agreed at run-time by the parties, and have been scheduled at T^{I}_{mod} and T^{II}_{mod} respectively, being of course $T^{II}_{mod} - T^{I}_{mod} < T_{slot}$.

Figure 6. Modification process timing

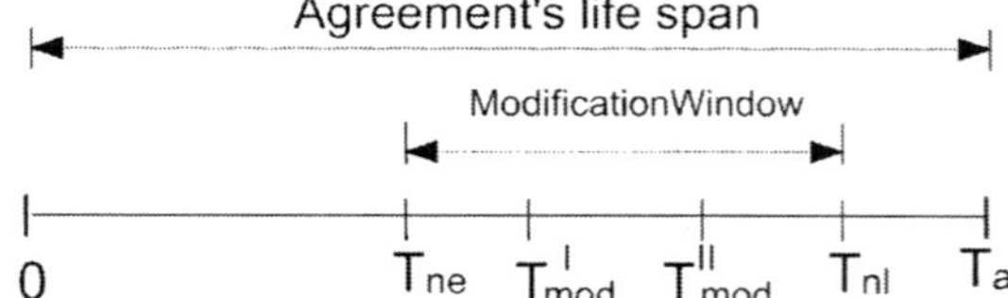

Enhancement of the Protocol

We have so far established the requirements and the criteria for the modification of an Agreement. Now we describe the means available to the parties of an Agreement to handle its modification.

The current WS-Agreement protocol provides only a single interaction. The Agreement Initiator (AI from now on) makes an Agreement offer and the Agreement Responder (AR from now on) is called to accept or reject it. We introduce a new form of interaction that enables both the parties to request modifications of the guarantees of an earlier signed Agreement. Either the AI or the AR, therefore, according to the above mentioned criteria, can make offers to modify one or more Agreement's SLOs; such modification becomes effective only after the other party has accepted the proposal.

We stress that after the issuing of an Agreement's modification offer, the service provisioning is not interrupted, nor the Agreement's monitoring is suspended. If the responding party accepts the proposal, the Service Provider will have to adjust the QoS to the new agreed levels; if the proposal is rejected, the service provisioning will continue according to the original QoS levels. The rejection of an Agreement's modification offer, in fact, does not invalidate the Agreement itself. The same applies to probable multiple modification offers: if the $(i+1)^{th}$ modification proposal is rejected, the guarantees agreed in the context of the ith proposal still apply.

In the following we detail the new Port Types and Operations that have been introduced for the integration of the described functionality.

First of all, in order to be able to accept modification offers, each party must provide the other with an ad-hoc contact point (or End Point Reference - EPR). We have introduced a new operation for the creation of Modifiable Agreements. Such an operation differs from the one provided in the current WS-Agreement specification (*CreateAgreement*) for the fact that the two parties exchange their EPRs that are specific for receiving WS-Agreement's modification proposals.

We thus have added the *CreateModifiableAgreement* operation to the "AgreementFactory" Port Type. Its signature is reported in Table 1.

Similarly, we added the *CreateModifiablePendingAgreement* operation to the "PendingAgreementFactory" Port Type.

Table 1. Signature of the CreateModifiableAgreement operation

wsag:CreateModifiableAgreement	
Input	**Result**
<wsag:CreateModifiableAgreementInput> <wsag:InitiatorAgreementEPR> <wsa:EndpointReference> wsa:EndpointReferenceType </wsa:EndpointReference> </wsag:InitiatorAgreementEPR> ? *<wsag:InitiatorAgModRequestEPR>* *wsa:EndpointReferenceType* *</wsag:InitiatorAgModRequestEPR>* <wsag:AgreementOffer> ... </wsag:AgreementOffer> <wsag:NoncriticalExtension> <xs:any>... </xs:any> </wsag:NoncriticalExtension> * <xs:any>... </xs:any> * </wsag:CreateModifiableAgreementInput>	<wsag:CreateModifiableAgreementResponse> <wsag:CreatedAgreementEPR> wsa:EndpointReferenceType </wsag:CreatedAgreementEPR> *<wsag:ResponderAgModRequestEPR>* *wsa:EndpointReferenceType* *</wsag:ResponderAgModRequestEPR>* <xs:any>... </xs:any> * </wsag:CreateModifiableAgreementResponse>

Let us focus back to a service composition scenario, like one of those depicted in Figures 4(a) and 5. Let us suppose that the AI acting on behalf of the Customer *C* has made his offer of Agreement's creation to the AR, which acts on behalf of SP_1, by invoking one of the two operations described above. In such a scenario this proposal triggers a number of consecutive proposals in a cascade fashion. If just one of this proposal got rejected, the original AI's proposal would be rejected. Let us suppose that all the Agreement's offers have been accepted, so that the AI gets its Agreement proposal accepted as well. From this moment on, each of the parties of this scenario is entitled to make a proposal of modification of the Agreements that it is involved in.

In the general case, for the provision of a given service a party signs as many Agreements as needed to provide that service. When that party for any reason wants to modify one of these Agreements, it first has to ask itself what the consequences of that modification might be, i.e., what that modification might bring for the rest of the Agreements in that scenario. After the modification of a given Agreement, in fact, the party might not be able to honor the rest of the Agreements signed with its chain's neighbors, and the neighbors, in their turn, might not be able to honor the Agreements signed with their own neighbors, and so on.

To make it clearer, let us refer to the tree structure depicted in Figure 5. Suppose that SP_5 wants to modify the Agreement signed with SP_3. It has first to verify whether, because of such a modification, it is no more able to honor both (or even one of) the Agreements respectively signed with SP_6 and SP_7. If SP_3 is not able to do that, then it has to choose between either to give up requesting the modification of the Agreement signed with SP_3 or checking whether SP_6 and SP_7 are willing in their turn to modify the Agreements that it would not be able to honor. Recursively, when receiving SP_5's proposal of Agreement modification, before accepting such proposal, SP_3 has to check whether, in the case that it decided to accept, it would still be able to honor the Agreement signed with SP_1. If not, it might test SP_1's willingness to modify that Agreement, and so on.

This is to say that a proposal of Agreement modification, wherever it is originated, can propagate throughout the Agreement's tree, theoretically affecting every Agreement. The acceptance of a given modification proposal is bound to the acceptance of other Agreements' modification proposals in the tree structure.

To support the dynamic modification of Agreements in the WS-Agreement specification, we introduce the "AgreementHandler" Port Type. This Port Type must be implemented by every party interested in taking part in the management of dynamic Agreements. Two operations are exposed through this Port Type: *ModifySLO* and *CondModifySLO*. The *ModifySLO* operation is defined as specified in Table 2.

The result parameter is just an acknowledgment for the reception of the modification offer; it does not represent the response to the offer itself. The input parameter SLOModificationOffer represents the offer of an Agreement where modifications have been introduced to any of the modifiable SLOs. The input parameter RequestExpirationTime represents the time-to-live for this specific request. The input parameter SLOModificationAcceptanceEPR represents the contact point of the party requesting the modification, to which the responding party will have to notify its decision of acceptance or rejection of the SLO modification proposal. To support such call-back mechanism, a new Port Type has been introduced. It has been named "SLOModificationAcceptance", must be implemented by both the parties and is in charge of receiving notifications for SLO modification proposals' acceptance or rejection. Two operations are exposed by this Port Type, respectively *Accept* and *Reject*. The signature of *Accept* is shown in Table 3.

By the time that the *Accept* operation is invoked, the modification of the SLO is effective,

Table 2. Signature of the ModifySLO operation

wsag:ModifySLO	
Input	Result
<wsag:ModifySLOInput> <wsag:SLOModificationAcceptanceEPR> <wsa:EndpointReference> wsa:EndpointReferenceType </wsa:EndpointReference> </wsag:SLOModificationAcceptanceEPR> <wsag:SLOModificationOffer> ... </wsag:SLOModificationOffer> <wsag:RequestExpirationTime> xs:dateTime </wsag:RequestExpirationTime> </wsag:ModifySLOInput>	<wsag:SLOModificationResponse> <xs:any>... </xs:any> * </wsag:SLOModificationResponse>

Table 3. Signature of the Accept operation

wsag:Accept	
Input	**Result**
<wsag:ModificationAcceptInput> <wsag:NoncriticalExtension/> * <xs:any>... </xs:any> * </wsag:ModificationAcceptInput>	<wsag:ModificationAcceptResponse> <xs:any>... </xs:any> * </wsag:ModificationAcceptResponse>

i.e., the Agreement has been modified and the Service Provider must adjust the QoS level to the new guarantee. As for the Reject operation, its signature is very similar to that of Accept, thus we omitted to report it.

For a better comprehension of the *ModifySLO* operation, in Figure 7 we report a very simple sequence diagram referred to the scenario depicted in Figure 4(a). The Service Provider SP_3 (or the AI on behalf of it) proposes SP_2 (or the AR on behalf of it) a modification of a SLO term of SLA_{32}. This proposal triggers other modification offers in the chain. In this case all the triggered offers are accepted, the original proposal is accepted as well. If just one of the involved actors rejected a modification offer, then the original proposal would not be accepted.

Let us now assume SP_1 be the party needing to modify the terms of one of its SLAs. This time the party originating the modification proposal has two SLAs with two different parties (two edges linking to two nodes). If for instance, according to the SP_1's needs, the modification of a given SLO in SLA_{21} would cause the need of a modification of a SLO in SLA_{1C}, SP_2 must check that both C and SP_2 agree with those modifications. Since the acceptance of one modification proposal is bound to the acceptance of the other, the ModifySLO operation is not appropriate to handle this situation. We need a *request-response-commit* interaction in order to first gather the willingness of both C and SP_2 to accept the proposed modifications, and then to confirm them (i.e., to commit the Agreements' modifications). To this end, to the "AgreementHandler" Port Type we have added the *ConditionalModifySLO* operation, whose input/result parameters' definition does not differ from those of the *ModifySLO* operation. The parties receiving a proposal of conditional modification, can respond by calling

Figure 7. Two-way interaction mechanism

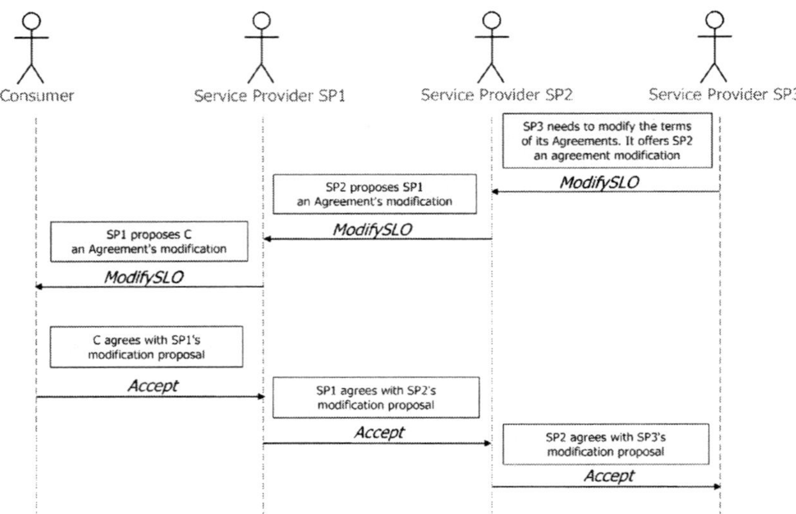

either a *ConditionalAccept* or a *ConditionalReject* (both of which have been added to the "SLO-ModificationAcceptance" Port Type) on the modification originator. The signature of *ConditionalAccept* is similar to that of *Accept*, but its meaning is different: the party invoking a *ConditionalAccept* communicates that it is just willing to accept the modification proposal, but a confirmation is still needed in order to consider the modification effective. When the modification proposal originator has gathered all the responses from the parties involved in the modification process, it can either confirm the commitment of the modifications, by calling the *Confirm* operation, or stop the entire modification process by invoking the *Cancel* operation (both the *Confirm* and the *Cancel* operations are accessible through the "SLOModificationAcceptance" Port Type). The signature of the *Confirm* operation is specified in Table 4.

In Figure 8 we show how the three-way interaction mechanism works.

CONCLUSION

Service level agreements are the most common mechanism used to establish agreements on the quality and the non-functional properties of services between a service provider and a service consumer. Today these SLAs are often created manually for each provisioned service. But, because of the dynamic nature of the requirements for service provisioning in modern service oriented architectures, new mechanisms are needed

Table 4. Signature of the Confirm operation

wsag:Confirm	
Input	**Result**
<wsag:ConfirmInput> <wsag:NoncriticalExtension/> * <xs:any>... </xs:any> * </wsag:ConfirmInput>	<wsag:ConfirmResponse> <xs:any>... </xs:any> * </wsag:ConfirmResponse>

Figure 8. Three-way interaction mechanism

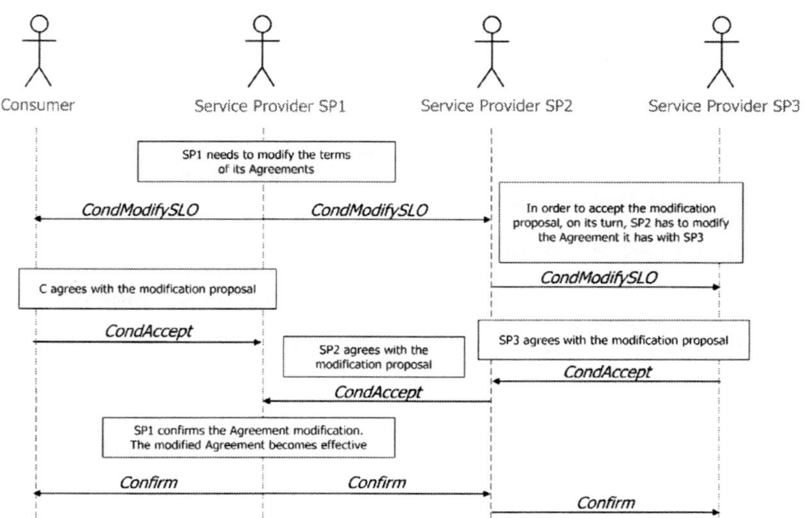

to dynamically create SLAs and to modify them at a later time.

This chapter has just focused on the requirements for the management of non-functional parameters arising in service composition scenarios. In such scenarios, it has been stressed the strong need for a mechanism enabling the management of flexible SLAs accounting for the dynamics of the interactions among the players (both providers and consumers of services). The state of the art for the discussed research topics has been thoroughly investigated. Finally, a framework for the management of dynamic SLAs has been presented.

Within the OGF, the GRAAP-WG is currently evaluating the opportunity of integrating re-negotiation into the WS-Agreement framework. This could foster the adoption of dynamic SLAs by the existing Grid systems. Recently, the concept of dynamic negotiation of QoS and SLAs has been embraced as one of the key points for cloud computing environments (Buyya et al., 2008), in which market-oriented resource management is necessary to regulate the supply and demand of resources.

REFERENCES

Andrieux, A., Czajkowski, K., Dan, A., Keahey, K., Ludwig, H., Nakata, T., et al. (2007). *Web Services agreement specification (WS-agreement)*. OGF proposed recommendation (GFD.107). Retrieved from http://www.ogf.org/documents/GFD.107.pdf

Angelov, S., & Grefen, P. (2001). B2B e-contract handling-a survey of projects, papers and standards. (Technical Report TR-CTIT-01-21), University of Twente.

Angelov, S., & Grefen, P. (2004). The business case for B2B e-contracting. In *Proceedings of the 6th International Conference on Electronic Commerce, (ICEC'04)*, Delft (The Netherlands).

Battre', D., Hovestadt, M., Kao, O., Keller, A. & Voss, K. (2007). Planning-based scheduling for SLA-awareness and Grid integration. In *Proceedings of The 26th Workshop of the UK Planning and Scheduling Special Interest Group (PlanSIG2007)*, Prague (Czech Republic).

Buyya, R., Yeo, C. S., & Venugopal, S. (2008). Market-oriented Cloud Computing: Vision, hype, and reality for delivering IT services as computing utilities, Keynote Paper. In *Proceedings of 10th IEEE International Conference on High Performance Computing and Communications (HPCC 2008)*, Dalian, (China).

Di Modica, G., Tomarchio, O., & Vita, L. (2009). Dynamic SLAs management in service oriented environments. *Journal of Systems and Software*, *82*(5), 759–771. doi:10.1016/j.jss.2008.11.010

Frankova, G., Malfatti, D., & Aiello, M. (2006). Semantics and extensions of WS-agreement. *Journal of Software*, *1*(1), 23–31. doi:10.4304/jsw.1.1.23-31

Joita, L., Rana, O. F., Chacn, P., Chao, I., & Ardaiz, O. (2005). Application deployment using Catallactic Grid middleware. In *Proceedings of the 3rd International Workshop on Middleware for Grid Computing (MGC05)*, Grenoble (France).

Keller, A. & Ludwig, H. (2003). The WSLA framework: Specifying and monitoring service level agreements for Web Services. *Journal of Network and Systems Management, Special Issue on e-Business Management, 11*(1).

Liu, Y., Ngu, A. H., & Zeng, L. Z. (2004). Qos computation and policing in dynamic Web service selection. In *WWW Alt. '04: Proceedings of the 13th international World Wide Web conference on Alternate track papers & posters*, (pp. 66–73), New York: ACM.

Ludwig, H., Dan, A., & Kearney, R. (2004). CREMONA: An architecture and library for creation and monitoring of WS-agreements. In *Proceedings of the Second International Conference on Service-Oriented Computing*, New York City.

Overton, C. (2002). On the theory and practice of Internet SLAs. *Journal of Computer Resource Measurement*, *106*, 32–45.

Papazoglou, M. P. (2003). Service-oriented computing: Concepts, characteristics and directions. In *Proceedings of 4th International Conference on Web Information Systems Engineering (WISE 2003)*, (pp. 3–12), Rome (Italy). IEEE Computer Society.

Papazoglou, M. P., & van den Heuvel, W.-J. (2007). Service Oriented Architectures: Approaches, technologies and research issues. *The VLDB Journal*, *16*(3), 389–415. doi:10.1007/s00778-007-0044-3

Sakellariou, R., & Yarmolenko, V. (2005). On the flexibility of WS-agreement for job submission. In *Proceedings of the 3rd International Workshop on Middleware for Grid Computing (MGC05)*, Grenoble (France).

Waeldrich, O., & Ziegler, W. (2006). *A WS-agreement based negotiation protocol*. Technical report, Fraunhofer Institute SCAI. VIOLA - Vertically Integrated Optical Testbed for Large Application in DFN. Retrieved from http://www.fz-juelich.de/zam/grid/VIOLA/

Ziegler, W., Waldrich, O., Wieder, P., Nakata, T., & Parkin, M. (2008). Considerations for negotiation and monitoring of service level agreements. (Technical Report TR-0167, CoreGRID).

Chapter 3
Quality of Service Monitoring, Diagnosis, and Adaptation for Service Level Management

Guijun Wang
Boeing Research & Technology, USA

Changzhou Wang
Boeing Research & Technology, USA

Haiqin Wang
Boeing Research & Technology, USA

Rodolfo A. Santiago
Boeing Research & Technology, USA

Jingwen Jin
Boeing Research & Technology, USA

David Shaw
Boeing Research & Technology, USA

ABSTRACT

A key requirement in Service Level Management (SLM) is managing the Quality of Services (QoS) demanded by clients and offered by providers. This managing process is complicated by the globalization and Internet scale of enterprise services and their compositions. This chapter presents two contributions to the QoS management task for SLM. First, instead of considering monitoring as an isolated service, it incorporates a monitoring service as an integral part of a comprehensive QoS management framework for SLM. Second, it includes a diagnosis service as an integral part of the QoS management framework. Using the data fed from monitoring service, diagnosis service detects system condition changes and reasons about the causes of detected degradation in networked enterprise system. With condition detection and situation understanding, the QoS management framework can then proactively activate adaptation mechanisms to maximize the system's ability to meet QoS contract requirements of concurrent clients. Using this framework, enterprise systems can provide real time automated QoS management to optimize system resources in meeting contract requirements. This approach is validated using QoS management services integrated in a publish/subscribe style of SOA. Benefits of QoS monitoring, diagnosis, and adaptation services for responsiveness SLM are demonstrated via experiments.

DOI: 10.4018/978-1-60960-493-6.ch003

INTRODUCTION

Traditionally, Service Level Management (SLM) relies on human analysts using monitoring tools (e.g., Microsoft SMS) and system management tools (e.g., HP OpenView). When enterprise services are interconnected as networked services in a Service Oriented Architecture (SOA) (Papazoglou & Georgakopoulos 2003), SLM becomes a complex process because of the dynamic, flexible, and compositional natures of SOA and the globalization of enterprise services. Globalization involves not only inter-enterprise collaboration and enterprise computing virtualization (e.g., grid computing), but also diverse physical locations of worldwide clients and computing systems. Global outsourcing adds additional demands for an integrated and comprehensive SLM framework. Instead of monitoring and reporting, this framework must establish service level agreements (SLA), monitor the execution of SLAs, and adapt autonomously whenever necessary to meet the constraints in SLAs. It will relieve human analysts from tedious repetitive work and let them focus on decision making.

A key requirement in SLM is managing the Quality of Services (QoS) demanded by clients and offered by providers in the SLAs. QoS management is critical for service-oriented enterprise architectures because services have different QoS characteristics and their interactions are dynamic and loosely coupled. In order to satisfy various QoS requirements from concurrent clients, QoS management in the networked enterprise systems needs to optimize system resources and activate computing mechanisms. These QoS requirements are expressed in terms of QoS characteristics such as performance, reliability, timeliness, and security. An integrated QoS management framework is desirable to provide comprehensive end-to-end QoS support in a consistent and coordinated fashion across all layers of enterprise systems, ranging from enterprise policies, applications, middleware platforms, and down to network layers. Under such an integrated QoS management framework, enterprise systems can bring policy management, SLA QoS contract management, monitoring and diagnosis, system management, resource management, and adaptations together for an autonomic SLM solution.

The publish/subscribe style of SOA has been widely adopted in the industrial and government enterprise systems. Examples include stock market applications using TIBCO publish/subscribe technology and the Joint Battlespace Infosphere concept well recognized in the US Air Force community (Combs, Hillman, Muccio & McKeel, 2005). In this chapter, we use the publish/subscribe style of SOAs to illustrate our QoS monitoring, diagnosis and adaptation approach. Specifically, different clients (publishers and subscribers) may have different QoS requirements in terms of performance, reliability, timeliness, and security. For instance, some publishers may have higher priority than others and may require their message deliveries to be guaranteed with correct ordering in faster response time. Similarly, some subscribers may be more critical than others and thus require shorter delays in receiving messages. Accordingly, the service provider, also called Information Broker or simply Broker in the following, must provide QoS guarantees to its publisher and subscriber clients. Clients and the Broker negotiate for mutually acceptable QoS contracts. The Broker must monitor not only the service levels agreed on in the contracts, but also the system health conditions of the server node, the network, and the client nodes. When contracts are violated or when contracts cannot continue to be honored due to system degradation, the Broker must also activate adaptation mechanisms to respond to these changes.

In this chapter, we present a policy based QoS management framework and its component services for SLM. This framework consists of QoS management services, including admission control, prognosis, resource management, monitoring, diagnosis, and adaptation. It uses policies to determine appropriate mechanisms, parameters and processes used in these component services. This framework is validated in a publish/subscribe style of SOAs, where publishers publish messages to one or more topics and interested parties subscribe to messages of certain topics. Publication and subscription are completely decoupled through the Information Broker which provides common services to both publishers and subscribers. These common services include discovery, registration, security, persistence, filtering, fusion, distribution, publication, and subscription as well as QoS management.

This chapter contributes to the QoS management for SLM in two aspects. First, the comprehensive QoS management framework incorporates enterprise system monitoring service with other interrelated enterprise infrastructure services, instead of considering monitoring in isolation. This enables automated QoS management using the real time monitoring information and reduces manual actions and human workload in SLM. The second contribution is the incorporation of a diagnosis service into the QoS management framework. The diagnosis service uses reasoning models and techniques to detect any condition changes and reasons about their causes in the networked enterprise system. With condition change detection and situation understanding, enterprise systems can proactively activate adaptation mechanisms to maximize the system's ability to meet QoS contract requirements of concurrent clients. This QoS management framework has been prototyped and validated via experiments.

The rest of the chapter is organized as follows. Section 2 introduces our policy based QoS management framework for SLM. Section 3 presents the monitoring approach; Section 4 focuses on the diagnosis approach; and Section 5 details the adaptation approach, all in our QoS management solution. Section 6 describes a case study using our prototype systems and reports some test results. Section 7 discusses some selected related work. Finally, Section 8 concludes with brief discusses on promising future works.

QoS MANAGEMENT FRAMEWORK AND ARCHITECTURE FOR SLM

Our QoS management framework (Wang, Chen, Wang, Fung, & Uczekaj, 2004; Wang et al., 2005) for SLM is developed based on key concepts in ISO (ISO/IEC, 1998, 1999; ISO/IEC JTC1/SC21, 1997), W3C (W3C, 2003), and OMG standards (OMG, 2003, 2004). A central concept in our framework is the QoS contract, which is a mutual agreement between the service requestor (called client hereafter) and the service provider (called server hereafter) on the guaranteed levels of various QoS characteristics. When a client first contacts a server, it specifies its requirements in terms of a set of QoS parameters. The server then consults policies to negotiate with the client for a QoS contract and allocate resources for supporting the agreed level of service. Since then, all client requests will be associated with a valid contract, and the server needs to provide the services at the agreed quality level. When no explicit QoS requirements are requested, a best-effort contract is used by default to provide services in a basic best-effort paradigm without any QoS measures.

We take an end-to-end integrated QoS management approach. By end-to-end, we mean both vertically from application systems to middleware to operating system down to the hardware, and horizontally between two end systems across the network in a distributed computing environment. Figure 1 illustrates our layered framework to achieve the end-to-end integration. On each host system, our QoS management service manages resources within the middleware and instructs the lower layer (network transport) to select appropriate QoS support, in order to provide QoS guarantees to applications on the upper layer. In addition, QoS management services on different host systems communicate with each other

Figure 1. End-To-End QoS management framework

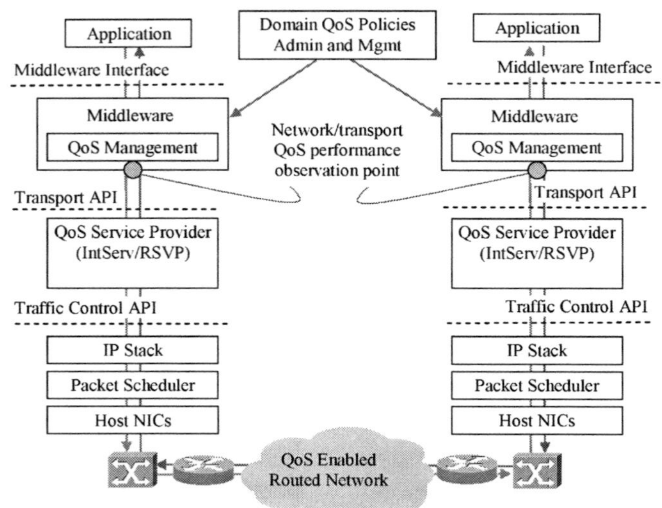

to orchestrate distributed resource management and collaborations between different QoS mechanisms.

Our integrated QoS management architecture implementing this framework consists of component services, their interactions, and interfaces with external services such as real-time host and network condition monitoring through Commercial Off-The-Shelf (COTS) monitoring tools as shown in Figure 2. Key component services include *QoS Manager, Establishment Service, Policy Manager, Resource Manager, Prognosis Service, Operation Service, Maintenance Service, Monitoring Service, Diagnosis Service* and *Adaptation Service*. Among these components, the *QoS Manager* is the orchestrator of overall QoS provision system. When a client initiates a QoS request to service provider, The *QoS Manager* triggers the *Establishment Service* with a QoS message that contains the QoS request and tries to establish a service contract with the client. The *Establishment Service* in turn consults with the *Policy Manager*, the *Resource Manager* and the *Prognosis Service* respectively, and returns a QoS contract to the *QoS Manager* if the service request can be met, based on whether or not the policies allow the level of requested service, resources are sufficient to meet the QoS request, and it is forecasted that there will not be future problems once the service is provided. The *QoS Manager* then triggers the *Operation Service* to start providing the service to the client. It also passes the QoS contract and operation context back to the client as their mutual service level agreement. The *Operation Service* is coupled with the *Monitoring Service* and the *Maintenance Service*, which keep aware of the system health condition and help provide a reliable service environment to meet the service level agreement.

The *Monitoring, Diagnosis* and *Adaptation* services are integral parts of the end-to-end QoS management framework. The role of the *Monitoring Service* is to monitor and aggregate QoS parameter values. It registers condition predicates with the *Diagnosis Service*, which notifies it when changes in the condition of the system cause certain predicates to become true. The *Diagnosis Service* is a vital service that uses formal reasoning models such as causal networks or Bayesian networks to aggregate low-level system signals into attributes that reflect current system conditions. It takes real-time inputs from monitoring

Figure 2. Integrated QoS management architecture and services

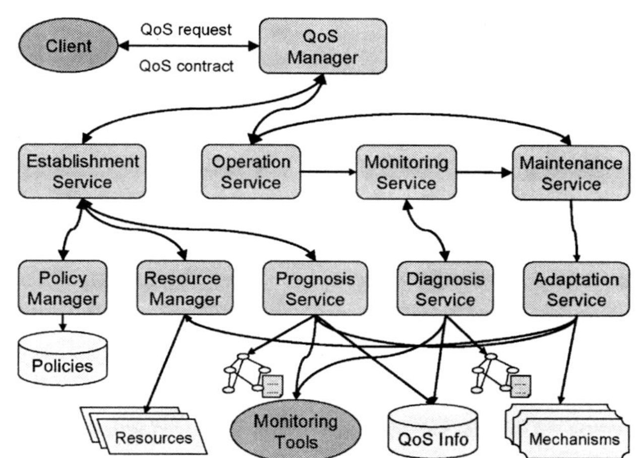

tools, aggregates data on the fly, and stores the data in a repository. It also evaluates any predicates registered on the monitored attributes when values of these attributes change, and sends notifications to the *Monitoring Service* when the registered conditions are satisfied. When the *Monitoring Service* receives the notifications, it updates the corresponding data in the *Maintenance Service*, which in turn activates some predefined adaptation mechanisms to address the situation through the *Adaptation Service*.

This QoS management architecture and their services have been implemented and integrated with several middleware platforms for service-oriented enterprise systems. For example, we have implemented and incorporated QoS management architecture and services to a publish/subscribe type of middleware, Infosphere, where one or more Information Brokers provide information collection, fusion, and dissemination for publishers and subscribers.

Figure 3 shows the role of QoS management and key services in a service provider, namely, Broker. Note that some component services interact closely with the host Broker service. For example, the *Resource Manager* manages resources that are in the Broker and the Adaptation mechanisms can change the status or sometimes the control flow of the Information Broker too.

In the following three sections, we describe in detail the Monitoring, Diagnosis, and Adaptation services. We then present a case study on these services using our prototype implementation and reports some test results that demonstrate the benefits of integrating these services in a comprehensive QoS management framework and its realization architecture.

Figure 3. Integration of QoS management architecture and services in infosphere services

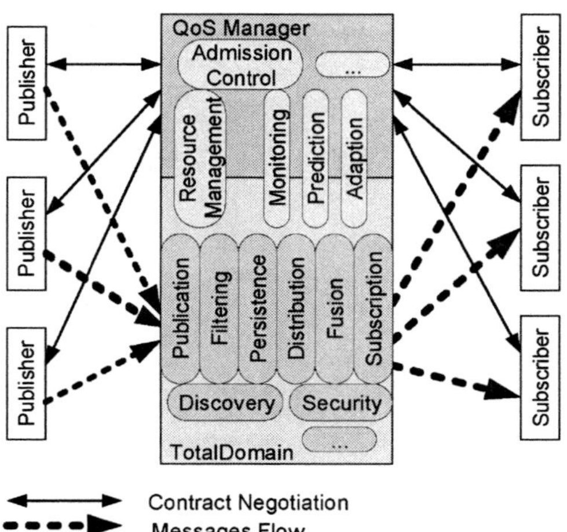

MONITORING APPROACHES IN QoS MANAGEMENT

The *Monitoring Service* is responsible for collecting statistics relating to system resource levels (e.g., current CPU utilization), application health status (e.g., a client application is slow in responding), and the clients' adherence to the QoS parameters in their contracts (e.g., volume rate exceeds upper bound). It provides input for other services, in particular the *Diagnosis Service* and the *Adaptation Service* for the QoS management system to understand the situation and determine whether and how to take actions in enforcing QoS contracts.

We use two types of monitoring approaches, namely, active reporting and passive polling. Correspondingly, communications between the monitored applications and the monitoring modules fall into two categories: proactive and passive. In the proactive style, the applications actively produce QoS related data and report them to the monitoring module. In this case, applications need to interface with the monitoring module. Hence legacy applications need to be refactored to support the monitoring task. In the passive style, applications passively wait for the monitoring modules to poll for QoS parameters. In this case, applications can be unaware of the monitoring module while the monitoring modules act as normal clients as far as the applications are concerned. Hence, legacy applications can be kept intact and treated as black boxes.

In Figure 4, the QoS monitor, shown as QoSM in the figure, is the monitoring module in the reporting approach that accepts information from the proactive applications. The directed arcs from the proactive applications to the QoSM indicate that the communication is one-way: from applications to the monitoring agent. The QoS prober, shown as QoSP in the figure, is the monitoring module in the probing approach that aggregates the acquired information from the applications. The bi- directional arc between the QoSP and the applications indicates that the communication is two-way: the QoSP sends the queries to the applications and then receives the answers from the applications.

Figure 4 also shows the high-level design of our QoS monitoring architecture in a typical

Figure 4. QoS monitoring architecture

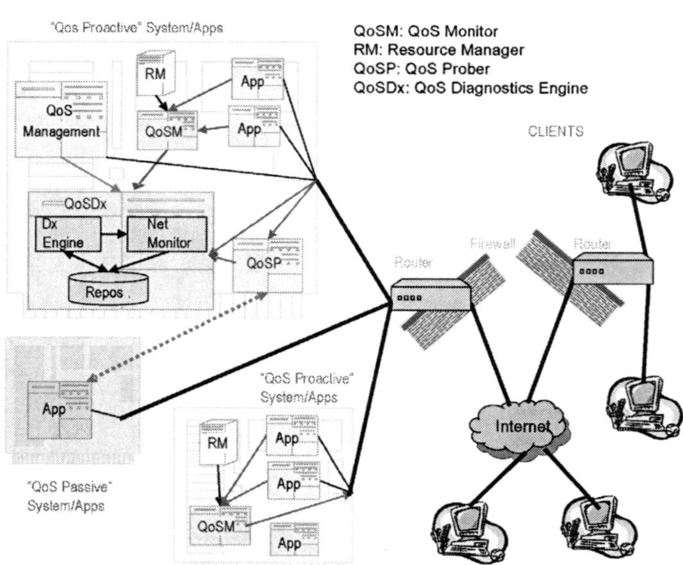

business-to-business Web service system. The monitored applications run on several machines connected by network segments. The segments are separated by firewalls into an enterprise service part (intranet) and an external client part (extranet). The clients access the services provided by the Web applications hosted within enterprise intranet through the Internet. In this case, the QoS monitors can be used to collect most of the QoS related parameters at the server side, and the QoS probers can be used for estimating the network packet delay and the network throughput between the server and the clients.

More specifically, the following components are needed to jointly provide the QoS monitoring capabilities.

- A set of resource monitors (shown as RM in Figure 4) which collect QoS performance data on the host machines and proactively send them to the corresponding QoS monitoring agents;
- A set of QoS monitoring agents which collect, aggregate, and process QoS related data produced by the resource monitors or the QoS proactive applications and send the processed information to the QoS diagnosis module (shown as QoSDx in Figure 4) for further analysis. The diagnosis approaches will be described in the next section.
- A set of QoS probing agents which periodically check the client health status and measure network traffic characteristics such as packet delay and throughput. They provide the processed QoS related information to the QoS diagnosis module in two modes. One is periodic mode, where a QoS prober sends the QoS information at a rate specified by the QoS diagnosis module; The other is on-demand mode, where a QoS prober only sends the QoS information to the QoS diagnosis module in response to the request from the module.

The *Monitoring Service* uses these components to monitor the QoS performance data related to system resources in host machines, networking elements and application status. For example, QoS monitor can be used to collect most of the QoS performance data within the host machines and the server applications, while QoS prober can be used to gather the perceived values of the transmission delay and the network throughput between the server application and the clients, e.g., between the Broker and the publishers or subscribers. In addition, more and more Commercial-Off-The-Shelf (COTS) tools have been adopted by enterprises to monitor the performance of Web services, networks, and computing resource utilization. These tools often use a non-intrusive passive polling approach without modifying the monitored entities. Our QoS monitoring architecture integrates these COTS monitoring tools in order to leverage their capabilities.

DIAGNOSIS APPROACHES IN QoS MANAGEMENT

The *Diagnosis Service* is responsible for detecting and isolating the most likely cause of any anomalous parameter values. It receives statistics on real-time raw system and network parameters from the *Monitoring Service* and makes diagnosis. The main use of QoS diagnosis is to find the root causes of degraded system performance, based on the network traffic measurements and the QoS related information produced by the QoS monitoring agents and the QoS probing agents. In addition, it stores these QoS information and analysis results into a repository for future retrievals by other relevant services such as the *Prognosis Service*. The diagnosis results are presented to other components of the QoS management framework through the *Monitoring Service* for further actions.

We take a model-based approach for QoS diagnosis. In particular, we use graphical models, specifically, causal networks, as our reasoning engine. Causal networks (Darwiche, 1995; Provan & Chen, 1999) are directed acyclic graphs, in which nodes represent variables of interest and arcs represent causal-effectual relationships between the variables. In the publish/subscribe paradigm, a node can be a publisher client, a subscriber client, an application, a publishing channel, etc. The arcs between nodes usually follow the information flow stream. For example, a message flows from its publisher to the publishing channel and ultimately to some subscribers. Therefore, there might be an arc from the publisher to the publishing channel, and arcs from the publishing channel to each of the subscribers.

Besides the graphical structure, a causal network also consists of a set of decision rules in if-then format to represent more specific dependence relationships between two connected nodes. For example, if a publisher is slow, all the subscribers that have subscription with this publisher must be slow in terms of message reception. Such condition-specific dependencies are encoded locally with individual nodes using the if-then rules.

A model-based reasoning mechanism is then applied on the causal network models to infer the diagnosis results given different evidence findings provided by the *Monitoring Services*. For the output, causal networks use a logical form (either in the conjunctive normal form or the disjunctive normal form) to represent the diagnosis results. Such results can then be used to evaluate, in a straightforward way, the logical predicates registered by *Monitoring Service* on system resource and contract health status, based on the diagnosis results.

Figure 5 shows an example of causal network models that used in QoS *Diagnosis Service*. It includes two computing machines (represented by Node_1 and Node_2 on the left), one runs an Information Broker and QoS prober and the other runs two publishers and two subscribers (represented by the six nodes to the right of the 2 machine nodes). Clearly, the status of each application (Broker, prober, publisher or subscriber) depends on the status of its host machine. The two subscribers each subscribes to both publishers. This is captured by the two publishing channels (represented by the Chan1Pub21 and Chan1Pub22 nodes) and the four specific connections (represented by the Chan1Pub21Sub21, Chan1Pub21Sub22, Chan1Pub22Sub21 and Chan1Pub22Sub22 nodes). The connection status depends on both the client (publisher or subscriber) status and the Broker status. In addition, the connection status also depends on the network (represented by Net1 node) status. The QoS prober probes all publishers and subscribers (represented by Pub21Probed, Pub21Probed, Sub21Probed and Sub22Probed). The probed node status depends on the status of the prober, the client and the network.

In general, each node in this example model has some input, output and mode attributes. The set of input and output attributes depends on the connections between nodes. The mode attribute usually indicates the health status of the node. For instance, a client node can have the mode of being normal, slow, or down; a system component can have a normal mode and a failed mode.

When an abnormal event occurs, the observed evidence is fed into the diagnostic model. The states of the involved nodes, typically the input and output attributes of the nodes in causal networks, are set accordingly. Then the reasoning algorithm is triggered to infer the root causes of the event based on the knowledge that has been encoded in the model, both in graph structure and in the decision rules. An example of the root cause can be the failure of network or the Broker. If a predicate (registered by the *Monitoring Service*) is evaluated to be true using the diagnosis result, the *Diagnosis Service* will raise an alarm to the *Monitoring Service* and pass the results over immediately. The *Monitoring Service* then informs the *Maintenance Service* which in turn triggers appropriate adaptation mechanisms to rescue the current situation through the *Adaptation Service*.

Thanks to the causal network model-based approach for diagnosis, partial inference can be

Figure 5. An example of causal network model for qos diagnosis

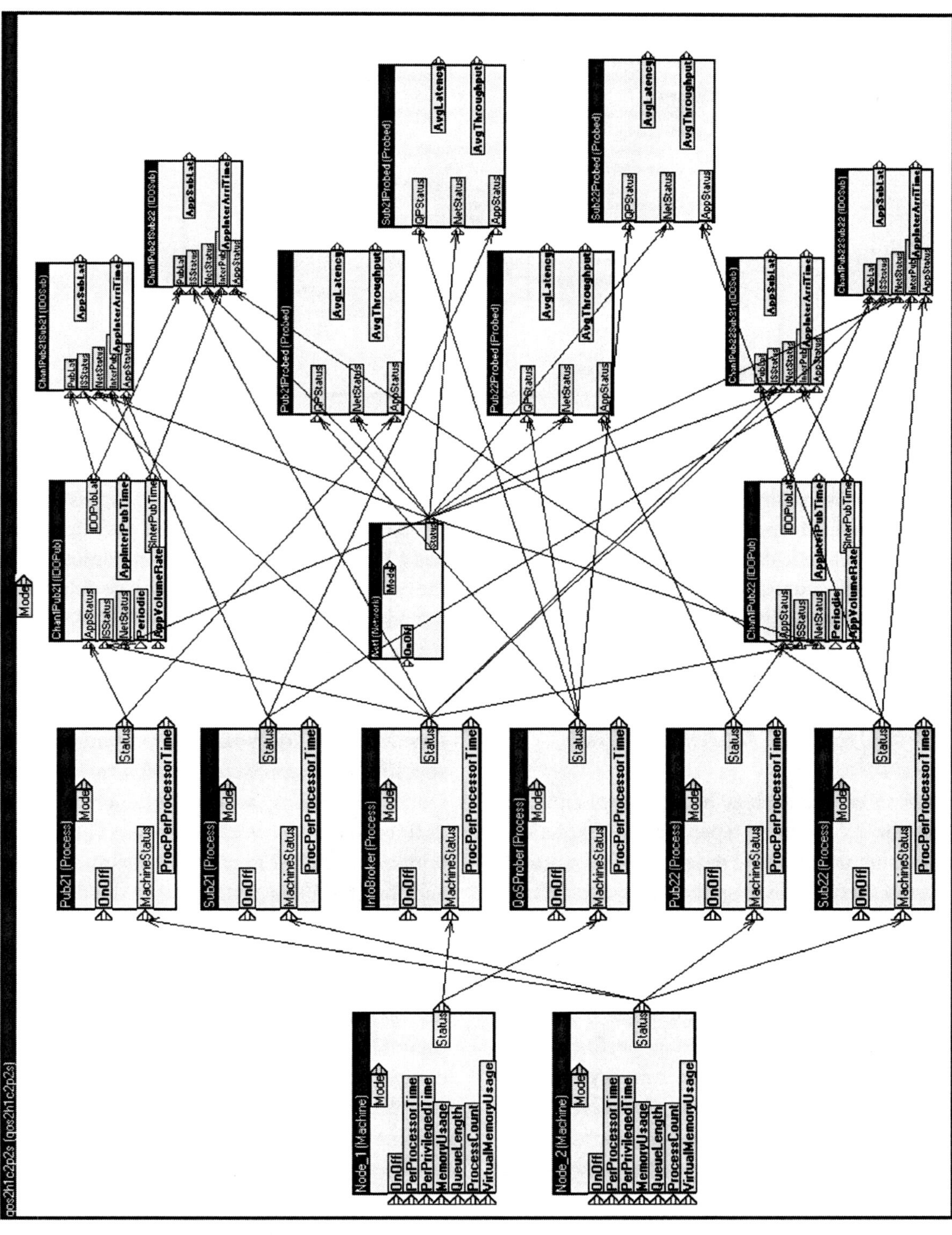

Figure 6. A snippet of the XML configuration for registering a predicate

```
<monitoring-service
    class="com.....MonitoringService">
  <monitor name="monitor"
           class="com.....DiagnosisMonitor" ... >
    <target
       predicate="Pub21Probed.AvgLatency==″long"′>
      <action
         class="com.....AdaptationAlertClientStatus">
        <parameter value="Pub21"
             type="java.lang.String" />
        <parameter value="slow"
            type="java.lang.String" />
        <parameter value="Pub21"
            type="java.lang.String" />
        <parameter value="Node_2"
            type="java.lang.String" />
      </action>
    </target>
  </monitor>
</monitoring-service>
```

performed even when the evidence is incomplete. In practice, observations are often limited, and the initial diagnosis results may be ambiguous to make a deterministic decision. As more and more evidences get accumulated, false causes can be ruled out gradually, leading to the discovery of root causes eventually.

CONFIGURABLE ADAPTATIONS

Depending on the system health status and the causes for its changes, appropriate adaptation mechanisms are triggered proactively to improve the system performance under the constraints of concurrent QoS contracts. When the *Monitoring Service* and the *Diagnosis Service* report abnormal events, the QoS *Maintenance Service* instructs the *Adaptation Service* to take appropriate actions accordingly to maintain system performance. The adaptation mechanisms are predefined and configurable to different situations. The system configuration defines system-resource-related predicates and corresponding adaptation mechanisms; the policy defines contract-related predicates and their corresponding adaptation mechanisms.

Figure 6 shows an example adaptation mechanism in a system configuration. In this example, the predicate of interest is that the client *Pub21* has a long average delay in communicating with the probing agent. When the average delay is long, the adaptation mechanism to call is *AdaptationAlertClientStatus*, which is implemented as a Java class. Also defined are the four parameter values that are used with the *AdaptationAlertClientStatus* function. Note that the adaptation mechanisms are specified in the context of the *Monitoring Service*. Other monitoring related parameters are also defined in the *Monitoring Service*. These include window size used to calculate the average value and threshold that distinguishes the delay being long or short.

Typically, the coordinator between the *Monitoring Service* and the *Adaptation Service* is the *Maintenance Service*. The *Maintenance Service* maintains some vital QoS parameters for QoS contracts and QoS clients. It activates the *Adaptation Service* upon threshold crossings in those parameters. In the above example, when a client is observed to be slow in communication, the *AdaptationAlertClientStatus* function is called to set the client status to reflect the situation. The updated client status can be used for further ad-

Figure 7. A snippet of adaptation mechanism specification

```
<create name="threshold" type="element">
    <create name="name" type="attribute">
        <constant>threshold</constant></create>
    <create name="value" type="attribute">
        <constant>5120</constant></create>
    <create name="cross-up" type="element">
        <create name="action" type="attribute">
            <create name="class" type="attribute">
                <constant>com.....AdaptationCompressionII
                </constant>
            </create>
            <create name="parameter" type="element">
                <create name="value" type="attribute">
                    <constant>5120</constant></create>
                <create name="type" type="attribute">
                    <constant>java.lang.Long</constant>
                </create>
            </create>
        </create>
    ......
    </create>
</create>
```

aptation on resource reallocation or computing mechanisms.

For example, the Information Broker may ask a slow publisher to compress its message before publishing, or compress the message before sending it to a slow subscriber. Ideally, whether or not to actually perform the compression action depends on whether the compression can help reduce the entire end-to-end delay. To balance the compression and decompression time versus the transmission time, we can develop a formula to estimate the compression benefit based on our empirical test data. In this formula, we can use message size and network throughput to estimate the message transmission time between the clients. We also need to take into account the compression and decompression time that is an extra computation overhead added to the clients when the compression adaptation is triggered. The current CPU utilization level is accounted for in the formula when determining if there is any benefit in applying the compression mechanism. It is only when the compression is beneficial for reducing the end-to-end delay based on balancing the compression/decompression time and network transmission time, that the compression adaptation mechanism is triggered in the appropriate situation. Otherwise, the message is sent out in its original format and size.

Figure 7 presents a policy snippet which specifies that the compression mechanism ("action") *AdaptationCompressionII* (implemented as a Java class) will be used on any messages that are larger than ("cross up") 5KB (threshold value). It is only when the message size is large enough that the compression mechanism is enabled. However, whether the compression action is eventually triggered or not is determined by the client status and the internal calculation of *AdaptationCompressionII* function.

When the client is in a normal state, the compression adaptation does nothing. Once the client exhibits slowness, the registered predicate in the system configuration, e.g. *Pub21Probed.AvgLatency=="long"*, becomes true. The *Diagnosis Service* raises the corresponding alarm to the *Monitoring Service*, which in turn interacts with the *Maintenance Service* to set the corresponding data flag, e.g. *clientStatus = slow*. When the client status is slow and the message size is large, the *AdaptationCompressionII* adaptation mechanism is run to calculate the benefit of compression. Only if there is a benefit will the compression actually take place. Once the client goes back to a normal state, the *AdaptationCompressionII* adaptation mechanism skips everything and essentially turns off the compression.

A CASE STUDY AND TEST RESULTS

In this section, we present a case study with an example application scenario to demonstrate the benefits of the integrated QoS management with monitoring, diagnosis and adaptation services. In the following, we describe the QoS management aspect of our publisher/subscriber prototype system, in particular, the monitoring, diagnosis and adaptation services for the end-to-end QoS in information processing and dissemination.

In our example, publishers send messages to the Information Broker on a specified channel with QoS requirements in terms of performance and reliability. The performance portion specifies its desired publishing volume rate and message payload size. The reliability portion specifies its required delivery guarantee (yes or no) and criticality level (Red, Yellow, or Green, where Red is most critical and Green is least critical). Similarly, subscribers register with the Information Broker for their interested channel with QoS requirements in terms of the two reliability parameters.

The QoS management framework incorporated in the Information Broker uses system configurations for the *Monitoring Service* to obtain client status from external QoS monitors (see Figure 6), and uses contract monitoring policies to configure a compression adaptation mechanism (see Figure 7), as discussed in Section 5. Specifically, the formula used to calculate the compression benefit is $s(1-r)/p-a(c+u)$, where s is the message size, r is the compression ratio, p is the throughput, $a\ (>=1)$ is an adjustable parameter defined in policy, c is the compression time and u is the decompression time. Here, r, c, and u are estimated by offline experiments on the compression methods, p is provided by *Monitoring Service*.

At run time, each client (publisher or subscriber) first negotiates with the QoS management framework incorporated in the Information Broker to obtain a QoS contract. This QoS contract includes both the agreed QoS requirements and the resource allocation, as well as monitoring and adaptation plans for maintaining the contract. The agreed QoS requirements might be different from the original proposed requirements by the client due to the runtime system resource constraints or business logics specified in the policies. For example, all "Combat" commands will have Red criticality while all "Reconnaissance" messages will have Green criticality.

The resource allocation plans characterize each type of Broker queues and threads allocated (exclusively or not) for each client. For example, Red clients will have dedicated queues while Green clients may share queues; clients with delivery guarantee will have larger queues than others, etc. The resource monitoring and adaptation plans specify the desired monitoring points and adaptation mechanisms to take when the monitored values (or their aggregations) cross some threshold values. Figure 8 shows part of the policy to create monitoring plans for triggering the compression mechanism (implemented by the *AdaptationCompressionII* Java class) when the predefined "payload-size" monitoring point on the "receiver" thread in the Broker detects its monitored value exceeds ("cross up") the upper bound ("threshold"), which is defined ("value") as twice the agreed payload size in the QoS contract. The receiver thread is a specific type of thread resource allocated for a publisher in the QoS contract. The Broker defines monitoring points for each type of resources or the whole system and provides implementation logic to actually monitor the corresponding values. The monitoring plan can target at the values or their aggregations (e.g., count, sum, or max).

Figure 8. A snippet of monitoring and adaptation plan

```
<create name="monitoring-points">
  <create name="monitoring-point">
    <create name="source"
type="attribute"><constant>receiver</constant></create>
    <create name="name" type="attribute"><constant>payload-
size</constant></…>
    <create name="facet"> <!-- payload size (default aggregation is
value) -->
      <create name="target" type="attribute"><varref name="payload-
size"/></…>
      <create name="threshold"> <!-- upper bound -->
        <create name="name" type="attribute"><constant>upper-
bound</constant></…>
        <create name="value" type="attribute">
          <function name="multiply">
            <varref name="payload-
size"/><constant>2</constant></function></…>
        <create name="cross-up">
          <create name="action" type="attribute">
            <constant>….AdaptationCompressionII</constant></create>
          <create name="parameter">
            <create name="value" type="attribute">
              <constant>5120</constant></create>
        </create>
      </create> …
    </create> …
  </create> …
</create>
```

After the contract is negotiated, it is maintained through the *Monitoring Service*, the *Diagnosis Service* and the *Adaptation Service*. When the communication with a publisher becomes slow (due to an emulated network stress loader in our experiment), the *Diagnosis Service* will find it out using the casual network with the inputs from installed (external) QoS probers, as discussed in Section 4. According to the system configuration in Figure 6, the *Monitoring Service* using the "*DiagnosisMonitor*" will evaluate the registered predicate and trigger the *AdaptationAlertClient-Status* mechanism, which in turn marks the client to be slow inside the Broker.

When a client becomes slow, key QoS parameters such as volume rate and delivery time in a contract may be violated. Therefore, some adaptation mechanisms need to be applied to correct the violation. If the slowness in transferring messages is caused by the slow network transmission (due to the network congestion introduced by other applications), instead of the slow processing speed in the client or the server host system (due to the fluctuating CPU load of concurrent applications), compression methods (appropriate for our experiments with text messages) can be used as adaptation mechanisms. Though compression adds extra overhead on computation, it may still be beneficial to overall end-to-end delay of message sending and receiving in our publish/subscribe message-based system, depending on message size, network throughput, and CPU utilization. In particular, when a large message is published, the "payload-size" monitoring point will detect the payload size cross the upper bound and trigger the *AdaptationCompressionII* mechanism, as specified in Figure 7. This *AdaptationCompressionII* mechanism will first check whether the communication with the client is slow. If so, it will calculate the benefit function to determine whether it is beneficial to compress the message before the publisher sends the message and decompress after the Broker or subscriber receives the same message.

We conducted test runs of these monitoring, diagnosis and adaptation services using our prototype system implemented in Java. The test runs were performed in a large enterprise intranet, with

Figure 9. Monitoring and diagnosis enable qos management to make intelligent adaptation decisions

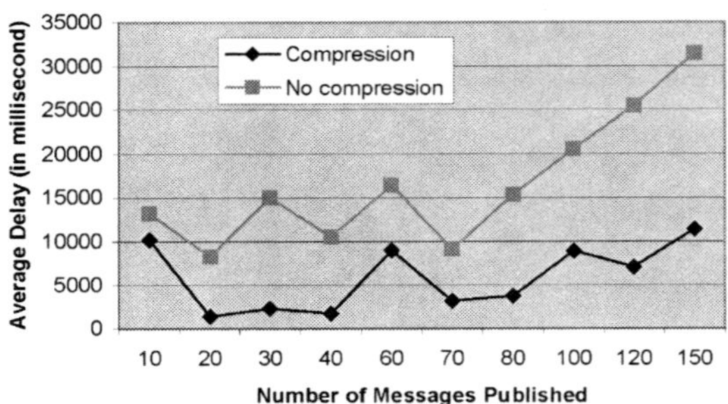

the Information Broker running on a desktop PC with Windows 2000 Pro on one campus and a publisher client and a subscriber client running on laptop PCs with Windows 2000 Pro on another campus. There are four routers between the two campuses, the network bandwidth is limited to 10Mbps due to the network settings for the client, and the network is shared with normal traffic in the enterprise. We ran two tests, one with the compression adaptation mechanism activated and the other without. In both tests, the publisher publishes messages of the same size and at the same rate. We recorded the average end-to-end delay for every 15 new messages published. The end-to-end delay of a message is measured as the time between the moment when the message is sent by a publisher and the moment when the same message is received by a subscriber.

Figure 9 shows that test difference between the end-to-end delays is significant in our tests. Typically the compression adaptation mechanism reduced the end-to-end delay by half or more. In addition, when the number of messages becomes large, the compression adaptation mechanism also helps to avoid unbounded growth in the end-to-end delay. We also tested this compression adaptation mechanism with multiple clients and different client / server deployment configurations and obtained similar results. Clearly, the monitoring, diagnosis and adaptation services provided situation awareness and proactive service contract maintenance. They enabled the QoS management system to make better use of resources, improved the system performance, responded to runtime situations as they occur, and achieved higher quality of service for concurrent contracts in an enterprise SOA.

RELATED WORK AND DISCUSSIONS

Traditional enterprise Service Level Management (SLM) approaches (Lewis & Ray, 1999) focused on service contract definition, monitoring and reporting. It is typically handled by enterprise system management tools (e.g., Microsoft's SMS, CA's Unicenter, Empirix's OneSight). These tools have been fragmented on market so far and have not yet integrated monitoring as part of a comprehensive QoS management framework such as the one we described in this chapter.

Recent work (Andrieux et al., 2007; Ludwig., Keller, Dan, King & Franck, 2003; Tosic, Pagurek, Esf, Patel & Ma, 2002), particularly from the Web service community, introduced standard languages to describe Service Level Agreements (SLAs) in generic senses. Our work presented in this chapter focused on the QoS aspects of publish/subscribe style of SOAs and provides specific parameters that can be used in the SLAs described by these standards.

Concepts and guidelines defined in specifications such as ISO/IEC QOS Framework (ISO/IEC, 1998) and RM-ODP (ISO/IEC JTC1/SC21, 1997) form the basis for the design and implementation of QoS management in networked enterprise architectures. For example, Aagedal and Milosevic (1998) presented a conceptual framework for modeling QoS in a command and control environment based on those QoS concepts defined in RM-ODP. OMG specifications (OMG, 2003, 2004) for real-time and enterprise systems provided conceptual framework for modeling QoS issues in enterprise systems and managing QoS in real-time systems. Our work shared a common root, but extended previous work with innovative features such as diagnosis.

Middleware QoS management research activities have been mostly around traditional middleware platforms such as CORBA and Java Messaging Service (JMS). Their real-time extensions add concepts such as Thread Pool, Scheduling Service and Predictable Memory Management to enable applications to manipulate some QoS parameters. For example, Quality Objects (QuO) (Krishnamurthy et al., 2001) is an extension to CORBA middleware with supports to QoS specification, measurement, and control. QuO consists of a Quality Description Language (QDL) for describing the QoS aspects of QuO applications, QuO Runtime Kernel, and Code Generator that weaves together QDL descriptions, the QuO kernel code and client code to produce a single application program. Monitoring, diagnosis and adaptation mechanisms can be injected into these platforms directly. For example, Scallan (2000) introduced four architectural components to monitor interactions among distributed components on CORBA platform: Profile for specifying interests, Probe to capture interested messages, Collector to aggregate data and Observer to respond.

Network QoS research has focused on providing prioritized transmissions of different types of data streams through labeling, scheduling, routing, and switching mechanisms (Wang, 2001). QoS management research for multimedia applications (Nahrstedt & Smith, 1995) extended traditional QoS research from the network communication area to the end systems (e.g., OS and devices) and applications. Application QoS requirements are described in terms of throughput, delay, and jitter. Resource management at the OS layer provides the scheduling, error-recovery mechanisms, and buffers to satisfy application QoS requirements.

Monitoring multimedia networks post some special challenges as outlined in Tham, Jiang and Ko (2000). Tham et al. (2000) introduced Relevant Monitor scheme and its improved version for this task, where real-time flows are assigned to relevant monitors which are registered to name servers. QualProbes (Li & Nahrstedt, 2000) took a further step to model applications as a dependent tree of task flows. In this model, observers monitor resource availability and application-specific parameters, and configurators use rules and runtime inputs to control application behavior.

QoS management in task-oriented systems and network communications supports computational applications to get high-priority tasks done in a timely manner in distributed environments. QoS management for message-oriented enterprise systems, on the other hand, emphasizes quality attributes for message collection, processing, and dissemination. The W3C specification on Web Services Reliability (WS-Reliability) Version 1.0 (W3C, 2003) addresses the Reliability aspect of QoS management for SOAP-based messages in Web services. Reliable message delivery means the ability to ensure delivery of a message with the desired level of QoS. Three reliability characteristics are defined: Guaranteed Delivery, Duplicate Elimination, and Message Ordering. Along with this specification, a WS-Reliability XML schema is defined to represent reliable message QoS characteristics. These characteristics are used, and other QoS characteristics defined by similar studies can be used, in our QoS management framework.

Others pursued QoS in enterprise distributed systems from the perspective of modeling and model transformations (Jonkers, Iacob, Lankhorst & Straiting, 2005; Poernomo, Jayaputera & Schmidt, 2005). QoS properties such as timeliness are expressed as constraints associated with UML-based system design models. Design time QoS analyses are performed through the models and their transformations. Runtime instrumentation code such as monitoring can be generated from the models. Abstract models can be transformed to platform specific models using OMG's Model Driven Architecture approach. We believe the model transformation approach will be helpful and complementary to our integrated QoS monitoring, diagnosis and adaptation framework.

CONCLUSION AND FUTURE WORK

Enterprise services are increasingly interconnected as networked services in a service-oriented architecture. Service Level Management (SLM) of the enterprise services is becoming a complex problem and can no longer be efficiently handled by traditional monitoring and reporting or system management tools. This chapter presents a comprehensive QoS management framework and implementation architecture for SLM. The presented approach integrates monitoring, diagnosis, and adaptation in managing QoS in Service Level Agreement (SLA).

This chapter has described in detail the monitoring, diagnosis, and adaptation services in the QoS management architecture. The result is a robust QoS management solution for network centric distributed systems. The monitoring service collects vital system and application parameters in two ways, one based on probing and the other based on proactive reporting. Monitors and probes are deployed throughout the networked application environment. The monitoring service feeds data collected to the diagnosis service. The diagnosis service uses a model-based approach, in which the system is modeled as a causal network. The diagnostic model is domain specific and represents entities (e.g., a client, an application, or a host machine), their attributes and their cause-effect relationships. A generic reasoning engine aggregates data and makes diagnosis based on the diagnostic model. The ability to integrate not only monitoring but also diagnosis into the QoS management framework improves the performance and robustness of a large scale networked system. We demonstrate the effectiveness of our solution by integrating it into a publish/subscribe style of the service-oriented architecture. We present a case study and discuss some of our test results showing benefits of improved situation awareness and robust adaptation based on diagnosis results.

In the future, we plan to integrate our QoS management framework with other SLM components to provide a full SLM solution suite. We will start initially in the domain of Web services by leveraging many existing and emerging standards in service level offering, negotiation, agreements and management. Our framework currently supports creation, negotiation, cancellation, and termination of contracts regarding the QoS guarantee. The integration work will involve consolidation of these functions.

Another area of our future work is to apply our QoS management framework to other styles of SOAs. Although our framework was designed for the general SOAs from the beginning, the focus was on the publish/subscribe style of SOA. To support other SOA styles including the client server based Web services, we plan to reuse the current framework and adapt it to fit into the target computing environment. For example, we can reuse most of the component services including the Monitoring, Diagnosis and Adaptation Services, and develop resource management and adaptation mechanisms to address specific QoS concerns in a (client-server based) method invocation paradigm. Further along this line is to extend our framework to support the peer to peer SOA style.

ACKNOWLEDGMENT

This paper is extended and updated based on our paper presented at the IEEE 9th International Enterprise Distributed Object Computing (EDOC) conference, September 2005. We thank the anonymous reviewers for their invaluable feedback.

REFERENCES

W3C. (2003). Web Services reliability (WS-reliability version 1.0). Retrieved from http://sunonedev.sun.com/platform/technologies/ws-reliability.v1.0.pdf

Aagedal, J., & Milosevic, Z. (1998). Enterprise modeling and QoS for command and control systems. *The Second International Enterprise Distributed Object Computing Workshop*, IEEE, November 3-5, 1998, (pp. 88-101).

Andrieux, A., Czajkowski, K., Dan, A., Keahey, K., Ludwig, H., Nakata, T., et al. (2007). *Web Services agreement specification (WS-agreement)*. Open Grid Forum. March 14, 2007.

Combs, V. T., Hillman, R. G., Muccio, M. T., & McKeel, R. W. (2005). Joint Battlespace Infosphere: Information management within a C2 enterprise. *Proceedings of the 10th International Command and Control Research and Technology Symposium*.

Darwiche, A. (1995). Model-based diagnosis using causal networks. In *Proceedings of International Joint Conference on Artificial Intelligence (IJ-CAI-95)*, (pp. 211-219).

ISO/IEC. (1998). International Standard 13236: Information Technology-Quality of Service: framework, 1st ed.

ISO/IEC. (1999). Technical Report 13243: Information Technology-Quality of Service: Guide to methods and mechanisms, 1st ed.

ISO/IEC JTC1/SC21. (1997). Working draft for open distributed processing-reference model-Quality of Service.

Jin, J. & Nahrstedt, K. (2002). Classification and comparison of QoS specification languages for distributed multimedia applications. UIUC CS Tech Report, 2002.

Jonkers, H., Iacob, M., Lankhorst, M., & Straiting, P. (2005). Integration and analysis of functional and non-functional Aspects in model-driven e-service development. *Proceedings of IEEE International Enterprise Distributed Object Computing (EDOC) Conference*, Enschede, Netherlands, September 19-23, 2005.

Krishnamurthy, Y., Kachroo, V., Karr, D., Rodrigues, C., Loyall, J., Schantz, R., et al. (2001). Integration of QoS-enabled distributed object computing middleware for developing next-generation distributed applications. *ACM SIGPLAN Notices, 36*(8).

Lewis, L., & Ray, P. (1999). Service level management definition, architecture, and research challenges. *Proceedings of the Global Telecommunication Conference 1999 (Globecom '99)*, (pp. 1974-1978).

Li, B., & Nahrstedt, K. (2000). QualProbes: Middleware QoS profiling services for configuring adaptive applications. J. Sventek and G. Coulson (Eds.), *Middleware 2000*, (LNCS 1795), (pp. 256-272). Springer-Verlag.

Ludwig, H., Keller, A., Dan, A., King, R. P., & Franck, R. (2003). *Web Service Level Agreement (WSLA) language specification*. IBM.

Nahrstedt, K., & Smith, J. (1995) The QoS broker. In *IEEE Multimedia Magazine, 2*(1), 53-67.

OMG. (2003). UML profile for modeling Quality of Service and fault-tolerance characteristics and mechanisms, revised submission. Retrieved on May 4, 2003, from http://www.omg.org/

OMG. (2004). Data distribution service for real-time systems, formal. Retrieved December 2004, from http://www.omg.org/

Papazoglou, M., & Georgakopoulos, D. (2003). Service-oriented computing. *Communications of the ACM*, 25–28.

Poernomo, I., Jayaputera, J., & Schmidt, H. (2005). Timed probabilistic constraints over the distributed management taskforce common information model. *Proceedings of IEEE International Enterprise Distributed Object Computing (EDOC) conference*, Enschede, Netherlands, September 19-23, 2005.

Provan, G., & Chen, Y.-L. (1999). Model-based diagnosis and control reconfiguration for discrete event systems: An integrated approach. In *Proceedings of 38th IEEE Conference on Decision and Control*, (pp. 1762-1768).

Scallan, T. (2000). Monitoring and diagnostics of CORBA systems. *Java Developers Journal,* 138-144.

Tham, C., Jiang, Y., & Ko, C. (2000a). Monitoring QoS distribution in multimedia networks. *International Journal of Network Management*, *10*, 75–90. doi:10.1002/(SICI)1099-1190(200003/04)10:2<75::AID-NEM355>3.0.CO;2-#

Tham, C., Jiang, Y., & Ko, C. (2000b). Challenges and approaches in providing QoS monitoring. *International Journal of Network Management*, *10*, 323–334. doi:10.1002/1099-1190(200011/12)10:6<323::AID-NEM382>3.0.CO;2-K

Tosic, V., Pagurek, B., Esf, B., Patel, K., & Ma, W. (2002). Web Service Offerings Language (WSOL) and Web Service composition management. In *Proceedings of of the Object-Oriented Web Services Workshop at OOPSLA 2002*.

Wang, G., Chen, A., Wang, C., Fung, C., & Uczekaj, S. (2004). Integrated Quality of Service (QoS) management in service-oriented enterprise architectures. *Proceedings of the 8th IEEE International Enterprise Distributed Object Computing Conference*, IEEE CS Press, Monterey, CA, September 2004, (pp. 21-32).

Wang, G., Wang, C., Chen, A., Wang, H., Fung, C., Uczekaj, S., et al. (2005). Service level management using QoS monitoring, diagnostics, and adaptation for networked enterprise systems. *Proceedings of the 9th IEEE International Enterprise Distributed Object Computing Conference*, IEEE CS Press, Enschede, the Netherlands, September 2005, (pp. 239-248).

Wang, Z. (2001). *Internet QoS: Architectures & mechanisms for Quality of Service*. Morgan Kaufmann Publishers.

Chapter 4
Supporting Service Level Agreement with Service Discovery

Andrea Zisman
City University, UK

ABSTRACT

Service Level Agreement (SLA) has been used as an effective way to evaluate and enforce the quality of services and their providers. However, despite the development in the area, the creation, maintenance, and evolution of SLAs are not easy tasks. This chapter presents an approach to support the creation of SLAs during the development of service-based systems. Said approach is based on an iterative service discovery process, in which services that can provide the functionalities and satisfy properties and constraints of service-based systems during their design phase are identified and used to (re-)formulate service level agreements between services participating in the system, as well as the design models of these systems. The discovery process is based on service requests expressing structural, behavioral, and quality characteristics of the system being developed. These requests are matched against different types of service specifications. The information represented in the service specifications of the matched services is used to generate service level agreements and the design models of the service-based systems.

INTRODUCTION

An important aspect of service oriented computing is concerned with quality of services, which allows for the differentiation between similar services and the assurance that the services used in an application can support its characteristics. Service Level Agreements (SLA), i.e. contracts that exist between two or more parties regarding the consumption and provision of services, has

DOI: 10.4018/978-1-60960-493-6.ch004

been used as effective ways to evaluate the quality of the services and its providers. However, despite its importance and the development in the area (Comuzzi & Pernici, 2005; Debusmann & Keller, 2003; Garofalakis et al., 2006; Gimpel et al., 2003; Keller & Ludwig, 2002; Mahbub & Spanoudakis, 2007), the creation, maintenance, and evolution of SLAs are not easy tasks.

The challenges associated with the creation of SLAs are concerned with the (a) specification of languages and formalisms that can represent SLAs in a clear and unambiguous way, (b) understanding and trusting of parties' capabilities, (c) reduction of cost and human intervention during SLA creation, (d) establishment of business relations in a flexible way, and (e) finding of balance between parties' risks and benefits. On the other hand, the challenges associated with the maintenance and evolution of SLAs are concerned with the (i) identification of services that can replace existing services in applications based on previously defined SLAs, (ii) need to change certain terms in existing SLAs due to changes in the way that participating services operate or changes of services in service-based applications, (iii) constant monitoring of services that are parties in SLAs in order to guarantee uphold of SLAs, and (iv) need to specify policies for cases of SLA violations.

Currently, the normal process associated with SLAs is to develop a service-based system, write SLAs based on negotiations between the parties participating in the system, enforce the agreement through monitoring, and substitute services in the system in case of violations of the agreement. However, as affirmed in (Keller & Ludwig, 2002), SLAs are manually produced and monitored which is very expensive and slow. The definition, negotiation, deployment, monitoring, and enforcement of SLAs should become an automatic process.

In this chapter, we present an approach to support the creation of SLAs in a more automatic way. Our approach is based on an iterative process in which SLAs are created during the development of service-based systems taking into consideration the characteristics of the system being developed and available services. More specifically, the approach consists of identifying services that provide functional and non-functional characteristics of service-based systems during the design phase of these systems. The identified services are used to formulate and amend SLAs between the services participating in the system, and the design models of these systems. The reformulations of the design models and SLAs trigger new service discovery iterations. The result of this process is not only a complete specification of the design models of the service-based system, but also the SLAs. In this way, the SLAs will be created based on the characteristics of the system being developed and familiarity with what available services can provide. In addition, the SLAs will be specified during the development of the system and not as a separate activity that is executed as an afterthought.

The work presented in this paper is based on our previous work for architecture-based service discovery (Kozlenkov et al., 2006; Kozlenkov et al., 2007; Spanoudakis et.a, 2005; Zisman & Spanoudakis, 2006). We extend this previous work to support the creation of service level agreements during the development of service-based systems.

The remaining of this paper is structured as follows. We discuss background works that have been proposed in the literature. We describe our service discovery approach including service queries, service discovery execution, and SLA generation. We discuss some future trends, and finalise with a summary of the work.

BACKGROUND

Service discovery has been the subject of research in both academia and industry and several approaches have been proposed to support the identification of services.

Some of the approaches are based on the use of graph matching techniques (Haussman et al.,

2004; Klein & Bernstein, 2004). The work in Haussman et al. (2004) uses graph transformation rules for specifying services and service discovery queries. In Klein and Bernstein (2004) the authors have also proposed the use of graph-matching for service discovery but very few details of the matching algorithm are available.

Other approaches use WordNet (Morato et al., 2004) to support similarity analysis (Kokash et al., 2006; Wang & Stroulia, 2003; Wu & Wu, 2005). The approach in Wu and Wu (2005) uses four similarity assessment methods for service matching, namely lexical, attribute, interface, and quality-of-service (QoS) similarity. These forms of similarity assessment can be used either separately or jointly. Wang and Stroulia (2003) combine WordNet-based techniques and structure matching for service discovery. The WSDL-M2 approach (Kokash et al., 2006) uses lexical matching to calculate linguistic similarities between concepts, and structural matching to evaluate the overall similarity between composite concepts. Moreover, this approach combines vector-space model techniques with synonyms based on WordNet and semantic relations of two concepts.

Approaches for service discovery based on behavioral matching have been proposed in Grigori et al. (2006), Hall and Zisman (2004), Mikhaiel and Stroulia (2006), and Shen and Su (2005). In Hall and Zisman (2004), the approach locates services, which satisfy task requirement properties expressed formally in temporal logic, by using a lightweight automated reasoning tool. In(Shen & Su, 2005), the authors propose a behavioral model for services, which associates messages exchanged between services with activities performed within services. A query language based on first-order logic that focuses on properties of behavior signatures is used to support the discovery process. These properties include temporal features of sequences of service messages or activities and semantic descriptions of activities. Mikhaiel and Stroulia (2006) suggest the use of BPEL specifications as a way of resolving ambiguities between requests and services and uses a tree-alignment algorithm to identify matching between request and services.

Various approaches based on semantic web matchmaking using logic reasoning of terminological concept relations represented as ontologies have been proposed to support service discovery (Aggarwal et al., 2004; Horrocks et al., 2003; Hoschek, 2002; Keller et al., 2005; Klein & Bernstein, 2004; Kokash et al., 2006; Li & Horrock, 2003; Wang & Stroulia, 2003; Wang et al., 2006). The METEOR-S (Aggarwal et al., 2004) system adopts a constraint driven service discovery approach in which queries are integrated into the composition process of a service-based system and are represented as a collection of tuples of features, weight, and constraints. In this approach, semantic, temporal, and security constraints are considered during service discovery. In (Horrocks et al, 2003), the discovery of services is addressed as a problem of matching queries specified as a variant of Description Logic (DL) with service profiles specified in OWL-S (OWL-S). The matching process is based on the computation of subsumption relations between service profiles and supports different types of matching (exact, plug-in, subsume, intersection, and disjoint matching). The work in (Klein & Bernstein, 2004) extends existing approaches by supporting explicit and implicit semantic by using logic based, approximate matching, and IR techniques. The work in (Wang et al., 2006) proposes QoS-based selection of services. In (Keller et al., 2005), the authors present a goal-based model for service discovery that considers re-use of pre-defined goals, discovery of relevant abstract services described in terms of capabilities that do not depend on dynamic factors (state), and contracting of concrete services to fulfill requesting goals.

Other approaches have been proposed to support quality-of-services aware composition in which services are composed to contribute to achieve quality of service characteristics and support service level agreements (Canfora et al.,

2006; Nguyen et al., 2006; De Paoli, et al., 2006). Although existing approaches have contributed to assist service composition an approach that uses these compositions as part of the development of service-based systems has not been proposed.

There have been proposals for specific query languages to support web services discovery (Beeri et al., 2006; Pantazoglou et al., 2006; Pantazoglou et al., 2007; Papazoglou et al.; Yunyao et al., 2005). In (Beeri et al., 2006), the authors propose BP-QL a visual query language for business processes expressed in BPEL. The query language proposed in (Papazoglou et al.) is used to support composition of services based on user's goals. NaLIX (Yunyao et al., 2005), which is a language that was developed to allow querying XML databases based on natural language, has also been adapted to cater for service discovery. In (Pantazoglou et al., 2006) the authors propose USQL (Unified Service Query language), an XML-based language to represent syntactic, semantic, and quality of service search criteria. An extension of USQL that incorporates the behavioral part of our query language has been proposed in (Pantazoglou et al., 2007).

Service Discovery Approach

Our work adapts an iterative process in which service discovery activity is based on the design of service-based systems, and the available services identified during this process are used to amend and reformulate (i) the design models of the system and (ii) the SLAs between the service-based system being developed and the services to be deployed in these systems. The design models and SLA generated in the iterations of the process may trigger new service discovery iterations. The result of this iterative process is a complete specification of the structural and behavioural design models of the service-based system and the SLAs between the service-based system and the services participating in the system.

In the approach, queries are derived from the design models and initial SLA being generated during the design of service-based systems. The approach uses structural and behavioural models of service-based systems expressed in UML class and sequence diagrams, and SLAs expressed in WS-Agreement (WS-Agreement).

The use of UML as the basis of the design models is due to the facts that (a) UML is the de-facto standard for designing software systems and can effectively support the design of service-based systems as it has been argued in (Deuble et al., 2005; Gardner, 2004; Kozlenkov et al., 2006). Furthermore, UML has the expressive power to represent the design models that we use, and can provide a basis for specifying queries. The adoption of WS-Agreement for representing SLAs is due to its flexibility, simplicity, and wide and successful use.

Figure 1 shows an overview of the process adopted in our approach. The process starts from the construction of initial service-based system design models and SLA templates by the system designers. These initial SLA templates are created based on the initial structural, functional, and non-functional characteristics of the system. The design models describe interactions between operations of a service-based system and the types of parameters and constraints for these operations that can be provided by web services, legacy systems, or software components. The initial design models, initial SLA templates, and some extra constraints support the specification of queries. Candidate services identified after the execution of queries are selected by designers of the system. The selected services are bound to the design models reformulating these models and are used to instantiate and reformulate the SLAs. Queries can also be reformulated and re-executed when the results of the discovery process are not adequate. It is also possible, that during the process, designers realise that part of the system cannot be fulfilled by available services. In this case, it may be necessary to use existing legacy software code or components, to evolve existing services, or to develop new services or software

Figure 1. Overview of the process

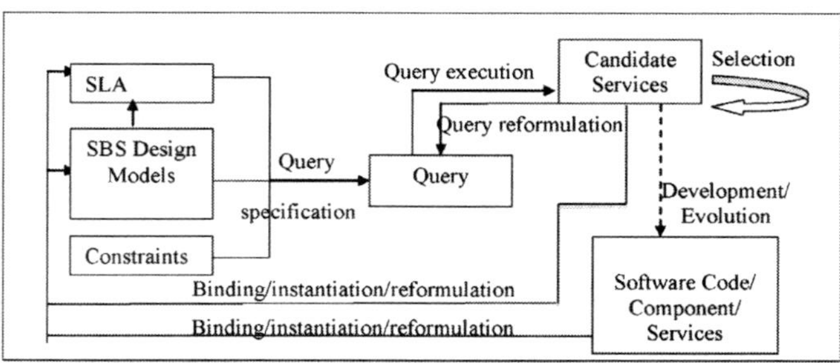

components. Designers may alter the design of the system and subsequent SLAs to reflect the above situations. The new versions of the design models and SLAs may be used to specify further queries to discover other services that can satisfy more elaborated functionality, properties, and constraints of the system. The process can be terminated by the designers at any time or when further queries cannot discover services that match the existing design models and SLAs.

Note that the initial step in the process can also be executed without the existence of constraints or SLA templates. In this case, the descriptions of initially selected services (e.g., QoS) are used to initialize the SLA template.

The discovery process is executed by searching for services in different registries. The search is based on similarities between service queries and service specifications. We adopt an approach in which the service specifications are composed by parts named facets, describing different aspects of the services. These facets include service interface specifications expressed in WSDL (WSDL), behavioural service specifications expressed in BPEL4WS (BPEL4WS), semantics service specifications expressed in OWL-S (OWL-S), WSMO (WSMO), or WSML (WSML), quality of service information, and other information types described in XML such as specific SLA metrics and measurement directives, and textual description.

In order to illustrate, consider an example of a PurchaseTransaction service-based system that allows its users to purchase services and goods online over the Internet. More specifically, the PurchaseTransaction scenario focuses on the design of an interaction for a user, who, after searching for an item to be purchased, requests information about the prices of the item and the delivery of the item, decides to purchase the item, and pays for the item by an online bank transfer transaction. The interaction can (i) search for a certain item on the Internet, (ii) display the results of the search on a web browser, (iii) allow for the selection of an item to be purchased, (iv) compare prices of a certain item, (v) support the purchase of an item, (vi) calculate the price to deliver the item, (vii) allow the user to check its bank account, and (viii) allow a purchased item to be paid by transferring money from the user's bank account.

Figures 2 and 3 show part of the initial behavioural (sequence diagram) and structural (class diagram) models for the PurchaseTransaction service-based system, respectively. The sequence diagram in Figure 2 describes the operations that a user can execute in order to realise some of the functionalities described above and placeholders for services to be discovered that may provide these functionalities. These placeholders are represented by interfaces (ISearchEngine, IPriceFinder, IBankService). The signatures and the types of the parameters of the operations in the sequence diagram are described in the class diagram in Figure 3.

Figure 2. Behavioral model for the PurchaseTransaction service-based system

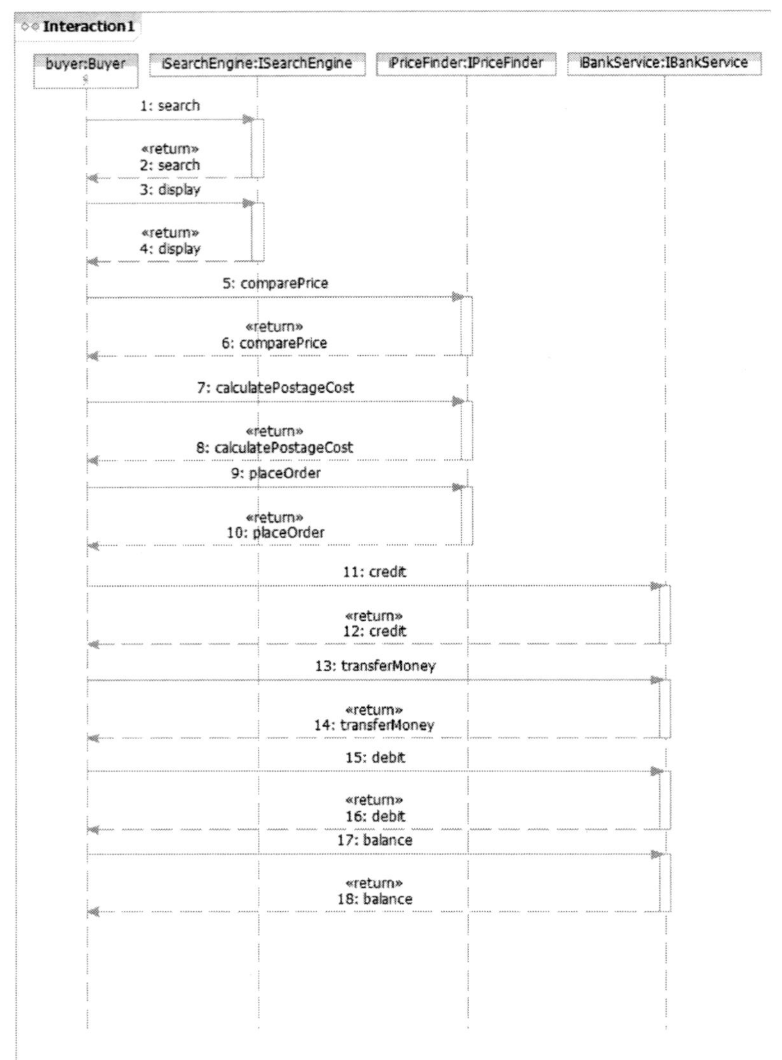

Figure 4 shows part of an initial (incomplete) SLA WS-Agreement (WS-Agreement)1 template for the PurchaseTransaction service-based system representing some extra quality characteristics of the system being developed that should be fulfilled by the services to be identified. Examples of these extra quality characteristics are concerned with the facts that (a) the response time to execute operations comparePrice, calculatePostageCost, placeOrder by a service to be discovered (represented by placeholder IPriceFinder in this case), should not take more than 5 seconds and (b) the cost to use the service should be between 5 and 10 Euros. As shown in Figure 4, these characteristics are described as terms in the agreement that should be supported by the service provider represented at this initial stage by placeholder IPriceFinder. The other terms in the agreement that are concerned with placeholders ISearchEngine and IBankService are not shown here for simplicity, but are defined in similar ways.

Figure 3. Structural model for the PurchaseTransaction service-based system

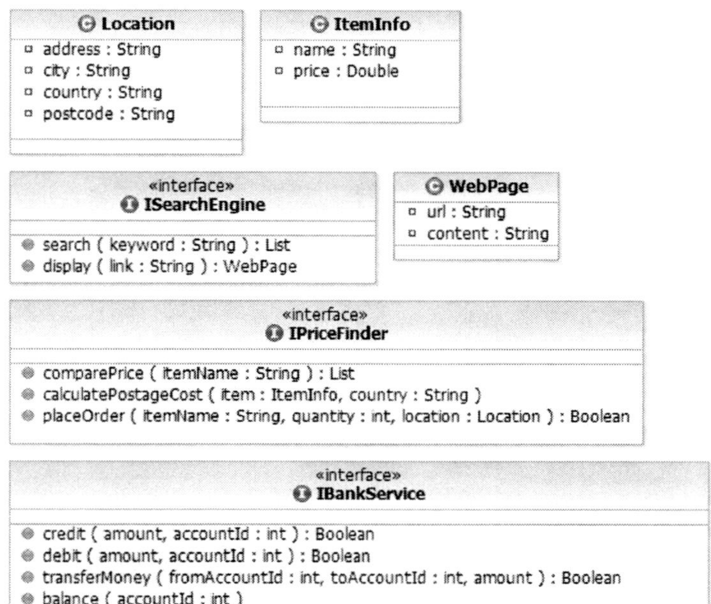

In the next subsections we describe the specification and execution of queries in the approach, the service discovery process, and the creation (amendment) of service level agreements based on discovered services.

Service Queries

In our approach, a query contains different types of characteristics concerning the service-based system being developed and the respective SLA. These characteristics include structural, behavioural, and non-functional (quality) aspects that are taken from the design models of the service-based system and the SLA template, and any other extra constraints. More specifically, a query is composed of three main parts, namely (a) structural, (b) behavioural, and (c) constraint. The structural and behavioural parts describe structural and functional aspects of the system being developed. The constraint part describes extra structural and behavioural conditions of the system being developed, non-functional characteristics of the system, and any necessary metric or computational characteristics to support the definition of SLAs. Examples of these extra constraints are the response time or cost to execute a certain operation in a service, the specific receiver of a message, the provider of a service, or the number of parameters in a service operation.

We adopt an XML-based query language named SerDiQueL (Service Discovery Query Language) (Zisman et al., review) to express service requests. More specifically, SerDiQueL is composed of three parts. The first part describes structural characteristics of the service-based application being developed. The second part expresses behavioural characteristics of the application representing the existence of a certain functionality or sequence of functionalities, the sequence and order in which certain functionalities should be executed, pre-conditions, and dependencies between functionalities. The third part represents the extra structural, behavioural, and non-functional constraints.

Figure 4. Initial SLA template for the PurchaseTransaction service-based system

```
<wsag:Agreement AgreementID="PT_Agg1">
...
<wsag:Terms>
  <wsag:All>
    <wsag:ExactlyOne>
      <wsag:All>
        <wsag:ServiceDescriptionTerm
          wsag:Name=ResponseTimeTerm"   wsag:ServiceName="IPriceFinder">
        </wsag:ServiceDescriptionTerm>
        <wsag:ServiceDescriptionTerm
          wsag:Name=MinCostTerm"   wsag:ServiceName="IPriceFinder">
        </wsag:ServiceDescriptionTerm>
        </wsag:ServiceDescriptionTerm>
        <wsag:ServiceDescriptionTerm
          wsag:Name=MaxCostTerm"   wsag:ServiceName="IPriceFinder">
        </wsag:ServiceDescriptionTerm>
    </wsag:ExactlyOne>
    <wsag:GuaranteeTerm
        wsag:Name="ResponseTimeReference"
        wsag:Obligated="ServiceProvider">
        <wsag:ServiceScope>
          <wsag:ServiceName>IPriceFinder</wsag:ServiceName>
        </wsag:ServiceScope>
        <wsag:ServiceLevelObjective>
         <wsag:KPITarget>
           <wsag:KPIName>ResponseTime</wasg:KPIName>
           <wasg:Target>5 seconds</wsag:Target>
         </wsag:KPITarget>
        </wsag:ServiceLevelObjective>
    </wsag:GuaranteeTerm>
    <wsag:GuaranteeTerm
        wsag:Name="CostReference"
        wsag:Obligated="ServiceProvider">
        <wsag:ServiceScope>
          <wsag:ServiceName>IPriceFinder</wsag:ServiceName>
        </wsag:ServiceScope>
        <wsag:ServiceLevelObjective xsi:type="sdtc:OpType">
         <Unit>Euros</Unit>
         <And>
          <SDT>MinCostTerm</SDT>
          <SDT>MaxCostTerm</SDT>
         </And>
        </wsag:ServiceLevelObjective
        <wsag:BusinessValueList>
         <wsag:Preference>
           <wsag:ServiceTermReference>MinCostTerm</wasg:ServiceTermReference>
           <wasg:Utility>5</wsag:Utility>
           <wsag:ServiceTermReference>MaxCostTerm</wasg:ServiceTermReference>
           <wasg:Utility>10</wasg:Utility>
         </wsag:Preference>
        </wsag:BusinessValueList>
    </wsag:GuaranteeTerm>
      . . .
  </wsag:All>
 </wsag:Terms>
    . . .
</wsag:Agreement>
```

Figure 5 presents a graphical representation of the overall XML schema of SerDiQueL2. As shown in the figure, a query has a unique identifier, a name, one or more elements describing different parameters for a query, and three other elements representing the structural, behavioural, and constraint parts. A parameter element is defined by a name and a value and can be used to limit the search space during the execution of a query, limit the number of services returned as a result of a query, define the type of a query, and define the author of a query.

Structural Part

The structural part is defined based on the structural and behavioural design models of the system being developed. More specifically, this part is represented as XMI document and makes use of a UML 2.0 profile that we have developed (Kozlenkov et al., 2007; Kozlenkov et al., 2007). The structural part is based on the selection by the application designer of messages in sequence diagrams that should be realized by operations of services to be discovered. The parts of the structural model representing the classes defining the types of the

Figure 5. Overview schema of SerDiQuel

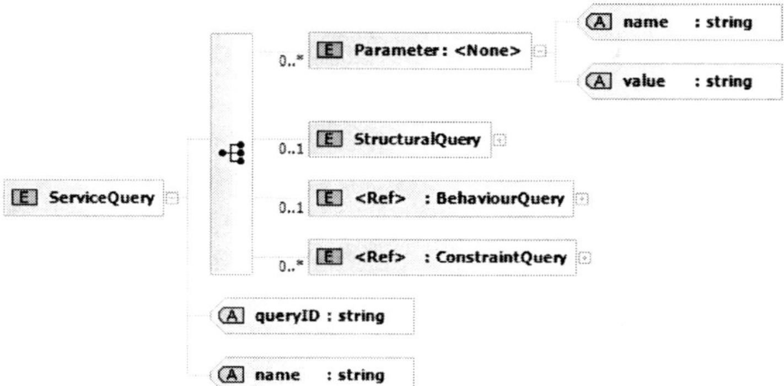

parameters of the selected messages are used to compose the structural part of a query.

The UML 2.0 profile defines stereotypes for different types of elements in class and sequence diagrams. More specifically, a message in the behavioural model of the application may be stereotyped as:

- query message (<<query_message>>) to indicate that the message invokes an operation that should be provided by a service that is to be discovered;
- context message (<<context_message>>) to indicate that the message defines additional constraints for the query messages (e.g. if a context message has a parameter p1 with the same name of a parameter p2 of a query message, then the type of p1 should be taken as the type of p2); or
- bound message (<<bound_message>>) to indicate that the message is bound to a concrete operation of a service that has been discovered by a query executed in some previous iteration.

All the messages in a behavioral model, which are not stereotyped by any of the above three stereotypes in a query, are not considered during the execution of the query (i.e., they are not related to the query). A more detailed definition of the stereotypes used in the profile can be found in (Kozlenkov et al., 2006; Kozlenkov et al., 2007)..

As an example of a portion of the structural part of a query specification, suppose the designer of PurchaseTransaction wants to specify a query (called PurchaseTransactionQuery1) to identify services that can provide the operations comparePrice, calculatePostageCost, and placeOrder in the sequence diagram shown in Figure 2. Suppose also that for this query the designer wants to restrict the number of candidate service operations that should be returned to 4 and the maximum number of services that should be searched in the registry to 100. Figure 6 shows the specification of this part of the query in SerDiQueL, with the respective parameters. As shown in the figure, messages comparePrice, calculatePostageCost, and placeOrder are stereotyped as <<query_messages>>.

Behavioural Part

The behavioural part of a query is based on temporal logic. It supports not only the representation of the sequence in which the operations should appear in a service, as specified in the sequence imposed by the sequence diagram, but also other characteristics. More specifically, the behavioural part allows the description of queries that verify: (a) the existence of a certain functionality, or a sequence of functionalities, in a service specifica-

Figure 6. Example of structural part of PurchaseTransactionQuery1

```
<?xml version="1.0" encoding="utf-8"?>
<tns:ServiceQuery xmlns:tns = … queryID="Q1" name="PurchaseTransactionQuery1">
 <tns:Parameter name="paramMaxCandidates" value="4" />
 <tns:Parameter name="paramMaxServices" value="100" />
 <tns:StructuralQuery>
  <?xml version="1.0" encoding="UTF-8"?>
  <uml:Model xmi:version="2.0" xmlns:xmi="http://www.omg.org/XMI"
      xmlns:xsi=http://www.w3.org/2001/XMLSchema-instance
      xmlns:Profile_77=http:///_yyMQkEF6Edu8RvZdbrrgBA.profile.uml2
      xmlns:uml=http://www.eclipse.org/uml2/1.0.0/UML
      xsi:schemaLocation="http:///_yyMQkEF6Edu8RvZdbrrgBA.profile.uml2
      pathmap://PROFILES/Profile.profile.uml2#_9BFthkF6Edu8RvZdbrrgBA"
      name="Models"
      appliedProfile="_wytb88G9Edul3rU0LuulHg _wytb9sG9Edul3rU0LuulHg _wytb">
       . . .
  <message xmi:id="_wzAKYsG9Edul3rU0LuulHg" name="comparePrice"
      receiveEvent="_wzAKlcG9Edul3rU0LuulHg"
      sendEvent="_wzAYIMG9Edul3rU0LuulHg" connector="_wzAKUMG9Edul3rU0LuulHg"
      signature="_wzAIScG9Edul3rU0LuulHg">
   <eAnnotations xmi:id="[illegible]" source="appliedStereotypes">
    <contents xmi:type="Profile_77:Profile__query_message"
          xmi:id="[illegible]"/> </eAnnotations> </message>
      <message xmi:id="[illegible]" name="comparePrice"
            messageSort="synchSignal"
            receiveEvent="[illegible]"
            sendEvent="[illegible]"
            connector="[illegible]"
            signature="[illegible]">
   <eAnnotations xmi:id="[illegible]" source="keywords">
     <details xmi:id="[illegible]" key="return"/> </eAnnotations>
   <eAnnotations xmi:id="[illegible]" source="appliedStereotypes">
     <contents xmi:type="Profile_77:Profile__query_message"
            xmi:id="[illegible]"/> </eAnnotations> </message>
       <message xmi:id="[illegible]"
             name="calculatePostageCost"
             receiveEvent="[illegible]"
             sendEvent="[illegible]"
             connector="[illegible]"
             signature="[illegible]">
   <eAnnotations xmi:id="[illegible]" source="appliedStereotypes">
      <contents xmi:type="Profile_77:Profile__query_message"
             xmi:id="[illegible]"/>
   </eAnnotations> </message>
  <message xmi:id="_wzAXbcG9Edul3rU0LuulHg"
          name="calculatePostageCost" messageSort="synchSignal"
          receiveEvent="[illegible]"
          sendEvent="[illegible]"
      connector="[illegible]" signature="[illegible]">
   <eAnnotations xmi:id="[illegible]" source="keywords">
     <details xmi:id="[illegible]" key="return"/> </eAnnotations>
   <eAnnotations xmi:id="[illegible]" source="appliedStereotypes">
      <contents xmi:type="Profile_77:Profile__query_message"
             xmi:id="[illegible]"/> </eAnnotations> </message>
  <message xmi:id="[illegible]" name="placeOrder"
          receiveEvent="[illegible]"
          sendEvent="[illegible]"
          connector="[illegible]"
          signature="[illegible]">

 . . .
</tns:StructuralQuery>
```

tion; (b) the order in which certain functionalities should be executed by a service; (c) dependencies between functionalities; (d) pre-conditions; and (e) loops concerning execution of certain functionalities.

Figure 7 shows a graphical representation of the SerDiQueL's XML schema for the behavioural part of a query3. As shown in the figure, behavioural parts of a query are defined as (a) a single condition, a negated condition, or a conjunction of conditions, or (b) a sequence of expressions separated by logical operators. It is also possible to define requires elements; i.e., elements that define one or more service operations that need to exist in service specifications, represented as members (element MemberDescription). These member elements are used in various conditions and expressions of a behavioural part of a query.

A condition can be negated and is defined as GuaranteedMember, OccursBefore, OccursAfter, Sequence, or Loop elements. A GuaranteedMember represents a member element (i.e., service operation) that needs to occur in all possible traces of execution in a service. The OccursBefore and OccursAfter elements represent the order of occurrence of two member elements (Member1 and Member2). They have two boolean attributes, namely (a) immediate, specifying if the two

Figure 7. XML schema for behavioural part of a query

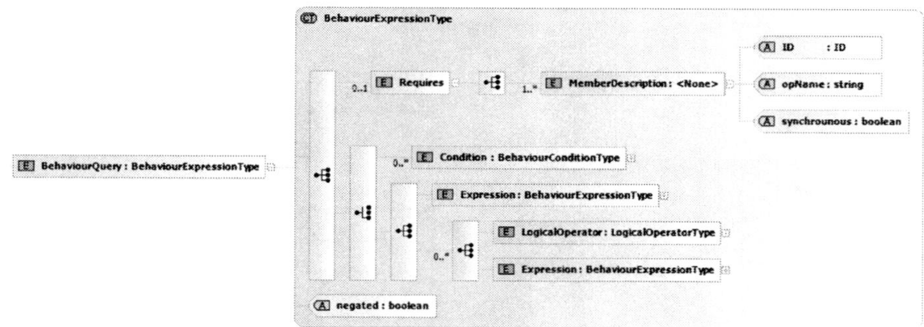

members occur in sequence or if there can be other member elements in between them, and (b) guaranteed, specifying if the two members need to occur in all possible traces of execution in a service. A Sequence element defines two or more members, which must occur in a service in the order represented in the sequence. It has an identifier attribute that can be used by the guaranteed member element. A Loop element specifies a sequence of members that are executed several times. Expressions are defined as a sequence of requires elements, conjunctions of conditions, or other nested expressions connected by logical operators AND and OR.

The behavioural part of a query is based on the behaviour expected by (i) an interface I representing a service placeholder described in the sequence diagram of a service-based system being developed, and (ii) any other functional characteristic that may be defined in a service level agreement. The behaviour expected by an interface is represented by the sequence of operations received by the interface.

Figure 8 shows the specification of the behavioural part of PurchaseTransactionQuery1 in SerDiQueL. As shown in the figure, the behavioural part of the query expresses the existence of messages comparePrice, calculatePostageCost, and placeOrder (Requires element) in this order (Sequence element).

Constraint Part

The constraints in a query can be hard or soft. A hard constraint must be satisfied by all discovered services for a query and are used to filter services

Figure 8. Example of behavioural part of PurchaseTransactionQuery1

```
<?xml version="1.0" encoding="utf-8"?>
<tns:ServiceQuery xmlns:tns = … queryID="Q1" name="PurchaseTransactionQuery1">
 <tns:Parameter name="paramMaxCandidates" value="4" />
 <tns:Parameter name="paramMaxServices" value="100" />
 <tns:StructuralQuery> . . . </tns:StructuralQuery>
 <tnsb:BehaviourQuery>
 <tnsb:Requires>
   <tnsb:MemberDescription ID="cprice" opName="comparePrice"
                           synchrounous="true" />
   <tnsb:MemberDescription ID="cpcost" opName="calculatePostageCost"
                           synchrounous="true"/>
   <tnsb:MemberDescription ID="porder" opName="placeOrder"
                           synchrounous="true" />
 </tnsb:Requires>
 <tnsb:Expression> <tnsb:Condition>
   <tnsb:Sequence ID="purchase">
       <tnsb:Member IDREF="cprice" />
       <tnsb:Member IDREF="cpcost" />
       <tnsb:Member IDREF="porder"/>
   </tnsb:Sequence></tnsb:Condition></tnsb:Expression>
</tnsb:BehaviourQuery>
```

Figure 9. XML schema for constraint part of a query

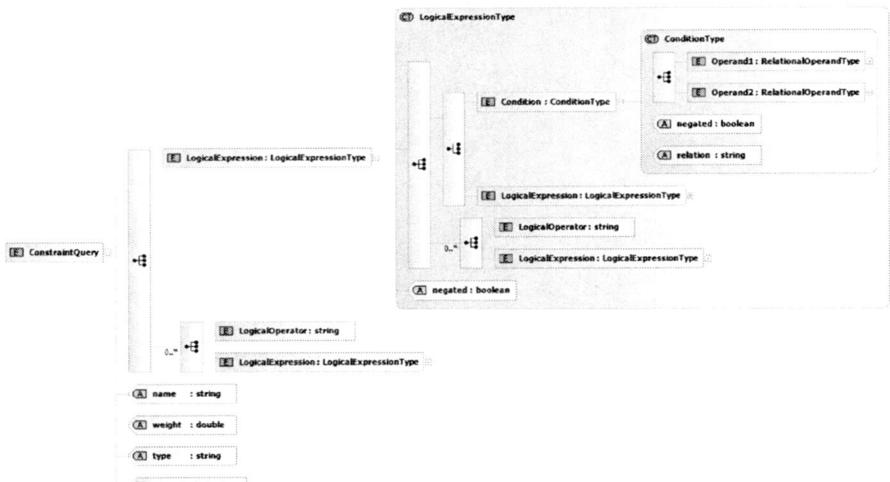

that do not comply with them. The soft constraints do not need to be satisfied by all discovered services, but are used to rank candidate services for a query (see Service Discovery Execution Section). The constraints in a query are generated either from the terms described in the template of an SLA (e.g., expected response time, cost) or directly specified by the application designer (e.g., provider of a service, receiver of a message, QoS characteristics).

Figure 9 shows a graphical representation of SerDiQueL's XML schema for specifying constraints4. As shown in the figure, a constraint sub-query is defined as a single logical expression, a negated logical expression, or a conjunction or disjunction of two or more logical expressions, combined by logical operators AND and OR.

A constraint sub-query has three attributes, namely (a) name, specifying a description of the constraint; (b) type, indicating whether the constraint is hard or soft; (c) weight, specifying a weight in the range of [0.0, 1.0]. The weight is used to represent prioritisations of the parameters in a query for soft constraints.

A logical expression is defined as a condition, or logical combination of conditions, over elements or attributes of service specifications. A condition can be negated and is defined as a relational operation (equalTo, notEqualTo, lessThan, greateThan, lessThanEqualTo, greaterThanEqualTo, notEqualTo) between two operands (operand1 and operand2). These operands can be query operands, constants, or arithmetic expressions.

A query operand has two attributes, namely (a) facetName, specifying the name of the service specification and (b) facetType, specifying the type of the service specifications to which the constraint will be evaluated. The operand contains an XPath expression indicating elements and attributes in the service specification referenced in facetName attribute. Therefore, the constraints can be specified against any element or attribute of any facet in the registries. Arithmetic expressions define computations over the values of elements or attributes in service specification or context information. A function supports the execution of a complex computation over a series of arguments. The results of these computations are numerical values that can be used as an operand in an arithmetic expression. A function has a name and a sequence of one or more arguments.

Figure 10. Example of constraint part of PurchaseTransactionQuery1

```
<?xml version="1.0" encoding="utf-8"?>
<tns:ServiceQuery xmlns:tns = … queryID="Q1" name="PurchaseTransactionQuery1">
 <tns:Parameter name="paramMaxCandidates" value="4" />
 <tns:Parameter name="paramMaxServices" value="100" />
 <tns:StructuralQuery> . . . </tns:StructuralQuery>
 <tnsb:BehaviourQuery> . . . </tnsb:BehaviourQuery>
 <tnsa:ConstraintQuery name="C1" type="HARD">
  <tnsa:LogicalExpression> <tnsa:Condition relation=" EQUAL-TO">
   <tnsa:Operand1>
     <tnsa:QueryOperand facetName="ServiceDescription" facetType="Textual">
      //serviceCharacteristic[Name="Provider"]/Constant</tnsa:QueryOperand>
   </tnsa:Operand1>
   <tnsa:Operand2><tnsa:Constant type="STRING">ProviderX</tnsa:Constant>
   </tnsa:Operand2></tnsa:Condition></tnsa:LogicalExpression>
 </tnsa:ConstraintQuery>
 <tnsa:ConstraintQuery name="C2" type="HARD" weight="0.5">
  <tnsa:LogicalExpression> <tnsa:Condition relation="LESS-THAN-EQUAL-TO">
   <tnsa:Operand1>
     <tnsa:QueryOperand facetName="QoS" facetType="QualityOfService">
      //QoSCharacteristic[Name="ResponseTime"]/Metrics/Metric[Name="Time"]
       [Unit="SECONDS"]
     </tnsa:QueryOperand></tnsa:Operand1>
   <tnsa:Operand2><tnsa:Constant type="NUMERIC">5</tnsa:Constant>
   </tnsa:Operand2></tnsa:Condition></tnsa:LogicalExpression>
 </tnsa:ConstraintQuery>
 <tnsa:ConstraintQuery name="C3" type="SOFT" weight="0.5">
  <tnsa:LogicalExpression> <tnsa:Condition relation="EQUAL-TO">
   <tnsa:Operand1>
     <tnsa:QueryOperand facetName="Cost" facetType="ServiceCost">
      //CostCharacteristic[Name="Value"]/Metrics[Unit="EUROS"]/MinValue
     </tnsa:QueryOperand></tnsa:Operand1>
   <tnsa:Operand2><tnsa:Constant type="NUMERIC">5</tnsa:Constant>
   </tnsa:Operand2></tnsa:Condition>
   <LogicalOperator>AND</tnsa:LogicalOperator>
   <tnsa:LogicalExpression> <tnsa:Condition relation="EQUAL-TO">
   <tnsa:Operand1>
     <tnsa:QueryOperand facetName="Cost" facetType="ServiceCost">
      //CostCharacteristic[Name="Value"]/Metrics[Unit="EUROS"]/MaxValue
     </tnsa:QueryOperand></tnsa:Operand1>
   <tnsa:Operand2><tnsa:Constant type="NUMERIC">10</tnsa:Constant>
   </tnsa:Operand2></tnsa:Condition></tnsa:LogicalExpression>
 </tnsa:LogicalExpression>
</tnsa:ConstraintQuery></tns:ServiceQuery>
```

The use of a specific language to represent constraints in a query instead of using WS-Agreement, for example, is (a) due to the need to represent not only quality constraints, but also extra structural and behavioural constraints that cannot be represented in the structural and bheavioural parts of a query; (b) to allow a general language to represent constraints and not to be dependent and restricted to a certain formalism; (c) to support the representation of more complex and expressive queries allowing for the representation of logical combinations of conditions, arithmetic expressions, functions, references to facets against which the conditions will be evaluated, and weights and types of constraints; and (d) to allow the specification of queries (and their constraints) independent of the existence of initial SLAs.

As an example consider the initial SLA schema template shown in Figure 4 specifying the facts that the response time to compare prices, calculate postage cost, and place an order should not take more than five seconds, and that the costs to execute these activities should be between five and ten Euros. Consider also another constraint that the service provider for the operations in query PurchaseTransactionQuery1 should be ProviderX5.

For this example, suppose that the designer (i) wants to select services that are only from ProviderX, (ii) does not want to consider services that may take more than five seconds to execute the above activities, and (iii) may consider services that cost less than five Euros or more than 10 Euros. Figure 10, presents the representation of the constraint part for PurchaseTransactionQuery. In this case, situations (i) and (ii) are represented as hard constraints (C1 and C2 in Figure 10), and situation (iii) is represented as soft constraint in the query (C3 in Figure 10).

For the above example, constraints C2 and C3 are generated from the guarantee terms described in the SLA in Figure 4, while constraint C1 is defined by the user. More specifically, constraint C2 represents the information described in ResponseTimeReference guarantee term in the SLA, while constraint C3 represents the information described in CostReference guarantee term. The term ResponseTimeReference is mapped to the XML schema of facet QoS. This schema and the information in element KPITarget in the SLA are used to support the specification of elements Operand1 and Operand2 in the constraint. A similar situation occurs to CostReference, which is mapped to the XML schema of facet Cost. In this case, the contents of elements ServiceLevelObjective and BusinessValueList are used to create the logical expressions with their respective operands for constraint C3 in the query.

Currently, we are implementing mapping rules to support automatic generation of constraints in the query from SLA guarantee terms. In this case, the application designer needs to select the guarantee terms in an SLA template that should be used as constraints in a query, and define which of these constraints should be considered as hard or soft during query evaluation.

Service Discovery Execution

In the approach, the discovery process is executed in two stages. The first stage is a filtering stage and is concerned with the search for candidate services that match the hard constraints in a query. These candidate services are used in the second stage of the process. The second stage is an optimization stage and is concerned with the evaluation of the candidate services returned by the first stage that match the structural, behavioral, and soft constraints of a query and the calculation of an overall distance. This overall distance takes into consideration structural, behavioural, and soft constraint distances calculated for each query message and service operations in the list of candidate services. After the overall distances are calculated, the optimal best operation matching for all query messages in a query is calculated, as well as the n-best operation matching for each query message. The optimal best operation matching is calculated as described in details in (SECSE A2.D12, 2008; SECSE A2.D8, 2006), using the Hungarian method (Papdimitrou & Steiglitz, 1982). In the approach, the n best candidate services (n-best operation matching) are specified in the maximum number of candidate services as a parameter element in a query (paramMaxCandidates). Otherwise, the approach assumes the value 10 when this parameter is not specified in a query.

When a query does not have hard constraints, the process is reduced to one-stage and the structural, behavioural, and soft constraints are calculated for all service operations in a service repository. When a query does not have behavioral or soft constraints, the computation of the overall distance does not consider the distances of the types of constraints not specified in a query.

The overall distance (OD) between a query message (qm) and a service operation (os) is specified as:

```
OD(qm, so) = (structural distance
(qm, os) + behavioral distance (qm,
os) +
soft constraint distance (qm, os)) /
3
```

The structural distance between a query message (qm) and a service operation (os) is calculated based on the linguistic distances of the signatures of qm and os, the distances between the input parameters of qm and so, and the distances between the output parameters of qm and os. The linguist distance is built on top of WordNet lexicon (Morato et al., 2004). The distances between the sets of input or output parameters of two operations is computed by finding the best possible morphism pm between the data types of the parameters of a service operation and a query message (Kozlenkov et al., 2007; Zisman & Spanoudakis, 2006). This distance requires the construction of a graph G representing the input and output parameters of a query message and service operation and uses a variant of the VF2 sub-graph isomorphism algorithm (SECSE A2.D12, 2008). More specifically,

More specifically, a graph G is constructed with (a) two disjoint sets of vertices: one set of vertices representing query operations (messages) and another set of vertices representing service operations of the services identified in the filtering stage; and (b) edges that connect each of the operations in the query with all the operations of the retrieved services, and vice versa. Each edge e(vi,vj) in graph G is weighted by a measure that indicates the overall distance between vertices vi and vj. This measure has a value between [0.0, 1.0] and is computed as the weighted sum of a set of partial distances quantifying the semantic differences between vi and vj, with respect to each facet in the description of vi and vj.

Following the computation of the distances between the vertices, the matching between the query and service operations is detected in two steps. In the first step, a subset S of the edges in graph G is selected, such that S is a total morphing between the vertices in G and has the minimal distance values (this subset is selected by applying an assignment problem algorithm as in Spanoudakis & Constantopoulos, 1996)6. In the second step, the subset S is restricted to include edges with distances that do not exceed a certain threshold value. The partial distances are computed based on functions that take into consideration the distance of the signature of two operations. These functions account for the linguistic distance of the names of the operations and distance between the set of input and output parameters. The distance between the set of parameters is computed by finding the best matching between the structures of the data types of these parameters.

The best matching is identified by comparing edges in the graphs representing the structure of the data types of the input and output parameters. The graph of the input and output parameters of an operation is constructed taking into consideration both primitive data types and non-primitive data types. In the graph, the operation name is represented as the root of the graph with immediate input_pi and output_po children nodes, for each input and output parameter in the operation, respectively. The data type associated with an input parameter or output parameter is added to the graph as a child node of the respective input_Pi node or output_po node (datatype_pi and datatype_po nodes). The name of the input and output parameters are represented in the graph as the name of the edges between input_pi and datatype_pi, and ouput_po and datatype_po. In the case of a data type datatype_i that is a non-primitive type, a sub-graph for this data type is constructed such that each data type of the attributes in the class representing datatype_i is added to the graph as a child of datatype_i with the name of the attribute as the name of the respective edge. If the data type of an attribute is also non-primitive the process is repeated for this data type. The process terminates when all the node edges of the graph has only primitive data types.

The behavioural distance between a query message (qm) and a service operation (os) is computed by matching paths (p) representing the behavioural part of the query (i.e., the behaviour expected by interface I that executed query message qm) and the state machine of the service that has operation os. The state machine of a service is generated from the BPEL specification of a service, as described in (Kozlenkov et al., 2006). The transitions in the paths represent operations in a query and services. The distance between a path p and the state machine of a service is computed by identifying a path q in the state machine that has the best possible match with p; i.e., a path q that has the minimum distance with path p. The identification of a path q that has the best possible match with a path p is computed based on the path transformation algorithm described in (Kozlenkov & Zisman, 2004). This algorithm attempts to

Figure 11. Architecture overview

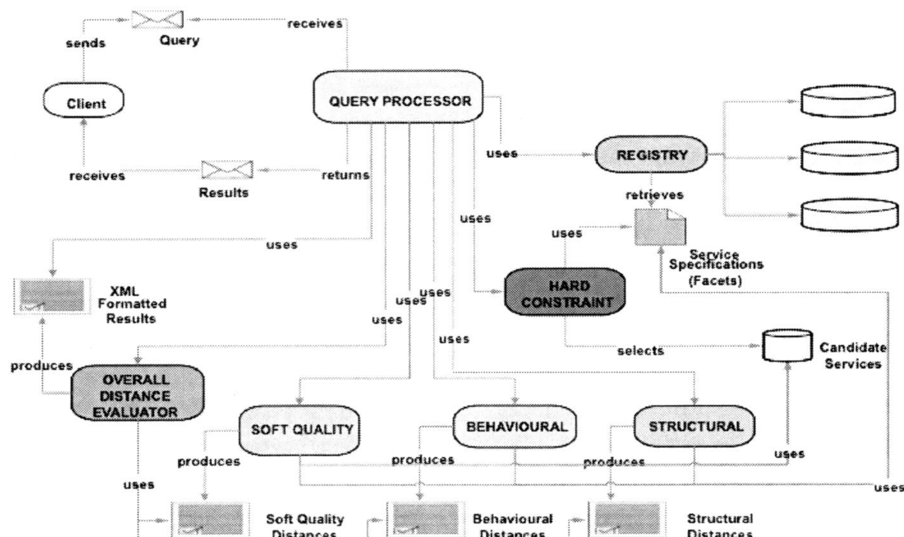

consume one by one all the transition (tpi) in path p by comparing them with the transitions (tqj) in path q, and verifying if (a) transition tpi can be accepted (when tpi matches tqj), (b) transition tpi can be removed (when tpi does not match tqj, but a transition tpi+x in p matches tpj), or (c) new transitions can be added (when tpi match tqj+x and the other following transitions in p can be consumed). The match between two paths p and q considers the structural distances between the operations in p and q (i.e., the operations represented in the label transitions of p and q).

The soft constraint distance between a query message (qm) and a service operation (os) is computed by the sum of the weights of the soft constraints that are applied to qm and are not satisfied by os, divided by the sum of the weights of all constraints in the query which apply to qm. A detailed description of the structural, behavioural, and soft constraint distances used in our approach can be found in (SECSE A2.D12, 2008; SECSE A2.D8, 2006).

The overall architecture of our approach to support service discovery is presented in Figure 11. As shown in the figure, the approach contains six main components, namely: (a) query processor, (b) hard constraint matcher, (c) structural matcher, (d) behavioral matcher, (e) soft constraint matcher, and (f) overall distance evaluator. In the following we describe each of these components.

- **Query Processor:** This component orchestrates the functionality offered by the other components. It is a web service component that (i) receives a query from a client, (ii) separates the various parts of a query to be processed, (iii) accesses the other components necessary to evaluate the various parts of a query, (iv) receives information about the candidate services that are compliant with a query, (v) organises the results of a query in an XML format, and (vi) returns these results to the client service. The query processor has been implemented as a web service. It can be deployed by any client that is able to produce service discovery queries expressed in SerDiQueL (see Service Queries Section). The deployment of the query processor as a web service allows the execution of service discovery queries independent of the use of a particular CASE tool.

- **Hard Constraint Matcher:** This component is responsible to parse the hard constraints of a query, when they exist, and evaluate these constraints against service specifications in the various service registries. The evaluated service specifications are concerned with the types of constraints (e.g., structural, behavioral, quality, textual). The component returns specifications of services that are compliant with the hard constraints in the query. These returned services are used by the structural, behavioral, and soft constraint matchers.
- **Structural Matcher:** This component performs the matching of the structural aspects of a query (signature of the messages in the models that are part of a query) against the signature of the operations of the services returned by the hard constraint matcher, when hard constraints where specified in a query, or against the signature of the operations of the services in the registries, when hard constraints were not specified in a query. The matching is performed after converting the WSDL specifications of a service and the signatures of the messages in a query into a set of data type graphs 0. The matching identifies the mapping and calculates the distances between the elements represented in the graphs. The component returns the structural distances between the messages and operations in the services.
- **Behavioral Matcher:** This component performs the matching of the behavioral aspects of aquery, when they exist, against behavioral specifications of services. These services are either the set of services returned by the hard constraint matcher component or services in the registries, when hard constraints have not been specified in a query. The matching is executed by (i) transforming behavioural service specifications into state machines, (ii) extracting all the possible paths from a service stetamachine, (iii) transforming the behavioural sub-query into a path, and (iv) verifying if the path representing the query can be matched against a path of the statemachine of a service. The matching of a query path and a service is calculated by a distance that computes the best mapping between the query path and all the paths in a service. The component returns the behavioral distances between the state machines of the services and a query. Given its popularity, we assume behavioural service specifications represented in BPEL4WS (BPEL4WS). However, the behaviour sub-query can be matched against other types of behavioural service specifications that can be represented as or transformed into statemachines.
- **Soft Constraint Matcher:** This component is responsible to parse the soft constraints of a query, when they exist, and evaluate these constraints against service specifications of the services returned by the hard constraint matcher or services in the registries, when hard constraints have not been specified in a query. As in the case of hard constraint matching, the types of service specifications used by this component are specific to the various types of constraints. The component also takes into consideration the weights of the soft constraints when they exist and returns the soft constraint distances between a query and the services.
- **Overall Distance Evaluator:** This component is responsible to compute the overall distance between a query and the candidate services. More specifically, this component computes the overall distances based on the structural, behavioral and soft constraint distances returned by the

Figure 12. Structure of the results of a query

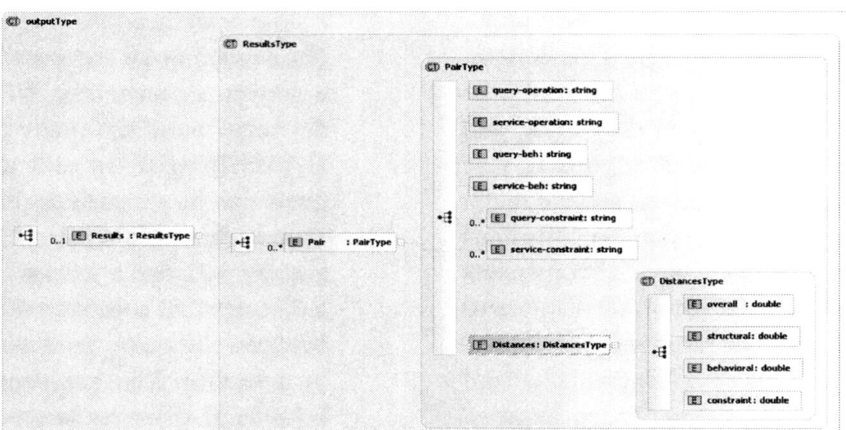

structural, behavioral, and soft constraint matchers, respectively. The component returns the best match between a query and the candidate services, as well as the n-best matches between each message in a query and an operation in a service, where n has a default value of 10 or is specified in a query by the designer of the system (parameter paramMaxCandidates). The results are represented in XML format and used by the query processor.

There may be some differences in the execution process of a query. These differences are due to the lack of hard, behavioral, and soft constraints in a query, or any combinations of the above constraints. In the case in which one or more of the constraint types are not present in a query, the corresponding component is bypassed and the overall distance evaluator computes the distance of the types of constraints specified in a query. Note that structural constraints are always present in a query and, therefore, at least distances based on structural constraints are calculated.

Query Results

The results of a query execution are used to reformulate the design models of the system and the service level agreements (SLAs). More specifically, the n-best candidate services are presented to the designer, together with the distances between the services and a query, who is supposed to choose a candidate service to be bound to the design models and be instantiated in the SLA templates. In the case of the SLA, it is also possible that some terms of the agreement are changed based on the services that have been found and the candidate service that has been chosen.

Figure 12 presents the structure of the XML schema for the results of a query in a graphical format7. According to this schema the results of a query are structured as pairs of (a) query operations (see element query_operation) and service operations (see element service_opeation); (b) behavioural of a query (see element query_behaviour) and service behaviour (see element service_behaviour); (c) constraint of a query (see element query_constraint) and service constraints (see element service_constraint). Each constraint in a query is represented by a different pair of query_constraint and service_constraint. The result also contains an associated distance element that has four sub-elements representing the overall, structural, behavioural and soft constraint distances between the relevant query and service, respectively.

Table 1. Sample of the results for PurchaseTransactionQ1

Query Operation (Q1)	**Service Operations (PurchaseService)**
comparePrice(itemName:String):List	Search(item:String):List
calculatePostageCost(item:ItemInfo, country:String):Real	calculateCost(item:String):Real
placeOrder(itemName:String, quantity:int, location:Location):Boolean	purchaseGoods(item:String, quantity:int, address:String):Boolean
Query Constraints (Q1)	**Service Constraints (Q1)**
ResponseTime = 5 seconds	ResponseTime = 5 seconds
5 Euros <= Cost <= 10 Euros	Cost = 8 Euros, 30 invocations per month

The information represented in the service_operation element will be used to re-formulate the design models while the information represented in the service_constraint element will be used to reformulate the SLA terms.

As an example, consider the PurchaseTransactionQuery1. Suppose that for this query the results of the best candidate service are shown in Table 1. For clarity, we present the results in a table format. We also do not present the information described in the service_behavioural element and the respective distances. As shown in Table 1, the operations search, calculateCost, and purchaseGoods from service PurchaseService (from ProviderX) are the best match for the query messages. In addition, according to the BPEL specification of PurchaseService, these operations are executed in the order shown in the table. Moreover, the response time for PurchaseService is the same as in the query, and the cost to use this service is eight Euros with a restriction of a maximum of 30 invocations of the service per month.

Suppose that the designer selects PurchaseService as the service to be bound to the design models and instantiated in the SLA. In this case, the sequence diagram of the service-based system is updated with the operations in the service, and placeholder IPriceFinder is instantiate as PurchaseService. The terms in the SLA are updated with the quality characteristics of the service.

Figure 13 shows part of the SLA with the instantiated information. As shown in the figure, the initial guarantee term ResponseTimeReference is maintained in the SLA, since the selected service has the same response time as requested (this was specified in the query as a hard constraint). However, the guarantee term CostReference is modified to represent the fact that the cost for using the service is eight Euros (instead of a range between five and ten Euros), and a new guarantee term TransactionReference is added to the SLA. This new term represents the fact that the cost of eight Euros to use PurchaseService is limited to 30 invocations of the service per month. In this case, the service consumer (PT_SBS service-based system) will be the party with the obligation to assure that the service will not be accessed for more than 30 times per month.

The decision of which party is obligated to guarantee a term (i.e., service provider or consumer) is based on (i) the meaning of the term, (b) any restriction imposed by a bound service, and (c) assistance from the application designer that is able to understand (i) and (ii) above and even negotiate with service providers, if necessary. Furthermore, the approach is supposed to be used in an interactive process in which the discovery activity relies on ongoing development of the design models of a service-based system and service level agreements, and the available services identified during the process can be used to amend and reformulate the design models of the systems and service level agreements by the application designer.

Figure 13. Part of instantiated SLA for the PurchaseTransaction service-based system and service PurchaseService

```
<wsag:Agreement AgreementID="PT_Agg1"> ...
<wsag:Terms>
  <wsag:All> <wsag:ExactlyOne>
      <wsag:All>
       <wsag:ServiceDescriptionTerm
         wsag:Name=ResponseTimeTerm"   wsag:ServiceName="PurchaseService">
       </wsag:ServiceDescriptionTerm>
       <wsag:ServiceDescriptionTerm
         wsag:Name=MaxCostTerm"   wsag:ServiceName="PurchaseService">
       </wsag:ServiceDescriptionTerm>
       </wsag:ServiceDescriptionTerm>
       <wsag:ServiceDescriptionTerm
         wsag:Name=TransactionTerm"   wsag:ServiceName="PT_SBS">
       </wsag:ServiceDescriptionTerm>
    </wsag:ExactlyOne>
    <wsag:GuaranteeTerm
        wsag:Name="ResponseTimeReference"
        wsag:Obligated="ServiceProvider">
       <wsag:ServiceScope>
         <wsag:ServiceName>PurchaseService</wsag:ServiceName>
       </wsag:ServiceScope>
       <wsag:ServiceLevelObjective>
        <wsag:KPITarget>
          <wsag:KPIName>ResponseTime</wasg:KPIName>
          <wasg:Target>5 seconds</wsag:Target>
        </wsag:KPITarget>
       </wsag:ServiceLevelObjective>
    </wsag:GuaranteeTerm>
    <wsag:GuaranteeTerm
        wsag:Name="CostReference"
        wsag:Obligated="ServiceProvider">
       <wsag:ServiceScope>
         <wsag:ServiceName>PurchaseService</wsag:ServiceName>
       </wsag:ServiceScope>
       <wsag:ServiceLevelObjective xsi:type="sdtc:OpType">
           <Unit>Euros</Unit>
           <SDT>CostTerm</SDT>
       </wsag:ServiceLevelObjective
       <wsag:BusinessValueList>
        <wsag:Preference>
            <wsag:ServiceTermReference>CostTerm</wasg:ServiceTermReference>
          <wasg:Utility>8</wsag:Utility>
        </wsag:Preference>
       </wsag:BusinessValueList>
    </wsag:GuaranteeTerm>
    <wsag:GuaranteeTerm
        wsag:Name="TransactionReference"
        wsag:Obligated="ServiceConsumer">
       <wsag:ServiceScope>
         <wsag:ServiceName>PT_SBS</wsag:ServiceName>
       </wsag:ServiceScope>
       <wsag:ServiceLevelObjective>
        <wsag:KPITarget>
          <wsag:KPIName>TransactionNumber</wasg:KPIName>
          <wasg:Target>30 invocations per month </wsag:Target>
        </wsag:KPITarget>
       </wsag:ServiceLevelObjective>
    </wsag:GuaranteeTerm> . . . </wsag:All> </wsag:Terms>. . .
</wsag:Agreement>
```

FUTURE TRENDS

Automatic support for the creation of service level agreements is important to assist with the development and wide use of service oriented computing. The approach described in this paper in which service level agreements are created concurrently with the development of service-based systems, based on identified services, and not after the system is developed, guarantees a better representation of the functional and non-functional characteristics of the systems and participating services. In addition, it provides a more realistic expectation of what available services that may be used in the system can really provide, instead of being based on requirements that may never be able to be fulfilled by service providers.

While the current approach assumes the existence of initial service level agreement templates, more work needs to be developed in order to support the creation of these initial agreement templates. More specifically, it is necessary to have methodologies and tools to derive the service level agreement templates from system design models, as well as requirements specifications. In addition, there is a need to support automatic (a) generation of queries expressed in SerDiQueL derived from the design models and service level agreement data, and (b) amendment of design models and SLAs based on the identified and chosen services.

The approach also needs to be extended to support service discovery and service level agreement creation based on service composition; i.e., the identification of operations from various services that together can fulfill a certain functionality of the system.

Another important extension for the approach is concerned with support for the creation or amendment of existing services based on the functional and non-functional demands of service-based systems. Service providers should consider changes to their services in order to fulfill the requirements of the systems being developed and, therefore, enhance the use of their services.

Other areas of research to be considered by the approach is the support for automatic generation of service-based system's workflow from its respective design models and automatic negotiation between service providers and consumers during the creation of the service level agreements.

CONCLUSION

In this chapter we have presented an approach to support creation of service level agreement and design models of service-based systems. More specifically, our approach is based on service discovery in which given initial structural and behavioural models of service-based systems and service level agreement templates, services that can fulfill the structural, functional, and quality characteristics of the system being developed represented by these models and SLA templates. The identified services are used to re-formulate the design models and to instantiate the SLA between the service-based system being developed (consumer) and the participating services (providers). The approach is iterative in which the re-formulated design models and service level agreement may trigger new service discovery iterations. An XML-base language is used to represent complex queries for identifying services.

A prototype tool for service discovery based on matching of structural, functional, and quality aspects of the service-based system has been developed. Initial evaluations of the tool in terms of recall and precision measurements, and performance of the matching process have been positive, as described in (Kozlenkov et al., 2007; Zisman & Spanoudakis, 2006; Spanoudakis & Zisman, review).

ACKNOWLEDGMENT

Part of the work reported in this paper has been funded by the European Commission under the Information Society Technologies Programme as part of the project SeCSE (contract IST-511680).

REFERENCES

Aggarwal, R., Verma, K., Miller, J., & Milnor, W. (2004). Constraint driven Web Service composition in METEOR-S. Proceedings of IEEE International Conference on Services Computing. New York, NY.

Beeri, C., Eyal, A., Kamenkovich, S., & Milo, T. (2006). Querying business processes. Proceedings of the 32nd International Conference on Very Large Data Bases. Korea.

Bormann, F., et al. (2005). Towards context-aware service discovery: A case study for a new advice of charge service. Proceedings of the 14th IST Mobile and Wireless Communications Summit. Dresden.

BPEL4WS. (2007). Specifications. Retrieved from http://www128.ibm.com/developerworks/ library/ specification/ws-bpel/

Broens, T., et al. (2004). Context-aware, ontology-based, service discovery. Ambient Intelligence, (LNCS 3295), (pp.72-83).

Canfora, G., Di Penta, M., Esposito, R., Perfetto, F., & Villani, M. L. (2006). Service composition (re)binding driven by application-specific QoS. Proceedings of the 4th International Conference on Service Oriented Computing. Chicago, USA.

Cardoso, J., & Sheth, A. (2003). Semantic e-workflow composition. *Journal of Intelligent Information Systems*, *21*(3), 191–225. doi:10.1023/A:1025542915514

Choonhwa, L., & Helal, S. (2003). Context attributes: An approach to enable context-awareness for service discovery. Proceedings of Symposium on Applications & the Internet. Orlando, USA.

CoDAMoS. (2008). Ontology. Retrieved from www.cs.kuleuven.ac.be/cwis/research/distrinet/projects/CoDAMoS/ontology/

Commuzi, M., & Pernici, B. (2005). An architecture for flexible Web Service QoS negotiation. Proceedings of the 9th IEEE Enterprise Computing Conference. The Netherlands.

Cuddy, S., Katchabaw, M., & Lutfiyya, H. (2005). Context-aware service selection based on dynamic and static service attributes. Proceedings of IEEE International Conference on Wireless and Mobile Computing, Networking and Communication. Montreal, Canada.

Debusmann, M., & Keller, A. (2003). SLA-driven management of distributed systems using the common information model. Proceedings of the 8th IFIP/IEEE International Symposium on Integrated Network Management. USA, March.

Deubler, M., Meisinger, M., & Kruger, I. (2005). Modelling crosscutting services with UML sequence diagrams. Proceedings of ACM/IEEE 8th International Conference on Model Driven Engineering Languages and Systems, Jamaica.

Doulkeridis, C., Loutas, N., & Vazirgiannis, M. (2006). A system architecture for context-aware service discovery. *Electronic Notes in Theoretical Computer Science*, *146*(1), 101–116. doi:10.1016/j.entcs.2005.11.010

Gardner, T. (2004). UML modelling of automated business processes with a mapping to BPEL4WS. Proceedings of the 2nd European Workshop on OO and Web Services. Oslo, Norway.

Garofalakis, J., Panagys, Y., Sakkopoulos, E., & Tsakalidis, A. (2006). Contemporary Web Service discovery mechanisms. *Journal of Web Engineering*, *5*(3), 265–290.

Gimpel, H., Ludwig, H., Dan, A., & Kearney, R. (2003). PANDA: Specifying policies for automated negotiations of service contracts. Proceedings of the 1st International Conference on Service Oriented Computing, Trento, Italy.

Grirori, D., Corrales, J. C., & Bouzeghoub, M. (2006). Behavioral matching for service retrieval. Proceedings of the International Conference on Web Services. USA.

Hall, R. J., & Zisman, A. (2004). Behavioral Models as Service Descriptions. International Conference on Service Oriented Computing. New York, USA.

Hausmann, J. R., Heckel, R., & Lohman, M. (2004). Model-based discovery of Web Services. Proceedings of the International Conference on Web Services. USA.

Horrocks, I., Patel-Schneider, P. F., & van Harmelen, F. (2003). From SHIQ and RDF to OWL: The making of a Web ontology language. *Journal of Web Semantics*, *1*(1), 7–26. doi:10.1016/j.websem.2003.07.001

Hoschek, W. (2002). The Web Service discovery architecture. Proceedings of the IEEE/ACM Supercomputing Conference. Baltimore, USA.

Jones, S., Kozlenkov, A., Mahbub, K., Maiden, M., Spanoudakis, G., Zachos, K., et al. (2005). Service discovery for service centric systems. eChallenges. Slovenia.

Keller, A., & Ludwig, H. (2002). Defining and monitoring service level agreements for dynamic e-business. Proceedings of the 16th System Administration Conference, USA.

Keller, U., Lara, R., Lausen, H., Polleres, A., & Fensel, D. (2005). Automatic location of services. Proceedings of the European Semantic Web Conference. Crete, Greece.

Khedr, M., & Karmouch, A. (2002). *Enhancing service discovery with context information*. Spain: Intelligent Tutoring Systems.

Klein, M., & Bernstein, A. (2004). Toward high-precision service retrieval. *IEEE Internet Computing*, 30–36. doi:10.1109/MIC.2004.1260701

Klusch, M., Fries, B., & Sycara, K. (2006). Automated Semantic Web service discovery with OWLS-MX. Proceedings of the International Conference on Autonomous Agents and Multiagent Systems. Japan.

Kokash, N., van den Heuvel, W. J., & D'Andrea, V. (2006). Leveraging Web Services discovery with customizable hybrid matching. Proceedings of the International Conference on Web Services. USA.

Kozlenkov, A., Fasoulas, V., Sanchez, F., Spanoudakis, G., & Zisman, A. (2006). A framework for architecture-driven service discovery. Proceedings of the International Workshop on Service Oriented Software Engineering. China.

Kozlenkov, A., Spanoudakis, G., Zisman, A., Fasoulas, V., & Sanchez, F. (2007). Architecture-driven service discovery for service centric systems. *International Journal of Web Services Research*, *4*(2). doi:10.4018/jwsr.2007040104

Kozlenkov, A., & Zisman, A. (2004). Discovering, recording, and handling inconsistencies in software specifications. *International Journal of Computer and Information Science*, *5*(2), 89–108.

Kramler, G., Kapsammer, E., Kappel, G., & Retschitzegger, W. (2005). Towards using UML 2 for modelling Web Service collaboration protocols. Proceedings of the 1st Conference on Interoperability of Enterprise Software and Applications. Geneva, Switzerland.

Li, L., & Horrock, I. (2003). A software framework for matchmaking based on Semantic Web technology. WWW Conference Workshop on e-Services and the Semantic Web. Budapest, Hungary.

Mahbub, K., & Spanoudakis, G. (2007). Monitoring WS-Agreements: An event calculus based approach. In Baresi, L., & diNitto, E. (Eds.), *Springer monograph on test and analysis of Web Services*. Springer Verlang. doi:10.1007/978-3-540-72912-9_10

Mikhaiel, R., & Stroulia, E. (2006). Interface- and usage-aware service discovery. 4th International Conference on Service Oriented Computing. Chicago, USA.

Morato, J., Marzal, M. A., Llorens, J., & Moreiro, J. (2004). WordNet application. Proceedings of The Second Global Wordnet Conference. Brno, Czech Republic.

Nguyen, X. T., Kowalczyk, R., & Han, J. (2006). Using dynamic asynchronous aggregate search for quality guarantees of multiple Web Services compositions. Proceedings of the 4th International Conference on Service Oriented Computing. Chicago, USA.

OWL-S. (2007). OWL-S version 1.0. Retrieved from www.daml.org/services/owl-s/1.0

Pantazoglou, M., Tsalgatidou, A., & Athanasopoulos, G. (2006). Discovering Web Services in JXTA peer-to-peer services in a unified manner. Proceedings of the 4th International Conference on Service Oriented Computing. Chicago, USA.

Pantazoglou, M., Tsalgatidou, A., & Spanoudakis, G. (2007). Behavior-aware, unified service discovery. In Proceedings of the Service-Oriented Computing: A look at the inside Workshop. Austria. De Paoli, F., Lulli, G. & Maurino, A. (2006). Design of quality-based composite Web Services. Proceedings of the 4th International Conference on Service Oriented Computing. Chicago, USA.

Papadimitriou, C., & Steiglitz, K. (1982). *Combinatorial optimisation: Algorithms and complexity*. Prentice-Hall Inc.

Papazoglou, M., Aiello, M., Pistore, M., & Yang, J. (2008). XSRL: A request language for Web Services. Retrieved from rom http://citeseer.ist.psu.edu/575968.html

Pawar, P., & Tokmakoff, A. (2006). Ontology-based context-aware service discovery for pervasive environments. Proceedings of the IEEE International Workshop On Service Integration in Pervasive Environment. Lyon, France.

SECSE A2.D8. (2006). Platform for architecture service discovery V2.0: specification.

SECSE A2.D12. (2008). Platform for architecture-time service discovery V3.0.

Shen, Z., & Su, J. (2005). Web Service discovery based on behaviour signatures. Proceedings of the IEEE International Conference on Service Computing. USA.

Spanoudakis, G., & Constantopoulos, P. (1996). Elaborating analogies from conceptual models. *International Journal of Intelligent Systems*, *11*(11), 917–974. doi:10.1002/(SICI)1098-111X(199611)11:11<917::AID-INT4>3.3.CO;2-V

Spanoudakis, G., & Zisman, A. (2006). UML-based service discovery tool. Proceedings of the 21st IEEE International Conference on Automated Software Engineering Conference. Japan.

Spanoudakis, G. & Zisman, A. (In press). Discovering services during hybrid service-based system design.

Spanoudakis, G., Zisman, A., & Kozlenkov, A. (2005). A service discovery framework for service centric systems. Proceedings of the IEEE International Conference on Service Computing. USA.

Wang, X., Vitvar, T., Kerrigan, T., & Toma, I. (2006). A QoS-aware selection model for Semantic Web Services. Proceedings of the 4th International Conference on Service Oriented Computing. USA.

Wang, Y., & Stroulia, E. (2003). Semantic structure matching for assessing Web-Service similarity. Proceedings of the International Conference on Service Oriented Computing. Italy.

WS-Agreement. (2007). Web Services agreement specification. Retrieved from http://force.gridforum.org/sf/projects/graap-ws

WSDL. (2009). TR. Retrieved from http://www.w3.org/TR/wsdl

WSML. (2009). Syntax. Retrieved from http://www.wsmo.org/wsml/wsml-syntax

WSMO. (2010). Submission. Retrieved from http://www.w3.org/Submission/2005/SUBM-WSMO-20050603.

Wu, J., & Wu, Z. (2005). Similarity-based Web Service matchmaking. Proceedings of the IEEE International Conference on Services Computing. USA.

Yunyao, L. Y., Yanh, H., & Jagadish, H. (2005). *NaLIX: An interactive natural language interface for querying XML*. Baltimore, USA: SIGMOD.

Zisman, A., & Spanoudakis, G. (2006). UML-based service discovery framework. Proceedings of the 4th International Conference on Service Oriented Computing. Chicago, USA

Zisman, A., Spanoudakis, G., & Dooley, J. (2008). A framework for dynamic service discovery. Proceedings of the IEEE International Conference on Automated Software Engineering. Italy.

Zisman, A., Spanoudakis, G. & Dooley, J. (In press). SerDiQueL: A Service Discovery Query Language.

ENDNOTES

1. A discussion about the WS-Agreement (WS-Agreement) language is beyond the scope of this paper.
2. In this graphical notation (i) E represents XML elements; (ii) A represents attributes of an element; (iii) sub-elements of an element are represented by associations; (iv) number of occurrences of an element is represented by cardinalities in associations.
3. The main concepts of this graphical representation are described in Footnote 2.
4. The main concepts of this graphical representation are described in Footnote 2.
5. To avoid any commercial issues, we use a fictitious service provider name.
6. When the number of operations is not the same between the query and candidate services, special vertices are added in the graph representing dummy operations, in order to make the number even.
7. The main concepts of this graphical representation are described in Footnote 2.

Chapter 5
Configuration of Non-Functional Properties in Embedded Operating Systems:
The CiAO Approach

Wanja Hofer
Friedrich–Alexander University Erlangen–Nuremberg, Germany

Julio Sincero
Friedrich–Alexander University Erlangen–Nuremberg, Germany

Wolfgang Schröder-Preikschat
Friedrich–Alexander University Erlangen–Nuremberg, Germany

Daniel Lohmann
Friedrich–Alexander University Erlangen–Nuremberg, Germany

ABSTRACT

In embedded operating systems (OSes), non-functional properties like reliability, performance, or memory footprint are of special importance. State-of-the-art OS product lines focus on the configurability of functional characteristics of the system. This chapter proposes an approach that aims at also making non-functional properties indirectly configurable and maintainable by the system configurator. In order to reach this goal, the CiAO OS product line used here has configurable architectural properties, which have no functional influence on the target system, but instead bear an impact on its non-functional properties. Additionally, the chapter develops a feedback approach that gains information about the non-functional properties of an already configured system to assist further configuration decisions, and presents and details the CiAO approach and evaluates it using two case studies from the CiAO operating system.

DOI: 10.4018/978-1-60960-493-6.ch005

MOTIVATION

In the domain of system software, non-functional properties (NFPs) are of fundamental importance to the end user. This is because system software never has a purpose and business value of its own, but it is rather a means to aid the *application* making use of it in fulfilling its (business-value-bringing) purpose. Hence, performance, for example, is an important non-functional criterion to select a suitable operating system (OS) to deploy an application on. In the sub domain of *embedded* operating systems, NFPs can even be mission-critical since some embedded systems applications depend on the fault tolerance or a given upper bound on the latency of the underlying embedded OS. Since the desired NFPs of a piece of system software are different from application scenario to application scenario (and sometimes reflect a trade-off decision), it is the task of the OS engineer to keep the NFPs *configurable*.

In our experience, though, the consideration of NFPs in system software causes problems because NFPs can never be made *directly* configurable. That is because most NFPs are *emergent* in their nature; that is, they have no direct representation in the system's implementation entities. Instead, they result from the orchestration of the properties available in the selected configuration. Hence, NFPs can only be made configurable via *indirect* configuration of other properties.

However, the set of *functional* properties to be selected is fixed, dependent on the application. Other properties, which we call *architectural* properties (APs), are transparent to the application, though, but they still have an enormous effect on the NFPs of the resulting end system. Examples of such APs of OSes include the chosen method of interrupt synchronization in the kernel, the available protection facilities (including memory protection, for instance), or the type of interaction between kernel modules. The latter has been under heavy discussion for decades now, arguing in favor of procedural interaction in monolithic systems versus message passing techniques in microkernels (Lauer and Needham, 1979, Liedtke, 1995). The early decision to adopt one of those alternatives has a significant impact on the NFPs of performance, latency, and memory footprint, among others.

The CiAO family of embedded OSes developed by our research group was designed with *architectural configurability* in mind; that is, even fundamental architectural properties are kept configurable in CiAO's design. Hence, the decision in favor of one or the other shape of an AP is postponed until the configuration stage and therefore left to the system configurator. He can then choose the one configuration option that has the best desired impact on the NFPs of the target system, effectively tailoring the OS (and its architecture) to the needs of the application scenario.

However, if the variability in a software product line exceeds a certain threshold (e.g., by offering architectural variability like in CiAO), the number of transparent configuration options left open to the configurator quickly becomes overwhelming. We therefore also propose a new kind of development process with a feedback approach, which gathers additional knowledge by analyzing product variants regarding their NFPs. It is thereby possible to assist the configurator in making his configuration decisions when aiming at optimizing a specific NFP.

The domain of embedded system software is one that has been concerned with non-functional properties for a long time being. Embedded systems engineers have gathered a lot of knowledge on how to deal with those properties, knowledge that the domain of service-oriented architecture can benefit from.

Structure of the Rest of the Chapter

The remainder of this chapter is structured in a top-down manner. First we give background information and definitions necessary for the understanding of the text. Then, an overview of our CiAO approach and, after that, its details are presented. The following section details the evaluation studies regarding the influence of APs on NFPs. We then present work that is related to our approach, and the chapter is concluded in the last section.

BACKGROUND

Our Understanding of Non-Functional Properties

To define what exactly non-functional properties (NFPs) are is a delicate task. There is no standard definition in the software engineering community available, and different groups inside the community have contradicting definitions. Moreover, even the nomenclature used is not uniform; for example, in different contexts the same kinds of software properties are termed NFPs, quality attributes (Bass, 2006), or soft goals (Cysneiros and do Prado Leite, 2004), among others. Amongst a myriad of examples of such properties, they include security, reliability, safety, performance, maintainability, usability, and code size, to just name a few.

Moreover, many of these terms are broad and generic; different stakeholders may have a varying understanding (and, therefore, expectations) of such properties. We believe that when dealing with such properties, it is necessary to define what is considered to be an NFP in that specific context. For this reason, we narrow NFPs down with the following definition.

Non-functional properties of a software system are those properties that do not describe the principal task or functionality of the software, but can be observed by end users in its run-time behavior (Lohmann et al., 2005).

This definition gives good insights into the type of properties that we see as NFPs. It is very well applicable to our domain of families of operating systems; however, it can also be applied to a number of other domains, especially those of infrastructure software (e.g., middleware, database systems, etc.).

The goal of our work is to show how we address the configuration of properties that fall under these definitions. Approaching such properties is a challenging task mainly due to two reasons. On one hand, a primary goal is to improve the understanding of NFPs already at the stage of software configuration. In a perfect scenario, this would be to provide the system configurator with means to express the non-functional requirements on the product. On the other hand, after having developed several families of operating systems, we have learned that many NFPs are *emergent*. That means that they are the result of the *interaction* of many components, which effectively hinders the possibility of *direct* configuration of such properties. Therefore, our techniques presented in this chapter aim at closing this gap. The complex interactions that will influence the system's NFPs cannot be appropriately predicted at design stage, which makes attempts of preparing configuration mechanisms during design not very reliable. As a result, we have decided to extend our approach to tackle NFPs not only during the design stage, but also in other development stages, and even *post* implementation. The idea is to learn from configured and running systems, and to gather information how the system's components are interacting, and how this interaction influences the investigated NFPs. Subsequently, this information should be used to improve the configuration of future systems.

The Classical and the SPL Software Development Processes

In order to be able to address NFPs in a thorough and holistic way, we have developed an own software development process, the CiAO development process, which is detailed in the main section of this chapter. It is based on the classical software development process and the process proposed for

Figure 1. The classical software development process

software product lines, both of which are briefly introduced here.

Figure 1 shows the main stages of the traditional software development process. The customer expresses his requirements on the desired product in an appropriate way; those requirements are then analyzed by the software engineer, enabling him to develop a software architecture. This design is then implemented using the languages and platforms that are appropriate for the target environment. If another customer asks for a similar, but different product, these stages are basically repeated, and the new product is developed from scratch.

This problem is tackled by the canonical software *product-line* (SPL) development process (see Figure 2). Here, not a single product is considered, but a whole family of products targeting a specific domain.

In the *domain engineering* process (upper half in Figure 2), the product line itself is developed, while in application engineering, a specific product is built from the outcome of the domain engineering without much effort. First, domain experts having comprehensive domain knowledge scope the domain and specify the desired variability and configuration options (domain analysis). This variability is often expressed in a feature model containing a feature diagram representing the configuration space. After this, a reference architecture is built during the domain design step, followed by the domain implementation. The assets that constitute the product-line implementation are stored and described by a family model.

In *application engineering* (lower half in Figure 2), the customer's demands on the product are first investigated in a requirements analysis step, which results in a feature selection in the feature model previously developed in the domain engineering process. This feature selection can then be used to automatically derive a final product variant using the family model and the product-line assets. Hence, those assets are then re-usable across multiple products in the product line, enabling an advance in important factors like time to market and product quality, for instance.

THE CiAO APPROACH

CiAO (CiAO is Aspect-Oriented) is a family of OSes targeting the embedded systems domain,

Figure 2. The software development process as proposed by the software product-line community. (adapted from (Czarnecki and Eisenecker, 2000))

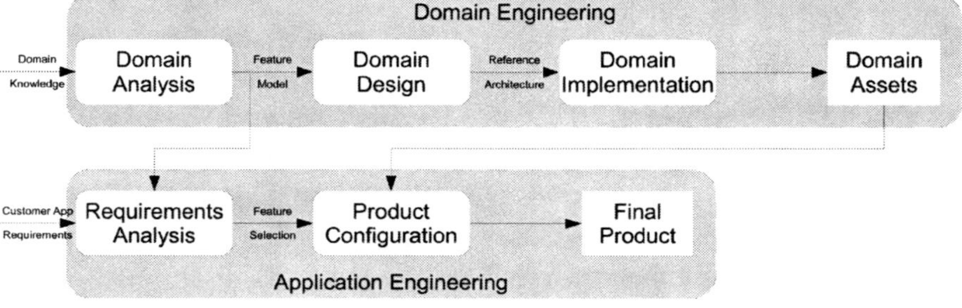

Figure 3. The CiAO software development process

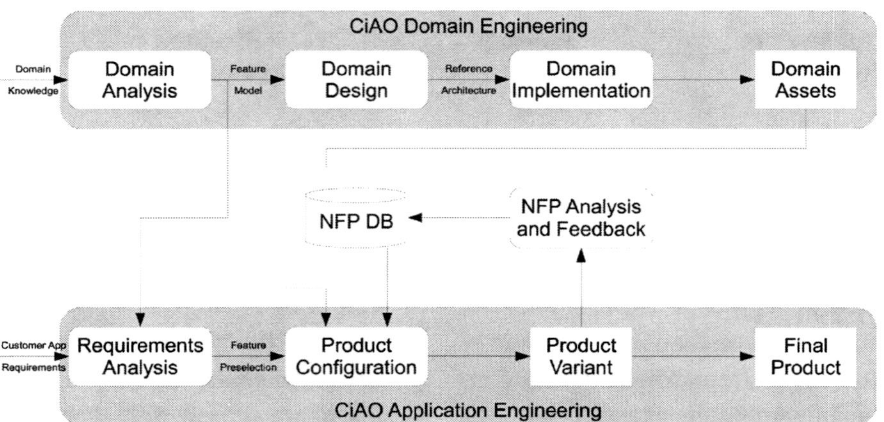

especially those systems deployed on microcontrollers in the automotive industry. The main goal of the project is to show that even fundamental architectural properties of an OS can be kept configurable, thereby effectively enabling the *indirect* configuration of non-functional properties. This goal is reached by using techniques from the field of software product-line engineering in the analysis stage, and by developing aspect-aware design patterns in order to be able to deploy aspect-oriented artifacts in the implementation. This way, CiAO reaches a very good separation of concerns while providing very fine-grained and deep configuration possibilities at the same time. By selecting a specific combination of architectural property configurations, it is possible to get an architecture that is optimized according to the non-functional requirements of a particular scenario. However, since those NFPs do not emerge until the production configuration stage, a specialized development process is needed to treat NFPs as "first-class citizens" in *all* development stages.

Overview of the CiAO Software Development Process

We have adapted the canonical software product-line development process (see also the previous section) to better address non-functional properties. The resulting CiAO software development process is depicted in Figure 3.

We enriched the steps in the layers of domain engineering and application engineering, which are described in the following two sub sections. Furthermore, we introduced additional steps in a feedback loop that has access to a database of non-functional properties of the product line. These additions are described in the remaining sub sections.

CiAO Domain Engineering

Domain engineering in the CiAO development process is similar to the steps proposed in software product-line engineering. However, those steps now encompass the consideration of non-functional properties from the very beginning. This is done by extending the domain knowledge by features that are *transparent* to the application developer—because it is mostly *those* features that have a significant *indirect* impact on the perceived non-functional properties of the target system. Thus, additional configuration options are considered in the domain analysis and offered in the feature diagram that would not be examined in the classical approach.

Figure 4. An excerpt of the CiAO feature diagram. Features that are functionally transparent to the application are depicted in gray color.

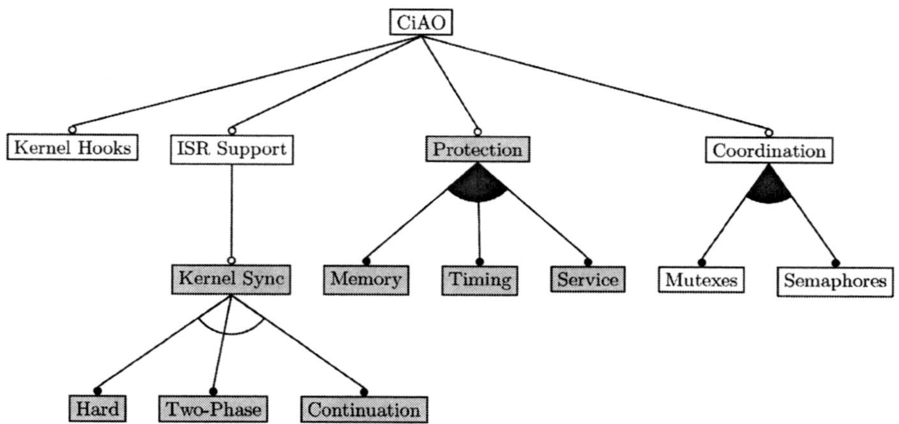

In the CiAO family of operating systems, most of those additional options refer to the configurability of CiAO's architecture. By keeping those architectural properties configurable in the domain design, the system configurator can still decide in favor of one flavor or the other, depending on the desired focus on the system's non-functional properties. Two of those properties—interrupt synchronization and memory protection—and their configurable influence on some non-functional properties is presented in the next section.

Another focus of the CiAO research project is to show that architectural configurability can still be maintainable in the implementation. In order to reach this goal and because many architectural properties are highly cross-cutting in the design and implementation, CiAO is implemented using aspect-oriented programming (AOP) techniques. In particular, the implementation language and aspect weaver AspectC++ (Spinczyk and Lohmann, 2007) is used, which is a superset of the C++ programming language. With this programming paradigm, we showed that is possible to have maintainable, concern-separated system software code that has configurable architectural properties in its domain implementation (Lohmann et al., 2007b, Lohmann et al., 2007a).

A small excerpt of the CiAO feature diagram, which resulted from the domain analysis step, is shown in Figure 4. It is referenced throughout the rest of the chapter to give examples of some of the steps performed in the development process.

CiAO Application Engineering

Application engineering in the CiAO development cycle also differs from the one in SPL engineering. The system configurator, who translates the customer requests into selections in the feature model provided by the domain analysis step, will not be able to make *all* configuration decisions. That is because CiAO aims at providing options that are transparent to the application, like those configuration options pertaining to the system architecture. Hence, the output of the requirements analysis step can only be a *pre*selection of features, and it is only a sample variant that is configured and generated first.

After that, our feedback approach comes into play. The generated sample variant is analyzed for its NFPs and checked against the NFP database, which results in an altered feature selection and therefore product variant. This iteration is repeated until the final product conforms to the desired non-functional requirements, or until the best solution is reached within given time constraints. The exact procedure of the CiAO configuration process, the feedback approach, and its application is discussed in the following sections.

The CiAO Configuration Process

As CiAO is a software product line, a member of this family of systems (i.e., a concrete solution) is derived according to a given specification (i.e., the feature selection) that conforms to the formal feature model. This transformation process is driven by a family model, which plays a central role. It is responsible for mapping the selected features to concrete implementations units. That is, according to the set of selected features, the corresponding components (e.g., classes, aspects, etc.) are customized (e.g., by conditional compilation, preprocessing, etc.) and then copied to another source-code tree, where it can be compiled to generate the required family member.

Feature models mostly correspond to a set of *functional* features (disclosed during domain engineering) that can be turned on and off, whereas the set of valid configurations is determined by the feature tree hierarchy and its extra interdependencies. However, it is often the case that several features define the same *interface* for a specific service, but derive different *implementations* for the service provided by the interface. This means that, from the user's perspective, the difference between the several features implementing the same service can only be distinguished by its effect on the system's NFPs. In traditional approaches, during the software configuration the system configurator either has to have strong knowledge about the internals of the system, or he has to have assistance from the developers in order to decide among features that implement the same interface. The root of the problem here is the missing information about the effect of otherwise identical features on the system NFPs.

In order to address this issue, we augment the feature model with non-functional information, which can be obtained from two different sources. First, from the system designers, who made the architectural decisions and are aware of the possible impact of features on NFPs. (Architectural decisions are often a trade-off between two or more NFPs). Second, from tests performed on generated family members. Even though the information provided by the system designers may be, to some extent, helpful, we believe that performing tests is the appropriate approach. Information from tests is not only able to assist the configuration process, but also assures that the implementation conforms to the expected behavior that motivated the design decisions. In short, it is real data, and it helps software *evaluation* and *evolution*, as it is able to reveal flaws in the design and the implementation.

THE FEEDBACK APPROACH

As we have detailed in the previous sections, many NFPs cannot be appropriately predicted at design time and, hence, not be directly configured at configuration time. Therefore, we believe that in order to get useful information about the system's NFPs, the use of tests on generated products is a promising alternative. The real behavior of many types of NFPs can not be detected until after the family member is configured and generated. That is, information regarding the interaction among the components that comprise the entire system can only be observed after the system is prepared to be deployed. For example, insights about the RAM footprint or code size can be gained from *static* tests performed after generation. Additionally, information about latency or performance can be captured by performing *dynamic* tests on the running system variants.

The feedback approach extends the traditional SPL development techniques in order to provide information regarding NFPs during product configuration. We introduced new structures and mechanisms so that the SPL infrastructure can be used to generate products that will be tested against the NFP that is to be investigated. This information is saved, organized, and re-inserted in the SPL process (see also Figure 3). It also enables the user to benefit from it in the configuration of *further* products. This feedback process is organized in three layers:

1. The SPL Repository comprises the software components that can be assembled together to generate products (see Figure 3, Domain Assets). Additionally, components that are used merely to *capture* non-functional information from generated products (like performance measurement aspects that instrument the product) are also available. We have shown that *aspects* are very adequate for this task (Gilani et al., 2007).
2. The User Configuration is responsible for providing the mechanisms for product configuration. Besides the traditional configuration process (selecting features from a feature model), we provide the user with non-functional information (see Figure 3, Product Configuration). As NFPs are very specific to each product, or even to each feature, this information can be displayed in different graphical ways, for example, sliders, graphs, charts, etc. Moreover, during configuration the user can select the aforementioned components that are responsible for measuring some of the NFPs of the product.
3. The Concrete Solution Domain encompasses the generated product, the compiling environment, and the run-time environment used to generate and test the product (see Figure 3, Product Variant).

The mechanisms described so far are appropriate for generating and testing single family members. That is, after the configuration process, the system configurator is able to confirm if the generated product meets his expectations regarding NFPs. Nevertheless, this is not enough if we want to use this information to guide the configuration process, because we would need information about the entire family, and not only about single configurations.

To solve this problem, the naive approach would be to generate all possible family members; this is not a feasible solution, though. Normally, system families have several hundreds of features, and they can generate several thousands of different family members. Therefore, an exhaustive study of all members is not computationally possible. However, important for our approach is how groups of features interact with each other to influence NFPs; in many cases, several features will not have any interaction at all. This means that many tests on different configurations will produce the same measurement results for a specific NFP that is investigated. In order to avoid redundant tests, and consequently to reduce the test space, a *metric* regarding *feature interaction* is to be defined so that only tests that reveal important information regarding how the feature interaction will influence the required NFP are performed. For examples of uses of these metrics, see the following section about the CiAO studies.

Ultimately, the organization of the SPL in this fashion aims at improving the *configuration experience* in the following ways:

1. Providing exact non-functional information about products that have been previously configured;
2. Using heuristics and regression techniques to provide approximated information about products that have only been partially configured;
3. If several software components implement the same functional behavior, the user should be able to select the most appropriate one depending on their non-functional characteristics;

RESTRICTING THE FEATURE MODEL FOR TESTING

An important characteristic of families of systems is that the code base does not only represent one system, but all valid family members. However, to perform tests on this code, specific members must first be configured and then generated. Moreover, aiming at understanding how features interact in different configurations requires whole sets of family members to be generated and tested. The strategy of testing the set of *all* family members is not practicable.

Therefore, our approach provides means for the application engineer to specify sets of products to be tested. The objective of specifying tests is to avoid generating members where interactions will not influence the desired NFPs. Of course, for some NFPs this definition may not be trivial. However, for others it may be pretty straightforward. For example, consider the scenario where the NFP represents the time required for the computation of a specific math algorithm. This algorithm may be configured in different ways by means of several features, and the math algorithm itself is a feature of a complex system comprised of other algorithms that can be configured independently. If those other algorithms do not share code with the investigated math algorithm, testing each of the algorithms separately (and not all of the combinations) would reduce the testing space, and the performance measurement results of each algorithm that is tested individually would not be altered.

In order to accomplish such kinds of restrictions on feature models, we came up with the idea of *partial configurations*. In traditional feature models, a feature selection is simply a list of features that are required to be present in the member to be generated. (The generation can only be performed when the selection is valid, though.) We have extended this concept, now enabling the user to set the features that must be present (*selected features*), the set of features that must not be present (*blocked features*), and other features that may be let open (*open features*). A list of such selections of features specifies a *partial configuration.* We developed a tool that is able to generate all valid configurations that conform to the specification of a partial configuration. Our tool transforms the feature model into a binary decision diagram (BDD) and by using the BuDDy library (BuDDy Developers, 2009) we are able to generate the set of valid configurations that conforms to the restrictions described by the partial configuration.

Using this tool, the engineer is able to set the features he wants to be present in all tests (of the test set) by defining them as *selected.* The ones that are known not to have an influence on the NFP to be tested are set to *blocked.* The features that actually represent the variability among the members of the test set are marked as *open.*

Applying the Feedback Approach

In order to explain how partial configurations can be used to generate a reduced set of tests and still produce meaningful results, we will illustrate an example using the feature model depicted in Figure 4. This feature model is only a small excerpt of the complete CiAO feature model, which has around 150 different features to be configured and represents about 10,000 different valid configurations. However, even this reduced subset of features (14 features) is able to represent 256 valid configurations. This fact shows that one should be very careful when defining the set of configurations to be tested; even a small number of features may represent a high number of configurations—and, consequently, can require a prohibitive testing time.

Nevertheless, one should also keep in mind that the testing process aims at capturing feature interactions that will influence a specific NFP. Interestingly, for many NFPs it is possible (with internal implementation knowledge) to determine the set of features that will influence the required NFP. For example, in the case of performance, or also latency, one could measure the time required for a certain computation by starting a timer at a specific point in the code, and stopping it at the point where the computation is finished. If this scenario represents our NFP *performance*, it is possible to determine which features insert code between these points (the *metric* that specifies *feature interaction*), or the ones that have their code called from within the code block having its *performance* measured. That is, when testing a specific NFP, it is often possible to describe the set of features that influence the desired NFP by using the concept of partial configurations. Moreover, in our experiments we have identified that normally the *critical* parts of the code, where, for example, *latency* is important, will not be composed of too many features, and therefore a testing process can be performed in a feasible amount of time. Likewise, when a feature specifies an *interface* and its sub features represents different *implementations*, testing can also be optimized in this manner, and only the variability represented by this sub tree must be tested.

The feature model depicted in Figure 4 can generate 256 different configurations; in this case, testing all possible configurations may be feasible. However, for some NFPs it would simply be a waste of time, since for many of those tests the output would be exactly the same and would not contribute to the understanding of how features interact to influence a specific NFP. For example, if one is interested in the performance of the different configurations of the *protection* mechanism, a test set can be defined by a partial configuration where the set of features to represent the minimal infrastructure are set as *selected*, the features under *protection* are marked as *open* (establishing the variability of the test set), and the rest is marked as *blocked*. By doing so, we can reduce the test set to 8 different combinations. These are basically all possible combinations of the features used for the configuration of the *protection* mechanism, namely *memory protection*, *timing protection*, and *service protection*.

In the evaluation of this work (see the following section), we deal with the NFPs of *latency* and *performance*; both of them are *measurable* NFPs. If one is interested in using the Feedback Approach for NFPs like *reliability* or *security*, a way to quantify these properties must be found. For example, for *security* one could take a set of different testing attacks and assign the number of failed and succeeded tests to the variant of interest. Regarding *reliability*, stress testing could be employed, and the time required for the crash (or success after a timeout) can be assigned to the variants under test.

CiAO STUDIES: THE EFFECT OF CONFIGURABLE APs ON NFPs

As outlined in the approach description, CiAO aims at making the system's NFPs configurable by indirectly keeping fundamental architectural properties configurable. In the domain of embedded operating systems, this includes the following concerns, amongst others.

- **Interrupt synchronization:** If control flows can be executed asynchronously *and* they can access critical kernel state, the consistency of that state has to be ensured by some synchronization mechanism. There are several ways to ensure synchronization, all of them bearing distinct advantages and disadvantages.
- **Component isolation:** In simple embedded systems, application components can influence each other; for instance, by accessing each other's memory areas. To increase robustness, isolation means can be deployed, including constructive isolation by using type-safe programming languages or memory protection using hardware support like memory protection units (MPUs). Other isolation techniques refer to *temporal* isolation so that applications in real-

time systems will not miss their deadlines because of other (potentially misbehaving) applications.

- **Kernel interaction:** The way components inside the kernel interact with each other has a significant impact on the perceived robustness and performance. Historically, suggested approaches range from monolith-like systems to microkernel systems (Liedtke, 1995).

Interestingly, the focus on configurability of those architectural concerns is increasing in the recent time. Proof for that is the specification of AUTOSAR OS (AUTOSAR, 2006a, AUTOSAR, 2006b), which aims to standardize the system software present on automotive microcontrollers. This specification includes several so-called *scalability classes*, which provide distinct isolation properties like memory protection and timing protection. Hence, those architectural properties are already prescribed to be implemented in a configurable way in this standard.

We have implemented two configurable architectural properties in CiAO—interrupt synchronization and memory protection—, which are presented in the following, together with an evaluation of their impact on different non-functional properties.

CASE STUDY 1: INTERRUPT SYNCHRONIZATION

Short Domain Analysis

Our first case study is based on the configurable architectural property of interrupt synchronization; that is, on how to keep the kernel state synchronous when possibly being accessed from within asynchronous events (e.g., interrupt handlers). After having analyzed the domain of operating systems, we found that there are three basic models to achieve interrupt synchronization, all of which are implemented (and therefore configurable) in CiAO.

1. **Hard synchronization:** This model lowers every critical section accessing kernel state to interrupt level, implemented by enabling and disabling interrupts or by setting the interrupt level accordingly. Hard synchronization has a very low performance overhead, but risks higher event-handling latency, depending on the length of the critical sections. This model is widely deployed in relatively simple embedded operating systems.
2. **Two-phase synchronization:** This model divides each interrupt handler into two different parts, named prologue and epilogue in CiAO. Prologues can be executed in a timely fashion with low latency, but they are not allowed to access critical kernel state. This is done in the corresponding epilogue, which can be delayed by the kernel when accessing critical state. Epilogues have priority over user threads, however, and user threads are only executed when no epilogues are pending. Two-phase synchronization is used in many desktop operating systems like Linux or Windows, but also in embedded OSes like OSEK OS (OSEK/VDX Group, 2005) or AUTOSAR OS (AUTOSAR, 2006b).
3. **Continuation synchronization:** This model enhances epilogues to full continuations (the thread abstractions in CiAO) with a context of their own. This way, user threads can be activated while interrupt handlers are waiting for a shared resource. This facilitates fine-grained locking of kernel components (having a positive impact on the perceived latency), but bears the highest performance and memory overhead of the three models. The Solaris OS uses a similar model to synchronize its kernel (Kleiman and Eykholt, 1995).

CiAO Design

We designed a generic driver model that leaves the driver developer unaware of the finally deployed interrupt synchronization method, which is not determined until the system configuration time. This way, the driver obeys common handler interfaces, and is adapted by aspects to fit the configured synchronization model. This configurability is designed and implemented with full separation of concerns, enabled by considering aspects as a design means from the beginning of the CiAO engineering process (*aspect awareness*). The design achieves a complete separation of concerns, separating the three dimensions of *what*, *where*, and *how* to apply interrupt synchronization.

For details concerning the aspect-aware design of configurable interrupt synchronization in CiAO and how the driver and OS components are integrated, please refer to (Lohmann et al., 2007b).

Influence on Non-Functional Properties

After having implemented the architectural property of interrupt synchronization to be configurable in CiAO, we investigated the impact of this variability dimension on the non-functional property of latency. Here, latency is understood as the elapsed time between the beginning of the hardware interrupt handler and interrupt termination (*iret* instruction). We also measured the time from the beginning of the handler until the first *prologue* instruction, and until the first *epilogue* instruction, respectively. The results are depicted in Table 1. We have tested only the features that can have its implementation code accessed (function call, data structure changes, etc.) from the *block of code* defined by the boundaries of our time measurement routines; in this case, those features are the different interrupt synchronization variants. This is the *metric* that represents the feature interaction for this NFP in order reduce

Table 1. Measurements of the non-functional property of latency for several configurable interrupt synchronization methods in CiAO. Measurements were performed on a TriCore TC1796b running at 50 MHz with a hardware trace analyzer (Lauterbach). The results were measured (and turned out to be stable) over 10 iterations.

ns	$t_{prologue}$	$t_{epilogue}$	t_{iret}
Hard Sync.	160	160	320
Two-Phase Sync.	160	800	1200
Continuation Sync.	320	1200	2160

the size of the test space (see also the previous section about the feedback approach).

One can clearly see that the chosen IRQ synchronization method has a significant impact on the latency of interrupt handlers in the system. This refers both to the time until completion and to the time until the first part (prologue) and the second part (epilogue) of the interrupt handler are executed. However, by choosing the continuation synchronization model, for example, it is possible to reach more fine-grained synchronization domains inside the kernel, leading to less contention and, therefore, to better performance in certain situations. Likewise, choosing two-phase synchronization over hard synchronization leads to lower interrupt locking times, which makes it less likely to lose interrupt signals, depending on the microcontroller architecture.

Hence, the architectural property of IRQ synchronization is transparent to the application developer *functionally*, but it has a significant impact on the emerging *non-functional* properties of the resulting system, latency being among them.

Case Study 2: Memory Protection

Short Domain Analysis

The second study we performed is concerned with an architectural property that is prescribed by the AUTOSAR embedded software standard: memory protection. This means of spatial isolation between applications is supposed to increase robustness by limiting the memory access of application components to legal ranges, disallowing access to the memory areas of other applications or the underlying system software. Depending on the chosen AUTOSAR scalability class, memory protection is to be provided by the operating system or not.

On the hardware side, memory protection is enforced by an MPU (memory protection unit), which bears reprogrammable range registers specifying the access rights to distinct memory areas. An MPU is a simplified variant of a full-featured memory management unit (MMU) known from PC systems, which can additionally perform paging. The MPU is only reprogrammable in the supervisor mode of the CPU so that only the OS and not the applications are able to alter memory protection properties.

During the domain analysis step, we found the following protection models to be suitable to be designed and implemented in CiAO.

1. **No protection:** This trivial variant does not feature any protection mechanism at all. However, there is no performance overhead either.
2. **Kernel protection:** This version separates the kernel from all applications by providing two separate protection domains.
3. **Application protection:** This model additionally separates the applications from each other, comprising *n* protection domains for *n* deployed applications, plus one domain for the kernel. This means that invocations of functions that are exported by another application involve some overhead for adjusting the access privileges.
4. **Task protection:** This most fine-grained model even protects task-local data like the task stack from the modification by other tasks or interrupt handlers in the same application.

CiAO Design

As with the configurable property of interrupt synchronization, the application developer is oblivious of the finally deployed memory protection method (if any) as chosen by the system configurator. Depending on the applied protection model, different points in the control flow in the CiAO system must be affected by an appropriate reprogramming of the MPU. Since CiAO's design is aspect-aware, those points are exposed as *join points* in the AOP sense, being advisable by configurably deployed aspects. This way, generic pointcuts representing the critical points like inter-application function calls, application—kernel transitions, interrupt handler invocations, or task dispatches can be supplied. An example control flow in a CiAO system is depicted in Figure 5.

The aspects implementing the protection method to be enforced are then implemented by advising the exposed join points in the form of the supplied pointcut expressions. The kernel protection aspect, for instance, reprograms the MPU to allow access to kernel state whenever entering the kernel and disallowing it upon exit from the kernel, including the first-time dispatch of tasks. Application protection, however, additionally needs to reprogram the MPU upon inter-application calls and upon inter-application task dispatches.

The CiAO reference hardware platform—the Infineon TriCore TC1796b—allowed us to provide an additional configuration variant called the *semi-trusted mode*. This variant exploits the peculiarity that on the TriCore platform memory protection is not implicitly disabled in supervisor mode. This allows applications to be run in supervisor mode with memory protection enforced without the need for kernel traps. An offline analysis can ensure that the applications do not reprogram the

Figure 5. Control flows and memory protection domains in an example CiAO system

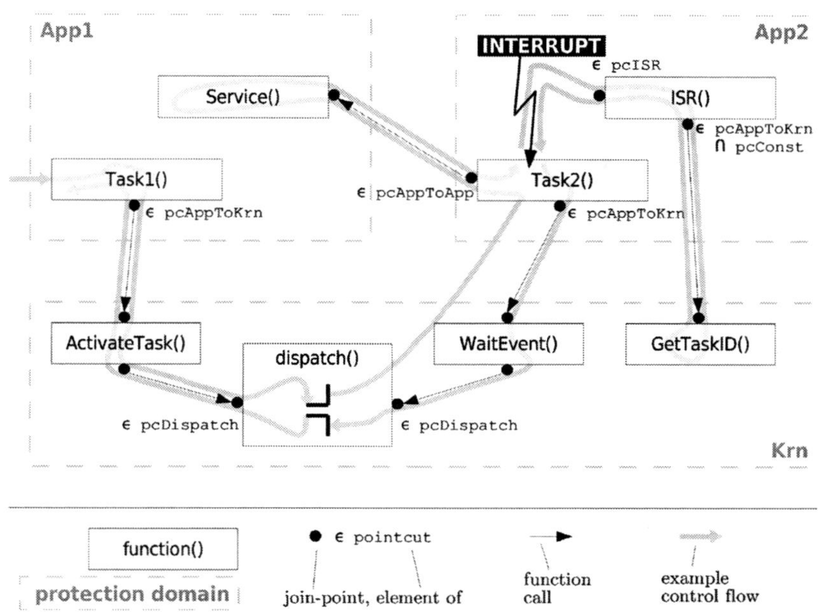

MPU in their code, thereby ensuring the safety of the system.

For a more detailed explanation of CiAO's memory protection design and the way applications interface with the OS components, and for implementation details of the generic pointcuts and the configurable aspects in AspectC++, please refer to (Lohmann et al., 2007a).

Influence on Non-Functional Properties

We evaluated the influence of the different memory protection models on the number of clock cycles needed for the execution of several characteristic functions; that is, the non-functional property of performance. All of those investigated functions either cross an inter-application boundary or the one between the kernel and an application (see Figure 5). The results are listed in Table 2 and shortly discussed here. The *metric* used to define feature interaction, and the corresponding test space, is analogous to the one presented in the previous section; that is, we tested the features that have its code accessed from the *blocks of code* that were measured. These features were the different kinds of memory protection in this case.

- Since GetTaskID() is a non-modifying kernel function, the memory protection domain is not switched in any of the protec-

Table 2. Measurements of the non-functional property of performance of selected representative function calls for several configurable memory protection variants in CiAO.

ns	GetTaskID()	ActivateTask()	dispatch()	Service()
No Protection	3	24	88	0
Semi-Trusted Mode	3	43	148	89
Full Protection	3	86	148	174

tion models. Hence, the clock cycles remain constant.

- The ActivateTask() system call, however, modifies kernel structures. No memory protection does not involve any overhead, whereas the semi-trusted variant needs 43–24=19 extra clock cycles to reprogram the MPU to allow write access to kernel space and disallow it after the call. A full trap with switch to supervisor mode and back to user mode costs 86–24=62 additional cycles.
- The kernel-internal dispatch() function switches the protection domain from one application to another in both protected modes, leading to a cost of 148–88=60 cycles. Since this function is invoked inside the kernel, there is no difference between the semi-trusted and the standard protected mode.
- An inter-application call like Service() does not cost anything without protection; the call can even be inlined. In the semi-trusted mode and the application protection configuration, the MPU is reprogrammed to the new application domain and back after the call, which is worth 89 cycles. The version that requires a full trap costs 174 cycles in total.

The architectural property of memory protection has a big influence on the performance of a system, as can be seen in the configurable implementation of the property in CiAO. The decision in favor of one of the protection methods and variants to be deployed is effectively a trade-off between the two non-functional properties of safety and performance.

RELATED WORK

As this work aims at tackling non-functional properties in *all* stages of development, there is a broad range of related work, which is discussed in the following.

Non-Functional Properties and Software Product Lines

Siegmund et al. propose the use of a *semi-automated derivation* (SAD) to assist developers in selecting product features in SPLs with a large number of features (Siegmund et al., 2008, Rosenmüller et al., 2008). The basic idea is to hide variation points that are irrelevant due to non-functional requirements that should be met. They claim that traditional approaches do not consider non-functional properties or alternatives for a feature implementation. To solve this problem, they present an integrated software product line model (ISPLM), which integrates code units and their non-functional properties into the feature model.

(Benavides et al., 2005) propose an extension to feature models (as proposed by Czarnecki and Eisenecker, 2000) to accommodate information about *extra-functional* features (NFPs, in our view). In this approach, attributes like price or development time can be assigned to features. The features and their attributes are transformed to a constraint satisfaction problem (CSP) so that an automated reasoning can be applied to it. Hence, optimal products can be generated according to a determined criterion (an extra-functional feature).

These methods take advantage of information about NFPs to improve product configuration. However, we think that both are more related to the field of variability *management* (Loesch and Ploedereder, 2007, Schirmeier and Spinczyk, 2007). They ease the configuration process in large SPLs but do not offer the ability to explicitly configure NFPs or to inform the user about the *real* influence of a feature on the required NFP.

(Etxeberria and Sagardui, 2008) present an approach for the quality evaluation of software product lines. In this approach, an extended feature model is used to identify the variability that has an impact on quality in order to reduce evaluation efforts. This technique is comparable to our idea of partial configuration. However, in contrast to our work, they state that the design stage is a good point to assure that the quality attributes are met.

TOOL SUPPORT

pure::variants (Beuche, 2003) is a tool that supports variant management of SPLs. It is independent of programming languages and it enables the definition of the problem domain by means of feature models, and the solution domain by family models. It also automates the process of product generation. Regarding the configuration of NFPs, the current version is able to assign bugs (from a bug-tracking system) to specific features. Therefore, during product configuration, the application engineer is informed about the *known* bugs that will be present in the final product.

Gears (Krueger, 2007b) is a tool and framework that enables the development and evolution of SPLs; it applies the three-tiered SPL methodology (Krueger, 2007a). In Gears, SPLs are comprised of three elements, software assets (source code, documentation, etc.), product feature profiles (to model each product in the portfolio), and the Gears configurator, which automatically assembles products based on their specifications.

FeaturePlugin (Antkiewicz and Czarnecki, 2004) is an open-source Eclipse plugin for designing and configuring feature models. It supports the concepts of staged configuration (Czarnecki et al., 2005b) and feature cardinalities (Czarnecki et al., 2005a). The tool focuses on providing advanced techniques of feature modeling and not on supporting the whole process of SPL development.

FAMA (FeAture Model Analyser) (Benavides et al., 2007) is an extensible framework for the automated analysis of feature models. It is able to denote feature models in several logic representations; therefore, different solvers can be used in the analysis process. Currently, it supports CSP, SAT (boolean satisfiability problem), and BDD (binary decision diagrams), but it is flexible enough to have other solvers added to it. Cardinality-based feature models are allowed and the following operations are supported: finding out if a feature model is valid (there exists a valid selection that satisfies all constraints), finding the total number of valid products, listing all valid configurations, and calculating the commonality of features (the number of valid products they appear in).

There are commercial, free, and open-source alternatives for the design of feature models. However, only pure::variants is able to provide non-functional information during product configuration; at the moment only at a very basic level, though.

REASONING IN FEATURE MODELS

Important to our work is also the process of *reasoning* in feature models. A seminal work by Benavides et al., (2006) presents the mapping from feature model components (e.g., optional features, mandatory features, and group features) to diverse logical representations, namely SAT, BDD, and CSP. Transforming feature models in these representations enables the use of off-the-shelf solvers that can perform several analyses that are relevant for feature models (e.g., validity, number of solutions, etc.).

The relation of feature models and grammars has also been studied (Batory, 2005). Batory, also motivated by the ability to use off-the-shelf satisfiability solvers, presented the mapping from feature models first to iterative tree grammars, and then to propositional formulas. However, his main goal was to simplify the laborious task of debugging feature models.

Recently, the relation of feature models and logic representation has been further explored. (Czarnecki and Wasowski, 2007) propose a method for the inverse transformation from propositional formulas to a feature model representation. (Janota and Kiniry, 2007) study the representation of feature models in higher-order logic. A formalized meta-model is presented; however, no tool support is provided.

Aspect-Oriented Programming and Operating Systems

There is some work describing the synthesis of operating system kernels and aspect-oriented programming already published; none of the projects target the configurability of architectural properties and, indirectly, of non-functional properties, however.

PURE is an operating-system family that aims to support even deeply embedded systems (Beuche et al., 1999). Its abstractions are designed in minimal extensions, providing for fine-grained configuration possibilities. However, it was originally designed in an object-oriented way, oblivious to AOP. Only after exploring the ability of AOP to modularize the cross-cutting concerns present in a PURE system, aspects were considered (Spinczyk and Lohmann, 2004), and only implemented for selected concerns like interrupt synchronization (Mahrenholz et al., 2002). Therefore, PURE was not designed to be aspect-aware from the beginning as is CiAO, and PURE does not have the (indirect) configurability of non-functional properties as an explicit goal.

The TOSKANA toolkit (Engel and Freisleben, 2005, 2006) enables the deployment of aspects into an OS kernel. The prototype is demonstrated using the NetBSD kernel; in general, the targeted OS domain is the PC domain and not embedded systems, where the consideration of non-functional properties is especially important (see also the motivation section). Furthermore, the toolkit *instruments* the kernel in order to be able to weave and unweave aspects *dynamically* at run time. The induced run-time and memory overhead is not tolerable in embedded computing; in this domain, static configuration and tailored implementations with distinct non-functional properties are needed.

Several studies were conducted on how to apply AOP ex post to existing kernels. Particularly, Coady et al. showed how to modularize prefetching in the FreeBSD operating system kernel (Coady et al., 2001), and sketched the design of an aspect-oriented page daemon and quota manager (Coady and Kiczales, 2003). However, the aspect weaver proposed for this task, AspectC, does not have a functioning implementation; the examples were hand-woven and therefore do not provide a real cost evaluation in terms of non-functional properties like performance or latency.

CONCLUSION

Non-functional properties are inherently complex to be dealt with, but nevertheless mission-critical in many systems. The main challenge in handling NFPs is that most of them are untraceable; that is, there is no line of code or implementation module that an NFP can be solely attributed to. Furthermore, NFPs are highly domain-specific in their nature.

Therefore, NFPs have traditionally often been assessed by the system architects, who have the expertise and experience to do that. When using a product-line approach, though, the requirements on the products are often very different between the desired variants, and the system configurator does not have that kind of knowledge about the product line that is to be configured.

That is why, in our opinion, NFPs have to be dealt with in a *holistic* way, approaching them on multiple levels both in domain engineering and application engineering, from analysis to implementation. Furthermore, the configurator has to be assisted in making his decisions regarding the NFPs of the final product by semi-automated means. The CiAO development process with its feedback approach, which was presented in this chapter, is a big step into that direction.

ACKNOWLEDGMENT

We would like to thank Christoph Elsner for giving valuable comments on a draft of this text.

This work was partly supported by the German Research Council (DFG) under grants no. SCHR 603/4 and SCHR 603/7.

REFERENCES

Antkiewicz, M., & Czarnecki, K. (2004). FeaturePlugin: Feature modeling plug-in for Eclipse. In *Proceedings of the 2004 OOPSLA workshop on Eclipse technology eXchange (Eclipse '04 at OOPSLA '04)*, (pp. 67–72). Vancouver, Canada.

AUTOSAR. (2006a). *Requirements on operating system (version 2.0.1). Technical report*. Automotive Open System Architecture GbR.

AUTOSAR. (2006b). *Specification of operating system (version 2.0.1). Technical report*. Automotive Open System Architecture GbR.

Bass, L. (2006). Principles for designing software architecture to achieve quality attribute requirements. In *SERA '06: Proceedings of the Fourth International Conference on Software Engineering Research, Management and Applications*, (p. 2), Washington, DC, USA. IEEE Computer Society.

Batory, D. S. (2005). Feature models, grammars, and propositional formulas. In *Proceedings of the 9th Software Product Line Conference (SPLC '05)*, (pp. 7–20).

Benavides, D., Ruiz-Cortés, A., & Trinidad, P. (2005). Automated reasoning on feature models. *Proceedings of Advanced Information Systems Engineering: 17th International Conference, CAiSE 2005*, (LNCS 3520), (491–503).

Benavides, D., Segura, S., Trinidad, P., & Ruiz-Cortés, A. (2006). A first step towards a framework for the automated analysis of feature models. In *Managing Variability for Software Product Lines*. Working With Variability Mechanisms.

Benavides, D., Segura, S., Trinidad, P., & Ruiz-Cortés, A. (2007). FAMA: Tooling a framework for the automated analysis of feature models. In *Proceeding of the First International Workshop on Variability Modeling of Software-Intensive Systems (VAMOS)*.

Beuche, D. (2003). *Variant management with pure variants*. Technical report, pure-systems GmbH. http://www.pure-systems.com/.

Beuche, D., Guerrouat, A., Papajewski, H., Schröder-Preikschat, W., Spinczyk, O., & Spinczyk, U. (1999). On the development of object-oriented operating systems for deeply embedded systems-the PURE project. In *Object-Oriented Technology: ECOOP '99 Workshop Reader*, Lisbon, Portugal. (LNCS 1743), (pp. 27–31). Springer-Verlag.

BuDDy Developers. (2009). *BuDDy project*. Retrieved from http://sourceforge.net/projects/buddy

Coady, Y., & Kiczales, G. (2003). Back to the future: A retroactive study of aspect evolution in operating system code. In M. Akşit (Ed.), *Proceedings of the 2nd International Conference on Aspect-Oriented Software Development (AOSD '03)*, (pp. 50–59). Boston:ACM Press.

Coady, Y., Kiczales, G., Feeley, M., & Smolyn, G. (2001). Using AspectC to improve the modularity of path-specific customization in operating system code. In *Proceedings of the 3rd Joint European Software Engineering Conference and ACM Symposium on the Foundations of Software Engineering (ESEC/FSE '01)*.

Cysneiros, L. M., & do Prado Leite, J. C. S. (2004). Nonfunctional requirements: From elicitation to conceptual models. *IEEE Transactions on Software Engineering*, *30*(5), 328–350. doi:10.1109/TSE.2004.10

Czarnecki, K., & Eisenecker, U. W. (2000). *Generative programming. Methods, tools and applications*. Addison-Wesley.

Czarnecki, K., Helsen, S., & Eisenecker, U. W. (2005a). Formalizing cardinality-based feature models and their specialization. *Software Process Improvement and Practice*, *10*(1), 7–29. doi:10.1002/spip.213

Czarnecki, K., Helsen, S., & Eisenecker, U. W. (2005b). Staged configuration through specialization and multilevel configuration of feature models. *Software Process Improvement and Practice*, *10*(2), 143–169. doi:10.1002/spip.225

Czarnecki, K., & Wasowski, A. (2007). Feature diagrams and logics: There and back again. In *Proceedings of the 11th Software Product Line Conference (SPLC '07)*, (pp. 23–34).

Engel, M., & Freisleben, B. (2005). Supporting autonomic computing functionality via dynamic operating system kernel aspects. In P. Tarr (Ed.), *Proceedings of the 4th International Conference on Aspect-Oriented Software Development (AOSD '05)*, (pp. 51–62). Chicago: ACM Press.

Engel, M., & Freisleben, B. (2006). TOSKANA: A toolkit for operating system kernel aspects. In Rashid, A., & Aksit, M. (Eds.), *Transactions on AOSD II, (LNCS 4242)* (pp. 182–226). Springer-Verlag.

Etxeberria, L., & Sagardui, G. (2008). Variability driven quality evaluation in software product lines. *Proceedings of the Software Product Line Conference, 2008. SPLC '08. 12th International*, (pp 243–252).

Gilani, W., Sincero, J., & Spinczyk, O. (2007). Aspectizing a Web server for adaptation. In *Proceedings of the Twelfth IEEE Symposium on Computers and Communications (ISCC'07)*, Aveiro, Portugal. IEEE Computer Society Press.

Janota, M., & Kiniry, J. (2007). Reasoning about feature models in higher-order logic. In *Proceedings of the 11th Software Product Line Conference (SPLC '07)*, (pp. 13–22).

Kleiman, S., & Eykholt, J. (1995). Interrupts as threads. *ACM SIGOPS Operating Systems Review*, *29*(2), 21–26. doi:10.1145/202213.202217

Krueger, C. W. (2007a). The 3-tiered methodology: Pragmatic insights from new generation software product lines. In *Proceedings of the 11th Software Product Line Conference (SPLC '07)*, (pp. 97–106).

Krueger, C. W. (2007b). BigLever software gears and the 3-tiered SPL methodology. In *OOPSLA '07: Companion to the 22nd ACM SIGPLAN conference on object-oriented programming systems and applications*, (pp. 844–845). New York: ACM.

Lauer, H. C., & Needham, R. M. (1979). On the duality of operating system structures. *ACM SIGOPS Operating Systems Review*, *13*(2), 3–19. doi:10.1145/850657.850658

Liedtke, J. (1995). On μ-kernel construction. In *Proceedings of the 15th ACM Symposium on Operating Systems Principles (SOSP '95)*, ACM SIGOPS Operating Systems Review. ACM Press.

Loesch, F., & Ploedereder, E. (2007). Optimization of variability in software product lines. In *Proceedings of the 11th Software Product Line Conference (SPLC '07)*, (pp. 151–162).

Lohmann, D., Spinczyk, O., & Schröder-Preikschat, W. (2005). On the configuration of non-functional properties in operating system product lines. In *Proceedings of the 4th AOSD Workshop on Aspects, Components, and Patterns for Infrastructure Software (AOSD-ACP4IS '05)*, (pp 19–25). Chicago, IL, USA. Northeastern University, Boston (NU-CCIS-05-03).

Lohmann, D., Streicher, J., Hofer, W., Spinczyk, O., & Schröder-Preikschat, W. (2007a). Configurable memory protection by aspects. In *Proceedings of the 4th Workshop on Programming Languages and Operating Systems (PLOS '07)*, (pp. 1–5). New York: ACM Press.

Lohmann, D., Streicher, J., Spinczyk, O., & Schröder-Preikschat, W. (2007b). Interrupt synchronization in the CiAO operating system. In *Proceedings of the 6th AOSD Workshop on Aspects, Components, and Patterns for Infrastructure Software (AOSD-ACP4IS '07)*, New York: ACM Press.

Mahrenholz, D., Spinczyk, O., Gal, A., & Schröder-Preikschat, W. (2002). An aspect-oriented implementation of interrupt synchronization in the PURE operating system family. In *Proceedings of the 5th ECOOP Workshop on Object Orientation and Operating Systems (ECOOP-OOOS '02)*, (pp. 49–54). Malaga, Spain.

OSEK/VDX Group. (2005). *Operating system specification 2.2.3*. OSEK/VDX Group. Retrieved from http://www.osek-vdx.org/

Rosenmüller, M., Siegmund, N., Schirmeier, H., Sincero, J., Apel, S., Leich, T., et al. (2008). FAME-DBMS: Tailor-made data management solutions for embedded systems. In *Proceedings of the Workshop on Software Engineering for Tailor-Made Data Management (SETMDM)*.

Schirmeier, H., & Spinczyk, O. (2007). Tailoring infrastructure software product lines by static application analysis. In *Proceedings of the 11th Software Product Line Conference (SPLC '07)*, (pp. 255–260). IEEE Computer Society Press.

Siegmund, N., Kuhlemann, M., Rosenmüller, M., Kästner, C., & Saake, G. (2008). Integrated product line model for semi-automated product derivation using non-functional properties. In *Proceedings of the International Workshop on Variability Modelling of Software-Intensive Systems (VAMOS)*, (pp. 25–23).

Spinczyk, O., & Lohmann, D. (2004). Using AOP to develop architecture-neutral operating system components. In *Proceedings of the 11th ACM SIGOPS European Workshop*, (pp. 188–192). New York: ACM Press.

Spinczyk, O., & Lohmann, D. (2007). The design and implementation of AspectC++. *Knowledge-Based Systems. Special Issue on Techniques to Produce Intelligent Secure Software*, *20*(7), 636–651.

Chapter 6
Adding Semantics to QoS Requirements

Ester Giallonardo
University of Sannio, Italy

Eugenio Zimeo
University of Sannio, Italy

ABSTRACT

To lead the software-service revolution and to make real the promise of Business to Business interactions, QoS and Semantics play key roles in every phase of Web processes' life-cycle. Ontology-based approaches for specifying QoS enable machines to reason autonomously and dynamically on QoS knowledge, aiding the development of open and large-scale distributed applications. This chapter presents the impact of Semantics for the management of QoS Requirements in Service-based Applications, focusing on the onQoS ontology, its role for specifying service requirements and to support queries for service discovery through the onQoS-QL language. The introduced concepts and the results presented in the chapter pave the way to new technology horizons where the semantics could represent the global glue for Web processes.

INTRODUCTION

In ITUT-T Recommendation E.800, Quality of Service (QoS) is defined as "*collective effect of service performance that determines the degree of satisfaction by a user of the service*". QoS information is a key aspect in order to design, identify, form, put in operation and dissolve service level agreements. It influences also the software components in charge to ensure service trust: the service providers with effectively "best" QoS can be more easily identified and preferred in future similar circumstances utilizing, for example, reputation-based mechanisms. So, QoS impacts on service selection, on business process modifications and refinements and reduces the enterprise risk associated to the adoption of Web service technologies.

DOI: 10.4018/978-1-60960-493-6.ch006

Figure 1. Phases of a Web process life-cycle

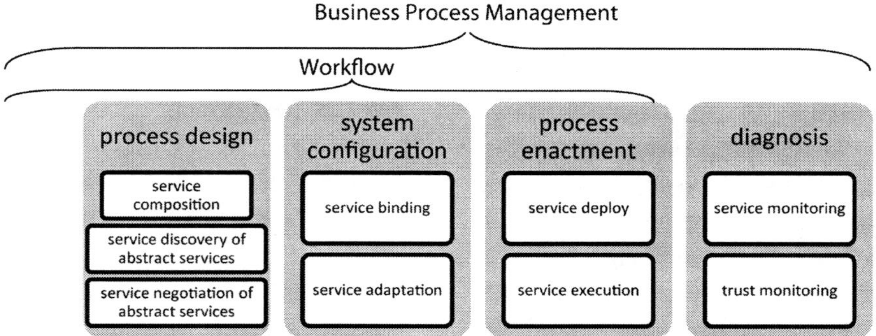

QoS needs to be taken into account in the overall life-cycle of a Web process. It guides a proper evolution of the process by continuously providing information about the actual behavior of each service/resource adopted. In particular, according to Van der Aalst et al. (2003), the business process life cycle presents the following phases: process design, system configuration, process enactment, and diagnosis. We retain that the *process design phase* objective is defining both the functional and non-functional aspects needed to getting a system to support requested business objectives.

Starting from business needs, *Composition, Discovery* and *Negotiation Components* can work for making an electronic model of the business processes. This model needs to specify *what are the services*, *the related control flow*, *what they have to do*, and *how they have to be supported,* but it is not always necessary to define also *who will perform them.*

Discovery systems use non functional requirements in order to reduce the search space by identifying only the Web services that guarantee the desired level of QoS, while negotiation systems utilizes standard protocols in order to create agreements between service consumers and providers, based also on QoS. These agreements can specify, in addition to other aspects, *when and how the service can be monitored (diagnosis points* and/or *monitoring tools).* So, service binding and service monitoring can be driven by service level agreements.

During the phase of system configuration, *Binding Components* set up the system, locating the concrete Web services to bind to the previously designed abstract processes. Instead, *Adaptive Components* can exploit semantics in order to configure the system for reducing human intervention during process execution.

In the *process enactment phase*, the software component in charge of executing the process (for example a *Workflow Engine* as in our case) is driven by abstract and concrete process specifications to deploy and execute processes. These specifications define also QoS requirements: when the *Enactment System* meets process activities abstractly modeled (and not yet concretized), the system configuration phase needs to be reactivated and the Engine can act as service requestor of *Discovery* or *Negotiation Systems*.

Process diagnosis, instead, regards the runtime evaluation of the satisfaction of QoS requirements specified at design-time in the process definition phase. The objective is to systematically examine the single service execution in order to determinate the satisfaction of QoS desiderata and the progress in achieving process objectives.

Semantic technologies can be used for improving interoperability between these different components, which can so exchange and use QoS information with semantic understanding.

Composition, Discovery and *Negotiation Components* can exploit semantic service descriptions in order to find the best services and create agreements between service consumers and providers. For example, the components in charge of implementing the discovery process can utilize semantic technologies to increase precision and recall of retrieved results and to address the scalability issue. In fact, a QoS model enriched with semantics for run-time support, can make scalable discovery systems that can so understand the queries and return the "right" answers even if the number of network available services increases.

During the system configuration phase, *Binding* components can perform their selections exploiting the semantics of the formulated queries, while *Adaptive* components can smartly configure systems in order to be able to reduce human intervention. The *Diagnosis Components* can exploit semantic descriptions to auto-configure themselves with the right monitoring tools. This way, the control process components can exploit the machine-understanding descriptions to modify or adapt processes in order to deal with highly dynamic and competitive environments. Finally, *Trust Monitoring Components* can utilize semantics for ensuring confidence on the quality of SOA systems, exploiting for example reputation-based mechanisms.

This chapter focuses on the role of semantics in QoS management. It is organized as follows. The "Background" section introduces the basic semantic concepts, languages and tools, and some QoS models. In section "Semantics in QoS" we present the motivations of our approach, the relative basic concepts, an ontology as QoS semantic model, a query language to specify QoS requirements in the discovery and the negotiation phases. Section "QoS-Aware Service Discovery" and "QoS Monitoring" presents the directions that we utilized during the matching and monitoring process. Section "onQoS Applications" explains how we have utilized semantics for managing Quality of Service in the QoS Discovery and in the QoS Monitoring process and how we intend to exploit them in ongoing research projects.

BACKGROUND

Basic Semantic Concepts, Languages and Tools

Semantics is the study of meanings of the message behind the words. Semantic computing addresses the problems of analyzing, defining, integrating and exploiting data at work in software systems. Semantics analysis of computational content has been addressed in different research areas, as in natural language processing, image and video analysis, audio and speech analysis, data and Web mining, analysis of behavior of software, services and networks and analysis of social networks. Once the semantics of the content has been derived, manually or automatically, it can be integrated in software applications exploiting, for example, semantic programming languages. In this section, we overview the most renowned Semantic Web Technologies: OWL, WSML, SPARQL, WSMO, OWL-S, and SAWDL.

The OWL language (Dean and Schreiber, 2003) has been created by the W3C Web Ontology Working Group. OWL 1 is built upon RDFs and has three dialects: OWL Lite, OWL Full and OWL DL. Recently OWL 2 has been designed to take advantage of the new XSD 1.1 datatypes, to facilitate ontology development and sharing via the Web, with the ultimate goal of making Web content more accessible to machines. Three different profiles are defined: OWL 2 EL, OWL 2 QL, and OWL 2 RL. They identify maximal OWL 2 sublanguages that are still implementable in Ptime. While OWL Full provides RDF-based semantics, but it is undecidable. OWL DL is decidable in N2ExpTime. OWL 2 EL enables polynomial time algorithms for all the standard reasoning tasks; OWL 2 QL is defined not only in terms of the set of supported constructs, but it also restricts the places in which these constructs are allowed to occur. OWL 2 QL enables conjunctive queries to be answered in LogSpace using standard relational database technology. Instead, OWL 2 RL is a rule subset of OWL 2. Rule-based reading simplifies modeling and implementation.

Also the Web Service Modeling Language, WSML (De Bruijn et other, 2005), is layered into dialects that correspond to the following different levels of logical expressiveness: Description Logics, First-Order Logic and Logic Programming. Furthermore, it has been influenced by F-Logic (Kifer et al., 1995) and frame-based representation systems. It is a language for the specification of ontologies and Web Services Semantic descriptions.

SPARQL (Prud'hommeaux, E.,& Seaborne, A., 2008) has been developed within the RDF Data Access Working Group of W3C. SPARQL is a SQL-like query language for getting information from RDF graphs. SPARQL provides facilities to extract information in the form of URIs, blank nodes, plain and typed literals; to extract RDF sub-graphs; and to construct new RDF graphs exploiting information in the queried graphs.

The Web Service Modeling Ontology (WSMO Group, 2004) is a conceptual model for Semantic Web Services. It presents the following four types of top-level elements: *Ontologies*, *Semantic Web Services*, *Goals*, and *Mediators*. *Ontologies* formally specify terminology; *Semantic Web Services* specify service capabilities and interfaces; *Goals* represent the objective that a client whishes to achieve by using Web Services, while *Mediators* provide facilities for handling heterogeneity of components.

OWL-S (Ankolekar and Burstein, 2004) is an upper level ontology for describing Web services in an unambiguous and computer-interpretable way. The OWL-S Service Profile describes the *Input*, *Output*, *Precondition* and *Effect* of the offered service; the *Service Grounding* specifies how to access the service; while the *Service Model* describes how the service works. OWL-S does not replace existing Web Services Standards, but it consents to extent them with explicit semantics.

According to the WSMO and OWL-S approaches, the ontological model has to semantically describe both the services aspects and the domain features. Instead, SAWSDL (Farrel, 2007) defines mechanisms to add semantic annotations to WSDL and XML-Schema components, with the use of ontologies only for the domain data.

A number of good semantic Web development tools are available, but here we present only the most popular Java-based ones. Protégé (2000) is a free, open source ontology editor and knowledge-base framework, based on a plug-and-play environment. Jena, instead, is an open source framework for building semantic Web applications. It provides a programmatic environment for RDF, RDFS, OWL, SPARQL. It includes a rule-based inference engine and supports external reasoners, such as RacerPro, Pellet and Fact++. Pellet is an open source Java-based OWL 2 DL reasoner. It has an excellent integration with Jena and its API provides functionalities to analyze the species validation, to check ontology consistency, to classify taxonomies, to check entailments and answer to a subset of RDQL queries. SHER, snorocket and ELLY are Java OWL EL reasoners, while Owlgres and QuOnto are OWL QL reasoners. Finally OWLIM and Jena are Java OWL RL reasoners.

QoS Models

In recent years, researchers dedicated much effort in developing formalized models to represent QoS in SOA environment. Most of them share the use of ontologies in order to define a model in a modular way, that can take advantage of the existing semantic tools. For example, Maximilien and Munindar (2004) concentrate on the definition of a QoS vocabulary and on the formalization of relationships between QoS attributes. The proposed ontological language is not rich enough to describe the QoS multifacets aspects. The main drawback is the lack of a metric model. Sycara et al. (2003) describe QoS offers or demands only through a rating attribute in the OWL-S ontology, one of the most used ontology for semantic resource description in the context of Web services. Kritikos and Plexousakis (2007) have extended their OWL-Q ontology with SWRL rules in order to support unit transformation, statistical metric value derivation, semantic property inference and matching of QoS Metric, achieving in this way a high-level of expressivity, able to capture different aspects of QoS-based Web service descriptions. The approach is also supported by a QoS-based Web service discovery framework.

Gramm A. et al. (2003), instead, support the runtime mapping of QoS requirements from Web Service layer onto the underlying network layer in terms of the Internet model. This mapping is achieved by the help of proxies (residing at the provider and consumer sides) and by the existence of a QoS-aware network. QoS network parameters are given as guidelines to QoS-aware routers while the client proxy calculates the network performance by taking into account the server performance information provided by the server proxy.

Oldham et al. (2006) semantically enrich the WS-Agreement language with different ontologies: (1) one for representing the WS-Agreement schema, (2) one for the QoS concepts used in guarantees, (3) one for the domain concepts and (3) an other one for the temporal constructs. The researchers use SWRL rules in order to manage the Semantics of Service Level Objectives (SLOs). However, the SLOs guarantees are expressed in terms of unary constraints and QoS metrics are not modeled at all. Tran et al. (2009) in the WS-QoSOnto ontology define QoS concepts and proprieties for supporting their AHP-based ranking algorithm. In particular they introduce QoS attributes like tendency, mandatory, weighting, relationship and grouping.

onQoS

Although the correct management of QoS directly impacts the success of organizations that have adopted a SOA approach, currently there are no comprehensive standards for expressing QoS. This section gives an overview of onQoS (*όνQoS,* i.e. QoS entity, ὄν in the early Greek, part. of εἶναι: to be), our ontological model for managing QoS during the whole process life-cycle. The first version of onQoS was developed with the objective of defining the semantics used in the QoS matching process (Giallonardo, E., & Zimeo, E., 2007). The model chosen for abstracting non-functional attributes was based on the Measurement Process. In fact, QoS are fundamental proprieties that have to be measured in many different ways by different service users. For example, service providers can declare QoS offered values during the service publication or negotiation phase; while service consumers can estimate the QoS values that they need or they can monitor them. Instead, to achieve a business QoS objective through the composition of different atomic services, their operational metrics have to be evaluated. Particular efforts are devoted to define a QoS model that considers as many as possible measures that can affect the quality of a service, and whose metrics can either be qualitative or quantitative, with the ultimate goal to semantically compute on the defined ontology.

The developed ontology is able to support QoS Management in the whole process life-cycle and it is able to cover the multi-facets of QoS in a variety of application domains. The latest version of onQoS defines a conceptualization regarding not only the QoS retrieval phase of the discovery process, but also the QoS ranking phase, the QoS monitoring and negotiation process performed during the service operation. The proposed ontological-based solution enables machines to reason on non-functional knowledge in order to derive services in matching, to compute the service ranks according to subjective user preferences, to monitor and to negotiate the Quality of Services.

onQoS has been formalized in OWL. It is able to support the reasoning power required to navigate the QoS terminology correctly and efficiently and it is able to formalize QoS knowledge, i.e. QoS parameters and their relationships. We utilize the ontology as the means to resolve terminology mismatches between the vocabularies, misunderstandings at message level, unsuccessful couplings between measurement processes, scales and units of measurement and as the means to derive knowledge utilizing the domain-dependent functions that can be specified between QoS metrics. The QoS model is able to cover the multi-facets of QoS in a variety of application domains, becoming the basis for the development of a knowledge-based middleware that enables SOA and BPM to work together.

onQoS presents three extensible levels: *upper*, *middle* and *low* ontology. The upper level defines the ontological language, i.e. the concepts identified as keys in QoS scenarios. The developers of these components can exploit the implemented upper level ontology reusing the concepts identified as keys in QoS scenarios. But they can also extend the middle ontology or they can introduce low ontologies in order to utilize QoS in specific application domains. In fact, in a distributed network of information, we cannot assume at any time that we have seen all the information in the network, or even that we know everything that has been asserted about any QoS aspect. New information might be discovered at any time. For this reason, onQoS can be extended and specialized with the new knowledge.

Figure 2 shows the main concepts and semantic relations between the onQoS Upper Ontology concepts. They derive from the analysis of process measurement (ISO 10012-1) and from its employment in the specification of each QoS entity. *Metric*, *Value*, *Measurement*, *Measurement Scale* are powerful concepts need to be defined in a domain independent ontology, i.e. in

Figure 2. The main onQoS upper ontology concepts and relationships

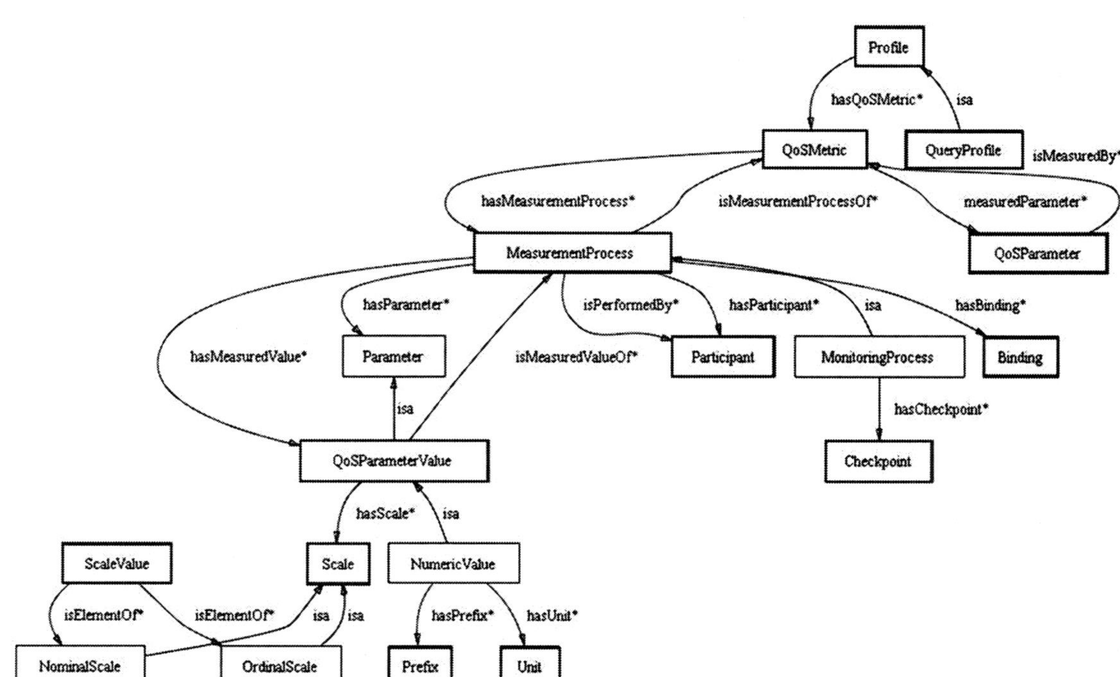

a high level conceptualization that allows for the definition of metrics for QoS parameters without dependence on the application domain. Metrics allows for defining how the parameters should be measured and a suitable tool that performs the specific measurement process for the parameter.

The onQoS *Profile* describes a QoS policy of a service endpoint through the definition of one or more QoS metrics. An onQoS profile is declared by a provider during the publishing or negotiation process for defining in a semantically computing way a set of metrics on QoS parameters. With an onQoS Profile, a provider informs the clients of the supported QoS parameter values and how he feels sure about them. When an e-contracting system creates an agreement and utilizes onQoS to describe non functional requirements, says that the provider promises to assure a service with the specified QoS Parameter values.

QoSMetric is a type of measurement tied to a QoS parameter. As we can see in Figure 3, according to the owl-based Protégé (2000) notation, something is a *QoSMetric* if it is in a relationship with two individuals, one of the class *MeasurementProcess* and another of the class *QoSParameter*. *QoSParameter* is a - measurable or quantifiable - QoS characteristic or feature. *MeasurementProcess* is the process by which numbers or symbols are assigned to QoS parameters according to clearly defined rules. *Scale* specifies the nature of the relationships among a set of values - *ScaleValue*. This is a number or symbol that identifies a category in which the QoS parameters can be placed. The *Participant* identifies the resource that performs the measurement process. The ontology identify the *Matchmaker*, the *Provider*, the *Requestor*, the *Monitor* and the *Negotiator* as typical participants of the QoS measurement process. The *QueryProfile,* instead, is a particular *Profile* that presents a unique QoS metric relating to the overall QoS of the desired services. Query profiles can be used by Web Service requestors. *QueryProfile* presents the single property *hasQoSMetric* on the range of *WSQoSMetric*. This is a metric relating to the overall QoS of a Web service. We

Figure 3. QoSMetric concept: Asserted hierarchy, logical and property views

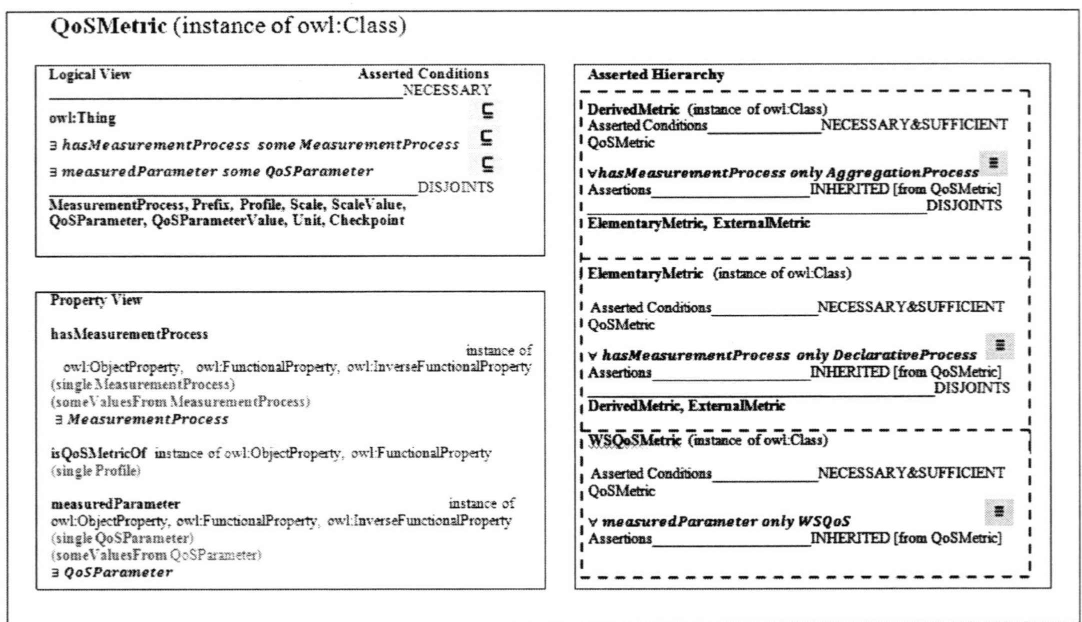

associate a *Profile* with a service advertisement, while a *QueryProfile* describes the QoS profile requested by a user. *Prefix* and *Unit* concepts, allows specifying for numeric values basic prefixes and unit of measure. While *Checkpoint* is a QoS inspection point of a *MonitoringProcess*. It fixes a monitoring scheduled time (*Scheduled Checkpoint*) or declares the provider availability to be monitored at any time (*Free Checkpoint*).

The *onQoS Middle Ontology* defines the onQoS domain-independent terminology. It presents the following modules: *QoS Parameters, QoS Measurement Processes, QoS Metric, QoS Scales, QoS Metric* and *QoS Unit. QoSParameter* links the upper ontology with the middle ontology and it is a common super class for the following concepts: *Availability, Integrity, Reputation, Negotiability, Flexibility, Capacity, Adaptability, Interoperability, Accessibility, Scalability, Accuracy, Adherence to specification, Observance to the specified requirements, Performance, Reliability, Robustness, Configuration, Security, Traceability,* and *WSQoS* (a measure of the whole QoS of Web Service functionality, calculated by means of a particular measurement process for a specific query).

MeasurementProcess, instead, is specialized by *EvaluationProcess, DeclarativeProcess*, *AggregationProcess*, *ReadingProcess*, and *MonitoringProcess*, as we can see in the related middle ontology (*Figure 4*). *Evaluation processes* are processes whose objective is to evaluate QoS constraints. These can be expressed utilizing different *Predicates*, i.e a specialization of the evaluation process (in our context), such as the comparison operators (<, >, =, !=, …) that operate on different scales. *DeclarativeProcesses* are direct measurement processes that enable statement on QoS parameter values. These do not present input parameters. They have to be utilized to specify the QoS service descriptions that the providers have to publish with the onQoS-based publishing model. *AggregationProcesses* are indirect measurement processes that reduce a set of measures into a unique representative one making a synthesis of different aspects. *Reading Processes* are processes that read data written in other sources and convert them into data which have meaning for the onQoS model. *MonitoringProcesses* describe the way for measuring a specified QoS parameter, they can require a periodic or a free measure of the QoS value *(Checkpoint)*.

Predicates and functions are measurement processes of *WSQoSMetric* and define how to measure (partial value of) the *WSQoS* parameters. The composition of evaluation and aggregation measurement process is driven by the compatibility of the input/output measured variables. onQoS defines a variable for each measurement scale, also for the *WSQoSScale*. The object property *hasMeasuredValue,* inherited from *MeasurementProcess* by class *Predicate,* has a range restriction on the *WSQoSValue* class. The properties *hasFirstArgument* and *hasSecondArgument* specialize the *hasParameter property* of *MeasurementProcess* and identify the arguments of a non-commutative predicate. The *Predicate*, instead, has restrictions on the subclass of *QoSParameterValue* corresponding with the scale (*NominalScale*, *OrdinalScale* or *RatioScale*) for which predicates are defined. For example, the *DoublePredicate* for the *RatioScale* has the inherited restriction *owl:allValueFrom* on *RatioValue,* specialized on *DoubleValues*. *WeightedMean*, *WSQoSOr* and *WSQoSAnd* are aggregation functions, that let a user to aggregate partial Web Services QoS evaluations to specify the wished measure in an expression.

Figure 5 reports, instead, the *QoS Metrics middle ontology*. The QoS metrics are classified basing on their measurement processes. *Derived Metrics* can only have aggregation processes as measurement processes; *Reading Metrics* can only have reading processes as measurement processes; *Declarative Metrics* can only have declarative processes as measurement processes and they present the *hasDirection* property for allowing to know their preferential direction. For

Figure 4. onQoS measurement process middle ontology

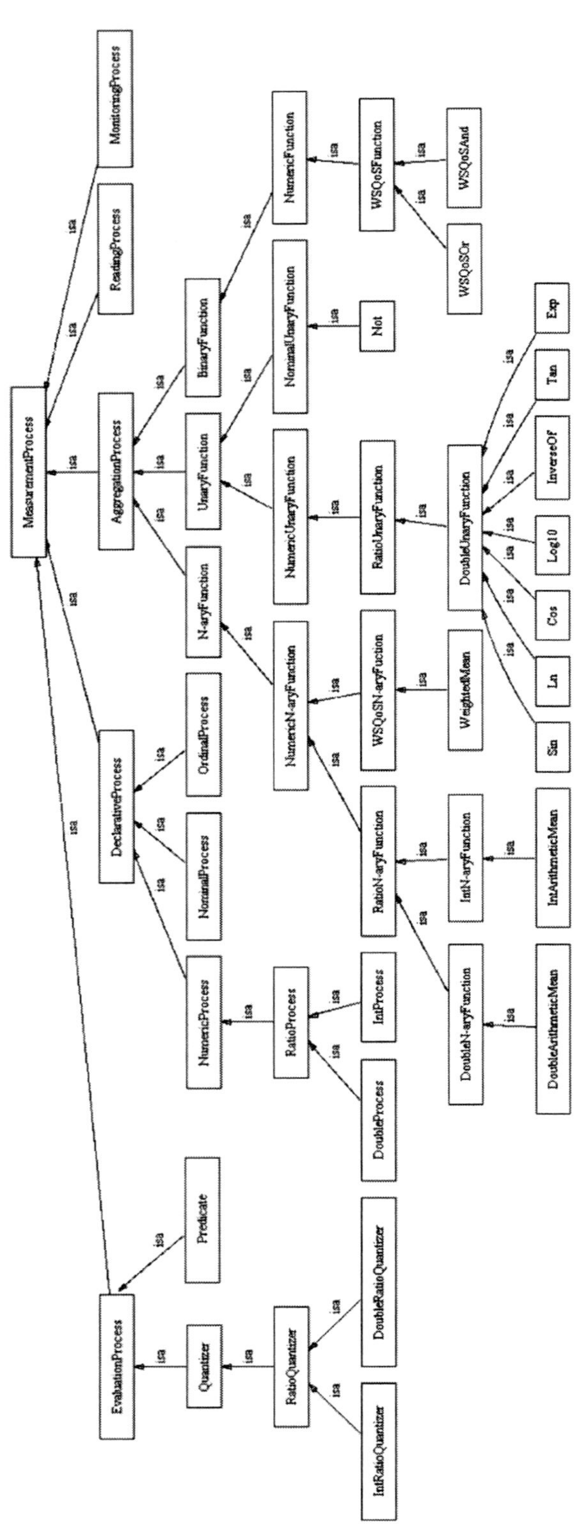

Figure 5. onQoS metrics middle ontology

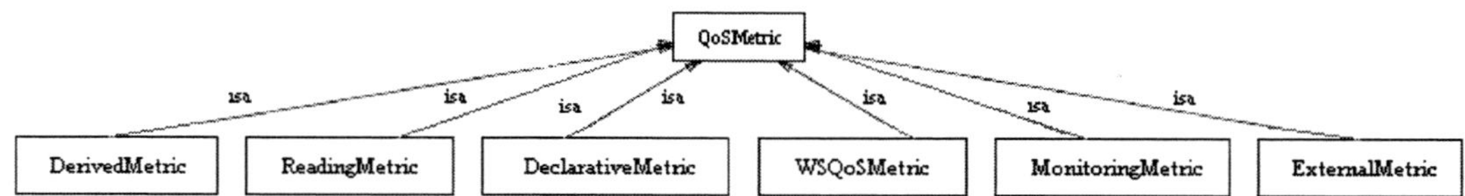

Figure 6. onQoS scales middle ontology

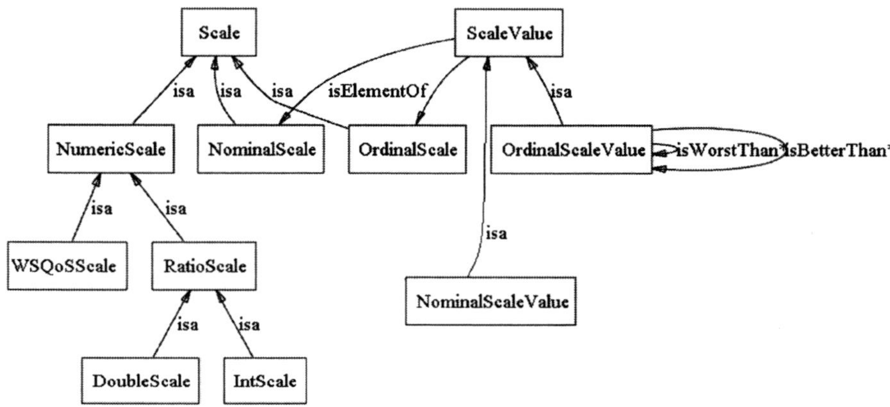

example, the throughput has a positive direction, while response time has a negative one. *Monitoring Metrics* can only have monitoring processes as measurement processes; *WSQoSMetric* can only have an aggregation process or an evaluation process as measurement process, and the object of the measurement process can be only the whole QoS of the Web Service. While, we specialize the Scale Concept into the following three types: *Numeric Scale, Nominal Scale*, and *Ordinal Scale* (*Figure 6*). *WSQoSScale* is defined as a numeric and totally ordered scale whose values span in the range [0, 1] of the real numbers. The object property *isMadeUpOf* of the *Scale* concept is restricted in a way that its values belong to the range *{hasWSQoSScaleValue}*. The data property *hasWSQoSScaleValue* links a float value in [0, 1] with a variable on the scale *WSQoSScale*. Formally, a variable whose values belong to *WSQoSScale* is represented with the class *WSQoSValue*, subclass of *NumericValue*. *WSQoSValue* also, defines the data property *hasWeight* that can be used to weight a QoS parameter constraint. Finally, the *onQoS Unit Middle Ontology* defines cardinality, percentage, frequency, information, money and counting units.

onQoS can be extended to include specific domain properties. It is not necessary to use the predefined parameters, one can define her own parameters by extending onQoS with specific low ontologies. At this level, for example, an individual of a desiderate *QoSMetricFunction*, specifying the properties of the component metrics and the properties of the resulting metric, can be instantiated. This way, a domain-dependent QoS knowledge can be directly specified in the ontology.

onQoS Query Language

Although service consumers need to communicate effectively their quality of service requests, today a standard QoS query language has not been defined yet.

Queries used during service discovery and negotiation have a direct influence on the results, since they are the means for the requestor to explicit the knowledge about its intention. Hence, to improve the quality of Web processes, the design of a specific and expressive QoS query language could be useful, as demonstrated by the focus on query and rule layers in the context of Semantic Web. An explicit formalization of QoS queries enables discovery and e-contracting components to base their execution on QoS queries semantics. In the design of a QoS Language we started from onQoS for the following main reasons:

- The queries need to be evaluated against a representation. onQoS is an expressive, stable and well-organized QoS model that can be used for semantically define QoS Profiles for SOA Software Components;
- The choose of an OWL ontology allows for re-use of software infrastructure, e.g. query parsers, query engines and reasoners;
- SPARQL can be used to query an OWL model and to filter out individuals with specific characteristics.

Although SPARQL is able to retrieve from a pool the services that satisfy a query, it does not provide a solution for ranking the retrieved services according to the desired non functional properties. So we decided to use it as basis for the implementation of a more expressive language able to capture user QoS desiderata and to rank services according to subjective QoS user preferences.

With the help of onQoS-QL (Damiano G. et al., 2007), service consumers can express (*Figure 7*) more effectively their QoS requests, so better formalizing their real intentions. In fact, these measures often depend on subjective expectations of the service or on context information and vary with the type of service and where it is used. Therefore, providing clients with a way to clearly and formally define QoS criteria and complex utility functions, the QoS discovery engine will be able to select automatically the proper service, reasoning not only on the QoS shared knowledge but also ranking the services according to the requestor criteria.

WSQoSMetric represents the main building block for query formulation. It measures the degree of compatibility between two descriptions on a scale that defines an ordinal relation. User formulates a query through several instances of

Figure 7. An example of onQoS-QL Query: RTT < 10 ms

```
<rdf:RDF ...
  xmlns:qosNet="http://address/ontology/qosNet.owl#"
  xmlns:onQoS="http://address/ontology/onQoS.owl#"     ...
<!-- (?RTT < 10.0) -->
  <onQoS:NumericProcess rdf:ID="RTTNumericProcessInd">
  <onQoS:hasMeasuredValue>
   <onQoS:DoubleValue rdf:ID="RTTValueInd">
    <onQoS:hasUnit rdf:resource="http://address/ontology/onQoS.owl#Seconds"/>
    <onQoS:hasPrefix rdf:resource="http://address/ontology/onQoS.owl#milli"/>
    <onQoS:isMeasuredValueOf rdf:resource="#RTTNumericProcessInd"/>
   </onQoS:DoubleValue>
  </onQoS:hasMeasuredValue>
  <onQoS:isMeasurementProcessOf>
   <onQoS:QoSMetric rdf:ID="RTTMetricInd">
    <onQoS:hasMeasurementProcess rdf:resource="#RTTNumericProcessInd"/>
    <onQoS:measuredParameter>
     <qosNet:RTT rdf:ID="RTTInd">
      <onQoS:isMeasuredBy rdf:resource="#RTTMetricInd"/>
      <onQoS:isPrivate rdf:datatype="http://www.w3.org/2001/XMLSchema#string"
      >false</onQoS:isPrivate>
     </qosNet:RTT>     </onQoS:measuredParameter>     </onQoS:QoSMetric>
  </onQoS:isMeasurementProcessOf>  </onQoS:NumericProcess>

<onQoS:DoubleLessThan rdf:ID="RTTDoubleLessProcessInd">
  <onQoS:hasSecondArgument>
   <onQoS:DoubleValue rdf:ID="RTTCostantValueInd">
    <onQoS:hasUnit rdf:resource="http://address/ontology/onQoS.owl#Seconds"/>
    <onQoS:hasPrefix rdf:resource="http://address/ontology/onQoS.owl#milli"/>
    <onQoS:hasDoubleScaleValue rdf:datatype=
"http://www.w3.org/2001/XMLSchema#double">10</onQoS:hasDoubleScaleValue>
   </onQoS:DoubleValue>   </onQoS:hasSecondArgument>
  <onQoS:isMeasurementProcessOf>
   <onQoS:QoSMetric rdf:ID="RTTEvaluationMetricInd">
    <onQoS:hasMeasurementProcess rdf:resource="#RTTDoubleLessProcessInd"/>
    <onQoS:isQoSMetricOf>
     <onQoS:QueryProfile rdf:ID="QueryProfileInd">
      <onQoS:hasQoSMetric rdf:resource="#RTTEvaluationMetricInd"/>
     </onQoS:QueryProfile>
    </onQoS:isQoSMetricOf>
    <onQoS:measuredParameter>
     <qosNet:WSQoS rdf:ID="WSQoSRTTInd">
      <onQoS:isPrivate rdf:datatype="http://www.w3.org/2001/XMLSchema#string"
      >false</onQoS:isPrivate>
      <onQoS:isMeasuredBy rdf:resource="#RTTEvaluationMetricInd"/>
     </qosNet:WSQoS>
    </onQoS:measuredParameter>
   </onQoS:QoSMetric>
  </onQoS:isMeasurementProcessOf>
  <onQoS:hasFirstArgument rdf:resource="#RTTValueInd"/>
  <onQoS:hasMeasuredValue>
   <onQoS:WSQoSValue rdf:ID="WSQoSRTTValueInd">
    <onQoS:isMeasuredValueOf rdf:resource="#RTTDoubleLessProcessInd"/>
   </onQoS:WSQoSValue>   </onQoS:hasMeasuredValue>  </onQoS:DoubleLessThan> ...
</rdf:RDF>
```

WSQoSMetric organized in hierarchical manner and according to a logical/arithmetic expression. The scope of a query is to capture the way in which users want to measure the quality of a Web service, represented by the class *WSQoS*, evaluating constraints defined on selected QoS parameters and aggregating these partial results. Aggregation can be performed only if a reference measurement scale exists for any value involved in this process and according to the operations it defines. The scale is represented through the class *WSQoSScale* and is a numeric and totally ordered scale whose values span in the range [0, 1] of the real numbers.

To clarify the role of onQoS-QL, we consider a simple example in the domain of networks to query for a service with a desired network QoS expressed in terms of Round Trip Time (RTT) and Jitter (if we are interested to a network service for transferring multimedia contents). The high level query could be expressed by using the following syntax:

$?WSQoSValue = (?RTTValue <_{WSQoS} y_1) \vee_{WSQoS} (?JitterValue <_{WSQoS} y_2)$

We associated to the $<_{WSQoS}$ operator an extended semantic. This means that the application of the operators not only returns a boolean value but also a value in the interval]0, 1[. This way, we not only determinate the existing services in match but also the distance from the desired QoS requirements. In particular, the value of *WSQoSValue* in the expression above could be calculated transforming it into the expression in *(1)*, considering k as constant on the same measurement scale of *?RTTValue* and *?JitterValue,* and the following extended semantics: $x \vee_{WSQoS} y$ is $max(x, y)$, while $?RTTValue <_{WSQoS} y_1$ is $\frac{2}{1+e^{\frac{y_1 - ?RTTValue}{k}}} - 1$.

$$?WSQoSValue = max\left(\frac{2}{1+e^{\frac{y_1 - ?RTTValue}{k}}} - 1, \frac{2}{1+e^{\frac{y_2 - ?JitterValue}{k}}} - 1\right) \quad (1)$$

Table 1 shows the extended semantics of the main onQoS-QL predicates and aggregation functions. The first two columns report the operators of the language and the operands with their measurement scales. The second two columns report retrieval and ranking semantics of each operator. The former means a service profile will be retrieved if and only if the logical condition it states is satisfied. The latter indicates the rank value of each satisfied operator, according to the mathematical expression provided in the table.

The sample expressions presented above and the metrics used are analyzed by the onQoS-QL reasoner that supports onQoS-QL query-answering. The onQoS-Reasoner has been implemented utilizing the Jena Framework and the internal Jena *SPAR-QL Engine*. The main reasoner component is the *onQoS-QL Engine* that manages and controls the *SPAR-QL Engine* and the *Ranking Engine.* The former selects from a pool the services that satisfy the query, whereas the latter establishes a ranking among the retrieved services. To this end, the *onQoS-QL Engine* rewrites the onQoS-QL query in a SPARQL one in order to pass it to the *SPAR-QL Engine*. The result set obtained from the SPAR-QL engine can be ranked according to the matching process defined in the query.

QoS-AWARE SERVICE DISCOVERY

Discovery engines are key architectural components of SOA. Service requestors have to use them to properly select the services to bind to a Web process during their design or system configuration. Human beings can perform the discovery process browsing services and their providers by several criteria. This manual approach is useful in order to reduce the learning curve required

Table 1. Main predicates and aggregation functions with their semantics

VOCABULARY TERM	ARGUMENT MEASUREMENT SCALE	RETRIEVAL SEMANTICS	RANKING SEMANTICS
Equal(x_i, x_j)	NominalScale $\{x\}_i=1\ldots N$	$i=j$	1
NotEqual(x_i, x_j)		$i \neq j$	1
BetterEqualThan(x_i, x_j)	OrdinalScale $\left\{x_i \mid x_i < x_j \Leftrightarrow i < j\right\}_{i=1\ldots N}$	$i \in \{j,\ldots,N\}$	$\frac{1}{N}(1+i-j)$
LessEqualThan(x_i, x_j)		$i \in \{1,\ldots,j\}$	$\frac{1}{N}(1+j-i)$
DoubleLessThan(x, y)	DoubleRatioScale $[X_{inf}, X_{sup}]$	$x<y$	$\frac{2}{1+e^{-\frac{y-x}{k}}}-1$
DoubleGreaterThan(x, y)		$x>y$	$\frac{2}{1+e^{-\frac{x-y}{k}}}-1$
WSQoSAnd(x, y)	WSQoSScale $\left\{p \equiv (x,w) \mid x \in [0,1] \wedge w \in [0, X_{sup}]\right\}$	$x \wedge y$	$min(x, y)$
WSQoSOr(x, y)		xy	$max(x, y)$
WeightedMean $(p_i)_{i=1,\ldots,N}$		$\exists p_l$, $l=1,\ldots,N$	$\sum_{i=1}^{N} w_i x_i \Big/ \sum_{i=1}^{N} w_i$

for developers not familiar with Web Services, but becomes not feasible when the number of services increases as it is happening in recent years in the Web.

Syntactical-based matching approaches produce results characterized by an insufficient precision degree. In fact, the probability that the requestor types the same keywords with the same meanings utilized by the providers is very low. Furthermore, as the UDDI case shows, a discovery system that does not take into account QoS features does not succeed easily. In fact, it returns also results characterized by very low QoS values that not only lack of QoS guaranties but in many cases make unfeasible their utilization.

In order to improve the service discovery process, Semantics and QoS are so essential features. Only a high level of accuracy of the discovery results allows for realizing automatic or semiautomatic service selections. In the next sections we present the directions that can be utilized during the matching process and how we exploit the introduced Derivation.

Directions in Semantic Matching

We identified *Specialization*, *Implication* and *Composition* as possible directions (Giallonardo, E., & Zimeo, E., 2007) to exploit the QoS knowledge in the matching process and we added the *Derivation* one. In the *QoS Specialization* dimension, discovery is performed by exploiting generalization/specialization relations to compute the matching degree between QoS descriptions. The

Figure 8. Derivation-based matching algorithm and QoS descriptions used for the testing

```
qosMatch(T, t) {
 effectiveConfidenceLeve l= 0;
 mappingList = empty;
 reasoner.check(T);
 reasoner.check(t);
 atomicMappingList = atomicMatch(T,t);
 nonMappedList = findNonMappedMetrics(atomicMappingList);
 aggregateMappingList = aggregateMatch(nonMappedList, t);
 mappingList = atomicMappingList.append(aggregateMappingList);
 score = weightedAverage(mappingList);
 effectiveConfidenceLeve l= getNumberOfSatisfiedMetric(T,t) /
                              getMetricNumber(T);
return;}
```

Confidence [%]	10	20	30	40	50	60	70	80	90	100
Precision derivation [%]	48	52	60	62	63	66	70	76	78	91
Precision no derivate. [%]	49	54	60	60	61	75	85	85	92	100
Recall derivation [%]	92	92	92	92	92	88	88	88	88	88
Recall no derivation[%]	85	85	81	81	81	77	77	73	73	69

D1 = { Authentication, Authorization, Cost <= 100€, ExecutionTime <= 0.5 ms, FaulRate <= 50%,Jitter<=0.3 ms, NetThroughput >= 200 kbps, RTT <= 14ms, Scalability >= 78%, TransmissionTime <= 7 ms,UpTime >= 90%, EncStand: RSA, PKI, OpenPGP, Triple-DES };

D2 = { Cost <= 121 €, ExecutionTime <= 0.6 ms,FaulRate <= 50%, Jitter <= 1.5 ms, Privacy, RTT <= 17ms, Scalability >= 43%, ThrLatRatio >= 3.5Mbps/s,UpTime >= 86%, EncStand: RSA, PKI, OpenPGP };

D3 = { Cost <= 140 €, Jitter <= 0.3 ms, NetLatency <= 24.9 ms, Privacy, UpTime >= 65%, EncStand: RSA, PKI };

D4 = { Authentication, Authorization, ExecutionTime <= 0.8ms, Jitter <= 2.6 ms, NetThroughput >= 10 kbps, RTT<=5ms, TransmissionTime <= 6 ms, UpTime >= 65%, EncStand: RSA, PKI, OpenPGP };

D5 = { Authentication, Authorization,ExecutionTime<=0.8 ms, Jitter <= 2.6 ms, NetThroughput >= 10 kbps, RTT<=5 ms, TransmissionTime <= 6 ms, UpTime >= 65%, EncStand: RSA, PKI, OpenPGP };

D6 = { NetLatency <= 22 ms };

D7 = { Authentication, Authorization }; **D8** = { RTT<=25ms}.

QoS Implication (or Correlation) dimension is typically linked to the domain. The last dimension is the *QoS Composition (or Aggregation among Web Services)* one.

We used onQoS to specify QoS requirements and QoS parameters as combination of other ones. By understanding, exploiting and reasoning on this knowledge we derive the semantic correspondences between syntactically different QoS descriptions and we increase the satisfaction of the retrieval engine users. In some domains, relationships among parameters are well known. For example, the network latency (L) presents shared definitions that can be exploited in order to increase the recall of matching process. As consequence *derivation* refers to the process of obtaining a QoS dimension from several QoS parameters of the same service through reasoning on formalized knowledge.

To validate the usefulness of the proposed dimension for QoS semantics, we performed some tests on a derivation-based strategy in the network domain (it is only an example for helping the reader). In particular, we exploited the common way ($L = RTT + t_e + t_t$) of measuring network latency that takes into account the following contributors: round trip delay (RTT), execution (t_e) and transmission times (t_t). So as humans immediately derive the formula $RTT = L - t_e - t_t$ and are able to reason on it and obtain the right pairs in matching, so this type of reasoning can be implemented in the matching algorithm by making inference on the QoS knowledge. Therefore a pair of descriptions apparently mismatched (template T and target t_1) can instead result as the optimal solution in the services space. In fact, if the RTT request value of the service template T is "≤ 10 seconds" and the latency L of the service target t_1 is "≤ 10 seconds", while the specified values in the target t_2 are "RTT=11s, t_e=8s, t_t=2s". The couple (T, t_1) is the best match and can be obtained by interpreting the semantic rule between the parameters.

We evaluated our ontology and algorithm (*Figure 8*) by using some descriptions both as template and targets, in every combination (each description is put in match with another description of the pool). The input of the matching algorithm is the QoS semantic descriptions and optionally the required level of confidence, i.e. the claimed degree of match (exact, plug in, subsume, intersection).

In the QoS query descriptions, the users can specify, by means of weights, the importance of each parameter in the matching process. A weight describes how the user prefers a particular characteristic rather than another. The algorithm includes two phases: atomic matching (1:1) and aggregated matching (1:N).

The outcome of the first phase is the *atomicMappingList* with the following information: required QoS metric, advertisement QoS metric, and matching score. We obtained these data utilizing the Pellet reasoner on the ontological descriptions. So we are able to understand the equivalence between measures expressed with different units. The second step recovers the *nonMappedList* template metrics that are not in atomic matching and, for each QoS template metric of the *nonMappedList*; it searches a mapping with more QoS target metrics exploiting the QoS knowledge of the ontology.

The results (*Figure 8*) showed that the recall is improved by using the proposed algorithm for each level of confidence given in input whereas the precision is not significantly decreased. 0% of confidence indicates the maximum level of flexibility of the matching algorithm (minimum level of precision). We can conclude that the proposed ontology and the introduction of functions to process derived QoS parameters significantly improve matching recall without degrading precision.

QoS Monitoring

However, although QoS influences the whole life-cycle of a process, the core phase around which QoS assumes the role of pillar in Web processes is *diagnosis*. It is fundamental for managing unexpected events during execution, correcting problems, avoiding process failure, increasing performance and improving resources exploitation. *Service monitoring* is intended as a planned or event-driven measurement of one or more properties of a service. Monitoring allows for verifying whether the QoS parameters specified in the contract are respected. It involves monitoring the QoS value status of the offered service and provides relevant information to service consumers. QoS monitoring is a specific example of measurement process for dynamically evaluating the values of QoS parameters. It works on QoS parameters that change continuously, it allows for observing them and to adapt the process behavior through the selection of services that meet the QoS requirements at execution time. Monitoring is useful in order to ranking service providers according to their reputation.

Both onQoS and onQoS-QL are used in the binding phase to discover the requested services. However, the selected services might not perform as expected for different reasons (tied to the execution context or simply to the reputation of the providers). Therefore, starting from onQoS, the SOA infrastructure should provide also some mechanism to verify at run-time the actual QoS offered by the providers by continuously monitoring the QoS parameters that characterize the selected services.

The QoS Monitoring component allows the process management system to acquire QoS values for the process binding, monitoring and redesign phases. It provides services with specific interfaces that enable the run-time evaluation of QoS expressions. The system so can promptly determinate violations of the Service Level Agreement, react when a quality parameter falls beyond a given threshold or decide to refine the process in future similar circumstances. onQoS can be utilized for specifying QoS requirements during the QoS negotiation in e-Contracting systems, so extending WS Agreement.

QoS Monitoring is a key architectural component, managing the fact that the values of QoS parameters change regularly during the process execution impacting on the quality of the whole process. It is utilized during the dynamic evaluation of the non functional expression ($?P_1$ && $?P_4$ in Figure 9) obtained by expanding the semantics of the onQoS-QL relational and logical operators on WSQoS scale.

The measures of QoS parameters can be automatically and dynamically performed by using measurement tools explicitly defined for the individuals of low-level onQoS by exploiting both the ontology and the attributes provided by the specific service under observation. The measures of the QoS parameters could be also acquired by the Monitoring Component retrieving the values from a monitoring repository (if the parameter has been previously monitored by the requestor) or directly from the service provider with a simple reading operation.

Figure 9 focuses on the QoS monitoring aspects of the system showing how SOA, BPM and Semantic Technologies can work together utilizing the following components: *Service Provider*, *Service Requestor*, *Web Service Discovery Engine*, *Semantic Workflow Engine*, *Ontologies* and *Service Registry*.

The capabilities available in the network are exposed via Web Services from the different providers that publish them in service registries. The Requestor-side system exploits a Semantic Workflow Engine in order to manage the desired processes. It can automatically bind an available capability to a managed process exploiting functional and non-functional semantic descriptions, ontologies, and a WS Discovery System. Figure 10 shows the main matching components of WS-Broogle, the discovery system developed at University of Sannio in Java for supporting the publishing of UDDI 2 services, the functional and non functional discovery capabilities for OWL-S, WSDL and onQoS-based services descriptions.

A requestor (simple client or a complex semantic workflow engine) sends a query to a mediator (WS Discovery Engine), which accesses to a space of services (WS_1, WS_2,... WS_n) and for each one builds an expression to pass to the monitor. This uses the knowledge formalized in the Non Functional Requirements (NFR) Ontology (linked to onQoS) to adopt the adequate

Figure 10. Reputation algorithm

```
reputation(P){
   reputation = 0
   C = contract subscribed with P
   forall c ∊ C do{
      Qs = qosparameters in c
      forall qs ∊ Qs do{
           GV = garanteedvalue of qs
            M = monitored_values
           median = computeMedian{GV-M}
           reputation+= evaluateMedian(median,F)
      }reputation/=|QS|
   }return reputation/=|C|}
```

Figure 9. QoS management system architecture

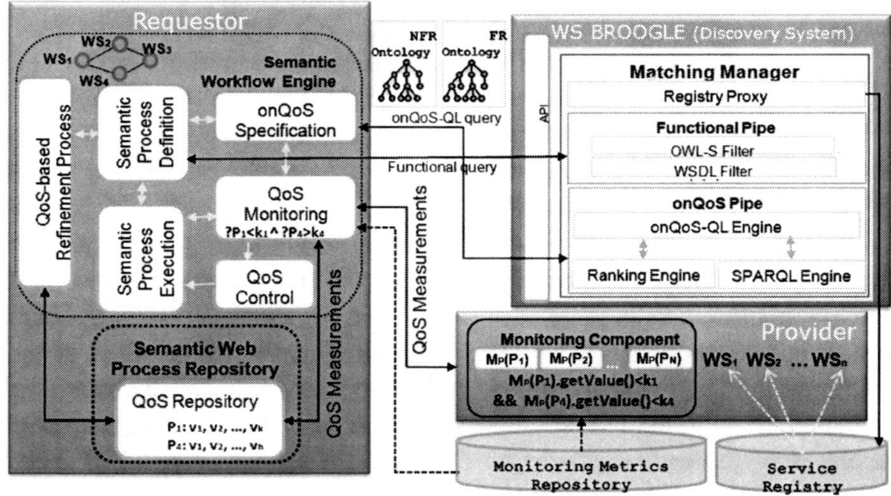

measurement processes for the parameters P_1 and P_4 (in the example). The measurement processes are implemented by the tools ($M_p(P_1)$ and $M_p(P_4)$) specified by the attributes of P_1 and P_4 (individuals) provided by the services under analysis according to onQoS. The matchmaker ranks the services by using the evaluation of the expression and returns the one(s) that better matches with the requestor's requirements.

Monitoring can be performed according diagnosis points (*checkpoints*) and monitoring tools specified in the agreement. QoS monitored measures have become fundamental elements to take into account for process refinement, for supporting decision making, and for incrementing trust in electronic contract establishment.

The ability to express QoS desiderata through complex and semantically enriched expressions enables sophisticated mechanisms for process monitoring based on event-driven evaluation of non-functional properties of running activities and processes. These mechanisms represent the main building blocks for enabling sophisticated computational models characterized by autonomic properties that aid processes and infrastructures to evolve and adapt to external stimuli and context changes. Moreover, if the values of monitored parameters are stored in requestors' repositories, dynamic and effective social adaptations of service networks become possible by introducing and evaluating the provider reputation as a global metric. This can be locally considered as the measure of the distance between the values exposed by a provider for a set of QoS parameters and the ones monitored by a service requestor. In order to compute the provider reputation, the implemented *Reputation Handler* component utilizes all provider QoS historical data stored in the Repository: QoS monitored values and SLA promised values. It takes into account also the preferential direction of the QoS metrics (exploiting the onQoS semantic description). The provider reputation value represents the median value of the differences between the QoS promised values and the monitored ones. Figure 10 shows the details of the reputation algorithm.

onQoS Application

onQoS, onQoS-QL, the Web Service Discovery Framework, the Workflow Engine and the Monitoring component were implemented and initially experimented in the context of an industrial project (LOCOSP) that aims at using SOA and Web Services technology for managing automotive supply chains during the design of a new vehicle. In this scenario, it is unlikely that anyone chooses a Web service supplier - a Web Service - without considering response time, availability, cost, security, standards compliance or quality of the products delivered, such as output correctness compared with the declared semantics of the related operation - CAD artifacts in the automotive domain.

The work on QoS is currently under experimentation in several ongoing projects. This way onQoS and the components for its management will pratically tested and improved in different domains and scenarios.

In the SIEGE (*Software Innovation for E-Government Expansion*) Project, we are planning to utilize the implemented Web Service Discovery Framework and the Monitoring tool in order to enable Governments to provide better public services to citizens and business organizations. In this case, onQoS-QL can enable Software E-Government Systems to measure the QoS of services (for example for emergency handling) they offer and to refine internal processes on measures that take into account the satisfaction of citizens.

The GLOBE (*Global Link Over Business Environment*) Project exploits QoS Semantics to manage the quality of streaming and location-based services in pervasive and mobile computing environments, where users queries their smart phones or handhelds to obtain touristic or public information related to the location of the device, with the support of cellular triangulation.

QoS and negotiation are instead exploited in the COSA (*Contract Oriented Service Architecture*) Project. Here, QoS is exploited in order to support differentiate forms of e-contracts by considering also a negotiation phase to achieve an agreement between a service provider and a service requestor. Hence, the implemented Web Service Discovery Framework can be used during the contract establishment phase in order to identify, among a set of potential service providers, the contract partner with whom to begin the negotiation phase. While, the Monitoring component can be used during the contract enacment phase in order to determinate its satisfaction.

The study of QoS, negotiation and monitoring are aimed at supporting a new model for highly dynamic workflows (for business, science and engineering domains), called *autonomic workflows*. These should be able to modify themselves autonomously according to QoS and monitoring information acquired during the execution. In the ARTDECO (*Adaptive InfrasTructures for DECentralized Organizations*) Project the QoS Semantics ingredient supports the autonomic features of the system that manages in a flexible and agile way an agribusiness network, formed by a collection of networked enterprises. Here, QoS management of the service level impacts also on reputation and trust between the involved parties.

CONCLUSION

In this chapter, we addressed, through a semantic-based approach, the following QoS issues: specification, computation and monitoring. Concerning the QoS specification level, we (1) identified the dimensions that we consider to be necessary parts of a QoS model for Web processes; (2) formalized our QoS model in onQoS; (3) defined the onQoS-QL language for formulating a query as a set of statements to retrieve and ranking Web Services by satisfying user defined QoS requirements.

Starting from the analysis of real world scenarios we support QoS heterogeneity, QoS complex descriptions and static and dynamic properties descriptions. We retain necessary for describing QoS to have a common way for expressing QoS dimensions. By reasoning on QoS Discovery, Negotiation and Monitoring, we identified as key aspect the importance of delivering measurable values to Service Consumers for advanced process handling. Such values are instances of concepts of a QoS Description Model that uses QoS metrics to share QoS knowledge between providers and consumers. OWL, the Ontology Web Language, has been utilized in order to define QoS semantics and to make it machine-processable during the whole process life-cycle.

onQoS concepts and relations can be used (1) for promising QoS parameter values, as declaring provider's availability to negotiate with a specific framework; (2) for declaring its availability to be monitored at run-time according to a defined QoS Monitoring Policy; and (3) for describing important QoS parameters features as for example the convenience direction. onQoS provides benefits in every phase of the processes' life-cycle. For example, during the Process Execution phase, it enables the late binding of resources to concrete services and the run time SLA Management, allowing for releasing human resources from the QoS negotiation and monitoring task. onQoS-QL, instead, tries to fill up the lack of a standard QoS query language giving the user a set of operators that merge retrieval constrains and ranking directives. As such, predicates and some aggregation functions have extended semantics to support both retrieval and ranking phases. onQoS-QL was tested through the WS-Broogle discovery system.

For the QoS Computation issues, we proposed a semantic derivation-based matching algorithm for service retrieval and we proposed an extension of the semantics of the onQoS-QL operators for a flexible service ranking. QoS Semantics descriptions make effective the automatic discovery not only enabling the easy reuse of the "right" available service among the many targets published on the Web, but also allowing automatic monitoring of QoS critical features, as for example, the availability. So, we directed our efforts on Monitoring by exploiting QoS knowledge for auto-configuring the related component with the necessary QoS monitoring tools.

QoS Semantics appears as a useful element for dealing effectively with the Web process complexity and as a main ingredient to use for the development of open systems, where services can dynamically be bound, invoked, monitored and changed. The idea is to use the knowledge stored in service queries, in advertisements, and in reputation management systems in order to enable semantic computing of agreements. Through a provider reputation model, we address the computation issue of preventing unsatisfactory chooses and predicting QoS values of the whole Web Process. This objective has been achieved analyzing the previously QoS monitored values stored in a QoS repository according to the different contexts of utilization.

In the future, we will extend the framework with the ability of performing negotiation between two parties of an e-contract in an automatic way.

ACKNOWLEDGMENT

This chapter has been partially supported by the following projects: FIRB - ArtDeco (Adaptive Infrastructure for Decentralized Organizations), COSA (Contract Oriented Service Architecture), SIEGE (Software Innovation for E-Government Expansion) of the Italian Minister of University and Research, POR 3.17 - GLOBE (Global Link Over Business Environments) of Campania Region.

REFERENCES

ART DECO. (2010). *Adaptative infrastructures for decentralised organizations*. Retrieved from http://artdeco.elet.polimi.it/

Brickley, D., & Guha, R. V. (2000). *Resource Description Framework (RDF) schemas*. W3C. Retrieved from http://www.w3.org/TR/2000/CR-rdf-schema-20000327/

Chia, L. T., Zhou, C., & Lee, B. S. (2004). DAML-QoS ontology for Web Services. *The International Conference on Web Services ICWS,* (p. 472-479). San Diego: IEEE Computer Society.

Damiano, G., Giallonardo, E., & Zimeo, E. (2007). OnQoS-QL: A query language for service selection and ranking. *Proceedings of ICSOC '07 Workshop on Non Functional Properties and Service Level Agreements*. Vienna, Austria.

De Bruijn, J., Lausen, H., Krummenacher, R., Polleres, A., Predoiu, L., Kifer, M., et al. (2005). *The Web Service Modeling Language WSML*. Retrieved from http://www.wsmo.org/TR/d16/d16.1/v0.21/

Dean, M., & Schreiber, G. (2004). *OWL Web ontology language reference*. W3C recommendation. Retrieved from http://www.w3.org: http://www.w3.org/TR/owl-ref/

Farrell, J., & Lausen, H. (2007). *Semantic annotations for WSDL and XML schema*. W3C recommendation. Retrieved from http://www.w3.org/TR/sawsdl/

Giallonardo, E., & Zimeo, E. (2007). More semantics in QoS matching. *IEEE International Conference on Service-Oriented Computing and Applications, SOCA '07,* (p. 163-171). Newport Beach, CA: IEEE Computer Society.

GLOBE, Global Link Over Business Environment. (2010). *Homepage information*. Retrieved from ttp://plone.rcost.unisannio.it:443/globe/

Gramm, A., Naumowicz, T., Ritter, H., Schiller, J., & Tian, M. (2003). A concept for QoS integration in Web. *Proceedings of the First Web Services Quality Workshop.* Rome: IEEE Computer Society.

JENA. (2010). *A Semantic Web framework for Java*. Retrieved from http://jena.sourceforge.net/

Kritikos, K., & Plexousakis, D. (2007). Semantic QoS-based Web Service discovery algorithms. *Proceedings of the Fifth European Conference on Web Services in ECOWS'07,* (p. 181-190). Halle, Germany: IEEE Computer Society.

LOCOSP. (2009). *LOCOSP*. Retrieved from http://plone.rcost.unisannio.it/locosp

Maximilien, E. M., & Singh, M. (2004). A framework and ontology for dynamic Web service selection. *IEEE Internet Computing*, *8*(5), 84–93. doi:10.1109/MIC.2004.27

Protégé. (2000). *The Protege project*. Retrieved from http://protege.stanford.edu

Prud'hommeaux, E., & Seaborne, A. (2008). *SPARQL query language for RDF.* W3C recommendation. Retrieved from http://www.w3.org/TR/rdf-sparql-query/

Sycara, K., et al. (2009). *OWL-S 1.2 release*. Retrieved from http://www.ai.sri.com/daml/services/owl-s/1.2/overview/

Taher, L., Basha, R., & El Khatib, H. (2005). QoS information & computation framework for QoS-based discovery for Web Services. *UPGRADE. The European Journal for the Informatics Professional*, *6*(4).

Tran, V. X., Tsuji, H., & Masuda, R. (2009). *A new QoS ontology and its QoS-based ranking algorithm for Web Services. Simulation modelling practice and theory*. Elsevier.

Van der Aalst, M. P. W., ter Hofstede, A. H. M., & Weske, M. (2003). Business process management: A survey. *In Proceedings of the Business Process Management: International Conference BPM'03.* WSMO working group. (2004). *WSMO homepage*. Retrieved from http://www.wsmo.org/f

Section 2
Service Composition

Service composition is the most straightforward method of managing complexity in SOA. However, service composition with respect to non-functional properties presents a new set of problems and challenges, some of which are treated in this section.

Chapter 7
Selective Querying for Adapting Hierarchical Web Service Compositions

John Harney
University of Georgia, USA

Prashant Doshi
University of Georgia, USA

ABSTRACT

Web Service compositions (WSC) often operate in volatile environments where the parameters of the component services change during execution. To remain optimal, the WSC could adapt to these changes by querying the participating providers for their revised parameters. Previously, the value of changed information (VOC) has been utilized in simple WSCs to selectively query only those services whose revised parameters are expected to bring about significant changes in the composition. In many cases, however, in order to promote scalability, a WSC is formulated as a more complex, nested structure – a higher-level WSC may be composed of WSs and lower-level WSCs – inducing a natural hierarchy over the composition. This chapter presents a novel approach that extends the capabilities of VOC-driven querying to address the problem of adapting hierarchical WSCs. It shows how to compose and adapt hierarchical WSCs by first deriving a model of volatility for lower-level WSCs and then by descending down the levels of nesting and computing the VOC for WSCs at each level. Experimental results demonstrate that this approach provides an effective and efficient solution for complex, hierarchical WSCs.

INTRODUCTION

Traditional approaches for composing Web Services (WS) assume that the parameters used to model the environment remain static and accurate throughout the composition's execution lifetime. This is especially true of approaches that use classical planning for composition. Web Service compositions (WSC) are built using a pre-defined,

DOI: 10.4018/978-1-60960-493-6.ch007

fixed model of the environment at design time, and executed. However, this fundamental assumption is often unrealistic as environments tend to be transient. For example, a product may go out of stock affecting its availability, the network bandwidth may fluctuate affecting the WS response time, or the cost of invoking a travel agent's service may increase. Many WSC techniques do not adapt compositions to such changes, leading to suboptimality.

Dynamism manifests in WSC environments in a variety of ways. For example, changes range from the operational level (such as a newly introduced task) to the organizational level, such as new company policies (Aalst & Jablonski, 2000; Han & Bussler, 1998). Indeed, these surveys classify a variety of changes in different ways. Solutions have been presented to address some of these changes ranging from exception handling techniques defined in Borgida and Murata (1999) to instituting protocol adaptations (as in Desai, Chopra, & Singh, 2006).

However, less attention has been paid to *data volatility* that exists during execution. As a concrete example, consider a mortgage loan acquisition process in which two title insurance agencies compete for orders from a large mortgage broker. The sequence in which the broker utilizes the services of the two insurers would depend on the probability with which the insurers usually satisfy the requests and the costs of using them. If the preferred insurer's rate of request satisfaction drops suddenly (due to say, a financial crisis), a cost-conscious broker should replace it with another insurer to remain optimal. Important non-functional service parameters such as cost, availability, or the rate of request satisfaction in the above example, often change during the lifecycle of a WSC. WSCs must be aware of the changing parameters of the participating services so as to optimize the composition. [1]

Thus, the WSC must possess up-to-date knowledge of the revised information during execution. To obtain this knowledge, an adaptive WSC may query services – typically their providers – for the services' revised parameter values. The revised values are then integrated into the model so that the composition is optimal.

Querying for component services' parameters, however, comes with its own attendant challenges. While revised information about some services may lead to changes in the WSC, changes to other services' parameters may have little or no impact on the WSC. Additionally, WSCs typically operate over an open and large scale system (the Web) due to which querying for information from service resources could get tedious, time consuming, and costly. Queries must therefore be carefully managed – we should query those services only whose parameter changes may potentially impact the WSC while minimizing any additional overhead introduced. Specifically, the adaptive WSC should know: (1) when is it cost effective to query for the changed information and, (2) which service(s) to query.

Previously, we introduced a method that guides intelligently query of revised service parameters using the *value of changed information (VOC)* (Harney & Doshi, 2009a). In particular, we compute the trade-off between the cost of querying for up-to-date information [2] and the value of expected change in the WSC that the revised information is expected to bring. We update the model parameters and compose the WSC again, only if the VOC is greater than the query cost. In computing the VOC, we utilize stochastic models of volatility of each of the services' parameters. We adopt a *myopic* approach in that we query only one service provider at a time and utilize the revised information for that WS which leads to the maximum VOC.

We previously demonstrated the usefulness of VOC in the context of simple WSCs (Harney & Doshi, 2009a). In this article, we generalize the applicability of VOC to a hierarchical WSC. To promote scalability a WSC may be often nested – a higher-level WSC may be composed of WSs and lower-level WSCs – which induces a natural hierarchy over the composition. In comparison to flat WSCs, a hierarchical decomposition introduces multiple challenges for adaptation: *(a)* Because only the parameters of the lower-level component services are known, we must derive the parameters of the composite service from these, and *(b)* we must derive a model of volatility for the composite service's parameters from the corresponding models of volatility of its component services. While approaches for aggregating parameters of component WSs exist (Zhao & Doshi, 2007, Cardoso, Sheth, Miller, Arnold, & Kochut, 2004), we investigate formulating the stochastic models of volatility of composite services. Given approaches that address both these challenges, we show how we may compose and adapt hierarchical WSCs by descending down the levels of nesting and computing the VOC for WSCs at each level. This procedure is further complicated if we decide to query a composite service. Here, we assume that the lower-level WSCs are sequential. In Harney and Doshi (2009b), this assumption is partially relaxed and the underlying compositions could have concurrent, conditional or looping flows.

We show that, though myopic, our approach performs well in the presence of WS data volatility, with reduced time and cost overhead caused by querying. In particular, our experiments demonstrate that the VOC mechanism avoids "unnecessary" queries in comparison to naive approaches of querying, say periodically. This translates to savings in overall costs for the WSC. For the purpose of evaluation, we utilize a realistic scenario of mortgage loan processing. Within our services-oriented architecture (SOA), we represent the mortgage broker's WSC using WS-BPEL (BPEL Specification, 2005), and the different provider services as well as a service for computing the VOC using WSDL (WSDL Specification, 2001).

RELATED WORK

Dynamism manifests in WSC environments in a variety of ways (Han & Bussler, 1998). Our work focuses on data volatility, which Aalst describes as dynamism in the information perspective (Aalst & Jablonski, 2000). Dealing with changes of this type constitute only a small portion of the general adaptation problem. Indeed, research into adaptation has been broad and encompasses many different types of volatility.

Earlier work focused on handling exceptions that occur in workflows (Strong & Miller, 1995, Brambilla, Ceri, Comai, & Tziviskou, 2005, Luo, Sheth, Kochut, & Miller, 2000). These events often result in task failures. Tasks that fail return an exception interpreted by an exception handler. The handler resolves these failures by using either manual correction techniques or the more advanced event-condition-action (ECA) paradigm, where pre-constructed rules trigger a change in the workflow when exceptions takes place (Chiu, Li, & Karlapalem, 1999, Muller, Greiner, & Rahm, 2004). Typically transaction constructs are employed such as task rollbacks and compensations (Narendra & Gundugola, 2006, Maamar, Narendra, Benslimane, & Sattanathan, 2007) to maintain correctness and consistent workflows (Reichert & Dadam, 1998, Borgida & Murata, 1999). However, changes to the task instance data was often overlooked in favor of guaranteeing that tasks interoperate.

Research in volatility in other aspects of the WSC has also received attention. Stohr and Zhao (1997) focus on changes in the organizational perspective. They devised a Business Process Adaptation Model, which seeks to decide how changes in business technologies may affect the needs of business process automation. Here, they focus on choosing new technologies that benefit the general needs of an organization. Desai et al. (2006a, 2006b) focus on adapting processes using handcrafted protocols. These business process protocols (set of rules that govern a business interaction) were created primarily to alleviate problems of heterogeneity and to support autonomy among different WS providers. Protocols may be changed to adapt to processes that require frequent changes in participating providers' heterogeneous business models. Van der Aalst et al. (2001) addressed the problem of "dynamic change" in workflows. The dynamic change problem finds solutions to handling old instances in new workflow process definitions. The dynamic change problem is not relevant to this chapter, as we only consider adapting compositions that are executed on an individual, case by case basis.

Only recently have researchers turned their efforts toward identification of change in the individual services' parameters (Sheth, Cardoso, Miller, & Kochut, 2002). In (Chafle, Dasgupta, Kumar, Mittal, & Srivastava, 2006, Chafle, Doshi, Harney, Mital, & Srivastava, 2007) several alternate plans are pre-specified at the logical level, physical level, and the runtime level. Depending on the type of changes in the environment, alternative plans from these three stages are selected. While capable of adapting to several different events, many of the alternative pre-specified plans may not be used making the approach inefficient. Further, there is no guarantee of optimality of the resulting WSCs. Paques et al. (2004) address changes by creating a WS "adaptation space". The adaptation space represents alternative logical WS compositions that may be used if a previous composition instance fails or is found to be suboptimal. While the adaptation space allows for WSCs to adapt to changes in the data, it does not consider the costs of obtaining the revised data. Doshi et al. (2005) adapt compositions using a technique that manages the dynamism of WSC environments through Bayesian learning. The process model parameters are updated based on previous interactions with the individual Web Services and the composition plan is regenerated using these updates. This method suffers from being slow in updating the parameters, and the approach may result in plan (process flow) re-computations that do not bring about any change in the WSC. Au et al. (2004, 2005, 2007) introduce a framework that composes processes in the presence of data volatility. Using a reactive querying policy, they obtain current parameters of the WSC by querying WS providers only when the parameters expire. While this is similar in concept to our approach, plan re-computation is assumed to take place irrespective of whether the revised parameter values are expected to bring about a change in the composition. This may lead to frequent unnecessary computations. Gotz and Mayer-Patel (2004) incorporate multidimensional data adaptation using a metric similar to the value of information to determine if new information may impact the utility of their application. The authors, however, primarily focus on multimedia applications rather than business processes.

Nanjangud et al. (2007) and Charfi et al. (2004) apply the aspect-oriented programming idea to WSCs. Aspects were used to adapt to changes in WS components dynamically and consistently. Analagous to the traditional exception-handling techniques, this line of work focuses on composition correctness and consistency. Gomadam et al. (2007) utilize semantic associations to identify events that may cause changes in a WSC. The focus, however, is on event identification as a precursor to adaptation. In a somewhat different vein, Verma et al. (2006) and Wu and Doshi (2007) explore adaptation in WSCs in the presence of coordination constraints between different WSs. This line of work is complementary as we do not consider such constraints here.

The composition of hierarchical WSCs is also a relatively new topic in the SOA literature. WSC tools such as SHOP2 (D. Wu, Parsia, Sirin, Hendler, & Nau, 2003) and HALEY (Zhao & Doshi, 2007) have been introduced to accomodate the hierarchies in WSCs. Both, however, focus on composition and assume the parameters used to model the environment remain static throughout execution.

Figure 1. A hierarchical mortgage loan process used by a mortgage broker. The broker may choose among multiple appraisal companies and title insurance companies at different levels in the composition. © 2009 IEEE (Harney & Doshi, 2009b)

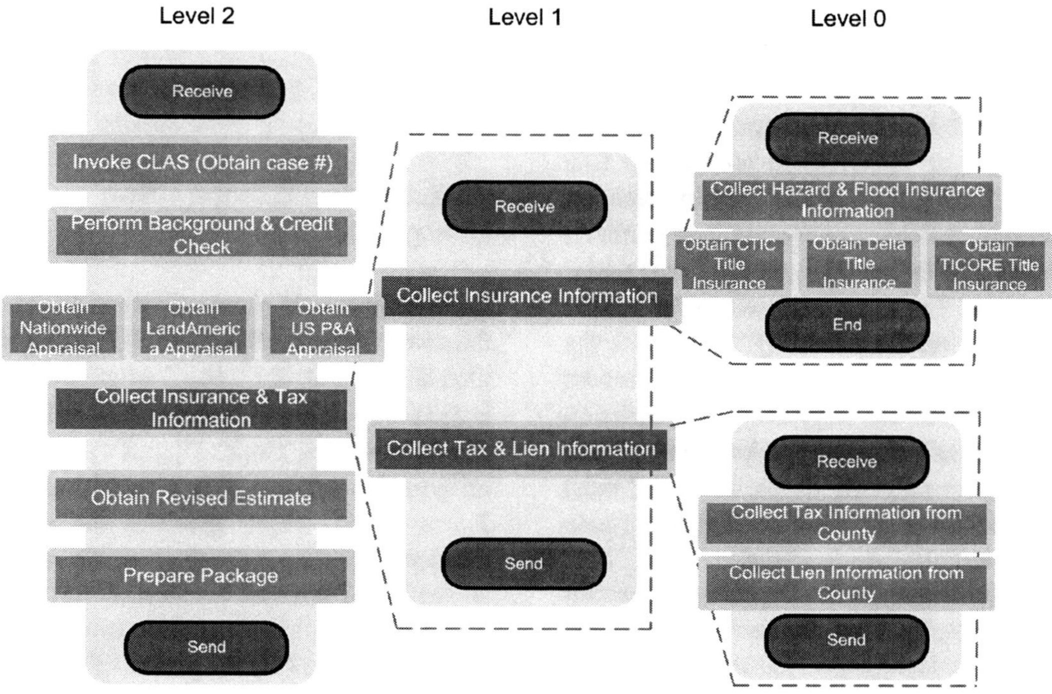

MOTIVATING SCENARIO: MORTGAGE LOAN PROCESSING

We utilize a simplified version of a mortgage loan acquisition process (Harney & Doshi, 2009b) as our running example. This process is typical of that used by broker businesses that service mortgage loans to individual clients. We presume that the broker is using a WSC to automatically process a mortgage loan request. The composition engages a variety of external WSs from multiple vendors to obtain information crucial to securing a suitable home mortgage loan for a client. Obviously, the broker aims to ensure a consistent and robust workflow while minimizing his or her expenditures.

In Figure 1, we illustrate the example process utilized by the broker. Most mortgage loan requests are handled by obtaining a case number followed by performing a background credit check and an appraisal of the value of the home. The case number is obtained by issuing a request to the CLAS (CHUMS Lender Access System) WS. Subsequently, the broker may choose between three different appraisal services: Nationwide, LandAmerica, and US P&A. The process chooses between them based on the cost and availability of the service. If a chosen service fails or is unable to perform the appraisal, one of the other appraisal services may be used instead. This steps are followed by collecting insurance and tax data for home insurance, tax and lien information. Finally, with all of this information on hand, the broker will complete an estimate of the loan and deliver the complete package to the client for reviewing.

We formulate the Insurance and Tax Information service (shown in red) as a composite service. The corresponding lower-level (level 1) composition consists of two services in sequence – one for collecting insurance information and the other for collecting tax and lien information. Observe that these services are themselves composite leading to a three level hierarchical process. The composite Insurance Information activity gathers data on both hazard and title insurances. Subsequently, the broker must decide on a vendor (CTIC, Delta, or TICORE) to provide the title insurance. Finally, the Tax and Lien Information service invokes home county services to obtain the tax and lien information on the home under consideration. The costs incurred to the broker hinge, in part, on the reliability with which the appraisal and the title insurance services process requests. For example, if the request completion rate of a previously chosen appraisal service (such as Nationwide) suddenly drops, the WSC must adapt (ie. utilize a different service) to remain cost-effective.

The example reveals two important factors for choosing optimally. First, the broker must know the rate at which the appraisal requests are satisfied by each of the agencies. Second, at each stage, rather than greedily selecting an action with the least cost, the broker must select the action which is expected to be optimal over the long term. We demonstrate that our approach addresses both concerns. First, we acquire up-to-date information about the services (such as an appraisal service's current rate of request satisfaction) by querying for their revised parameters only when we expect the revised imformation to impact the WSC. Second, we utilize a principled composition method capable of making decisions that are optimal in the long term in the presence of a volatile environment given the updated information.

BACKGROUND

For purposes of illustration, we select a decision-theoretic planning technique for composing WSs (Doshi et al., 2005) although our approach is compatible with any model-based service composition technique such as (Agarwal et al., 2005) (for example, see (Chafle et al., 2007)). We then briefly review the definition and formulation of the *value of changed information* (VOC) of participating WSs, and refer the reader to (Harney & Doshi, 2009a) for more details.

Web Service Composition Using MDP

Decision-theoretic planners such as MDPs model the composition environment, *WP*, using a sextuplet: $WP = (S, A, T, C, H, s_0)$ where $S = \Pi_{i=1}^{n} X^i$, S is the set of all possible states factored into a set, X, of n variables, $X=\{X^1,X^2,\ldots,X^n\}$; A is the set of all possible actions; T is a transition function, $T:S\times A\rightarrow\Delta(S)$, which specifies the probability measure over the next state given the current state and action; C is a cost function, $C : S \times A \rightarrow \Re$, which specifies the cost of performing each action from each state; H is the period of consideration over which the plan must be optimal, also known as the horizon, $0<H\leq\infty$; and

$$Q^n(s,a) = \begin{cases} C(s,a) + \sum_{s'\in S} T(s' \mid a,s) V^{n-1}(s) & \text{n} > 0 \\ 0 & \text{n} = 0 \end{cases}$$

is the starting state of the process.

In order to understand our planning-based composition, let us model the problem of composing the component WSs of the Insurance Information composite service at level 1 of the mortgage scenario in Figure 1 as a MDP. The state of the composition is captured by the random variables. – **hazard and flood insurance information available**, **CTIC title insurance available**, **Delta insurance available**, and **TICORE title insurance available**. A state is then a conjunction of assignments of either *Yes*, *No*, or *Unknown* to each random variable. Actions are WS invocations, A={Hazard and Flood Insurance Information, CTIC Title Insurance, Delta Insurance, and TICORE Title Insurance}. For readability, let us abbreviate the variable names above to **HF Avail**, **CTIC Avail**, **Delta Avail**, and **TICORE Avail**, respectively, and the WSs that are invoked as HF, CTIC, Delta, and TICORE, respectively.

The transition function, *T*, models the non-deterministic effect of each action on some random variable(s). For example, invoking the WS CTIC will cause **CTIC Avail** to be assigned *Yes* with a probability of *T* (**CTIC Avail**=*Yes* | CTIC, **CTIC Avail**=*Unknown*). This rate of order satisfaction depends on two probabilities: (1) the probability that CTIC is able to provide the insurance, and (2) the availability of the CTIC's WS interface. If the two availabilities are independent of one another *, we may view *T* as a product of these two probabilities: *T* (**CTIC Avail**=*Yes* | CTIC, **CTIC Avail**=*Unknown*) = *Pr* (**CTIC Product Avail**=Yes) × **WS Availability**. Similarly, the **CTIC Avail** will be assigned *No* with a probability of *T* (**CTIC Avail**=*No* | CTIC, **CTICAvail**=*Unknown*) = *Pr* (**CTIC Product Avail**=No) × **WS Availability**, and *Unknown* with a probability of *T* (**CTIC Avail**=*Unknown* | CTIC, **CTIC Avail**=*Unknown*) = 1-**WS Availability**. Note that the latter occurs when the WS fails or is not available.

Multiple WS parameters may be relevant in defining the cost function, *C*. In our scenario, we model the cost function as a sum of the cost of invoking, say, the CTIC WS, and the cost of the insurance itself. However, the formulation of cost tends to be domain specific and may include intangible costs such as waiting for a response from a WS and the risk of interacting with a less trustworthy WS.

We let *H* be some finite value which implies that the broker is concerned with getting the most optimal WSC possible within a fixed number of steps. Since no information is available at the start state, all random variables will be assigned the value *Unknown*.

Once the mortgage broker has modeled its WS composition problem as a MDP, it may apply standard MDP solution techniques to arrive at an optimal process. These solution techniques revolve around the use of stochastic dynamic programming (Puterman, 1994) for calculation of the optimal policy using *value iteration*:

$$V^n(s) = \min_{a \in A} \; Q^n(s,a)$$

where:

$$Q^n(s,a) = \begin{cases} C(s,a) + \sum_{s' \in S} T(s' \mid a,s) V^{n-1}(s) & \text{n} > 0 \\ 0 & \text{n} = 0 \end{cases}$$

The value function $V^n : S \rightarrow \Re$ quantifies the minimum long-term expected cost of reaching each state with *n* actions remaining to be performed. It is a minimization of the action-value function $Q^n(s,a)$, which represents the long-term expected cost from *s* on performing action *a*.

Note that $Q^n(s,a)$ is derived from the previously defined MDP model. $Q^n(s,a)$ is a sum of both the immediate cost, $C(s,a)$, of invoking a service *a*, and the expected cost (due to the probability of failure of a WS) of subsequent WS invocations (the $\sum_{s' \in S} T(s' \mid a,s) V^{n-1}(s)$ term) in the WS composition. For example, $Q^n(s,a)$ for, say, the Nationwide Appraisal WS, is a sum of both the cost incurred from using and invoking the Nationwide Appraisal WS and the expected cost of the subsequent WS invocations that would occur later in the WSC such as invoking the Revise Estimate WS. Thus, $Q^n(s,a)$ is of the same type as $C(s,a)$ obtained from the model.

Once we know the expected cost associated with each state of the process, the optimal action for each state is the one which results in the minimum expected cost.

Figure 2. Algorithm for translating a policy into a WSC. Note the interleaving of WSC composition and execution.

```
Algoithm for generating the WSC

Input: Optimal policy π*, initial state s0
Assign to state s ← s0
while goal state is not reached
     Assign to action a ← π*(s)
     Execute Web Service a
     Get response of a and formulate next state, s'
     Assign to state s ← s'
end while
end algorithm
```

$$\pi^*(s) = \underset{a \in A}{argmin}\ Q^n(s,a)$$

In the above equation, π^* is the optimal policy which is simply a mapping from states to actions, $\pi^*: S \rightarrow A$. The WSC is composed by performing the WS invocation prescribed by the policy given the state of the process and observing the results of the actions.

How does an optimal policy such as π^* translate to an optimal composition? In Figure 2, we give an algorithm that addresses this question. It takes the optimal policy, and the starting state of the composition as input, and interleaves composition and execution of the process. For each state encountered during the execution of the WSC, we refer to the policy of the MDP to recommend the current WS to invoke. The response of the service is integrated into the random variable set, effectively transitioning into a new state. This process is repeated until the desired goal state is reached.

Value of Changed Information

As discussed previously, the parameters of the participating services and providers may change during the life-cycle of a WSC. For example, the cost of using the Delta Title Insurance provider's services may increase or the probability with which Delta can process a request may reduce. The former requires an update of the cost function, C, while the latter requires an update of the transition function, T, in the MDP model. In this article, we focus on a change in the transition function T, though our approach is generalizable to fluctuations in other model parameters as well.

Not all updates to the model parameters cause changes in the WSC. Furthermore, the change effected by the revised information may not be worth the cost of obtaining it. In light of these arguments, we need a method that will suggest a query, only when the queried information is *expected* to be sufficiently valuable to obtain. We provide one such methodology next.

As we mentioned before, we adopt a myopic approach to information revision, in which we query a single provider at a time for new information. In the Insurance Information composite service in the mortgage acquisition processing example, this would translate to asking, say, only the CTIC provider for its current rates of request satisfaction (insurance and WS availability), as opposed to both the CTIC and TICORE providers, simultaneously. The revised information may change the following transition probabilities, T(**CTIC Avail** = *Yes* | CTIC, **CTIC Avail** = *Unknown*), T(**CTIC Avail** = *No* | CTIC, **CTIC Avail** = *Unknown*), and T(**CTIC Avail** = *Unknown* | CTIC, **CTIC Avail** = *Unknown*).

Let $V_{\pi^*}(s \mid T')$ denote the expected cost of following the optimal policy, π^*, from the state s when the revised transition function, T' is used. Since the actual revised transition probability is not known unless we query the service provider, we average over all possible values of the revised transition probability, using our current belief distributions over the values. These distributions may be provided by the service providers through pre-defined service-level agreements or they could be learned from previous interactions with the service providers. Formally,

$$EV(s) = \int_{\mathbf{p}} Pr(T'(\cdot \mid a, s') = \mathbf{p}) V_{\pi^*}(s \mid T') d\mathbf{p}$$

where $T'(\cdot \mid a, s')$ represents the distribution that may be queried and subsequently may get revised, $\mathbf{p} = \langle p_1, p_2, \ldots, p_m \rangle$ represents a possible response to the query (revised distribution), *m* is the number of values that the variable under question may assume, and $Pr(\cdot)$ is our current *belief* over the possible distributions.

As a simple illustration, let us suppose that we intend to query the CTIC WS provider for its current rate of order satisfaction. The above equation becomes,

$EV(s) = \int_{\langle p_1, p_2, 1-p \rangle} Pr(T'$ **(CTIC Avail**=Yes/No/Unknown | CTIC, **CTIC Avail** = Unknown)= *Contract Oriented Service Architecture* $p_1, p_2, 1-(p_1+p_2)\rangle\ V_{\pi^*}(s \mid T')dp$

assuming that the random variable **CTIC Avail** assumes either *Yes*, *No*, or *Unknown* on checking the status of the title insurer.

Let $V_{\pi}(s \mid T')$ be the expected cost of following the original policy, π, from the state, *s*, in the context of the revised model parameter, T'. We recall that the policy, π is optimal in the absence of any revised information. We formulate the *value of change* (VOC) due to the revised transition probabilities as:

$$VOC_{T'(\cdot|a,s')}(s) = \int_{\mathbf{p}} Pr(T'(\cdot \mid a, s') = \mathbf{p})[V_{\pi}(s \mid T') - V_{\pi^*}(s \mid T')]d\mathbf{p}$$

The subscript to *VOC*, $T'(\cdot \mid a, s')$, denotes the revised information inducing the change. Intuitively, the equation represents how badly, on average, the original policy, π performs in the changed environment as formalized by the MDP model with the revised T'.

We point out that the VOC shares its conceptual underpinnings with the value of perfect information (VPI) (Russell & Norvig, 2003). Indeed, both of them may be seen as special cases of the value of information idea, which determines whether new information is useful to a particular process. However, there is an important difference between the two concepts. VPI computes the value of *additional* information, while the VOC provides the value of *revised* information. We illustrate this distinction using the following example.

In the mortgage acquisition process, the VPI provides a way to gauge the expected impact of knowing additional (previously unknown) parameters of WSs such as say, time to service failure and time to service repair, on the composition. In comparison, the VOC measures the expected impact of revised values of parameters that were previously considered while forming the initial composition, such as request satisfaction rate and service cost.

Analogous to VPI, the following theorem holds for VOC, whose proof is in (Harney & Doshi, 2009a).

Theorem 1. $\forall s \in S$, $VOC(s) \geq 0$.

Querying for information from service providers may often be tedious, time consuming and subsequently, expensive. We define $QueryCost(T'(\cdot \mid a, s'))$, where $T'(\cdot \mid a, s')$ represents the distribution we want to query, as the cost of querying service *a* for its distribution. Analogous to the cost function, *C*(*s*,*a*), *QueryCost* tends to be domain specific as well, and may depend on a number of different costs. In general, *QueryCost*could be a combination of the monetary cost incurred in issuing the query due to say, network bandwidth and provider's subscription costs, and the intangible cost of the delay until the response arrives. Typically, process analysts have some knowledge of these costs. Subscription costs may be mentioned in a predefined service-level agreement between the composer and the individual service providers.

We must undertake the querying only if we expect it to pay off. In other words, we query for revised information from a state of the WSC only if the VOC due to the revised information in that state is greater than the query cost. More formally, we query if

$$VOC_{T'(\cdot|a,s')}(s) > QueryCost(T'(\cdot \mid a, s'))\,.$$

Adapting Hierarchical WSC Using VOC

In order to promote scalability and understanding, large WSCs may often be decomposed into a hierarchy. Specifically, a WSC may include component services that are themselves WSCs. Such a nesting could be repeated down to any level, *ad infinitum*. We refer to a WS that is itself implemented as a lower-level WSC as a *composite* WS. Before we present an approach that queries WSs guided by VOC in a hierarchical WSC, we need a way to compose the WSC because we interleave adaptation with composition and execution.

Zhao and Doshi (2007) provide a method of composition that exploits a hierarchical decomposition. In that work, each level of the hierarchy is modeled using a MDP. Specifically, the lowest levels of the hierarchy (leaves) are modeled using a MDP containing *primitive* actions, which are invocations of the WSs. Higher levels of the composition problem are modeled using MDPs that contain *abstract* actions, which represent the execution of lower-level WSCs. While formulating the lowest-level MDPs is straightforward because the component WS parameters are given and proceeds as in the previous section, the parameters of the composite WS must be derived to permit the formulation of the MDP that models the composition problem at the higher-level WSCs.

In this context, Zhao and Doshi derive the transition and cost parameters for the *abstract* services from those of the corresponding lower-level services. We may then use the derived parameters to compose the hierarchical WSC. As we focus on *adapting* compositions, we complement Zhao and Doshi's approach by deriving the *distribution of the parameters* for the composite WSs. Thus, a major point of distinction is that the focus of Zhao and Doshi was on the hierarchical WS *composition* problem, while *adapting* the hierarchical WSCs is the focus of this chapter.

Parameters and Volatility of Composite Web Services

A higher-level MDP is so far not well-defined because meaningful parameters for the abstract actions in the model are not given. For example, in the mortgage scenario, the composite WS, Insurance Information, at level 1 is composed of primitive WSs: Hazard and Flood Insurance Information, and one or multiple WSs among CTIC, Delta and TICORE. Transition probabilities associated with the abstract action Collect Insurance Information are not available, but instead must be derived from the transition probabilities associated with the primitive actions.

Zhao and Doshi (2007) utilize the correspondence between the high level abstract actions and the corresponding low level primitive actions. Let the abstract action, $\bar{a}$, represent the sequential execution, in some order, of primitive actions, $\{a_1, a_2\}$, of the underlying primitive MDP. Because the order in which the primitive actions a_1 and a_2 are performed is not known from beforehand, there may be multiple ways to achieve the composition – start from the state s_p and reach the state, s_e. Let $s_p \xrightarrow{a_1} s_1 \xrightarrow{a_2} s_e$ be one such path, where s_1 is an intermediate state of the WSC, then, $T(s_1 \mid a_1, s_p) \times T(s_e \mid a_2, s_1)$ is the probability of following this path, where *T* is the transition function of the primitive MDP. The required probability, $Pr(s_e|s_p)$, is the sum of the probabilities of following all such paths. Analogously, the cost of performing the abstract action is the average of the cost of following each of the possible paths that achieve the composition weighted by the probability of that path.

Figure 3. Example probability density functions representing the mortgage broker's beliefs over the (a) Hazard and Flood Insurance WS and (b) Title Insurance WSs' probabilities of satisfying requests.

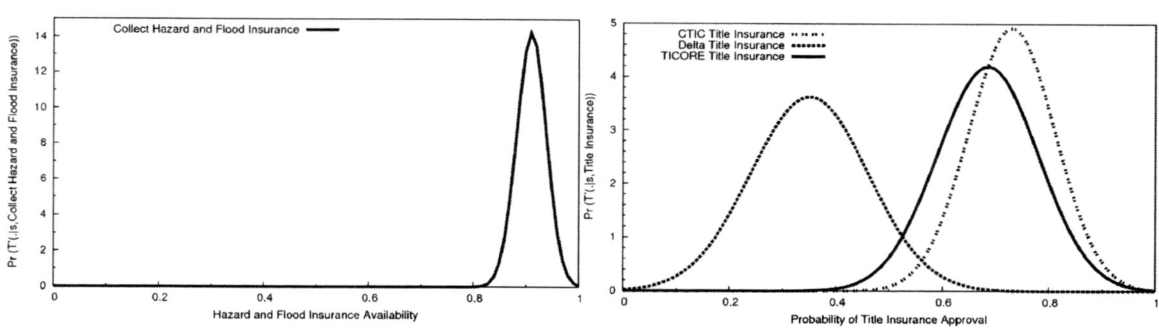

(a) Hazard and Flood Insurance

(b) Title Insurance

In addition to the model parameters previously introduced by Zhao and Doshi, we must also model the mortgage brokers' beliefs over the *volatility* of the parameters. We may model this mortgage broker's beliefs over the possible parameters of primitive WSs, ($Pr(T'(\cdot| a, s') = \mathbf{p}$)) using probability density functions. We let the densities for the WSs take the form of *Gaussian* density functions †. Figure 3 shows examples of such densities, defined for the Hazard and Flood Insurance Information WS (Figure 3(a)) and the title insurance WSs (Figure 3(b)). Other WSs in the mortgage loan process are assumed to have analogous densities. We emphasize that these densities are marginalizations of the more complex ones that would account for all the factors that may influence, for example, a service's rate of request satisfaction.

Notice that the means of the densities reveal that the Delta WS tends to be less reliable in satisfying requests than the other title insurers' WSs. Note also that the Hazard and Flood Insurance Information WS is very reliable, as its mean is close to 1 and its standard deviation is relatively small.

Modeling beliefs over the volatility of parameters of the composite services is more complex. Previously, we mentioned that the transition function of the composite service may be obtained by taking the product of the transition probabilities of the corresponding individual services. We use this in forming beliefs over the volatility of parameters of composite services. For example, let us obtain the belief for the Insurance Information composite WS at level 1. The availability of the Insurance Information service is the sum of the products of the availability of Hazard and Flood Insurance service and one or more of the different Title Insurance services. *Therefore, the belief density over the availability of* Insurance Information, *will be the summation of functions over the product space: availability of* Hazard and Flood Insurance *WS* ×availability of a Title Insurance *service.*

Although we model the densities over availability of individual WSs as Gaussians (for example Figures 3(a) and (b)), the function over the product space is not a Gaussian but rather a modified *Bessel function* of the second kind (Glen, Leemis, & Drew, 2004). Because generating the Bessel function exactly is complex, we utilize a sampling scheme to generate the density over the product space, which converges to the exact as the number of samples approaches infinity. These densities will be summed to obtain the broker's belief over the aggregate parameter of the composite WS Insurance Information.

Figure 4. Algorithm for executing and adapting a hierarchical WSC to revised information using VOC

Algorithm for adaptive Web Service compositions - AWSC

```
Input: Optimal policies at different levels ⟨π*_l, π*_{l-1}, ..., π*_0⟩
Initial state s_0 depth l, horizon H
1.  Assign to state s ← s_0
2.  Assign to s ← H
3.  while horizon n > 0
4.    if VOC*(s) > QueryCost(T(·|a*,s'))
5.      if service to query a* is composite
6.        a*_k ← findWS(l-1,A,s)
7.        Query primitive WS a*_k
8.        T' ← UpdateModel(Level l, Level k)
9.        Calculate policy π*_l using the new MDP with T'
10.   a ← π*_l (s)
11.   If a is composite
12.     Recursively call AWSC for a at level l-1 and π*_{l-1}
13.   Else
14.     Execute primitive Web Service a
15.   Get response of a and construct next state s'
16.     Assign to state s ← s'
17.     Decrease horizon n ← n-1
18. end while
end algorithm
```

Algorithm

We modify the algorithm outlined in Figure 2 to utilize VOC in a hierarchical setting. We look up the current state of the WSC in the policy and execute the WS prescribed by the policy for that state. The response to the WS invocation determines the next state of the WSC. We adapt the composition to consider fluctuations in the model parameters by interleaving the formulation with VOC-based selective querying.

For each state encountered during the execution of the WSC at some level *l*, we find the WS whose revised information is expected to bring about the greatest change in the WSC. In other words, we select the provider associated with the WS invocation, *a*, to possibly query for whom the VOC is maximum:

Figure 5. Function findWS recursively finds a primitive WS that yields the highest VOC*

Algoithm for *findWS(k,A, s^k)**

```
Input: Current level k , action set A, state at level k s^k
s*_k ← argmax_{a∈A} VOC_{T(·|a,s')}(s_k)
if a*_k is a primitive service then
  return a*_k
else // a*_k is a composite service
  Assign to state s^{k-1} ← initial state of the WSC at level k-1
  return findWS*(k,A, s^k)
end algorithm
```

$$VOC^*(s) = \max_{a \in A} VOC_{T(\cdot|a,s)}(s)$$

The algorithm for an adaptive WSC is shown in Figure 4. If a^* is a composite WS at level *l*, we must find the WS at level *l*-1 to query (lines 5-7). This procedure recurses down the nesting level until we select a primitive WS to query. We outline this recursive procedure in Figure 5.

After querying a_k^*, where *k* represents the level at which the queried WS resides, we must formulate a new transition, T', and policy, π^*, for the level *k* WSC. Subsequently, the new transition function (for the corresponding composite WS) and policies must be computed at all levels up to the top-most level, *l* (lines 8-9). For example, if the CTIC is being queried, we reformulate the policy at level 0 given the revised information, and recompute the aggregate parameters of the composite WS, Insurance Information at level 1. We subsequently revise the transition function, T' and resolve π^* at level 1. This recursive procedure is presented in Figure 6.

The *AWSC* algorithm displayed in Figure 4 consists of recursive procedure calls to both *findWS** (Figure 5) and *UpdateModel* (Figure 6). The number of recursive calls are determined by the number of levels contained in the composition. For example, our mortgage scenario requires two recursive calls when evaluating the VOC of the

Figure 6. Recursively update the transition probabilities and policies in the hierarchical composition using the revised information

Algoithm for ***UpdateModel(l,k)***

Input: Depth k, l *current level*

1. **If** $l > k$ **then**
2. Assign to $T' \leftarrow$ ***UpdateModel(l,k)***
3. Calculate new policy π^*_{l-1} using the MDP with revised T'
4. Formulate new T_c for composite WS given T'
5. **return transition function** T_c
6. **else**
7. Integrate revised information from query to form T'
8. Calculate new policy π^*_k using the MDP with T'
9. **return** T

end algorithm

Collect Insurance and Tax Information WS. The algorithm will call *findWS**, which would be called again for both the Collect Insurance Information and Collect Tax and Lien Information WSs. *UpdateModel* recurses analagously, but also requires the formation of T_c (Line 4 in Figure 6) for each level *l*, which involves finding all possible paths between two states and performing a weighted average of the probabilities of those paths.

An analysis of the *AWSC* algorithm reveals that the complexity of the algorithm will grow exponentially as the number of levels increases in the WSC. As we demonstrate later, this additional overhead should be seen in the context of significant overall savings in cost that our approach brings. Furthermore, our analysis is limited to hierarchies where lower-level compositions are sequential. Of course, this is not always the case in practice. Harney and Doshi (2009b) theoretically show how we may aggregate parameters and volatility of WSs for different types of underlying compositions.

EXPERIMENTAL RESULTS

We outline our SOA, in which the VOC computations are performed within a WSDL based internal WS. Then, we present experimental results on the performance of the adaptive WSC. The results were compared to approaches that use a static, unchanging policy, query random WSs and other heuristics.

Architecture

The algorithm described in Figure 4 is implemented as a WS-BPEL (BPEL Specification, 2005) flow and all WSs were implemented using WSDL (WSDL Specification, 2001).

BPEL Implementation of Mortgage Acquisition Process

To the WS-BPEL flow, we give the optimal policy, π^*, of the top level WSC, the start state, and horizon as input. Our experiments utilized the ActiveBPEL engine for executing the BPEL process and AXIS 2 as the container for the WSs. We show our SOA in Figure 7(a).

Within our SOA, we provide internal WSs for solving the MDP model of the composition problem and generating the policy, and for computing the VOC. If the VOC exceeds the cost of querying a particular service provider (this cost is also provided as an input), the WS-BPEL flow queries the service provider's information-providing WSs for revised information. This information is used to formulate and solve a new MDP and the output policy is fed back to the WS-BPEL flow. This policy is used by the WS-BPEL flow to invoke the prescribed external WS at the current state of the composition if it is not a composite one, and the response is used to formulate the next state of the process. If the WS to invoke is composite, the procedure is recursively repeated for the lower-level WSC. This procedure continues until the goal state is reached or the total number of steps are exhausted.

As we utilize WS-BPEL in a somewhat non-standard way, we provide some details on how we implement the WS-BPEL flow in Figure 7(b).

Figure 7. SOA for implementing our adaptive WSC. (a) demonstrates the interaction of the composition with internal services. In (b), we show a sample of the BPEL markup for the mortgage acquisition process. Labels (1) (2) and (3) in (a) correspond to its associated markup in (b).

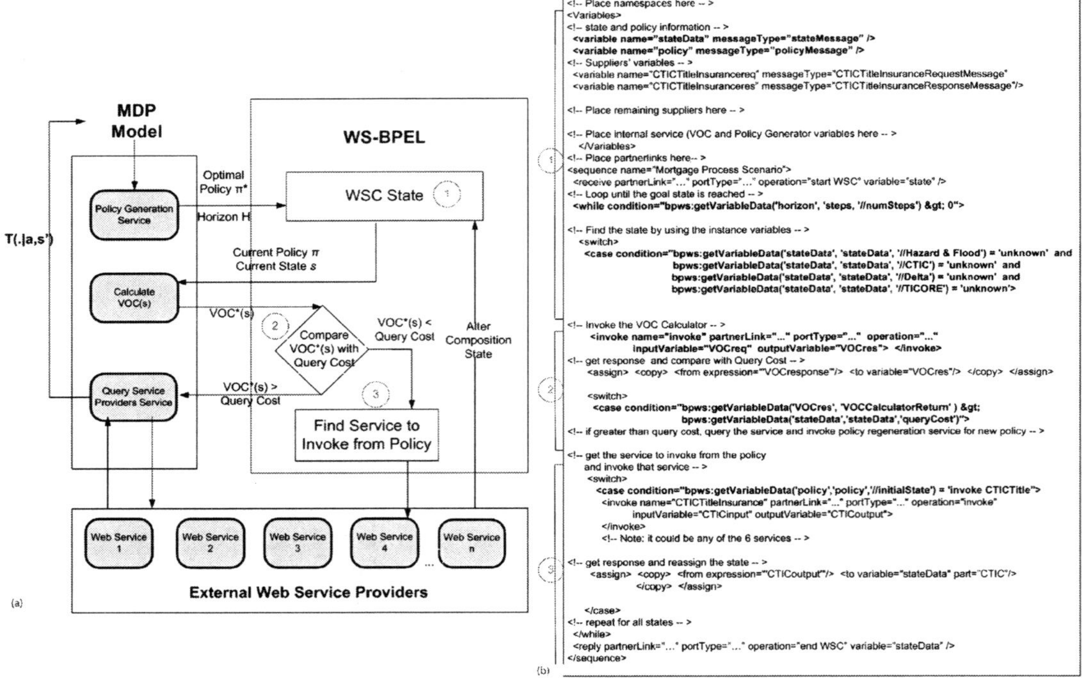


```
<!-- Place namespaces here -- >
<Variables>
<!-- state and policy information -- >
 <variable name="stateData" messageType="stateMessage" />
 <variable name="policy" messageType="policyMessage" />
<!-- Suppliers' variables -- >
 <variable name="CTICTitleInsurancereq" messageType="CTICTitleInsuranceRequestMessage"
 <variable name="CTICTitleInsuranceres" messageType="CTICTitleInsuranceResponseMessage"/>

<!-- Place remaining suppliers here -- >

<!-- Place internal service (VOC and Policy Generator variables here -- >
   </Variables>
<!-- Place partnerlinks here-- >
<sequence name="Mortgage Process Scenario">
 <receive partnerLink="..." portType="..." operation="start WSC" variable="state" />
<!-- Loop until the goal state is reached -- >
 <while condition="bpws:getVariableData('horizon', 'steps, '//numSteps') &gt; 0">

<!-- Find the state by using the instance variables -- >
   <switch>
    <case condition="bpws:getVariableData('stateData', 'stateData', '//Hazard & Flood') = 'unknown' and
                     bpws:getVariableData('stateData', 'stateData', '//CTIC') = 'unknown' and
                     bpws:getVariableData('stateData', 'stateData', '//Delta') = 'unknown' and
                     bpws:getVariableData('stateData', 'stateData', '//TICORE') = 'unknown'>


<!-- Invoke the VOC Calculator -- >
      <invoke name="invoke" partnerLink="..." portType="..." operation="..."
             inputVariable="VOCreq" outputVariable="VOCres"> </invoke>
<!-- get response and compare with Query Cost -- >
     <assign> <copy> <from expression="'VOCresponse"/> <to variable="VOCres"/> </copy> </assign>

     <switch>
      <case condition="bpws:getVariableData('VOCres', 'VOCCalculatorReturn' ) &gt;
                       bpws:getVariableData('stateData','stateData','queryCost')">
<!-- if greater than query cost, query the service and invoke policy regeneration service for new policy -- >

<!-- get the service to invoke from the policy
     and invoke that service -- >
     <switch>
       <case condition="bpws:getVariableData('policy','policy','//initialState') = 'invoke CTICTitle">
        <invoke name="CTICTitleInsurance" partnerLink="..." portType="..." operation="invoke"
              inputVariable="CTICinput" outputVariable="CTICoutput">
        </invoke>
        <!-- Note: it could be any of the 6 services -- >

<!-- get response and reassign the state -- >
      <assign> <copy> <from expression="'CTICoutput"/> <to variable="stateData" part="CTIC"/>
              </copy> </assign>

    </case>
<!-- repeat for all states -- >
 </while>
 <reply partnerLink="..." portType="..." operation="end WSC" variable="stateData" />
</sequence>
```
(b)

First, note that the following constructs must be added to implement the VOC algorithm:

- state and policy data structures,
- tasks that will invoke a VOC computation service, compare the VOC to a given query cost, and regenerate the policy, and
- a task that will invoke the external services providers as recommended by the policy.

As outlined by section (1) in Figure 7(a), state is stored in the BPEL document by creating a complex message type, *staeMessage* and stored in the *stateData* variable. Similarly, complex message type *policyMessage*, is stored in the *policy* variable, and used to represent the given policy.

The *<while>* condition corresponds to the while loop in Figure 4. Each state has an associated *<switch>* *<case>* construct. In each *<case>*, the WSC invokes the compute VOC WS, which upon completion, returns VOC^* (section (2)). The VOC^* value is compared to a *QueryCost* variable. If the returned VOC^* is greater than the *QueryCost*, then the associated service is queried. The queried parameters are integrated into the MDP, which invokes the policy generator service, returning the new optimal policy thereby replacing the old policy of the WSC. The policy is then used to recommend the optimal service to invoke in the state. This process repeats until the composition has terminated (i.e. all steps have been exhausted).

Performance Evaluation

We utilized the mortgage loan processing scenario for our evaluations. We simulated querying the different WSs for their current percentage of request satisfaction (availability). [3]

Figure 8. Comparisons of the VOC based adaptive WSC with the static policy and other querying approaches for the mortgage loan acquisition. Lower average cost indicates better performance. © 2009 IEEE (Harney & Doshi, 2009b)

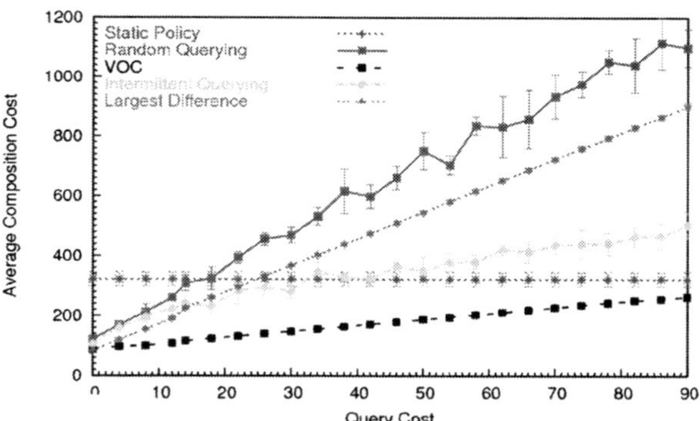

We model the mortgage broker's beliefs over the possible parameters of the individual WSs, ($Pr(T'(\cdot| a, s') = \mathbf{p})$) using *Gaussian* density functions. For composite WSs, we derive the densities over the aggregated parameters as shown previously.

Mortgage Acquisition Process

In Figure 8 we compare the VOC-driven selective querying with four other strategies with respect to the average cost incurred from the execution of the adapted hierarchical WSCs, as the cost of querying the WSs for information is increased. Our methodology consisted of running a trial of 150 independent instances of each composition within a simulated volatile environment, where the queried parameters of the services were distributed according to the corresponding density plots (see Figure 3 for example). We ensured a uniform testing environment for the compositions so that each of the five strategies received similar responses from the services.

We utilized the following four other approaches for adaptation:

1. **Static policy.** This is our baseline approach that ignores adaptation and the initial policy is utilized unchanged for executing the composition in each instance.
2. **Random query.** In this approach, we randomly select a service each time for querying for revised information.
3. **Intermittent querying.** We begin by querying services every alternate instance and as the costs of querying increase, we reduce the frequency with which we query services.
4. **Largest difference.** This approach utilizes the distributions of the services parameters shown in Figure 3. It selects a service to query whose existing parameter value is most different from the mean as obtained from the corresponding distribution.

We note that each of the approaches mentioned above are naive analogies of certain aspects of the VOC-based approach. Thus, the approaches provide an effective testbed with which to compare our VOC-based WSC adaptation.

Intuitively, as we increase the cost of querying, the VOC based approach performs less queries and adapts the WSC less. For large query costs, its performance is similar to using a WSC with an unchanging policy. For smaller query costs, a VOC based approach will query frequently, though not as much as a strategy that always

Table 1. Running times of the various querying strategies for different query costs. We used Linux platform on Xeon 3.8GHz with 2.0GB memory. © 2009 IEEE (Harney & Doshi, 2009b

Query strategies	Time (ms)		
	Query cost = 0	Query cost = 40	Query cost = 80
Static Policy	609 ± 50	609 ± 50	613 ± 47
Random query	759 ± 72	755 ± 66	759 ± 72
VOC	2112 ± 196	1800 ± 136	1650 ± 116
Intermittent querying	653 ± 4	540 ± 20	470 ± 20
Largest difference	535 ± 8	535 ± 12	541 ± 11

queries a provider, such as *random query*. As we increase the query costs, the VOC based approach will allow a query for revised information only if its value exceeds the cost. Though *intermittent querying* naively seeks to emulate this behavior, it performs worse because it does not utilize the value of a potential change in the composition in deciding when to query. We note that the *largest difference* approach performs well for lower query costs, though worse than the VOC based approach. This is because the service exhibiting the largest difference from the mean in its parameter value is often the one that brings about the largest change in the composition. However, this is not always the case – for example, a large change in the parameter of a mandatory service, such as the Credit Check service in the mortgage process, does not affect the composition though the approach will query it and incur the query cost. In addition, the difference in parameter values is not compared to query costs because it is not comparable. In summary, a WSC that is adapted using VOC performs better (incurs less average cost) because only significant changes to the WSC are carried out while simultaneously avoiding frequent costly queries.

Undoubtedly, the additional computational overhead imposed by the VOC algorithm comes at a computational price. In Table. 1 we give the run times for each of the comparative strategies used previously. We first observe that an adaptive WSC that uses VOC runs two to three times slower than a WSC that does not adapt (static policy). However, the difference in time with other strategies for adapting WSCs is less. The additional runtime of the VOC is primarily due to the intense computations required for its calculations. All of the adaptive approaches suffer from a lag time in receiving the query response from the WSs. Notice, however, that as the query cost increases, the time required by the VOC based approach decreases, because it issues less queries.

FUTURE TRENDS

The focus of our future work will be to improve upon our current model of volatility of a process environment. This will enable the development of more efficient approaches for adaptation. We also intend to focus on non-myopic approaches, which may enhance querying strategies that use VOC. Furthermore, we will investigate approximate ways of introducing revised values to the model, when applicable, so as to avoid full recomputations of the policies.

CONCLUSION

Often, real world process environments are volatile – parameters of the services and providers such as costs and reliability vary over time. In such environments, WSCs must adapt to the revised information to remain cost-effective. The value of changed information (VOC) has been used to gauge the value of the expected change that revised information may bring to the WSC, and it is compared with the cost of obtaining the information. If the probable revised information is worth the cost of obtaining it, the providers are queried for their WS's current parameters and we reformulate the WSC using the revised information.

While previously, the VOC was applied toward adapting simple flat WSCs, in this article, we extend its applicability to hierarchical WSCs. Specifically, we showed how to address the two important challenges in adapting complex hierarchical WSCs in order to preserve optimality. First, we sought to let the composer (i.e. the mortgage broker in our scenario) know the reliability with which requests to composite WSs would be satisfied. This was accomplised by deriving beliefs over the volatility of composite WSs' parameters. Using these beliefs, we then applied the VOC methodology to determine if a query should be issued to any WS for their revised parameters. Once the revised parameters were received, we updated the composition accordingly. Second, we selected the WS at each stage of the process that was expected to be optimal over the long term. Using the revised model, we applied standard solution techniques that guaranteed optimal decisions with the newly acquired information over the long term. By resolving these challenges, we were able to create and manage self-adaptive, hierarchical WSCs operating in the context of volatile environments.

ACKNOWLEDGMENT

This work was supported by a grant from the UGA Research Foundation. A substantially expanded version of this work appeared in the IEEE International Conference on Web Services (Harney & Doshi, 2009b). Some images and tables appear here with permission from IEEE.

REFERENCES

Aalst, W. M. P. V. D. (2001). Exterminating the dynamic change bug: A concrete approach to support workflow change. *Information Systems Frontiers*, *3*(3), 297–317. doi:10.1023/A:1011409408711

Agarwal, V., Chafle, G., Dasgupta, K., Kamik, N., Kumar, A., & Mittal, S. (2005). Synthy: A system for end to end composition of Web Services. *Journal of Web Semantics*, *3*, 311–339. doi:10.1016/j.websem.2005.09.002

Au, T. C., Kuter, U., & Nau, D. S. (2005). Web Service composition with volatile information. In *Proceedings of the International Semantic Web Conference (ISWC),* (pp. 52-66).

Au, T. C., & Nau, D. (2007). Reactive query policies: A formalism for planning with volatile external information. In *Proceedings of the IEEE Symposium on Computational Intelligence and Data Management (CIDM),* (pp. 243–250).

Au, T. C., Nau, D. S., & Subrahmanian, V. S. (2004). Utilizing volatile external information during planning. In *Proceedings of the European Conference on Artificial Intelligence (ECAI),* (pp. 647-651).

Borgida, A., & Murata, T. (1999). Tolerating exceptions in workflows: A unified framework for data and processes. In *Proceedings of the International Conference on Work Activities Coordination and Collaboration (WACC),* (pp. 59–68).

Brambilla, M., Ceri, S., Comai, S., & Tziviskou, C. (2005). Exception handling in workflow-driven Web applications. In *Proceedings of the World Wide Web conference (WWW),* (pp. 170–179). New York: ACM.

Cardoso, J., Sheth, A., Miller, J., Arnold, J., & Kochut, K. (2004). Quality of service for workflows and Web Service processes. *Journal of Web Semantics*, *1*(3), 281–308. doi:10.1016/j.websem.2004.03.001

Chafle, G., Dasgupta, K., Kumar, A., Mittal, S., & Srivastava, B. (2006). Adaptation in Web Service composition and execution. In *IEEE International Conference on Web Services (ICWS),* (pp. 549-557).

Chafle, G., Doshi, P., Harney, J., Mital, S., & Srivastava, B. (2007). Improved adaptation of Web Service compositions using value of changed information. In *Proceedings of the IEEE International conference on Web Services (ICWS)* (pp. 784-791).

Charfi, A., & Mezini, M. (2004). Aspect-oriented Web Service composition with ao4bpel. In *European Conference on Web Services,* (pp. 168-182).

Chiu, D. K. W., Li, Q., & Karlapalem, K. (1999). A meta modeling approach to workflow management systems supporting exception handling. *Information Systems, 24*(2), 159–184. doi:10.1016/S0306-4379(99)00010-1

Desai, N., Chopra, A. K., & Singh, M. P. (2006a). Business process adaptations via protocols. In *IEEE Conference on Services-Centered Computing (SCC),* (pp. 601-608).

Desai, N., Mallya, A. U., Chopra, A. K., & Singh, M. P. (2006b). Owl-p: A methodology for business process modeling and enactment. In *Proceedings of Agent-Oriented Information Systems-iii,* (LNCS 3529), (pp. 79-94).

Doshi, P., Goodwin, R., Akkiraju, R. & Verma, K. (2005). Dynamic workflow composition using Markov decision processes. *Journal of Web Services research (JWSR), 2*(1), 1–17.

Glen, A. G., Leemis, L., & Drew, J. H. (2004). Computing the distribution of the product of two continuous random variables. *CSDA*, *44*(3), 451–464.

Gomadam, K., Ranabahu, A., Ramaswamy, L., Sheth, A. P., & Verma, K. (2007). A semantic framework for identifying events in a Service Oriented Architecture. In *Proceedings of the IEEE International Conference on Web Services (ICWS,)* (pp. 545-552).

Gotz, D., & Mayer-Patel, K. (2004). A general framework for multidimensional adaption. In *Proceedings of the International Conference on Multimedia and Expo (ICME),* (pp. 612-619).

Han, A. S. Y., & Bussler, C. (1998). A taxonomy of adaptive workflow management. In *Proceedings of the CSCW-98 Workshop, Towards Adaptive Workflow Systems.*

Harney, J., & Doshi, P. (2009a). Selective querying for adapting Web Service compositions using the value of changed information. *IEEE Transactions on Services Computing*, *1*(3), 169–185. doi:10.1109/TSC.2008.11

Harney, J., & Doshi, P. (2009b). Selective querying for adapting hierarchical Web Service compositions using aggregated volatility. In *Proceedings of the IEEE International Conference on Web Services (ICWS),* (pp. 43-50). IEEE©.

IBM. (2005). *Business process execution language for Web Services version 1.1.* Retrieved from http://www-128.ibm.com/developerworks/library/specification/ws-bpel/

Luo, Z., Sheth, A. P., Kochut, K., & Miller, J. A. (2000). Exception handling in workflow systems. *Applied Intelligence*, *13*(2), 125–147. doi:10.1023/A:1008388412284

Maamar, Z., Narendra, N. C., Benslimane, D., & Sattanathan, S. (2007). Policies for context-driven transactional Web Services. In *Proceedings of the International Conference on Advanced Information Systems Engineering (CAiSE),* (pp. 249-263).

Muller, R., Greiner, U., & Rahm, E. (2004). Agentwork: A workflow system supporting rule-based workflow adaptation. *Journal of Data and Knowledge Engineering*, *51*(2), 223–256. doi:10.1016/j.datak.2004.03.010

Narendra, N. C., & Gundugola, S. (2006). Automated context-aware adaptation of Web Service executions. In *Proceedings of the ACS/IEEE International Conference on Computer Systems and Applications (AICCSA),* (pp. 179–187).

Narendra, N. C., Ponnalagu, K., Krishnamurthy, J., & Ramkumar, R. (2007). Run-time adaptation of non-functional properties of composite Web Services using aspect-oriented programming. In *Proceedings of the International Conference on Services-Oriented Computing (ICSOC),* (pp. 546-557).

Paques, H., Liu, L. & Pu, C. (2004). Adaptation space: A design framework for adaptive Web Services. *Journal of Web Services research (JWSR), 1*(3), 1-24.

Puterman, M. L. (1994). *Markov decision processes.* NY: John Wiley & Sons.

Reichert, M., & Dadam, P. (1998). Adeptflex-supporting dynamic changes of workflows without losing control. *Journal of Intelligent Information Systems*, *10*(2), 93–17. doi:10.1023/A:1008604709862

Russell, S., & Norvig, P. (2003). *Artificial Intelligence: A modern approach* (2nd ed.). Prentice Hall.

Sheth, A., Cardoso, J., Miller, J., & Kochut, K. (2002). Qos for service-oriented middleware. In *Proceedings of the World Multiconference on Systemics, Cybernetics and Informatics (SCI),* (pp. 528-534).

Stohr, E., & Zhao, J. (1997). A technology adaptation model for business process automation. In *Proceedings of the Hawaii International Conference on System Sciences (HICSS),* (pp. 405).

Strong, D. M., & Miller, S. M. (1995). Exceptions and exception handling in computerized information processes. *ACM Transactions on Information Systems*, *13*(2), 206–233. doi:10.1145/201040.201049

van der Aalst, W. M. P., & Jablonski, S. (2000). Dealing with workflow change: Identification of issues and solutions. *International Journal of Computer Systems Science and Engineering*, *15*(5), 267–276.

Verma, K., Doshi, P., Gomadam, K., Miller, J., & Sheth, A. (2006). Optimal adaptation in Web processes with coordination constraints. In *Proceedings of IEEE International Conference on Web Services (ICWS),* (pp. 257-264).

Web Services Description Language (WSDL) 1.1. (2001). *TR*. Retrieved from http://www.w3.org/TR/wsdl

Wu, D., Parsia, B., Sirin, E., Hendler, J., & Nau, D. (2003). Automating daml-s Web Services composition using shop2. In *Proceedings of the International Semantic Web Conference (ISWC),* (pp. 195-210).

Wu, Y., & Doshi, P. (2007). Regret-based decentralized adaptation ofWeb processes with coordination constraints. In *Proceedings of IEEE Services-Centered Computing (SCC),* (pp. 262-269).

Zhao, H., & Doshi, P. (2007). Haley: A hierarchical framework for logical composition ofWeb Services. In *Proceedings of IEEE International Conference on Web Services (ICWS),* (pp. 312-319).

ENDNOTES

* The two probabilities could be dependant on each other depending on the underlying business logic of the WS. For example, insurance

availability may influence CTIC's decision to keep the WS active. For simplicity in our scenario, however, we assume that they are independent.

† Note that other density functions (such as betas and polynomials) may also be used

1 For the sake of simplicity, we assume that changes in the composition do not upset the consistency of the WSC. See Aalst, 2001 for work along this line.

2 Often, contractual agreements are required to obtain the revised parameters from the service providers. Nevertheless, we also consider the case that the revised information may be obtained at no cost.

3 Of course, the rate of request satisfaction, for example, would depend on the amount of the loan and other factors; we assume that these will be provided.

Chapter 8
Aggregating Functional and Non-Functional Properties to Identify Service Compositions

Eduardo Blanco
Universidad Simón Bolívar, Venezuela

Yudith Cardinale
Universidad Simón Bolívar, Venezuela

María-Esther Vidal
Universidad Simón Bolívar, Venezuela

ABSTRACT

This chapter presents an aggregated metric to estimate the quality of service compositions, and two algorithms to select the best compositions based on this metric. Both algorithms follow different strategies to prune the space of possibilities while minimizing the evaluation cost. The first algorithm, DP-BF, combines a best first strategy with a dynamic-programming technique. The second one, PT-SAM, adapts a Petri-net unfolding algorithm and tries to find a desired marking from an initial state. An experimental study was conducted in order to evaluate the behavior of DP-BF and PT-SAM compared to SAM and to the exhaustive solution. The experiments show that the quality of the compositions identified by the presented algorithms is close to the optimal solution produced by the exhaustive algorithm, while the optimization time is close to the time required by SAM to identify a solution.

INTRODUCTION

A Service-Oriented Architecture (SOA) (Erl, 2005) is essentially a collection of loose coupled services, that interoperate based on a formal language which is independent of the platform and the programming language used to implement each service. SOA relies on a set of policies, practices, and frameworks by which it ensures that the appropriate services are provided and consumed, and enhances services inter-connectivity. Hence, rather than leaving developers to discover individual services and execute them independently, SOA provides the Business Service Bus that

DOI: 10.4018/978-1-60960-493-6.ch008

works across multiple SOA applications in the same domain.

Flexible SOA connections between services, as well as software components that pass simple data among other services or that coordinate simple activities, are seen as services which can be combined with other services to achieve specific goals. Thus, SOA provides a scalable and robust framework to integrate heterogeneous software agents and enhance reliability of isolated software components.

In systems engineering as well as in SOA applications, requirements are partitioned into functional and non-functional. Functional requirements specify the functions that a system or its components must be capable of performing. These software requirements define the system behavior, i.e., fundamental processes or transformations performed by software and hardware components of the system on its inputs to produce the correct outputs. In contrast, non-functional requirements are constraints that allow the description of an application in terms of quality attributes or transactional behavior, e.g., performance-related, reliability, availability issues, or fault tolerance capability. These types of requirements are often classified into execution and evolution quality requirements or parameters. The former parameters are observable at run time, while the latter are embodied in the static structure of the software system. It is well known that functional and non-functional requirements constrain each other, and therefore, they should be considered together to completely specify a user request.

As SOA applications become popular and Web Services proliferate, it becomes more dificult to find a specific service that can meet a user request expressed in terms of a set of functional and non-functional requirements, and combinations of several heterogeneous services may be required to satisfy the user request.

Heterogeneity, which means diffrent non-functional requirements (response time, cost, reliability, throughput, trust, fault tolerance capability), granted by multiple distributed services delivering the same functionality, must be adequately managed to ensure effcient implementations of user requests. In this sense, machine-readable knowledge about the parameters whose values describe the execution quality or transactional properties of the available services, play an important role to decide if a given service composition satisfies the user non-functional requirement, and services with the highest quality will produce more efficient compositions.

In this chapter, we consider the problem of identifying a service composition that best meets functional and non-functional user requirements (the WSC problem). Related problems have been studied in different areas, for example, query optimization (Florescu, Levy, Manolescu, & Suciu, 1999; L. Haas, Kossmann, Wimmers, & Yang, 1997; Levy, Rajaraman, & Ordille, 1996; Papakonstantinou, Gupta, & Haas, 1996; Ouzzani & Bouguettaya, 2004; Srivastava, Munagala, Widom, & Mot-wani, 2006; Zadorozhny, Bright, Raschid, Urhan, & Vidal, 2000; Zadorozhny, Raschid, Vidal, Urhan, & Bright, 2002), and service discovery (Bansal & Vidal, 2003; Paolucci, Kawamura, Payne, & Sycara, 2002; Al-Masri & Mahmoud, 2008b; Bachelechner, Siorpaes, Lausen, & Fensel., 2006).

The complexity of the WSC problem depends on the number of available services; thus, the definition of techniques that efficiently identify optimal service compositions is a challenging problem, particularly in large-scale environments where services are in the range of 1,000 to 100,000. Diverse solutions that take advantage of AI techniques and Search Meta-Heuristics, have been proposed (Brogi, Corfini, & Popescu, 2008; Kuter, Sirin, Nau, Parsia, & Hendler, 2004; Rainer, 2006). However, none of the existing approaches simultaneously consider functional and non-functional requirements to efficiently produce optimal service compositions. Recently, researchers have considered non-functional requirements to identify the services that can be used to rewrite a given business Process Model or workflow (see Berardi, Calvanese, Giacomo, Hull, & Mecella, 2005; Berardi, Giacomo, Mecella, & Calvanese, 2006; Berardi, Cheikh, Giacomo, & Patrizi, 2008; Cardellini, Casalicchio, Grassi, & Presti, 2007; Constantinescu, Faltings, & Binder:, 2004; Wada, Champrasert, Suzuki, & Oba, 2008; Ho mann, Ingo Weber, Kaczmarek, & Ankolekar, 2008; Meyer & Weske, 2006; Ko, Kim, & Kwon, 2008; Rahmani, GhasemSani, & Abolhassani, 2008; Traverso & Pistore, 2004). Compositions of the selected services maximize the satisfaction grade of the QoS parameter permissible values. Although these solutions are able to efficiently solve this optimization problem, they are not suitable to identify the service compositions that, given a set of input attributes, produce a specific set of outputs. To overcome the limitations of existing approaches, we propose a hybrid cost-based approach that receives and considers at the same time, a functional user request expressed by a pair of input and output attribute sets, and a non-functional condition represented by a set of QoS parameter permissible values; thus, the returned composition satisfies the functional request and best meets the non-functional restrictions.

We developed two algorithms that follow different strategies to travese the space of possible service compostions that meet the user functional conditions while the satisfaction of the non-functional requirements is maximized. Both algorithms use a utility function that combines the functional requirements expressed in the output attributes of the user request, and the QoS parameter permissible values specified in the non-functional conditions. This utility function expresses an aggregated metric or cost model that guides the service composition process. The first algorithm combines a Best-First strategy with a Dynamic-Programming technique and produces efficient service compositions by exploring a small portion of the search space; only intermediate solutions that may lead to an optimal composition are considered during the search. Optimality is measured in terms of the aggregated metric or cost model; thus, the algorithm identifies a service composition that satisfies the functional requirements and best meets the non-functional conditions among the space of traversed service compositions. The second algorithm adapts a Petri-Net unfolding approach and performs a Best-First search which stops when a desired marking, reachable from an initial marking in the Petri-Net, is found. The initial marking represents the input attributes of the functional requeriments, the desired marking represents the outputs attributes of the functional requirement, and the Petri-Net models the services and their dependencies. The unfolding method is guided by the aggregated metric or cost model, therefore, the identified sequence of transitions, fired to reach the final marking, corresponds to a composition of services that satisfies the functional and non-functional user request. Since, the metric may not be an admissible heuristic, the solution could not be optimal.

We empirical studied the quality of our proposed approach. We report on the predictive capability of the response time cost model; the execution time of the cost-based service composition techniques; and the quality of the compositions identified by our techniques with respect to optimal compositions. Initial results of this work have been reported in Blanco, Cardinale, Vidal, and Graterol (2008).

The rest of this chapter is organized as follows. First we illustrate the problem using real-world examples. Then we present our approach. First, we define the background knowledge and formalize the Web Service composition problem and the service functional and non-functional requirements descriptions. We propose a cost-model that approximates the non-functional parameters values of a given service composition. Second, we present two algorithms and proofs of their properties. Finally, we summarize the main advantages of both algorithms. Next, we report on the predictive capability of the cost model and empirically evaluate the quality of the proposed

Table 1. Service capabilities

Service Name	Input	Output
S_1	(AuthorCod,Inst)	(PubCod)
S_2	(AuthorName)	(PubCod)
S_3	(PubCod)	(Title)
S_4	(PubCod)	(ConfCod)
S_5	(PubCod)	(ConfCod,ConfName)
S_6	(ConfCod)	(ConfName,ConfDate)
S_7	(Inst)	(AuthorCod)
S_8	(ConfCod)	(ConfPlace)
S_9	(AuthorCod)	(ConfCod)

techniques. The execution time of the cost-based optimization techniques is studied. The quality of the compositions identified by our techniques are reported. Finally, we analyze existing state-of-the-art approaches and outline the advantages and limitations of each approach; then we present our conclusions and future work.

MOTIVATING EXAMPLES

We illustrate the problem of efficiently identifying a service composition that minimizes/maximizes execution quality parameters and meets non-functional user requirements with two examples:

Example 1. Consider a scientist who needs to process and combine some datasets to perform an in silico experiment in the least amount of time. First, she/he needs to identify the protocol to be followed and the tasks that have to be executed. Then, she/he has to identify the services that are suitable for each task. However, by 2007, at least 3,000 bioinformatics services have been reported (K. Wolstencroft et al., 2007), and she/he may need to manually discover these services.

Some of these services are replicas of the same analysis tools, but they are located on dfferent sites. Also, some services can execute at least two activities simultaneously, while others are only able to perform one of them. Finally, these services may be characterized by different quality parameters, e.g., some of them may be described by a low amount of time to transfer data across the network, while others, may require large delays. Thus, to avoid a costly evaluation, this scientist must solve two complex tasks. First, she/he has to identify the services that fulfill her/his requirements and second, she/he has to combine them in a way that her/his functional and non-functional requirements are met. ◇

Example 2. Consider Web Services in Table 1 which are annotated with their functional capabilities expressed by input and output attributes. Input attributes represent data that need to be bound or provided to invoke the service, while outputs attributes correspond to data returned when the service is invoked.

The functional capabilities induce relationships among the services in terms of Inputs and Outputs. Figure 1 shows the graph generated in terms of these capabilities. Nodes in the graph are of two types: one type of nodes represents services, while the other corresponds to Inputs and Outputs. Arcs in the graph relate a service with its input and output attributes. In other words, if **t** is an attribute and **s** is a service, then:

- *if(**t, s**)is in the service graph, thentcorresponds to an input parameter of the services.*

Figure 1. Dependency graph of services

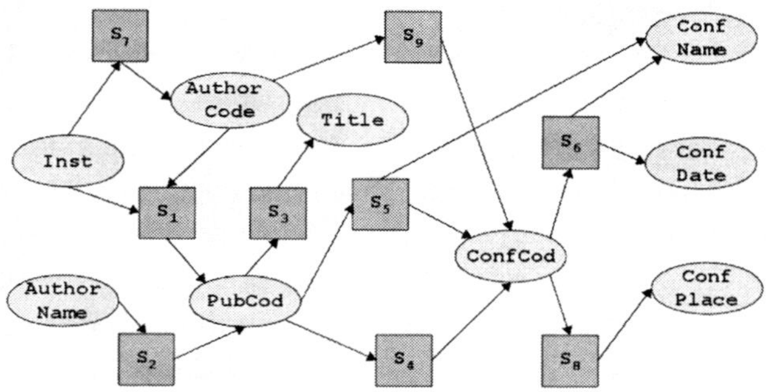

- *if(s, t)is in the service graph, then elements of the attributetare produced by the services.*

Suppose that we have the following request **Q**= "Name and Date of conferences where researchers affiliated to the Simón Bolívar University (USB) have attended". Functional requirements are expressed as a pair of Input and Output parameters: **Inputs = {Inst}** and **Outputs = {ConfName, ConfDate}**.

Figure 2 shows one of the solutions for **Q** (depicted by the colored nodes). Note that, for this functional requirement, some services are not needed to answer the request and they should not be included in the solution:

- $\mathbf{S_2}$ is a non-useful service because **AuthorName** is not available (it is not given in the Inputs and is not produced by any service).
- $\mathbf{S_3}$ and $\mathbf{S_8}$ are non-useful services because there is not a path from any of these services to any of the Output nodes.
- $\mathbf{S_5}$ produces one of the Output; however it will not be selected because there is another service ($\mathbf{S_6}$) that in addition to produce this attribute, returns one more Output attribute.
- $\mathbf{S_4}$ and $\mathbf{S_9}$ belong to the solution, however, one of them is a redundant service because both produce the same Output attribute.

In this example, with nine services it is relatively easy to exhaustively enumerate the solutions.

Figure 2. One possible non-optimal solution

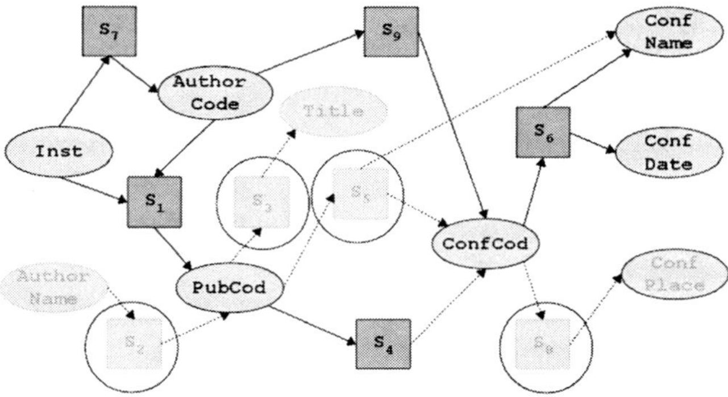

However, in case of a larger number of services, the number of solutions can be extremely large.

Lemma 1. (Upper bound of the search space size) Let **n** be the number of available services. An upper bound on the number of possible solutions for a user request, is given by the expression in Equation 1:

$$\sum_{i=1}^{n} \binom{n}{i} \quad * \quad i! \quad * \tag{1}$$

Proof: The first term denotes all ways of picking **i** unordered services from a set of **n** services, and it counts the number of compositions of different sizes; the second term counts all possible orderings of service compositions of length **i**; and the third term is a Catalan number and counts the number of compositions containing **i − 1** parenthesis which are correctly matched.

In environments with a large number of available services, service compositions cannot be manually enumerated. We present a framework that is able to effciently identify service compositions which minimize/maximize the non-functional requirements, while the functional requirements are satisfied.

OUR APPROACH

In this section we define the framework of our approach. First some initial definitions.

Definition 1. t-norm[1]**:** A mathematical function $\mathbf{T}: \cup_{n \in N} [0, 1]^n \to [0, 1]$ that is commutative, associative, monotonic, and the (n-1)-tuple **(1, · · ·, 1)** acts as the identity element, i.e., **T (a, 1, · · ·, 1) = a**. Examples of t-norm are the functions minimum, maximum, average and product.

Definition 2. Query: A Query **Q** is a pair **(F, NF)**, where **F** and **NF** represent functional and non-functional requirements, respectively. The functional requirement **F** is represented by a pair **(I, O)**, where **I** is a set of input attributes and **O** is the set of attributes that need to be produced as the result of the Query. The non-functional requirement **NF** is represented by a set of triples, **(p, op, va)**, where, **p** corresponds to a **QoS** parameter, **op** to a relational operator, **va** to a value. The evaluation of the Query **Q** has to respect the conjunction of the conditions expressed in the set **NF**.

For each **QoS** parameter **p** there exists a t-norm **t** that will be used to combine values of **p**.

Definition 3. Service Graph[2]**:** A Service Graph **G = (V, E)** is a directed acyclic bipartite graph. Nodes in **V** are of two types: attributes and services. Arcs in **E** represent relationships between attributes and services, such that, if **t** is an attribute and **s** is a service, then:

- if **(t, s) ∈ E**, then **t** corresponds to an input attribute of the service **s**,
- if **(s, t) ∈ E**, then values of the attribute **t** are produced by the service **s.**

Definition 4. Service Graph Description: Let **G = (V, E)** be a Service Graph. A Service Graph description for **G** is a five-tuple $(\mathbf{nf}, \mathbf{I^b}, \mathbf{I^f}, \mathbf{O^b}, \mathbf{O^f})$. **nf** is a set of pairs **(p, v)** representing the non-functional properties of **G**, where **p** represents a **QoS** parameter and **v** corresponds to a permissible value of **p** in **G**. $\mathbf{I^b}$, $\mathbf{I^f}$, $\mathbf{O^b}$, and $\mathbf{O^f}$ are sets of attributes, and $\mathbf{I^b} \subseteq \mathbf{V}$, $\mathbf{I^f} \subseteq \mathbf{V}$, $\mathbf{O^b} \subseteq \mathbf{V}$, and $\mathbf{O^f} \subseteq \mathbf{V}$, where:

- $\mathbf{I^b}$ represents the set of attributes that are bound in **G**.
- $\mathbf{I^f}$ represents the set of attributes that are unbound or free in **G**.
- $\mathbf{O^b}$ represents the set of attributes that are produced by **G**.
- $\mathbf{O^f} \cup \mathbf{O^b}$ represents the set of attributes that could be produced by **G**, if the attributes in $\mathbf{I^b} \cup \mathbf{I^f}$ were all bound.

We illustrate these definitions in the following example.

Figure 3. Example of definition 4: Service graph description. (a) two service graphs (b) the service graph that answers the query

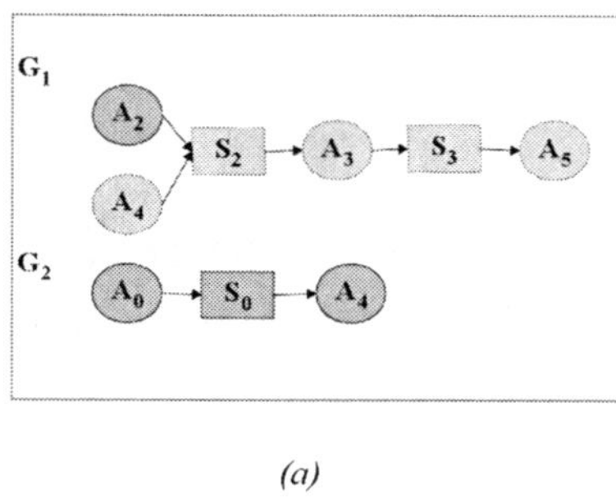

(a)

(b)

Example 3. *Suppose an attribute* $\mathbf{A_5}$ *needs to be produced when the attributes* $\mathbf{A_0}$ *and* $\mathbf{A_2}$ *are bound. Additionally, there is a restriction that at most five services can be executed and the answer needs to be generated in less than 50sec. Suppose the dependency graphs* $\mathbf{G_1}$ *and* $\mathbf{G_2}$ *in Figure 3(a) are available. Nodes with dotted lines represent either attributes that are unbound or services that cannot be invoked because their input attributes are unbound. Consider that services* $\mathbf{S_0}$, $\mathbf{S_2}$, *and* $\mathbf{S_3}$ *require 10, 15, and 5 seconds to be executed, respectively.* $\mathbf{G_1}$ *has the potential to return values of attributes* $\mathbf{A_3}$ *and* $\mathbf{A_5}$, *when the attribute* $\mathbf{A_4}$ *is bound, and* $\mathbf{G_2}$ *is able to return values of attribute* $\mathbf{A_4}$. *Hence, if these two graphs,* $\mathbf{G_1}$ *and* $\mathbf{G_2}$, *are combined into graph* $\mathbf{G_3}$ *(as shown in Figure 3(b)), the Query can be answered.*

Using the previous definitions, we can formalize this request as a Query **Q = (F, NF)**, s.t.:

- ***F= (I, O)***
  - $I = \{A_0, A_2\}$
  - $O = \{A_5\}$
- ***NF={(ExecutionTime, ≤, 50sec), (ServiceNumber, ≤, 5)}***

The Service Graphs $\mathbf{G_1 = (V_1, E_1)}$ and $\mathbf{G_2 = (V_2, E_2)}$ where

- $V_1 = \{A_2, S_2, A_3, S_3, A_4, A_5\}$
- $E_1 = \{(A_2, S_2), (A_4, S_2), (S_2, A_3), (A_3, S_3), (S_3, A_5)\}$
- $V_2 = \{A_0, S_0, A_4\}$
- $E_2 = \{(A_0, S_0), (S_0, A_4)\}$

and the Service Graph descriptions for Service Graphs $\mathbf{G_1}$ and $\mathbf{G_2}$:

G_1:

$\mathbf{SD_1} = (\mathbf{nf_1} = \{(\textbf{ExecutionTime, 20sec}), (\textbf{ServiceNumber, 2})\},$
$I_1^b = \{A_2\}$,
$I_1^f = \{A_3, A_4\}$,
$O_1^b = \varnothing$,
$O_1^f = \{A_3, A_5\})$

G_2:

$\mathbf{SD_2} = (\mathbf{nf_2} = \{(\textbf{ExecutionTime, 10sec}), (\textbf{ServiceNumber, 1})\},$
$I_2^b = \{A_0\}$,
$I_2^f = \varnothing$,
$O_2^b = \{A_4\}$,
$\mathbf{O_2^f = \varnothing)}$ ◇

Now, we define the concepts necessary to formally identify solutions to a Query.

Definition 5. Satisfiability: Let **Q = (F, NF)** be a Query. Let **G = (V, E)** be a Service Graph and $(\mathbf{nf, I^b, I^f, O^b, O^f})$ be the Service Graph Description of **G**. The set **nf** satisfies **NF** iff for each triple **(p, op, va)** in **NF**, exists a pair **(p, v)** in **nf** and the expression **v op va** holds.

Definition 6. Execution Plan: Let $\mathbf{Q} = (\mathbf{F}, \mathbf{NF})$ be a Query. An Execution Plan for $\mathbf{Q}$ is a Service Graph $\mathbf{G} = (\mathbf{V}, \mathbf{E})$ annotated with a Service Graph Description $(\mathbf{nf}, \mathbf{I^b}, \mathbf{I^f}, \mathbf{O^b}, \mathbf{O^f})$, s.t.,

- if $\mathbf{F} = (\mathbf{I}, \mathbf{O})$, then $\mathbf{I^b} \subseteq \mathbf{I}$ and $\mathbf{O} \subseteq \mathbf{O^b}$,
- **nf** satisfies **NF**.

In our work, an Execution Plan for a Query **Q** corresponds to a service composition.

Example 4. Using the formalization in Example 3, we can see that $\mathbf{nf_1}$ and $\mathbf{nf_2}$ both satisfy the non-functional requirements in **Q**, but neither $\mathbf{G_1}$ nor $\mathbf{G_2}$ are Execution Plans for **Q** because they do not produce the answer to **Q**, i.e., $\mathbf{O} \not\subseteq \mathbf{O_1}^b$ and $\mathbf{O} \not\subseteq \mathbf{O_2}^b$.

On the other hand, we can intuitively note that $\mathbf{G_3}$ has the following Service Graph Description:

$\mathbf{SD_3}$=($\mathbf{nf_3}$ = {(**ExecutionTime, 30sec**), (**ServiceNumber, 3**)},
$I_3^b = \{A_0, A_2\}$,
$I_3^f = \varnothing$,
$O_3^b = \{A_3, A_4, A_5\}$,
$O_3^f = \varnothing$)

In this case, $\mathbf{O} \subseteq \mathbf{O_3}^b$ and $\mathbf{nf_3}$ satisfies **NF**. Thus, $\mathbf{G_3}$ is an Execution Plan for Query **Q**, i.e., $\mathbf{G_3}$ represents the composition of services that can be used to evaluate the Query **Q**. ◇

DEDUCTION SYSTEM

In this section we provide a deductive framework that supports the inference tasks illustrated in Figure 3. We formalize the reasoning process by using the following deductive system to combine two service graphs.

Axiom 1. *Let* $\mathbf{Q} = (\mathbf{F}, \mathbf{NF})$ *be a Query. Let* $\mathbf{SD_1} = (\mathbf{nf_1}, \mathbf{I_1}^b, \mathbf{I_1}^f, \mathbf{O_1}^b, \mathbf{O_1}^f)$ *and* $\mathbf{SD_2} = (\mathbf{nf_2}, \mathbf{I_2}^b, \mathbf{I_2}^f, \mathbf{O_2}^b, \mathbf{O_2}^f)$ *be the Service Graph Descriptions of* $\mathbf{G_1}$ *and* $\mathbf{G_2}$*, respectively. If* $\mathbf{nf_1}$ *and* $\mathbf{nf_2}$ *both satisfy* **NF**, *then* $\mathbf{nf_3} = \mathbf{nf_1} \bullet \mathbf{nf_2}$, *where* $\mathbf{nf_3}$ *is a set of pairs* $(\mathbf{p_i}, \mathbf{v_{i3}})$, *such that,* $\mathbf{v_{i3}}$ *is the result of applying a t-norm* $\mathbf{t_i}$ *to* $\mathbf{v_{i1}}$ *and* $\mathbf{v_{i2}}$ *in the pairs* $(\mathbf{p_i}, \mathbf{v_{i1}})$ *and* $(\mathbf{p_i}, \mathbf{v_{i2}})$ *of the sets* $\mathbf{nf_1}$ *and* $\mathbf{nf_2}$*, respectively.*

The t-norm functions $\mathbf{t_i}$ *are defined in terms of the* **QoS** *parameters.*

Axiom 2. Let $\mathbf{SD_1} = (\mathbf{nf_1}, \mathbf{I_1}^b, \mathbf{I_1}^f, \mathbf{O_1}^b, \mathbf{O_1}^f)$ **and** $\mathbf{SD_2} = (\mathbf{nf_2}, \mathbf{I_2}^b, \mathbf{I_2}^f, \mathbf{O_2}^b, \mathbf{O_2}^f)$ be two Service Graph Descriptions. If $\mathbf{I_2}^f \subseteq \mathbf{O_1}^b$, then $\frac{SD_1 \;\ominus\; SD_2}{SD_3}$ where $SD_3 = (\mathbf{nf_3}, \mathbf{I_3}^b, \mathbf{I_3}^f, \mathbf{O_3}^b, \mathbf{O_3}^f)$ and the following conditions hold:

- $\mathbf{I_3}^b = \mathbf{I_1}^b \cup \mathbf{I_2}^b$
- $\mathbf{I_3}^f = \mathbf{I_1}^f$
- $\mathbf{O_3}^b = \mathbf{O_1}^b \cup \mathbf{O_2}^b \cup \mathbf{O_2}^f$
- $\mathbf{O_3}^f = \mathbf{O_1}^f$
- $\mathbf{nf_3} = \mathbf{nf_1} \bullet \mathbf{nf_2}$

Axiom 3. *Let* $\mathbf{SD_1} = (\mathbf{nf_1}, \mathbf{I_1}^b, \mathbf{I_1}^f, \mathbf{O_1}^b, \mathbf{O_1}^f)$ *and* $\mathbf{SD_2} = (\mathbf{nf_2}, \mathbf{I_2}^b, \mathbf{I_2}^f, \mathbf{O_2}^b, \mathbf{O_2}^f)$ *be two Service Graph Descriptions, then* $\frac{SD_1 \;\ominus\; SD_2}{SD_3}$, where $\mathbf{SD_3} = (\mathbf{nf_3}, \mathbf{I_3}^b, \mathbf{I_3}^f, \mathbf{O_3}^b, \mathbf{O_3}^f)$ *and the following conditions hold:*

- $\mathbf{I_3}^b = \mathbf{I_1}^b \cup \mathbf{I_2}^b$
- $\mathbf{I_3}^f = \mathbf{I_1}^f \cup \mathbf{I_2}^f$
- $\mathbf{O_3}^b = \mathbf{O_1}^b \cup \mathbf{O_2}^b$
- $\mathbf{O_3}^f = \mathbf{O_1}^f \cup \mathbf{O_2}^f$
- $\mathbf{nf_3} = \mathbf{nf_1} \bullet \mathbf{nf_2}$

Inference Rule 1. *Any substitution of an axiom is an axiom.*

Inference Rule 2. *If* **r:** $\frac{SD_1 \;\ominus\; SD_2}{SD_3}$ *is an axiom, then* $\mathbf{G} \vdash_r \mathbf{G'}$ *if the following conditions hold:*

- $\mathbf{G_3} \subseteq \mathbf{G'}$ *and* $\mathbf{SD_3}$ *is the Service Graph Description of* $\mathbf{G_3}$.
- $\mathbf{G_1} \subseteq \mathbf{G}$ *and* $\mathbf{SD_1}$ *is the Service Graph Description of* $\mathbf{G_1}$
- $\mathbf{G_2} \subseteq \mathbf{G}$ *and* $\mathbf{SD_2}$ *is the Service Graph Description of* $\mathbf{G_2}$

Inference Rule 3. *Given the following Service Graphs* **G** *and* **G'**, *then* $\mathbf{G} \vdash \mathbf{G'}$ *iff there exists a finite number of Service Graphs* $\mathbf{G_1}, \mathbf{G_2}, \ldots, \mathbf{G_{n-1}}, \mathbf{G_n}$, *such that,*

$G \vdash_r G_1$
$G_1 \vdash_r G_2$
. . .
$G_{n-1} \vdash_r G_n$
$G_n \vdash_r G'$

Definition 7. Union Operator ⊕: $\mathbf{G_3}$ *is the result of the union operator between* $\mathbf{G_1}$ *and* $\mathbf{G_2}$, *i.e.,* $\mathbf{G_1} \oplus \mathbf{G_2} = \mathbf{G_3}$ *if there exists a Service Graph* **G**, *such that,* $\mathbf{G} \vdash_r \mathbf{G_3}$ *and* $\mathbf{G_1} \cup \mathbf{G_2} = \mathbf{G}$.

Definition 8. Closure of the Union Operator $\oplus^*$: *Let* $\mathbf{G = (V, E)}$, $\mathbf{G_1 = (V_1, E_1)}$ *and* $\mathbf{G_2 = (V_2, E_2)}$ *be Service Graphs, then* $\mathbf{G_1} \oplus^* \mathbf{G_2} = \mathbf{G'}$ *if the following conditions hold:*

- $\mathbf{G \vdash G'}$
- $\mathbf{G = G_1 \cup G_2}$
- $\mathbf{V = V_1 \cup V_2}$
- $\mathbf{E = E_1 \cup E_2}$

Using this deductive system we can establish how Execution Plans can be combined into a new and more useful Execution Plan. For instance, the process we have followed to generate Service Graph $\mathbf{G_3}$ in Figure 3(b) makes use of the Service Graphs $\mathbf{G_1}$ and $\mathbf{G_2}$ in Figure 3(a), e.i., $\mathbf{G_3 = G_1 \oplus^* G_2}$. This is done using Inference Rule 1 and Axioms 2 and 1.

A dependency graph **G** can be seen as a Petri-Net as follows: places correspond to attributes and transitions represent services.

Definition 9. Petri-Net: *A directed, bipartite graph in which nodes are either Places (represented by circles) or Transitions (represented by rectangles). In other words, a Petri-Net is a Service Graph* $\mathbf{G = (P \cup T, F)}$, *where:*

- **P** *is a finite set of nodes, called Places.*
- **T** *is a finite set of nodes, called Transitions, disjoint from* **P**, $\mathbf{(P \cap T = \emptyset)}$.
- $\mathbf{F \subseteq (P \times T) \cup (T \times P)}$ *is a set of directed edges called arcs, known as the flow relation. If a pair* **(p, t)** *belongs to* **F**, **p** *is an Input Place of* **t**. *If a pair* **(t, p)** *belongs to* **F**, **p** *is an Output Place of* **t**.

Definition 10. Marking: *A marking of a Petri-Net G =*$\mathbf{(P \cup T, F)}$, *is a mapping* $\boldsymbol{M{:}P \rightarrow N}$, *suct that, for* $\boldsymbol{p} \in \boldsymbol{P}$ *and predecessor(*$\boldsymbol{p}$*)* $\neq \Phi$, *if exists a transition* $\boldsymbol{t} \in$ *predecessors(*$\boldsymbol{p}$*) and* $\boldsymbol{t}$ *is fired then* $\boldsymbol{M(p)}$ *=* |*sucessors(*$\boldsymbol{p}$*)* | + *1;*$\boldsymbol{M(p)}$ *= 0, otherwise. If predecessor(*$\boldsymbol{p}$*) =* Φ*,*$\boldsymbol{M(p)}$ *=* | *sucessors(*$\boldsymbol{p}$*)* | *+ 1, i.e.,*$\boldsymbol{p}$ *is part of the initial marking. A transition is fired when all its Input Places have at least one token.*

The dependency graph in Figure 1 can also be seen as a Petri-Net. Using this representation, a service (Transition) can be invoked (fired) when all its Input attributes (Places) have been marked, this causes its Output attributes (Places) to be marked. Then, a Marking refers to a specific set of marked Places. Concepts of Petri-Net are based on definitions in (Khomenko, Koutny, & Vogler, 2002).

Definition 11. Cut-off Service: *Let* $\prec$ *be an adequate order of Transitions in a Petri-Net and* $\boldsymbol{\beta}$ *be a prefix, i.e., a path in the Petri-Net. Let* **e“** *be a Transition in the Petri-Net, and Marking(***e“***) is a Marking induced when the Transition* **e“** *is fired. A Transition* **e** *is a cut-off Transition in* $\boldsymbol{\beta}$ *with respect to* $\prec$ *iff* $\boldsymbol{\beta}$ *contains some event* **e′**, *such that, Marking(***e***) = Marking(***e′***) and* $\mathbf{e'} \prec \mathbf{e}$.

Cut-off Transitions refer to Transitions where a Petri-Net unfolding algorithm can stop and all possible Markings are reached.

PROBLEM DEFINITION

We assume that the relationships among the available services and attributes are given in an input

Service Graph **G**. Thus, given a Query **Q**, our problem is to generate a new service graph **G´**, so that, nodes in **G´**correspond to the services in **G** required to evaluate **Q**, and edges in **G´** induce a partial order in which the services need to be evaluated to satisfy the functional requirements and to bind the input restrictions of each selected service. Additionally, the cost associated with the Execution Plan that describes **G´**, needs to be minimized.

In consequence, we define the **WSC** problem as follows:

Definition 12. The Web Service Composition Problem-(WSC) Given a Query **Q = (F, NF)**, a Service Graph **G = (V, E)** that represents the relationships among the available services and the attributes, the WSC problem is to identifying a Service Graph **G´= (V´, E´)** associated with a Service Graph description **(nf, I^b, I^f, O^b, O^f)**, such that, **G´** corresponds to an Execution Plan for **Q** i.e., if **F = (I, O)**, then $I^b \subseteq I$ and $O \subseteq O^b$ and the values of the **QoS** parameters in **nf** satisfy the constrains expressed in **NF**.

Solutions to the WSC Problem

We have extended the greedy Service Aggregation Matchmaking (SAM) (Brogi et al., 2008) algorithm with meta-heuristics to guide the composer into a portion of the search space where efficient service compositions can be found. We present the algorithms, Dynamic-programming Best-First (DP-BF) and Petri-Nets SAM (PT-SAM) to solve the WSC problem (see Definition 12). They use different criteria to prune the space of service composition, while minimizing/maximizing QoS values specified in the non-functional requirements. Additionally, they avoid the generation of service compositions with redundant services. An aggregated function that reflects the QoS values is used to guide the exploration of the search space.

Before defining our solutions, we will proceed to summarize the most important aspects of the SAM algorithm.

Service Aggregation Matchmaking (SAM)

SAM (Brogi et al., 2008) is an extension to a basic discovery algorithm (defined in (Bansal & Vidal, 2003)) that uses the information of the services contained in the Profile Model as well as in the Process Model of an OWL-S ontology. SAM receives a query expressed as a pair of input and output attributes, i.e., SAM only considers functional requirements. SAM starts with a preliminary phase during which, it builds a tree for each Process Model of the services stored in an OWL-S registry in order to establish service restrictions. When a single service that satisfies the query cannot be found, SAM tries to coordinate a set of services where the functional requirements hold. The functional capabilities of a service are defined in its input and output attributes using an OWL ontology. If such a coordination cannot be generated, SAM tries to combine sets of failed sub-plans.

SAM has two main phases: first, it builds a dependency graph, then it analyzes this graph to select the services that can answer the query. We briefly describe the most important phases of **SAM**. For more specific information refer to (Brogi et al., 2008).

Construction of the Dependency Graph

SAM defines a bipartite graph comprised of nodes that represent services, annotated with ontology concepts, and nodes that represent the concepts used for describing the service functional capabilities. This graph is similar to the one shown on Figure 1, except that instead of containing all the available services and attributes, it contains attributes and services relevant to a given query, i.e., there is a path from one of the attribute associated with an input to the attribute associated with an output of the query. The algorithm iterates over the service descriptions to identify the ones that satisfy the match criteria.

Figure 4. SAM: Yellow coloring step

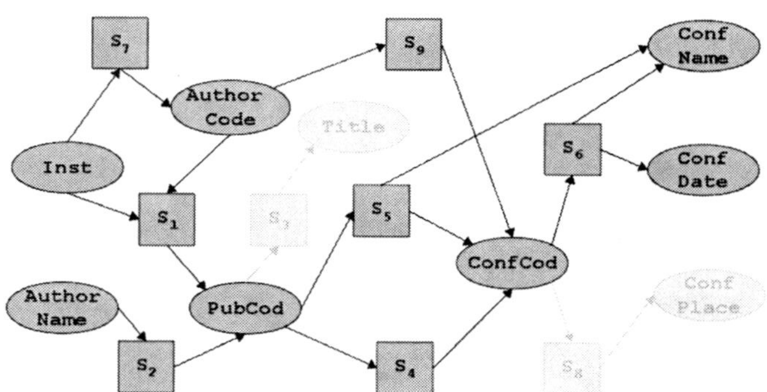

Analysis of the Dependency Graph

This phase focuses on finding a solution to the query. SAM traverses the dependency graph and in each iteration, it adds a service to the sub-plan until a solution is found or no more services can be added. This is done in five steps:

1. *Step 1 (Reachability of query outputs)*: It verifies that all nodes corresponding to the query output have incoming arcs. In such case, the algorithm can proceed to the next step. Otherwise, it means that the output in the query cannot be produced.
2. *Step 2 (Yellow Coloring)*: The goal of this step is to identify the services that may be useful to produce the query output. SAM paints in yellow the query outputs, and then recursively, for each yellow node, it colors all its predecessors. At the end of this step, the nodes that were not colored, are *non-useful* and can be eliminated from the graph. Figure 4 shows the result of this step for the query in Example 2. Note that services $\mathbf{S_3}$ and $\mathbf{S_8}$ are *non-useful* to produce the query output; thus, they will be eliminated from the graph.
3. *Step 3 (Red Coloring)*: The goal of this step is to identify which services can produce the query output. To describe this step, it is convenient to introduce the notion of *firable* service. A service is *firable*, if it is colored yellow and all its inputs have been already colored red. This step begins by coloring red all nodes associated with the query input. Then, while there is a yellow node that corresponds to the query output and there is at least a firable service, a firable service is randomly selected and colored red. All its successors are also colored red. At the end of this step, if the set of red nodes contains all the query output, then all the red services comprise an Execution Plan. Figure 5 shows the final state of the dependency graph. At the end of this step, services in the Execution Plan which are still yellow, like $\mathbf{S_2}$, are *non-useful* for the query. Note that this solution considers $\mathbf{S_4}$ and $\mathbf{S_9}$ as part of the Execution Plan. As we pointed before, one of these services becomes redundant.
4. *Step 4 and 5 (Analysis and additional inputs suggestions)*: On the case that an Execution Plan has not been identified in the previous step, SAM tries to find a combination of failed sub-plans that together can answer the query. If this cannot be done, a suggestion to relax the functional requirements can be given to the user.

The following sequence of services corresponds to a simple enumeration of an Execution Plan identified by **SAM** for the query in Example 2: $\mathbf{S_7}$, $\mathbf{S_1}$, $\mathbf{S_4}$, $\mathbf{S_5}$, $\mathbf{S_9}$, $\mathbf{S_6}$. In this case, SAM can identify this solution in Step 3.

Figure 5. SAM: Red coloring step

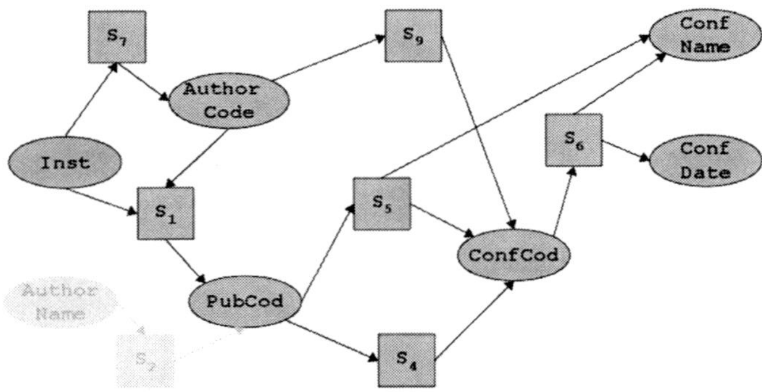

Lemma 2 (complexity of SAM) Let **n** be the number of available services. SAM time complexity is lineal in the size of the dependency graph[3].

Proof SAM iterates until an Execution Plan is found or no more services can be added. The number of iterations is limited by the maximum number of services. Hence, SAM is **O(n)**.

We can summarize that SAM uses a greedy heuristic to produce solutions which may contain services that might be redundant. SAM only focuses on satisfying the functional requirements of a Query. To consider the non-functional requirements, SAM has to be extended as follows:

- It needs to explore a larger portion of the search space.
- It needs to consider cost models to drive the search into portion of possibly optimal solutions.
- It needs to avoid Execution Plans with *non-useful* and *redundant* services.

Our approaches consist on extending **SAM**'s red coloring phase (Step 3) to expand the search space and guide the composition considering non-functional requirements. Steps 4 and 5 are not needed in our approaches.

Following sections present the detailed description of our algortihms.

Dynamic-Programming Best-First (DP-BF) Algorithm

DP-BF follows a Best-First strategy using a Dynamic-Programming technique and expands the top sub-compositions of services identified so far, until an Execution Plan that fulfills the Query requirements is identified. DP-BF produces efficient Execution Plans by traversing a small portion of the search space.

DP-BF resembles the Dynamic-Programming based optimization algorithm presented in (Florescu et al., 1999). A Dynamic-Programming approach is proposed to solve the problem of query optimization in the presence of limited access patterns; this algorithm receives a select-project-join query that represents the functional requirements and the relational tables that will be rewritten with the selected sources. Similarly, DP-BF traverses the space of possibly Web Service combinations and prunes the search space based on an aggregated metric or cost model that estimates the quality of a particular solution. Thus, only solutions with the highest quality seen so far, survive at the end of one iteration.

In each iteration the sub-combination associated with the highest quality is combined with those sub-plans that can improve or maintain that quality level in a more complete sub-plan; combination is done by following Definition 7.

The quality of an Execution Plan can be defined in different ways depending on which non-functional parameters should be minimized/ maximized. In this approach, we define the Execution Plan quality based on a function quality that aggregates functional and non-functional requirements in a Query **Q = (F, NF)**. The quality function of an Execution Plan **G** of a Query **Q** is defined as follows:

Quality(G, Q) = Cost(G, NF) × (1 + ReachedOutputs(G, F)) × Combinables(G) (2)

where:

- **G** is an Execution Plan.
- **ReachedOutputs(G, F)** is the number of Query outputs that are already produced by **G**.
- **Combinables(G)**: represents the number of Execution Plans that can be combined with G.
- **NF** is the set of non-functional properties as shown in Definition 2.

Then, the cost of an Execution Plan is a combination of the values related to its non-functional parameters. The expression that defines this cost is shown in Formula 3-5:

$$Cost(G, NF) = \frac{f_{NF}(NF)}{f_g(p_1, p_2, \ldots, p_n)} \quad (3)$$

$$f_{NF}(NF) = t(v_1, v_2, \ldots, v_n) \quad (4)$$

$$f_G(p_1, p_2, \ldots, p_n) = t(ev_1, ev_2, \ldots, ev_n) \quad (5)$$

where

- $\mathbf{NF} = \{ (\mathbf{p_1}, \mathbf{op_1}, \mathbf{v_1}), (\mathbf{p_2}, \mathbf{op_2}, \mathbf{v_2}) \ldots (\mathbf{p_n}, \mathbf{op_n}, \mathbf{v_n}) \}$
- $f_G(p_1, p_2, \ldots, p_n)$ maps a sub-plan **G** and the values of the **QoS** parameters $\mathbf{p_1}, \mathbf{p_2}, \ldots \mathbf{p_n}$ to an overall value.
- $\mathbf{ev_i}$=estimateCost($\mathbf{p_i}$, **G**), i.e., $\mathbf{ev_i}$ represents the estimated value of the **QoS** parameter $\mathbf{p_i}$ in the sub-plan **G**.
- $\mathbf{f_{NF}}$ corresponds to an overall benefit of the **QoS** parameters $\mathbf{p_1}, \mathbf{p_2} \ldots \mathbf{p_n}$ in the Query.
- **t** represents a t-norm function that combines the values of the **QoS** parameters that describe a sub-plan **G** (See Definition 1).

In the experimental study, we will empirically show the quality of the proposed metric by reporting on its predictive capability. This aggregated metric could be used by other approaches to produce solutions that meet functional and non-functional requirements.

DP-BF is presented in Figure 6. On each iteration, **DP-BF** chooses the best sub-plan according to its quality. Steps 1 to 4 initialize the data structures. Step 5 is the core of the **DP-BF** algorithm. Once the best sub-plan $\mathbf{G_1}$ is found (Step 5), **DP-BF** chooses, from the sub-plans generated so far, the set of Combinables for $\mathbf{G_1}$ (Step 6) i.e., sub-plans that satisfy at least one of the following conditions:

1. At least one input free on $\mathbf{G_1}$ matches an output bound on **G**.
2. At least one input free of **G** matches an output bound on $\mathbf{G_1}$.
3. The amount of outputs reached from $\mathbf{G_1}$ plus the amount of outputs reached from **G,** is smaller than the outputs reached from $\mathbf{G_3} = \mathbf{G_1} \oplus^* \mathbf{G}$.
4. The estimated quality of $\mathbf{G_3}$, defined in terms of a t-norm function that combines the **QoS** parameters values of $\mathbf{G_1}$ and **G**(Definition 7), is higher than the quality of **G** and $\mathbf{G_1}$.

The best sub-plan $\mathbf{G_1}$ is combined with each sub-plan in its combinable set[4] (Step 8). Each resulting sub-plan $\mathbf{G_3}$ is added to the list, if there does not exist an equivalent sub-plan $\mathbf{G_4}$ already in the list (Step 11) or there exists one whose quality is lower than the quality of $\mathbf{G_3}$ (Step 10).

Figure 6.

Algorithm 1: DYNAMIC-PROGRAMMING BEST-FIRST (DP-BF)

```
   Input: Query Q = (F, NF), where F = (I, O) with I is the set of inputs and O is the set of outputs and NF is a
          set of non-functional properties (See Definition 2).
   Input: OT: Ontology describing the domain
   Input: OWS: Ontology of Web Services
   Output: G: an execution plan that satisfies Q
   begin
       Create dependency service graph Depen_Graph = (V_dep, E_dep), as shown in Figure 1
       Plans_new ← {G = ({v}, ∅) : v ∈ V_dep}
1      forall G ∈ Plans_new do create service a graph description SD_G:
2          if v ∈ I then SD_G = (nf_1, ∅, ∅, {v}, ∅)
3          if v ∈ O then SD_G = (nf_1, ∅, {v}, ∅, ∅)
4          if v ∈ OWS then SD_G = (nf_2, ∅, {d : (d, v) ∈ E_dep}, ∅, {d : (v, d) ∈ E_dep})
           where
           nf_1 = {(p_i, val_i) : val_i is the identity value of the t-norm for QoS parameter p_i}
           nf_2 = {(p_i, val_i) : val_i is the value of the parameter p_i for service v}
       Found ← false
       repeat
           Plans ← Plans_new
5          Select a G_1 ∈ Plans_new s.t.: (∀G_i ∈ Plans_new − {G_1}: Quality(G_1) ≥ Quality(G_i))
6          Combinables ← {G_c : G_c ∈ Plans_new ∧
                              (∃G_n = G_1 ⊕* G_c ∧ Quality(G_n) > Quality(G_c))}
7          foreach G_2 ∈ Combinables do In descending order by the value of Quality of G_2
8              G_3 ← G_1 ⊕* G_2
               if ∃G_4 ∈ Plans_new such that AreEquivalent(G_4, G_3), then
9                  if (Quality(G_3) ≤ Quality(G_4)) then
                       Ignore G_3
                   else
                       if nf_3 satisfy NF then
10                         Plans_new ← Plans_new ∪ {G_3}
                           forall G_5 ∈ Plans_new that contains G_4 do
                               Replace G_4 by G_3 in G_5
                               Calculate again Quality(G_5)
               else
11                 Plans_new ← Plans_new ∪ {G_3}
               Found = Found OR (G_3 is an Execution Plan for Q AND nf_3 satisfies NF)
12     until (Found or Plans = Plans_new)
       if Found then
13         Return G ∈ Plans_new that satisfies Q and ∄ G_j ∈ Plans_new s.t., G_j satisfy Q and
           Quality(G_j) ≤ Quality(G)
       else
           Return ERROR
   end
```

In this case, if $\mathbf{G_4}$ is part of another sub-plan $\mathbf{G_5}$ in the list, it is replaced by $\mathbf{G_3}$ in $\mathbf{G_5}$ and its quality is recomputed. This process is repeated until a combination that satisfies the Query is found, this condition is represented on Step 12.

Figure 7 shows the Execution Plan that **DP-BF** generates for the Query presented on the Example 2. Note that *non-useful* or *redundant* services like $\mathbf{S_2}$, $\mathbf{S_3}$, $\mathbf{S_8}$, and $\mathbf{S_9}$ were not considered for different reasons: $\mathbf{S_2}$ and $\mathbf{S_3}$ cannot help to generate the Query output with the provided inputs. $\mathbf{S_8}$ would not be useful regardless of the input. In contrast, $\mathbf{S_9}$ can be useful but it generates the same output as $\mathbf{S_4}$, **DP-BF** will select from these two services, the one that maximizes the quality of the resulting Execution Plan.

Lemma 3. *(complexity) Let* **n** *be the number of available services. The* **DP-BF** *time complexity is polynomial in the size of the dependency graph.*

Proof: DP-BF *iterates until an Execution Plan is found or no more sub-plans can be generated by combining current sub-plans (Step 12). Inside there is a loop controlled by the number of combinable sub-plans of the sub-plan selected in Step 5, in the worse case, this number is* **n** *(Step 7). Inside this loop there is a computation of the closure over the graphs (Step 8), this operation is known to be*$\mathbf{O(n^3)}$. *Hence, we can say that* **DP-BF** *is* $\mathbf{O(n^5)}$.

Lemma 4. *(termination) If the number of services on the dependency graph is finite, then* **DP-BF** *terminates in a finite number of steps.*

Figure 7. DP-BF phase 2

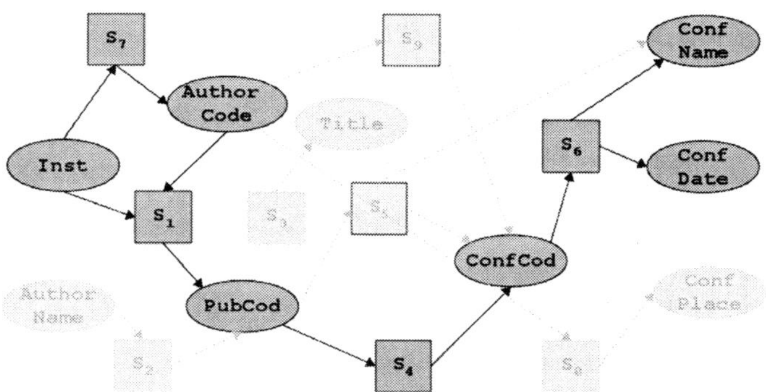

Proof: *The number of services, as well as the the number of attributes (**I** and **O**) in the Query, are finite, hence the initial number of graphs is finite. The algorithm iterates combining these graphs (or combination of them) until it finds a solution or it cannot combine more new sub-plans. The latter is the worse case, and when the algorithm reaches a fix point, it will end indicating that an answer could not be found.*

Lemma 5. *(soundness) Let* **G** *be an Execution Plan generated byDP-BFfor the Query* **Q = (F, NF)**, *then* **G** *answers* **Q**, *and* **G** *is the best Execution Plan among the space of traversed compositions.*

Proof: *Let* $\mathbf{SD_G} = (\mathbf{nf}, \mathbf{I^b}, \mathbf{I^f}, \mathbf{O^b}, \mathbf{O^f})$ *be the service description for* **G**. *As* **G** *is an Execution Plan for* **Q**, *then we know that* $\mathbf{I^b} \subseteq \mathbf{I}$ *and* $\mathbf{O} \subseteq \mathbf{O^b}$ *(Definition 6). We knowDP-BFverified that* **G** *satisfied* **Q**, *i.e.,* **nf** *satisfied* **NF** (Step 10 and 12 in Figure 6). *By definition of the operator*$\oplus$***and using axioms 2 and 3,* $\mathbf{O^b}$ *is generated by applying Inference Rule 3, successively, over pairs of sub-plans until the first iteration where* $\mathbf{Plans_{new}} = \{\mathbf{G(V, E)}: |\mathbf{V}| = 1 y \mathbf{E} = \varnothing\}$, *i.e., a fixed point is reached, or there is plan* **G** *that satisfies the functional and non-functional requirements. If such as Execution Plan G was found, the output bound of G, i.e.,* $\mathbf{O^b}$, *was generated using* **I** *by moving attributes from* $\mathbf{O^f}$ *of a sub-plan* $\mathbf{G_1}$ *to the* $\mathbf{O^b}$ *of the resulting graph (using Axiom 3). This guarantees that the functional restriction* **F** *are satisfied by* **G**. *Then, we can effectively say that* **G** *answers* **Q**. *On the other hand, suppose* **G** *is not the best plan in the traversed space, i.e., there exists another Execution Plan* $\mathbf{G'}$ *generated byDP-BFand* $\mathbf{Quality(G')} > \mathbf{Quality(G)}$. *However, in Step 9 if this condition holds* **G** *would have been replaced by* $\mathbf{G'}$ *and* **G** *would not be produced byDP-BF.*

Lemma 6. *(completeness) Let* **Q = (F, NF)** *be a Query. If there exists an Execution Plan for* **Q** *in a given dependency graph, thenDP-BFcan find the Execution Plan.*

Proof: *If an Execution Plan exists, then it is a sub-graph of the global dependency graph. Let us supposeDP-BFcannot find a solution.DP-BFuses all services that are in a path in the dependency graph from any of the* $\mathbf{i} \in \mathbf{I}$ *to any of the* $\mathbf{o} \in \mathbf{O}$. *In each iteration,DP-BFcombines partial sub-plans and it stops when an Execution Plan is found or when no more new sub-plans can be generated.*

In the first case, done. In the second case, if no more combinations can be generated, it means that there are no sub-plans that mutually satisfy conditions established in Axioms 2 and 3, i.e., there is no a combination that yields to a solution; however, we know that by combining all these graphs. Therefore, we can generate the dependency graph where there exists a solution.

Lemma 7. *(Correctness) TheDP-BFalgorithm is correct.*

Figure 8.

```
Algorithm 2: PETRI-NETS SAM (PT-SAM)
  Input: Query  Q = (F, NF), where F = (I, O) with I is the set of inputs and O is the set of outputs and NF is a
         set of non-functional properties (See Definition 2).
  Input: OT: Ontology describing the domain
  Input: OWS: Ontology of Web Services
  Output: G: an execution plan that satisfies Q
  begin
      Create service graph Dependence_Graph = (V_dep, E_dep)
      define G(V, E) s.t.: V = I and E = ∅ Candidates ← {v ∈ V_dep : ∃ w ∈ I and (w, v) ∈ E_dep}
      repeat
          G_old ← G
1         Select v ∈ Candidates s.t.: (∀w ∈ Candidates: Quality(v) ≥ Quality(w))
2         if ¬ isCutOff(v) then
              Let G(V, E) = G_old(V_old, E_old)
3             V ← V ∪ {v} ∪ successors(v, Dependence_Graph)
              E ← E ∪ {(x, v) : x ∈ V_old} ∪ {(v, y) : y ∈ successors(v, Depen_Graph)}
4             foreach v_s ∈ {v_s : v_s ∈ successors(v, Depen_Graph) ∧
              predecessors(v_s, Depen_Graph) ∈ V} do
                  Candidates ← Candidates ∪ successors(v_s, Depen_Graph)

          Candidates ← Candidates − {v}
5     until Candidates = ∅ or (∀o ∈ O : o is Marked in G)

      if ∀o ∈ O : o is Marked in G then
6         Return G
      else
          Return ERROR
  end
```

Proof: *Follows directly from Lemmata 4, 5, and 6, and the fact that the number of services is finite.*

Petri-NETs SAM (PT-SAM) Algorithm

The Petri-Net directed unfolding algorithm, presented in (Bonet, Haslum, Hickmott, & Thiébaux, 2008), extends the algorithm ERV (Esparza, Romer, & Vogler, 1996). It is used to solve the problem of whether a desired Marking is reachable from an initial Marking. It orders a set of Transitions that are to be *fired* according to an heuristic that estimates how close to the desired Marking will be the sub-plan produced by adding that Transition.

In the same way, PT-SAM adapts that Petri-Net unfolding algorithm and tries to find a desired Marking from an initial Marking. The Initial marking refers to a Petri-Net where the Places that correspond to the Query Inputs are marked (nodes in **I**) while the desired Marking corresponds to the state where Query Output are marked (nodes in **O**). In order to find a sequence of transitions that generates the desired Marking, PT-SAM keeps a list of all services that can be added to the sub-plan. This list is ordered according to a quality metric as the one defined in Equation 2. On each iteration of PT-SAM only one sub-plan is generated. PT-SAM is defined in Figure 8.

PT-SAM starts by creating a Petri-Net and marks the Places that correspond to the Input attributes in the Query. **PT-SAM** iterates until the desired Marking has been reached or there is no more services to be added to the sub-plan (Step 5). Each iteration begins by selecting a firable service with the highest quality; thus, the quality of the Petri-Net, induced by the resulting Marking, will be closer to the quality of the desired solution (Step 1).

Then, it filters out the services that are *cutoff* (Step 2), because they will not produce new Markings. The services that represent new information will be added to the sub-plan, improving the sub-plan quality (Step 3). Then, the successors of the output attributes of the chosen service will be added to the list of services to be considered in future iterations if they became firables in this step. At the end of the iteration, the chosen service is eliminated from the list of the Candidates services (Step 4).

Figure 9 shows the desired Marking generated by PT-SAM for the Query in Example 2. Note that PT-SAM does not consider services $\mathbf{S_2}$, $\mathbf{S_3}$ and $\mathbf{S_8}$ because they are *non-useful*, i.e., they will not contribute in the creation of a better Marking.

Figure 9. PT-SAM generated execution plan

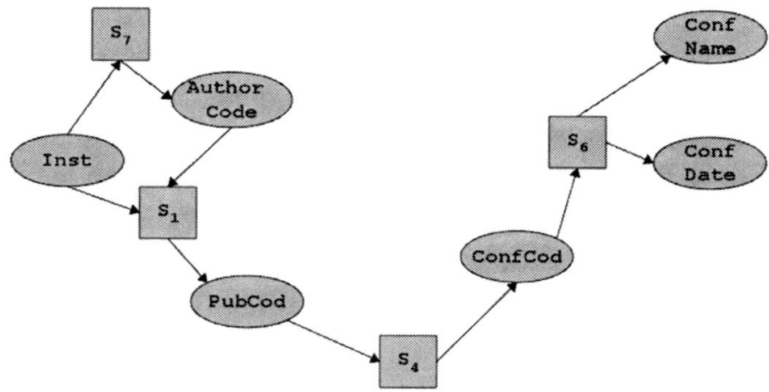

Finally, services S_5 and S_9 are relevant; however, they are not in the resulting Marking because service S_4 has an equivalent functionality and higher quality.

Lemma 8. *(complexity) Let* **n** *be the number of available services.PT-SAMtime complexity is linear in the size of the Petri-Net.*

Proof: *PT-SAMonly builds one Petri-Net until it finds a solution to* **Q** *or such a solution cannot be generated. In each iteration,PT-SAMfires a single service and generates a new Marking. Considering that* **n** *is the number of available services,PT-SAMperforms up to* **n** *iterations. Hence, we can conclude thatPT-SAMis* **O(n)**.

Lemma 9. *(termination) If the number of services on the Petri-Net is finite, then* **PT-SAM** *terminates in a finite number of steps.*

Proof: *PT-SAMfires a service in each iteration, this service is selected from the set ofCandidates. The cardinality ofCandidateschanges in each iteration and the number of services that can be added to this set is limited by* **n**. *Hence, the number of iterations performed by the algorithm is finite.*

Lemma 10. *(soundness) Let* **G** *be an Execution Plan generated byPT-SAMfor the Query* **Q = (F, NF)**, *then* **G** *answers* **Q**.

Proof: PT-SAM *stops when no more services can be fired or the Petri-Net reaches the desired Marking. A service is added to theCandidatesset when all its Inputs Places (attributes) have been marked. When a candidate service is fired, all its Output Places are marked. Then, if all the attributes in* **O** *are marked, it is because the Petri-Net can produce them from the attributes in* **I**. *Hence,* **G** *is the desired Marking and corresponds to an Execution Plan for* **Q**.

Lemma 11. *(completeness) Let* **Q = (F, NF)** *be a Query. If there exists an Execution Plan* **G** *for* **Q** *for a given Petri-Net* **P**, *thenPT-SAMcan find* **G**.

Proof: *If an Execution Plan* **G** *exists, then it is a sub-graph of* **P**. *This sub-graph has the nodes in* **I** *as sources, and because there exists a solution, then there is a sequence of services (and attributes) that can be fired (or marked) until all the attributes in* **O** *are marked. Therefore,PT-SAMfinds* **G**, *which is a desired Marking.*

Lemma 12. *(correctness) ThePT-SAMalgorithm is correct.*

Proof: *Follows directly from Lemmata 9, 10, and 11, and the fact that the number of services is finite.*

Experimental Study

We present the results of our experimental study. We report on the predictive capability of the proposed response time model, and on the quality of the proposed algorithms.

Experiment Design

DataSets

We have conducted our experiments on two datasets: the QWS (Al-Masri & Mahmoud, 2007a, 2007b, 2008b) and DS. The QWS dataset includes a set of 2,507 Web Service interfaces (WSDL documents) collected using the Web Service Crawler Engine (WSCE). Each service is annotated with a set of **QoS** parameters. In this experiment we consider the parameter that represents the response time of a service. It measures the time in miliseconds taken by the service to response a request.

DS is a synthetic dataset comprised of 50 services randomly generated following a uniform distribution. We created a base ontology to describe the concepts of our domain. We also generated a set of OWL-S Web Service definitions for the 50 services. The atomic processes are described by the attributes that correspond to their **Inputs** and **Outputs** arguments. Services were replicated with different response time as if they were mirrors on different sites.

Hardware and Software

The experiments were executed on a SUN workstation with 2 GBytes of memory, two Dual Core AMD Opteron processors 180 with 2.4 GHz and running Ubuntu 8.04 operating system. JDK 1.5.0 06 virtual machine was used to develop and run the programs. The OWL-S API (Sirin, 2004) was used to parse the Web Services definitions and to deal with the OWL classification process.

Cost Model

As we show in previos section, the quality of an Execution Plan is defined in terms of its aggregrated metric or cost model; this metric approximates the execution cost of the composition evaluation (Equations 2 and 3). This cost model is based on the estimates of the response time of the services that comprise the Execution Plan. This estimation can be performed by using sampling techniques as the ones proposed in (P. Haas & Swami, 1992; Hou et al., 1991; Ling & Sun, 1992; Lipton & Naughton, 1990; Lipton et al., 1990; Ruckhaus et al., 2008). However, in the reported experiments, the estimated evaluation cost of each service corresponds to the response time parameter of the dataset QWS. The formula used to estimate the response time of a sub-plan composed of two services $\mathbf{S_1}$ and $\mathbf{S_2}$, where $\mathbf{S_2}$ requires attributes generated by $\mathbf{S_1}$ to bind its input attributes; the response time is estimated as follows:

$$\text{responseTime}(S_1, S_2) = \text{responseTime}(S_1) + \text{card}(S_1) \times \text{responseTime}(S_2) \quad (6)$$

where, $\mathbf{card(S_1)}$ corresponds to the number of answers produced during the evaluation of service $\mathbf{S_1}$. This expression resembles the formula used to estimate the cost of evaluating a *dependent join* between two web sources (Zadorozhny et al., 2002). In a *dependent join* between two services $\mathbf{S_1}$ and $\mathbf{S_2}$ it is assumed that $\mathbf{S_1}$ will be evaluated first and then, for each answer produced by $\mathbf{S_1}$, $\mathbf{S_2}$ will be evaluated. This operator is needed when the output produced by $\mathbf{S_1}$ is required to bind inputs attributes of $\mathbf{S_2}$. The first term of Formula 6 estimates the response time of evaluating service $\mathbf{S_1}$, while the second term computes the response time of evaluating $\mathbf{S_2}$ for each of the answers produced by $\mathbf{S_1}$.

Predictive Capability of the Cost Model

To study the predictive capability of the proposed cost model, we have generated 50 compositions of services in the dataset **QWS**. Table 2 describes the set of the compositions considered in our study. For each composition, we have computed the estimated cost using Formula 6 and its actual response time.

Table 2. Composition descriptions

Number of Services	Number of Compositions
1	8
2	9
3	9
4	8
5	8
6	7
7	1

Figure 10 plots the actual response time versus the estimated cost of each composition; actual response time was computed by executing the service compositions. We can observe a positive trend between the estimated and actual cost, which indicates a linear relation between these two values. We also have computed the correlation; the value is 0.98. Both results suggest that the proposed cost model is able to accurately predict the non-functional parameter response time of a composition of services.

Quality of the Proposed Algorithms

We compare DP-BF and PT-SAM to SAM and to an exhaustive Dynamic-Programming solution, called DP-First. The latter is called DP-First because it expands all sub-plans in each iteration, but it stops when the first Execution Plan G is found for a Query Q. We also implemented an algorithm (DP-All) that finds, using a Dynamic-Programing approach, all possible solutions to each Query; thus, it is able to identify the optimal solution.

We studied the behavior of the algorithms **SAM**, **DP-BF**, **PT-SAM**, **DP-First**, and **DP-All** on a set of synthetic queries. This set is comprised of 240 queries randomly generated over the dataset **DS** following a uniform distribution. These queries are classified according to their size: the number of services in the optimal Execution Plan. The sizes range from one to twelve services, and there are twenty queries for each size.

We present the results of our experiments considering three measures: optimization time, the estimated and the actual response time of an Execution Plan.

Optimization Time

Figure 11 presents the time required by the algorithms to produce an Execution Plan. We can observe that the time consumed by DP-First is at least two orders of magnitude greater than the time required by the other algorithms for compositions of more than six services. The behavior exhibited by **DP-First** is not monotonic, because even if a

Figure 10. Correlation of estimated cost to actual cost of service compositions in the dataset QWS

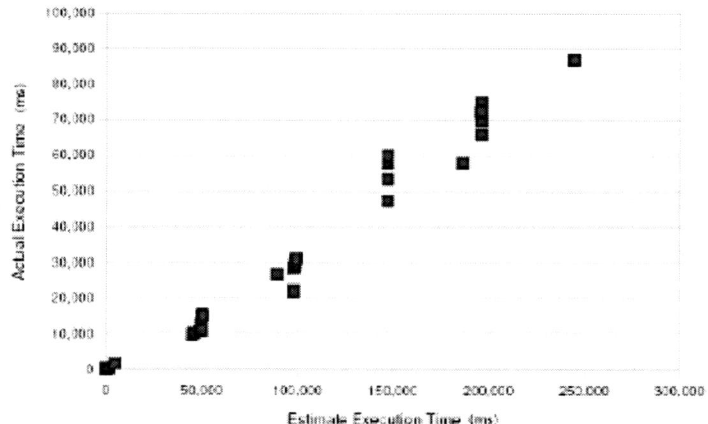

Figure 11. Optimization time

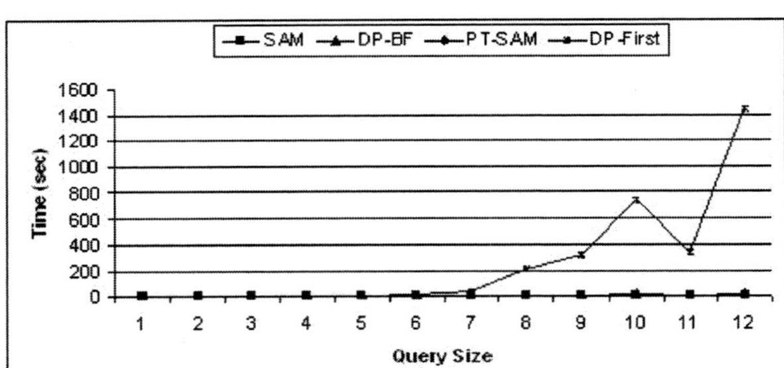

Figure 12. Optimization time (SAM, DP-BF, and PT-SAM)

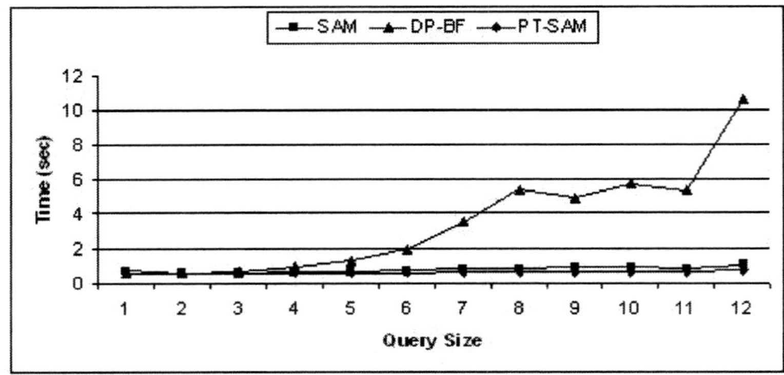

Query is larger, the search space may be shorter than the search space of a shorter Query.

Figure 12 shows these results only for the algorithms SAM, DP-BF, and PT-SAM. We note that SAM is more scalable. It produces solutions to queries in less than 2 seconds. Time consumed by DP-BF goes up to 10 seconds, while PT-SAM can produce answers in less time than SAM. This behavior could be explained by the fact that SAM may waste time considering *redundant* services, and DP-BF may produce a large number of subplans, because it explores a larger portion of the search space.

Execution Plan Quality

Figure 13 reports on the estimated response time of the Execution Plans identified by each algorithm. We can observe that the Execution Plans generated by SAM have very low quality compared to those generated by DP-BF and PT-SAM.

In Figure 14, we just report on estimated response time of that DP-BF and PT-SAM. We can observe that DP-BF and PT-SAM identify solutions that are close to the ones produced by the **DP-First** algorithm, which is close to the optimal.

Percentile Analysis

In Table 3 we present the percentile analysis of the costs of the Execution Plans identified by SAM, DP-BF, PT-SAM and DP-First compared to the costs of the optimal Execution Plans generated by DP-All.

The results clearly show that, DP-BF and PT-SAM are able to produce Execution Plans that

Figure 13. Estimated response time for generated execution plans

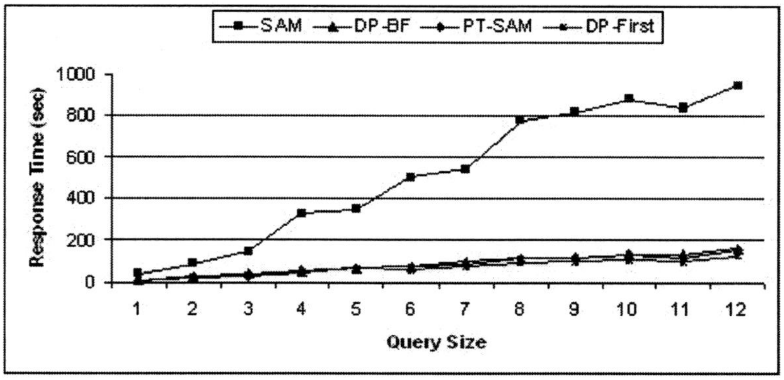

Figure 14. Estimated response time for generated execution plans (DP-BF, PT-SAM, and DP-First)

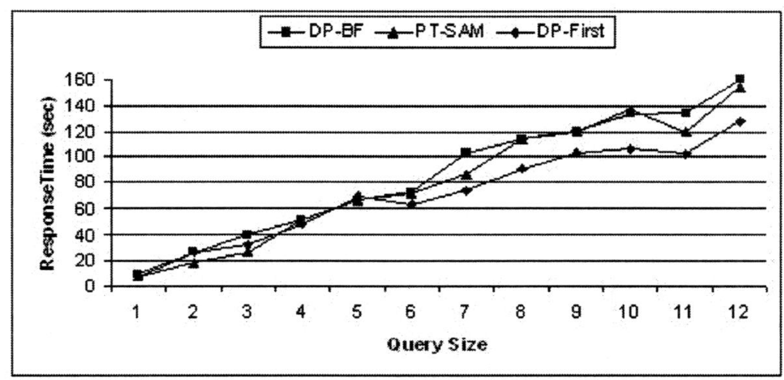

Table 3. Percentile range of estimated costs

Query Size	1	2	3	4	5	6
SAM	46,3	71,8	49,4	51,6	45,6	41,4
DP-BF	88,3	90,0	93,2	93,9	96,1	96,5
PT-SAM	93,2	94,1	96,6	93,9	95,6	97,0
DP-First	95,7	90,9	95,4	94,60	95,8	97,4

outperform those produced by SAM, while the optimization time remains in the same order of magnitude. The percentile analysis shows that our proposed algorithms are able to produce Execution Plans close to the optimal Execution Plans, i.e., close to the best Execution Plans produced by **DP-All**. Percentiles were computed by identifying the position of a plan produced by a particular algorithm, with respect to the ranked set of plans produced by DP-All.

RELATED RESEARCH

The problem of identifying combinations of services that meet a given set of non-functional and functional requirements is related to problems that have been studied in query optimization, service matching and discovery, service selection, and Web Service composition. This section presents a review of the state-of-art in these concerns.

Query Optimization

The query optimization problem is to identify an execution plan, such that, the cost of evaluating the execution plan is minimized. In order to solve this problem, a model that estimates the cost of evaluating the execution plan or the benefits, needs to be defined; additionally, because the size of the search space, strategies are required to traverse the space effciently.

In the context of the Web, queries usually need to be rewritten in terms of web limited query processing data sources. This restriction on the source functionally impacts on the size of search space of possibly rewritings of the query in the sources, and new approaches have been proposed to scale up the traditional solutions. The query rewriting and optimization tasks identify not only a low evaluation cost ordering of the sub-goals of the query; additionally, query sub-goals need to be implemented by the available sources and the identified ordering has to satisfy the limited processing capabilities of each considered web source (Srivastava et al., 2006; Duschka & Levy, 1997; Florescu et al., 1999; Friedman & Weld, 1997; L. Haas et al., 1997; Levy et al., 1996; Papakonstantinou et al., 1996; Tomasic, Raschid, & Valduriez, 1998; Zadorozhny et al., 2002; Ouzzani & Bouguettaya, 2004; Srivastava et al., 2006; Zadorozhny et al., 2000).

Typically, existing approaches represent source's limited capabilities as binding patterns, and implement search meta-heuristics which ensure that the identified solutions, in addition to be effcient, they meet the binding restrictions with the query constants or with the attributes produced by previous sources in the execution plan. Functional requirements are represented as conjunctive or select-project-join (SPJ) queries, and the length of the paths are limited by the number of sub-goals in the query.

Similarly, to compose Web Services and meet a given set of non-functional and functional requirements, the input and output restrictions that describe the services need to be satisfied. In addition, cost models need to be defined to estimate how well the non-functional user requirements are satisfied by the chosen services. These cost models need to be used to conduce the search into the space of optimal solutions and avoid visiting *non-relevant* solutions. Optimal compositions of services can be of any length, and there is not a length bound established by the size of the query. Thus, approaches proposed to optimize Web queries, are not suitable to compose services because they limit the search to execution plans whose number of nodes is bound by the number of sub-goals in the query.

Example 5 illustrates the main drawbacks of the query optimization approaches in the context of Web Service Composition.

Example 5. *Consider the following relational tables composed of attributes that define the parameters of the services shown inFigure 1:*

```
Conference(ConfCod,ConfName,ConfDate,
ConfPlace)
Researcher(AuthorCod,AuthorName,Work
sFor)
Attend(AuthorCod,ConfCod)
Suppose the following SPJ query rep-
resents a user functional request:
Select C.ConfName, C.ConfDate
From Conference C, Researcher R, At-
tend A
Where
     R.WorksFor = ''USB'' and
     A.AuthorCod = R.AuthorCod
     and A.ConfCod = C.ConfCod
```

Based on the service descriptions presented inFigure 1, the following compositions $\mathbf{c}_1$ *and* $\mathbf{c}_2$*, can be used to evaluate the query:*

$\mathbf{c}_1$: $\mathbf{S}_7$, $\mathbf{S}_9$, $\mathbf{S}_6$
$\mathbf{c}_2$: $\mathbf{S}_7$, $\mathbf{S}_1$, $\mathbf{S}_4$, $\mathbf{S}_6$

By using the approach proposed by (Florescu et al., 1999), composition $\mathbf{c}_1$ *could be generated. However, because of the length of the query, the composition* $\mathbf{c}_2$ *will not be generated. Thus, in case of* $\mathbf{S}_1$ *or* $\mathbf{S}_4$ *being more effcient than* $\mathbf{S}_9$*, the service composition* $\mathbf{c}_2$ *could not be identified following this approach.* ◇

Service Matching and Discovery

Given a set of functional requirements or query, the problems of service discovery and service matching for the query is to identify a service that best meets the requirements.

Algorithms to matching and discovery sources range from keyword-based search engines to ontology-based frameworks for discovering semantically heterogeneous Web Services. On one hand, keyword-based search languages as well as category browsing such us Google, provide a significantly higher number of WSDL files for a given keyword-based user request (Al-Masri & Mahmoud, 2008a; Bachelechner et al., 2006). However, Google is not well suitable for Web Service discovery because, services are selected in terms of how "good" are these services for a given set of keywords, and they are ranked by using link-based metrics that do not necessarily reflect the satisfaction grade of the solutions with respect to the user functional and non-functional requirements.

On the other hand, the majority of resource discovery approaches use Request Functional Profiles to represent user requirements. These approaches usually rely their computations on reasoning engines that depending on the service semantic descriptions, offer a semantic-based solution.

First, matchmaking algorithms proposed in Paolucci et al. (2002) make use of information published in the Service Profile to identify the resources that satisfy a set of functional constraints. A Service Profile is part of an **OWL-S** ontology, where a service can be associated with zero or more Service Profiles. A Service Profile specifies the service functionality in terms of inputs, outputs, preconditions, and effects. Inputs and outputs refer to OWL classes describing the types of the instances to be sent to the service and the type of the expected answer. The main disadvantage of these algorithms arises from the limited capability of the Service Profiles to describe the properties of a service. Information of the control structures used in a service is not available; thus, incorrect matches can be identified (Bansal & Vidal, 2003).

Extensions to previous matchmaking algorithms are presented in Bansal and Vidal (2003). In addition to consider Service Profile, this approach takes into account information specified on the Process Model, i.e., the restrictions and control structures that are used to define the service and to decide which attributes can be produced as output during the evaluation of the service. Al-Masri and Mahmoud (2007c) and Reddy et al. (2009) propose mechanisms that consider **QoS** parameters as constraints when searching for relevant services.

In a similar way, to identify the compositions of services that satisfy a given set of functional and non-functional requirements, information represented in the Service Profile and Process Model could also be used. However, existing service discovery and matching approaches focus their search on single services, thus, they will not be able to identify solutions for the query in Example 5. Our proposed solution is defined on the basis that services have been already discovered and their descriptions (capabilities and **QoS** parameters) are kept in a local catalog.

The Web Service Composition: The WSC Problem

The **WSC** problem has been extensively treated in the literature, and diverse solutions that take advantage of AI techniques, Search Meta-Heuristics, and Linear Programming have been proposed. In this section we will describe approaches that select services based on functional user requirements, and then, we will present state-of-the-art techniques to select services which can be composed in a way that a set of non-functional requests is satisfied. Functional requirements are usually specified in terms of the set of input attributes that will be bound in the query, and the set of attributes that will be returned as the output (Brogi et al., 2008; Constantinescu et al., 2004; Fernández & Ossowski, 2007; Kuter et al., 2004; Rainer, 2006); also, some approaches orchestrate available services in terms of the pre-conditions and the effects of the service composition (Ho mann et al., 2008; Meyer & Weske, 2006; Rainer, 2006; Traverso & Pistore, 2004). However, approaches based on non-functional requirements, often receive a business Process Model or workflow comprised of abstract processes that meet the functional user request, and the order in which they must be evaluated; the problem is to identify concrete services for each of the abstract processes in a way the grade of satisfaction of the non-functional requirements is maximized (Berardi et al., 2005, 2006, 2008; Cardellini et al., 2007; Wada et al., 2008; Ko et al., 2008; Rahmani et al., 2008). In this work, we propose a hybrid solution that takes advantages of search meta-heuristics techniques to consider functional conditions expressed as input and output attributes, and non-functional constraints represented by a set of **QoS** parameters and their permissible values. Functional and non-functional requirements are considered at the same time, to compute in relatively short time, "good" service compositions; goodness is measured in terms of the combination of functional and non-functional degrees of satisfaction. Thus, this is a novel and efficient solution to the WSC problem that in contrast to existing approaches, does not require the execution of two independent techniques to first identify the services that satisfy the functional requirements, and then, the compositions that meet the non-functional constraints.

Composing Services in Terms of Functional Requirements

In the context of AI, the WSC problem has been represented as a planning problem; actions to be taken by the planner are defined in a theory of temporal formulas that represent functional service properties in terms of their preconditions and effects. This information is used by a reasoner to take actions that ensure the consistency of the inferred knowledge in a way that temporal formulas need to be true in a semantic model (Constantinescu et al., 2004). The performance of this solution is based on the quality of existing planning algorithms that are able to generate execution plans effciently and can deal with large search spaces. However, since the complexity of the model enumeration problem is exponential in the number of rules, this solution may be impractical in real-world domains. In addition, no cost is considered during the model enumeration process, so the identified solution may not correspond to the one that best meets the non-functional requirements.

To overcome the limitations of basic planning solutions, Hierarchical Task-Network planning techniques have been proposed (HTN) (Kuter et al., 2004). HTN planning incorporates and exploits domain-independent control knowledge to improve the performance (Au, Kuter, & Nau, 2005; Martinez & Lesperance., 2004; Kuter et al., 2004). The description of a planning domain includes a set of planning operators and methods that establish the way a task can be decomposed into smaller subtasks. The description of a planning problem contains an initial state as in classical planning. Instead of a goal formula, there is a partially-ordered set of tasks to be accomplished. Planning proceeds by decomposing tasks recursively into smaller subtasks, until primitive tasks, which can be performed directly using one planning operator, are reached. For non-primitive tasks, the planner chooses an applicable method, instantiates it to decompose the task into subtasks, and then, it chooses and instantiates other methods to decompose the subtasks even further. If the constraints on the subtasks or the interactions among them prevent the Execution Plan from being feasible, the planning system backtracks and tries other methods. The main advantage of HTN planning lies in its ability to deal with very large problem domains by decomposing goal into smaller manageable subtasks, which can be solved directly. Hence, the computational cost of finding correct sequence of actions is reduced significantly. However, a domain expert is needed in order to formalize the tasks to be achieved. This may become a disadvantage if such expert is not available when new requirements arise. Additionally, as in general planning solutions, information about **QoS** parameters is not used during the planing tasks.

An approach that uses *Answer Set Programming (ASP)* is presented in Rainer (2006). It shows that service descriptions can be expressed as a theory by using a rule-based first order logic language. The formalization of the problem is defined in a way that models of the theory correspond to service compositions that satisfy the restrictions imposed in the query and in the service descriptions. Models of the theory are exhaustible enumerated. Thus, ASP ensures the optimality of the identified Execution Plan. However, if there is a large number of restrictions of services, this exact solution may not scale up.

To scale up to a large number of services, Fernández and Ossowski (2007) propose a two-fold technique. In the first step, the initial set of services is partitioned into classes of equivalent services based on a given criterion. Each class is associated with a service that is characterized by the capabilities of the services in the class. In the second step, only representatives of classes are considered to identify a composition that meets the user functional requirements. The quality of the generated solution relies on the criteria used to partition the services. In addition, QoS parameters are not considered.

In the context of Search Meta-Heuristics, the Service Aggregation Matchmaking (SAM) algorithm is defined (Brogi et al., 2008). It makes use of an OWL-S ontology, and explicitly returns a sequence of atomic processes that need to be executed in order to achieve the desired result. When no full match is possible, SAM features a flexible matching by returning partial matches and by suggesting additional inputs that would produce a solution that fulfill the query constraints. SAM follows a greedy approach in which only one sub-plan is generated in each iteration. In terms of time, SAM is able to scale up in environments with a moderated number of services (e.g., in the range of 100 to 200 services). However, since SAM does not consider any cost metric or optimization criteria to compose the services, plans produced by SAM may be costly. To exacerbate this problem, SAM may add services to the plan that are *non-useful* to satisfy the non-functional and functional user requirements, and *non-relevant* and redundant services may be part of the generated solutions. In consequence, the quality of the identified plans may be far from optimal.

Composing Services in Terms of Non-Functional Requirements

The problem of identifying a set of concrete services that implement a graph or workflow of abstract processes and best meet a set of non-functional requirements is known as the QoS-aware WSC problem, and has been shown to be NP-hard (Wada et al., 2008); a survey of existing approaches can be found in Claro, Albers, and Hao (2006) and Yu and Rei -Marganiec (2008). This problem is a combinatorial optimization problem and several heuristics have been proposed to find a relatively effcient solution in a reasonably short period of time. In (Rahmani et al., 2008), it is defined a heuristic distance metric to drive a backward search algorithm; this metric induced an order of the services in a way that sink nodes are unlikely to be visited. In Berardi et al. (2005, 2006, 2008), services are described in terms of deterministic finite state machines, and a client specification that corresponds to the composition tree that the user would like to evaluate using the available services, is also expressed as a non-deterministic finite state machine; all finite state machines are encoded in a Description Logic theory and the problem of identifying an optimal rewriting of the client specification is reduced to the satisfiability of the resulting theory; this approach benefits the composition of small number of simple services. Ko et al. (2008) propose a constraint-based approach that encodes the non-functional permissible values as a set of constraints whose violation needs to be minimized; to traverse the space of possibly optimal solutions, a hybrid algorithm that combines the tabu search and simulating annealing meta-heuristics is implemented; experimental results show that the proposed solution is able to scale up to a large number of services and abstract processes. In Cardellini et al. (2007) the QoS-aware WSC problem is encoded as a Linear Programming problem providing a scalable solution to the problem. In Wada et al. (2008) this problem is defined as a multi-objective optimization problem where the different QoS parameters are considered equally important and there is not an aggregated function to combine all of them; a genetic based algorithm is proposed to identify a set of non-dominated service compositions that best meet all the QoS parameters. Although all these solutions are able to effciently solve the optimization problem and scale up to a large number of abstract processes, they are not suitable to identify the set of services that satisfy a given user functional request. Barreiro, Licchelli, Albers, and Arájo (2008) propose a two-fold solution to compose services in terms of functional and non-functional requirements. In the first step a planning algorithm is performed, and services that meet the functional request are identified; in the second step, QoS parameters are considered to select the services that best meet the non-functional requirements among the ones chosen in the first step. In contrast, we propose a hybrid approach that receives and considers at the same time, a functional user request expressed by a pair of input and output attributes, and a non-functional condition represented by a set of **QoS** parameter permissible values; thus, the returned composition satisfies the functional request and meets the non-functional restrictions.

CONCLUSION AND FUTURE WORK

Web Services are quickly raising as a standard for publishing data and operation for loosely coupled heterogeneous systems. The current trend proposes that applications should not be manually developed but integrated from an adequate set of already existing and available Web Services. Transparent service composition has a great potential to facilitate the integration of applications among different organizations. Existing solutions are focused on the inherent challenges associated with the tasks of service discovery and service composition, and take into account functional and non-functional requirements independently.

There exist some approaches that intend to produce a service composition that fulfills a particular set of functional requirements (Brogi et al., 2008; Beco, Cantalupo, N.Matskanis, & Surridge, 2005; Chen et al., 2003; Majithia, Walker, & Gray, 2004; Au et al., 2005; Martinez & Lesperance, 2004). SAM is one of such approaches. It takes as input a query and a set of services and returns a coordination of services that can produce the desired result. SAM traverses the space of possibly combinations by using a greedy approach, and it focuses on finding a solution (if such a solution exists) regardless of its quality.

In order to estimate the quality of a composition in terms of functional and non-functional requirements, we have proposed an aggregated metric. To overcome SAM limitations, we have presented two algorithms DP-BF and PT-SAM that use two search meta-heuristics strategies to traverse the space of compositions, and they make use of this metric to guide the search into portions of possibly optimal compositions.

DP-BF extends SAM by combining a Best-First strategy with a Dynamic-Programing technique to produce effcient Web Service compositions; only intermediate solutions that may lead to an effcient composition are considered during the search. On the other hand, PT-SAM adapts a Petri-Net unfolding algorithm and tries to find a desired Marking from an initial Marking. Both algorithms identify compositions that satisfy the functional and non-functional requirements specified in the Query. Our experimental results indicate that the proposed cost model used to estimate the quality of a composition in terms of its response time, is able to accurately predict the values of this non-functional parameter. Additionally, they show that our heuristics provide an effcient and effective solution to the WSC problem.

We are planning to enrich DP-BF and PT-SAM with costs models adapted to the dynamic properties of grids platforms and to other non-functional parameters that characterize these platforms. In particular, we will address the problem of generating effcient service compositions that satisfy some of the constraints present in the GRID.

REFERENCES

Al-Masri, E., & Mahmoud, Q. (2007c). QoS-based discovery and ranking of Web Services. In *Computer Communications and Networks,* 529–534.

Al-Masri, E., & Mahmoud, Q. (2008a). Discovering Web Services in search engines. *IEEE Internet Computing, 12*(3), 74–77. doi:10.1109/MIC.2008.53

Al-Masri, E., & Mahmoud, Q. (2008b). *Investigating Web Services on the World Wide Web* (pp. 795–804). WWW.

Al-Masri, E., & Mahmoud, Q. H. (2007a). Discovering the best Web Service. In *WWW '07: Proceedings of The 16th International Conference on World Wide Web,* (pp. 1257–1258). New York: ACM.

Al-Masri, E., & Mahmoud, Q. H. (2007b). *QoS-based discovery and ranking of Web Services* (pp. 529–534). ICCCN.

Au, T.-C., Kuter, U., & Nau, D. S. (2005). Web Service composition with volatile information. In *Proceedings of the International Semantic Web Conference (ISWC),* (p. 52-66).

Bachelechner, D., Siorpaes, K., Lausen, H., & Fensel, D. (2006). Web Service discovery-a reality check. In *Demos and Posters of the 3rd European Semantic Web Conference.*

Bansal, S., & Vidal, J. M. (2003). Matchmaking of Web Services-based on the DAML-S service model. In *Proceedings of the II International Joint Conference on Autonomous Agents and Multiagent Systems,* (pp. 926–927).

Barreiro, D., Licchelli, O., Albers, P., & de Araújo, R.-J. (2008). *Personalized reliable Web Service compositions*. WONTO.

Beco, S., Cantalupo, B., & Matskanis, N. L. G. & Surridge, M. (2005). OWL-WS: A workflow ontology for dynamic Grid Service composition. In *Proceedings of the First International Conference on e-Science and Grid Computing.*

Berardi, D., Calvanese, D., Giacomo, G.D., Hull, R. & Mecella, M. (2005). Automatic composition of transition-based Semantic Web Services with messaging. *Journal of Very Large Data Bases.*

Berardi, D., Cheikh, F., Giacomo, G. D., & Patrizi, F. (2008). Automatic service composition via simulation. *International Journal of Foundations of Computer Science, 19*(2), 429–451. doi:10.1142/S0129054108005759

Berardi, D., Giacomo, G. D., Mecella, M., & Calvanese, D. (2006). *Composing Web Services with nondeterministic behavior* (pp. 909–912). ICWS.

Blanco, E., Cardinale, Y., Vidal, M.-E., & Graterol, J. (2008). Techniques to produce optimal Web Service compositions. In *Proceedings of 2008 IEEE Congress on Services 2008 - Part I (SERVICES-1 2008),* (pp. 553–558). Honolulu, HI: IEEE Computer Society.

Bonet, B., Haslum, P., Hickmott, S., & Thiébaux, S. (2008). *Directed unfolding of petri nets* (pp. 172–198).

Brogi, A., Corfini, S., & Popescu, R. (2008). Semantics-based composition oriented discovery of Web Services. *ACM Transactions on Internet Technology, 8*(4), 1–39. doi:10.1145/1391949.1391953

Cardellini, V., Casalicchio, E., Grassi, V., & Presti, F. L. (2007). Flow-based service selection for Web Service composition supporting multiple QoS classes. In *Proceedings of IEEE 2007 International Conference on Web Services.*

Chen, L., Shadbolt, N. R., Goble, C. A., Tao, F., Cox, S. J., Puleston, C., et al. (2003). Towards a knowledge-based approach to semantic service composition. In *2nd International Semantic Web Conference (ISWC),* (pp. 319-334).

Claro, D. B., Albers, P., & Hao, J.-K. (2006). Web Services composition. In *Semantic Web Services* (pp. 195–225). Processes and Applications.

Constantinescu, I., Faltings, B., & Binder, W. (2004). *Large scale, type-compatible service composition* (pp. 506–513). ICWS.

Duschka, O., & Levy, A. (1997). Recursive plans for information gathering. In *Proceedings IJCAI-97.*

Erl, T. (2005). *Service-Oriented Architecture: Concepts, technology, and design.* Prentice Hall PTR.

Esparza, J., Romer, S., & Vogler, W. (1996). An improvement of McMillan's unfolding algorithm. In *Tools and algorithms for construction and analysis of systems,* (p. 87- 106).

Fernández, A., & Ossowski, S. (2007). Semantic service composition in service-oriented multiagent systems-a filtering approach. In Huang, J. (Eds.), *Service-oriented computing: Agents, semantics, and engineering* (pp. 78–91). Springer. doi:10.1007/978-3-540-72619-7_6

Florescu, D., Levy, A., Manolescu, I., & Suciu, D. (1999). Query optimization in the presence of limited access patterns. In *Proceedings of ACM SIGMOD Conference on Management of Data,* (pp. 311–322).

Friedman, M., & Weld, D. (1997). Efficiently executing information-gathering plans. In *Proceedings of IJCAI-97.*

Haas, L., Kossmann, D., Wimmers, E., & Yang, J. (1997). Optimizing queries across diverse data sources. In *Proceedings of VLDB Conference.*

Haas, P., & Swami, A. (1992). Sequential sampling procedures for query estimation. In *Proceedings of VLDB Conference.*

Hoffmann, J., Weber, I., Kaczmarek, T., & Ankolekar, A. (2008). *Combining scalability and expressivity in the automatic composition of Semantic Web Services* (pp. 98–107). ICWE.

Hou, W., Ossoyoglu, G. & Doglu. (1991). Error-constrained count query evaluation in relational databases. In *Proceedings of SIGMOD.*

Khomenko, V., Koutny, M., & Vogler, W. (2002). Canonical prefixes of petri net unfoldings. In *CAV '02: Proceedings of the 14th International Conference on Computer Aided Verification,* (pp. 582–595). London: Springer-Verlag.

Ko, J. M., Kim, C. O., & Kwon, I.-H. (2008). Quality-of-Service oriented Web Service composition algorithm and planning architecture. *Journal of Systems and Software, 81*(11), 2079–2090. doi:10.1016/j.jss.2008.04.044

Kuter, U., Sirin, E., Nau, D. S., Parsia, B., & Hendler, J. A. (2004). Information gathering during planning for Web Service composition. In *Proceedings of the International Semantic Web Conference (ISWC),* (p. 335-349).

Levy, A., Rajaraman, A., & Ordille, J. (1996). Querying heterogeneous information sources using source descriptions. In *Proceedings of the VLDB Conference.*

Ling, Y., & Sun, W. (1992). A supplement to Sampling-based methods for query size estimation in a database system. *SIGMOD Record, 21*(4), 12–15. doi:10.1145/141818.141820

Lipton, R., & Naughton, J. (1990). Query size estimation by adaptive sampling (Extended Abstract). In *PODS '90: Proceedings of the 9th ACM SIGACT-SIGMOD-SIGART Symposium on Principles of Database Systems,* (pp. 40–46).

Lipton, R., Naughton, J., & Schneider, D. (1990). Practical selectivity estimation through adaptive sampling. In *Proceedings of SIGMOD,* (pp. 1–11).

Majithia, S., Walker, D. W., & Gray, W. A. (2004). Automated composition of Semantic Grid services. In *Proceedings of AHM.*

Martinez, E., & Lesperance, Y. (2004). Web Service composition as a planning task: Experiments using knowledge-based planning. In *ICAPS-P4WGS.*

Meyer, H., & Weske, M. (2006). *Automated service composition using heuristic search.* (LNCS 4102), (pp. 81-96).

Ouzzani, M., & Bouguettaya, A. (2004). Query processing and optimization on the Web. *Distributed and Parallel Databases, 15*(3), 187–218. doi:10.1023/B:DAPD.0000018574.71588.06

Paolucci, M., Kawamura, T., Payne, T. R., & Sycara, K. P. (2002). Semantic matching of Web Services capabilities. In *Proceedings of the International Semantic Web Conference,* (p. 333-347).

Papakonstantinou, Y., Gupta, A., & Haas, L. (1996). Capabilities-based query rewriting in mediator systems. In *Conference on Parallel and Distributed Information Systems.*

Rahmani, H., GhasemSani, G. & Abolhassani, H. (2008). Automatic Web Service composition considering user non-functional preferences. *Next Generation Web Services Practices, 0,* 33–38. doi:10.1109/NWeSP.2008.27

Rainer, A. (2006). Web Service composition using answer set programming. In *PuK.*

Reddy, K. K., Maralla, K., Kumar, R., & Thirumaran, M. (2009). A greedy approach with criteria factors for QoS-based Web Service discovery. In *COMPUTE '09: Proceedings of the 2nd Bangalore Annual Compute Conference,* (pp. 1–5).

Ruckhaus, E., Ruiz, E., & Vidal, M.-E. (2008). Query evaluation and optimization in the Semantic Web. *TPLP, 8*(3), 393–409.

Sirin, E. (2004). *OWL-S API.*

Srivastava, U., Munagala, K., Widom, J., & Motwani, R. (2006). Query optimization over Web Services. In *VLDB'2006: Proceedings of the 32nd International Conference on Very Large Data Bases,* (pp. 355–366). VLDB Endowment.

Tomasic, A., Raschid, L. & Valduriez, P. (1998). Scaling access to distributed heterogeneous data sources with Disco. *IEEE Transactions On Knowledge and Data Engineering.*

Traverso, P., & Pistore, M. (2004). Automatic composition of Semantic Web Services into executable processes. In *Proceedings of the International Semantic Web Conference (ISWC).*

Wada, H., Champrasert, P., Suzuki, J., & Oba, K. (2008). Multiobjective optimization of SLA-aware service composition. In *Proceedings of IEEE Congress on Services, Workshop on Methodologies for Non-functional Properties in Services Computing.*

Wolstencroft, P. A., Hull, D., Wroe, C., Lord, P., Stevens, R., & Goble, C. (2007). The myGrid ontology: Bioinformatics service discovery. *International Journal of Bioinformatics Research and Applications*, *3*(3), 303–325. doi:10.1504/IJBRA.2007.015005

Yu, H.Q. & Rei -Marganiec, S. (2008). Non-functional property-based service selection: A survey and classification of approaches. In *Proceedings of the Non-Functional Properties and Service Level Agreements in Service Oriented Computing Workshop co-located with The 6th IEEE European Conference on Web Services.*

Zadorozhny, V., Bright, L., Raschid, L., Urhan, T., & Vidal, M.-E. (2000). *Web query optimizer.* International Conference on Data Engineering, (p. 661).

Zadorozhny, V., Raschid, L., Vidal, M., Urhan, T., & Bright, L. (2002). Efficient evaluation of queries in a mediator for WebSources. In *Proceedings of the ACM SIGMOD Conference on the Management of Data.*

ENDNOTES

1 This definition is taken from (Kyselov, 2006).

2 We use a similar definition as the one presented in (Brogi et al., 2005).

3 For the purpose of this work, we will assume that SAM finds solutions in Step 3. If SAM reaches Step 4, the problem becomes NP-hard, because sub-sets of failed solutions need to be combined (Step 4 of the algorithm).

4 The calculation of this set is based on the condition previously stated i.e., there is no need to calculate G1 $\oplus*$ G for every possible G.

Chapter 9
Web Services Composition Problem:
Model and Complexity

Fahima Cheikh
Université de Toulouse, France

ABSTRACT

In the approach taken in this chapter, the composition problem is as follows: given a client service, a goal service and a set of available services, determine if there exists a mediator service that enables the communication between the client and the existing services in order to satisfy the client request, represented by the goal service. In this chapter's model, available services that have access control constraints are considered. To formally capture these constraints, the chapter defines Web Services as Conditional Communicating Automata (CCA) in which communication is done through bounded ports. This chapter gives a detailed presentation of said model and gives complexity results of the composition problem.

INTRODUCTION

Service oriented computing (Singh & Huhns, 2005) is a programming paradigm which allow the realization of distributed applications by composing existing services. In particular, in order to realize a client request that is not realizable by the existing services, an eventual solution is to combine/compose the available services.

Several approaches are investigated for the composition problem. A survey can be found in Dustdar and Schreiner (2005) and Hull and Su (2005), using formal methods. Other authors use a planning method (Pistore, Marconi, Bertoli & Traverso, 2005; Pistore, Traverso & Bertoli, 2005), a theorem prover method (Rao, Küngas & Matskin, 2004), and a method based on propositional dy-

DOI: 10.4018/978-1-60960-493-6.ch009

namic logic (Berardi, Calvanese, De Giacomo & Micelle, 2006; Berardi, Calvanese, De Giacomo, Hull & Mecella, 2005). In section 3, we discuss in detail all these approaches. More precisely, for each of them, we answer the following questions:

- How services are defined?
- How the request/goal is defined?
- How services are composed?

In our approach, the composition problem is as follows: given a client service, a goal service and a set of available services, to determine if there exists a mediator service which allows the communication between the client and the existing services in order to obtain a system with a behavior equivalent to the goal service. To represent equivalence between two systems, we use one of these relations: trace inclusion, trace equivalence, simulation and bisimulation. Further, in our model, each available service has a security policies. These policies describe the conditions the user of the service should satisfy. For example, conditions can be about the value of credentials/certificate attributes. In our model, services are represented by Conditional Communicating Automata (CCA) in which both communicating actions and internal actions are possible. The communication is done through bounded ports. Moreover, the transitions are augmented by guards that ensure the system security (Cheikh, De Giacomo & Mecella, 2006; Mecella, Ouzzani, Paci & Bertino, 2006).

The chapter is organized as follows. In section 3 we discuss the related works cited above and compare them with our model. In section 4, we give basic definitions on automata. Then, in section 5, we define the notion of conditional communicating automata (CCA). In section 6, we present our model of services and we formally define the composition problem in section 7. Section 8 provides complexity results about the composition problem. We finally conclude in section 9.

RELATED WORKS

Several formal approaches investigated the issue of Web services composition. These approaches differ in several aspects. In fact, they do not use the same formal model to represent services and they do not consider the same definition of the composition problem. In this section, we briefly overview some of these approaches. For each one, we give the answer to the following questions:

- How services are defined?
- How the request/goal is defined?
- How services are composed?

In the approach proposed by Pistore, Traverso and Bertoli (2005), the authors propose a model where Web services are BPEL files. Formally, Web services are defined as State Transition Systems where communicating and internal actions are possible. However, the internal actions of the available services are non-observable. The goal is defined as an EaGLe formula (Dal Lago, U., Pistore, M., & Traverso, 2002) to satisfy and the composition problem is defined as follows: given a set of available services and a goal, synthesize a process that interacts asynchronously with the available services and satisfies the requirements. Formally, the asynchronous product of the available services is the planning domain, the goal represents the formula to satisfy and the composite service is obtained from the solution plan. The authors present their experimental results with different applications. However, they do not give neither an upper bound nor a lower bound complexity of the problem.

In the approach proposed by Rao, Kungas and Matskin (2004), the authors consider semantic Web services. In practice, they are described by the DAML-S language. Formally, Web services are described as axioms of the Linear Logic (LL). Whereas the goal is represented by a sequent of this logic. The composition problem is defined as follow: given a set of available Web services, find a composition of the available services that satisfies the client requirement. Formally, given a set of axioms and a sequent prove the theorem. To solve the problem, the authors use a theorem prover of LL. In particular, if the sequent is proved then a process calculus is extracted from the proof. This process represent the composed services. The proposed method is correct and complete.

In the approach proposed by Mitra, Kumar and Basu (2007), the authors consider Web service interfaces. In practice, interfaces use the WS-BPEL, OWLS and WSDL. Formally, services and the goal are defined as I/O automata. The composition problem is defined as follows: given a goal service and available services, does there exist a choreographer such that the goal service is simulated by the asynchronous product of the available services and the choreographer. Two restrictions are considered in this approach. Services communicate only with the choreographer and the choreographer is not able to produce inputs. The authors do not give complexity results concerning the proposed method. This approach is different from our, because internal actions are not considered. In addition, there is neither guards nor effects in transitions.

In the approach proposed by Berardi, Calvanese, De Giacomo, Hull and Mecella (2005), the authors consider semantic Web services. Formally, Web services are defined as guarded automata. In these automata communication can be performed through ports and internal actions are also possible. Moreover, in order to perform a transition, conditions should be satisfied. The authors consider a database shared by the available services and the goal service and the composition problem is defined as follows: given a goal service, a client service and a set of available services, select a family of services (from the existing set) and synthesize a mediator service such that: the asynchronous product of the goal service and the client service is isomorphic, modulo communicating actions, to the asynchronous product of the client service, the mediator service and the available services. In order to solve this problem, the authors proposed a reduction to the satisfiability problem of a propositional dynamic logic formula. However, they considered the following restrictions:

- strict mediation: the available services communicate only with the mediator,
- the mediator has a bounded number of internal variables and a bounded number of states,
- the available services are deterministic,
- blocking behavior: when available services send messages, they block or they wait for a message receive and
- bounded access: the number of messages sent by the clients are bounded by the number of messages received by them. In addition, the number of Key-based research done by the goal are bounded by the number of messages sent by the client.

The authors proved that, when these restrictions are considered, the problem can be solved in double exponential time.

In the approach proposed by Pathak, Basu, Lutz and Honavar (2006), the authors propose a model where Web services are BPEL files. This approach is inspired by the COLOMBO model. More precisely, services are defined as Symbolic Transition Systems (STS). An STS is a transition system with guards. In these systems, both communicating actions and internal actions can be performed. Furthermore, the goal is also defined as an STS. The composition problem is defined as follows: given a goal service and a set of available services, identify a subset of the available services and synthesize a choreographer that orchestrate the necessary interactions among the selected services, such that the product of the available services and the choreographer is bisimilar to the goal service. Here, the product is asynchronous with respect to internal actions and synchronous with respect to communicating actions. The authors proposed a correct and complete algorithm to solve the composition problem. The proposed algorithm takes an exponential time.

Comparison of our Approach with the Existing Ones

In the approaches described above, two categories can be distinguished. In the first one (Pistore, Traverso & Bertoli, 2005; Rao, Kungas & Matskin 2004), the aim is to create a new service that orchestrate the existing services in order to satisfy a logical formula, where a formula represents, for example, client requirements. In the second category (Mitra, Kumar & Basu, 2007; Berardi, Calvanese, De Giacomo, Hull & Mecella, 2005; Pathak, Basu, Lutz & Honavar, 2006), the composition is based on a desired service model, called a goal service. More precisely, the objective is to orchestrate existing services in order to obtain a behavior equivalent to the goal service behavior. Our approach belongs to the second category, and is inspired from the work done by (Berardi, Calvanese, De Giacomo, Hull & Mecella, 2005).

The approach proposed by Mitra, Kumar and Basu (2007) belongs to our category. Simulation relation between automata also interests the authors. However, the main difference between us is that they do not consider internal actions. In their model, services can only communicate. Another difference is that they consider the restriction of strict mediation. This means that the communication is not possible between existing services.

Since our approach is close to the one proposed by (Berardi, Calvanese, De Giacomo, G., Hull & Mecella, 2005), it would be interesting to compare them. Like the COLOMBO model, we consider that Web services perform both communication and internal actions. Notions of client service, goal service and mediator service are also inspired from the COLOMBO model. The difference between our model and the COLOMBO model is that we do not consider a shared data base. The reason is that we suppose that services are independent and do not necessary use the same data. However, we consider a shared set of propositionnel variables. Intuitively, this set represents informations about the client (his age, the credit card he owns...). From a technical point of view, our results remain valid if we consider that this set is an abstraction of the COLOMBO data base. The second difference is that the authors consider some restrictions such as: "bounded access", "blocking behavior", "bounded mediator ", "strict mediator " and that services are deterministic. These restrictions are not considered in our model. Finally, we do not consider the same equivalence relations. In (Berardi, Calvanese, De Giacomo, G., Hull & Mecella, 2005) the authors consider an isomorphism between two systems. This equivalence relation is more restrictive than the equivalences we consider. Indeed, in our approach the purpose is to make services able to execute action sequences executed by the goal service, but not necessary with the same number of states. Nevertheless, in the approach proposed by (Pathak, Basu, Lutz & Honavar, 2006), the authors propose a model close to the COLOMBO model. In this model, instead the isomorphism relation they consider the bisimulaiton relation. But, they consider the COLOMBO model restrictions.

Finite Automata

The model we consider, to represent Web services, is based on automata. In this section, we first give the needed background on automata. More precisely, we define four equivalences and preorder relations between automata namely: the trace inclusion, the trace equivalence, the simulation and the bisimulation.

Definition. (Automaton) An *automaton* over a finite set of actions Σ is a structure $A=(Q,q_0\rightarrow)$ such that:

- Q is a finite set of states,
- q_0 is the initial state and
- $\rightarrow\subseteq Q\times\Sigma Q$ is the transition relation.

For all $\Sigma' \subseteq \Sigma$, the relation $\rightarrow_A^{\Sigma'} \subseteq Q \times Q$ describes how the automaton can move from one state to another in 1 step under some action in Σ'. Formally, $(q, q') \in \rightarrow_A^{\Sigma'}$ iff there exist $a \in \Sigma'$ such that $(q, a, q') \in \rightarrow$. We denote $(q, q') \in \rightarrow_A^{\Sigma'}$ by $q \rightarrow_A^{\Sigma'} q'$. Furthermore, let $\rightarrow_A^{\Sigma'^*}$ be the reflexive and transitive closure of $\rightarrow_A^{\Sigma'}$. For all $\Sigma' \subseteq \Sigma$, we shall say that A loops over Σ' iff for all $a \in \Sigma'$, $\rightarrow_A^{\{a\}} = Id_Q$. The automaton will be represented by a graph. The nodes of the graph are the states of the automaton and the arcs are its transitions.

Definition. (Trace of automaton) Let Σ' be a finite set of actions and $A=(Q,q_0,\rightarrow)$ an automaton over Σ. A *path* for A modulo Σ' is a finite sequence of the form (q_0,a_1,q_1), $(q_1,a_2,q_2),\cdots,(q_{n-1},a_n,q_n)$ such that:

$$q_i \rightarrow_A^{\Sigma'^*} \circ \rightarrow_A^{\{a_{i+1}\}} \circ \rightarrow_A^{\Sigma'^*} q_{i+1} \text{ where } i \in \{0,\ldots,n\text{-}1\}.$$

The word $a_1 \ldots a_n$ is its trace. The empty word is represented by ε. The set of all words traces for A modulo Σ' is denoted $Tr_{\Sigma'}(A)$. Here, modulo Σ' means when actions in Σ' are non-observable.

Example. Let us consider the following finite automaton $A^1 = (\{q_0^1, q_1^1, q_2^1, q_3^1\}, q_0^1 \rightarrow_{A^1})$ over $\Sigma=\{a,b\}$ such that:

- $(q_0^1, a, q_1^1) \in \rightarrow_{A^1}$,
- $(q_0^1, a, q_2^1) \in \rightarrow_{A^1}$ and
- $(q_2^1, b, q_3^1) \in \rightarrow_{A^1}$.

The automaton A^1 is represented by the graph in Figure 1. The set of A^1 traces modulo the empty set is $Tr_{\varnothing}(A^1)=\{\varepsilon,a,ab\}$.

Definition. (Synchronous product of automata) Let $A^1 = (Q^1, q_0^1, \rightarrow_{A^1})$ and $A^2 = (Q^2, q_0^2, \rightarrow_{A^2})$ be automaton over Σ. By $A^1{\times}A^2$, we denote the synchronous product of A^1 and A^2 and is defined by the structure $A=(Q,q_0,\rightarrow)$ over Σ such that:

Figure 1. Finite automaton A^1

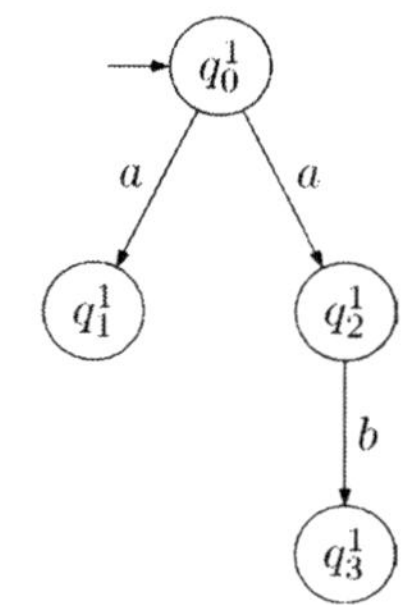

- $Q=Q^1{\times}Q^2$,
- $q_0 = (q_0^1, q_0^2)$ and
- $\rightarrow \subseteq Q{\times}\Sigma Q$ is the transition relation defined by: $\left((q_1^1, q_1^2), a, (q_1^1, q_2^1)\right) \in \rightarrow$ iff $(q_1^1, a, q_2^1) \in \rightarrow_{A^1}$ and $(q_1^2, a, q_2^2) \in \rightarrow_{A^2}$.

In the synchronous product of automata, an action is executed from a state (q_1^1, q_1^2), iff this action is executed in A^1 from q_1^1 and in A^2 from q_1^2. This notion of synchronous product of automata is used in order to describe the controller synthesis problem.

Example. Consider the automata A^1 and A^2 from Figure 2. The synchronous product of these automata is represented in Figure 3.

Figure 2. From top to bottom, finite automaton A^1 and A^2

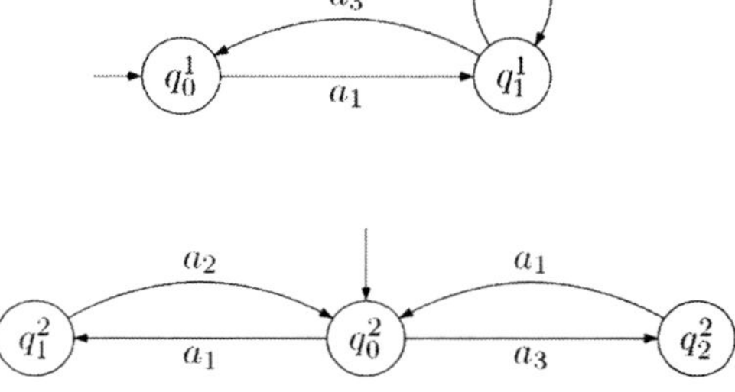

Figure 3. Finite automaton $A^1 \times A^2$

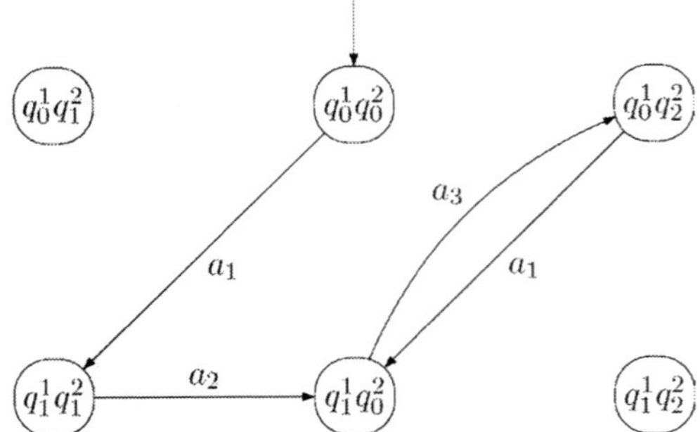

Equivalences and Preorders

In order to define the composition problem we need to compare two systems. In one hand, we consider the system representing the client goal. On the other hand, we consider the system representing the available services. Thus, it is important to define formally the equivalence and/or the preorder we choose. In our approach, we are interested in the most used equivalences and preorders: trace inclusion (Hoare, 1978, 1985), trace equivalence (Hoare, 1978, 1985), simulation (Park, 1981; Milner, 1989) and bisimulaition (Park, 1981; Milner, 1989). In the following definitions the set Σ' represents the set of non-observable actions.

Definition. (Trace inclusion) Let $A^1 = (Q^1, q_0^1, \rightarrow_{A^1})$ and $A^1 = (Q^1, q_0^1, \rightarrow_{A^1})$ be automaton over.ΣFor all $\Sigma' \subseteq \Sigma$, we shall say that A^1 is trace included in A^2 modulo Σ', denoted $A^1 \subseteq_{tr} A^2(\Sigma')$, iff $Tr_{\Sigma'}(A^1) \subseteq Tr_{\Sigma'}(A^2)$

Example. Let us consider the automata A^1 and A^2 represented in Figure 4. In this case, $Tr_{\varnothing}(A^1)=\{\varepsilon,a,ab\}$ et $Tr_{\varnothing}(A^2)=\{\varepsilon,a,c,ab\}$. Consequently, $Tr_{\varnothing}(A^1) \subseteq Tr_{\varnothing}(A^2)$ Hence, the automaton A^1 is trace included in A^2, when all the actions are observable Consequently, all action sequences executed by A^1 can also be executed by A^2. However, one can observe that A^2 can execute more sequences than A^1. Indeed, A^1 cannot execute the sequence containing the single action "c"

Figure 4. From left to right, automata A^1 and A^2

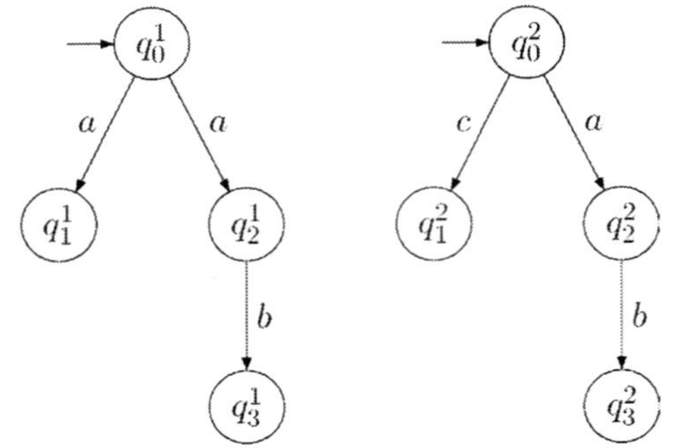

Definition. (Trace equivalence) Let $A^1 = (Q^1, q_0^1, \rightarrow_{A^1})$ and $A^2 = (Q^2, q_0^2, \rightarrow_{A^2})$ be automaton over Σ. For all $\Sigma' \subseteq \Sigma$, we shall say that A^1 and A^2 are trace equivalent modulo Σ', denoted $A^1 \equiv_{tr} A^2(\Sigma')$, iff $Tr_{\Sigma'}(A^1) = Tr_{\Sigma'}(A^2)$

Example. Let us consider the case where A^1 and A^2 are represented in Figure 5. In this case, the automata are trace equivalent. Indeed, $Tr_{\varnothing}(A^1)=Tr_{\varnothing}(A^2)=\{\varepsilon,a,ab\}$. Intuitively, action sequences are executable in A^1 iff they are executable in A^2.

In this example, it is possible for the automaton A^1 to reach a locked state after the execution of a, this is not the case for the automaton A^2. If we are intersted by a comparison, based on states, between the behavir of automata then the appropriate relations are the simulation and the bisimulation

Figure 5. From left to right, automata A^1 and A^2

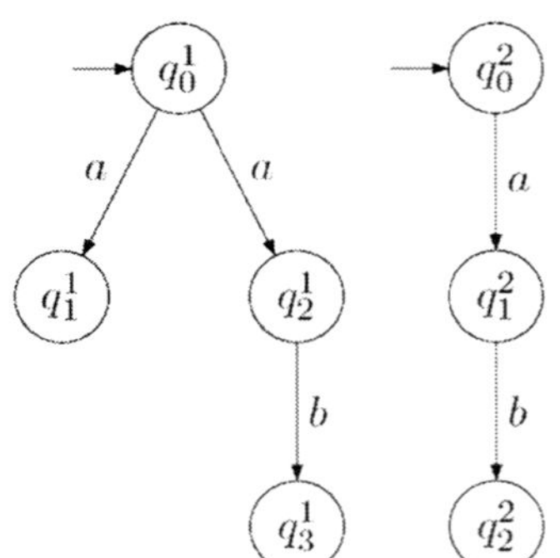

Figure 6. From left to right, automata A^1 and A^2

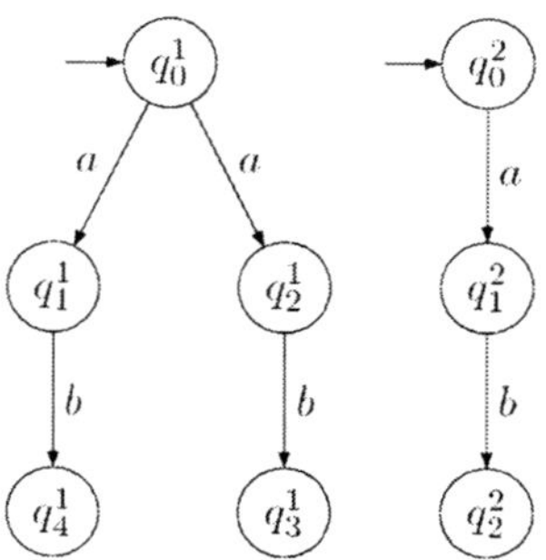

Definition. (Simulation) Let $A^1 = (Q^1, q_0^1, \rightarrow_{A^1})$ and $A^2 = (Q^2, q_0^2, \rightarrow_{A^2})$ be automaton over Σ. For all $\Sigma' \subseteq \Sigma$, a relation $Z \subseteq Q^1 \times Q^2$ such that $(q_0^1, q_0^2) \in Z$ (also denoted $q_0^1 \; Z \; q_0^2$) is called simulation between A^1 and A^2 modulo Σ' iff for all $(q_1^1, q_1^2) \in Z$ and for all $a \in \Sigma \setminus \Sigma'$ the following conditions are satisfied:

For all $q_2^1 \in Q^1$, if $q_1^1 \rightarrow_{A^1}^{\Sigma'^*} \circ \rightarrow_{A^1}^{\{a\}} \circ \rightarrow_{A^1}^{\Sigma'^*} q_2^1$ then there exists $q_2^2 \in Q^2$ such that $q_1^2 \rightarrow_{A^2}^{\Sigma'^*} \circ \rightarrow_{A^2}^{\{a\}} \circ \rightarrow_{A^2}^{\Sigma'^*} q_2^2$ and $(q_2^1, q_2^2) \in Z$.

Moreover, for all $\Sigma' \subseteq \Sigma$ if there is a simulation between A^1 and A^2modulo Σ' then we shall write $A^1 \leq_{si} A^2(\Sigma')$ and we shall say that A^1 is *simulated* by A^2 modulo. Σ'

Definition. (Bisimulation) A relation $Z \subseteq Q^1 \times Q^2$ such that $(q_0^1, q_0^2) \in Z$ is said to be bisimulation between A^1 and A^2 modulo Σ' iff Z and Z^{-1} are simulation between A^1 and A^2 modulo Σ'.

Moreover, for all $\Sigma' \subseteq \Sigma$, if there is a bisimulation between A^1 and A^2 modulo Σ' then we shall write $A^1 \leftrightarrow_{bi} A^2(\Sigma')$ and we shall say that A^1 and A^2 are bisimilar modulo Σ'.

Recall that in the case of deterministic automata, the trace inclusion (resp. the trace equivalence) and the simulation (resp. bisimulation) are the same relations. It is not the case when the automata are non deterministic. Indeed, the simulation (resp. bisimulation) relation is more restrictive than the trace inclusion (resp. equivalence).

Example. In Figure 5, the automaton A^1 is simulated by the automaton A^2. On the other hand, these automata are not bisimilar. Once the automaton A^1 performed action a it is possible to be in a state where it is impossible to execute action b, it is not the case of the automaton A^2. In Figure 6, the automata A^1 and A^2 are bisimilar.

CONDITIONAL COMMUNICATING AUTOMATA (CCA)

Representing Web services by formal methods is not new (Foster, Uchitel, Magee & Kramer, 2007; Pistore, Traverso & Bertoli, 2005; Berardi, Calvanese, De Giacomo, G., Hull & Mecella, 2005). There exist several works that propose methods to transform Web service from given files to formal structures. Web services are able to: communicate, to verify conditions before an action execution and to change the value of variables after an action execution. In order to model these three key aspects, we use what we call CCA. In our approach, we suppose that services are already transformed into CCA. The CCA are an extension of automata. They contain specific actions called communicating actions and they contain preconditions and effects in their transitions. In our model, the preconditions and effects are represented by sets of literals over a finite set of atomic formulas, denoted *At*. We consider two kinds of communicating actions; message received through a port and message sent through a port. Without loss of generality and for technical reasons, we suppose that a port can contain at most one message at a time. Let *Port* be the finite set of ports that services can share.

Definition. (Literals) The set of literals over *At* is defined by $Li(At) = At \cup \{\neg p : p \in At\}$.

Definition. (Consistent set) A set $J \in 2^{Li(At)}$ is consistent iff for all $p \in At$, $p \notin J$ or $\neg p \notin J$.

Figure 7. Conditional communicating automaton Ac^1.

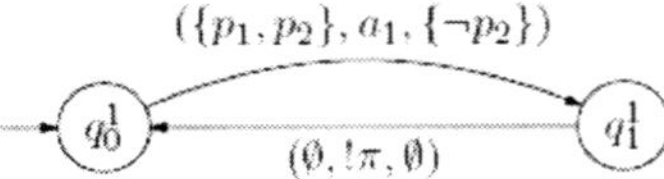

Definition. (Maximal set) The set $J \in 2^{Li(At)}$ is maximal iff for all $r \in At$, $r \in J$ or $\neg r \in J$.

Definition. (Conditional communicating automata) A conditional communicating automaton over $\Sigma \cup (\{!,?\} \times Port)$ and At is a structure $Ac=(Q,q_0,\delta)$ such that:

- Q is a finite set of states,
- q_0 is the initial state,
- $\delta \subseteq 2^{Li(At)} \times Q \times (\Sigma \cup (\{!,?\} \times Port)) \times Q \times 2^{Li(At)}$ is the transition relation.

For all literal sets $J, J' \in 2^{Li(At)}$, for all states $q, q' \in Q$ and for all actions $a \in \Sigma \cup (\{!,?\} \times Port)$, $(J, q, a, q', J') \in \delta$ means that the conditions for the execution of a from q to q' are represented by the set J and the effects of this execution are represented by the set J'. In order to simplify the notation, elements $(?,\pi)$ (resp. $(!,\pi)$) in $\{!,?\} \times Port$ are denoted $?\pi$ (resp. $!\pi$). The action $?\pi$ means that a message is received through the port π. The action $!\pi$ means that a message is sent through the port π.

Example. As an example, let us consider the CCA Ac^1 over $\Sigma \cup (\{!,?\} \times Port)$ and At, represented in Figure 7, where $\Sigma=\{a_1,a_2\}$, $Port=\{\pi\}$ and $At=\{p_1,p_2\}$.

Products of CCA

Products of CCA are used to represent systems composed of several CCA. The product can be synchronous or asynchronous. The asynchronous product is used when the concerned CCA are independent (or concurrent), whereas, the synchronous product is used when each CCA have

Figure 8. Conditional communicating automaton Ac^2

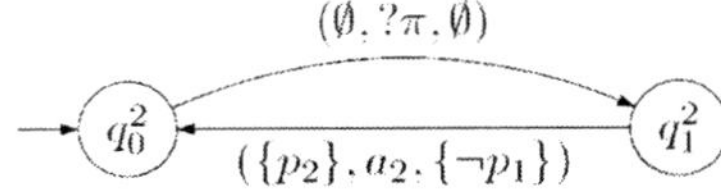

to be synchronized with others. In our model the appropriate product is the asynchronous one.

Definition. (CCA asynchronous product) Let $Ac^1 = (Q^1, q_0^1, \delta^1)$ and $Ac^2 = (Q^2, q_0^2, \delta^2)$ be two conditional communicating automata over $\Sigma \cup (\{!,?\} \times Port)$ and At. The asynchronous product of Ac^1 and Ac^2 is denoted $Ac^1 \otimes Ac^2$, and is defined by the structure $Ac=(Q,q_0,\delta)$ over $\Sigma \cup (\{!,?\} \times Port)$ and At such that:

- $Q=Q^1 \times Q^2$,
- $q_0 = (q_0^1, q_0^2)$ and
- $\delta \subseteq 2^{Li(At)} \times Q \times (\Sigma \cup (\{!,?\} \times Port)) \times Q \times 2^{Li(At)}$ is the relation defined by $(J,(q_1^1,q_1^2),a,(q_2^1,q_2^2),J') \in \delta$ iff $(J,q_1^1,a,q_2^1,J') \in \delta^1$ and $q_2^2 = q_1^2$ or $(J,q_1^2,a,q_2^2,J') \in \delta^2$ and $q_2^1 = q_1^1$.

Example. Consider the sets Σ+{a_1,a_2}, Port={π}, At={p_1,p_2} and the *CCA* Ac^1 and Ac^2 *over* $\Sigma \cup (\{!,?\} \times Port)$ and At, respectively represented in Figure 7 and Figure 8. The asynchronous product of Ac^1 and Ac^2 is represented in Figure 9. The dashed arcs are the transitions

Figure 9. Conditional communicating automaton $Ac^1 \otimes Ac^2$

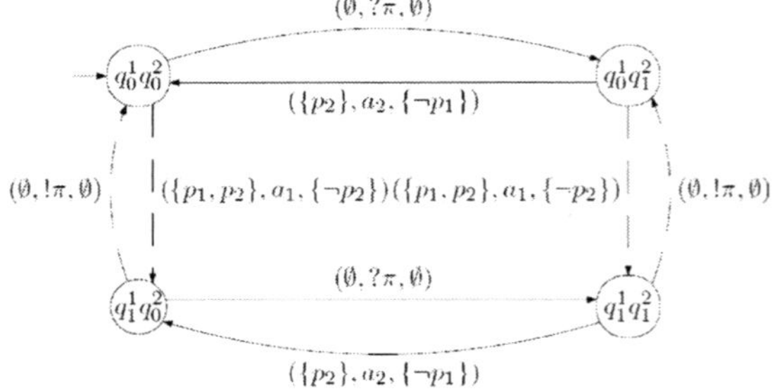

performed by Ac[1] and the rest of the arcs are the transitions performed by Ac[2].

The Execution of CCA

In order to characterize the dynamic aspect of a CCA, i.e., the evolution of the atomic formulas and the ports content, we use the finite automata. We suppose that ports are initially empty. In addition, the initialization of the atomic formulas is represented by a maximal consistent set of literals $I_0 \subseteq Li(At)$.

Definition. (Execution of CCA). Let $Ac=(Q,q_0,\delta)$ be a CCA over $\Sigma \cup (\{!,?\} \times Port)$ and At. We call execution of Ac, the automaton $Exec(Ac, I_0) = (Q', q_0', \rightarrow')$ defined over $\Sigma \cup (\{!,?\} \times Port)$ such that:

- $Q' = \{(q,\gamma,I) \mid q \in Q, \gamma : Port \rightarrow N$ and $I \subseteq Li(At)$ is a maximal consistent set $\}$,
- $q_0' = (q_0, \gamma_0, I_0)$ where $\forall \pi \in Port, \gamma_0(\pi)=0$ and
- $\rightarrow' \subseteq Q' \times \Sigma \cup (\{!,?\} \times Port) \times Q'$ is the transition relation defined by $((q,\gamma,I), a, (q',\gamma',I')) \in \rightarrow'$ iff there exist a transition $(J, q, a, q', J') \in \delta$ such that $J \subseteq I$ and $I' = (I \setminus \neg J') \cup J'$ where : $\neg J' = \{p \neg p \in J'\} \cup \{\neg p : p \in J'\}$: and one of the following conditions is satisfied
    - $a \in \Sigma$ and $\gamma = \gamma'$,
    - $a=?\pi$, $\gamma(\pi)=1$, $\gamma'(\pi) = 0$ and $\gamma'(\pi') = \gamma(\pi)$ for $\pi' \neq \pi$ and
    - $a=!\pi$, $\gamma(\pi)=0$, $\gamma'(\pi) = 1$ and $\gamma'(\pi') = \gamma(\pi)$ for $\pi' \neq \pi$.

Intuitively, in the definition of $Exec(Ac,I_0)$, for all ports π, $\gamma(\pi)$ represents the actual number of messages in π and I represent the actual value of the atomic formulas. The set of all possible γ functions is denoted Γ. Concerning the transitions. From a state (q,γ,I) to a state (q',γ',I'), it is possible to perform a transition labelled by a only if:

Figure 10. Finite automaton $Exec(Ac^1,I_0)$

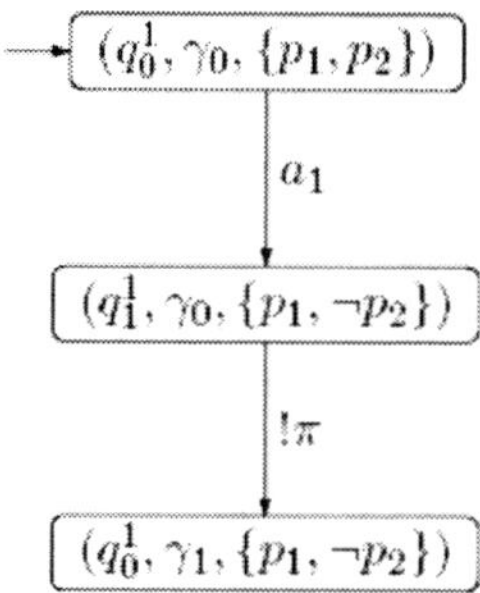

conditions to execute a are satisfied and the effects of a are considered in the state (q',γ',I'). Moreover, the implicit conditions of communicating actions are satisfied and their implicit effects are considered. More precisely, the implicit condition of the action $!\pi$ (resp. $?\pi$) is that π is empty (resp. full). The implicit effect of the action $!\pi$ ($?\pi$) is that π is full (resp. empty).

Example. Let us consider the CCA Ac^1 in Figure 7. The finite automaton that represent the execution of Ac^1 is in Figure 10. In this figure, $\gamma_0(\pi)=0$ and $\gamma_1(\pi)=1$ is initialized by $I_0=\{p_1,p_2\}$. Actions a_1 and$!\pi$ cannot be performed more than once. The reason is that the condition to perform $a=1$ is no longer satisfied after its execution and the execution of$!\pi$ depend of those of a_1. Observe, that the non accessible states are not represented in the figure. The total number of states is 16.

Web Services Model

In an open communication, as it is the case in the internet, the service providers and their clients do not know each other. Thus, it is necessary to find a way to establish trust between them. As example, in one hand, providers need a guarantee that they will be paid. On the other hand, clients need a guarantee that their personnel information will not be reused without their permission. Among the existing methods to establish a trust relationship providers/clients, there is the use of credentials (certificates). Credentials represent assertions about a service. This service can be a client or a provider. These credentials (Mecella, Ouzzani, Paci & Bertino, 2006) are issued by an authority certification that sign the credential with a private key. Credentials are authenticated using the public key of their issuer.

Definition. (Credential) A credential is a structure *Cred=(Attr, Issuer)* such that:

- *Attr* is an attribute (name, date of birth, ...) and
- *Issuer* is the name of the service that issued the credential.

Example. Consider the set of credentials $Cred=\{C_1,C_2\}$ such that $C_1=(MasterCr, SGBank)$ and $C_2=(VisaCr, CLBank)$. These credentials are credit cards. They have as attributes: the type of the card and the name of the bank which has issued the card.

Our model is inspired by the COLOMBO model (Berardi, Calvanese, De Giacomo, G., Hull & Mecella, 2005). The model components are the following:

- available services $Ac^1,\ldots,Ac^n$,
- a goal service Ac^{gaol},
- a client service Ac^{client} and
- a mediator service Ac^{med}.

Web Services

Services perform internal actions and communicating actions. In order to execute these actions, some conditions can be required. For example, a possible condition concerns either the value of a credential attribute or the value of an internal variable. Furthermore, when actions are performed, effects are taken into account ?. To simplify our model, we represent all these conditions and effects by atomic formulas over the set *At*. In addition, the set of internal actions in denoted by the set Σ and the communication is done through the set *Port* of ports.

Example. The example we consider is inspired from (Pistore, Traverso & Bertoli, 2005). The example concerns the purchase and the delivery of books. The set of internal actions is Σ={ CheckAvail, Payment, Cancel, Complete} such that:

- *CheckAvail*: Check the book availability.
- P*ayment*: accept the payment.
- *Cancel*: Cancel the transaction.
- *Complete*: complete the transaction.

The set of ports is *Port*={ SelectPr, BInfo, SendPrice, BPrice, AnsPurch, ConfPurch, Fail, BFail, Success Description, DInfo, DeliveryPrice, DPrice, AnsDelivery, DConf, SucDelivery}. The ports are used for:

- *SelectPr, BInfo*: send/receive the book identification.
- *SendPrice, BPrice*: send/receive the book price.
- *AnsPurch,ConfPurch*: send/receive the confirmation of the book purchase.
- *Fail, BFail*: send/receive a message of transaction failure.
- *Success*: send/receive a message of transaction success.
- *Description, DInfo*: send/receive the type of the delivered product, the date and the place of delivery.
- *DeliveryPrice, DPrice*: send/receive the delivery price of a product.
- *AnsDelivery, DConf*: send/receive the confirmation that the product price is accepted.
- *SucDelivery*: send/receive a message of delivery success.

We consider the credentials of the previous example. Hence, the set of atomic formula *At*={Available, Acpt, MasterCr, VisaCr, SGBank, CLBank, Pay, AcptDelivery} such that:

- *Available*: is "true" if the book is available.

Figure 11. BookSell service

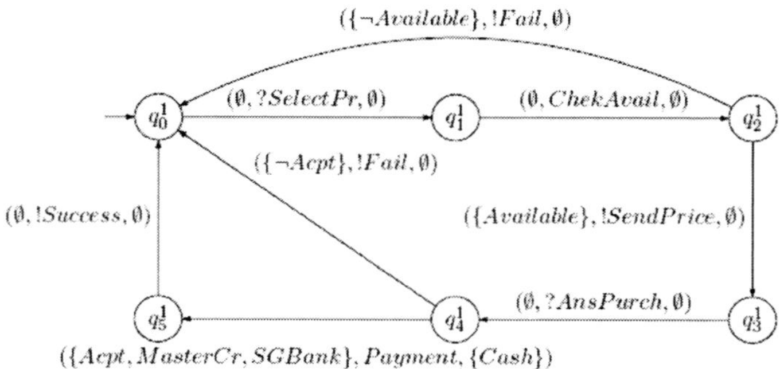

- *Acpt*: is "true" if the client accepts to pay the book.
- *MasterCr*: is "true" if the client own a card with the type *Master Card.*
- *VisaCr*: is "true" if the client own the card with the type *Visa Card.*
- *SGbank*: is "true" if the issuer of the credit card is the bank named *SGBank*.
- *CLbank*: is "true" if the issuer of the credit card is the bank named *CLBank*.
- *Cash*: is "true" if the payment of the book is accepted.
- *AcptDelivery*: is "true" if the client accepts to pay the delivery.

Definition. (Web service) A Web service is a CCA $Ac=(Q,q_0,\delta)$ over $\Sigma \cup (\{!,?\} \times Port)$ and *At*

Example. In this example, we consider that Σ, *Port* and *At* as in the previous example. Let us consider a service that sells books denoted *BookSell* and represented by the CCA Ac^1 (represented in Figure 11) defined over $\Sigma \cup (\{!,?\} \times Port)$ and *At*. In order to execute the *Payement* action, it is necessary that the client accepts to pay with a credit card of the type Master Card and the issuer *SGBank*. Formally, it means that the atomic formulas Acpt, MasterCr and SGBank must be satisfied. Once the payment is accepted the atomic formula *Cash* becomes true.

Example. Let us consider the service Delivery which allows the delivery of several kind of products in different places. This service is represented by the CCA Ac^2 of Figure 12.

Goal Service

When a programmer creates a new service, it is better for him to reuse existing services, to avoid wasting time. This programmer has a model of a desired service, called a goal service. This service is a virtual service, not referenced in the UDDI.

Figure 12. Delivery service

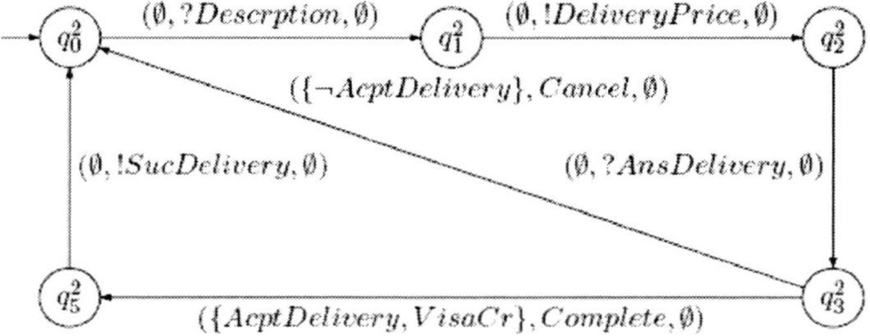

Figure 13. Goal service

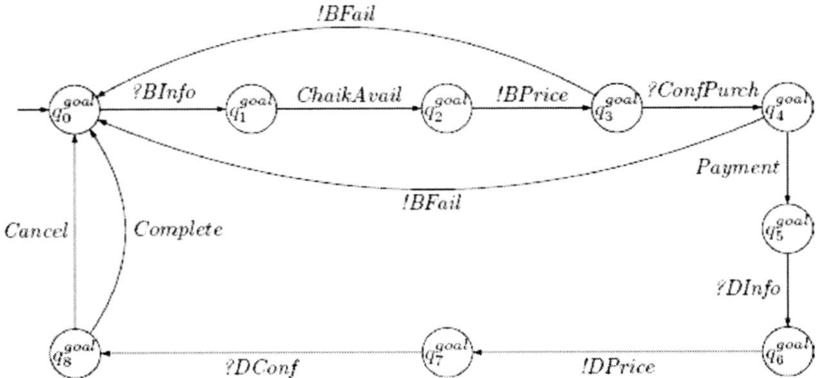

However, in ideal situation, it is possible to find among the available services, a service equivalent to the goal service. Generally, to realize this goal service it is necessary to use a mediator service that orchestrates existing services. When a client gives a request to the mediator service, he has the illusion that he communicate with a single service. Actually, the mediator will transfer this request to the adequate service, among the available services.

Definition. (Goal service) A goal service is aCCA $Ac^{goal} = (Q^{goal}, q_0^{goal}, \delta^{goal})$ over $\Sigma \cup (\{!,?\} \times Port)$ and At.

Example. Consider the goal service in Figure 13. It is a service that sells books and delivers products.

Client Service

The client service represents the user of the goal service and the mediator service. In our model, we do not need the complete description of the clients. It is enough to describe their interactions with services. Consequently, the CCA representing the client service contains only communicating actions possibly with conditions and effects.

Definition. (Client service) A *client service* is a CCA $Ac^{client} = (Q^{client}, q_0^{client}, \delta^{client})$ over $\{!,?\}\times Port$ and At, such that $Q^{client} = \{q_0^{client}, q_1^{client}\}$ and for all $\pi \in Port$ and all sets $J, J' \subseteq Li(At)$ we have:

- $(J, q_1^{client}, !\pi, q_i^{client}, J') \notin \delta^{client}$ where $q_i^{client} \in Q^{client}$, $i \in \{0,1\}$ and
- $(J, q_0^{client}, ?\pi, q_i^{client}, J') \notin \delta^{client}$ where $q_i^{client} \in Q^{client}$, $i \in \{0,1\}$.

Example. We consider a client who wants to purchase a book and to be delivered. We suppose that this client owns the credential of the previous examples. This client can be represented by the CCA from Figure 14. In this figure, observe that the label: (∅,!BInfo,∅)/(∅, !DInfo,∅)/(∅,!ConfPurch, ∅)/ (∅,!DConf, ∅) between q_0^{client} and q_1^{client} represents three different transitions.

Mediator Service

In our model the mediator service represents the composite service. His role is to orchestrate the available services in order to realise the goal service. Mediators play the role of an intermedi-

Figure 14. Client service

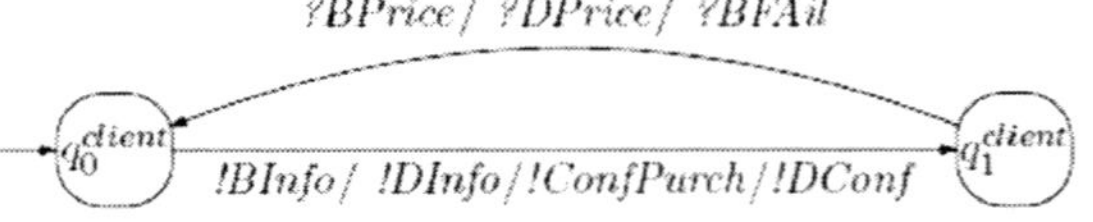

Figure 15. Mediator service

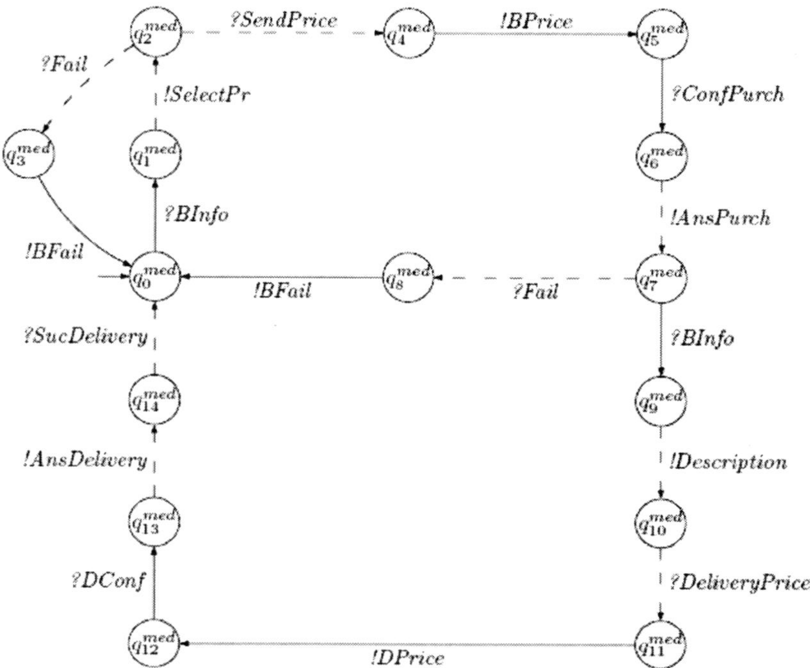

ate between the client service and the available services, by sending the information from one to another. Mediator services perform only exchanges of messages. They have conditions in their transitions, but they do not have effects.

Definition. (Mediator service) A mediator service is a CCA $Ac^{med} = (Q^{med}, q_0^{med}, \delta^{med})$ over $\{!,?\}\times Port$ and At such that $\delta^{med} \subseteq 2^{Li(At)} \times Q^{med} \times (\{!,?\} \times Port) \times Q^{med} \times 2^{\varnothing}$.

Example. Consider the mediator service from Figure 15. In this figure, the dashed arcs are the communications done between the client service and the mediator service. Whereas the plain arcs are the communications done between the mediator service and the available services, these actions are not observable for the client

Web Service Composition Problem

When a client wants to perform some operations and no available service of the community can execute all these operations, a possible solution is to combine the services of the community. Thus, Web services composition problem consists of linking services between them. Sometimes, a mediator service is required to enable this linkage. Some works as (Pistore, Marconi, Bertoli & Traverso, 2005), are interested in the linkage of services in order to verify some properties, for example "avoid the locked states". Also, several works (Berardi, Calvanese, De Giacomo, G., Hull & Mecella, 2005) are interested in the linkage of services in order to obtain a new service similar or equivalent to a predefined service. Our work belongs to the second category. More precisely, our composition problem is a decision problem defined as follows. Let $\approx \in \{\subseteq_{tr}, \equiv_{tr}, \leq_{si}, \leftrightarrow_{bi}\}$.

CP($\approx$)**problem: Composition problem**

Instance: a finite set of actions Σ, a finite sets of ports *Port* and $Port' \subseteq Port$, a finite set of atomic formulas *At*, a maximal consistent set of literals I_0 over *At*, a CCA Ac^{client} over $\{!,?\}\times Port$ and At and CCA Ac^{goal}, $Ac^1,\ldots,Ac^n$ over $\Sigma \cup (\{!,?\} \times Port)$ and *At*.

Question: does there exist a CCA Ac^{med} over $\{!,?\}\times Port$ and At, such that

$$Exec(Ac^{client} \otimes Ac^{goal}, I_0) \approx Exec(Ac^{client} \otimes Ac^{1} \otimes \ldots \otimes Ac^{n} \otimes Ac^{med}, I_0)(\{!,?\} \times Port')$$

In this definition, I_0 represents the initial value of the atomic formulas over At and $Exec(Ac,I_0)$ the execution or the behavior of a CCA Ac. Intuitively, the composition problem is to decide wether for a given client service, goal service and available services, there exists a mediator service such that when combined to the available services and the client service he has the same behavior as the client service combined with the goal service. We suppose that the communication between the mediator and the services is unobservable for the client service. For this reason, we consider an equivalence modulo $\{!,?\} \times Port'$, where $Port'$ is the set of ports used by the available services. The *CP* problem represents four different problems depending on the assignment of $\approx$ to $\subseteq_{tr}$, $\equiv_{tr}$, $\leq_{si}$, or $\leftrightarrow_{bi}$. Intuitively, having as purpose the trace inclusion means that all possible action sequences performed by the first system (client service and goal service) are also possible for the second system (client service, mediator service and available services). The second system can eventually execute more sequences. In the case of trace equivalence, it is prohibited for the second system to execute more sequences than the first system. This can be used to guarantee the system security. Indeed, some action sequences can enable the deduction of a confidential information. With trace equivalence, it is possible to prohibit this sequence by deleting it from the first system. The notions of simulation and bisimulation are based on the system states. When both systems ares non-deterministic, the bisimulation (resp. simulation) is more restrictive than trace equivalence (resp. trace inclusion).

Two systems are bisimilatr means that all accessible states, in the first system are bisimilaire to accessible states in the second one. Consequently, all the actions performed from accessible states, in the first system are performed from the corresponding states, in the second one (the converse is also true). Concretly, if the first system do not contain an accessible locked state, then the second system verify this property.

Example. Consider the client service, the goal service and the available services BookSeller and Delivery respectively represented in Figure 13, Figure 14, Figure 11 and Figure 12. In this example there exists a mediator service for the $CP(\leftrightarrow_{bi})$ problem. This mediator is represented in Figure 15. In Figure 16 all the services are represented with their different interactions 2. The dashed arcs are the unobservable actions, from the client point of view.

COMPLEXITY RESULTS

Now we present the complexity results concerning the composition problems $CP(\subseteq_{tr})$, $CP(\equiv_{tr})$, $CP(\leq_{si})$and $CP(\leftrightarrow_{bi})$.

Upper Bound

In what follows, we show that the composition problem can be solved in exponential time for the simulation, in polynomial space for trace inclusion and in double exponential time for bisimulation. In order to solve $CP(\leq_{si})$ and $CP(\subseteq_{tr})$, we will employ procedures used to solve respectively the simulation (Hütel & Shukla, 1996) and trace inclusion (Garey & Johnson, 1979) problem between finite automata. In addition, we show that these procedures cannot be adapted to solve $CP(\leftrightarrow_{bi})$ and $CP(\equiv_{tr})$. For this reason, we propose another method to solve $CP(\leftrightarrow_{bi})$ which use a procedure that solves the controller synthesis problem (Arnold, Vincent & Walukiewicz, 2003). Unfortunately, we do not know if there is a procedure to

Figure 16. Overview of the model

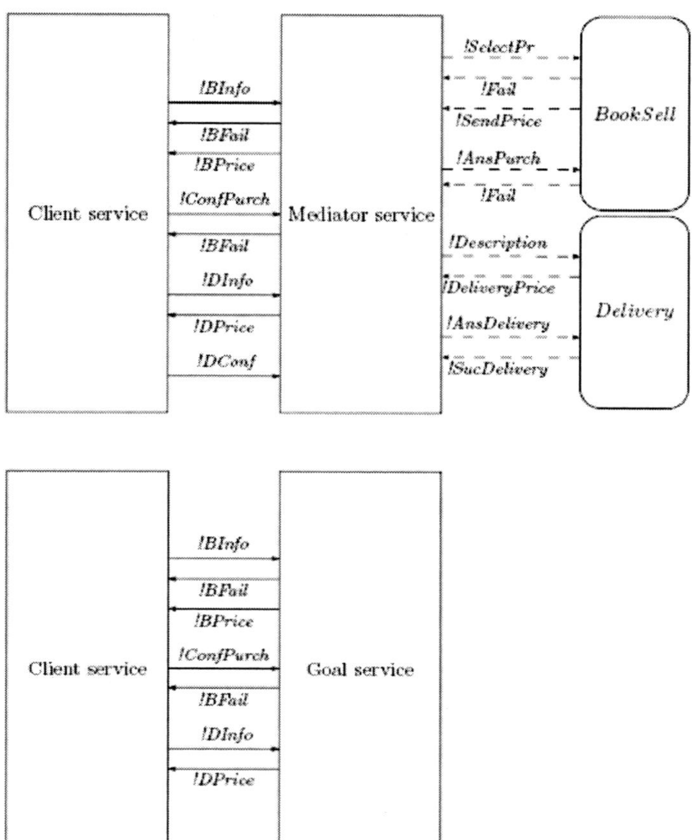

solve $CP(\equiv_{tr})$. Hence, we do not know if $CP(\equiv_{tr})$ is decidable.

The Results for CP($\leq_{si}$) *and* CP($\subseteq_{tr}$)

Let us consider a mediator Ac^{Lmed} able to execute all the communicating actions in $\{!,?\}\times Port$. Suppose that this mediator contains only one state, the initial state.

Definition. (Large mediator service) A large mediator service for a set ***Port*** is a CCA $Ac^{Lmed} = (Q^L, q_0^L, \delta^L)$ over **{!,?}×*Port*** and ***At*** such that:

- $Q^L = \{q_0^L\}$ and
- $\delta^L = \{(\varnothing, q_0^L, a, q_0^L, \varnothing) \mid a \in \{!,?\} \times Port\}$

Example. Let us consider the mediator service represented in Figure 17. This service is the large mediator for the set *Port* considered in the privious examples.

It is easy to prove the following lemma. Let $\subseteq \in \{\leq_{si}, \subseteq_{tr}\}$.

Lemma. Let the CCA Ac^{client} be a client service, a CCA Ac^{goal} be a goal service, the CCA $Ac^1,\ldots,Ac^n$ be available services and I_0 be a maximal consistent set of literals. There exists a mediator service Ac^{med} such that

$$Exec(Ac^{client} \otimes Ac^{goal}, I_0) \subseteq Exec(Ac^{client} \otimes Ac^1 \otimes \ldots \otimes Ac^n \otimes Ac^{med}, I_0) ((\{!,?\} \times Port'))$$

Figure 17. Large mediator service Ac^{Lmed}

$!SelectPr, ?SelectPr, \ldots, !SucDelivery, ?SucDelivery$

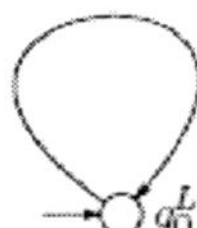

if

$$Exec(Ac^{client} \otimes Ac^{goal}, I_0) \subseteq Exec(Ac^{client} \otimes Ac^{1} \otimes \ldots \otimes Ac^{n} \otimes Ac^{Lmed}, I_0) ((\{!,?\} \times Port'))$$

Proof. A detailed proof can be found in (Cheikh, 2009).

From this lemma, we obtain that the following algorithm, that solve $CP(\leq_{si})$, is correct and complete.

This algorithm has as input a set of actions Σ, a set of ports *Port* a set of non-observable ports $Port'$, a client service Ac^{client}, a goal service Ac^{goal} and available services $Ac^1, \ldots, Ac^n$. The procedure named Solve- $CP(\leq_{si})$ returns "True" iff there exists a mediator service such that the system composed by the client service and the gaol service is similar to the system composed by the client service, the available services and the mediator service. In line 2, the function *LargeMed* returns the large service mediator for Port. This operation can be done in a linear time with respect to the size of the set *Port*. In line 3, the algorithm compute a finite automaton A from Ac^{client}, Ac^{goal} and I_0. This operation can be done in an exponential time with respect to the size of I_0. In line 4, the operation that compute Ac can be done in an exponential time with respect to the number n of the available services. As for the construction of A, in line 3, the construction of A', in line 5 can be done in an exponential time with respect to the size of I_0. In line 6, the time needed to determine if $A \leq_{si} A'(\{!,?\} \times Port')$ is polynomial with respect to the size of the input (Hütel & Shukla, 1996). Consequently, in order to return a solution, the algorithm take an exponential time with respect to the size of the inputs. As a result.

Theorem 1. The - $CP(\leq_{si})$ problem is in EXPTIME.

The same method used to solve - $CP(\leq_{si})$ can be used to solve $CP(\subseteq_{tr})$. More precisely, in order to obtain an algorithm to solve $CP(\subseteq_{tr})$, it is enough to change the line 6, from Figure 18. In order to return a solution, Figure 19 need an exponential space. The reasons are: (1) the operation of line 6 need a polynolial space (Garey & Johnson, 1979). (2) the size of A and A' are exponential on the size of I_0 and n. Consequently.

Theorem 2. The $CP(\subseteq_{tr})$ problem is in EXPSPACE.

The Results for $CP(\leftrightarrow_{bi})$

One can ask: is it possible to modify line 6 of Figure 18, in order to solve $CP(\leftrightarrow_{bi})$ (resp.

Figure 18.

Algorithm 1 Algorithm for the resolution of $\mathcal{CP}(\leq_{si})$

1: **procedure** SOLVE-$\mathcal{CP}(\leq_{si})(\Sigma, Port, Port', I_0, Ac^{client}, Ac^{goal}, Ac1, \ldots, Ac^n)$
2: $Ac^{Lmed} \leftarrow LargeMed(Port)$
3: $A \leftarrow Exec(Ac^{client} \circledast Ac^{goal}, I_0)$
4: $Ac \leftarrow Ac^{client} \circledast Ac^1 \circledast \ldots \circledast Ac^n \circledast Ac^{Lmed}$
5: $A' \leftarrow Exec(Ac, I_0)$
6: **if** $A \leq_{si} A'(\{!,?\} \times Port')$ **then return** True
7: **else return** False
8: **end if**
9: **end procedure**

Figure 19.

Algorithm 2 Algorithm for the resolution of $\mathcal{CP}(\subseteq_{tr})$

procedure SOLVE-$\mathcal{CP}(\subseteq_{tr})(\Sigma, Port, Port', I_0, \mathcal{A}c^{client}, \mathcal{A}c^{goal}, \mathcal{A}c1, \ldots, \mathcal{A}c^{n})$
  $\mathcal{A}c^{Lmed} \leftarrow LargeMed(Port)$
  $\mathcal{A} \leftarrow Exec(\mathcal{A}c^{client}, I_0)$
  $\mathcal{A}c \leftarrow \mathcal{A}c^{client} \circledast \mathcal{A}c^{1} \circledast \ldots \circledast \mathcal{A}c^{n} \circledast \mathcal{A}c^{Lmed}$
  $\mathcal{A}' \leftarrow Exec(\mathcal{A}c, I_0)$
  if $\mathcal{A} \subseteq_{tr} \mathcal{A}'(\{!, ?\} \times Port')$ **then return** True
  else return False
  end if
end procedure

$CP(\equiv_{tr})$)? The answer, is: the obtained algorithm will be correct but not complete. This means that, if the algorithm returns "False" then it does not imply that the answer of $CP(\leftrightarrow_{bi})$ (resp. $CP(\equiv_{tr})$) is "False". In other words, it is possible to be in a situation where the algorithm returns "False" but there exists a mediator service such that: the system composed of the client and the goal is bisimilar (resp. trace equivalent) to the system composed by the client, the mediator and the available services. Let us consider an example.

Example. Let us consider a set of actions $\Sigma=\{a,b\}$, sets of ports $Port = Port' = \{\pi_1\}$, an empty set of atomic formulas, a client service such that $\delta^{client}=\varnothing$, the goal service represented in Figure 19 and only one available service. This service is also represented in Figure 20. It is clear that the system composed by the large mediator service, the client service and the available service is not bisimilar to the system composed by the client service and the goal service. Consequently, the algorithm will return "False". However, if we consider a mediator service such that $\delta^{med}=\varnothing$, then the system composed by this mediator, the client service and the available service is bisimilar to the system composed by the client service and the goal service.

Now, let us present a method to solve $CP(\leftrightarrow_{bi})$. This method is based on controller synthesis techniques. Intuitively, to control a system means that it is possible to prohibit some transitions. The idea of this method is to find a controller for the large mediator, in order to obtain a bisimulation between the system composed by the client service and the goal service and the system composed by the client service, the large mediator and the available services, when this latest system is controlled. We know that the actions executed by the client service and the available services are not controllable. Thus, we need to distinguish between the actions executed by the large mediator (which are controllable) and the actions executed by the client service and the available services. Let us consider a set of ports *Port*. We associate to port a set $Ren(Port)=\{\pi^{\circ} | \pi \in Port\}$. This set is disjoint from $\Sigma \cup Port$ and has the same size as *Port*. For simplicity reason, we denote by *Action* the set $\Sigma \cup (\{!,?\} \times (Port \cup Ren(Port)))$. In what follows, the large mediator will be defined over $\{!,?\} \times Ren(Port)$. In the algorithm we pro-

Figure 20. From left to right a goal service and an available service

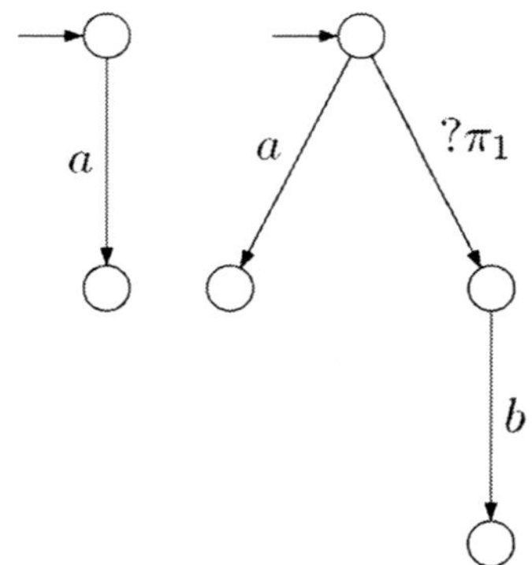

pose, we use two functions Del° and $Exec^{\circ}$. More precisely:

- the input of Del° is a CCA over *Action* and the output is a new CCA defined over $\Sigma \cup (\{!,?\} \times Port)$. The returned CCA is obtained by renaming transitions of the input CCA. All transitions labeled by$!\pi^{\circ}$ (resp.$?\pi^{\circ}$) in the input CCA are labeled by$!\pi$ (resp.$?\pi$) in the returned CCA. Thus, in the returned CCA we do not distinguish between the communicating actions executed by the large mediator service and those executed by other services.
- the input of $Exec^{\circ}$ is a CCA over *Action* and the output is an automaton over *Action*. The differences between the functions *Exec* and $Exec^{\circ}$ are the following:
  - in Exec the condition to execute $?\pi^{\circ}$ (resp. $!\pi^{\circ}$) is that π° is full (resp. empty), whereas in Exec° the condition is that π is full (resp. empty),
  - in Exec the effect of the execution of $?\pi^{\circ}$ (resp. $!\pi^{\circ}$) is that π° is empty (resp. full), whereas in Exec° the effect is that π is empty (resp. full).

Let us give some preliminary definitions concerning the controller synthesis. Let Σ be a finite set of actions. This set is partitioned on a set of observable actions denoted Σ_{ob} and a set of non-observable actions denoted Σ_{nob}. Also, Σ is partitioned on a set of controllable actions denoted Σ_{ct} and a set of non-controllable actions denoted Σ_{nct}.

Definition. (Observability and controllability constraints) Let *C* be a finite automaton. The observability constraints denoted C_{obs} and the controllability constraints denoted C_{ctr} for the automaton *C* are defined as follows:

- for all state *q* in *C* and for all non-observable action $a \in \Sigma_{nob}$, there exists a transition from *q* labeled by *a* then this transition is a loop over *q*.
- for all state *q* in *C* and for all non-cotrollable action $a \in \Sigma_{nct}$, there exists a transition from *q* labelled by *q*.

Let us consider the following decision problem: Controller synthesis problem:

Instance: a finite set of actions Σ and $\Sigma' \subseteq \Sigma$, finite automata *A* and *G* over Σ and constraints C_{obs} and C_{ctr}

Question: does there exist a controller *C* over Σ that satisfies C_{obs} and C_{ctr} and such that: $A \leftrightarrow_{bi} Del^{\circ}(G \times C)(\Sigma')$?

Consider the following lemma:

Lemma. Let us consider the CCA Ac^{client}, the CCA Ac^{goal}, the CCA $Ac^{1},\ldots,Ac^{n}$ and the set I_0. There exists a mediator service Ac^{med} such that

$$Exec(Ac^{client} \otimes Ac^{goal}, I_0) \leftrightarrow_{bi} Exec(Ac^{client} \otimes Ac^{1} \otimes \ldots \otimes Ac^{n} \otimes Ac^{med}, I_0)((\{!,?\} \times Port'))$$

iff there exists a controller *C* over *Action* that satisfies C_{obs} and C_{ctr}, when

$$\Sigma_{nct} = \Sigma_{nob} = \Sigma \cup (\{!,?\} \times Port),$$

and such that

$$Exec(A^{client} \otimes A^{but}, I_0) \leftrightarrow_{bi} Del^{\circ}(Exec^{\circ}(Ac^{client} \otimes Ac^{1} \otimes \ldots \otimes Ac^{n} \otimes Ac^{Lmed}, I_0) \times C)(\{!,?\} \times Port')$$

Proof. A detailed proof can be found in (Balbiani, Cheikh & Feuillade, 2008a; Balbiani, Cheikh & Feuillade, 2008b).

From this lemma, we obtain that the following algorithm, that solve $CP(\leftrightarrow_{bi})$, is correct and complete. In this algorithm, for the sets of actions Σ, Σ', Σ^{nct} and Σ_{nob} and the finite automaton *A* and A' the function

Figure 21.

Algorithm 3 Algorithm for the resolution of $\mathcal{CP}(\longleftrightarrow_{bi})$

procedure SOLVE-$\mathcal{CP}(\longleftrightarrow_{bi})(\Sigma, Port, Port', I_0, \mathcal{A}c^{client}, \mathcal{A}c^{goal}, \mathcal{A}c1, \ldots, \mathcal{A}c^{n})$
  $\mathcal{A}c^{Lmed} \leftarrow LargeMed(Port)$
  $\mathcal{A}c^{RLmed} \leftarrow Ren(\mathcal{A}c^{Lmed})$
  $\mathcal{A} \leftarrow Exec(\mathcal{A}c^{client} \circledast \mathcal{A}c^{goal}, I_0)$
  $\mathcal{A}c \leftarrow \mathcal{A}c^{client} \circledast \mathcal{A}c^{1} \circledast \ldots \circledast \mathcal{A}c^{n} \circledast \mathcal{A}c^{RLmed}$
  $\mathcal{A}' - Exec^{\circ}(\mathcal{A}c, I_0)$
  $\Sigma_{nct} \leftarrow \Sigma \cup (\{!, ?\} \times Port)$
  $\Sigma_{nob} \leftarrow \Sigma \cup (\{!, ?\} \times Port)$
  if $(Controller(Action, \{!, ?\} \times Port', \Sigma_{nct}, \Sigma_{nob}, \mathcal{A}, \mathcal{A}') = \text{True})$ **then**
return True
  else return False
  end if
end procedure

$$Controller(\Sigma, \Sigma', \Sigma_{nct}, \Sigma_{nob}, A, A')$$

returns "True" iff there exists a controller C over *Action* that satisfies C_{obs} and C_{ctr} and such that $A \leftrightarrow_{bi} Del^{\circ}(A' \times C)(\Sigma')$. The same reasoning as the one used to determine the time needed to return a solution by Figure 18, can be used to determine the time needed by Figure 21. It is easy to see that the size of A and A' is exponential with respect to n and I_0. In addition, the function *Controller* takes an exponential time with respect to the size of its inputs (Arnold, Vincent & Walukiewicz, 2003). Consequently, Figure 21 returns a solution in double exponential time with respect to n and I_0. As a result.

Theorem 3. The CP$(\leftrightarrow_{bi})$ problem is in 2-EXPTIME.

Lower Bounds

First, let us consider a decision problem with a set of inputs. Remind that this problem is EXPSPACE-hard (resp. EXPTIME-hard) if we can reduce/transform all the problems that are in *EXPSPACE* (resp. in EXPTIME) to this problem. However, the reduction must be done in a reasonable time 3. In order to prove that a decision problem is *EXPSPACE*-hard (resp. EXPTIME-hard), it is enough to prove that there exists an *EXPSPACE*-hard (resp. EXPTIME-hard) decision problem that can be reduced to him. For the interested readers, they can find all the formal definitions in (Papadimitriou, 1994). Intuitively, if we prove that a decision problem is *EXPSPACE*-hard (resp. EXPTIME-hard) it means that there does not exist an algorithm that solve this problem using a space (resp. a time) lower than exponential with respect to the input size. Hence, if we know that the problem is *EXPSPACE*-hard (resp. EXPTIME-hard) and we have an algorithm that solves the problem in a space (resp. time) exponential with respect to the size of the input, then we are sure that this algorithm is optimal in space (resp. time). Concerning the composition problems $CP(\subseteq_{tr})$, $CP(\leq_{si})$, $CP(\leftrightarrow_{bi})$ and $CP(\equiv_{tr})$, we proved the following results.

Theorem 4. *The* composition problem CP$(\subseteq_{tr})$ is EXPSPACE-har.

Proof. The proof is based on a reduction from the universal problem for regular expressions with squaring, known to be *EXPSPACE*-hard (Meyer & Stockmeyer, 1972) to $CP(\subseteq_{tr})$ problem. A detailed description of the universal problem for regular expressions and a detailed proof can be found in (Cheikh, 2009).

Theorem 5. The composition problem $CP(\leq_{si})$ is EXPTIME-hard.

Proof. The proof is based on a reduction from a simulation problem between a finite automaton and the asynchronous product of n automata,

Table 1. Summary table of results

Problem	Lower bound	Upper Bound
$CP(\subseteq_{tr})$	*EXPSPACE*	*EXPSPACE*
$CP(\equiv_{tr})$	*EXPSPACE*	?
$CP(\leq_{si})$	*EXPTIME*	*EXPTIME*
$CP(\leftrightarrow_{bi})$	*EXPTIME*	*2-EXPTIME*

known to be EXPTIME-hard ? to $CP(\leq_{si})$ problems. A detailed proof can be found in (Cheikh, 2009; Balbiani, Cheikh & Feuillade, 2007).

Theorem 6 The composition problem CP$(\leftrightarrow_{bi})$ is EXPTIME-hard.

Proof. The proof is based on a reduction from the bisimulation problem of 1-safe Petri nets, known to be EXPTIME-hard (Jategaonkar & Meyer, 1996) to the $CP(\leftrightarrow_{bi})$ problem. A detailed description of the 1-safe Petri nets and of the proof can be found in (Balbiani, Cheikh & Feuillade, 2008b).

Theorem 7 The composition problem CP$(\equiv_{tr})$ is EXPSPACE-hard.

Proof. There are two methods to prove that $CP(\equiv_{tr})$ is EXPSPACE -hard. The first one is to use the same reduction as the one used to prove Theorem 4. The second method is to use the reduction used in the proof of Theorem 6. Knowing that the trace equivalent problem of 1-safe Petri nets is EXPSPACE-hard (Jategaonkar & Meyer, 1996), we obtain that $CP(\equiv_{tr})$ is also EXPSPACE-hard. A detailed proof can be found in (Cheikh, 2009).

From this results and those presented in the Theorem 4 and Theorem 5. We deduce that Figure 18 and Figure 19 are respectively optimal in time and space.

CONCLUSION

In this chapter, we presented a formal model for Web services, in which both communicating actions and internal operations are performed. We formalized services by Conditional Communicating Automaton (CCA) in which communication is done through bounded ports. We described Web services composition problem for the trace inclusion, trace equivalence, simulation and bisimulation. The complexity results are summarized in Table 1. Concerning the composition problem when the trace inclusion and the simulation are considered, we proposed optimal algorithms that are correct and complete. Moreover, when the simulation is considered, the proposed algorithm returns a solution in an exponential time, with respect to the input size. Whereas, when trace inclusion is considered, the algorithm proposed uses an exponential space, with respect to the input size, in order to return a solution. We also proved that the composition problem is EXPSPACE-hard for the trace equivalence and EXPTIME-hard for bisimulation. In addition, we proposed a procedure to solve the problem for bisimulation in a double exponential time, according to the size of the problem input. All the procedures proposed in this chapter require the generation of the asynchronous product of the services. This step is expensive on time, when a high number of services is considered. However, the lower bounds show that no algorithm exists with a lower complexity, at least for trace inclusion and simulation. It is instructive to notice, from Table 1 that: (1) the decidability of the composition problem, when trace equivalence is considered is unknown. (2) we do not have the exact complexity of the composition problem when bisimulation is considered. Namely, wether the problem is in EXPTIME or is 2-EXPTIME-hard. Furthermore, different restrictions are considered in our model, such as: messages do not contain attributes, variables are Boolean and operations are atomic. As future works, it would be interesting to first extend our model in order to be closer to the real model of services. Then to answer the open questions, namely what is the upper bound for the trace equivalence? And is the composition problem in EXPTIME or 2-EXPTIME, for the bisimulation?. As future work, we intend to establish an experimental study, in order to analyse the procedures performance. In the procedures proposed, the explicit computation of the available service product need an exponential time. Consequently, to reduce this complexity, we think that it would be interesting to use heuristics as in (Bertoli, Pistore & Traverso, 2006).

ACKNOWLEDGMENT

The work described here has been conducted within the french project COPS and the european project AVANTSSAR. It would have not been realised without help of Philippe Balbiani and Guillaume Feuillade.

REFERENCES

Arnold, A., Vincent, A., & Walukiewicz, I. (2003). Games for synthesis of controllers with partial observation. *Theoretical Computer Science*, *303*(1), 7–34. doi:10.1016/S0304-3975(02)00442-5

Balbiani, P., Cheikh, F., & Feuillade, G. (2007). Considérations relatives à la décidabilité et à la complexité du problème de la composition de services. In *Journées Francophones modèle formels de l'interaction,* 261–268. Annales du LAMSADE.

Balbiani, P., Cheikh, F., & Feuillade, G. (2008). Composition of interactive Web Services based on controller synthesis. In *Proceedings of the 2nd International Workshop on Web Service Composition and Adaptation*. Honolulu, USA: IEEE.

Balbiani, P., Cheikh, F., & Feuillade, G. (2008). Composition of Web Services: Algorithms and complexity. In *Proceedings of The 1st Interaction and Concurrency Experience*. Reykjavik, Iceland: ENTCS.

Berardi, D., Calvanese, D., De Giacomo, G., Hull, R., & Mecella, M. (2005). Automatic composition of transition-based Semantic Web Services with messaging. In *Proceedings of the 31st International Conference on Very Large Data Bases,* (pp.613–624). Trondheim, Norway: ACM.

Berardi, D., Calvanese, D., De Giacomo, G., & Mecella, M. (2006). Composing Web Services with nondeterministic behavior. *In Proceedings of the IEEE International Conference on Web Services,* (pp. 909-912). Chicago: IEEE Computer Society.

Bertoli, P., Pistore, M., & Traverso, P. (2006). Automated Web Service composition by on-the-fly belief space search. In *Proceedings of the Sixteenth International Conference on Automated Planning and Scheduling*, (pp. 358–361). Cumbria, UK: AAAI.

Cheikh, F. (2009). Problème de la composition: Modèle et complexité. PhD thesis, Université de Toulouse.

Cheikh, F., De Giacomo, D., & Mecella, M. (2006). Automatic Web Services composition in trustaware communities. In *Proceedings of the 3rd ACM Workshop On Secure Web Services,* (pp. 43-52). Alexandria, VA: ACM.

Dal Lago, U., Pistore, M., & Traverso, P. (2002). Planning with a language for extended goals. In *Proceedings of the 18th National Conference on Artificial Intelligence and 14th Conference on Innovative Applications of Artificial Intelligence,* (447–454). Alberta, Canada: AAAI Press.

Dustdar, S., & Schreiner, W. (2005). A survey on Web Services composition. *International Journal of Web and Grid Services*, *1*(1), 1–30. doi:10.1504/IJWGS.2005.007545

Foster, H., Uchitel, S., Magee, J., & Kramer, J. (2007). WS-Engineer: A model-based approach to engineering Web Service compositions and choreography. In *Test and analysis of Web Services*, (pp. 87–119). Springer.

Garey, M. R., & Johnson, D. S. (1979). *Computers and intractability: A guide to the theory of NP-completeness*. New York: Freeman and Company.

Hoare, C. (1978). Communicating sequential processes. *Communications of the ACM, 21*(8), 666–677. doi:10.1145/359576.359585

Hoare, C. A. (1985). *Communicating sequential processes*. New Jersey: Prentice-Hall.

Hull, R., & Su, J. (2005). Tools for composite Web Services: A short overview. *SIGMOD Record, 34*(2), 86–95. doi:10.1145/1083784.1083807

Hütel, H., & Shukla, S. (1996). *On the complexity of deciding behavioural equivalences and pre-orders, a survey. Basic Reasearch in Computer Science (RS-96-39)*. Aahrus, Denmark: University of Aarhus, Department of Computer Science.

Jategaonkar, L., & Meyer, A. R. (1996). Deciding true concurrency equivalences on safe, finite nets. *Theoretical Computer Science, 154*(1), 107–143. doi:10.1016/0304-3975(95)00132-8

Mecella, M., Ouzzani, M., Paci, F., & Bertino, E. (2006). Access control enforcement for conversation-based Web Services. In *Proceedings of the 15th International World Wide Web Conference,* (257-266). Edinburgh: ACM.

Meyer, A., & Stockmeyer, L. (1972). The equivalence problem for regular expressions with squaring requires exponential space. In *Proceedings of the 13th Annual Symposium on Switching and Automata Theory,* (125–129). Maryland, USA: IEEE.

Milner, R. (1989). *Communication and concurrency*. New Jersey: Prentice-Hall.

Mitra, S., Kumar, R., & Basu, S. (2007). Automated choreographer synthesis for Web Services composition using I/O automata. In *proceedings of IEEE International Conference on Web Services,* (pp. 364–371). Utah, USA: IEEE Computer Society.

Muscholl, A., & Walukiewicz, I. (2008). *A lower bound on Web Services composition*. Computing Reasearch Repository.

Papadimitriou, C. H. (1994). *Computational complexity*. Addison-Wesley.

Park, D. (1981). Concurrency and automata on infinite sequences. In *proceedings of the 5th GI Conference,* (pp. 167-183). Karlsruhe, Germany: Springer.

Pathak, J., Basu, S., Lutz, R., & Honavar, V. (2006). Parallel Web Service composition in MOSCOE: A choreography-based approach. In *proceedings of the Fourth IEEE European Conference on Web Services,* (pp. 3-12). Zürich, Switzerland: IEEE Computer Society.

Pistore, M., Marconi, A., Bertoli, P., & Traverso, P. (2005). Automated composition of Web Services by planning at the knowledge level. In *the proceedings of the Nineteenth International Joint Conference on Artificial Intelligence,* (pp. 1252-1259). Scotland: Professional Book Center.

Pistore, M., Traverso, P., & Bertoli, P. (2005). Automated composition of Web Services by planning in asynchronous domains. *In the proceedings of the Fifteenth International Conference on Automated Planning and Scheduling,* (pp. 2–11). California: AAAI.

Rao, J., Küngas, P., & Matskin, M. (2004). Logic-based Web Services composition: From service description to process model. In *proceedings of the IEEE International Conference on Web Services*, (pp. 446-453). California, USA: IEEE Computer Society.

Singh, M., & Huhns, M. (2005). *Service-oriented computing. Semantics, process, agents*. Wiley.

ENDNOTES

[1] Id_Q represents the identity relation on Q.

[2] This figure represents an outside overview of the model.

[3] Reasonable time means a polynomial time with respect to the input size.

APPENDIX

Table of notations

Σ	Set of actions.
Σ'	Set of observable actions.
Σ_{obs}	Set of observable actions (with respect to a controller).
Σ_{nobs}	Set of non-observable actions (with respect to a controller).
Σ_{ctr}	Set of a controlable actions (with respect to a controller).
Σ_{nctr}	Set of non-controlable actions (with respect to a controller).
A	Automaton.
Q	Set of states.
q_0	Initial state.
$\rightarrow$	Transition function of automaton.
$\times$	Synchronus product of automata.
$Tr_{\Sigma}(A)$	Trace of A modulo Σ'.
$\subseteq_{tr}$	Trace inclusion.
$\equiv_{tr}$	Trace equivalence.
$\leq_{si}$	Simulation.

$\leftrightarrow_{bi}$	Bissimulation.
At	Finite set of atributs.
Li(At)	Litterals over At.
Port	Finite set of Ports.
$?\pi$	Message received through a port π.
$!\pi$	Message sent through a port π.
Ac	Conditional Communicating Automaton (CCA).
δ	Transiton function of CCA.
$\otimes$	Asynchronus product of CCA
$Exec(Ac,I_0)$	Execution of Ac when the initial set of litérals is I_0.
Cert	Finite set of credentials/certificates.
$Ac^1 \ldots Ac^n$	n CCA representing available services.
Ac^{goal}	CCA representig the goal service .
Ac^{client}	CCA representing the client service.
Ac^{med}	CCA representing the mediator service.
Ac^{Lmed}	CCA representing the large mediator service.
$CP(\approx)$	The composition problem for $\approx \in \{\subseteq_{tr}, \equiv_{tr}, \leq_{si}, \leftrightarrow_{bi}\}$.

Chapter 10
Specification of Non-Functional Requirements and their Trade-Offs in Service Contracts in the NGOSS Framework

Xiaoqing (Frank) Liu
Missouri University of Science and Technology, USA

Nektarios Georgalas
British Telecom GCTO, UK

ABSTRACT

The community of Operation Support Systems (OSS) for telecom applications defined a set of fundamental principles, processes, and architectures for developing the Next Generation OSS through the TeleManagement Forum TMF. At the heart of NGOSS lies the notion of a "Contract" which embodies the specification of services offered by an OSS component for quality management and product evaluation. However, TMF does not provide any method (or process) for specification of the non-functional part in the NGOSS contract specification. This chapter develops a systematic approach for specifying non-functional requirements of telecom OSS applications for contracts in the NGOSS framework for quality management and evaluation. Specifically, two categories of non-functional specification techniques are explored: qualitative and quantitative. Furthermore, two quantitative non-functional requirements specification methods are introduced: crisp and elastic to expand the capability of the current NGOSS contract specification method since only qualitative non-functional specification is currently available from TMF. In addition, a technique is developed for specification of trade-offs between non-functional requirements.

DOI: 10.4018/978-1-60960-493-6.ch010

INTRODUCTION

Background

Service Oriented Architecture (SOA) (Margolis, 2007; Leymann & Karastoyanova, 2008; Erl, 2005) is gaining momentum in information technology applications. It is a loosely-coupled architecture designed to meet business needs of an organization and allow systems group functionality around business processes. In response to challenging goals of improving quality, reducing cost, increasing agility, improving inter-operability, and managing IT and Telco resources effectively, the community of Operation Support Systems (OSS) for telecom applications, has defined a set of fundamental principles, processes, and architectures for developing the Next Generation OSS – NGOSS (TeleManagement Forum, 2004a, 2004b, 2005) based on SOA through the TeleManagement Forum TMF.

Related Work

Unlike Functional Requirements (FR) whose significance has been widely recognized, Non-Functional Requirements (NFRs) are poorly understood (Paech & Kerkow, 2004). Research of non-functional requirements has focused on their analysis instead of specification (Cysneiros & Leite, 2004; Mylopoulos et. al, 1992). In fact, neglecting non-functional requirements has been counted as one of the top risks of requirement engineering. The problem of incorrect specification of non-functional requirements often leads to disputes in business contracts, wrong design and implementation, wrong trade-off decisions, poor customer satisfaction, and loss in competition.

Specification of non-functional requirements for SOA has attracted attentions of researchers recently. It is necessary to specify non-functional requirements in addition to functional requirements in SOA since they play an important role in development and selection of services. It still has many open and challenging issues which need to be investigated (Tsai et. al, 2007). Several modeling methods have been developed to specify non-functional requirements. UML profiles have been used to model non-functional requirements in SOA (Ortiz & Hernändez, 2006; Wada, Suzuki, & Oba, 2006; Wada, Suzuki, & Oba, 2007). A goal-oriented modeling method is used to represent non-functional requirements in SOA (Xiang et. al, 2007). However, non-functional requirements are specified to be crisp and they can be either satisfied or not, or they are specified to be qualitative in these non-functional requirements modeling methods. They are difficult to be used for trade-off analysis in service selection when multiple non-functional requirements cannot be satisfied at the same time and a trade-off among them is needed.

Service Level Agreements (SLAs), which are widely used in telecom industry and increasingly become popular in e-commerce and SOAs, stipulate service level requirements from external customers due to contractual or other reasons. In order to develop an OSS which satisfies service level requirements in a SLA, NGOSS introduce a notion of a "Contract", which serves as an internal contract between intermediate phases in a development process and embodies the specification of services offered by an OSS component for quality management and product evaluation in a specific phase (TeleManagement Forum, 2005). However, TMF does not provide any method (or process) for specification of the non-functional part in the NGOSS service contract specification except the exemplary list of fields. In addition, TMF does not provide any trade-off specification mechanisms for resolving conflicts between non-functional requirements in the service contract, which exist in many Telco applications.

Objective

In this book chapter, we present a systematic approach for specifying non-functional requirements and their trades of telecom OSS applications for contracts in the NGOSS framework. Specifically, two categories of non-functional specification techniques are explored: qualitative and quantitative. Furthermore, we introduce two quantitative non-functional requirements specification methods: crisp and elastic to expand the capability of the current NGOSS contract specification method since only qualitative non-functional specification is currently available from TMF. Non-functional requirements trade-off specification techniques are developed to resolve conflicts and achieve consensus among stakeholders. An example of non-functional requirements and their trade-off specification for exemplary NGOSS contracts are presented based on qualitative, and crisp and elastic quantitative non-functional requirements specification techniques.

NGOSS: LIFE CYCLE METHODOLOGY AND CONTRACT SPECIFICATION

The OSS community in the global telecom industry has defined a set of fundamental principles for architecting the Next Generation OSS – NGOSS through the TMF. In a nutshell, NGOSS (TeleManagement Forum, 2004a) applies a top-level approach for the specification of an OSS architecture where:

Technology Neutral and Technology Specific Architectures are separated. The more dynamic "business process" logic is separated from the more stable "component" logic.

Components present their services through well defined "contracts" with clear semantics. A Contract defines interaction between internal functionalities within an enterprise in order to satisfy an external Service Level Agreement (SLA), as discussed later.

Policies are used to provide a flexible control of behavior in an overall NGOSS system.

The infrastructure services such as naming, invocation, directories, transactions, security, persistence, etc are provided as a common deployment and runtime framework for use by all OSS components and business processes over a service bus.

A common Shared Information and Data Model – SID, where all data used by components, processes and policies will follow an agreed standard format.

A business process framework eTOM (TeleManagement Forum, 2004c) is a framework where business processes encompassing all aspects of operating an IT enterprise from fulfillment to assurance and billing activities are mapped from top level abstract description to more detailed decompositions. Furthermore, NGOSS specifies a rigorous methodology for architecting an OSS.

The NGOSS life cycle is depicted in Figure 1. There are four views of an OSS. The Business view captures business requirements irrespective of how automated computerised system will realise them. The System view describes the automated system capabilities in a technology neutral manner. The Implementation view describes technology specific system capabilities; and finally the deployment view captures the run-time components of the system.

The notion of views was used to specify software architecture and other artifacts from multiple perspectives in the past. For example, a model of "4+1 views" was developed to specify software architecture (Kruchten, 1995). It focuses on object-oriented software architecture while the NGOSS model focuses on development life cycle of service oriented software systems in telecom industry.

The key to a NGOSS architecture is the notion of "contract" in each of the four views of the lifecycle: business, system, implementation, and deployment view as discussed above. A contract specification includes the functional aspect of an OSS capability (such as billing, trouble ticketing, order handling, etc.) as well as non-functional

Figure 1. NGOSS life cycle

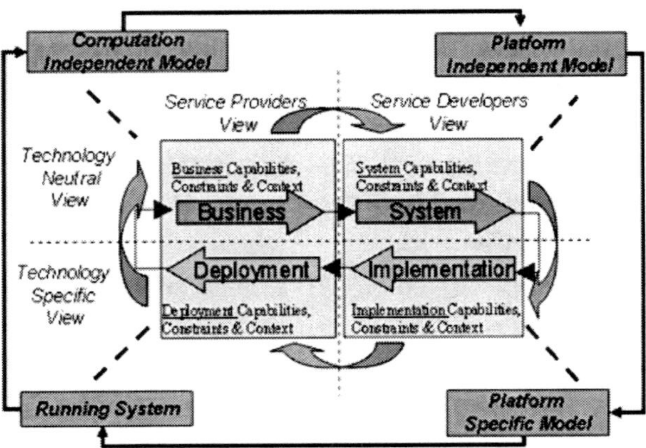

requirements to aid procurement of third party components as well as guiding design decisions for developing an OSS application. While this approach to automation of life cycle of an OSS can be applied to functional aspects of the overall system, non-functional requirements of an OSS system are largely expressed as rather vague qualitative statements which are not amenable to further analysis and have little value while making design decisions in subsequent phases in the life cycle (Georgalas & Azmoodeh, 2004a, 2004b).

The basic description of a NGOSS contract, no matter the view being represented is made up of five main parts: general contract view, functional part, non-functional part, management part, and view specific model part (TeleManagement Forum, 2004b, 2005). Please note that a contract is used to help developers to design and implement services of an operation support system for satisfaction of the service requirements and select services either manually or automatically. The non-functional part defines aspects which govern or restrict the bounds of operation of the capabilities specified a contract, examples of them include external influences such as technological limitations, legal, regulatory limitations and organization limitations, as well as other considerations (e.g., cost). The number of fields in a non-functional part of a contract can be changed. An exemplary list of fields is provided for non-functional part of a business view contract in the NGOSS documents by the TMF as shown in Table 1 (TeleManagement Forum, 2005).

Approaches to Non-Functional Requirements Specification for NGOSS Contracts

No examples of non-functional parts of a contract have been given by TMF in the NGOSS contract specification yet (TeleManagement Forum, 2004b; TeleManagement Forum, 2005). TMF does not provide any method (or process) for specification of a non-functional part in the NGOSS contract specification except providing a list of examples of fields (TeleManagement Forum, 2005). In the list of examples, all fields are in text, and they are qualitative. The reason that qualitative non-functional requirements specification is often used in practice is that it is easy to develop. It is sometimes difficult to identify metrics to quantify a non-functional characteristic, or it is too complex and time-consuming to use metrics to quantify them. However, qualitative non-functional requirements specified in text sometimes may be hard to use for making design decisions and selecting reusable components in the product development process, and very difficult to validate since they may be

Table 1. Non-Functional Part of Business View Contract

Field	Type
Deployment Related	
Availability limitations	Textual attribute
Safety limitations	Textual attribute
Organization Related	
Business environment	Textual attribute
Organizational limitations	Textual attribute
Market limitations	Textual attribute
Financial limitations	Textual attribute
Legal Related	
Regulatory limitations	Textual attribute
Legal limitations	Textual attribute
Miscellaneous	
Stakeholders	Textual attribute
Assumptions	Textual attribute
Offering period	Textual attribute

ambiguous and subject to different interpretations by different stakeholders. For example, assume that we have a qualitative non-functional requirement for a billing system in a telecom company:

R_1 "the performance of the billing system shall be high".

First, how to measure the performance may be unclear to developers. Second, "high" is qualitative and can be interpreted differently by different people.

Therefore, we propose that quantitative non-functional requirements specification needs to be used instead if precise requirements specification is needed in NGOSS specifications. Below is an example of quantitative performance requirements specification:

R_2: The response time of search of a customer account in a billing system is no more than one (1) second.

This requirement is precise and can be easily validated. An implementation of the billing system either satisfies it or not since it is crisp. However, in telecom industry, a billing system which slightly violates the requirement is usually considered to be fine. It leads to the development of elastic quantitative non-functional requirements specification in NGOSS discussed below.

TOWARDS ELASTIC QUANTITATIVE NON-FUNCTIONAL REQUIREMENTS SPECIFICATION IN NGOSS

In this section, we further propose to enhance capability of existing NGOSS contract specification which currently is limited to be only qualitative by developing elastic quantitative non-functional requirements specification which enables trade-offs in a development process. Non-functional requirements enforce constraints on a system or service. Clarity of non-functional requirements, such as availability, is vital to for efficient business operation and product development.

We propose two methods for quantitative specification of a non-functional requirement in NGOSS: 1) crisp, and 2) elastic. A crisp quantitative non-functional requirement imposes a rigid constraint on a non-functional characteristic of a system or service. It is either satisfied or dissatisfied. Considering the following crisp quantitative non-functional requirement:

R_3: The worst-case latency of billing must be less than one (1) second.

If the billing of a system takes 1.05 seconds for a test case in the testing process, it does not satisfy the above requirement, and the system realization is not acceptable. Crisp quantitative requirements are easy to validate. The crisp quantitative non-functional requirement specification is used widely in industry. Actually, the British Telecom has adopted it in specification of performance of operations for its telecom capabilities.

Elastic quantitative non-functional requirements specification for NGOSS is based on works on imprecise requirements specification (Liu & Yen, 1996). An elastic quantitative non-functional requirement imposes an elastic constraint on a

Figure 2. Satisfaction function for requirement R_4

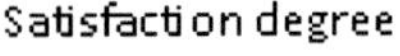

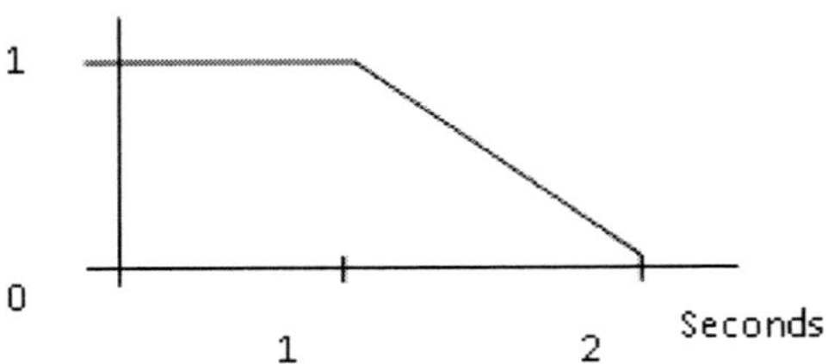

non-functional characteristic of a system or service using a membership function of a qualitative term to characterize its satisfaction. A membership function for a fuzzy set characterizing a qualitative term represents a degree of membership of item in a fuzzy set (Zimmermann, 1991). Below is an example of an elastic quantitative non-functional requirement:

R_4: The worst-case latency of billing must be SHORT,

where SHORT is a linguistic term in fuzzy logic whose membership function characterizes satisfaction of the above requirement as shown in Figure 2.

In the figure, one (1) represents the highest level of requirement satisfaction by a realization of system or service, and zero (0) represents the lowest level of requirement satisfaction by a system realization or service. If the billing of a system realization takes 0.8 seconds in the worst case in the testing process, its satisfaction degree is one which is the highest. It indicates that it completely satisfies the requirement. If it takes 1.5 seconds in the worst case, its satisfaction degree is around 0.5 and it partially satisfies the requirement although it is acceptable. In the elastic non-functional requirement specification, a minimal threshold for its metric value is usually specified. It indicates that a system realization whose metric value is below this threshold is not acceptable. For example, if the billing of a system realization takes three (3) seconds in the worst case which is greater than the threshold of two (2) seconds, its satisfaction degree is zero (0) and it is completely unacceptable.

Elastic quantitative non-functional requirements specification enables trade-offs in the design of a system and selection of reusable components, which is impossible if crisp quantitative non-functional requirements specification method is used. This is absolutely important when a design trade-off decision for resolving a conflict among non-functional requirements, which often exists in many applications, needs to be made. For example, suppose that we need to select a reusable billing component for a new product. Assume that there is a reusable component $COMP_1$ which provides the functionality needed for the new product, and its worst case latency of $COMP_1$'s billing is 1.01 seconds. Different results can be obtained using crisp and elastic requirements specification techniques.

We discuss crisp non-functional requirements specification for the new product first. Assume that crisp requirement R_3 is its latency requirement. $COMP_1$ can not be reused for the new project since it violates the above requirement.

Now we discuss how to use elastic non-functional requirements specification technique for the new product. Assume that the elastic requirement R_4 is its latency requirement. Based on this requirement, $COMP_1$ can be reused for the new project since it has a satisfaction level which is close to one (1) which is the highest and far greater than the minimal threshold of satisfaction based on its satisfaction function in Figure 2. This result is much more desirable and practical than the one obtained using crisp non-functional requirement specification discussed above in many applications. In addition, the elastic quantitative non-functional requirements specification also makes non-functional requirements easily evaluated and validated than qualitative non-functional requirements specification.

To overcome problem of the lack of guidance and example for specification of non-functional requirements for a NGOSS contract in NGOSS standard documents, a complete contract example, CRM-SM&O Customer Problem Handling, is developed by adding its non-functional part in a incomplete contract provided by NGOSS (TeleManagement, 2005) using qualitative, crisp quantitative, and elastic quantitative non-functional requirements specification techniques discussed above. Please note that adjectives expressing qualitative requirements, such as High, Short, Minimal should have their satisfaction functions defined and included in a contract to specify respective elastic quantitative non-functional requirements.

SPECIFICATION OF TRADE-OFFS BETWEEN NON-FUNCTIONAL REQUIREMENTS FOR A NGOSS CONTRACT

Two non-functional requirements in a contract may not be satisfied at the same time since they may conflict with each time. In Telco environments, their trade-offs are highly desirable. Trade-offs between crisp non-functional requirements can be achieved using two methods: 1) they are revised through negotiations so that a compromise can be found; 2) one of the conflicting non-functional requirements needs to be removed since no compromise is possible.

The two methods used to resolve trades between crisp non-functional requirements can be also used for trade-off analysis between elastic non-functional requirements. In addition, trade-offs between elastic non-functional requirements can be achieved can be achieved using more methods than those available for crisp non-functional requirements. In general, their trade-offs can be provided using four methods: adjusting, withdrawing, compromising, and prioritizing.

The "adjusting" is established by revising their membership functions to resolve their conflicts. It usually relaxes or strengthens elastic non-functional requirements.

The "withdrawing" technique is used to resolve the conflict between mutually exclusive conflicting requirements. It usually withdraws one of conflicting requirements.

The "compromising" of elastic non-functional requirements is achieved by combining conflicting requirements using fuzzy compromise operators in fuzzy logic.

The "prioritizing" is used to assess relative importance of the conflicting requirements so that more important one could carry more weight in a trade-off based conflict resolution.

In this chapter, let's focus on specification of trade-offs among elastic non-functional requirements. There exist many ways to combine multiple criteria in fuzzy logic (Chen & Hwang, 1991). Different aggregation operators can be used to aggregate multiple elastic non-functional requirements. Compromise operators can be developed to aggregate conflicting requirements to achieve effective trade-offs. An aggregation rule is provided to compute the satisfaction degree of the combined requirement in terms of the satisfaction degree of individual requirements.

Averaging (Dubois & Prade, 1984) and compensatory (Zimmermann, 1991) operators are often used to combine multiple criteria in fuzzy multi-criteria decision making. The resulting trade-offs of an average operator lie between the most optimistic lower bound and the most pessimistic upper bound. It can be formally defined as follows (Dubois & Prade, 1984).

Definition (averaging operator)

An operator **M** is said to be an averaging operator if and only if it satisfies:

Min (Sat (R_i, s), …, Sat (R_n, s)) <= **M** (Sat (R_i, s), …, Sat (R_n, s));

M (Sat (R_i, s), …, Sat (R_n, s)) <= **Max** (Sat (R_i, s), …, Sat (R_n, s));

M is different from either **Min** or **Max**.

M (1, 1, …, 1) = 1; and M(0, 0, …, 0) = 0;

For all $x_1, \ldots, x_n$; $y_1, \ldots, y_n$; if (for all j, $x_j >= y_j$), then

$\mathbf{M}(x_1, \ldots, x_n) >= \mathbf{M}(y_1, \ldots, y_n)$.

The examples of averaging operator include arithmetic mean and geometric mean. The arithmetic mean of a list of numbers is the sum of all of the numbers in the list divided by the number of items in the list. In the calculation of geometric mean, instead of adding the set of numbers and then dividing the sum by the count of numbers in the set, n, the numbers are multiplied and then the nth root of the resulting product is taken.

For a compensatory operator, a decrease in one operand can be compensated by an increase in another operand. The compensatory operator can be formally defined as follows:

Definition (compensation)

Suppose that $x_1, x_2, \ldots, x_n$ be real numbers in [0, 1] and **f** be a function that maps to a real number in [0, 1]. We say **f** is compensatory iff given $f(x_1, x_2, \ldots, x_n) = k$, for any $1 <= i <= n$, for any Δ such that $0 <= x_i + \Delta_{xi} <= 1$, there exists $1 <= j <= n$, which is not equal to i, and Δ_{xj} such that

$$0 <= x_j + \Delta_{xj} <= 1, \text{ and}$$

$$f(\ldots, x_i + \Delta_{xi}, \ldots, x_j + \Delta_{xj}, \ldots) = k.$$

In requirement engineering, a trade-off between conflicting elastic non-functional requirements usually is a compromise which is compensatory. Thus the compromise operator is developed to combine elastic non-functional conflicting requirements for trade-off analysis.

Definition (compromise)

An operator is said to be a compromise operator if and only if it is both averaging and compensatory operator.

In the following context, C denotes a compromise operator. It realizes the trade-offs by allowing compensation between requirements. The resulting compromise is between the minimal and maximal degree of membership of the aggregated fuzzy sets. The arithmetic mean is an example of the C operator.

If all of individual elastic non-functional requirements need to be satisfied at the same time, they can be aggregated using a fuzzy conjunctive operator $\cap$ (Dubois & Prade, 1984; Zimmermann, 1991). "Min" is an example of a fuzzy conjunctive operator and it takes the minimum of operands. If one of individual elastic non-functional requirements needs to be satisfied, they can be aggregated using a fuzzy disjunctive operator $\cup$ (Dubois & Prade, 1984; Zimmermann, 1991). "Max" is an example of fuzzy disjunctive operator and it takes the maximum of operands.

AN EXAMPLE OF NON-FUNCTIONAL SPECIFICATION FOR A NGOSS CONTRACT

In the draft of examples of a NGOSS contract provided by the TMF (TeleManagement Forum, 2005), a contract in NGOSS business view contains multiple capabilities. A capability in turn contains multiple processes.

We now extend a contract example, CRM-SM&O Customer Problem Handling, in the draft (TeleManagement Forum, 2005) by adding its non-functional part to illustrate the above framework. It deals with both customer order and service order handling. Here is a description of its business capabilities (TeleManagement Forum, 2005).

This Contract defines interaction between Customer Relationship Management and Service Management areas within an enterprise (as represented by the relevant eTOM CRM and SM&O processes (TeleManagement Forum, 2004c). It directly interacts with two processes in eTOM for this Contract, at eTOM level 2 (TeleManagement Forum, 2004c):

Order Handling (in OPS-CRM)

Service Configuration & Activation (in OPS-SM&O).

The functionalities at eTOM level 2 used in this example are very generic. But they can be decomposed into eTOM level 3 processes in a CRM and SM&O fulfillment process flow, such as *validate customer order* and *activate service*, which are primitive functionalities specified in a clear and precise way (TeleManagement Forum, 2005). However, since NGOSS does not provide a contract example using primitive functionalities, we use the functionalities at eTOM level 2.

Next, we are going to complete the non-functional part for the contract example. It will contain examples of three specification techniques: qualitative, crisp quantitative, and elastic quantitative non-functional requirements specification. It must be noted that it is deliberately restricted to a simple scenarios and simple data since it is intended to illustrate principals. Actual requirements may vary from company to company. In the specification of non-functional part for the following example of contract, we still use the categorization of non-functional requirements recommended by TMF (TeleManagement Forum, 2004b) although we would suggest replacing the category of deployment with category of quality in a business view contract since it is supposed to be deployment independent.

NGOSS Contract Example: CRM-SM&O Fulfillment Information Handling

Other parts in the contract (TeleManagement Forum, 2005)

Business View – Non-Functional

Deployment-Related Availability

A crisp non-functional requirement for availability can be developed as follows:

ER_1: Availability of all business capabilities specified in the contract must not be lower than 99.99%.

An elastic non-functional requirement about reliability can be specified as follows:

ER_2: The MTTF (Mean Time To Failure) Should be MINIMAL.

An example of satisfaction function can be defined for SHORT of ER_2 in Figure 3. In this figure, one (1) represents total satisfaction and zero (0) represents total dissatisfaction. Basically, it indicates that if the mean time to failure for a capability realization is less than or equal to 1000 hours, it is totally unacceptable; if it is more than or equal to 4000, it achieves the highest level of

Figure 3. Satisfaction function for latency requirement ER_2

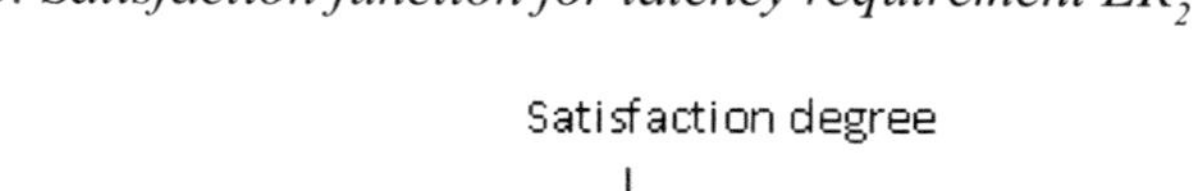

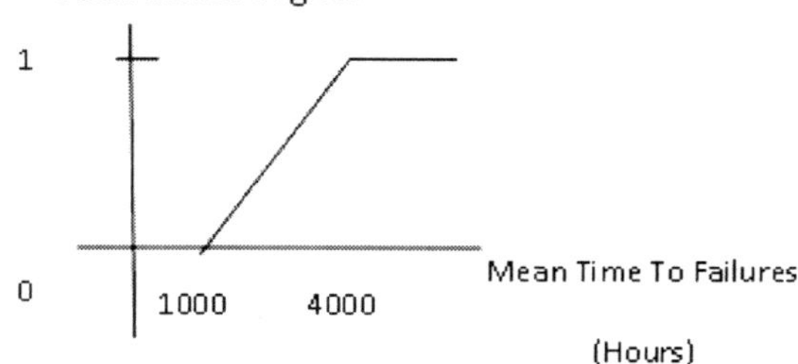

satisfaction; and if it takes between 1000 and 4000 hours, its satisfaction level is gradually increased as number of hours is increased. The numbers used in this example are for illustration only.

Performance

ER_3: Performance of all business capabilities specified in the contract must be good.

This requirement is specified qualitatively, and in many cases it may be appropriate although it may have different interpretations from different stakeholders and may be hard to validate. We can transform it into more precise requirements if the qualitative requirements specification is not appropriate. Performance is usually characterized by sub-characteristics, such as time-efficiency and resource-efficiency. ER_2 can be transformed into lower level requirements based on its sub-characteristics. An example of such requirements may look as follows:

$ER_{3,1}$: The time-efficiency of all business capabilities specified in the contract must be good.

Once again, this requirement is qualitative and is not precise. The time-efficiency is usually characterized by several metrics, such as response time, latency and throughput. Non-functional requirements can be derived from $ER_{3,1}$ based on these metrics. An example of these derived non-functional elastic requirements is shown here:

$ER_{3,1,1}$: The average response time for processing of an inquiry of a customer order should be SHORT.

An example of satisfaction function can be defined for SHORT of $ER_{3,1,1}$ as follows:

In this figure, one (1) represents total satisfaction and zero (0) represents total dissatisfaction. Basically, it indicates that if a capability realization takes more than ten seconds to process of an inquiry of a customer order, it is totally unacceptable; if it takes no more than five seconds, it achieves the highest level of satisfaction; and if it takes between five and ten seconds, its satisfaction level is gradually decreased as number of seconds is increased. The numbers used in this example are for illustration only.

Another example of the derived non-functional requirements is shown below:

$ER_{3,1,2}$: The throughout for service activation should be HIGH.

An example of satisfaction function can be defined for *HIGH* of $ER_{3,1,2}$ as follows:

Safety

There is no safety requirement for business capabilities in this contract.

Organization-Related Business Environment

ER_4: Some of business processes may be business environment specific. It is specified as a qualitative non-functional requirement.

Organization Limitations

ER_5: Some of business processes may be organization specific. It is specified as a qualitative non-functional requirement.

Figure 4. Satisfaction function for latency requirement $ER_{3,1,1}$

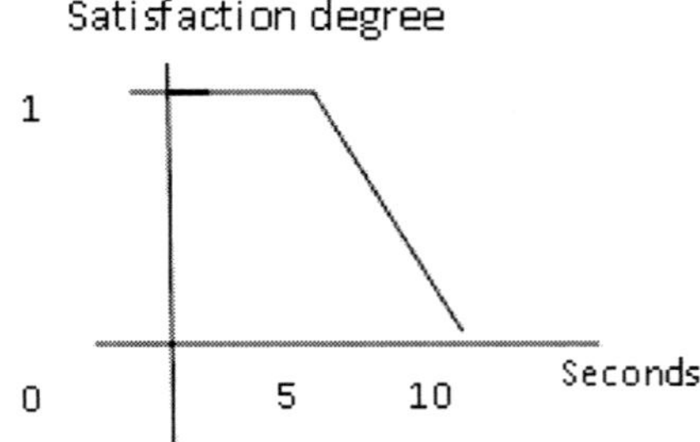

Market Limitations

$ER_{6:}$ *Some of business processes may be market specific.* It is specified as a qualitative non-functional requirement since no quantitative constraints are specified.

Financial Limitations

$ER_{7:}$ Financial loss from cancellation of customer orders due to service delay must be MINIMAL.

An example of satisfaction function can be defined for MINIMAL of ER_4 in Figure 4. In this figure, one (1) represents total satisfaction and zero (0) represents total dissatisfaction. Basically, it indicates that if percentage of revenue lost from cancelled orders due to service delay is no more than two (2) percent, it achieves the highest level of satisfaction; if percentage of revenue lost from cancelled orders due to service delay is equal to or more than five (5) percent, it is totally unacceptable; and its satisfaction level is gradually decreased when percentage of revenue lost from cancelled orders due to service delay is increased from two (2) to five (5) percent. The numbers used in this example are for illustration only.

Legal-Related

Regulatory Limitations

None identified

Legal limitations

ER_8: Customer order data must not be released for public usage without consent.

Miscellaneous

None identified

Trade-Offs

Many trade-offs can be formulated in the contract. One example of such trade-offs is that between reliability and performance of services since they usually conflict with each other and it is difficult

Figure 5. Satisfaction function for latency requirement $ER_{3,1,2}$

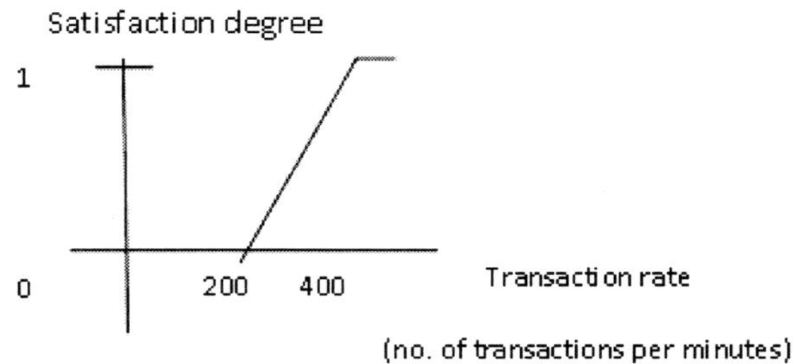

Figure 6. Satisfaction function for minimal financial loss due to service delay

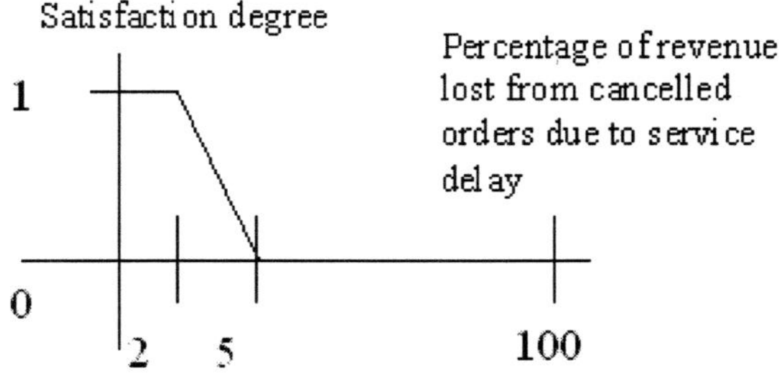

to achieve their highest satisfaction levels at the same time. This trade-off can be represented as the following formula using a fuzzy compromise operator. Please note that elastic non-functional requirements $ER_{3,1,1}$, $ER_{3,1,2}$ are combined using a fuzzy conjunctive operator since they usually can be satisfied at the same time.

$$C\ (ER_{2}, ER_{3,1,1} \cap ER_{3,1,2}).$$

Assume that "*Min*" is selected for the fuzzy conjunctive operator to aggregate $ER_{3,1,1}$ and $ER_{3,1,2}$, the satisfaction degree of $ER_{3,1,1}$ is 0.8, and satisfaction degree of $ER_{3,1,2}$ is 0.6 based on their satisfaction functions, the result of $ER_{3,1,1} \cap ER_{3,1,2}$ is 0.6. Assume *arithmetic mean* is selected to be the compromise operator for aggregating service requirements of reliability and performance. Please note that *arithmetic mean* is both the *averaging* and *compensatory* operators. In addition, assume that the satisfaction degree of ER_2 is 0.9 based on its satisfaction function. The satisfaction degree of aggregated requirement $C\ (ER_{2}, ER_{3,1,1} \cap ER_{3,1,2})$ is 0.75.

CONCLUDING REMARKS

The quality problems, increased cost, and lack of agility in building OSS applications are caused by lack of standards, methodologies, and data / component / process description languages and implementations that are often technology specific and are constantly subject to change, and hence creating a barrier to business agility and quality management as requirements change as well as new middleware's are introduced. NGOSS of TMF has already laid out the foundations for a rigorous methodology which enables high level and more abstract business focused models of OSS applications be designed for a given software platform based on Service Oriented Architecture (SOA). A key enabler for increased use of NGOSS is the concept of a "contract". In this chapter, we developed a method for contract based non-functional requirements specification using qualitative, crisp quantitative, and elastic quantitative non-functional requirements specification techniques. An example of non-functional specification of a NGOSS contract has been presented based on these techniques. The quantitative non-functional requirements specification techniques, especially elastic non-functional requirements specification which enables trade-offs in a development process, enhance capability of current NGOSS contract specification which is only qualitative currently.

Future works include service selection based on evaluation of satisfaction of non-functional requirements using both crisp and elastic non-functional requirements specification in service oriented architecture and integration of the proposed approaches with other methods in valued based software engineering (Huang & Boehm, 2006).

REFERENCES

Chen, S., & Hwang, C. (1991). *Fuzzy multiple attribute decision making: Method and applications. (LNEMS 375)*. New York: Springer-Verlag.

Cysneiros, L., & Leite, J. (2004). Nonfunctional requirements: From elicitation to conceptual models. *IEEE Transactions on Software Engineering*, *30*, 328–350. doi:10.1109/TSE.2004.10

Dubois, D., & Prade, H. (1984). Criteria aggregation and ranking of alternatives in the framework of fuzzy set theory. *Studies in the Management Sciences*, *20*, 209–240.

Erl, T. (2005). *Service-Oriented Architecture (SOA): Concepts, technology, and design*. Prentice-Hall.

Georgalas, N., & Azmoodeh, M. (2004a). Using MDA in technology-independent specifications of NGOSS architectures. *Proceedings of the 1st European Workshop on MDA (MDA-IA 2004)*, Enschede, Netherlands.

Georgalas, N., Azmoodeh, M., Clark, T., Evans, A., Sammut, P., & Willans, J. (2004b). MDA-driven development of standard-compliant OSS components: The OSS/J inventory case study. *Proceedings of the 2nd European Workshop on Model Driven Architecture with emphasis on Methodologies and Transformations (EWMDA 2004)*, Canterbury, UK, 7-8 September 2004.

Huang, L., & Boehm, B. (2006). How much software quality investment is enough: A value-based approach. *IEEE Software*, (September/October): 2006.

Kruchter, P. (1995). The 4+1 view model of architecture. *IEEE Software*, *6*(12), 42–50. doi:10.1109/52.469759

Leymann, F. & Karastoyanova, D. (2008). Service Oriented Architecture–overview of technologies and Standards. *Information Technology, 50.*

Liu, X., & Yen, J. (1996). An analytic framework for specifying and analyzing imprecise requirements. *Proceedings of the 18th IEEE International Conference on Software Engineering (ICSE-1996)*, (pp. 60-69). Berlin.

Margolis, B. (2007). *SOA for the business developer: Concepts, BPEL, and SCA*. Mc Press.

Mylopoulos, J., Chung, L., & Nixon, B. (1992). Representing and using non-functional requirements: A process-oriented approach. *IEEE Transactions on Software Engineering, 18*, 483–497. doi:10.1109/32.142871

Ortiz, G., & Hernändez, J. (2006). Toward UML profiles for Web Services and their extra-functional properties. *Proceedings of the 2006 IEEE International Conference on Web Services*, September 2006.

Paech, B., & Kerkow, D. (2004). Non-functional requirements engineering-quality is essential. *Proceedings of REFSQ'04*.

TeleManagement Forum. (2004a). *New generation operations systems and software*. Retrieved from http://www.tmforum.org/browse.asp?catID=1911

TeleManagement Forum. (2004b). *NGOSS architecture technology neutral specification: Contract description: Business and system views*.

Telemanagement Forum. (2004c). *TMF eTOM process framework*. Retrieved from www.tmforum.org

TeleManagement Forum. (2005). *NGOSS contract examples: Examples of the NGOSS lifecycle and methodology for NGOSS contract definition.*

Tsai, W. T., Jin, Z., Wang, P., & Wu, B. (2007). Requirement engineering in service-oriented system engineering. *Proceedings of the 2007 IEEE International Conference on e-Business Engineering*, (pp. 661-668). Hong Kong, China, October 2007.

Wada, H., Suzuki, J., & Oba, K. (2006). Modeling non-functional aspects in Service Oriented Architecture. *Proceedings of the 3rd IEEE International Conference on Services Computing (SCC)*, Chicago, IL, September 2006.

Wada, H., Suzuki, J., & Oba, K. (2007). A feature modeling support for non-functional constraints in Service Oriented Architecture. *Proceedings of the 4th IEEE International Conference on Services Computing (SCC)*, Salt Lake City, UT, July 2007.

Xiang, J., Liu, L., Qiao, W., & Yang, J. (2007). SREM: A Service Requirements Elicitation Mechanism based on ontology. *Proceedings of the 2007 IEEE International Conference on Computer Software and Applications*, (pp. 196-203). Beijing, China, July, 2007.

Zimmermann, H. (1991). *Fuzzy set theory and its applications*. Boston: Kluwer Academic.

Chapter 11
Applying Concept Reuse for Adaptive Service Composition

Onyeka Ezenwoye
South Dakota State University, USA

S. Masoud Sadjadi
Florida International University, USA

ABSTRACT

Web Services are gaining acceptance as the predominant standards-based approach to building open distributed systems. Business Process Execution Language (BPEL) allows for the composition of existing Web Services to create higher-level Web Services. There is a need to deliver reliable service compositions with precise Quality of Service (QoS) attributes covering functional correctness, performance and dependability, especially since the current BPEL standard provides limited constructs for specifying exceptional behavior and recovery actions. This chapter presents a language-based approach to transparently adapting BPEL processes to improve reliability. This approach addresses reliability at the business process layer (i.e., the language layer) using a code generator, which weaves fault-tolerant code to the original code and an external proxy. The chapter also explains the software patterns present in this approach. These patterns constitute abstract reusable concepts that will facilitate rapid model-driven development of adaptive service compositions that can be easily configured for a range of situations.

INTRODUCTION

In *component-based architectures*, the functionality of a whole system is divided into smaller functions, each encapsulated in *components* that can work together. As an extension of the component-based architecture, in a *distributed system*, components may reside in different physical locations (*e.g.*, client/server architecture; Nickull, 2005). Web Services are gaining acceptance as the predominant standards-based approach to building open distributed systems. With Web Services, distributed applications can be encapsulated as self-contained, discoverable

DOI: 10.4018/978-1-60960-493-6.ch011

Figure 1. Service composition

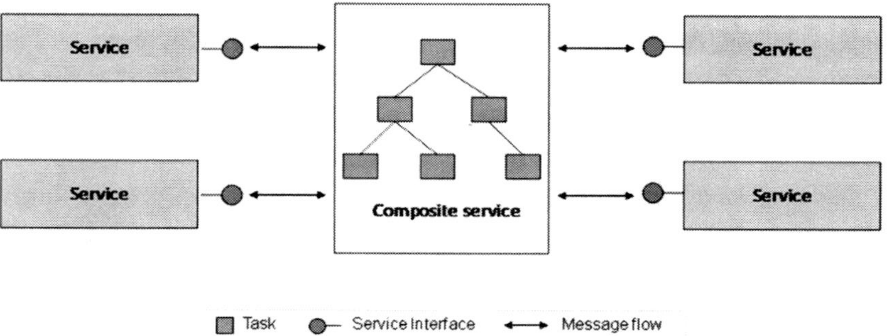

and Internet-accessible software components that can be integrated to create other applications. The fundamental aspects of Web Services can be summarized as follows: (1) strict separation of service interface description, implementation, and binding; (2) declarative policies and Service Level Agreements (SLAs) to govern service interactions; and (3) loosely coupled, standards-based and message-centric interactions between autonomous and replaceable service components (Erradi, Maheshwari, & Tosic, 2006).

The family of specifications that makes up the Web service standards includes a specification for service composition known as *Business Process Execution Language* (BPEL; Ezenwoye & Sadjadi, 2005). BPEL allows for the composition of existing Web Services to create new higher-level Web Services. BPEL is used to define abstractions that represent composite services. As depicted in Figure 1, these executable abstractions constitute centralized applications that model the interaction between the integrated distributed services. The composite service is modeled as a graph where the nodes represent *tasks* and the edges represent some *composition constraints* in the form if inter-task dependencies, data flow or flow control. Figure 2 shows the Service Composition Model. In this model, the composite service is an aggregation of tasks and the tasks may be implemented by

Figure 2. The service composition model

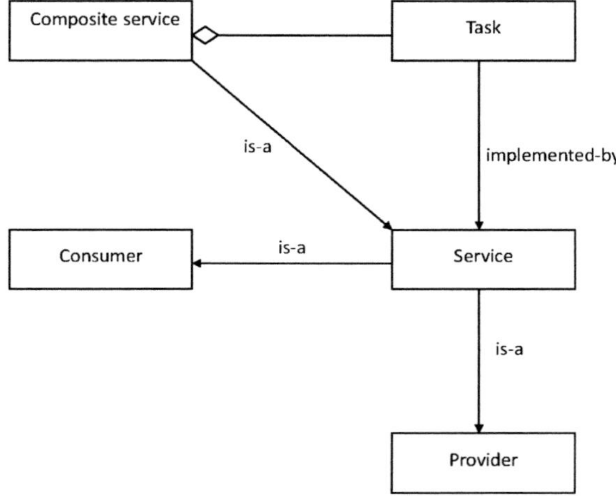

the integrated services. The composite service itself is a service.

In Grid computing, the resources available on disparate distributed computing environments are harnessed to create a parallel infrastructure that allows for applications to be processed in a distributed manner. The goal is to create an accessible virtual supercomputer by integrating distributed computers with the use of open standards (Foster, Kesselman, & Tuecke, 2001). To achieve this, OGSA (The Open Grid Services Architecture) defines an architecture for service-oriented Grid computing. Under OGSA, computational and storage resources that exist within autonomous collaborating institutions are exposed as an extensible set of networked Grid services that can be integrated to create higher-function applications (Foster, Kesselman, Nick, & Tuecke, 2002). As illustrated in Figure 3, this service integration that is achieved through composite services are used to create applications for coordinated problem solving in areas such as Bioinformatics and Meteorology. These highly available applications need to remain operational and rapidly responsive even when failures disrupt some of the nodes in the system (Birman, Renesse, & Vogels, 2004). Thus, there is a need to deliver reliable service compositions with precise Quality of Service (QoS) attributes covering functional correctness, performance and dependability (Ouzzani & Bouguettaya, 2004), especially since current Web Services standards provide limited constructs for specifying exceptional behavior and recovery actions.

While it is relatively easy to make an individual service fault-tolerant, addressing reliability and availability of Web Services collaborating in multiple application scenarios is a challenging task (Dialani, Miles, Moreau, Roure, & Luck, 2002). This is because the integration of multiple services introduces new levels of complexity in management. Due to the autonomy of services involved in a composition, the management of composite services cannot extend into the administrative boundaries of individual services (Vogels, 2003). Thus the composed service has no influence over the factors affecting QoS provision. Also, since services interacting in a composition are distributed, there is the added problem of Internet latency and its unmanaged nature. More-

Figure 3. Grid service interaction

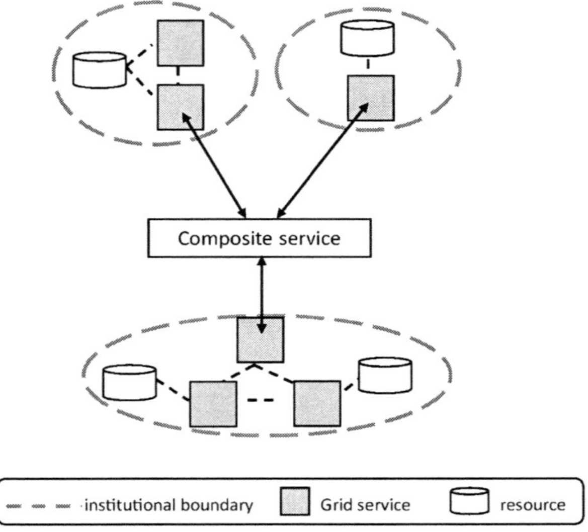

over, services may fail because of problems in their execution such as network faults, overload and lack of resources (Erradi, Maheshwari, & Tosic, 2006).

Given the unreliability of communication channels, the unbounded communication delays, and the autonomy of the interacting services, it is difficult for developers of composite services to anticipate and account for all the dynamics of such interactions. There is therefore a need for adaptability in composed services to make them more robust and dependable. Besides, ensuring the reliability of composite Web Services that are expected to dynamically discover and assemble components, configure themselves, and operate securely and reliably in a completely automated manner calls for the development of new reliability techniques that introduce *autonomic* functionality to address these challenges (Birman, Renesse, & Vogels, 2004; Erradi, Maheshwari, & Tosic, 2006).

Autonomic computing (Kephart & Chess, 2003) promises to solve the management problem by embedding the management of complex systems inside the systems themselves, freeing the users from potentially overwhelming details. The ultimate goal of autonomic computing is to create *self-managing* systems that are able to function with little direct human intervention. A Web service is said to be autonomic if it encapsulates some autonomic attributes (Gurguis & Zeid, 2005). Autonomic attributes include: (1) *Self-Configuration*, for the automatic configuration of components; (2) *Self-Optimization*, for automatic monitoring and control; (3) *Self-Healing*, for automatic discovery, and management of faults; and (4) *Self-Protection*, for automatic identification and protection from attacks or failure.

In this chapter, we present an approach to transparently incorporating autonomic behavior in BPEL processes. Our approach does not require the processes to be redeveloped from scratch nor is there a need for any manual modification to the code of the *existing* processes. The adaptation is done in a manner that the code for business logic is kept separated from the code for robustness of the process to avoid these different concerns to result in entangled code that is difficult to maintain and evolve. We explain design patterns (Gamma, Helm, Johnson, & Vlissides, 1995) present in the approach. These patterns constitute abstract reusable concepts that will facilitate the rapid development of adaptive service compositions that can be easily configured for a range of situations.

The rest of this chapter is structured as follows. In Section 2, we introduce reliability in composite services and survey possible approaches to providing reliability in composite services. We finish this section by identifying where our approach, TRAP/BPEL, fits in the introduced taxonomy. In Section 3, we provide an overview of our approach to instrumenting BPEL processes. In Sections 4, we explain the various design patterns available in our approach. Section 5 contains some related work. Finally, some concluding remarks are provided in Section 6.

ADDRESSING RELIABILITY IN COMPOSITE COMPONENTS

Structurally, a system is a set of *interrelated* components that are *interacting* in an *interdependent* manner to accomplish a set of goals. In this view, a component is in itself another system and embodies the interrelations of its member components. This recursion stops when a system is considered as being atomic and thus any further decomposition cannot be perceived, or is ignored (Laprie, 1995). Although a system does not necessarily have to interact with an external entity, in the context of distributed systems, the service delivered by a system is the behavior of the system as *perceived* by the other systems with which it is interacting (Laprie, 1995; Avizienis, Laprie, Randell, & Landwehr, 2004).

A service delivered is said to be correct, only if it implements the system's function. A *failure* is an event that occurs *when* the delivered service does not meet the specification of expected system function or the specification does not adequately capture the functional requirements of the system. The *failure domain* of distributed services can be classified as follows:

- **Content:** Content failure happens when the information delivered at the service interface is different from what is expected, as defined by the specification (Avizienis, Laprie, Randell, & Landwehr, 2004)
- **Timing:** When the delivery of information at the service interface does not meet the required timing constraints, a timing failure is said to have occurred (Avizienis, Laprie, Randell, & Landwehr, 2004)
- **Availability:** A system can become unavailable through the cessation of service or the system is just not reachable. Cessation of service can occur during a *halt failure.* When this happens, the external state becomes constant and system activity is no longer perceptible.

So failure occurs because part of the system has assumed an erroneous state that does not correspond to the correct service state (*i.e.*, the logical state of the system differs from the intended value). The error itself is the manifestation of a *fault* (an anomalous physical condition) in the system (Nelson, 1990). Faults can be internal or external. Internal faults reside within the system and can be caused by improper specification or implementation. External faults are those that occur in the environment of the system and are caused by external disturbances such as harsh environmental conditions, unanticipated inputs, or system misuse.

The goal of *fault-tolerance* is to improve *dependability* in a system by enabling it to perform its intended functions in the presence of a given number of faults (Nelson, 1990). There exist several definitions of dependability (Avizienis, Laprie, Randell, & Landwehr, 2004). These definitions often depend on the attributes (*e.g.*, availability, reliability and safety) of the system that are being defined as a criterion to decide whether or not a system is dependable. The attribute defined may depend on the intended use of the system.

In general, dependability is based on the notion of *reliance* in the context of interacting components. It associates to the relation *depends upon*, where a component *A* depends upon a component *B* if the correctness of *B's* service delivery is necessary for the correctness of *A's* service delivery (Avizienis, Laprie, Randell, & Landwehr, 2004). This relationship is typical of composite services since they are entirely dependent on interaction with partner services. An error may propagate from a partner to the composite thereby creating new errors. As illustrated in Figure 4, an error can propagate from component *A* to component *B* since *B* receives service from *A*. The error propagation happens when an error reaches the service interface of component *A* and service delivered by *A* to *B* becomes incorrect. The failure of *A* becomes an external fault to *B* and propagates the error into *B* through its use interface.

Our work focuses on the *reliability* attribute of dependability with a specialization on *robustness* as a *secondary attribute*. Avizienis (Avizienis, Laprie, Randell, & Landwehr, 2004) defines

Figure 4. Error propagation (software fault tolerance: fundamental concepts)

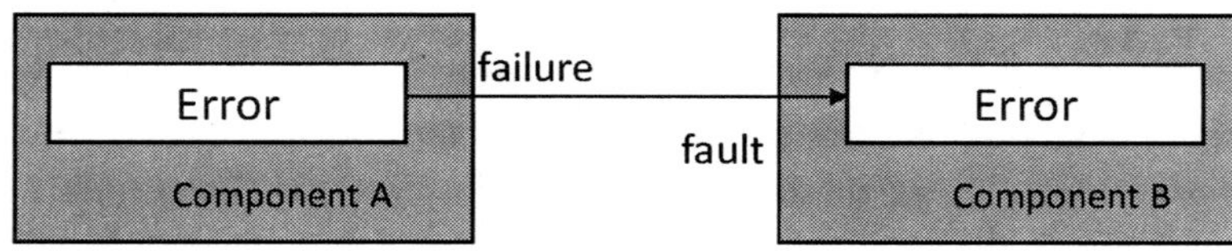

reliability as the continuity of *correct* service; it defines robustness as dependability with respect to *external* faults. Reliability is a key requirement for building dependable systems. The means to achieving dependability can be classified into four groups: (1) *fault avoidance*, through rigorous design and implementation to prevent the occurrence or the introduction of faults; (2) *fault removal*, through verification, validation and diagnosis to reduce the number or the severity of faults; (3) *fault forecasting*, to estimate the presence and consequences of faults; and (4) *fault tolerance*, to provide correct service in spite the presence of faults (Laprie, 1995; Erradi, Maheshwari, & Tosic, 2006). These techniques that are applied at development time are not sufficient enough for ensuring the reliability of composite Web Services that are expected to dynamically discover and assemble components, configure themselves, and operate securely and reliably in a completely automated manner. This calls for the development of new reliability techniques that introduce *autonomic* functionality to address these challenges (Birman, Renesse, & Vogels, 2004; Erradi, Maheshwari, & Tosic, 2006).

New reliability techniques for service compositions can be developed at four layers. Figure 5 shows the different layers at which reliability techniques can be applied.

Figure 5. Layers to apply reliability techniques

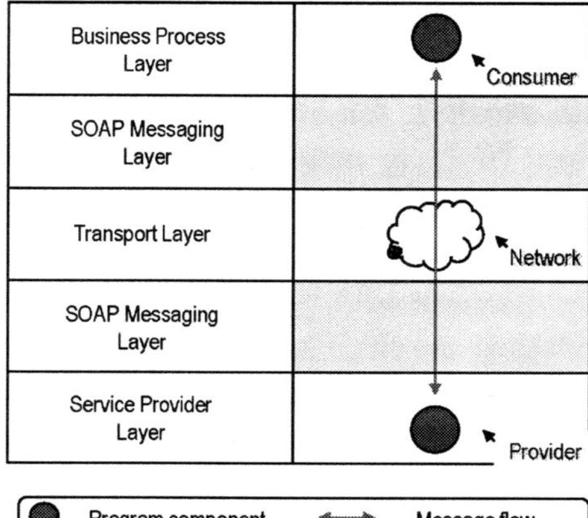

Service provider layer: At this level, reliability focuses on the service hosting environment. Here, reliability can be achieved by techniques that provide redundancy of computation and data, load sharing to improve performance and fault tolerance, and clustering which interconnects multiple servers to avoid single point of failure (Erradi, Maheshwari, & Tosic, 2006).

Transport layer: At this level, the focus is on implementing reliable messaging for Web Services at the transport layer. SOAP messaging can take different forms of reliability depending on the underlying transport service (Tai, Mikalsen, & Rouvellou, 2003). Therefore, techniques in this layer center on using message-oriented middleware (MOM; Goel, Sharda, & Taniar, 2003) to ensure reliability and robustness of message traffic. Example technologies are reliable transport protocols such as HTTPR (HTTPR Specification) and messaging infrastructures such as IBM WebsphereMQ (Gilman & Schreiber, 1996), which have built-in transactional support for business processes (Erradi, Maheshwari, & Tosic, 2006).

SOAP messaging layer: Addressing reliability at this layer focuses on extending SOAP messages to include reliability properties that allow messages to be delivered reliably between services in the presence of component, system, or network failures. Using recently proposed SOAP-based protocols such as WS-Reliability (WS-Reliability 1.1, 2004), "extended SOAP" messages can carry relevant reliability information. However, the extended SOAP messages must be understood and supported by a messaging infrastructure (Erradi, Maheshwari, & Tosic, 2006; Tai, Mikalsen, & Rouvellou, 2003; Ferguson, Storey, Lovering, & Shewchuk, 2003).

Business process layer: Reliability at this layer aims to provide dependable composition of Web Services through advanced failure handling and compensation-based transaction protocols (Erradi, Maheshwari, & Tosic, 2006; Tai, Mikalsen, Wohlstadter, Desai, & Rouvellou, 2004). Efforts in this layer can be categorized into two groups; *language-based* and *non language-based* approaches. *Language-based* techniques provide advanced failure handling and adaptability by augmenting the process logic with additional language constructs while *non-language* based approaches focus specifically on the process supporting infrastructure such as the execution engine. Our work fits into this category by enabling adaptability in BPEL process to address the concerns raised above. One might argue that BPEL should be extended with constructs to handle those concerns. However, this would increase the complexity of the language and it is also against the principle of separation of concerns (Charfi & Mezini, 2005). Constructs for specifying exceptional behavior and recovery actions should be modularized and externalized and not scattered and tangled with the service implementation. Entangling the logic for exceptional behavior and recovery actions with the business logic of the application negatively impacts maintainability and adaptability. To address these requirements for adaptable BPEL process execution, we propose an approach that uses the transparent shaping programming model to transparently adapt their behavior.

Failure Handling Techniques

There are several factors that can cause failure in the execution of the workflows that define composite services in distributed environments; they include network failure, resource overload, or non-availability of required components. It is therefore important for workflow management systems to be able to identify and handle failures and support reliable execution in the presence of concurrency and failures. Workflow failure handling techniques are classified into two groups, *task-level* and *workflow-level* (Yu & Buyya, 2005; Yu & Buyya, 2005).

Task-level techniques mask the effects of the execution failure of individual tasks in the workflow. Task-level techniques include *retry, alternate resource, alternate task, checkpoint/restart* and *replication*. The *retry* technique tries to execute the same task on the same resource after failure. The *alternate resource* technique (also known as migration) submits failed task to another resource while the *alternate task* technique executes another implementation of a certain task if the previous one failed. The *checkpointing* technique attempts to continue workflow execution from the point of failure, this may involve moving failed tasks transparently to other resources. The *replication* technique runs the same task simultaneously on different resources to ensure successful task execution provided that at least one of the replicas does not fail (Yu & Buyya, 2005).

Workflow-level techniques manipulate the workflow structure such as execution flow to deal with erroneous conditions. Workflow-level techniques include *user-defined exception handling* and *rescue workflow*. *User-defined exception handling* allows users to specify a fault-handling behavior for a certain failure of a task in the workflow; the fault-handling strategy may be specified as part of the process logic. The *rescue workflow* technique executes a rescue workflow, which performs a set of recovery actions/tasks. The rescue workflow can be used, for instance, where the failure was due to lack of disk space that can be reclaimed or in cases where totally new resources need to be assigned for continued execution (Thain, Tannenbaum, & Livny, 2003; Yu & Buyya, 2005.

Adaptive Service Composition

As the standard for creating composite Web Services, BPEL in increasingly being used for commercial and scientific applications. However, BPEL as a composition language mainly concentrates on modeling the interaction between autonomous services and does not consider the behavior of such models at runtime. BPEL specification does not consider how to enforce or simply probe the constraints on the composition (Baresi, Ghezzi, & Guinea, 2004) and this presents some challenges to reliable service composition, especially in Grid environments (Leymann, 2006; Ezenwoye, Sadjadi, Carey, & Robinson, 2007). For scientific Grid applications, when a Grid service partner fails, the application fails and either has to be recomposed or restarted even though there are other nodes in the Grid that can substitute for the failed service. This problem is made more severe by the fact that such applications are often long running and complex; hence, ensuring their high availability and reliability, in spite of service or infrastructure failures, becomes a critical issue. Also, making such applications dynamically recomposable would alleviate the problem of frequent redevelopment and improve reliability.

The highly-level nature of BPEL is intended to provide a level of abstraction that is suitable for domain specialist to easily orchestrate the interaction between services. Therefore any technique for addressing reliability and adaptability need not increase the complexity of the language while maintaining the separation of concerns (Kiczales, et al., 1997). Constructs for specifying exceptional behavior and recovery actions should be modularized and externalized and not scattered and tangled with the composite service implementation. Entangling the logic for exceptional behavior and recovery actions with the business logic of the application negatively impacts maintainability and adaptability. TRAP/BPEL (Ezenwoye & Sadjadi, 2007) is an approach that addresses these requirements by using the transparent shaping programming model (Sadjadi, McKinley, & Cheng, 2005) to transparently adapt the behavior of BPEL process execution. The Transparent Shaping programming model provides dynamic adaptation in existing applications. The goal is to respond to dynamic changes in their non-functional requirements. In transparent shaping, an application is augmented with code that intercepts and redirects interaction to *adaptive code*. The adaptation is transparent because it preserves the original functional behavior and does not tangle the code that provides the new behavior (adaptive code) with the application code.

By adapting *existing* applications, transparent shaping aims to achieve a separation of concerns (McKinley, Sadjadi, Kasten, & Cheng, 2004). That is, enabling the separate development of the functional requirements (the business logic) from the non-functional requirements of an application[1]. In TRAP/BPEL, *transparency* ensures that the adaptation preserves the original behavior of the process and does not tangle the code for *autonomic* behavior with that of the business process and its original functionality. Adaptive code is encapsulated in external components that use a set of extensible recovery policies to declaratively specify how to handle exceptional behavior and how to recover from typical failures.

There are two steps to creating an adaptable BPEL composite service during the transparent shaping process. The first step involves statically transforming an existing service composition to produce an *adapt-ready* application at development time. During this first step, generic interceptors (called *hooks*) are woven into an application. At the second step, the hooks are used to intercept and redirect interaction to *adaptive code*, thereby making the adapt-ready application adaptable. The adaptive code provides the new autonomic behavior. Since a BPEL process is an aggregation of tasks performed by services, the most appropriate place to insert interception hooks is at the point of interaction between the composite service and its partner services. Therefore, tasks which require monitoring are identified and hooks are inserted at their point of invocation (as illustrated in Figure 6).

In BPEL processes, the point of interaction with partner services is at the *invoke* instruction. The inserted code is in the form of standard BPEL constructs to ensure the portability of the modified process. This adaptation permits for the BPEL workflow behavior to be modified at runtime by redirecting interaction through the Proxy, which provides adaptive behavior.

Figure 6. Workflow fault tolerance classification

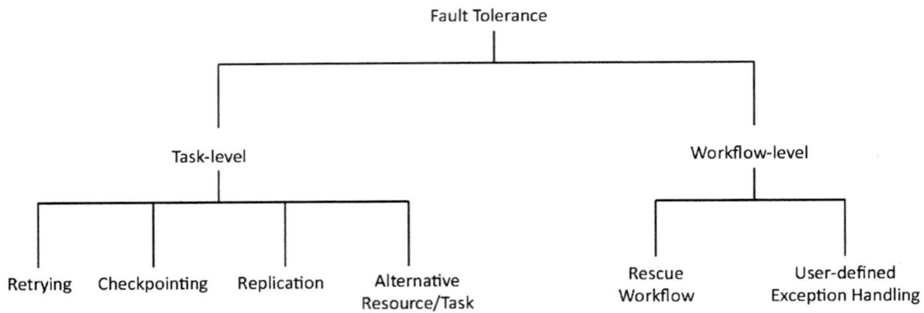

Figure 8 depicts the main players in the system. For runtime failure management and adaptability of the workflow, we use a Generic Proxy. The Proxy sits between the BPEL engine and the partner services of the workflow, and intercepts calls in both directions. The BPEL engine is a virtual machine that takes a workflow defined in BPEL, converts it into a BPEL process and exposes the process as a web service. The process enacts the business logic of the workflow. The Generic Proxy comprises two distinct components: (1) a Monitoring component that monitors each invocation; and (2) a Recovery component that kicks in when a failure is detected. To intercept calls transparently from the BPEL engine (i.e., imposing no changes to the BPEL engine), all calls to partner services originating from in the BPEL workflow are replaced with calls to the Proxy. The BPEL workflow needs to go through an adaptation process for the Proxy to be able to intercept the calls between BPEL engine and partner services. After the adaptation process is complete, the adapted BPEL document is then deployed on the BPEL engine for enactment. Upon a failure, the proxy has to detect and handle the failure based on the recovery policy specified for the workflow. Recall that in Section 2, the failure domain of distributed services is classified into content, timing and availability. The monitor module detects the occurrence of a failure and triggers the Recovery module. The recovery module refers to the Policy file for the corresponding recovery action to perform. A recovery policy is used in the proxy to dictate the adaptive behavior for each monitored service. The policies themselves can be changed at runtime. This design of the Proxy allows developers to dynamically define new failure handling.

The TRAP/BPEL framework currently supports failure recovery at the task-level, and at that

Figure 7. Adaptable service composition

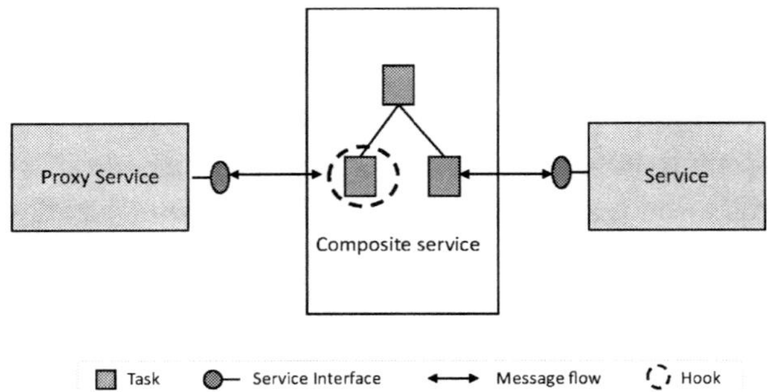

Figure 8. Overview of system and its components

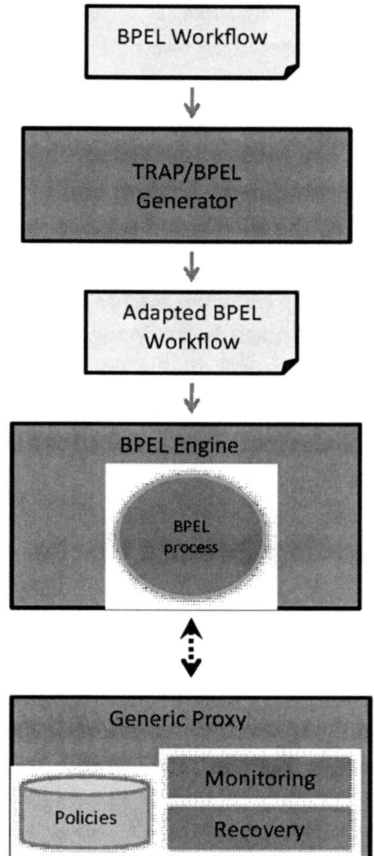

only *retrying* and *alternative resource* (see Figure 6) solutions are available. The framework was designed to work with stateless and idempotent services and applications. However, the framework can be extended to support other failure handling techniques especially for Grid environments where statefull service call for more sophisticated failure handling (Kalayci, Ezenwoye, Viswanathan, Dasgupta, Sadjadi, & Fong, 2008).

High-Level Architecture

In this section, we show the high-level architecture of the generic proxy and the generation process. Figure 9 illustrates the architectural diagram of TRAP/BPEL at run time. As can be seen from the figure, several adapt-ready BPEL processes can be assigned to one generic proxy, which augments the BPEL processes with self-management behavior. The generic proxy uses a look-up mechanism to query a registry service at runtime for services that can be used to replace failed services. Also, generic proxy has a standard interface which bears no relation to the interfaces of the monitored services. The generic proxy in Figure 9 has as interface pt_g that is able to accept requests for the any monitored Web Services

Figure 9. Architectural diagram showing the sequence of interactions among the components in TRAP/BPEL during runtime

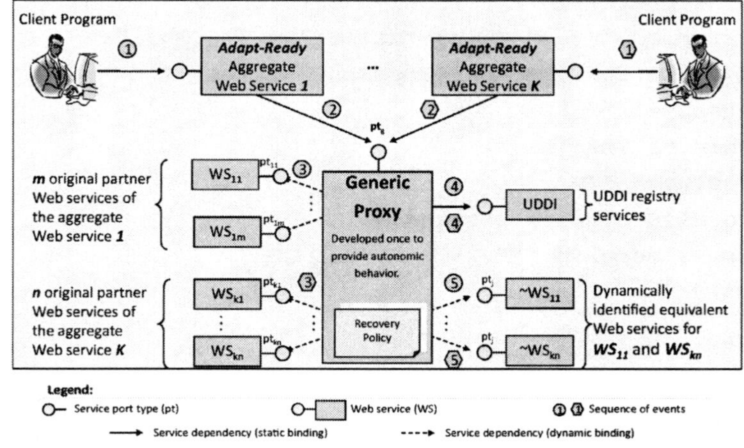

(*e.g.*, WS_{11} and WS_{kn} partner Web Services) with different port types. As can be followed in the figure, a recovery policy can be used to forward the intercepted calls to original services (labels 1, 2, and 3) and use a substitute service in case an original service fails (labels 4 and 5)

The generic proxy can provide self-management behavior either common to all adapt-ready BPEL processes or specific to each monitored invocation using some high-level policies. These high-level policies are specified in a configuration file that is loaded at startup time into the generic proxy. We plan to allow runtime modification to these high-level policies in the future versions of TRAP/BPEL. Box 1 shows an example policy file where each unique monitored invocation can have a policy specified under a <service> element. The <InvokeName> element (line 4) has a value that uniquely identifies a monitored invocation in an adapt-ready BPEL process. The generic proxy checks all intercepted invocations and tries to match these invocations with the specified policies. If it finds a policy for that invocation, the proxy behaves accordingly; otherwise it follows its default behavior. If a policy exists, the generic proxy may take one of the following actions according to the policy: (1) invoke the service being recommended in the policy (line 6); (2) find and invoke another service to substitute for the monitored service; and (3) retry the invocation of the monitored service in the event of its failure (line 10). The policy also specifies the time interval between retries (line 12).

Box 1The default behavior of the proxy is to consult the registry to find a service that implements the same port type as the monitored invocation. This service is then invoked as a substitute service.

Incorporating Generic Hooks

As mentioned before, following the Transparent Shaping programming model (Sadjadi, McKinley, & Cheng, 2005), we first need to incorporate some generic hooks at *sensitive joinpoints* in the original BPEL process. For the TRAP/BPEL framework,

Box 1. A portion of a policy file for the generic proxy

```
1. <Policy>
2.  <Service>
3.   <!--a unique name for monitored invocation-->
4.   <InvokeName value="WS-Invoke"/>
5.   <!--WSDL for a preferred alternative service-->
6.   <WsdlUrl preferred="true" value="http://.../WS.wsdl"/>
7.   <!--timeout value for the monitored invocation-->
8.   <Timeout seconds="2"/>
9.   <!--the number of retries-->
10.   <MaxRetry value="2"/>
11.   <!--time to wait between retries-->
12.   <RetryInterval seconds="5"/>
13.  </Service>
14.  <Service>
15.  ...
16.  </Service>
17. </Policy>
```

Box 2. Left, an invocation in the original BPEL; Right, an invocation in the adapt-ready BPEL

```
<invoke name="InvokeWS11"
 partnerLink="..."
 portType="pt11"
 operation="operation1"
 inputVariable="..."
 outputVariable="...">
</invoke>
```

```
<invoke name="ProxyInvokeWS11"
 partnerLink="..."
 portType="pxns:proxyPT"
 operation="genericInvocation"
 inputVariable="..."
 outputVariable="...">
</invoke>
```

as listed in Box 2, an invocation that is selected for monitoring is replaced with an invocation to the generic proxy. This approach allows more flexibility as to what kind of adaptive behavior to provide. We note that as the port type of the proxy is generic, all the contents of the original method invocation are serialized in the input variable. Therefore, the process of replacing the target invocation with the proxy invocation involves identifying all the messages that are needed to create the input message for the proxy. Also, the sequence of activities needed to deserialize the output message from the proxy need to be created. This is done in a way that does not affect the original execution sequence of the BPEL process.

To better understand the need for serialization and deserialization, we provide a section of the WSDL of the generic proxy Web service in Box 3. As can be seen from its description, the interface for the proxy has two operations: genericInvocation and extract (lines 22-25 and 26-29 respectively). The input message for the proxy genericInvocation operation (lines 1-6) has four parts: (1) invokename, which is used to identify the monitored service; (2) porttype, which identifies the port type of the monitored invocation (this variable is the unique key used to query the UDDI registry for services that implement the same interface); (3) operation, which identifies the exact operation of the port type being called; and (4) variables, which contains the serialized input message for the monitored service. When the proxy generic-Invocation operation called with the genericInputMessage, the proxy identifies which service is being monitored and the necessary details about its invocation. The proxy can then take one of several actions as specified in the policy file.

At runtime the input message for each monitored service is serialized and used as part of the input message for the proxy genericInvocation operation. The proxy invokes any equivalent service with that same input message. Service invocation from within the proxy is done with the Web Service Invocation Framework (WSIF; Duftler, Mukhi, Slominski, & Sanc). A reply from the substitute service is serialized into the genericOutputMessage (lines 8-10) and sent back to the adapted BPEL process from the proxy. We need to serialize the input and output messages (for the monitored invocations) because the proxy needs to have standard interface through which messages for any service can be sent.

When the genericOutputMessage arrives at the adapted BPEL process, it will need to be deserialized for further processing within the BPEL process, as part of the original execution. Since BPEL is not a general-purpose programming language, it lacks the necessary constructs that would be needed to deserialized the generic output message (genericOutputMessage) of the generic proxy. One solution to this problem, without extending the BPEL language, is to use a partner Web service to perform more complicated data manipulation. To this end, we have decided to use the generic proxy to deserialize the genericOutputMessage.

Box 3. A section of the WSDL description of the interface of the generic proxy

```
1. <message name="genericInputMessage">
2.  <part name="invokename" type="xsd:string"/>
3.  <part name="porttype" type="xsd:string"/>
4.  <part name="operation" type="xsd:string"/>
5.  <part name="variables" type="xsd:string"/>
6. </message>
7.
8. <message name="genericOutputMessage">
9.  <part name="reply" type="xsd:string"/>
10. </message>
11.
12. <message name="extractInputMessage">
13.  <part name="values" type="xsd:string"/>
14.  <part name="param" type="xsd:string"/>
15. </message>
16.
17. <message name="extractReply">
18.  <part name="value" type="xsd:string"/>
19. </message>
20.
21. <portType name="proxyPT">
22.  <operation name="genericInvocation">
23.   <input message="tns:genericInputMessage"/>
24.   <output message="tns:genericOutputMessage"/>
25.  </operation>
26.  <operation name="extract">
27.   <intput message="tns:extractInputMessage"/>
28.   <output message="tns:extractReply"/>
29.  </operation>
30. </portType>
```

Since a WSDL message can comprise of one or more parts (Christensen, Curbera, Meredith, Weerawarana, & W3C, 2001), the deserialzation would have to extract the value for each message part. Therefore, after the adapted BPEL process receives the genericOutputMessage, it then make a call to the generic proxy's extract operation for each part of the reply message. The input message (extractInputMessage, lines 12-14) for the proxy's extract operation has two parts, values and param. The values part contains the serialized generic-Output-Message and the param parts specifies which parameter value to extract from the generic-Output-Message. The proxy then sends this value back to the BPEL process.

The Generation Process

The adapt-ready BPEL processes are generated by the TRAP/BPEL generator. The only input to this generator is a configuration file. First, the Parser reads the information needed for generating adapt-ready BPEL process and sends them to the adapt-ready BPEL compiler. Next, the generator uses the information provided by the parser and retrieves the required files from the local disk and starts its compilation process. The primary information the generator needs are the original BPEL file, the list of which invocation to monitor and the WSDL files for all the partner Web Services. The WSDL files are needed so that the generator can get details about the specification of the messages that are exchange by the monitored services. This information is used for the serialization and deserialization of messages. Figure 10 depicts at a high-level the architecture of the generator.

4. REUSABLE CONCEPTS

Software Patterns constitute abstract reusable concepts that can be configured for a range of situations. The reuse of these abstract concepts is facilitated by the fact that applications in the same domains are similar and carry out comparable functions (Sommerville, 2006). Workflows are currently being used for various applications both in industry and academia. The ability to rapidly create an application by orchestrating predefined tasks based on some modifiable set of rules, offers great advantages to the traditional programming model. In industry workflows are being used to enhance business process management, while allowing business partners to integrate applications. The advent of Service-Oriented Computing (SOC) has further facilitated the integration of distributed components available on heterogeneous platforms. Grid computing is one paradigm that takes advantage of workflows, SOC and distributed components to create a class of applications that are long-running and resource intensive. In academia, workflows permit domain specialist to declaratively model scientific applications for grid environments without the need to master the underlying technical details of the computing infrastructure. However, the complex nature of such applications, their distributed execution environments and inherent dependability issues, coupled with the deficiencies of workflow languages such as BPEL means that the dream of separating design from architecture for the domain specialist is far from reality.

There is a need for architectures that support adaptive workflows. This is especially true for scientific workflows in Grid environments. Such workflows must not only be semantically rich

Figure 10. Inputs and outputs of the TRAP/BPEL generator

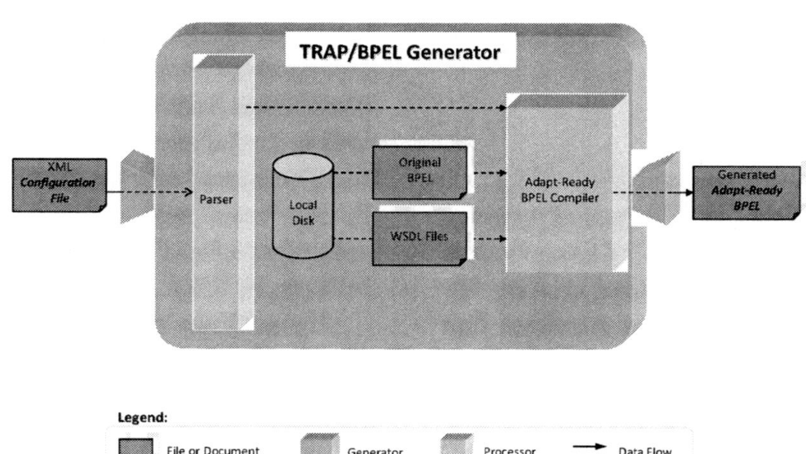

enough to allow for adequate representation of the business logic of the application, it should permit the abstraction of program semantics at a level that is easy for domain specialist to use. Such architectures should permit the separate development of the functional and non-functional requirements of the application as well as be dynamic enough to permit the alteration of the workflow at runtime for optimization. Part of the solution for this problem must employ a model-driven approach to development of applications. In Model-driven architecture (MDA), application functionality is defined in a manner that is platform-independent using models and other domain-specific abstractions. The goal of MDA is to separate design from architecture by promoting interoperability, concept reuse, and standardization of models for application domains (Stahl & Voelter, 2006). Domain knowledge can thus be used to model the specification of software, and application generators used to produce new systems from those high-level abstractions. For the rest of this section, we identify the software patterns (reusable concepts) that are present in our TRAP/BPEL framework for adaptive BPEL processes. By identifying these patterns, program generators that capture such reusable domain knowledge can be developed. Domain experts can then specify software by selecting which reusable concepts patterns are to be used (Sommerville, 2006). The use of a generator in this case would facilitate separation of concerns, that is, the separate addition of fault tolerant concerns to the workflow.

Adapter

When a monitored service fails, part of recovery action by the proxy could be to find an equivalent service to substitute for the failed service. We assume that *equivalent* services are those that implement the same interface (and consequently implement the same business logic) as that of the monitored services. So, when two Web Services implement the same port type, we assume that they provide the same functionality and they may be different only in the quality of the service they provide. This is especially true in grid environments where standardized interfaces are the norm. We expect that in the near future, standard organizations will specify standard service interface definitions for different business domains that different service providers can use to expose their semantically equivalent services through the corresponding specified standard interfaces (Kreger & IBM Software Group, 2001). In the case where the interfaces of semantically equivalent services are not the same, all needs to be done is to go through an extra step of mapping the interfaces of the equivalent services to those of the monitored services. By using the adapter design pattern (Gamma, Helm, Johnson, & Vlissides, 1995), one can expose the equivalent services with the same interface to those of the monitored services.

Figure 11 illustrates the Adapter pattern. The intent of the pattern is to convert the interface of a component into another interface clients expect. Adapter lets components work together despite incompatible interfaces (Gamma, Helm, Johnson, & Vlissides, 1995). The participants in the pattern are the *Workflow* (Client), *Proxy* (Target), *Adapter*, and the partner *service* (Adaptee).

Mediator

A Mediator is a component that encapsulates how a set of other components interact with it. Mediators promote loose coupling by keeping components from interacting explicitly while allowing for independent variations in interaction. Mediators localize behavior that would otherwise be distributed among several objects, making easier for the behavior to evolve (Gamma, Helm, Johnson, & Vlissides, 1995).

Figure 12 models the Mediators pattern. In the model, the *Proxy* acts as a mediator between the partner services (Colleagues), and the Workflow. By being able to dynamically discover and bind to partner services, the proxy promotes loose

Figure 11. The adapter pattern

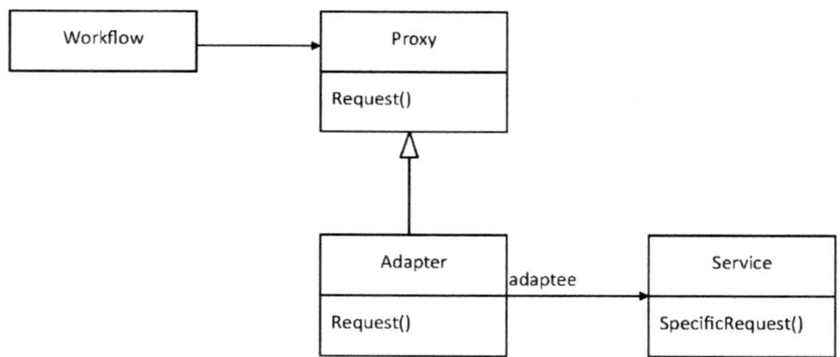

coupling. Also, the ability to provide adaptive behavior, the proxy encapsulates and externalizes behavior that would otherwise be hard-coded into the Workflow or the partner services.

Proxy

Interaction between the workflow and partner services is redirected through a *proxy Web service*, which monitors the interaction and applies failure recovery and adaptability in a transparent manner. The interaction between the components here exhibits the *Proxy* software pattern. The Proxy pattern, illustrated in Figure 13, provides a surrogate for another component to control access to it. The participants in this pattern are the *Workflow* (Client), *Proxy*, and the partner *service* which is the real component that the proxy represents (Gamma, Helm, Johnson, & Vlissides, 1995).

Observer

The Observer behavioral pattern allows for dependency between object to be specified so that when one component changes state all dependent components are notified and updated (Gamma, Helm, Johnson, & Vlissides, 1995). The TRAP/BPEL framework can be extended with a notification interface to support this behavioral pattern (Kalayci, Ezenwoye, Viswanathan, Dasgupta, Sadjadi, & Fong, 2008). This pattern of behavior is especially important in grid environments where services are stateful and long-running. Grid services also provide notification interfaces that allow for observers to be updated about state change. In Figure 14, the *Proxy* is the observer and registers for state change notification with the monitored partner service.

Figure 12. The mediator pattern

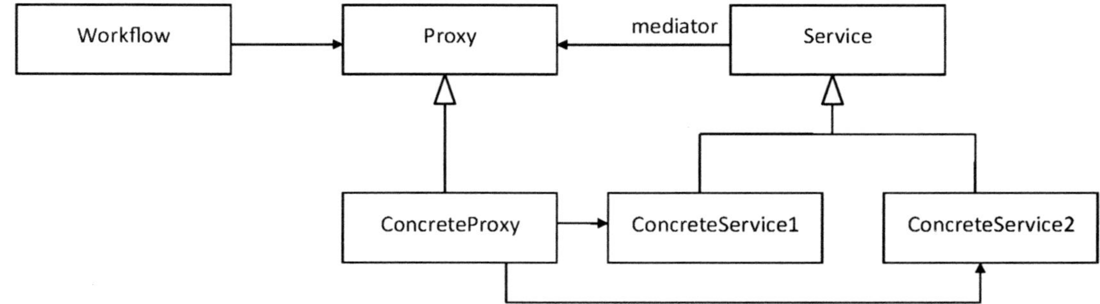

Figure 13. The proxy pattern

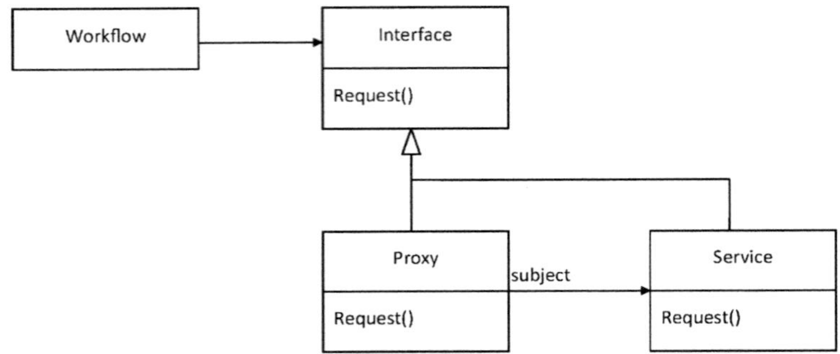

Strategy

In the TRAP/BPEL framework, the proxy encapsulates and externalizes adaptive behavior outside of the Workflow definition. This behavior that is captured in the monitory, recovery and dynamically modifiable policy components of the proxy, represents strategies for adaptability and failure recovery. This behavior is akin to the Strategy behavioral pattern as depicted in Figure 15. The Strategy pattern facilitates the definition of a set of interchangeable algorithms. The pattern lets the algorithm vary independently from the client (in this case the Workflow) that uses it (Gamma, Helm, Johnson, & Vlissides, 1995).

Figure 14. The observer pattern

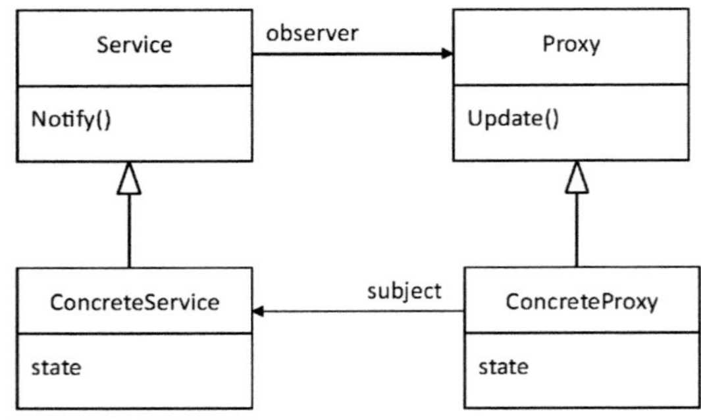

Chain of Responsibility

The Chain of Responsibility pattern avoids the coupling of the sender and the receiver of a request by giving more than one component the opportunity to handle the request. In this pattern, the component that provides the service isn't explicitly known to the component that initiated the request (Gamma, Helm, Johnson, & Vlissides, 1995). In Figure 16, the *Proxy* acts as the handler of the request and provides the interface for the request. The *concrete handlers* in this case are the

Figure 15. The strategy pattern

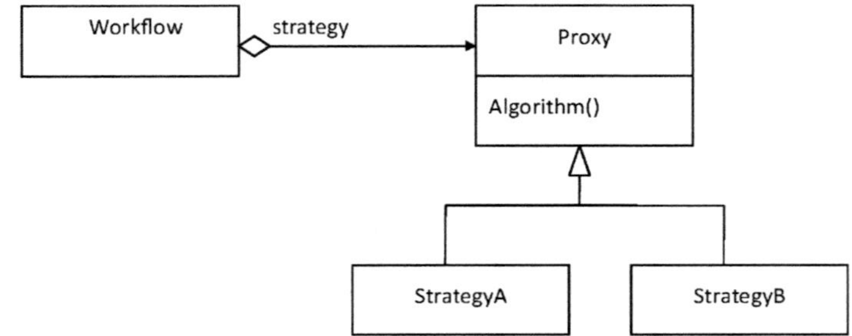

Figure 16. The chain of responsibility pattern

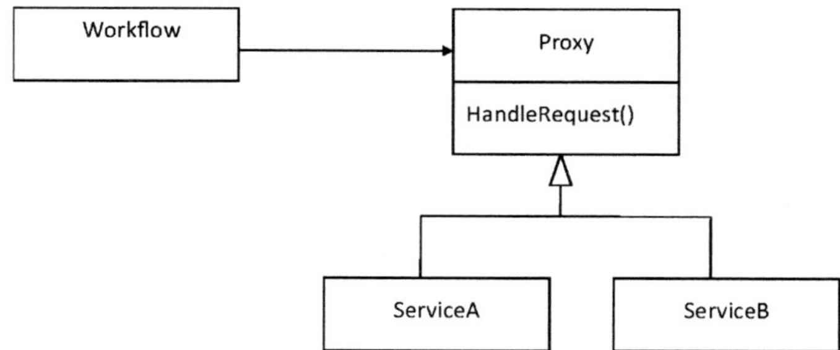

dynamically discovered services that implement the requested task.

Composite

Finally, the workflow is a Composite pattern, since the workflow is an aggregation of other services (see Figure 2). In Composite patterns, clients treat the compositions in the same way as they would treat the individual components. Clients interact with the components in the composite through some component interface. The Composite forwards requests from the client to its child components and possibly performing other operations before or after forwarding (Gamma, Helm, Johnson, & Vlissides, 1995).

RELATED WORK

Since Web Services technology is still emerging, most of the work that aim to address the requirements for reliable and fault tolerant Web Services execution are still in their infancy (Erradi, Maheshwari, & Tosic, 2006). These efforts can be distinguished by their focus on different layers (see Figure 5) of the Web Services infrastructure. We note that our work is focused on the business process layer and as a result the work in the other layers are complementary to ours.

SOAP Messaging Layer

Some works aim to address the reliability of Web Services from the *SOAP messaging layer* by addressing the issues concerning reliable transport-independent messaging. To this end, SOAP-based protocols like WS-ReliableMessaging (Web Services Reliable Messaging) and WS-Reliability (WS-Reliability 1.1, 2004) strive to standardize message delivery by specifying rules for acknowledgment, message correlation, ordered delivery and so on. Such a protocol does however contribute to inefficiency if the underlying transport layer does use protocols that address reliable message delivery (Erradi, Maheshwari, & Tosic, 2006).

Transport Layer

Other approaches and technologies focus on implementing reliable massaging for Web Services at the transport layer. The reliability of SOAP messaging largely depends on the underlying transport chosen. Since SOAP-over-HTTP is not reliable, attempts are being made to build messaging middleware that accept messages from sending processes and delivers them reliably to receiving processes. Reliable messaging implementations communicate across a network on behalf of senders and receivers, and have built-in transactional support to manage message conversations in the context of a larger business process (Erradi, Maheshwari, & Tosic, 2006).

Examples of message-oriented middleware are IBM WebsphereMQ (Gilman & Schreiber, 1996) and MSMQ (Microsoft. Microsoft Message Queuing). These implementations support their own proprietary messaging APIs and protocols, as well as the standard Java Message Service (JMS) API (Hapner, Burridge, & Sharma, 1999). Open standards for reliable messaging include the ebXML Message Service and the HTTPR protocol. These approaches however do not guarantee reliability for multi-hop messaging over different protocols as they assume that reliable transport protocols will be available for the entire path of the message (Erradi, Maheshwari, & Tosic, 2006; Tai, Mikalsen, & Rouvellou, 2003).

Service Provider Layer

At this layer, approaches focus on the service hosting container. Here, approaches aim to achieve reliability by using techniques that provide redundancy of computation and data, load sharing to improve performance and fault tolerance, and clustering to avoid single point of failure (Erradi, Maheshwari, & Tosic, 2006). Dialani et al. (Dialani, Miles, Moreau, Roure, & Luck, 2002) provide an approach to enabling fault tolerance in *stateful* Web Services by requiring the developer to implement an interface for rollback and checkpoint. An extension is made to the SOAP communication layer so that messages can be logged and replayed.

Birman et al. (Birman, Renesse, & Vogels, 2004) propose extensions to the Web Services architecture to support mission-critical applications. They propose extensions to achieve such things as: (1) track the health of individual Web service; and (2) Consistent and Reliable Messaging.

Business Process Layer

We further categorize works that focus on the business process layer into two groups: *language-based* and *non language-based*.

Non-language based approaches focus specifically on the process supporting infrastructure such as the execution engine. They include wsBus (Erradi & Maheshwari, 2005; Erradi, Maheshwari, & Tosic, 2006), which is a lightweight service-oriented middleware for transparently enacting recovery action in service-based processes. The wsBus is a mediation layer that intercepts the execution of composite services and transparently provides recovery services based on an extensible set of recovery policies. This approach is modular and separates the business logic of the process from the QoS requirements; however, this approach requires the installation of additional middleware.

AdaptiveBPEL (Erradi, Maheshwari, & Padmanabhuni, 2005; Erradi & Maheshwari, 2005) is a related platform to wsBus. The goal of AdaptiveBPEL is to enable adaptability in composite services in a decoupled, modularized and reusable way. To achieve this, AdaptiveBPEL proposes to augment an *existing* BPEL engine with aspect weaving capabilities to address QoS concerns and adapt BPEL processes through predefined extensions.

Charfi et al. (Charfi & Mezini, 2005) use an aspect-based container to provide middleware support for BPEL. The process container is the runtime environment for the BPEL process. All interactions go through the container which plugs in support for non-functional requirements. The process container uses AO4BPEL (Charfi & Mezini, 2004) aspects. This framework is different from ours because it requires a purpose built BPEL engine.

Language-based techniques provide advanced failure handling and adaptability by augmenting the process logic with additional language constructs. These approaches include BPEL for Java (BPELJ), an effort from IBM and BEA Systems to combine the capabilities of BPEL and the Java programming language. This combination is achieved by extending the BPEL to allow for sections of Java code, called *Java snippets*, to be included in BPEL process definitions. The snippets are meant to improve the capabilities of BPEL by enhancing the logic of business functions, message preparation, data manipulation and looping conditions. BPELJ, however, requires an extended BPEL engine that understands the additional constructs. This limits the portability of BPELJ processes. Also, exception handling logic in BPELJ often gets tangled with the process logic, thus hampering maintainability.

Other language-based techniques include the work done by Baresi et al. (Baresi, Ghezzi, & Guinea, 2004). In their approach, BPEL processes are monitored at run-time to check whether individual services comply with their contracts. Monitors are automatically defined as additional services and linked to the service composition. Their approach to monitoring involves the use of annotations that are stated as comments in the source BPEL program and then translated to generate a target monitored BPEL program. This approach achieves the desired separation of concern, however, it requires manually modifying the original BPEL process and the monitoring code is entangled with the process logic. The manual modification of BPEL code is not only difficult and error prone, but also hinders maintainability.

SUMMARY

We presented an approach to transparently incorporating self-management behavior into existing BPEL processes. We have introduced the TRAP/BPEL framework and its generic proxy, and demonstrated how a generic proxy can be used to encapsulate autonomic behavior through the use of policies.

For distributed applications, where there is a large number of orchestrated resources, having to develop and maintain long-running and resource intensive applications is quite cumbersome. The highly dynamic and heterogeneous nature of such environments calls for a more flexible architecture for specifying exceptional behavior.

We presented a solution to this problem by introducing the use of policy-based *generic* proxies. We showed how with the use of generic proxies and some externalized and extensible recovery policies we are able to extend the autonomic capabilities of adapted BPEL processes. The *generic* proxies intercept all the invocations to the monitored partner Web Services and may choose to forward the invocations to substitute services even before the original service. This approach allows for the specification of more diverse task-specific exceptional behavior. Also, externalizing the behavioral policy permits the specifications for the application logic and mechanism for exceptional behavior to evolve separately. We showed the design of the generic proxy and some details of its adaptation process.

We explained design patterns present in the approach. These patterns constitute abstract reusable concepts that will facilitate the rapid development of adaptive service compositions that can be easily configured for a range of situations.

ACKNOWLEDGMENT

This work was supported in part by IBM, the National Science Foundation (grants OCI-0636031 and HRD-0833093). Any opinions, findings and conclusions or recommendations expressed in this material are those of the author(s) and do not necessarily reflect those of the NSF and IBM.

REFERENCES

Avizienis, A., Laprie, J.-C., Randell, B., & Landwehr, C. (2004). Basic concepts and taxonomy of dependable and secure computing. *IEEE Transactions on Dependable and Secure Computing*, *1*(1), 11–33. doi:10.1109/TDSC.2004.2

Baresi, L., Ghezzi, C., & Guinea, S. (2004). Smart monitors for composed services. *ICSOC '04: Proceedings of the 2nd international conference on Service oriented computing,* (pp. 193-202). ACM Press.

Birman, K. P., Renesse, R. v., & Vogels, W. (2004). Adding high availability and autonomic behavior to Web Services. *Proceedings of the 26th International Conference on Software Engineering (ICSE 2004),* (pp. 17-26). Edinburgh: IEEE Computer Society.

Charfi, A., & Mezini, M. (2004). Aspect oriented Web Service composition with AO4BPEL. *Proceedings of The European Conference on Web Services.*

Charfi, A., & Mezini, M. (2005). An aspect based process container for BPEL. *Proceedings of The First Workshop on Aspect-Oriented Middleware Developement.* Genoble, France.

Christensen, E., Curbera, F., Meredith, G., Weerawarana, S. & W3C. (2001). *Web Services Description Language (WSDL) 1.1.*

Dialani, V., Miles, S., Moreau, L., Roure, D. D., & Luck, M. (2002). Transparent fault tolerance for Web Services based architectures. *Proceedings of the Eighth International Europar Conference (EURO-PAR '02).* Padeborn, Germany: Springer-Verlag.

Duftler, M.J., Mukhi, N.K., Slominski, A. & Sanc. (2009). *Web Services Invocation Framework (WSIF).*

Erradi, A., & Maheshwari, P. (2005). *AdaptiveBPEL: A policy-driven middleware for flexible Web Services composition.* Enschede, The Netherlands: Proceedings of Middleware for Web Services.

Erradi, A., & Maheshwari, P. (2005). WSBus: QoS-aware middleware for relaible Web Services interaction. *Proceedings of the IEEE International Conference on e-Technology, e-Commerce and e-Service.* Hong Kong, China.

Erradi, A., Maheshwari, P., & Padmanabhuni, S. (2005). Towards a policy driven framework for adaptive Web Services composition. *Proceedings of International Conference on Next Generation Web Services Practices.*

Erradi, A., Maheshwari, P., & Tosic, V. (2006). A policy-based middleware for enhancing Web Services reliability using recovery policies. *Proceedings of the 2006 IEEE International Conference on Web Services.* Chicago, USA.

Ezenwoye, O., & Sadjadi, S. M. (2005). *Composing aggregate Web Services in BPEL.* Miami: School of Computing and Information Science, Florida International University.

Ezenwoye, O., & Sadjadi, S. M. (2007). TRAP/BPEL: A framework for dynamic adaptation of composite services. *Proceedings of the International Conference on Web Information Systems and Technologies (WEBIST 2007).* Barcelona, Spain.

Ezenwoye, O., Sadjadi, S. M., Carey, A., & Robinson, M. (2007). Grid Service composition in BPEL for scientific applications. *Proceedings of the International Conference on Grid computing, high-performAnce and Distributed Applications (GADA'07).* Vilamoura, Algarve, Portugal.

Ferguson, D., Storey, T., Lovering, B. & Shewchuk, J. (2003). *Secure, reliable, transacted Web Services.*

Foster, I., Kesselman, C., Nick, J. M., & Tuecke, S. (2002). Grid Services for distributed system integration. *Computer, 35*(6), 37–46. doi:10.1109/MC.2002.1009167

Foster, I., Kesselman, C. & Tuecke, S. (2001). *The anatomy of the Grid: Enabling scalable virtual organizations.* (LNCS 2150).

Gamma, E., Helm, R., Johnson, R., & Vlissides, J. (1995). *Design patterns: Elements of reusable object-oriented software.* New York: Addison-Wesley Publishing Company.

Gilman, L., & Schreiber, R. (1996). *Distributed computing with IBM MQSeries*. Wiley.

Goel, S., Sharda, H., & Taniar, D. (2003). Message-oriented-middleware in a distributed environment. *Third International Workshop on Innovative Internet Community Systems*, (pp. 93-103).

Gurguis, S., & Zeid, A. (2005). Towards autonomic Web Services: Achieving self-healing using Web Services. *Proceedings of DEAS'05*. Missouri, USA.

Hapner, M., Burridge, R., & Sharma, R. (1999). *Java message service specification*. Sun Microsystems.

Kalayci, S., Ezenwoye, O., Viswanathan, B., Dasgupta, G., Sadjadi, S. M., & Fong, L. (2008). Design and implementation of a fault tolerant job flow manager using job flow patterns and recovery policies. *Proceedings of the 6th International Conference on Service Oriented Computing (ICSOC'08)*. Sydney, Australia.

Kephart, J. O., & Chess, D. M. (2003). The vision of autonomic computing. *IEEE Computer*, *36*(1), 41–50.

Kiczales, G., Lamping, J., Mendhekar, A., Maeda, C., Lopes, C. V., Loingtier, J. M., et al. (1997). Aspect-oriented programming. *Proceedings of the European Conference on Object-Oriented Programming (ECOOP)*. (LNCS 1241). Springer-Verlag.

Kreger, H. & IBM Software Group. (2001). *Web Services Conceptual Architecture (WSCA 1.0).*

Laprie, J.-C. (1995). Dependable computing and fault tolerance: Concepts and terminology. *25th International Symposium on Fault-Tolerant Computing (FCTS-25), 3*. Pasadena, California.

Leymann, F. (2006). Choreography for the Grid: Towards fitting BPEL to the resource framework: Research articles. *Concurrent Computing: Practical Experience*, *18*(10), 1201–1217. doi:10.1002/cpe.996

McKinley, P.K., Sadjadi, S.M., Kasten, E.P. & Cheng, B.H. (2004). Composing adaptive software. *IEEE Computer*, 56-64.

Nelson, V. P. (1990). Fault-tolerant computing: Fundamental concepts. *IEEE Computer*, *23*(7), 19–25.

Nickull, D. (2005). *Service Oriented Architecture*. White Paper.

Ouzzani, M., & Bouguettaya, A. (2004). Efficient access to Web Services. *IEEE Internet Computing*, *8*(2), 34–44. doi:10.1109/MIC.2004.1273484

Sadjadi, S. M., McKinley, P. K., & Cheng, B. H. (2005). Transparent shaping of existing software to support pervasive and autonomic computing. *Proceedings of the 1st Workshop on the Design and Evolution of Autonomic Application Software 2005*. St. Louis, Missouri.

Sommerville, I. (2006). *Software engineering* (8th ed.). Addison-Wesley.

Stahl, T., & Voelter, M. (2006). *Model-driven software development: Technology, engineering, management*. Wiley.

Tai, S., Mikalsen, T., & Rouvellou, I. (2003). Using message-oriented middleware for reliable Web Services messaging. *Proceedings of Second International Workshop of Web Services, E-Business, and the Semantic Web*, (pp. 89-104).

Tai, S., Mikalsen, T., Wohlstadter, E., Desai, N., & Rouvellou, I. (2004). Transaction policies for service-oriented computing. *Data & Knowledge Engineering*, *51*(1), 59–79. doi:10.1016/j.datak.2003.03.001

Thain, D., Tannenbaum, T., & Livny, M. (2003). *Grid computing: Making the global infrastructure a reality*. John Wiley and Sons.

Vogels, W. (2003). Web Services are not distributed objects. *IEEE Internet Computing*.

Yu, J., & Buyya, R. (2005). A taxonomy of scientific workflow systems for grid computing. *SIGMOD Record*, *34*(3), 44–49. doi:10.1145/1084805.1084814

Yu, J., & Buyya, R. (2005). A taxonomy of workflow management systems for Grid computing. *Journal of Grid Computing*, *3*(3-4), 171–200. doi:10.1007/s10723-005-9010-8

ENDNOTE

[1] *Functional requirements* describe the interaction between the system and its actors (*e.g.*, end users and other external systems) while *non-functional requirements* are constraints on the system that are not directly related to the functional requirements (*e.g.*, reliability, security, scalability, performance and fault-tolerance).

Section 3
Reliability and Fault Tolerance

In the world where on-demand and trustworthy service delivery is one of the main preconditions for successful business, service and business process availability is of the paramount importance and cannot be compromised. For that reason, service availability is coming into central focus of the IT operations and management research and practice. This section presents approaches for estimating service reliability and designing fault-tolerant SOA systems.

Chapter 12
Prediction of Non-Functional Properties of Service-Based Systems:
A Software Reliability Model

Adel Taweel
King's College London, UK

Gareth Tyson
King's College London, UK

ABSTRACT

From the outset, service-based systems offer several advantages, including the promise of shortening the development life cycle, reducing the costs of software development and faster utilisation of recent technical improvements in the software industry in terms of capability, reliability, compatibility, performance, and so forth. However, this is rarely realised in practice. An important issue of service-based systems is that they are likely to be (or perhaps already being) used in domains where human life and/or economic loss are possible and the need for a highly reliable system is a must. However, would it be possible to build reliable service-based systems that meet such domains' requirements? Does it necessarily mean that composing a system from highly reliable services produce a highly reliable system? Is it possible to predict quality attributes of a service-based system from its services before building it? In this chapter, the complexity of this issue is highlighted, focusing on reliability, in an attempt to answer some of these questions. The chapter outlines various approaches that attempt to address this issue, and proposes a possible way forward for predicting the reliability of service-based systems from its individual services.

INTRODUCTION

Traditionally, software systems are constructed from individual parts, which are then integrated to produce a system that meets certain functional and non-functional specifications. The produced system, as a whole, is then tested to check whether these specifications are met. Systems in this case are therefore normally viewed as a whole and thus tagged by these specifications, rather than as

DOI: 10.4018/978-1-60960-493-6.ch012

individual parts. Although changes may need to be done on certain parts of the system to improve a non-functional property, the whole system will have to be re-tested to check whether or not that improvement has been achieved.

In service-oriented architectures, however, systems are constructed or integrated from individual services. These individual services are combined together, normally based on a defined architecture or framework, to produce a system that meets certain functional and non-functional specifications or properties. These individual services, on the other hand, have their own functional profile, run-time environment, and functional and non-functional properties. Which leads to the question: *whether the properties of individual services can be used or extended to determine the system-level properties of the composed system?*

One way to determine the properties of the composed system is to re-test this composed system as whole. However, in service-based systems, this method is not always feasible and is not preferable for several reasons. Firstly, with services that are expected to be bought (or obtained) individually, possibly from different vendors, it is unlikely that developers (or integrators[1]) would commit themselves to buying a service that they might later discover to not achieve the specific purpose that it was originally bought for. Secondly, even if it were possible to acquire a service (or a use of a service) without buying it, perhaps through a provided evaluation period, it is less likely that integrators would be happy to waste their time and effort on incorrectly selected services. Thirdly, the longer the service selection process takes, the less economical it becomes for integrators as they are expected to meet deadlines and budget.

In reality, integrators are unlikely to choose a service to test or evaluate for their system unless it stands a fair chance of success. The selection of a service can therefore be a complex task, and a mechanism that facilitates the selection, even to a certain degree, would greatly reduce the complexity of the process and thus the development of the system. One mechanism could be envisaged from enabling developers (or integrators) to determine or predict the system-level properties of the resultant composed system from the properties of its individual services. The potential and importance of prediction theories for service-based and component-based systems has been recognised early in the software engineering research community. In fact, special teams have shown special interest in this field, such as [Bachmann et al, 2000, Crnkovic et al, 2001, Wallnau, 2003].

The chapter first presents the background, related issues and complexities of the prediction of non-functional properties. It then presents related work outlining general approaches and potential approaches to address these issues. The rest of the chapter proposes a model to predict the software reliability of service-based systems from their individual services as a potential method to address other non-functional properties.

BACKGROUND

Large scale distributed service oriented systems are increasingly becoming used in industry and commercial settings. They are offering the rapid development throughput that software industry needs to stay competitive. However, one of the main issues is creating re-usable services that can be used to serve different purposes and different types of systems in different domains. Standardisation is a key issue for providing standard interfaces to enable flexible integration [Wallnau, 2003]. As different domains have different demands and expectation, it is becoming critical that services not only meet functional requirements but also non-functional requirements. Domains such as banking, retail and manufacturing require systems to provide real-time, highly reliable, secure, and safe functionality where potentially human-life or economic loss is possible. In such environments, non-functional requirement specifications are not a commodity but necessity.

In a commercially supported service oriented architecture, it is becoming less likely that developers will buy a physical version of the service, but more likely they will buy a 'use of the service' possibly over a period of time, within agreed licensing constraints. Further, services themselves can potentially be running remotely on the supplier's run-time environment and only be providing the requested service. In the service oriented architecture paradigm, systems can comprise or be built from locally run or remotely run services. These can be locally developed or remotely provided, thereby enabling more flexible system building process. This, however, adds further complexities regarding how functional and non-functional properties are specified. Service oriented architectures therefore provide a defined approach and a generic framework that can be used to enable a system building and integration environment, in which systems can be built from autonomous services. They generally incorporate standardised interfaces, message exchange, discovery protocols [Cerami, 2002] and a workflow management engine [Oinn et al, 2004, Taylor et al, 2007] to enable and specify how services can be integrated and /or executed to achieve specific system functionalities. Most of these environments require individual services to be autonomous dependable services that provide pre-defined functionalities (or services). This gives the opportunity to derive system-level non-functional properties from service-level non-functional properties.

Figure 1 depicts a typical service-based system. The composed system is typically composed using a composition framework running in its own operational profile or environment. It is composed of local services or components that run within the same operational profile and remote services that run within their own operational profile. These remote services may potentially use their own local services or other remote services. In this chapter, we define components as physical self-contained software entities that have specific interfaces and provide a system, process or workflow function to complete or aid the composed system functional process and are only accessible locally within the operational environment.

Several approaches have been proposed to enable predicting non-functional properties of component-based and service-based systems [Roshandel et al, 2004, Crnkovic et al, 2005, Grassi, 2005, Grassi et al, 2006, Trivedi et al, 1994, Sato et al, 2007, Muppala et al, 1994, Bachmann et al, 2000, Hamlet et al, 2001, Klein et al, 1999,

Figure 1. A typical service-based system

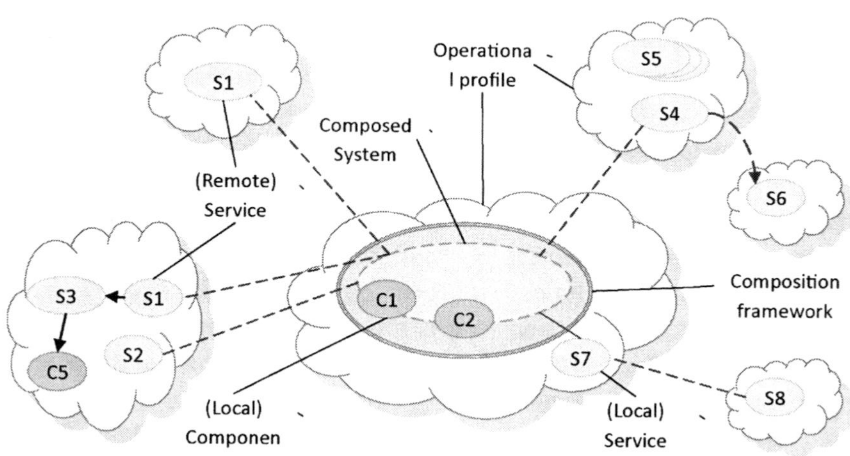

Crnkovic et al, 2001, Wang et al, 1999, Stafford et al, 2002]. These models generally flow a *white-box* or *black-box* approach (see below), each demanding constraints on how systems are composed or different levels of knowledge about the services (or both) [Shooman, 1991, Grassi, 2005, Dolbec et al, 1995]. Architecture-based approaches [Grassi, 2005, Roshandel et al, 2004, Wang et al, 1999, Bachmann et al, 2000] propose to predict quality attributes from individual services that conform to an architecture pattern, for example. However, in practice, services are rarely built conformant to a fixed architectural pattern. Other approaches (such as [Hamlet et al, 2001, Klein et al, 1999]) demand internal knowledge about each of the services and their development process. This type of knowledge is usually unavailable, especially in off-the-shelf services. In cases where it is available, some service suppliers, such as in the software industry, would rarely make it available to users as it may affect their services' 'saleability'. Also coming from different vendors, the amount and representation of the collected information will vary from one service supplier to another and is potentially provided incomplete which may make it unusable. These approaches tend to take into consideration the non-functional properties of the 'whole' service, although the composed system may only use some of the service operations or functions rather than all of them. In practice, however, service-oriented systems tend to use only specific operations or functions of the whole service, despite the fact that the whole service may get incorporated into the composed system. The proposed approach in this chapter focuses on considering that each service has quality properties tagged to its operations or functions, rather than to the service as a whole. It takes the analogy of hardware component specifications, where each component has functional related quality attributes and usually each function is tagged with a relevant non-functional property value. What distinguishes this approach is that it provides a middle approach between *black-box* and the *white-box* approaches, imposing a minimal need for internal knowledge and less influence on the development process. Since composed systems often use only a subset of the 'whole' service functions, using the values of the quality properties of individual functions would potentially enable a more precise measure or prediction of the system-level quality properties, opposed to using the values of the quality properties of the 'whole' service'. It also provides a more practical approach for software service suppliers where they are expected only to tag individual functions of the 'whole' service with a respective quality attribute. In addition, since most common functional units are easier to quantify than the 'whole' service, tagging individual functions is more feasible and practical. Measuring interconnected functionalities is more complex but remains more quantifiable than the 'whole' service approach. The proposed model is discussed below in detail.

ISSUES AND COMPLEXITIES

There are several obstacles and issues related to service-based systems that should be addressed by any approach that attempts to predict final system properties. These are briefly discussed below.

Non-functional properties representation: as mentioned above one of the main difficulties that will be faced in addressing these questions, will be determining how the non-functional properties are represented. Bachmann et. Al (2000). highlight this problem through asserting the importance of certifying components [Bachmann et al, 2000]. Certification does not only provide tangible representation of the non-functional properties, but also provides *minimal guarantees,* in a way, how services will behave (i.e. functionality) [J. Voas in Crnkovic et al, 2001]. Therefore, it is essential to study different *certification* techniques and various representations of the values of these non-functional properties before envisaging possible techniques that can be applied on these representations. Although Bachmann et. Al, (2000). express the need for certification; they also assert that until there exists a strong *theory* that utilises certification results to predict composed system properties, industry would not be enthusiastic about certifying their services.

Composition architecture/framework: In service-based systems, services are *integrated* together to form a complete system. Since these services are expected to be self-contained, autonomous and standalone, they must have or provide an interface capability through which they can be invoked or accessed. Integrating these services together may thus follow a particular architecture; this is also referred to as *glue logic*. This architecture can be very intelligent, potentially supporting multiple types of interfaces and have the capability of defining various *glue* methods between services and defining constraints on its services deployment or use. It can be seen as an operating system or a motherboard that supports *plug and play*, in which services can be plugged in to form a system, with its operations being decided, controlled or provided through a microprocessor or 'main' service. Figure 2 depicts such architecture. Several frameworks of this type have been proposed, providing different levels of sophistication [Zeng et al, 2003, Zeng et al, 2004, Liu et al, 2004, Lin et al, 2005, Cotroneo et al, 2003]. Generally, they attempt to enable dynamic binding with services based on a limited set of defined functional and non-functional properties. Most of these frameworks assume a formal definition or representation of these properties, or assume services provide mechanisms to deduce these properties. However, because there are no formal standardised definitions, representations or mechanisms, these frameworks are less widely used. But they represent important steps towards developing this type of composition frameworks.

On the other hand, this *glue* architecture can function as a traditional "main program" or 'execution workflow' that includes instructions that defines the sequence of how services are invoked (see Figure 3). Web Services standards around compositions, such as the Business Process Execution Language (BPEL), allow the composition of existing web services into higher-level services; typical examples of this are [Ezenwoye et al, 2007, Ezenwoye et al, 2005, Erradi et al, 2005, Milanovic et al, 2005]. These composition architectures are becoming more often referred to as workflow management systems in service-oriented architectures. Taverna and Triana are two examples of workflow management systems that can be seen to represent this type of composition framework [Oinn et al, 2004, Taylor et al, 2007].

Taverna [Oinn et al, 2004] provides a composition engine in which services are combined in a specified workflow that defines the sequence of execution for the selected services. The outcome of one service is fed as input to one or more services for further processing and so forth until a final output is obtained. For services that do not

Figure 2. Component-driven composition framework

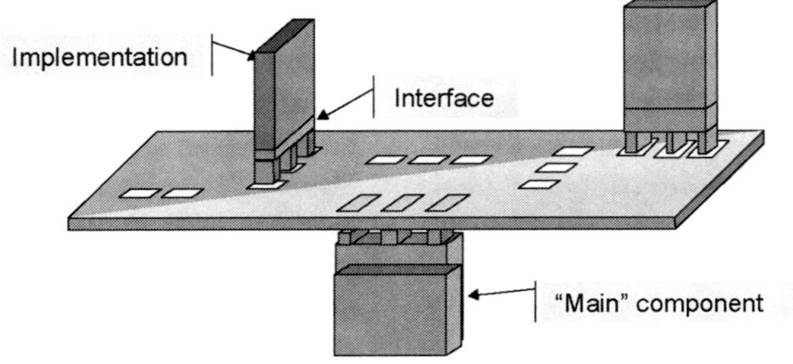

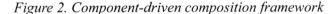

Figure 3. 'Workflow' driven composition framework

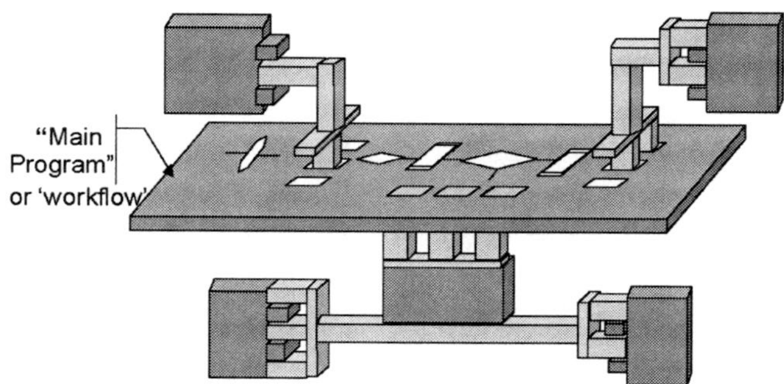

have matching interfaces, Taverna provides a mechanism to build adapters, referred to as *Shims*, to translate or match between their interfaces. Taverna provides a good example of a composition engine to compose systems from services, that uses a 'main program' or 'workflow' analogy, however, it soon became more sophisticated, incorporating a complex mesh of its own components to meet user needs, such as the need for handling provenance information at run-time. All such additions add to the complexity of quantifying the composition framework's effects on the calculation of the non-functional properties of the composed system.

Triana [Tayler et al, 2007] is another example of a composition framework. It provides a more dynamic graphical interface to find, select and integrate services. However Triana adapters are bespoke and go through a more complex process to build. Also provenance handling is limited and is not supported as it is in Taverna.

In both of the composition frameworks or *glue* architectures mentioned above, further constraints and additional overheads are added, which are bound to affect the final composed system properties. For example, reliability of the final system will be affected by how services interact, which is determined by the *glue* architecture. Several questions arise, such as, which architecture adds fewest overheads, and how can these overheads be calculated or evaluated etc. Therefore, any theory that attempts to predict final system properties should as well address the composition architecture properties and their effect on the final system. Several researchers highlighted the need for addressing the properties of the employed composition architecture or framework [Bachmann et al, 2000, Lycett et al, 1999, Klein et al, 1999]. Interconnection and communication mechanisms are examples of the properties of the underlying composition architecture or framework that are bound to affect and/or determine the properties of the composed system. Bachmann et. al (2000) suggest that it could also be necessary to study the composition framework's internal properties, types of composition frameworks and their attributes. In addition, improving the non-functional properties of the composition framework may as well contribute more to the composed system than those of its individual services [Lycett et al, 1999].

Operational profile defines the run-time environment that services or components operate in, and the input data that these services use to complete their operations. In one case, systems could be built from services that are designed to work in different environments, forming for example distributed systems on different operating and/or hardware systems. In another case, systems could be built from components and services that can work under the same environment. In either case, services are affected by their operational profile. How they are affected and how these contribute or affect the final system properties are important aspects and should be addressed in a more quantifiable or measurable way by predication theory. In a commercially supported service oriented architecture environment, some of the used services will be running remotely on the supplier infrastructure and in their own operational profile. This therefore provides a strong need for suppliers to provide and quantify quality attributes relating to their services and individual functions.

The run-time environment also adds others factors, such as communication overheads between the composed system and its services or between the remote services themselves. Such factors would affect some of the quality attributes of the composed system, such as reliability and performance, should the communication network have bandwidth constraints or behave abnormally for example. The main complexity here is quantifying these additional factors or overheads. One way, for example, would be to consider them as other services, providing particular functions that have their own non-functional properties.

Level of dependency between services: although in service-based systems, services are, generally, expected to be autonomous and self-contained, services can depend on each other within a system to complete their operations. Services can be distinguished as composite services or standalone services [Grassi et al, 2006]. Standalone or autonomous services are independent and do not require any other service or resource to provide their services, although complete independence may not seem possible if the run-time environment is taken into account. Composite services depend on other resources or use other services or certain functions provided by other services to provide their service. Composite services can be seen to form architecture of composite services that depend on other composite services. If a service or one of its functions within a composite service fails, that composite service may fail as a whole. How often that composite service fails to provide a particular functionality would depend on how dependent is it on the failed service. Thus, the level of dependency between services eventually affects the composed system being able to provide its system-level functionalities. Therefore predicting the reliability, for example, of a composed system would depend on how well this dependency (or level of dependency) is captured by the prediction theory. However, for the proposed model in this chapter, the dependency is considered at a higher granularity, looking at the specific functions within each service, rather than the composite service as a whole. In other words, the dependency is identified between functions rather than services. Thus the dependency points of composite services become more clearly identified in this case and potentially easier to quantify.

Level of knowledge required to develop a "sufficient" prediction theory: the different models discussed below require different levels of knowledge about the services of the composed system to be able to provide a reasonable predication. However, for any theory to become practical and widely adopted, it should be applicable to various types of available services with various levels of knowledge available about them. Off-the-shelf services, for instance, exist in the market place in different forms, with most as closed-source and many others as open-source. Some services have reasonable documentation, but many do not. But, in general, the knowledge available about these services is very limited indeed. On the other hand, services provided by a supplier or those locally developed or under development for a particular composed system could consider this requirement and hence could be packaged with sufficient level of knowledge to meet most predication models. In fact, some of these models demand services to be designed according to certain architectural styles to be applicable [Klein et al, 1999]. Predication models might demand high levels of (internal) knowledge about the services, but in general they should also be developed with reasonable assumptions that consider the state of the existing reality of the market.

Frequency of services usage in a system: The workflow of services within a system determines how often services are used to contribute to a particular system-level functionality. Services that have a higher frequency of usage within a composed system thus determine how often a system can provide its system-level functionalities compared to services that have lower a frequency of usage. It is logical therefore to expect that the properties of these services should have a higher influence on the final composed system properties. Determining these services as well as their corresponding degree of influence may prove very advantageous. For example, assuming high reliability services, if in a composed system, 80% of its operations depend on a particular service, the reliability of this service is expected to contribute more to the final system reliability than a service that only used in only 5% of its operations. A similar example can be made on the performance property.

General Approaches

As mentioned above, there are two general approaches to predicting non-functional properties. These can be classified as *black-box* (or macroscopic) approaches and *white-box* (or microscopic) approaches [Shooman, 1991]. In *black-box* approaches, the (system-level) properties of a service-based system are predicted from (high level) properties of its individual services, dealing with each service or component as a "black-box". These approaches examine the (high level) properties of these individual services and study their impact on system-level properties, attempting to predict an equivalent property of the system while avoiding the details of how these properties are obtained. *Model checking* is an example of a black-box approach [Clark et al, 1989]. Model checking is normally used for automatic model verification and validation against requirement specifications. It employs LTL (Linear temporal logic) and CTL (Computational Temporal logic) to check, what is normally referred to as, the correctness of the model. However, it can be extended to also deduce system properties from their own services' properties by using additional interface processes for establishing correctness of (system) properties [Clark et al, 1989, Abadi et al, 2003]. Clark et. al (1989) proposes a theory that employs CTL (Computation Tree Logic) logic to deduce system properties out of the properties of its services. The authors refer to service-level (or component-level) properties as local properties and systems-level properties as global properties. However, to enable preserving these local properties at a global level they suggest using additional interface processes to model the environment for services or components. Composing these components with added interface processes should then create an integrated system that enables preserving properties of individual services at a global level. Abadi et. al (2003) on the other hand, proposes a theory for automating the composition of specifications. It can be used to prove that specifications of 'lower-level systems' are used to implement specifications (of the same form) of 'higher-level systems'. This is mainly developed for verifying system-level specifications of systems composed of sub-systems, thus implying that the specifications, of the same form, of the 'higher-level systems' can be deduced from its lower-level systems or sub-systems. However, this theory does not necessarily hold for quality properties, especially for properties that are a function of different types of properties.

In *white-box* approaches, however, not only the (high-level) properties of individual services are taken into consideration but also details of these properties are studied to examine their impact on system-level properties. Some of these approaches specify how services should be designed; others demand specific details that should be collected during services' development cycle to enable better prediction of system-level properties. *Compositional reasoning* theory is an example of this approach [Bachmann et al, 2000]. Compositional reasoning theory employs mainly algebra and logic to predict the end-system properties. This theory is based on the belief that end-system properties are most often attributable to interacting services (and components) within the system and thus the properties of these services can be "composed" to predict properties of the end-system. ABAS is an example that uses compositional reasoning to deduce system performance out of its services' (or components') performance [Klein et al, 1999]. It is based on the assumption that a specific architecture (or design) is employed for the services used. It also defines a set of architecture styles and design guidelines that services (or components) should use. Based on these guidelines, it sub-classifies system attributes and then reasons the impact of changes in architecture design on these attributes. In other words, it tries to formalise architecture design as an engineering method that should be followed for developing services.

Towards a Solution

A solution for predicting non-functional properties of composed system from properties of their individual services could be envisaged from prediction theories, such as compositional reasoning [Bachmann et al, 2000]. However, existing compositional reasoning theories, such as ABAS, imply that services and components should have been developed according to pre-defined architecture styles and design guidelines, which would make them inapplicable to existing (off-the-shelf) services. Although a significant number of these services exist as open-source, few will be tempted to dig into them and look closely at how it was designed. The majority of users will be interested in simply using off-the-shelf services, rather than completely comprehending their designs or re-developing them. On the other hand, there is recent emerging research that has led to the creation of service-based (SOA: Service Oriented Architectures) and component-based software engineering (CBSE) that attempt, in one way or another, to "formalise" the engineering of services and components so that it eventually enables the development of prediction-enabled systems [Bachmann et al, 2000, Crnkovic et al, 2001]. These include several models that have been proposed, which demand certain (internal) knowledge about services and put constraints on their designs [Hamlet01, Klein99]. Nevertheless, a successful service-based prediction theory should take in consideration the amount of effort needed to be spent on assessing potential services before selection.

The process of predicting system-level non-functional properties can be envisaged as depicted in the following figures. Figure 4 views this process as a compositional process, where the same properties of each service are composed or collapsed to produce the equivalent property for the whole system. This is similar to the compositional reasoning and model checking views. For example, in ABAS, the performance property of individual services (or components) are composed to produce the equivalent performance property for the whole system, though it adds some constraints on how the system should be designed and which architecture it should use.

Figure 5 views this process as a network aggregation process where an output system-level property is seen as a contribution of not just the equivalent service-level property but also other service-level properties. This forms a network-like skeleton that at one end has the service-level properties and on the other end system-level

Figure 4. Compositional-based solutions

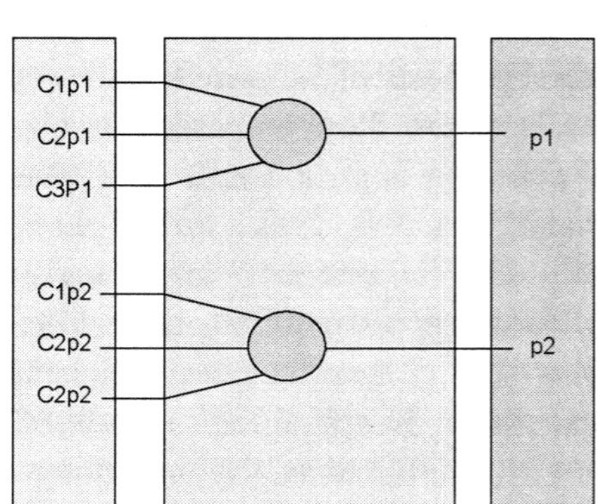

Figure 5. Network-based solutions

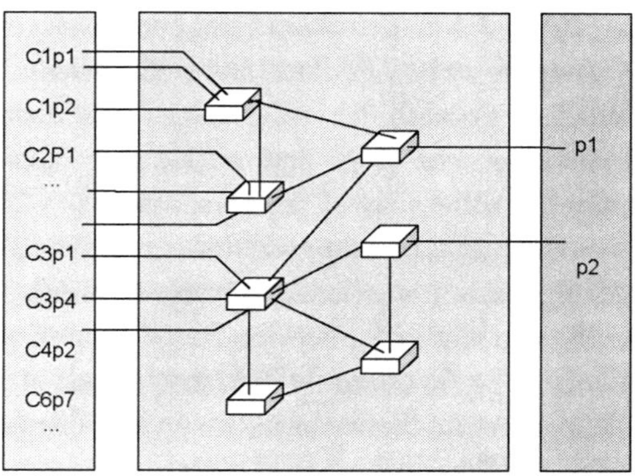

Figure 6. Aggregation-based solutions

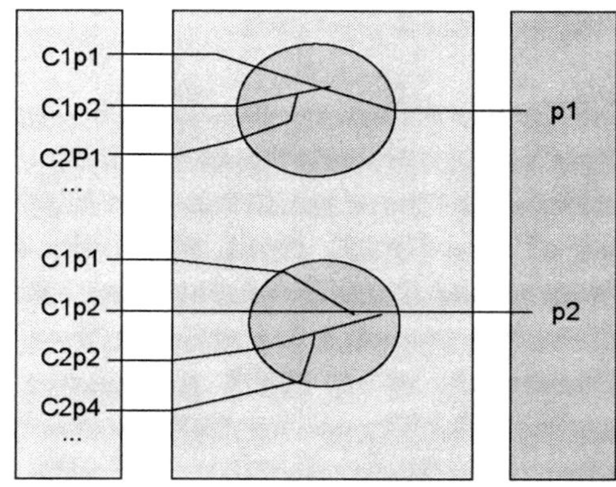

properties. For example, to find out the reliability of a system, we may need not just to look at the reliability of individual services, but also at their fault tolerance and recoverability attributes. Petri Nets is one of the network theories that can probably be recalled that addresses similar problems. Petri nets, although used to aggregate processes, can probably be seen as a potential method to aggregate non-functional properties especially when the process is depicted as a network.

The prediction process can as well be viewed as a conversion process (see Figure 6), where a relevant or equivalent set of service-level properties are aggregated or converted to an equivalent system-level property. For example, the reliability of a system can be seen to be made up of the reliabilities of its individual services. In another view, the reliability of a system can be seen as the reliabilities of its system-level functions, where the reliability of each system-level function is an aggregation of the reliabilities of contributing service-level functions. This yields chains-like structure for each system level property for each function. Theories based on stochastic Markovian chains are used for this type of process [Muppala et al, 1994, Trivedi et al, 1994]. Such theories attempt to aggregate each Markovian chain within a system into a single value.

Since, however, measuring all non-functional properties of systems, services or components does not follow a particular method, metric or a standard, addressing all of the non-functional properties of a composed system using the same theory is not feasible [Bachmann et al, 2000, Klein et al, 1999]. In fact, measuring non-functional properties of individual services or systems (as a whole) still poses a challenge to the computing community. Most of the existing methods or theories from metrics or formal methods disciplines offer only prediction and not accurate measurement. Therefore, addressing each non-functional property individually may not just enable extending existing predictive methods or theories but also enable using theories from other disciplines and potentially simplify the complexity of the problem. For example, as discussed above, theories from stochastic process algebra, aggregation of Markovian chains and Petri nets, address similar problems and may be extended to offer a better solution to this problem.

Therefore, the rest of the paper focuses on theories that attempt to predict reliability of service-based systems. The proposed model follows an approach as that depicted in Figure 6.

Prediction of Reliability of Service-Based System

Reliability of a software system is defined as the ability of a system or service to perform its required functions under stated conditions for a specified period of time [IEEE, 1990]. Reliability of a software system is also defined as its probability of failure free operation in a given environment [Krishnamurthy et al, 1997]. Approaches for measuring reliability can be similarly classified into two main types: *black-box* and *white-box* [Dolbec et al, 1995]. *Black-box* approaches attempt to measure or estimate reliability of a software system while dealing with it as a "back-box" and not needing any internal knowledge of the software system. However *white-box* or microscopic approaches use the data gathered during the development stage of a software system and attempts to estimate its reliability. Nevertheless both approaches have been criticised as fraught with risk and not entirely satisfactory for use in practical software development environments [Horgan et al, 1995, Gokhale et al, 1997]. However, estimating or knowing software reliability measures can be very useful. Such measures help users and developers alike not only to be selective about the services they want to use but also help them to estimate or predict such measures for their composed system. For example, if services with very low reliability have been used, what chance would the final system have a high reliability?

Several approaches that have been proposed to measure software reliability can be considered of relevance to service-based systems [Dolbec et al, 1995, Woit et al, 1998, Krishnamurthy et al, 1997, Grassi et al, 2006, Sato et al, 2007, Wang et al, 1999, Grassi et al, 2005, Hamlet et al, 1996, Hamlet et al, 2001, Muppala et al, 1994]. Dolbec's (1995) and Kirshnamurthy's (1997) approaches can be considered black-box approaches, while Hamlet's approach can be seen as a microscopic approach. The first five approaches use the reliability measures of individual services to predict the reliability of the final system; Wang et al (1999) and Grassi et al (2005) demand architectural constraints and the latter, however, demand internal knowledge of services through the collection of data during the development stage and utilise this data to predict the reliability of the final system. While this model might be more accurate (as claimed by Hamlet), it is not practical and in most cases inapplicable especially for service-based system and unlikely to be favoured by industry. Grassi et. al. (2006) propose a theory based on an architectural framework for service-based systems. It assumes different levels of knowledge available about each service and defines the format in which this knowledge should be available. The approach of Grassi et. al. (2006) can be seen to fall within the white-box and black-box approaches, as it tries to adapt to the different levels of knowledge available about each service. Krishnamurthy's and Dolbec's models are black-box approaches that attempt to predict systems' reliability out of their services (or modules). Although such models might produce less accurate results, they are applicable to a wider range of (especially off-the-shelf) services or components and are more likely to be favoured or used by practitioners. However, due to the low accuracy of such models in their current state, they are unlikely to be widely adopted.

OUR APPROACH

Krishnamurthy's and Dolbec's models deal with each service (or module) as a "black-box" and use the reliability associated with a service as whole to predict the reliability of the system. However, in service-based systems, since services are expected to be self-contained and can, in many cases, operate autonomously to provide certain functions and since these functions will not necessarily all be used (as the composed system may utilise only part of these functions), it would be more precise to associate properties with the functions of a service rather than to it as a 'whole'. Consequently, the values of properties will be associated with the functions provided by the composed system. This model is not completely a black-box approach, since it considers reliability of individual functions provided by each service opposed to the service as a 'whole'. In this case, the reliability of a system-level function provided by the composed system can be derived from reliabilities of the used respective service-level functions. Thus a service-based system can be viewed as made up of system-level functions (or sub-services) and these system-level functions are made up of execution paths that run across the services' service-level functions that make up the system. We refer to this approach as a *Service-Based Reliability Estimation* (SBARE) model.

In addition, since functions can be considered as (behavioural) subparts of services, theories used in Krishnamurthy's and Dolbec's models can be modified or extended to apply to this model. Although both models follow the same general concept, their approach to deriving the theory is different. Therefore, based on these two models, two corresponding models can result. Further, theoretical and empirical research can then be further applied to evaluate when and which model provides more accurate results. The following derivation assumes that the composition architecture is as depicted in Figure 3, where a "main program" or "execution workflow" defines the sequence of how services are invoked. The behaviour of the system is determined by the functions or services it provides. SBARE attempts to tag each function of each service with its own reliability measure. In this case, the main workflow is considered as a "service" that provides this function of execution and is part of the execution paths of each system-level service. In addition, in a typical service-based system, as depicted in Figure 1, remote services are likely to be used in the composed system. These remote services add additional communication reliability measure to the system-level functions that utilise those services. These are also dealt with as a service that provides a specific function.

Extending Dolbec's Model

The following derivation is based on Dolbec's model. Dolbec's model is based on a structure based software reliability model proposed by Shooman, (1991). In Shooman's model, the number of failures (i.e. does not complete the function) in a software system can be found by the following equation.

$$n_f=Nu_1q_1+Nu_2q_2+...+Nu_lq_l \tag{1}$$

where N is the number of software system tests, u_i is the usage ratio of the execution path i, q_i is the probability of failure of path i and l is the number of execution paths. This equation (1) suits very well the SBARE model view, as it views the system as made up of execution paths. Obviously, the probability of failure (unreliability) of the software system can be found as

$$Q_s=\frac{n_f}{N}=\sum_{i=1}^{l} f_i q_i \tag{2}$$

and the reliability of the software system can be found as

$$R_s=1Q_s \tag{3}$$

Equation 2 represents the unreliability of a software system as equal to the sum of the probability of failure of every execution path within this system weighted by its corresponding usage ratio.

To extend this theory on a similar basis to Dolbec's model, however, for service-based reliability estimation, consider the following.

C_{iF_jK} = is event that function F_j in service C_i of path K executes successfully.

$p(C_{iF_jK})$ = is the probability that function F_j in service C_i of path Kdoes not fail.

$q(C_{iF_jK})$ = is the probability that function F_j in service C_i of path K fails.

E_{KF} is event that execution path K within function F is successfully executed.

$p(E_{KF})$ = is the probability that execution path K within function F does not fail.

$q(E_{KF})$ = is the probability that execution path K within function F fails.

Since each system-level function can be made up of one or more execution path, the reliability of each execution path can be found by multiplying the reliability of service-level functions used within that path. However to avoid complications in the calculation, it is assumed that these execution paths are independent and failure of one function in a standalone service or component does not cause a failure in another function with the same standalone service or component.

Thus the probability that execution path K within function F does not fail can be found as

$$p(E_{KF}) = \prod_{i=1,j=1}^{n_K,m_K} p(C_{iF_jK}) \tag{4}$$

Where n_K is the number of standalone services or components and m_K is the number of functions within path K (n_K and m_K have the same value, i.e. n_K=m_K).

Equation (4) can also be expressed as

$$p(E_{KF}) = \prod_{i=1,j=1}^{n_K,m_K} 1 - q(C_{iF_jK}) \tag{5}$$

Consequently, the probability of failure of execution path K within function F can be found as

$$q(E_{KF}) = \prod_{i=1,j=1}^{n_K,m_K} 1 - p(C_{iF_jK}) = \prod_{i=1,j=1}^{n_K,m_K} q(C_{iF_jK}) \tag{6}$$

However, if the reliabilities of service/component-level functions within execution path K are high, then Equation (5) can be approximated (as shown in [Misra, 1992]) to the following equation

$$p(E_{KF}) \approx \sum_{i=1,j=1}^{n_K,m_K} q(C_{iF_jK}) \tag{7}$$

Consequently, the probability of failure can be written as

$$q(E_{KF}) \approx \sum_{i=1,j=1}^{n_K,m_K} q(C_{iF_jK}) \tag{8}$$

Using this Equation (8) in equation (1), the number of failures of a given system-level function F_{w^s} can be found as

$$\begin{aligned} n_{fF_{w^s}} &\approx Nu_1(\sum_{i=1,j=1}^{n_1,m_1} q(C_{iF_j1})) + Nu_2(\sum_{i=1,j=1}^{n_2,m_2} q(C_{iF_j2})) \\ &+ \ldots + Nu_K(\sum_{i=1,j=1}^{n_K,m_K} q(C_{iF_jK})) + \ldots + Nu_l(\sum_{i=1,j=1}^{n_l,m_l} q(C_{iF_jl})) \end{aligned} \tag{9}$$

Where l is the number of execution paths within Function F_{w^s} and w is the function number within the system s.

Therefore the unreliability of F_{w^s} can be found as

$$\begin{aligned} Q_{F_{w^s}} &\approx \frac{n_{fF_{w^s}}}{N} \approx u_1(\sum_{i=1,j=1}^{n_1,m_1} q(C_{iF_j1})) + u_2(\sum_{i=1,j=1}^{n_2,m_2} q(C_{iF_j2})) \\ &+ \ldots + u_K(\sum_{i=1,j=1}^{n_K,m_K} q(C_{iF_jK})) + \ldots + u_l(\sum_{i=1,j=1}^{n_l,m_l} q(C_{iF_jl})) \end{aligned} \tag{10}$$

In general, the same functions could be executed or utilised by different paths within the same system-level function. Therefore, $C_{1F_1 1}$ and $C_{3F_{23} 2}$ can be the same function. Thus, some functions will have higher usage rates than others. Consequently, if we combine the same standalone or autonomous services by adding their individual usage ratios, Equation (10) can be re-written as

$$Q_{F_{w^s}} \approx U_1 Q_1 + U_2 Q_2 + \ldots + U_y Q_y \tag{11}$$

Where y is the number of standalone or autonomous service-level functions used in the execution of the system-level function F_{w^s}. U_y is the usage ratio of the standalone service -level function y in N tests. Q_y is the probability of failure of the standalone service -level function y. Equation (11) can be re-written as

$$Q_{F_{w^s}} \approx \sum_{i=1}^{y} U_i Q_i \tag{12}$$

Consequently reliability of function F_{w^s} can be found as

$$R_{F_{w^s}} = 1 - Q_{F_{w^s}} \approx 1 - \sum_{i=1}^{y} U_i Q_i \tag{13}$$

This equation implies that the reliability of a system-level function can be found from the sum of un-reliabilities of the used standalone service -level functions weighted by their corresponding usage ratios. These usage ratios also can be used as a useful indication of the standalone service-level functions that have a higher impact on the corresponding system-level function. In Dolbec's model, he defines the usage ratio as equal to the standalone service execution time divided by the total system execution time. However, on a function level, we can redefine this usage ratio as the number of times a given (service-level) function is used in the execution of a system-level function divided by the total number of times all other (service-level) functions are used, i.e.

$$U_{F_j} = \frac{N_{C_{F_j}}}{N_{F_{w^s}}} \tag{14}$$

Where is the number of times a standalone service-level function F_j is used in the execution of the system-level function F_{w^s}. $N_{F_{w^s}}$ is the number of times all other (standalone service-level) functions are used in the execution of the system-level function F_{w^s}.

This is a reasonable assumption, since we are only interested in knowing whether a function completes its function or not and not necessarily how long it takes to complete it. In addition, in practice, it will be hard to find out individual standalone services' execution times because this time is also dependent on which functions are used and their operational profile.

Of course, it is also possible that some standalone service-level functions are used in more than one execution paths across different system-level functions. Although we have assumed execution paths are independent, standalone service-level functions that have higher usage ratios across system-level functions can provide a useful indication of their impact on system-level functions and thus indicate their importance to the whole system.

Extending Krishnamurthy's Model

The above derivation is base on Shoorman's model and further has used the same approach followed in Dolbec's model. The SBARE model can also be derived in a similar way as Krishnamurthy's model. As an addition to Krishnamurthy's model, an approach is suggested to represent the dependence between standalone services, although, as reported case studies indicate, it is not always accurate. This is mainly due to the fact that system structure is not taken into account and the type of functionality of standalone components is not considered as related to the degree of dependency between these services. However, SBARE model can reuse a similar experimental set up noted in Krishnamurthy's model to compare both derivations and provide a suitable evaluation for both.

The above derivation is based on the assumption that standalone service functions have high reliability, thus for functions with low reliability, Equation (7) to (14) are not applicable. However, Equation (6) is still applicable. In fact, Krishnamurthy's model builds on a similar equation. However, he assumes that a number of tests that should be carried out on a system vary and a sufficient number of tests should be carried out to eventually converge on a *near true* reliability.

Repeating Equation (4), the probability that execution path K within function F does not fail can be found as

$$p(E_{KF}) = \prod_{i=1,j=1}^{n_K,m_K} p(C_{iF_jK})$$

If this execution path is tested by a given test case t, then using the above equation the reliability of execution path K can found as

$$R^t_{E_{KF}} = \prod_{i=1,j=1}^{n_K,m_K} R^t_{C_{iF_jK}} \tag{15}$$

Therefore, based on Krishnamurthy's model, if all execution paths within the system-level function F are tested with respect to a test set T, its reliability can be found as

$$R_{F_{w^s}} = \frac{\sum_{\forall t\in T,k=1}^{K} R^t_{E_{kF}}}{|T|} \tag{16}$$

Where K is the number of execution paths within system-level F_{w^s}. The error ℓ in this estimation can be found as

$$e = \frac{\left|R_{F_{w^s}} - R_{TF_{w^s}}\right|}{R_{TF_{w^s}}} \tag{17}$$

Where $R_{TF_{w^s}}$ is the *true* reliability for function F_{w^s}. If $R_{TF_{w^s}}$ is achieved through $N_{F_{w^s}}$, where $N_{F_{w^s}}$ is the number of tests or executions of function F_{w^s} to arrive at $R_{F_{w^s}}$ and $N_{TF_{w^s}}$ is the number of tests or executions of F_{w^s} to arrive at $R_{TF_{w^s}}$ then the δ-efficiency of this estimate for $e \leq \delta$ can be found as

$$\eta_\delta = 1 - \frac{N_{F_{w^s}}}{N_{TF_{w^s}}} \tag{18}$$

η_δ can be used as a measure of how fast $R_{F_{w^s}}$ can be obtained compared to $R_{TF_{w^s}}$.

In Krishnamurthy's model dependency between standalone services is handled by their degree of independence. This degree of independence (DOI) of a standalone service determines the number of times its reliability is used in Equation (15) compared to the number of its occurrence in an execution path or paths of the system-level function F_{w^s}.

VALIDATION AND EVALUATION

Another part of this research is the validation and evaluation of the above models. The main purpose of this evaluation is to examine the accuracy and efficiency of the SBARE model, i.e. to examine the SBARE reliability ($R_{F_{w^s}}$) estimates with respect to the true reliability ($R_{TF_{w^s}}$) observed over a test set T using Equation 17 and to examine the efficiency of SBARE reliability estimates with respect to true reliability estimates over a test set T using Equation 18 of the SBARE model extension to Krishnamurthy's model. An extensive evaluation with detailed analysis of both extensions is beyond the scope of this chapter.

Experimental Setup

We used a general experimental setup as noted in Krishnamurthy's work, with several variations. A service-based system was used with a focus on predicting the reliability of a chosen set of functions from each service with the system. The overall system, named searchMService, included 20 remote services and 9 local services in addition to the workflow framework to provide more than 73 system-level functions, as shown in Figure 7 (it shows only the services that have been used in the experiment). These included 5 off-the-shelf remote services, 3 off-the-shelf local services and 21 purpose built services. The purpose-built services are designed with varied complexities, each providing 5 to 23 functions. A Simple workflow framework has been built specifically for evaluating the SBARE model. This composition framework is based on the "main program" or "workflow" concepts depicted in Figure 3.

We chose three (of the purpose built) services and one or two functions of each service for seeding faults based on their complexity measured in the number of computational units, their lines of code density and potential frequency of occurrence in the system shown in Figure 4. These three services provide functions to perform searches and data presentation and formatting with varied complexity and destinations depending on the input parameter. In addition, we built four specific workflows in BPEL: WF1 & WF2 runs functions from service S1, WF3 runs functions from services S1 and S2 and WF4 runs functions from services S2 and S3. Table 1, Table 2 and Table 3 show the lines of code count (LOCC) for the workflow enactor, services and their respective functions and workflows. One or two functions of each service are seeded with faults as shown in Table 2, and the overall faulty workflows of the system are shown in Table 4. These functions were chosen to meet the required fault density of 0.01.

RESULTS AND DISCUSSION

The first step we obtained reliabilities of the selected individual faulty functions using a test set,

Figure 7. System experiment setup

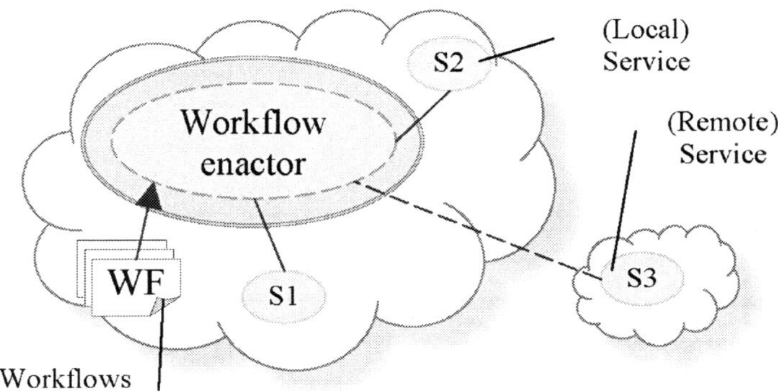

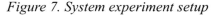

Table 1. Services seeded with faults

Service	LOCC	Total Faults
S1	1336	5
S2	1234	5
S3	1876	6
WFEncator	4300	

Table 2. Functions seeded with faults

Functions	LOCC	Faults
S1: F1	202	2
S1: F2	173	2
S2: F1	198	2
S2: F2	389	4
S3: F2	312	3

Table 3. Workflows

Workflow	LOCC	Faults
WF1	12	
WF2	20	
WF3	20	
WF4	20	

the results are shown Table 5 with reliabilities of S1, S2 and S3 are 0.51032, 0.375 and 0.394 respectively. SBARE reliability estimates were then derived as shown in Table 6 for the searchMService system for each workflow assuming that the degree of independence is 1 and the reliabilities of workflow enactor, its interfaces and the communication as 1.

Table 5. Reliabilities of faulty functions

Function	Reliability
S1F1	0.697
S1F2	0.724
S2F1	0.391
S2F2	0.331
S3F2	0.362

Table 6 shows that the relative error between the true reliability $R_{TF_{w^s}}$ and the predicted reliability $R_{F_{w^s}}$. The relative error for WF1, WF2 and WF4 is relatively small compared to WF3's. These high accuracy values indicate that the $R_{F_{w^s}}$ estimate appears a good predicator for true reliability $R_{TF_{w^s}}$, however, for WF3 it is not as good a predictor of true reliability. Table 6 also shows the 0.01-efficiency and 0.05-efficiency values. These are calculated before the reliability estimates converged to true reliability, thus a high value of is obtained. These indicate that reliability estimates reach the true reliability very fast. Despite the high efficiency for WF3 to reach true reliability, it has poor accuracy, which indicates reliability estimate values do not converge as illustrated in Figure 8.

These results however are insufficient to make any general conclusions about the effectiveness of the SBARE model; however, they help to bring other factors to the surface. Other factors, such as dependency, operational profile, composition framework, service interface, communications and so forth also need to be considered within the

Table 4. Faulty services, functions, workflows

Workflow/ Functions	Total LOC	Faults	Fault Density= faults/LOCC
WF1:S1F1	4514	2	0.000443
WF2:S1F1+S1F2	4695	4	0.000852
WF3:S1F1+S2F2	5001	6	0.0012
WF4:S2F1+S3F2	4830	5	0.001035

Table 6. SBARE reliability estimates

Faulty Workflows	Reliability		Accuracy (Error *e*)	Efficiency	
	$R_{TF_{w^s}}$	$R_{F_{w^s}}$		δ= 0.01	δ= 0.05
WF1:S1F1	0.6541	0.6422	1.819%	0.98	0.97
WF2:S1F1+S1F2	0.5103	0.5033	1.375%	0.96	0.89
WF3:S1F1+S2F2	0.3127	0.3875	23.920%	0.94	0.90
WF4:S2F1+S3F2	0.3712	0.3842	3.502%	0.99	0.98

prediction model carefully. The difference here, however, is in the granularity of the SBARE model, being that these results are reflected at the system-level function and the contributing service service-level functions rather than the 'whole' system or the 'whole' service. Given the higher granularity of the SBARE model, these results potentially provide higher efficiency and accuracy covering a wider spectrum of execution paths across the horizontal and the vertical dimensions of the composed system.

CONCLUSION

Predicting non-functional properties of service-based systems from properties of their individual services faces many challenges with a complicated mix of obstacles and related issues, yet, if successful, promises significant potential benefits to users, developers, integrators and industry. These promises include shortening the development life cycle of integrating or building a composed system, reducing the amount of effort needed for the service selection process, potentially enabling dynamic service binding frameworks, and potentially contributing to the quality of the resultant system.

This chapter explored potential complexities, issues, and possible theories. It then presented a generic approach and model to predict the reliability of a composed system. It highlighted differences between different models, and the importance of such models for service-based systems. The chapter proposed a model for estimating the reliability of service-based systems. The proposed

Figure 8. True & SBARE reliabilities for WF2 and WF3

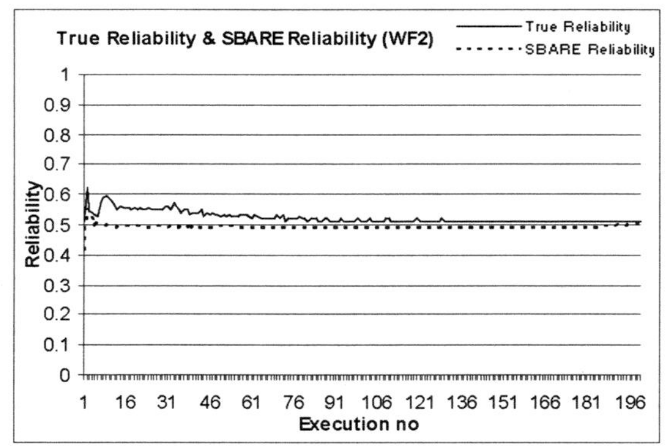

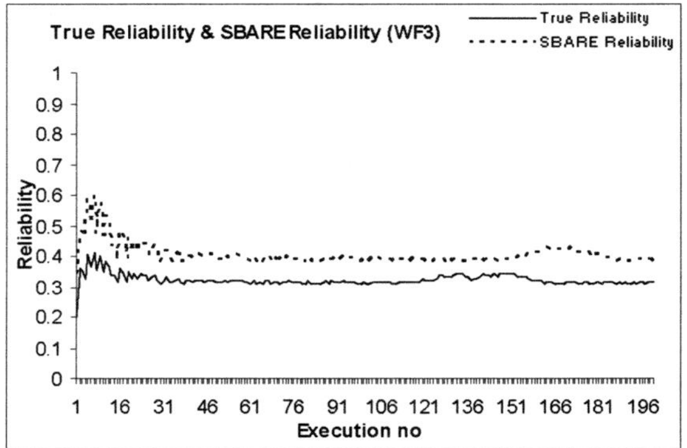

model, SBARE, provides a practical mid-way mid-detailed approach between the white-box and the black-box approaches. SBARE model assumes each service-level functions or sub-services are tagged with a reliability attribute value, which can consequently be used to derive the reliability of the composed system system-level function. This effectively, for example, provides the composed system (S1) system-level functions (sysF1, sysF2…sysFn) with reliability values (sysF1R, sysF2R…sysFnR) estimated from contributing service-level functions. The authors believe this model provides a more practical approach that has a higher chance to be adopted by industry enabling tagging each system-level function with quality attribute values, opposed to the overall system, thus providing a more detailed map of the quality attributes of the system. On the other hand, the model has limitations and makes assumptions on dependency, interfaces and communication issues. Also it does not support complex service interactions by multiple clients, or more complex representations of non-functional properties, which in complex service-based systems may need to be considered.

Although, the chapter focused on reliability prediction models, it also presented a generic approach to predicting non-functional properties of composed systems, which the authors believe can be used to derive theories for predicting other non-functional properties, the most obvious of which is performance, for example.

The chapter concludes that while many researchers have proposed many prediction models and significant progress has been made in this direction, there are several challenges that need to be overcome before prediction theories becomes widely used and adopted by industry.

ACKNOWLEDGMENT

This work is in part funded by the EU CLARiFi project. The authors would like to thank Prof. Pearl Brereton and other members of the CLARiFi consortium for their input.

REFERENCES

Abadi, M. & Lamport, L. (2009). Composing specifications. *ACM Transactions of Programming Language Systems, 15*(1).

Bachmann, F., Bass, L., Buhman, C., Comella-Dorda, S., Long, F., Robert, J., et al. (2000). *Volume II: Technical concepts of component-based software engineering*. (Technical Report, CMU/SEI-2000-TR-008, 2000).

Cerami, E. (2002). *Web services essentials*. O'Reilly.

Clarke, E. M., Long, D. E., & McMillan, K. L. (1989). *Compositional model checking*. In Proceedings of the 4th Symposium on Logic in Computer Science, (pp. 353-362).

Cotroneo, D., Di Flora, C. & Russo, S. (2003). *An enhanced Service Oriented Architecture for developing Web-based applications. Journal of Web Engineering*.

Crnkovic, I., Larsson, M., & Preiss, O. (2005). *Concerning predictability in dependable component-based systems: Classification of quality attributes*. In de Lemos et al. (Eds.), *Architecting dependable systems III*, (LNCS 3549), (pp. 257 -278).

Crnkovic, I., Schmidt, H., Stafford, J., & Wallnau, K. (2001). *Proceedings of the 4th ICSE Workshop on Component-Based Software Engineering: Component Certification and System Predication*, 2001

Dolbec, J., & Shepard, T. (1995). *A component based software reliability model*. Ontario: Department of Electrical and Computer Engineering, Royal Military College of Canada.

Erradi, A., & Maheshwari, P. (2005). WSBus: QoS-aware middleware for reliable Web Services interaction. *Proceedings of the IEEE International Conference on e-Technology, e-Commerce and e-Service*. Hong Kong, China.

Ezenwoye, O., & Sadjadi, S. M. (2005). *Composing aggregate Web Services in BPEL*. Miami: School of Computing and Information Science, Florida International University.

Ezenwoye, O., & Sadjadi, S. M. (2007). TRAP/BPEL: A framework for dynamic adaptation of composite services. *Proceedings of the International Conference on Web Information Systems and Technologies (WEBIST 2007)*. Barcelona, Spain.

Ezenwoye, O., Sadjadi, S. M., Carey, A., & Robinson, M. (2007). Grid Service composition in BPEL for scientific applications. *Proceedings of the International Conference on Grid computing, high-performance and Distributed Applications (GADA'07)*. Vilamoura, Algarve, Portugal.

Gokhale, S., & Trivedi, K. S. (1997). Structure-based software reliability prediction. In *Proceedings of Fifth International Conference on Advanced Computing*, Chennai, India, December 1997.

Gokhale, S., Wong, W. E., Trivedi, K. S., & Horgan, J. R. (1998). *An analytical approach to architecture-based software reliability prediction*, (p. 13). IEEE International Computer Performance and Dependability Symposium (IPDS'98), 1998.

Grassi, V.(2005). Architecture-based dependability prediction for service-oriented Computing. ACM SIGSOFT Software Engineering Notes, 30*(4)*.

Grassi, V. & Patella, S. (2006). *Reliability prediction for service oriented computing environments*. Internet Computing, 2006.

IEEE Computer Society. (1990). *IEEE standard glossary of software engineering terminology*. (IEEE Std 610.12-1990). The Institute of Electronical and Electronics Engineers, Inc, 1990.

Klein, M., & Kazman, R. (1999). *Attribute-based architectural styles*. (Technical Report CMU/SEI-99-TR-022), Software Engineering Institute, Carnegie Mellon University, Pittsburgh, PA, 1999.

Krishnamurthy, S., & Mathur, A. P. (1997). On the estimation of reliability of a software system using reliabilities of its components. *Proceedings ISSRE '97*, November 02-05, 1997.

Lin, M., Xie, J., & Guo, H. (2005). Solving Qos-driven Web Service dynamic composition as fuzzy constraint satisfaction. *Proceedings of the 2005 IEEE Conference*.

Liu, Y., Ngu, A. H. H., & Zeng, L. (2004). QoS computation and policing in dynamic Web Service selection. *Proceedings of the 13th International Conference World Wide Web*, 2004.

Lumpe, M., Achermann, F., & Nierstrasz, O. (2000). A formal language for composition. In Leavens, G., & Sitaraman, M. (Eds.), *Foundations of component based systems* (pp. 69–90). Cambridge University Press.

Lumpe, M., Schneider, J. G., Nierstrasz, O., & Achermann, F. (1997). *Towards a formal composition language. Proceedings of ESEC '97 Workshop on Foundations of Component-Based Systems*, September 1997, (pp. 178-187).

Lycett, M. & Paul, R.J. (1998). *Component-based development: Dealing with non-functional aspects of architecture*. ECOOP, 1998.

Milanovic, N., & Malek, M. (2005). *Architectural support for automatic service composition-services computing*. IEEE International Conference on Service Computing, 2, (pp. 133-140).

Misra, K. B. (1992). *Reliability analysis and prediction*. Elsevier.

Muppala, J., Ciardo, G., & Trivedi, K. (1994). *Stochastic reward nets for reliability prediction.* Communications in Reliability. *Maintainability and Serviceability*, *1*(2), 9–20.

Oinn, T., Addis, K., Ferris, J., Marvin, D., Senger, M., & Greenwood, M. (2004). Taverna: A tool for the composition and enactment of bioinformatics workflows. *Bioinformatics (Oxford, England)*, *20*(17). doi:10.1093/bioinformatics/bth361

Plakosh, D., Smith, D., & Wallnau, K. (1999). *Builder's guide for WaterBeans components.* (Technical Report CMU/SEI-99-TR-024), Software Engineering Institute, Carnegie Mellon University, Pittsburgh, PA, 1999.

Roshandel, R., & Medvidovic, N. (2004). Toward architecture-based reliability estimation. In *Proceedings of the Twin Workshops on Architecting Dependable Systems, International Conference on Software Engineering* (ICSE 2004), Edinburgh, UK, May 2004, and *The International Conference on Dependable Systems and Networks* (DSN-2004), Florence, Italy, June 2004

Sato, N. &. Trivedi, K.S (2007). *Accurate and efficient stochastic reliability analysis of composite services using their compact Markov reward model representations.* Services Computing, 2007.

Shooman, M. L. (1991). A micro software reliability model for prediction and test apportionment. *Proceedings 1991 International, Symposium on Software Engineering* (Austin, Texas), (pp. 52-59). May 1991.

Stafford, J., & McGregor, J. D. (2002). Issues in predicting the reliability of composed components. *Proceedings of the 5th ICSE CBSE Workshop*, Orlando, Florida, May 2002.

Taylor, I., Shields, M., Wang, I., & Harrison, A. (2007). The Triana workflow environment: Architecture and applications. In I. Taylor, E. Deelman, D. Gannon, and M. Shields, (Eds.), *Workflows for e-science.* (pp. 320-339). New York, Secaucus, NJ: Springer.

Trivedi, K., Malhotra, M., & Fricks, R. (1994). *Markov reward approach to performability and reliability analysis.* In the 2nd International Workshop on Modeling, Analysis, and Simulation of Computer and Telecommunication Systems, 1994.

Wallnau, K. (2003). *Volume III: A technology for predictable assembly from certifiable components.* (Technical Report, CMU/SEI-2003-TR-009), 2003.

Wang, W. L., Wu, Y., & Chen, M. H. (1999). *An architecture-based software reliability model.* IEEE Pacific Rim International Symposium on Dependable Computing, Hong Kong, 1999.

Woit, D., & Mason, D. (1998). Software system reliability from component reliability. *Proceedings of 1998 Workshop on Software Reliability Engineering* (SRE '98), July, 1998.

Zeng, L., Benatallah, B., Ngu, A. H. H., Dumas, M., & Kalagnanam, J. (2003). Quality driven Web Services composition. *Proceedings of the 12th International Conference World Wide Web*, 2003.

Zeng, L., Benatallah, B., Ngu, A. H. H., Dumas, M., Kalagnanam, J., & Chang, H. (2004). QoS-aware middleware for Web Services composition. *IEEE Transactions on Software Engineering*, *30*(5).

ENDNOTE

1 The terms developers and integrators are used interchangeably throughout the chapter

Chapter 13
Model-Based Methodology and Framework for Assessing Service and Business Process Availability

Nikola Milanovic
Model Labs - Berlin, Germany

Bratislav Milic
Humboldt University, Germany

ABSTRACT

In the world where on-demand and trustworthy service delivery is one of the main preconditions for successful business service and business process, availability is of the paramount importance and cannot be compromised. This chapter presents a framework for modeling business process availability that takes into account services, the underlying ICT-infrastructure and people. Based on a fault model, the chapter develops the methodology to map dependencies between ICT-components, services and business processes. The mapping enables automatically derived appropriate availability models and analytically assessed steady-state, interval and user perceived availability at all levels, up to the level of the business process. The chapter demonstrates the applicability of the mapping using two case studies. Finally, it defines a roadmap towards model-based service management and position this work within its context.

INTRODUCTION

Service Oriented Architecture (SOA) is the paradigm that pretends to play a dominant role in the shaping of the Information Technology (IT) landscape in the coming decades. It represents a logical and evolutionary step initiated by development in the areas of distributed computing, business process modeling, and the increased ubiquity of networking technologies. The main goal of SOA

DOI: 10.4018/978-1-60960-493-6.ch013

is to introduce standard methodologies, architectures, tools, languages and protocols for development and integration of distributed applications based on the loosely coupled, independent and autonomous software artifacts, thus supporting the large-scale composability, reusability and agility.

Trustworthy service delivery in SOA is at present one of the main preconditions for the successful and sustainable business operations. Therefore, service and business process availability cannot be compromised. Even today, services are simply expected to be delivered reliably and on demand, and this requirement will be even more important in the near future. The unreliable and incorrect services (Amazon EC-2 Support Team, 2007) can corrupt business processes causing an impact such as lost opportunity or money. Common understanding of the service and business process availability properties is rather sketchy, limited and mostly empirical.

Several methodologies can be used to assess service and business process availability: quantitative, qualitative and analytical. Quantitative assessment is based on the real-time measurement and monitoring. Whereas it has proven itself in several areas (e.g., hardware benchmarks and testing), it is difficult to apply to services because of the lack of adequate metrics and instrumentation. Qualitative availability assessment is performed informally (e.g., through the questionnaires and interviews) and assigns an availability class to the system (service). The qualitative results are easy to misinterpret, difficult to compare and depend heavily on the consultant performing the analysis. The analytical methods are used to attempt to model services and their behavior and calculate or simulate their availability. Up to now, however, classical analytical methods have been applied to determine service availability with mixed success and relative low industry penetration due to the scalability, complexity and evolution problems.

DEFINITIONS

In this section we present the basic (and informal, that is, non-mathematical) definitions of reliability and availability, as well as definitions of services and business processes, as all these terms are used very colloquially today, and also frequently outside of the strict computer science vocabulary and context. Such definitions will suffice to comprehend the overall context of the proposed framework, for a deeper mathematical treatment of the subject many of the references in this section provide enough detailed information.

The events that lead to the system malfunction have intrinsic probabilistic nature. Therefore, the lifetime or time to failure of a system can usually be represented by a random variable. A phenomenon is considered random if its future behavior is not exactly predictable. An example is tossing a pair of dice or measuring the time between particle emissions by a radioactive sample. A function that associates a number with every possible outcome of an event is called a random variable. Let the random variable X represent the lifetime or time to failure of a system. The continuous random variable X can be characterized by the cumulative distribution function $F(t)$, the probability density function $f(t)$ and the hazard rate function $h(t)$, also known as the instantaneous failure rate. The CDF represents the probability that the system will fail before a given time, the PDF describes the rate of change of the CDF, and the hazard rate function represents the conditional probability that a system that has survived until time t will fail in the given subsequent interval.

Time to failure or lifetime of a system may follow different distributions, such as exponential, Weibull, geometric, Erlang etc. These distributions are parameterized, e.g., with parameters such as failure or repair rate.

Reliability

One of the basic definitions of reliability is the recommendation E.800 of the International Telecommunications Union (ITU-T) which defines reliability as

the ability of an item to perform a required function under given conditions for a given time interval. (International Telecommunications Union, 2008)

In (Siewiorek and Swarz, 1982) reliability is defined as

a function of time, R(t), representing the conditional probability that the system has survived the interval [0,t], given that it was operational at time t = 0.

In the seminal work in this field (Avizienis, Laprie, Randell and Landwehr, 2004), reliability is defined as the attribute of dependability. Dependability is the ability to deliver a service that can justifiably be trusted. It has the following attributes: availability, reliability, safety, integrity and maintainability. Hence, in this context reliability is perceived as

the continuity of correct service.

Finally, in Grottke, Sun, Fricks and Trivedi (2008) reliability is defined as

the function R(t), which is the probability that the system continues to function until time t.

We will adopt the following definition of reliability:

Definition 1: For any time interval (z, z+t], reliability function R(t|z) is the conditional probability that the system does not fail in this interval, assuming it was working at time z. We will observe the intervals starting at z = 0, where reliability R(t) = R(t|0) is the probability that the system continues to function until time t.

The mean time to failure (MTTF) represents the expected time that a system will operate before the first failure occurs, and is equal to the inverse failure rate for the exponential distribution. For example, the system will on the average operate for MTTF time units and then encounter its first failure. MTTF can be calculated as the mean of the system's lifetime distribution.

Availability

Availability is closely related to, but also very often confused with reliability. According to the ITU-T recommendation E.800 (International Telecommunications Union, 2008), availability is defined as

the ability of an item to be in a state to perform a required function at a given instant of time, or at any instant of time within a given time interval, assuming that the external resources, if required, are provided.

In Siewiorek and Swarz (1982), availability is defined as

a function of time A(t), which represents the probability that the system is operational at the instant of time t. If the limit of this function exists as t goes to infinity, it expresses the expected fraction of time that the system is available to perform useful computations.

Analogously to reliability, Avizienis, Laprie, Randell and Landwehr (2004) treats availability as an attribute of dependability and defines it as:

the readiness for the correct service.

Finally, in Sahner, Trivedi and Puliafito (2002) availability is defined as:

the probability that system is working at the instant t, regardless of the number of times it may have failed and been repaired in the interval (0,t).

The main difference between reliability and availability is that reliability requires that no failures have occurred during the entire observed interval. Availability, on the other hand, focuses on failure-free operation at a given instant of time, allowing that a system may have broken down in the past and has been repaired. If the system is not repairable however, definition and meaning of availability and reliability are equivalent. Let us introduce availability definitions that we will be using:

Definition 2: Instantaneous availability of a system is the probability that the system is operational (delivers the satisfactory service) at a given time instant.

Definition 3: Steady state availability of a system is a fraction of lifetime that the system is operational.

Steady-state availability is the long-term probability that the system is available. It can be shown that steady-state availability does not depend on the nature of the failure or repair time distribution, but only on the average time required to repair system failure and average time to system failure. This well-known relationship is given as A = MTTF/(MTTF+MTTR).

Definition 4: Interval availability of a system is the probability that the system is operational (delivers satisfactory service) during a period of time.

In other words, interval availability is the expected proportion of time the system is operational during the given time interval and can be calculated as $A_I = E[U(t)]/t$, where $U(t)$ is the random variable representing the expected system uptime and t is duration of the observed interval.

Services and Business Processes

Services are the basic building blocks of service oriented architectures (SOA). SOA is an architectural attempt to describe and understand distributed systems which have minimal shared understanding among the systems components. SOA is characterized with the following properties: logical view, message orientation, description orientation, large and complex messages, network orientation and platform neutrality (W3C Working Group, 2004). An important consequence of the above properties is the profiling of the main SOA roles: requester, provider and broker (discovery agency).

The term service itself is heavily overloaded, and generally not exclusively used in the context of the IT systems or the computer science only. For the start, Merriam Webster Online defines a service as

a facility supplying some public demand that does not produce a tangible commodity. (Merriam Webster Online, 2008)

The first part of this definition implies that a service can be performed by nearly anyone (e.g., a craftsman or an enterprise as well as hardware or software systems), as long as the service provider (supplier) and the service consumer (public demand) are defined. The second part of the definition however, restricts certain activities, namely those that produce physical artifacts, from being considered as a service. The IT focus is stricter in the following definition, where a service is described as

a meaningful activity that a computer program performs on request of another computer program. (Krafzig, Banke and Slama, 2004)

Similar is one of the earliest definitions of a service in the computational context where service is *a loosely-coupled computing task communicating over the internet, that plays the growing part in business-to-business interaction. (Burbeck, 2000)*

The above definition does not specify that service consumers must necessarily be other services. Also, it clearly states that the service focus is business-to-business communication, implicitly disqualifying services used internally in an enterprise. Another technical-oriented definition states that a service is

characterized by three parts: offered functionality, input and output messages, and interface address or port reference. (Vogels, 2003)

Services can also be observed from a business perspective, as in (Weske, 2007):

A service captures functionality with a business value that is ready to be used. Services are made available by service providers. A service requires a service description that can be accessed and understood by potential service requestors. Software services are services that are realized by software systems.

Apart from introducing the business aspect of the service functionality, this definition is important because it also requires standardized and interpretable service description and allows services to be of a nature other than just software. If we focus on the IT-services, the predominant technology that is used today to implement them is the Web Service Architecture (Alonso, Casati, Kuno and Machiraju, 2004). The W3 consortium defines a Web service as

a software system designed to support interoperable machine-to-machine interaction over a network. It has an interface described in a machine-processable format (specifically WSDL). Other systems interact with the Web Service in a manner prescribed by its description using SOAP-messages, typically conveyed using HTTP with an XML serialization in conjunction with other Web-related standards. (W3 Consortium, 2004)

In (Polze, Milanovic and Schoebel, 2006) the following service types are distinguished: basic, intermediary, process-centric and enterprise services. Basic services are stateless and can be data- or logic-centric. The former handle persistent data (storage, retrieval, locking etc.) for one major business entity and provide strict interfaces to access its data. The latter encapsulate atomic implementation of the business rules and processing (calculation). In practice there is a smooth transition between the two types as data-centric services may also use logic to check, validate or process the data. Intermediate services are used to enforce micro consistency rules, performing gateway, adapter, facade and similar functions. They are often implemented as the simple business workflows (so called microflows) and are application-specific. More complex business tasks are realized using the process-centric services which are often stateful. They call the basic and intermediate services and thus encapsulate the knowledge and functionality of the organization's processes. Enterprise services are composed out of the process-centric services across the company boundaries. Their interfaces have the granularity of the business documents and are consequently very coarse grained. Their behavior is described by the service level agreements (SLA).

Based on the previous considerations, in the remainder of this chapter we will be using the following definition of a service and accordingly investigate service availability:

Definition 5: Service is an abstraction of the infrastructure-, application- or business-level functionality. It consists of a contract, interface and implementation. The contract provides a description of constraints, functionality, purpose and usage of the service. The formal contract description can provide technology-independent abstraction suitable for verification and validation.

The contract also imposes detailed semantics on the functionality. The service interface provides means for the clients to connect to the service, possibly but not mandatory via the network. Finally, business logic and business data are parts of the service implementation that fulfills the service contract. Consequently, a service encapsulates business entity of a differing granularity and functional meaning.

Contrary to the service definition, business process definition is fairly established and understood. We will be using a definition from (Vogels, 2003) and (Aalst, Hofstede and Weske, 2003):

Definition 6: Business process consists of a set of activities that are performed in coordination in an organizational and technical environment. These activities jointly realize a business goal. Each business process is enacted by a single organization, but it may interact with business processes performed by other organizations. A business process is represented by a business process model. It consists of a set of activities and execution constraints between them. A set of activities building a business process is organized in a workflow; therefore a business process is described using a workflow. Process activities are enacted by services, which are also elements of workflows.

For expressing workflows, modeling languages such as Business Process Modeling Notation (Object Management Group, 2008) are used.

Reference Architecture and the Fault Model

In the research community, service availability was treated either too broadly or in a very specialized context which is difficult to reuse and generalize. We will first cite some examples of the latter. In (Dahlin, Baddepudi, Chandra, Gao, and Nayate, 2003) the authors investigate service availability in the wide area networks. They assume that service is available as soon as the client and the server are able to communicate and ignore other requirements that a service has to fulfill apart from connectivity. In (Bulka, 1992) reliability of the optical token ring is analyzed using fault trees, completely ignoring services deployed in such networks. Voice over IP (VoIP) service availability has been investigated in numerous works, such as (Jiang and Schulzrinne, 2003) or (Wang and Trivedi, 2005). The former evaluates VoIP using several metrics, such as the call success rate or the call abortion rate, but they cannot be generalized to the other types of services. The latter uses manual modeling methods to capture both the system and the user behavior, but ignores client availability and network topology.

In the context of IT-services or Web services, there exist only specifications and design frameworks targeted for development and they are not applicable to availability evaluation or modeling. Furthermore, as they are based on the middleware concepts, they do not provide means for analytical and quantitative analysis of service availability. For example, Service Availability Forum (SAF) (Service Availability Forum, 2008) is a consortium that develops high availability and management software interface specifications, specifically tailored to the telecommunications sector. In (Buskens and Gonzalez, 2007), a high availability middleware is presented, while (Immonen and Niemela, 2008) surveys the existing methodologies for reliability predictions of component based software architectures. The Web Service Reliable Messaging specification (WS-R) (Web Service Reliable Messaging Protocol, 2008) is used to guarantee SOAP message delivery for Web services architecture, but also does not provide a fault model or availability quantification. Some works expand on the WS-ReliableMessaging to include stochastic models for calculating optimal restart time for improving service performance, again without generality or quantifiable (model-based) availability assessment (Reinecke, Moorsel and Wolter, 2006) (Moorsel and Wolter, 2006). There are experimental approaches to determine Web service dependability using measurement, such as described in (Chan, Lyu and Malek, 2007).

Finally, a recent interesting trend in the community can be observed, where concepts from the field of dependable embedded systems, such as (Pataricza, Majzik, Huszerl and Varnai, 2003) or (Majzik, Domokos, and Magyar, 2007), are being reused at the service level, e.g., see (Gonczy, Chiaradonna, Giandomenico, Pataricza, Bondavalli, and Bartha, 2006). However, the work is mostly based on the analysis of error propagation and testability, and not on the rigorous availability assessment.

In the (business) process management area, service and process availability is not explicitly mentioned or investigated. Instead, broader dependability concepts are used to estimate partial service availability. Most of the process management frameworks (some of which will be mentioned in the following section) use real-time or historical availability and performability indicators and data, such as transaction throughput, processor or server load, to predict availability and performance trends of particular services. They, however, neither define service availability explicitly nor provide a consistent fault model.

The examples above indicate that, in order to understand service availability, an appropriate fault model has to be defined first. We argue that service availability should be perceived as a function of the underlying ICT-layer availability. This layer comprises of:

- Hardware (e.g., servers, clients, workstations, clusters, grids)
- Software (e.g., operating systems, database services, web services, custom applications, configuration)
- Network (e.g., routers, switches, network cables, topology)
- Supporting infrastructure (e.g., air-conditioning, power supply, physical security)
- People (e.g., users, administrators, maintenance)

A successful approach to assess service and business process availability has to be able to determine (possibly functional) dependency between the ICT-layer availability (including the elements listed above) on one side, and the service and business process availability on the other side. To define a comprehensive and consistent fault model, we introduce an additional layer to the well known hierarchy describing the relationship between services and business processes (shown in Figure 1).

The new layer is based on the ICT-layer components which are elements of topologies. The topologies implement atomic services, and atomic services are based on one or more ICT-layer components. The components themselves belong either to the technical infrastructure (hardware, network, supporting infrastructure), software or IT-personnel categories. Atomic services can further be composed into composite services. Services are elements of workflows (possibly expressed as some BPMN derivative or formal

Figure 1. Reference architecture comprising business process, service and ICT-layer.

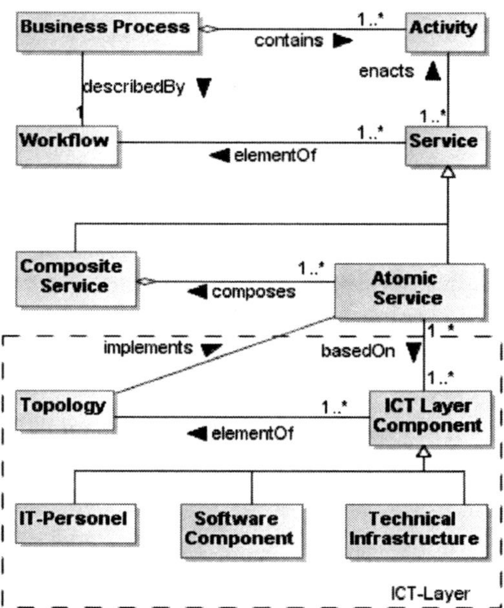

notation such as Petri net) and they enact business process activities at the same time. A business process comprises one or more activities and is described by the appropriate workflow. This will be the reference architecture and the premise of our further investigation. We will now define service and business process availability.

The first step in this direction is to distinguish between faults, symptoms, errors and failures. The fault is incorrect state of a service, not necessarily leading to the observable incorrectness or failure. The symptom is observable out-of-norm parameter behavior. The error is a manifestation of a fault (e.g., by observing symptoms) observed by a fault detector. A failure is then defined:

Definition 7: The failure is an event caused by errors which occurs when the service or business process deviates from the specified service or business process.

As defined in (Avizienis, Laprie, Randell and Landwehr, 2004), correct service, in the most general form, is delivered when the service implements the system function or process. A service failure is an event that occurs when the delivered service deviates from the correct service. A service can fail either because it does not comply with its functional specification, or because the specification did not adequately describe the system function required by the service users. A service failure is transition from the correct to the incorrect service. The period of incorrect service is service outage. The transition from incorrect to correct function is service restoration. The deviation from correct service may assume different forms that are called service failure modes. In this context, availability can be simplified as the readiness for correct service. We will refine this understanding presently.

In order to define a service fault model, we have to investigate four attributes that characterize incorrect services: failure domain, detectability of failures, consistency of failures, and consequences of failures. The failure domain comprises content and timing failures. With content failures, the output information delivered by the service deviates from the correct output. Timing failures are characterized by the incorrect time offset of the service result delivery. Timing failures can be early and late. When combined, these two classes produce halting (potentially silent) failures and erratic failures. Failure detectability is related to the signaling of service failure to the environment or to the user, and failures can be classified as signaled or unsignaled. Problematic issue is the user-perceived correctness, where the service may have been executed according to its specification and no failure signals will be emitted, however user is not satisfied with the results, as the service description did not correctly describe the required functionality from the user's perspective. With respect to the failure consistency, service failures can be either consistent (the incorrect service is perceived identically by all users, assuming there is more than one user), or inconsistent (where users perceive differently incorrect services, and some even the correct service). The detectability and consistency of service failures will lead us to define user-perceived service availability later. Finally, with respect to consequence, service failures can be either minor (the harmful consequence of a failure is of a similar cost when compared with the benefit of a correct service) or catastrophic (cost of the harmful consequence is orders of magnitude higher than the benefit provided by correct delivery). Service failures, their domains, detectability, consistency and consequences are summarized in Figure 2.

Based on these preliminaries and the layered architecture from the Figure 1, we define the following service and business process failure modes.

Defintion 8: Temporal service failure mode describes failures which cause the service to miss a deadline. A service will not respond in time if 1) a subset of ICT-components in a topology it is based on does not respond in time; 2) all ICT-components respond on time, but topology synchronization exceeds the deadline; 3) the topology has a deadlock.

Figure 2. Service failure modes.

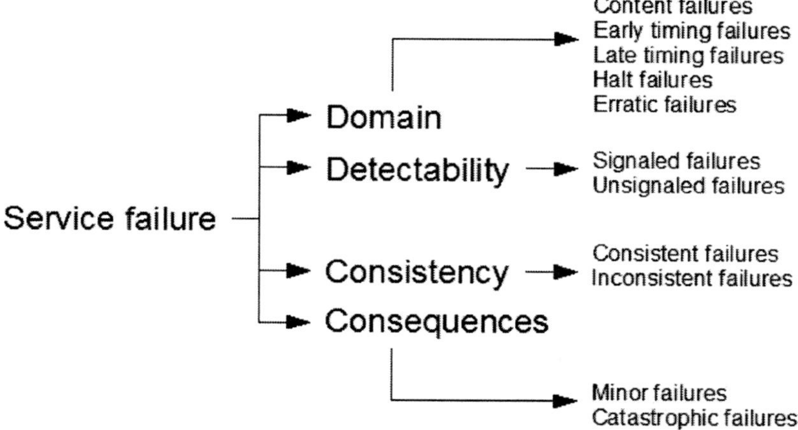

Definition 9: Temporal business process failure mode describes failures which cause the business process to miss a deadline. A business process will not respond in time if 1) a subset of services in a workflow does not respond in time; 2) all services respond in time, but workflow synchronization exceeds the deadline; 3) the workflow has a deadlock.

Definition 10: Value service failure mode describes failures which cause the service to return incorrect value or perform incorrect function. A service will respond with incorrect value if 1) a subset of ICT-components in a topology delivers incorrect values; 2) data and control flow in a topology are incorrect.

Definition 11: Value business process failure mode describes failures which cause the business to perform the incorrect business operation. A business process will perform incorrect business operation if 1) a subset of services in a workflow delivers incorrect values; 2) workflow orchestration description is incorrect.

The value failure mode is not restricted to the pure functional correctness, but may comprise non-functional properties expressed as service guarantees (or service level agreements) in the service contract. Thus a service may operate with reduced capacity or quality and still be considered correct. Additional details on non-functional capabilities and service contracts can be found in (Milanovic, 2006) or (Wada, Suzuki and Oba, 2006). Based on the above failure modes, we define the following types of service availability.

Definition 12: Instantaneous service or business process availability is the probability that the service or business process is in the correct state and ready to perform its function at a specified time.

Definition 13: Interval availability is the probability that the service or business process is operating correctly during the given time interval. It is the expected proportion of time the service or business process is operational during the given time interval. It can also be estimated as the number of correct service or business process invocations over a number of total invocations for the given time interval.

Definition 14: Steady state availability is the long-term probability that the service or business process is available. It can be calculated as the expected service or business process uptime over its lifetime.

Definition 15: User-perceived availability is the number of correct service or business process invocations for a specified time interval (interval user-perceived availability) or over service or business process lifetime (steady-state user-perceived availability), calculated for a particular user of a service or a business process.

We will now briefly investigate what tools are currently available for the service and process reliability/availability modeling.

Availability Assessment Tools

There are many formalized, well known and proven modeling methodologies for the evaluation of dependable systems, such as Markov chains, reliability block diagrams, fault trees, Petri nets, or stochastic activity networks. Numerous academic and industrial general purpose availability assessment tools, such as Reliability Workbench (IsoGraph, 2008), Moebius (Sanders, 2007), SHARPE (Trivedi, 1999), or OpenSesame (Walter, 2007), offer model solution techniques for these methodologies. We made a detailed survey of the existing methodologies and studied more than 60 reliability/availability modeling tools; the results of this investigation can be found in (Malek, Hoffmann, Milanovic, Bruening, Meyer and Milic, 2007).

The existing methods and tools are powerful but difficult to apply directly for modeling service and business process availability. The historical development of reliability/availability models has associated them with mission-critical systems that rarely change during their lifetime, such as real-time embedded systems, avionics, or telecommunication systems. The availability assessment procedures they offer are unable to adapt to fast-paced changes that are observed in the modern IT systems: it is sufficient to install a new router within the network to invalidate existing availability models. Standard models are also very complex and manually built. Each time the IT infrastructure or business process changes, it is required to manually intervene and update, verify and evaluate the new model. This process is imprecise, slow and costly. Furthermore, modern service-based systems are just too complex, and standard modeling methodologies simply do not scale to that level. Therefore, only isolated and relatively small portions of the enterprise infrastructure can be feasibly and realistically modeled using state-of-the-art general purpose availability assessment tools.

Due to these reasons, impact and penetration of traditional tools and methodologies in service industry is limited. Instead, process management tools such as Fujitsu Interstage (Fujitsu, 2007), IBM Tivoli (IBM, 2007), or HP Mercury (HP, 2007) are used. They perform online tracking and monitoring of deployed systems and services running on them, using the configuration management database (CMDB) principles. They do not use formal modeling methodologies, but implement best industry practices like CobiT (IT Governance Institute, 2007) or ITIL (IT Infrastructure Library, 2007), covering wide area of topics intended to improve overall business operations. In the segment that is used for availability management, they focus on actual performance indicators and prompt problem resolution. Often, methods that they support in this respect are rudimentary, based on thresholds – an alarm is raised only if an indicative parameter exceeds a certain value. They are built for large enterprises and require considerable resources to acquire, install and run. Small and medium enterprises can use open source solutions such as ECDB (ECDB, 2007) that are not as complete in business coverage as commercial solutions but provide acceptable basis for IT management.

Our goal is to combine both approaches: to use the existing, enterprise-ready solutions for flexible and automated extraction of the ICT-infrastructure description, and then employ formal methods to automatically generate reliability/availability models which enable us to reason about the availability of the services and business processes deployed on the existing infrastructure.

Service and Business Process Availability Assessment Procedure

Business processes and services are based on the ICT-layer components; their availability therefore depends directly on the availability properties of the underlying ICT-components. We introduce a mapping process that describes dependencies between the ICT-layer, services and business processes. Essentially, process and service availability is a function of the ICT-layer components' availability. The result of the mapping process is an availability model that is resolved analytically or through simulation. The mapping and availability assessment comprise the following steps:

1. Business process is identified and described using a process modeling language, such as BPMN (in this chapter) or UML activity diagram. Optionally, the required (target) process availability is defined.
2. For each business process activity, services enacting it are iteratively described using the same process modeling formalism, until all activities are represented as compositions of atomic services. Similarly to step 1, required availability of each service can be also defined.
3. Infrastructure data is collected by a network management system that may be integrated in a larger configuration management database (CMDB) system. In this step, communication and computation topology is extracted in form of the infrastructure graph. Information on the supporting-infrastructure, such as power supply or air-conditioning devices, are either taken from specialized tools (e.g., GSTool) or added manually to the infrastructure graph.
4. Services are iteratively mapped to the infrastructure elements contained in the infrastructure graph, in a process that is inversion of the step 2: atomic services are mapped first, followed by the composite services. Each step of atomic or composite service execution has a source S and destination D in the graph. The task is to find all paths between S and D. The paths are then transformed into Boolean expressions by applying operator AND between nodes that belong to the same path. If more than one path between source and destination exist, the operator OR is applied to the expressions defining single paths. If two nodes are executing concurrently in the service description, they are serialized using operator AND, however if only one or k-out-of-n have to be executed, they are joined with the operator OR or expanded to the combination of AND-OR operators (in k-out-of-n case). The resulting expressions are then minimized. The Boolean equations thus minimized represent communication paths.
5. Step 4 is repeated for the business process. Effectively, Boolean equations are derived that express functional dependency between business process, service and ICT-layer availability, analogously to service-ICT mapping from the Step 4.
6. The expressions obtained in the steps 4 and 5 are transformed to an appropriate model for availability assessment. In the following sections it is demonstrated how to transform Boolean expression into reliability block diagrams (RBD)/fault trees (FT)[1].
7. Availability of the business process, composite service or atomic service is calculated by solving/simulating the model generated in the previous step, using an existing solver. The provided availability of each service and business process can be compared with the required availability, if one was defined in steps 1-2.

Steps 4 and 5 require identification of all paths between two nodes in a given graph. In the worst case of a complete connectivity graph, the space/time complexity of a recursive algorithm reaches prohibitive *O(n!)*. However, real intranets are mostly tree structures, where loops may be created only by routers whose number in a network is limited. Networks are designed such that a moderate number of switches are connected to the routers and numerous hosts are then connected to the switches, creating a tree (see infrastructure figures in the Case Study sections). Such sparse structure limits the algorithm complexity, and it remains polynomial (for a tree it is linear as there is only one path for each pair of nodes).

The first two steps are human-dependant but they are performed only once per process/service, when it is added to the enterprise or when its definition is changed. Furthermore, process and service modeling can be supported using template-based mechanisms and service description repositories. The steps three through seven can be automated and they can autonomously adapt to changes: e.g., a change in the infrastructure triggers the update of the CMDB which initiates the availability assessment.

We will now cover the algorithm steps in more detail, explaining how to define business process/service mappings, that is, who performs which task in a BPMN model (step 4), how to perform infrastructure graph generation (step 3), how to define communication paths (steps 4 and 5) and finally how to generate the appropriate availability model (step 7).

Mapping BPMN activities

For each deployed (observed) instance of a BPMN model, a deployment descriptor is generated, similar in structure and purpose to BPEL deployment descriptors. Each activity in a BPMN model is tagged with a <partnerLink> element, which can either specify a composite service, atomic service or ICT-layer element (or several of them) which implement this activity. The only constraint is that atomic service activities must reference ICT-level elements. In this way, hierarchical tagging of processes/services is performed. A deployment descriptor reads the activities from an abstract BPMN model (persisted in XMI format) and generates a set of <provide> and <invoke> elements for each <partnerLink> element. Every <partnerLink> used with a <receive> activity must be matched with a <provide> element, and every <partnerLink> used in an <invoke> activity must be matched with an <invoke> element in deployment descriptor. The root element, <deploy>, contains a list of all deployed processes, that is, single deployment descriptor can be used for more than one process (BPMN) model:

```
<deploy>
 <process...>*
 { other elements }
 </process>
</deploy>
```

Each process is identified by its qualified name and specifies bindings for provided and invoked composite/atomic services or ICT-layer elements:

```
<process name = QName fileName =
String? implName = String? >
 (<provide> | <invoke>)*
 { other elements }
</process>
```

Each process element must provide a name attribute with the qualified name of the BPMN process. This is parsed from XMI file. Optionally, a fileName attribute can be used to specify the location of the BPMN process definition. The implName attribute is used to specify an endpoint which implements a particular partnerLink. Each <process> element must further enumerate services or components provided by the process and bind each service or component to an endpoint. This is done through <provide> elements which associate partnerLink with endpoint. Essentially, in this step it is determined which components implement a certain BPMN activity and this information is stored in an endpoint:

```
<provide partnerLink = NCName>
 <service name  =  QName port  =
pName?>*
</provide>
```

However, whereas in the BPEL deployment descriptor a partnerLink can be implemented only with a WSDL endpoint, we do not impose this restriction. The partnerLink can be implemented by any class from Figure 1 derived from the class ICTLayerComponent. Some of these information can be extracted manually and bound to the information extracted from the infrastructure graph (see next section), for example if a software component is deployed in an application server, this information can be extracted by looking into component deployment descriptor (usually web. xml file). In some cases however, manual deployment descriptor generation is required (see the Publishing Case Study, where manual activities of editors must be defined by hand in the mapping process).

Let us observe a business process where client initiates the process with an input which is forwarded to serviceA, it computes a value which is asynchronously sent in parallel to serviceB and serviceC, and finally, a selection between the two computed values is performed. The following is the XML (BPEL exported) representation of such a business process:

```
<process name = "test">
<partnerLinks>
<partnerLink name = "client"/>
<partnerLink name = "serviceA"/>
<partnerLink name = "serviceB"/>
<partnerLink name = "serviceC"/>
</partnerLinks>
<variables>
<variable name = "procesInput"/>
<variable name = "AInput"/>
<variable name = "AOutput"/>
<variable name = "BCInput"/>
<variable name = "BOutput"/>
<variable name = "COutput"/>
<variable name = "processOutput"/>
<variable name = "AError"/>
</variables>
<sequence>
<receive name = "client" variable =
"processInput"/>
<assign><copy><from variable = "pro-
cessInput"/>
<to variable = "AInput"/></copy></as-
sign>
<scope>
<faultHandlers>
<catch faultName = "faultA" fault-
Variable = "AError"/>
</faultHandlers>
<sequence>
<invoke name = "invokeA" partnerLink
= "serviceA"`
inputVariable = "AInput" outputVari-
able = "AOutput"/>
</sequence>
</scope>
<assign><copy><from variable =
"AOutput"/><to variable = "BCInput"/>
</copy></assign>
<flow>
<sequence>
<invoke name = "invokeB" partnerLink
= "serviceB"
inputVariable = "BCInput"/>
<receive name = "receive_
invokeB"partnerLink = "serviceB"
variable = "BOutput"/>
</sequence>
<sequence>
<invoke name = "invokeC" partnerLink
= "serviceC"
inputVariable = "BCInput"/>
<receive name = "receive_invokeC"
partnerLink = "serviceC" variable =
"COutput"/>
</sequence>
</flow>
```

```
<switch><case>
<!-- assign value to processOutput
-->
</case></switch>
<invoke name = "reply" partnerLink =
"client" inputVariable = "processOut-
put"/>
</sequence>
</process>
```

This is a general business process model which can be deployed in numerous infrastructures. The task of the mapping is to determine those elements in a given infrastructure that implement particular tasks. The corresponding deployment descriptor would have the following form:

```
<deploy>
<process name = "test">
     <provide partnerLink = "client">
          <service name = "clientWeb-
Form" port = "foo:8080/client"/>
     </provide>
     <invoke partnerLink = "servi-
ceA">
          <service name = "SAPSer-
vice" port = "BOR.IDOC.SEGMENT.abc/>
          <service name = "BackupSer-
vice" port = "jdbc:storedProc"/>
     </invoke>
     <invoke partnerLink = "ser-
viceB">
          <service name = "WS1" port
= "foo:serviceB.wsdl"/>
          <service name = "auth" port
= "foo:auth.wsdl"/>
     </invoke>
     <invoke partnerLink = "servi-
ceC">
          <service name = "EJB1" port
= "jndi:serviceC"/>
          <service name = "auth" port
= "foo:auth.wsdl"/>
     </invoke>
     <invoke partnerLink = "client">
          <service name = "Client-
File" port = "ssh user@host/>
          <service name = "Client-
File" port = "ftp user@host/>
     </invoke>
</process>
</deploy>
```

It can be seen that initial client activity is performed by a manual input using a Web form, serviceA is implemented as a combination of a SAP IDOC (structured file) call and a JDBC backup stored procedure, serviceB and serviceC are implemented as a Web service and an Enterprise Java Bean respectively, and delivery of the results to the client is peformed as a file transfer using ssh and ftp protocols. Note how client definitions differ in the <provide> and <invoke> roles. Also, the component auth is used to invoke both ServiceB and ServiceC. This shows that, although the process description specifies parallel execution of both services, internally (when deployed) they both depend on a single component, which represents a single point of failure. This information is neither obvious nor possible to include in the process/service description. Finally, note that deployment descriptor is not limited to WSDL endpoints only.

After activities have been mapped, all process/service activities are associated with the underlying infrastructure graph elements, this information is persisted in the deployment descriptor, and the process of communication path generation can now take place.

Infrastructure Graph and Communication Path Generation

One of the prerequisites for successful availability modeling of services and business processes is the accurate information on characteristics of infrastructure components, their organization and mutual relationships. Services and business processes are deployed on the infrastructure layer that comprises the technical infrastructure (hardware, network, supporting infrastructure), software and IT-personnel categories (Figure 1).

In modern enterprises, the number of components in the infrastructure and their diversity makes manual management of this information difficult, if not impossible. Network monitoring/configuration management database (CMDB) systems are used for easier and more accurate information collection (e.g., they may automatically detect the changes at a node or in network's configuration). The monitoring tools are primarily used to track status of services and devices in the network. They may be configured to raise alarms if a device or service becomes unavailable, thus improving the time to repair. The data on service and device availability is preserved and can be used for MTTF and MTTR parameter estimation that is required for availability assessment.

Automatic network discovery is a desirable property of network monitoring systems, but it is not supported by all of them: for instance, a popular open source monitoring tool Nagios requires tedious manual configuration process in which a user defines monitored devices and services. The process is lengthy, inflexible in presence of changes and it does not provide network's Layer 2 topology.

CMDB systems are considerably more powerful, enterprise-ready solutions (e.g., IBM Tivoli, HP OpenView, Fujitsu Interstage). They are capable of automatic device, application and service discovery. They additionally manage configurations and their histories, allowing expedite problem resolution. Compared with open source solutions, they have wider set of tools at their disposal, such as the agent-less scanning of hosts in the network and built-in support for numerous vendor-dependent protocols and applications. Agent-less configuration and performance management is performed from a centralized server that locally runs software which accesses nodes in the network and gathers predefined data. For successful agent-less scanning, it is necessary that data collection server has credentials of managed devices and that a managed device supports some form of remote access (e.g., SSH). Agent-less collection is performed in part through SNMP protocol (SNMP, 2009), but in order to gather data about the application configuration, specialized software must be deployed at the server. The custom plug-ins considerably improve the detail level of collected data. For instance, HP Discovery and Dependency Mapping (HP, 2009) is capable of gathering application specific information, such as the configuration of a WebSphere server or a tablespace configuration in Oracle.

Agent-based approach, on the other hand, requires installation of specific software agents on target nodes, but in addition to status monitoring, they frequently provide node and application management. For instance, IBM Tivoli Monitoring provides custom agents for SAP solutions that monitor the system and detect predefined exception conditions (e.g., exceeding of a performance threshold), investigate the causes of the exception and schedule work/automate some manual tasks.

Collecting configuration of nodes and services deployed in the network is important for the later step in the availability assessment process: the construction of communication paths. For example, a large organization hosts a set of mail servers. Each of the mail clients is associated with one of them. It is not possible to say which server is responsible for the assessed client and to evaluate the impact of network availability on their communication, based only on the general BPMN description of the email service. It is the task of the configuration collection modules (agent or agent-less) to provide the actual information that is used to instantiate the abstract BPMN service description with the accurate data. If a configuration collection system does not exist in the organization, it is the task of the user of the assessment tool to specify this data.

As an example of a network monitoring system, we will briefly describe OpenNMS, which an open source network monitoring system that we use in our prototypical implementation (see Section: Tool Prototype), capable of automatic node, topology and service discovery. It employs IP-range scan to discover devices and then performs port scan of discovered nodes to determine services activated at them. The discovery rate can be altered, in order to avoid network overloading. The data is preserved in PostgreSQL database for later use by OpenNMS or other applications.

Figure 3 shows a part of the database structure that is used by OpenNMS. The table node holds the basic information about nodes, such as their identification, operating system and domain name. Each node has one or more network interfaces (table atinterface) and belongs to a LAN network (table vlan). Different types of LAN networks are supported, such as Ethernet, token-ring, FDDI. Services are deployed on nodes (tables ifservices and service). The service status is periodically polled. Data about node and service outages and restorations are preserved in form of events.

OpenNMS is also capable of the Layer 2 topology discovery, although it is not enabled by default. The topology discovery requires activation and configuration of the additional modules. In order to function properly, the topology discovery process requires that network devices (bridges, routers) support SNMP. It discovers routers (data about their interfaces is saved into table iprouteinterface) and bridges (table stpnode). Table datalinkinterface stores data about network structure and inter-node connections.

OpenNMS is conceptually an excellent tool, but our experiences exposed the issues related to older network devices – although they deliver SNMP data to the linkd module of the OpenNMS, data was not interpreted correctly.

It is obvious that discovery of data about the technical infrastructure and people working in an enterprise is not fully automatable. However, there are other tools which are used for collection and management of this data. If such tools are employed in the enterprise, their data can be also used to improve accuracy of the proposed availability assessment process. We will illustrate this on the example of GSTool (GSTool, 2009), which primarily supports users in preparing, administrating and updating IT security concepts that meet the IT Baseline Protection Manual defined by the German Federal Office for Information Security (BSI). In addition to the security-related information, the tool manages information about technical infrastructure and personnel that is highly relevant for the availability assessment.

Figure 4 shows how the tool captures information about building, rooms, IT systems and employees. In comparison with network monitoring tools, the level of details about the IT systems is considerably reduced, but on the other side we can

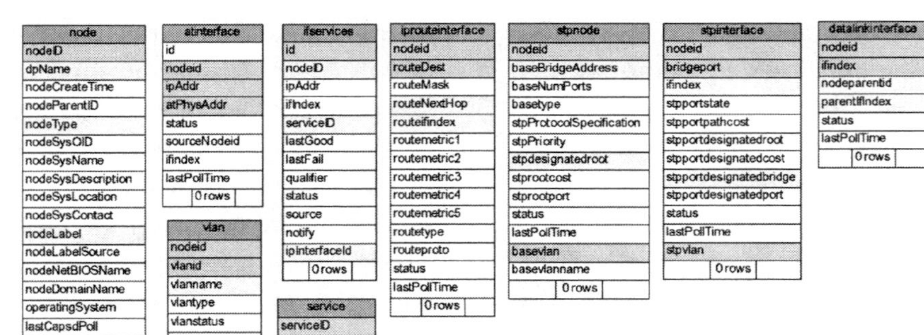

Figure 3. Partial database schema of the OpenNMS.

Figure 4. Hierarchical organization of the ICT infrastructure elements in GSTool.

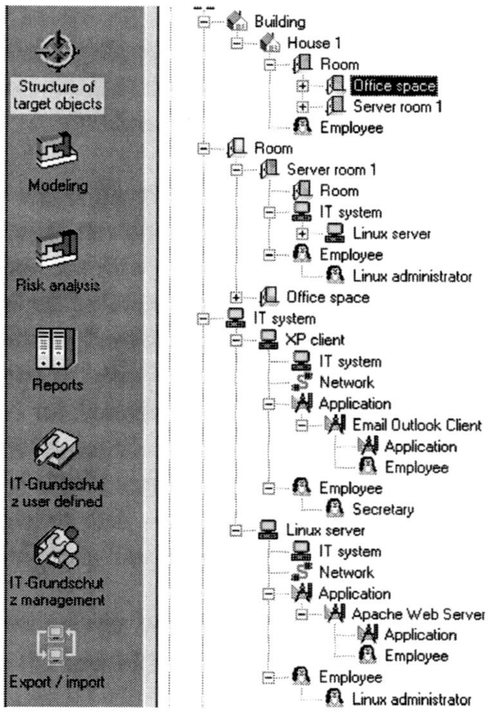

now clearly see that the Linux server is placed in the server room, which has a specialized administrator associated with it. Server room is located in Building 1 of the organization. A secretary is working in the ordinary office space within the same building. The secretary uses a client with the Windows XP operating system and the Outlook mail client.

The tool can collect additional data on technical infrastructure elements. As we can see in Figure 5, server rooms in Building 1, where our sample Linux server is located, have overvoltage protection, emergency circuit breakers, local UPS and a redundant air-conditioning system that is connected to an independent UPS (indicated by the green color in the figure). On the other hand, a study of technical and organizational requirements for server rooms and the support for remote reporting of system malfunction do not exist (indicated by the red color). Finally, the redundancy of the technical infrastructure is only partially implemented (indicated by the yellow color). Similar data may be defined at organization level. Same as in the OpenNMS, data is preserved in a relational database and it can be easily accessed from other applications, such as our tool prototype.

Automatic Generation of Availability Models

Based on the minimized Boolean equations obtained in the previous steps of the algorithm,

Figure 5. Technical infrastructure description in GSTool.

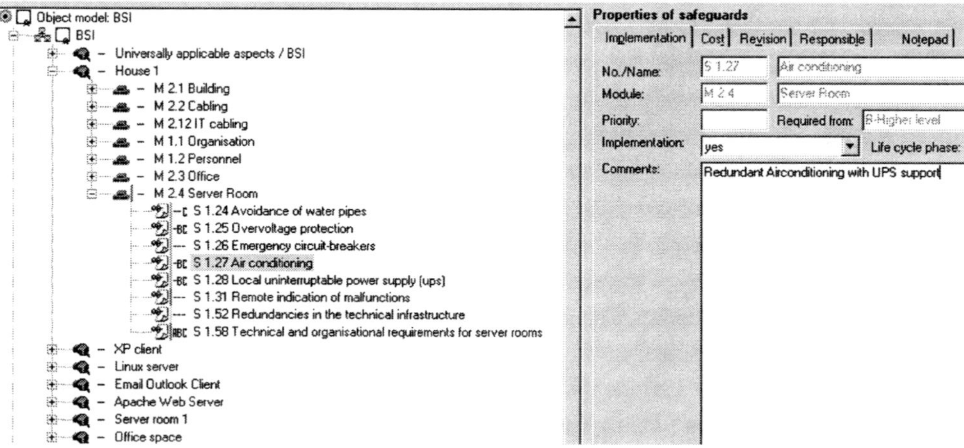

availability models are generated. We currently support combinatorial models: reliability block diagrams and fault-trees.

Reliability block diagrams (RBD) are used to represent the logical structure of a system, with respect to how the reliability of its components affects the overall system reliability and availability. The basic configurations in which components of a diagram may be combined are series, parallel and k-out-of-n configurations. It is further assumed that components are independent, that is, failure information for one component provides no information about (i.e. does not affect) other components in the system. In a series configuration, a failure of any component results in a failure of the entire system. In other words, for the whole system to work, all serial components must also work. In a parallel configuration, at least one of the components must succeed for the system to succeed. In other words, the system will function if any one (or more) of the components is working. The components in parallel are also referred to as the redundant units. The third basic configuration is *k-out-of-n*, and it includes both series and parallel configurations as special cases. This type of configuration requires that at least *k* components succeed out of the total n parallel components for the system to succeed. When $k = n$, we have *n-out-of-n* which is equivalent to the series configuration, and when $k = 1$ we have *1-out-of-n*, which is equivalent to the parallel configuration. Fault trees, similar to reliability block diagrams, represent all sequences of individual component failures that may cause the system to stop functioning. Fault trees apply deductive logic to produce a fault-oriented pictorial diagram which allows one to analyze system safety and reliability. The main difference between the fault trees and RBDs is that with RBD one is working in the success space, that is, looking at the success combinations of the system components. Contrary, a fault tree diagram is generated in the "failure space", identifying all possible system failure combinations. Hence, fault trees are also a design aid for identifying the general fault classes of a fault tolerant system. Examples of both reliability block diagrams and fault trees are shown in Case Studies, and here we give a very simple procedure to transform Boolean equations into RBD (there exists a bijection between RBD and FT):

- The blocks of the RDB are all terms appearing in the minimized Boolean equation
- Ii two terms are connected with the operator & , RBD blocks are generated for both terms and placed into serial configuration
- If two terms are connected with the operator ||, RBD blocks are generated for both terms and places into parallel configuration
- The process is performed in a single pass, parsing the equation from left to right, obeying operator priorities and grouping

Using this model, steady state service availability and reliability (*Definition* 14 and 15) can be calculated.

In the following sections we will demonstrate our approach. We first show how to assess availability of an e-mail service and how far can we go with the assessment if data needed for it is only partially available (e.g., a service description exists, but infrastructure topology is unknown). Then, the approach is generalized to a business process from the publishing and media sector, demonstrating effects of technical infrastructure and personnel to the availability.

CASE STUDY: E-MAIL SERVICE AVAILABILITY ASSESSMENT

The proposed approach is demonstrated on the example of steady-state user-perceived availability assessment of the e-mail service. The example is based on the SMTP protocol defined in RFC 2821 (Klensin, 2001). The e-mail service is chosen because of its ubiquity and presence in almost every modern enterprise. The availability of the

Figure 6. Email service description.

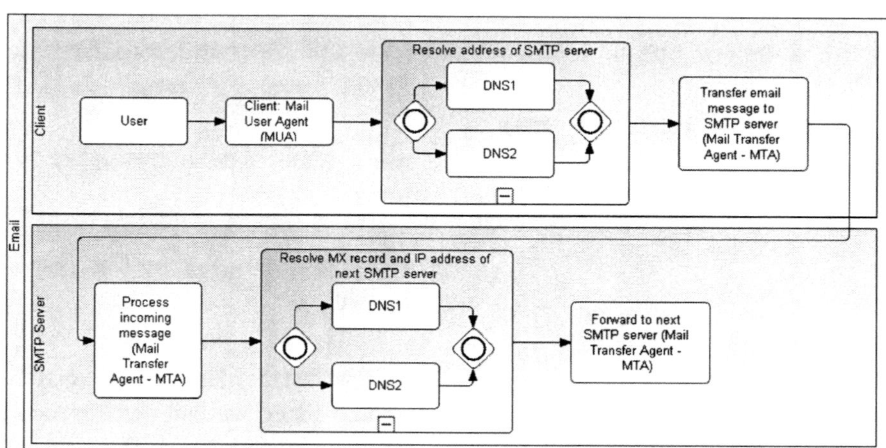

Table 1. Evaluation parameters for the e-mail service

	Router	Channel	DNS	Mail	Client	Out1	Out2
MTTF	9000	45000	4500	4000	4500	13500	5400
MTTR	1	3	2	2	2	4	6

e-mail service is evaluated for two users in order to show that availability is not only the function of component availability but also of infrastructure topology and user location within the topology.

Service Description and Mapping

The first step in availability estimation is to define the service of interest and its required availability. Let us assume that required availability of the e-mail service should be above 0.9985. BPMN service description is given in Figure 6.

Service description is then mapped to the existing infrastructure elements. CMDB provides the infrastructure graph and component availability statistics (Table 1). The next step is to transform the infrastructure graph to the connectivity graph. If CMDB provides sufficient detail level, there is no need for this transformation – data from the CMDB can be used directly. Figure 7 shows both representations of the infrastructure.

The abbreviations have the following meaning: Client i–CL_i, Mail Server–MS, Routers–R_i, Channel–CH_i, Out_1 and Out_2 are redundant connections to Internet Service Providers of the enterprise. A channel is an abstraction that includes switches and/or network adapters/links that are placed between routers and hosts. The channels are introduced for simplicity reasons— the goal of this example is to demonstrate the approach without going into unnecessary details. In the next section an example is given with much more accurate and detailed network topology graph. The channels are depicted in Figure 7 by dotted lines.

Based on the SMTP description from Figure 6 and connectivity graph from Figure 7, we map the service execution steps to paths in the connectivity graph. In order to send an e-mail, client has to resolve address of the mail server. It is common that hosts in a network use two DNS servers, primary and secondary:

```
CL1 → DNS: (CL1 & CH1 & R1 & CH2 &
DNS1) ||
(CL1 & CH1 & R1 & CH2 & CH3 & DNS2)
=
CL1 & CH1 & R1 & CH2 & (DNS1 || (CH3
& DNS2)
```

and

```
CL2 → DNS: (CL2 & CH9 & R2 & CH3 &
CH4 & DNS1) ||
(CL2 & CH9 & R2 & CH4 & DNS2)  =
CL2 & CH9 & R2 & CH4 & (DNS2 || (CH3
& DNS1)
```

The clients now establish a connection with the SMTP server and send the e-mail:

```
CL1 → MS: CL1 & CH1 & R1 & CH2 & CH3
& CH4 & R2 & CH5 & MS
CL2 → MS: CL2 & CH9 & R2 & CH5 & MS
```

In case that the e-mail recipient is within the enterprise, the following steps would not be performed, as the e-mail would be stored directly to a disk system by the SMTP server, waiting there for a local client to access it. In this example, we assume that a recipient is outside the enterprise and local SMTP server has to determine the forward SMTP server. This requires a DNS query:

```
MS → DNS: (MS & CH5 & R2 & CH4 &
DNS2) ||
(MS & CH5 & R2 & CH4 & CH3 & DNS1) =
MS & CH5 & R2 & CH4 & (DNS2 || CH3 &
DNS1)
```

The last step is to dispatch e-mail to the outside server. Since we can neither measure nor influence the availability of the Internet and outgoing (receiving) SMTP server, we evaluate availability up to the point where e-mail leaves the network of the enterprise[2]:

```
MS → OUT: (MS & CH6 & R3 & CH7 &
OUT1) ||
(MS & CH6 & R3 & CH8 & OUT2)  =
MS & CH6 & R3 & (CH7 & OUT1 || CH8 &
OUT2)
```

For the successful e-mail service execution, all these steps must be performed in series. The resulting expressions are simplified by applying

Figure 7. Infrastructure graph and transformation to communication graph.

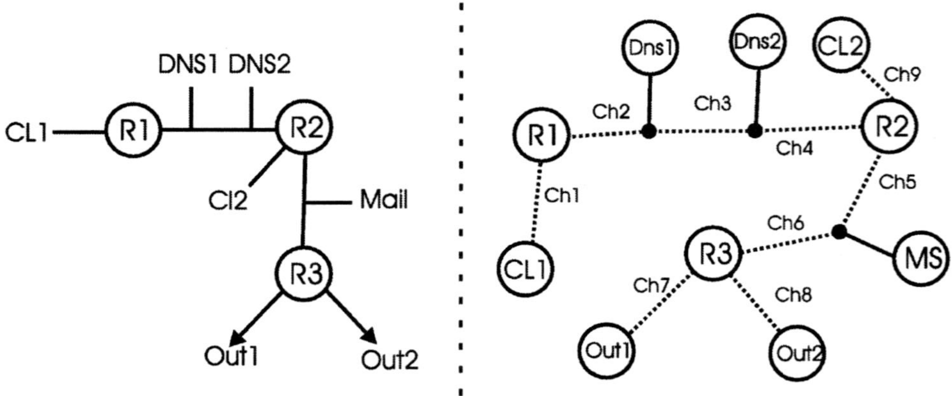

the idempotence, associativity and distributivity rules of operators & and ||:

```
CL1:(CL1 → DNS) & (CL1 → MS) & (MS →
DNS) & (MS → OUT) =
CL1 & MS & R1 & R2 & R3 &
CH1 & CH2 & CH3 & CH4 & CH5
& CH6 & (DNS1 || DNS2) & (CH7 &
OUT1 || CH8 & OUT2)
CL2: (CL2→ DNS) & (CL2→ MS) & (MS →
DNS) & (MS → OUT) =
CL2 & MS & R2 & R3 & CH9 & CH4 & CH5
& CH6 & (CH3 & DNS1 || DNS2) & (CH7 &
OUT1 || CH8 & OUT2)
```

After generating the minimal communication paths, we can proceed and, based on the two expressions given above, derive the corresponding availability model which will enable user-perceived availability assessment of the e-mail service.

Availability Assessment

As already explained, the obtained expressions can be directly transformed into Fault Trees (FT) or to Reliability Block Diagrams (RBD). In this example, we use RBD (Figure 8). The evaluation parameters are in Table 1. The model was solved in Isograph's Reliability Workbench and it assumes exponential distributions for failure and repair processes. The failure and repair rates are constant and they are calculated from MTTF and MTTR. The evaluation results are in Table 2.

Required and user-perceived provided availability can be compared now. The provided availability of Client 1 (calculated as 1 - Unavailability) is 0.99834, and provided availability of Client 2 is 0.99858. As our required availability is 0.9985, it is clear that e-mail service does not provide required availability to Client 1.

Since measurement-based methods are already used to evaluate availability of individual infrastructure elements, like routers or servers, it could be tempting to claim that the same, measurement based approach should be used for service availability. However, as the user-perceived availability is network topology dependant and differs from one client host to another, it implies a monitoring application should be installed on every client host in the network for every monitored service. The overhead introduced through installation and maintenance of monitors on each client host, for every service the client is using, would be rather extensive and not very practical. Furthermore, for some IT services, such as e-mail where responsibility for service execution is delegated through the network, it is not straightforward to estimate the availability by counting the success rates since measurements at individual points (server or client) ignore the unavailability introduced by the other infrastructure elements. If the e-mail service success ratio is measured on the client-side only, the availability monitor cannot detect event where e-mail cannot leave the server because the Internet connection is not functional. Similarly, if a monitor is placed on the SMTP server only, it is not possible to detect events where client cannot connect to the server due to network failures. Therefore, precise service availability assessment through measurement requires careful monitoring of progress of individual e-mails through the whole IT infrastructure (outgoing e-mail is served once it leaves the enterprise, incoming e-mail once it reaches a client).

Our approach requires less effort for maintenance and provides an additional advantage: in case of planned changes in the IT infrastructure, the impact of changes on availability can be estimated prior to implementation. For instance, if DNS1 server is moved to the same sub-network as the mail server, availability of the first client remains the same but the availability of the second client increases to 0.99865. Pure measurement-based approach is not able to predict the impact of infrastructure changes on availability, before the actual change takes place.

Figure 8. Reliability block diagram for the e-mail service.

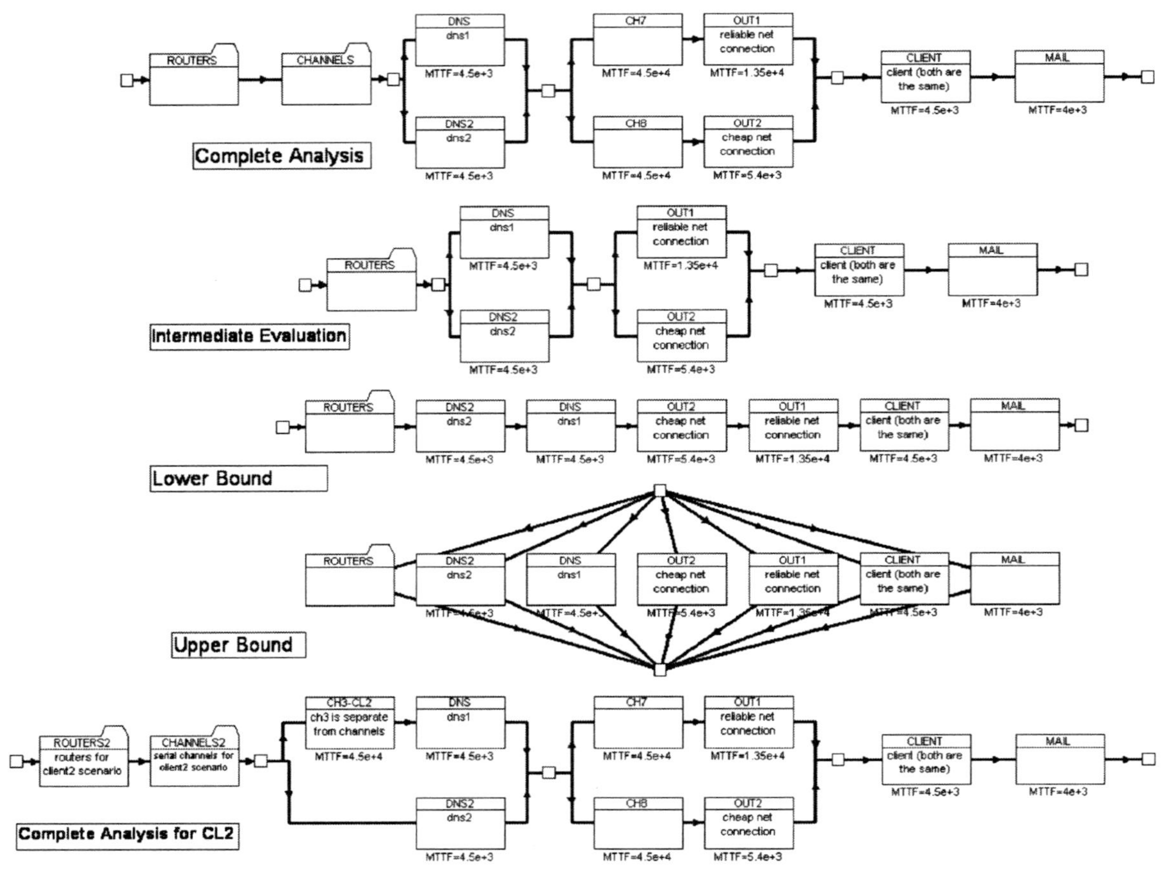

Table 2. Evaluation results for the e-mail service

	Precise CL1	Precise CL2	Lower bound	Intermediate	Upper bound
MTTF	1060	1280	662	1240	6.1 e+22
MTTR	1.79	1.83	2.37	1.59	0.293
Unavailability	0.00166	0.00142	0.00322	0.00127	3.5 e-24

Working with Incomplete Data

An implicit assumption of the proposed method is that complete network topology, as well as availability of individual components, is known. Although many methods for determining service availability make this assumption, in practice this is frequently not the case. In such situations it is possible to estimate availability. The following cases of incomplete data can be distinguished.

Incomplete service description or network topology. If service description (functionality) or the network topology are unknown, but the ICT-components on which the service depends are known as well as their availabilities, the lower availability bound can be determined assuming that all components are placed in series:

LOWER: CL & MS & DNS1 & DNS2 & R1 & R2 & R3 & OUT1 & OUT2

This model is unaware of communication channels and it does not include them. Similarly, the upper availability bound can be estimated assuming that all elements are placed in parallel:

UPPER: CL || MS || DNS1 || DNS2 || R1 || R2 || R3 || OUT1 || OUT2

Finally, if the service description and component availabilities are known, but the exact topology of the network is unknown, availability can be estimated as:

INTERMEDIATE: CL & MS & (DNS 1|| DNS2) & R1 & R2 & R3 & (OUT1|| OUT2)

The approximate service availabilities are in Table 2. The upper availability bound is of no practical use since it is very close to one. Lower bound is considerably lower than the actual availability, as expected. Intermediate model slightly overestimates the availability but it is very close to precise values, considering that it does not utilize the network topology information. Still, this particular intermediate model example should be taken with caution since the difference may be much larger for other, more complex infrastructure configurations.

Unknown availability of some components in the network. In case that it is not possible to determine availability of one or more components in a network that are used by the evaluated service, clearly, the exact service availability cannot be calculated. Assuming that availability is unknown for n components, the availability can be observed as an n-variable function and it can be evaluated in n-dimensional space. It is necessary to assume the component availability distribution type or to take a distribution based on previous experience (e.g., if the availability distribution for one router type is known, in absence of better data it is to expect that the new router from same producer will have similar behavior), to vary the distribution parameters and to observe the availability. This approach is applicable to precise and approximate models, but it is highly dependent on human experience and actual behavior of unknown components.

Quantitative system data do not exist. It is sometimes required to make availability assessment even if we are unable to determine/measure IT component availabilities, services are not described and network topology is unknown. In such extreme conditions, our and other analytical or simulation based approaches are not applicable. One possibility is to use qualitative assessment, based on the best-practice guides like CobiT (IT Governance Institute, 2007), ITIL (IT Infrastructure Library, 2007), BITKOM (BITKOM Consortium, 2007). The best practices cover various aspects of IT management, therefore it is necessary to extract segments that are of importance for the availability, clearly define questions, interview the personnel in the enterprise and finally interpret the answers. The interpretation can be quantitative or qualitative:

- **Quantitative:** (BITKOM Consortium, 2007) lists the expected downtime per year in data centers as a function of environmental factors. For example, if a data center has no redundant power supplies for equipment and air-conditioning, and no power generator, it can be expected that it may experience more than 72 hours of unplanned downtime per year. Another example is the CobiT process DS1 (Deliver and Support) that defines a metric that gives the percent of users satisfied with service delivery levels. As the CobiT specification does not define how to measure this percentage, the metric requires careful interpretation.
- **Qualitative:** Existence of formally defined RACI (Responsible, Accountable, Consulted, Informed) charts (IT

Governance Institute, 2007) clearly improves information flow in an enterprise and increases service availability. However, it is not possible to quantify the availability improvement.

Best practices can be promptly implemented, providing coarse guidelines where to aim for availability improvement. Still, they are imprecise in comparison with analytical and simulation methodologies.

CASE STUDY: PUBLISHING BUSINESS PROCESS AVAILABILITY ASSESSMENT

In this section, availability will be exemplary assessed for the business process from the publishing and media sector, which describes the scenario where an editor is accepting and approving a new manuscript (the business process is shown in Figure 9).

Business Process Description and Mapping

The process is initiated when the editor receives a new manuscript. She then initiates the editorial tasks (art, marketing and finances) and delegates the procedures to junior editors which perform their operations concurrently. The editor waits until all tasks are completed, evaluates the results, and makes a decision whether to approve the manuscript for printing or to return corrections. Once the editor is satisfied, manuscript goes to print and the business process ends.

Each activity of the business process is enacted by one or more services. Figures 10, 11 and 12 describe the following activities (composite

Figure 9. Business process describing the acceptance of a new manuscript.

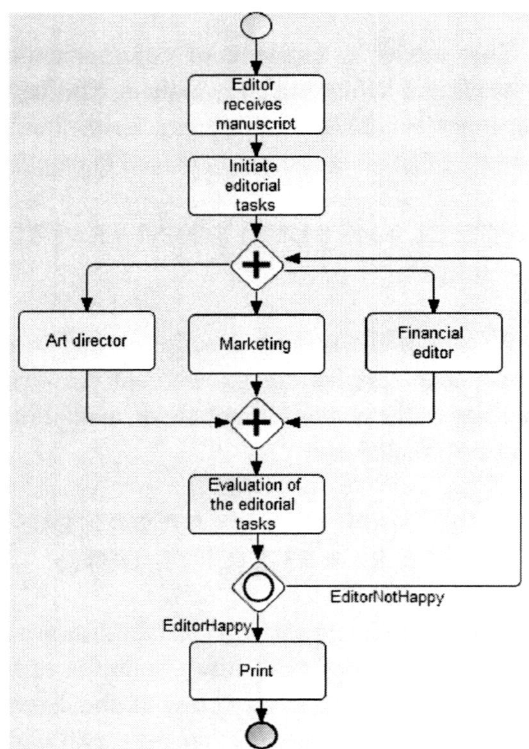

Figure 10. Initiating editorial tasks service.

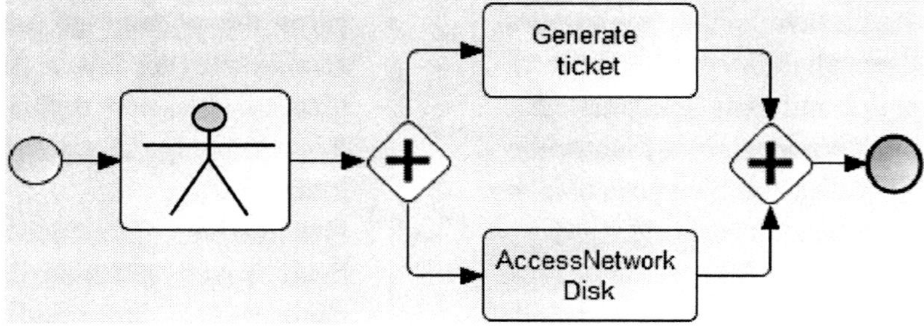

Figure 11. Editorial tasks evaluation service.

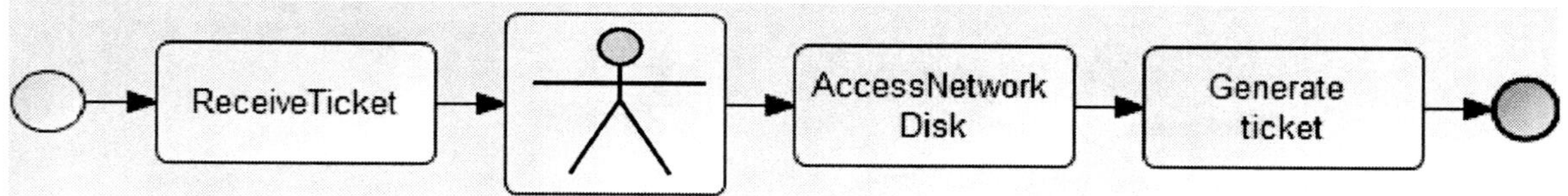

Figure 12. Junior-editors task service.

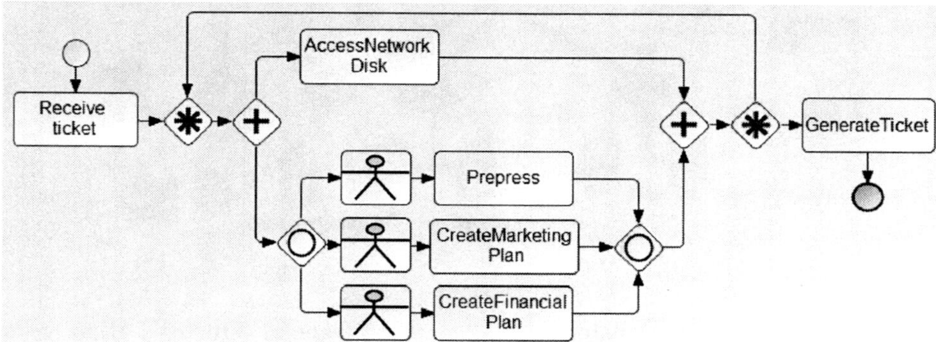

services) of the business process respectively: initiating editorial tasks, junior editors' tasks and evaluation of the junior editorial-tasks (acceptance/rejection) by the editor.

The following atomic services are available to the business process: Generate Ticket, Access Network Disk, Receive Ticket, Prepress, Create Marketing Plan, and Create Financial Plan. In order to initiate editorial tasks, the editor generates tickets (addressed to junior editors) and uses network disk access service to make the manuscript available to the junior editors. Junior editors use the read ticket service to receive tasks, access network disk service to obtain the manuscript copy, and then process the manuscript (prepress, marketing and financial plan services). Parallel to these activities, they repeatedly access network disk. Finally, all junior editors generate tickets once they have finished their tasks. In order to evaluate the results, editor has to receive tickets from all junior editors, access network disk to inspect the results, and generate the ticket, either to approve the print or to return relevant corrections. BPMN activities that are denoted with the UML use case actor symbol imply that manual activity is performed at that point in the workflow.

The described business process is executed on the infrastructure shown in Figure 13. It is assumed that the infrastructure data is provided by a CMDB system (step 3 of the algorithm). Routers *R1* to *R3* form the core of the network. Subnetworks are connected to the core via switches *S1* to *S7*. The subnetworks are divided by the intended usage: there is a subnetwork for editor's (CL_e) and directors' (financial CL_f, marketing CL_m and art CL_a) client computers, a subnetwork for other employees, for *DNS* and web servers, etc. Other infrastructure components important for the availability assessment are the ticket server *TS*, file server *FS*, financial server *SAP*, and server running the graphical applications (print prepare) *PP*.

The core routers are placed at considerable distance and cables (*C1* to *C3*) interconnecting them are included in the availability evaluation as they are more likely to be damaged and their repair time is non-negligible. Cabling within local

Figure 13. Infrastructure/communication graph for business process of accepting a new manuscript.

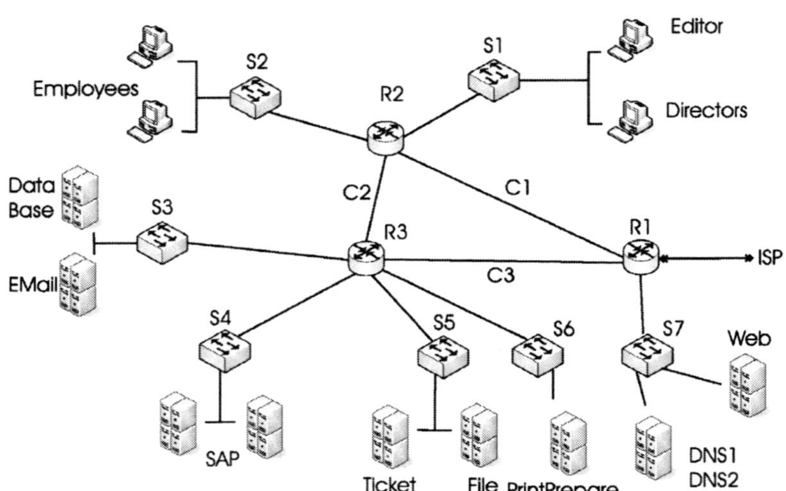

subnetworks is considered highly available (unlikely to be damaged, rather easy to diagnose and repair) and ignored in this analysis. In case that local cabling is also considered to be of high relevance for the availability, it can easily be added to the evaluation process.

The first task in the step 4 of the algorithm is to describe the individual communication paths that are used by atomic services: e.g., access of a client computer to a DNS server. In order to successfully communicate, initiator (source), executor (destination) and the infrastructure between them need to be active and functional. Atomic services can be also described directly, but derivation of equations for communication paths simplifies that task and encourages reuse of equations – typically each communication path is used by multiple services.

The key communication paths are:

- Editor's client computer to DNS:
  CLe → DNS: CLe & S1 & R2 & (C2 & R3 & C3||C1) & R1 & S7 & (DNS1||DNS2)
- Editor's client computer to ticket server:
  CLe → TS: CLe & S1 & R2 & (C2||C1 & R1 & C3) & R3 & S5 & TS
- Financial director's client computer to financial server:
  CLf → SAP: CLf & S1 & R2 & (C2||C1 & R1 & C3) & R3 & S4 & SAP
- Art director's client computer to print preparation server:
  CLa → P: CLa & S1 & R2 & (C2||C1 & R1 & C3) & R3 & S6 & PP
- Ticket server to DNS:
  TS → DN: TS & S5 & R3 & (C2 & R2 & C1||C3) & R1 & S7 & (DNS1||DNS2)
- Ticket server to editor's client:
  TS → CLe: TS & S5 & R3 & (C2||C1 & C3 & R1) & R2 & S1 & CLe
- Print preparation server to file server:
  PP → FS: PP & S6 & R3 & S5 & FS
- Financial server to file server:
  SAP → FS: SAP & S4 & R3 & S5 & FS

For brevity, we do not write down all communication paths. The omitted paths can be easily generated: for instance, access of art director's client computer to DNS servers is essentially the same as for the editor's client as they belong to the same subnetwork. Of course, for evaluation of the service/business process availability, all activities have been included.

Equations describing atomic and composite services are derived iteratively from the description of communication paths, repeating step 4 of the mapping algorithm. If a service has more than one user (e.g., generate ticket service), the user of the service is marked in superscript (e.g., editor's generate ticket service is marked as GT_s^e while art director's generate ticket service is marked as GT_s^a). The atomic services are:

- Generate Ticket service:
  GT_s^e :(CLe → DNS) & (CLe → TS)
- Access Network Disks service:
  ANDs:(CLe → DNS) & (CLe → FS)
- Ticket Reception service is initiated by the ticket server:
  TRs:(TS → DNS) & (TS → CLe)
- Print Preparation service, after initiation by the arts director is executed on PreparePrint servers:
  PPs:(PP → DNS) & (PP → FS)
- Financial Calculation service:
  FCs:(CLf → DNS) & (CLf → SAP) & (SAP → DNS) & (SAP → FS)
- Marketing Plan service:
  MPs:(CLm → DNS) & (CLm → SAP)

In addition to the ICT-components, persons (editor ED, art director AD, financial director FD and marketing director MD, all marked with UML actor symbol) are involved in the composite services execution:

- Initiate Editorial Tasks composite service (Figure 10):

$$IETs\text{: } ED \,\&\, AND_s^e \,\&\, GT_s^e \qquad (1)$$

- Junior-editor Tasks composite service (Figure 12):

$$JETs\text{:}(TR_s^a \,\&\, AD \,\&\, AND_s^a \,\&\, PPs \,\&\, GT_s^a) \,\&\, (TR_s^f \,\&\, FD \,\&\, AND_s^f \,\&\, FCs \,\&\, GT_s^f) \,\&\, (TR_s^m \,\&\, MD \,\&\, MPs) \qquad (2)$$

- Evaluation of the Editorial Tasks composite service (Figure 11):

$$EETs\text{: } TR_s^e \,\&\, ED \,\&\, AND_s^e \,\&\, GT_s^e \qquad (3)$$

Figure 14. Reliability block diagram corresponding to the business process from Figure 9.

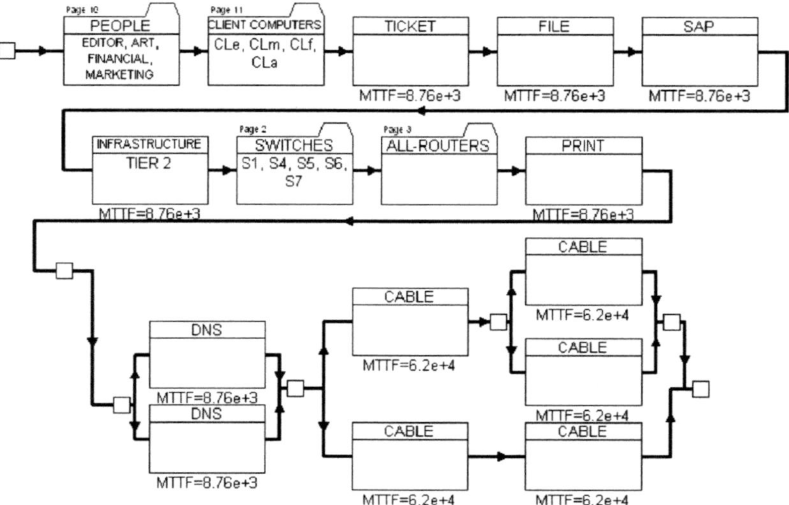

Table 3. ICT-layer component parameters for the business process example

	Routers	Switches	Cables	DNS, File, Ticket	SAP	Clients	Print-Prepare
MTTF	83220	100740	62000	8760	8760	8760	8760
MTTR	48	48	3	1.73	0.6	8.9	1.44

Finally, the composite services are used to describe availability of the business process (step 5 of the mapping algorithm):

Print: IETs & JETs & EETs (4)

Expressions (1), (2) and (3) are substituted in (4) and then further expanded with atomic service and communication path descriptions. At the end, mapping of the business process on the ICT-component layer is obtained as follows:

ED & Cle & AD & MD & FD & CLa & CLf & CLm & FS & TS & SAP & PP & (DNS1||DNS2) & S6 & S4 & S1 & S7 & S5 & R1 & R2 & R3 & ((C1 & (C2||C3))||(C2 & C3)) & INF (5)

Business Process Availability Assessment

In the step 6 of the algorithm formal availability model is created from expression 5. Same as in the previous example, equations are transformed to reliability block diagram (RBD) using the rule that & symbol is transformed to serial while || is transformed to parallel connection of RBD blocks. Figure 14 shows the RBD corresponding to the expression (5).

RBD from Figure 14 is solved using an external tool in the step 7. We have used Isograph Reliability Workbench. Table 3 shows the availability parameters of individual infrastructure components. The parameters are taken from industrial studies performed by the Yankee group (Yankee Group, 2008) and Schweitzer Engineering Laboratories (Scheer and Dolezilek, 2004). We assume that DNS and file servers operate on RedHat Linux, SAP on AIX, personal client computers are running Microsoft Windows (due to unavailability of data for Windows desktop systems, we are using data for Microsoft Server 2003), print prepare runs on Solaris. For cabling we had to use our own estimation based on the various sources, interviews with technical staff and personal experience. For routers and switches we use data from (Scheer and Dolezilek, 2004), assuming that enterprise uses standard routers. In solver, failure and repair rates are modeled as exponentially distributed.

Human errors are not described by the exponential failure distribution, like it is common for the IT components. They have a fixed failure rate instead. The data for errors introduced by human operators is taken from (Kirwan, 1994) for trained personnel. The impact of human errors on availability is set to be 0.1%.

Observing the hardware, software and network availability ignores the impact of supporting infrastructure that, according to numerous industry experiences, has significant impact on the system availability. The Uptime Institute has defined four classes (tiers) of infrastructure that define additional downtime that supporting infrastructure adds to IT systems (Turner, Seader and Brill, 2005). In our example we assume that publishing company running the business process has implemented the Tier 2 infrastructure: the redundancy of power supply, UPS and air conditioning is limited, while maintenance of critical parts of the infrastructure requires processing shutdown. The Tier 2 infrastructure *INF* increases downtime of systems by 22h annually.

Table 4. Evaluation results for the composite service and the business process (unavailability)

	IETs/EETs	JETs	BP
IT only	0.0027	0.0049	0.0059
IT+infrastructure	0.0052	0.0074	0.0084
IT+people	0.0037	0.0079	0.0099
IT+people+Inf.	0.0062	0.0104	0.0124

Table 4 shows the evaluation results of steady-state availability for the composite services and the business process. Four cases are investigated, differentiating whether the impact of people and support infrastructure is included in the evaluation.

If it is assumed that people and support infrastructure are ideal ('IT only' entry in the table), availability of the business process is 0.9941. More precise models that include human (IT + people) or supporting infrastructure (IT+infrastructure) failures show decrease in availability to 0.9901 and 0.9916 respectively. Failures that are introduced jointly by humans and support infrastructure double the unavailability, reducing availability of the business process to 0.9876.

Tool Prototype

In order to support the business process and service mapping, we are developing a tool which enables the mapping of ICT-layer components to services and business processes, as well as the calculation of service and process availability. For that purpose, we use a model-based approach based on Meta Object Facility (Object Management Group, 2004). The concepts of failure modes, availability and necessary transformations are described at the metamodel (MOF M2) level, while the instances are described at the model (MOF M1) level. MOF levels are shown in Figure 15.

The tool architecture is shown in Figure 16. As an input, the tool accepts service or business

Figure 15. Model-based architecture for the mapping and availability assessment.

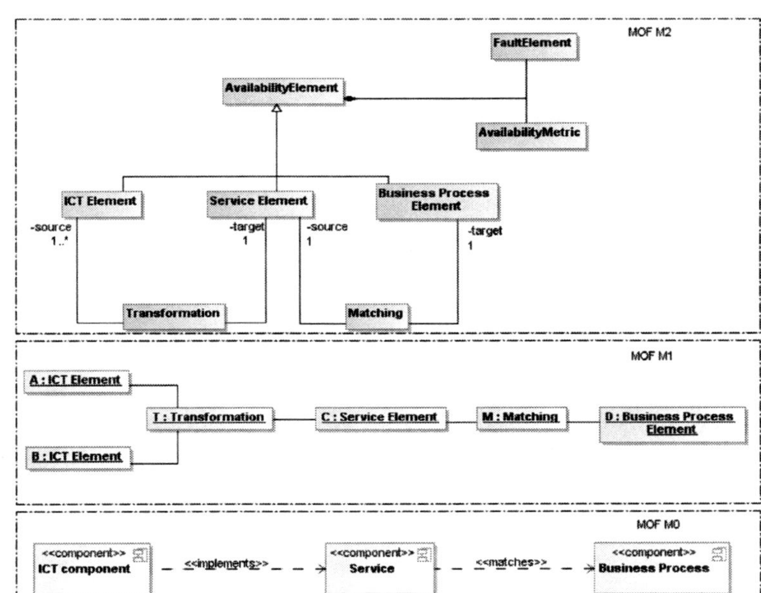

Figure 16. Mapping and availability assessment tool architecture.

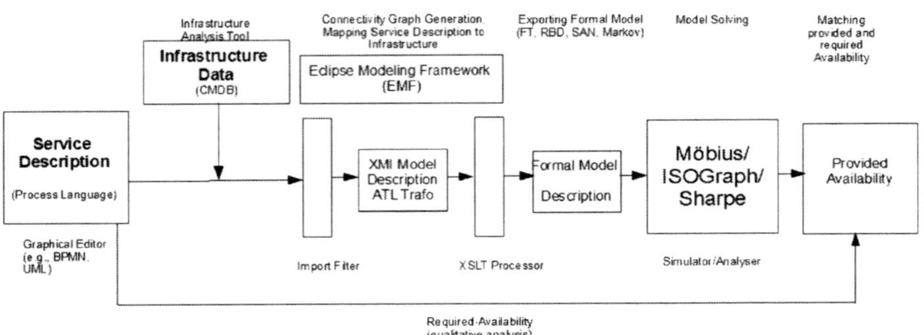

process description in high-level process language (currently BPMN and UML activity diagrams) and infrastructure data collected from a network monitoring/CMDB system (we currently use OpenNMS). This requires graphical BPMN/UML editor and OpenNMS installation. The main tool is realized as an Eclipse Rich Client Platform (RCP) application (Eclipse Foundation, 2008a) using Eclipse Modeling Framework (EMF) (Eclipse Foundation, 2008b) and Graphical Modeling Framework (GMF) (Eclipse Foundation, 2008c). It generates infrastructure graph, and enables (graphical) mapping of the business process and service description elements to the ICT infrastructure elements, which results in a connectivity graph. Based on the transformation rules specified in Atlas transformation language (ATL) (LINA & INRIA Atlas Group, 2006), transformation is performed on the connectivity graph using Eclipse M2M project (Eclipse Foundation, 2008d), transforming it into formal model description required for the external solver. Currently, we support transformations to reliability block diagrams and fault trees. The resulting model is then used as an input to an existing solver (currently we support Isograph Reliability Workbench and SHARPE 2002), which computes provided business process and service availability. Required and provided service availability are then matched, and if discrepancies are found, adequate action can be taken.

It is also planned to develop a repository supporting the tool which will store service and process templates, as well as information required for model parameterization (e.g., MTTR and MTTF or frequently used system components). The basic idea is to provide a comprehensive collection of availability data for the known components at the ICT-layer, similarly to the way that standard availability assessment modeling tools manage part catalogues such as MIL-HDBK-217 or Telcordia SR-332. For this purpose, however, a deeper understanding of the nature of the fault characteristics of component types other then hardware, such as software, supporting infrastructure and particularly people (human faults), is required.

THE ROADMAP TO SERVICE MANAGEMENT

In this chapter the approach for business process and service availability assessment was presented, based on the availability properties of the underlying ICT-components, with special focus on mapping dependencies between those layers and automatic generation of availability models.

One of the main benefits of the proposed solution is independence from a particular formal model required for the availability assessment. We demonstrated how to transform process and service descriptions into reliability block diagrams and fault trees, using collected data and topology of the ICT-components. Separation of the business process description and the ICT-components used to implement it enables automatic updates of service or process availability when the underlying components change. Just the ability to map parts of the business process to the existing infrastructure, and identify critical points, e.g., single points of failure, is already a benefit. Furthermore, cost-benefit or risk-impact analysis can be performed by simulating changes in the ICT-infrastructure, and observing how the availability of the process or particular services changes. The model may be extended with additional factors, such as cost or power utilization, to obtain more specific analysis, e.g., cost can influence the decision to improve the level of availability for the cost-critical employees or services, or power consumption may be leveraged with the increased availability. Using these models, we were already capable to calculate other metrics apart from availability, such as to determine the impact of infrastructure elements to the overall service availability with Fussel-Veseley metric (Fussell, 1975).

Furthermore, we see the proposed approach as a first step to establish a comprehensive model-based service management infrastructure, with the goal to complement existing measurement and empirical-based process management frameworks (e.g., Tivoli or Mercury) with precise fault models and analytical capabilities. The elements of such service management roadmap are:

- *Automatic generation of new reliability/availability models.* In this chapter we demonstrated use of relatively simple combinatorial models. However, to determine other properties of interest and to model more complex systems, state-space models may be required, such as Markov chains, Petri nets, stochastic activity networks or Markov reward models. Such additional models (and the corresponding solvers) may be dynamically incorporated in the proposed framework.
- *Model parameterization.* It is still not clear how to parameterize all elements of the ICT-infrastructure. Frequently, it is not possible either to measure or to obtain availability parameters of a system. Qualitative methods have to be investigated further which may help in estimating the missing parameters. It is not only the parameterization problem, but also more fundamental problem of choosing the adequate distribution to describe a physical occurrence such as operating system, custom application, network cable or human operator failure. In this chapter we used only exponential distribution and introduced fixed rate failures for human operators and infrastructure. We are currently experimenting with other distributions (such as Weibull, Erlang, normal, Gamma, Bayesian etc.) and applying them to different ICT-layer elements.
- *Monitoring tools.* The essential part of the solution for service management is elaborate runtime monitoring capability, such as built in into the existing process management tools. Interoperability of such tools is, however, very limited. As the fundamental property of any SOA system is high dynamicity and absence of central controlling entities, this drawback has to be resolved as the monitoring data from heterogeneous systems will have to be pulled together and aggregated in order to perform high-quality availability prediction.
- *Performability models.* Services do not necessarily fail right after an infrastructure failure has occurred, but may continue working in the degraded performance mode (e.g., reduced bandwidth, lower transaction throughput). This phenomenon and its consequences are captured by performability models, such as Markov re-

ward chains, which can be generated as additional output of the proposed framework.

- *Availability of Business to business (B2B) interactions*. The case study in this chapter involved an in-house business process, described using orchestration. The issue of monitoring tool interoperability becomes even more important when choreographed business processes have to be evaluated, as frequently not enough data and/or control is available to perform a qualified availability assessment. Bound estimation methods, such as demonstrated for the E-mail service with incomplete topology knowledge, have to be developed to enable treatment of such scenarios. Furthermore, parameterization and modeling of best-effort environments, such as the Internet, also play an important role in understanding availability properties of cross-enterprise processes.
- *Mapping of availability metrics to concrete business tasks and objectives*. It is important to understand properties such as SLA parameterization or calculation of costs that are imposed on the enterprise by service and business process unavailability. Coarse grain approaches such as (Patterson, 2002), where costs of downtime are calculated under assumption that either all processes in an enterprise operate within their specifications or neither of them, can be considerably refined.
- *Education*. The general knowledge about modeling, fault-tolerance and service-oriented architecture has to be improved in order to understand the acuteness of the problems facing the still small community trying to address dependability aspects of modern service-oriented systems. The proposed approach addresses availability at different layers, providing awareness of it at different levels of enterprise management and giving a clear message which ICT components or services are of critical value for the overall business stability and prosperity.

REFERENCES

W3 Consortium. (2004). *Web Services glossary*. Retrieved from www.w3.org/ TR/2004/ NOTE-ws-gloss-20040211

W3C Working Group. (2004). *Web Services Architecture*. Retrieved from http://www.w3.org/TR/ws-arch/

Alonso, G., Casati, F., Kuno, H., & Machiraju, V. (2004). *Web Services: Concepts, architectures and applications*. Springer-Verlag.

Amazon, E. C-2 Support Team. (2007). Amazon EC-2 outage report. Retrieved from http://developer.amazon webservices.com/ connect/message.jspa?message ID = 56849#56849

Avizienis, A., Laprie, J., Randell, B. & Landwehr, C. (2004). Basic concepts and taxonomy of dependable and secure computing. *IEEE Transactions on Dependable Secure Computing*.

BITKOM Consortium. (2007). Betriebssichere Rechnenzentren. Retrieved from http://www.bitkom.org

Bulka, D. (1992). Fault tree models for reliability analysis of an FDDI token ring network. *Proceedings of the 30th Annual Southeast Regional Conference*.

Burbeck, S. (2000). *The Tao of e-business services. Emerging Technologies*. IBM Software Group.

Buskens, R., & Gonzalez, O. (2007). *Model-centric development of highly available software systems*. Springer-Verlag.

Chan, P. W., Lyu, M. R., & Malek, M. (2007). *Reliable Web Services: Methodology, experiment and modeling*. IEEE International Conference on Web Services.

Dahlin, M., Baddepudi, B., Chandra, V., Gao, L., & Nayate, A. (2003). End-to-end WAN service availability. *IEEE/ACM Transactions on Networking*, *11*(2). doi:10.1109/TNET.2003.810312

ECDB. (2007). An open source approach to configuration management. Retrieved from http://www.cmdb.info

Eclipse Foundation. (2008a). Rich client platform. Retrieved from http://www.eclipse.org/ home/ categories/ rcp.php

Eclipse Foundation. (2008b). Eclipse modeling framework. Retrieved from http://www.eclipse.org/ modeling/emf/ ?project = emf

Eclipse Foundation. (2008c). Graphical modeling framework. Retrieved from http://www.eclipse.org/ modeling/gmf/

Eclipse Foundation. (2008d). M2M project. Retrieved from http://www.eclipse.org/m2m/

Fujitsu. (2007). Fujitsu inter-stage business process manager. Retrieved from http://www.fujitsu.com /global/services/ software/interstage/ bpm/ index.html

Fussell, J. (1975). How to calculate system reliability and safety characteristics. *IEEE Transactions on Reliability*, *24*(3). doi:10.1109/TR.1975.5215142

Gonczy, L., Chiaradonna, S., di Giandomenico, F., Pataricza, A., Bondavalli, A., & Bartha, T. (2006). Dependability evaluation of Web Service-based processes. *Proceedings of European Performance Engineering Workshop*.

Grottke, M., Sun, H., Fricks, R. M., & Trivedi, K. S. (2008). Ten fallacies of availability and reliability analysis. *Proceedings of the 5th International Service Availability Symposium*.

GSTool. (2009). Home index. http://www.bsi.de/gstool/index.htm

HP. (2007). Mercury business technology optimization enterprise. Retrieved from http://www.mercury.com /us/products/

HP. (2009). An insider's view to the HP universal CMDB. A technical white paper, HP. Retrieved from http://www.rubik solutions.com/ Admin/ Public/ DWSDownload.aspx? File = %2FFiles% 2FFiler%2FPDF +UCMDB% 2FUcmdb_white paper.pdf

IBM. (2007). IBM Tivoli availability process manager. Retrieved from http://www-306. ibm.com/ software/tivoli/ products/ availability-process-mgr/

Immonen, A., & Niemela, E. (2008). *Survey of reliability and availability prediction methods from the viewpoint of software architecture*. Software and System Modeling.

International Telecommunications Union. (2008). Final draft of revised recommendation. *E (Norwalk, Conn.)*, *800*, Retrieved from http://www.itu.int/ md/T05-SG02-080506 -TD-WP2-0121/en.

IsoGraph. (2008). *Reliability workbench technical specification*. Retrieved from http://www.isograph- software.com/ _techspecs/ wk32tech spec.pdf

IT Governance Institute. (2007). CobiT 4.1. Retrieved from http://www.itgi.org/cobit

IT Infrastructure Library. (2007). *Official site*. Retrieved from http://www.itil-officialsite.com

Jiang, W., & Schulzrinne, H. (2003). Assessment of VoIP service availability in the current Internet. *Proceedings of the Passive and Active Measurement Workshop*.

Kirwan, B. (1994). *A guide to practical human reliability assessment*. London: Taylor and Francis Ltd.

Klensin, J. (2001). *Simple mail transfer protocol*. (RFC 2821).

Krafzig, D., Banke, K., & Slama, D. (2004). *Enterprise SOA: Service-Oriented Architecture best practices*. Prentice Hall PTR.

LINA & INRIA Atlas Group. (2006). ATL: Atlas Transformation Language user manual. Retrieved from http://www.eclipse.org/ m2m/atl/doc/ATL User Manual[v0.7].pdf

Majzik, I., Domokos, P., & Magyar, M. (2007). *Tool-supported dependability evaluation of redundant architectures in computer based control systems*. Formal Methods for Automation and Safety in Railway and Automotive Systems.

Malek, M., Hoffmann, G., Milanovic, N., Bruening, S., Meyer, R., & Milic, B. (2007). Methods and tools for availability assessment (Methoden und Werkzeuge zur Verfuegbarkeitsermittlung). Retrieved from http://edoc.hu-berlin.de/ series/ informatik -berichte/ 219/PDF/219.pdf

Merriam Webster Online. (2008). *Dictionary service*. Retrieved from http://www.merriam-webster.com/ dictionary/ service

Milanovic, N. (2006). *Contract-based Web Service composition*. Berlin: Humboldt University.

Object Management Group. (2004). Meta Object Facility (MOF) 2.0 core specification. Retrieved from http://www.omg.org/ cgi-bin/ apps/ doc?ptc/ 03-10-04.pdf

Object Management Group. (2008). Business process modeling notation specification. Retrieved from http://www.bpmn.org/ Documents/OMG Final Adopted BPMN 1-0 Spec 06-02-01.pdf

Pataricza, A., Majzik, I., Huszerl, G., & Varnai, G. (2003). *UML-based design and formal analysis of a safety-critical railway control software module*. Formal Methods for Railway Operation and Control Systems.

Patterson, D. (2002). A simple way to estimate the cost of downtime. *Proceedings of the 16th System Administrator Conference-LISA'02*. Retrieved from http://roc.cs. berkeley.edu/ papers/Cost_ Downtime_ LISA.pdf

Polze, A., Milanovic, N., & Schoebel, M. (2006). *Fundamentals of service-oriented engineering*. HPI, University of Potsdam.

Reinecke, P., van Moorsel, A. P. A., & Wolter, K. (2006). The fast and the fair: A fault-injection-driven comparison of restart oracles for reliable Web Services. *Proceedings of the 3rd International Conference on the Quantitative Evaluation of Systems*.

Sahner, R. A., Trivedi, K. S., & Puliafito, A. (2002). *Performance and reliability analysis of computer systems*. Kluwer Academic Publishers.

Sanders, W. (2007). *Moebius manual*. University of Illinois.

Scheer, G. W., & Dolezilek, D. J. (2004). *Comparing the reliability of ethernet network topologies in substation control and monitoring networks*. (Schweitzer Engineering Laboratories Technical Report 6103).

Service Availability Forum. (2008). *General information*. Retrieved from http://www.saforum.org/

Siewiorek, D., & Swarz, R. (1982). *The theory and practice of reliable system design*. Digital Press.

SNMP. (2009). An architecture for describing Simple Network Management Protocol (SNMP) management frameworks–RFC 3411. Retrieved from http://www.ietf.org/rfc/rfc3411.txt

Trivedi, K. S. (1999). *SHARPE 2000 GUI manual*. Duke University.

Turner, W. P., Seader, J., & Brill, K. (2005). *Industry standard tier classification define site infrastructure performance*. White paper, The Uptime Institute.

van der Aalst, W., Hofstede, A., & Weske, M. (2003). *Business process management: A survey*. International Conference on Business Process Management.

van Moorsel, A. P. A., & Wolter, K. (2006). Analysis of restart mechanisms in software systems. *IEEE Transactions on Software Engineering*, *32*(8). doi:10.1109/TSE.2006.73

Vogels, W. (2003). Web Services are not distributed objects: Common misconceptions about the fundamentals of Web Service technology. *IEEE Internet Computing*, *7*(6).

Wada, H., Suzuki, J., & Oba, K. (2006). Modeling non-functional aspects in Service Oriented Architecture. *Proceedings of the 3rd IEEE International Conference on Services Computing (SCC).*

Walter, M. (2007). OpenSESAME-simple but extensive structured availability modeling environment. Retrieved from http://www.lrr.in.tum.de/ ~walterm/ opensesame/

Wang, D., & Trivedi, K. S. (2005). Modeling user-perceived service availability. *Revised selected papers from the Second International Service Availability Symposium.*

Web Service Reliable Messaging Protocol. (2008). WSRMP. Retrieved from http://download. boulder. ibm.com/ ibmdl/pub/ software/dw/ specs/ ws-rm/ ws-reliable messaging 200502.pdf.

Weske, M. (2007). *Business process management: Concepts, languages, architectures*. Springer-Verlag.

Yankee Group. (2008). Global server operating system reliability survey 2007-2008. Retrieved from http://www.yankeegroup.com/ Research Document. do?id = 16063

ENDNOTES

1. There is a bijection between RBD and FT models (for standard configurations/gates).
2. We will come back to the challenge of end-to-end service availability in B2B interactions and best-effort environments in the last section of this chapter.

Chapter 14
Complexity Analysis at Design Stages of Service Oriented Architectures as a Measure of Reliability Risks

Muhammad Sheikh Sadi
Curtin University of Technology, Australia

D. G. Myers
Curtin University of Technology, Australia

Cesar Ortega Sanchez
Curtin University of Technology, Australia

ABSTRACT

Tremendous growth in interest of Service oriented Architectures (SOA) triggers a substantial amount of research in its reliability assurances. To minimize the risks of these types of systems' failure, it is a requirement to flag those components of SOA that are likely to have higher faults. Clearly, the degree of protection or prevention of faults mechanism is not same for all components. This chapter proposes the usage of metrics that are simply heuristics and are used to scan the system model and flag complex components where faults are more likely to take place. Thus the metric output is some priority or it is a measure of likelihood of faults in a component. This chapter then suggests the designers for possible changes in the design if there remains any risk(s) of degradation of desired functionalities.

INTRODUCTION

Service Oriented Architecture (SOA), which is prompting a variable shift in the distributed computing history, is subsisted in modern computing environments and is at critical risks due to permanent and transient faults in computing structures (Lakhal, Kobayashi, & Yokota, 2006). Permanent faults such as node stuck-at-1/0, transistor open, shorted transistors, etc., arise during fabrication or result from aging, and destroy the intended function of the circuit (Timor, Mendelson, Birk,

DOI: 10.4018/978-1-60960-493-6.ch014

& Suri, 2008). Transient faults, in contrast, do not damage the chips physically but are catastrophic for desired functionalities of the system (Mukherjee, Emer, & Reinhardt, 2005), (F. Wang, 2008), (Iyer, Nakka, Kalbarczyk, & Mitra, 2005). Both of these faults are severe for those SOA where reliability is a great concern(Narayanan & Xie, 2006), (Tosun, 2005). For example, online banking transactions where a single bit change (1→0) in the most significant bit of the data storing register, may cause a huge difference in balance. Due to processor scaling, reduction in operation voltages, exponential growth of number of transistors in a single chip, increase in clock frequencies, and/or device shrinking, the rate of these faults are moving upwards day by day (Saggese, Wang, Kalbarczyk, Patel, & Iyer, 2005), (Crouzet, Collet, & Arlat, 2005).

Prior research to cope with transient faults (which in turn create soft errors) mostly focuses on post-design phases, such as circuit level solutions, logic level solutions, spatial redundancy, temporal redundancy, and/or error correction codes. Early detection and correction of such problems during the design phase is much more likely to be successful than detection once the system is operational (Cortellessa et al., 2005). Estimating reliability (or at least identifying failure-prone components) early in the life-cycle of a design is therefore preferable (Jurjens & Wagner, 2005), (A. Bondavalli, 2001). From a pure dependability viewpoint, complex components attract more attention of soft errors tolerant approaches than others do, since reliability of a system is correlated with the complexity of the system (Khoshgoftaar, 1996), (Yacoub & Ammar, 2002). To minimize the risks of system failure, it is a requirement to flag those components of SOA that are likely to have higher faults. Clearly, the degree of protection or prevention of faults mechanism is not same for all components. Hence, an approach is needed at the design stage to highlight those complex components and suggest the designers for possible changes in the design if there remains any risk of affecting desired functionalities.

This chapter flags complex components at early design stage and investigates how to encourage the designer to explore changes that could be made in the existing model. For example, how the complexities of the components could be minimized, or how these components could be replaced with alternatives and/or with less complex components are examined. The objective is to keep the functionality and other constraints of the system unaffected or to make a trade-off between them, with the goal to minimize the reliability risks. Case studies illustrate the effectiveness of the proposed approach in determining components' complexity ranking and then lowering their complexities. The model is expressed in Unified Modeling Language (UML) since this allows the modeler to describe different views on a system, including the physical layer (Wood, Akehurst, Uzenkov, Howells, & McDonald-Maier, 2008), (L. Wang, Wong, & Xu, 2007).

EXISTING WORK ON SOFT ERRORS RISKS MINIMIZATION

Software based approaches to tolerate soft errors include redundant programs to detect (Mukherjee, Kontz, & Reinhardt, 2002), (Reinhardt & Mukherjee, 2000), (Rotenberg, 1999), (Smolens et al., 2004) and/or recover from the problem (Vijaykumar, Pomeranz, & Cheng, 2002), duplicating instructions (Oh, Shirvani, & McCluskey, 2002), (Reis, Chang, Vachharajani, Rangan, & August, 2005), task duplication (Xie, Li, Kandemir, Vijaykrishnan, & Irwin, 2004), dual use of super scalar data paths (Ray, Hoe, & Falsafi, 2001), and Error detection and Correction Codes (ECC) (Chen & Hsiao, 1984). Chip level Redundant Threading (CRT) (Mukherjee et al., 2002) used a load value queue such that redundant executions can always see an identical view of memory. Although the load value queue produced an identical view of memory for both leading and trailing threads, integrating this into the chip multiprocessor environment requires significant changes. In (Reinhardt & Mukherjee, 2000), the authors described the concept of sphere of replication in aiding the design and discussion of fault tolerant Simultaneously and Redundantly Threaded (SRT) processors. The parts of the computer system that fall outside the sphere are not replicated and must be protected by other means such as information redundancy. AR-SMT (Active-stream/Redundant-stream Simultaneous Multithreading) (Rotenberg, 1999) increases the memory requirement and bandwidth pressure two times, since both threads required accessing the cache and individual memory. Doubling the memory may stress the memory hierarchy and degrade performance. Walcott et al. (Walcott, Humphreys, & Gurumurthi, 2007) used redundant multi threading to determine the architectural vulnerability factor, and Shye et al. (Shye, Blomstedt, Moseley, Janapa Reddi, & Connors, To be Appeared) used process level redundancy to detect soft errors. In redundant multi threading, two identical threads are executed independently over some period and the outputs of the threads are compared to verify the correctness. EDDI (Oh et al., 2002), and SWIFT (Reis et al., 2005) duplicated instructions and program data to detect soft errors. Both redundant programs and duplicating instructions create higher memory requirements and increase register pressure. Error detection and Correction Codes (ECC) (Chen & Hsiao, 1984) adds extra bits with the original bit sequence to detect error. Using ECC to combinational logic blocks is complicated, and requires additional logic and calculations with already timing-critical paths.

Hardware solutions for soft errors mitigation mainly emphasize circuit level solutions, logic level solutions and architectural solutions. At the circuit level, gate sizing techniques (Park & Kim, 2008), (Miskov-Zivanov & Marculescu, 2006), (Quming & Mohanram, 2004) increasing capacitance (Oma, Martin, Rossi, & Metra, 2003), (STMicroelectronics, 2003), resistive hardening (Rockett, 1992) are commonly used to increase the critical charge (Q_{crit}) of the circuit node as high as possible. However, these techniques tend to increase power consumption and lower the speed of the circuit. Logic level solutions (S. Mitra, 2006), (Ming Zhang, 2006), (M. Zhang et al., 2006) mainly propose detection and recovery in combinational circuits by using redundant or self-checking circuits. Architectural solutions mainly introduce redundant hardware in the system to make the whole system more robust against soft errors. They include dynamic implementation verification architecture (DIVA) (Austin, 1999), and block-level duplication used in IBM Z-series machines (Meaney, Swaney, Sanda, & Spainhower, 2005). DIVA (Austin, 1999) in its method of fault protection assumed that the checker is always correct and it proceeds using the checker's result in case of a mismatch. So, faults in the checker itself must be detected through alternative techniques.

Hardware and software combined approaches (Gold et al., 2005), (Krishnamohan, 2005), (Vijaykumar et al., 2002), (Mohamed, Chad, Vijaykumar, & Irith, 2003), (Xie et al., 2004), (Srinivasan, Adve, Bose, & Rivers, 2004), (Rashid, Tan, Huang, & Albonesi, 2005) use the parallel processing capacity of chip multiprocessors (CMPs) and redundant multi threading to detect and recover the problem. (Mohamed et al., 2003) shows Chip Level Redundantly Threaded Multiprocessor with Recovery (CRTR), where the basic idea is to run each program twice, as two identical threads, on a simultaneous multithreaded processor. One of the more interesting matters in the CRTR scheme is that there are certain faults from which it cannot recover. If a register value is written prior to committing an instruction, and if a fault corrupts that register after the committing of the instruction, then CRTR fails to recover from that problem. In Simultaneously and Redundantly Threaded processors with Recovery (SRTR) scheme (Vijaykumar et al., 2002), there is a probability of fault corrupting both threads since the leading thread and trailing thread execute on the same processor. Others (Krishnamohan, 2005), (Xie et al., 2004), (Srinivasan et al., 2004), (Rashid et al., 2005) have followed similar approaches. However, in all cases the system is vulnerable to soft error problems in key areas. In software-based approaches, the complex use of threads presents a difficult programming model. In hardware-based approaches, duplication suffers not only from overhead due to synchronizing duplicate threads, but also from inherent performance overhead due to additional hardware. Moreover, these post-functional design phase approaches can increase time delays and power overhead without offering any performance gain.

Few approaches (Chidamber & Kemerer, 1994), (Harrison, Counsell, & Nithi, 1998) dealt with the static complexities of the system as a risk assessment methodology to minimize the risks of faults. (McCabe, 1976) introduced Cyclomatic complexity, which is measured based on program graphs. However, these static approaches do not deal with the matter of how a module functions in its executing environment. A fault may not manifest itself into a failure if never executed. (Cortellessa et al., 2005), and (Yacoub & Ammar, 2002) defined dynamic metrics that include dynamic complexity and dynamic coupling metrics to measure the quality of software architecture. To assess the severity of the components they have defined only three levels of system failure. However, in real life scenarios, only three severity levels are not sufficient to represent several possible failure modes. Criticality analysis at the sub-system level along with failure Mode and Effect Analysis (FMEA) is also becoming popular in fault tolerant research. A few common methods for assessing criticality in FMEA are Risk Priority Number (RPN) (Bowles, 2004), the MIL_STD 1629A Criticality Number ranking (author, 1984), and the multi-criteria Pareto ranking (Bowles, 1998). However, difficulties in calculating failure rate values or probability of failure make Criticality Number ranking, and the multi-criteria Pareto ranking unpopular to researchers. (Sherer, 1988) has shown a risk assessment methodology by measuring the consequences of errors in different modules. However, the high complexity of the method in real-life applications makes it obsolete. Moreover, the method is applied at the later stages of the system design, which can mean a huge cost increase.

A METHODOLOGY TO MEASURE AND REDUCE COMPONENT'S COMPLEXITY

Complexity analysis does not measure the impact of components in system functionality, but rather shows the rank of likelihood of encountering errors among the components. Some empirical studies have found a correlation between the number of errors in a system and the complexity of the system (Khoshgoftaar, 1996), (Ammar, Nikzadeh, & Dugan, 1997). (Cortellessa et al., 2005) also pointed out that the probability of encountering errors is proportional to the complexity of the system. To minimize the reliability risks, it is therefore necessary at the early design phase to flag complex components that are likely to have higher faults. This paper highlights these components by an assessment of execution time via simulation and the Message-In-and-Out frequency. The details of these metrics are given below.

Execution Time during Simulation

The Failure-In-Time (FIT) of a system due to soft error is proportional to the fraction of time in which the system is susceptible to soft error if the circuit type, transistor sizes, node capacitances, temperature and so forth are kept constant (Nguyen, Yagil, Seifert, & Reitsma, 2005). Hence, the fractional time that a component uses in the execution of a system can flag the soft error proneness of that component. Using Execution Time

(ET) during simulation to measure a component's complexity is a novel approach. Components are executed for a specific operation. Users can specify any operation that seems to be involved with all components. The longer duration to perform the selected operation implies that the component is being used more frequently and/or that it is experiencing many state changes. A soft error occurs at any access point of these components can spread towards all communicating components through the large number of behavioural linkages until the soft error affected component remains in execution. Hence, the likelihood of soft error may be increased if the component takes a longer ET. The method of measuring ET during simulation (to perform an operation by a component) can be shown as follows. Component state S is a function of time: S (t) where t denotes time. An external function F () is required to be executed to perform the operation $F(S(t_i)) \rightarrow S(t_j)$: where $S(t_i)$ is the state of a component at t_i and $S(t_j)$ is the state of that component at t_j. Hence, ET, to execute the function F () that changes the state of the pth component from $S(t_i)$ to $S(t_j)$, is:

$$ET_p\ (F\ (S\ (t_i))\ \rightarrow\ S\ (t_j)) = \sum_{j=1}^{n} d_{pj} \qquad (1)$$

where n is the total number of state changes in the pth component's behaviour execution and d_{pj} is the duration in the jth slot of changing states of pth component.

Since UML does not specify an action model, Telelogic Rhapsody (Telelogic, 2009) is used to gain execution data via simulation. The model is executed in tracing mode. Several tracing commands are used to execute the model. The state transition times for the components are saved to a log file. At the end of the simulation, that log file is analysed to calculate the total ET of the components to perform a selected operation.

Message-In-And-Out Frequency

In object-oriented designs, components are often interdependent. Hence, a failure or error can easily propagate to other components. The malfunctioning behaviour of a component in a high interdependent design cannot be easily isolated. Therefore, this dependence is considered as a valuable measurement for both "a posteriori" and "a priori" analysis (Hitz & Montazeri, 1995). A posteriori analysis is conducted to trace those design aspects that were more likely to produce errors and hence correlate errors with design quality metrics. A priori analysis makes use of this dependence measurement to assess the reliability of designs in an early development phase. This research accepts a priori analysis since it saves both costs and time. In a system model (assumed in UML), components communicate with each other by message passing among them. The number of messages from and to a component shows the measure of dependence with other components. Components with more dependence could easily manifest themselves into failure of the system because services of these components are frequently accessed by other components (Yacoub & Ammar, 2002).

To determine the error proneness, a component's Message-In-and-Out frequency (MIO), which is the ratio of number of messages from and to a component in a scenario and the total number of messages in that scenario, is calculated. More specifically, a component with higher Message-In-and-Out frequency (MIO) is more likely to cause changes in the whole system if there arise any architectural or behavioral change in that component. Define MIO_{i_k} as the MIO for ith component in kth scenario. $M_{(i,j)}$ is the message between component i and component j (where j=1,….,m, $i \neq j$, and m is the number of messages from ith component to other components) in kth scenario, and n_k is the total number of messages, communicating among all the components, in that scenario. Then, MIO_i can be derived as:

$$MIO_{i_k} = \frac{|\sum_{j=1}^{m} M_{(i,j)} \mid i \neq j|}{n_k} \qquad (2)$$

For each component, Total MIO (TMIO) in all possible different scenarios can be calculated using (3). TMIO for ith component is:

$$TMIO_i = \sum_{k=1}^{n'} P(Sc_k) MIO_{i_k} \qquad (3)$$

where n' is the total number of scenarios in Handset system, $P(Sc_k)$ is the probability of kth Scenario in that system, and MIO_{i_k} is the MIO for ith component in kth scenario.

Overall Complexity

The Overall Complexity of the ith Component (OCC_i) is the summation of different complexity factors for that component. The equation is:

$$OCC_i = ET_i + TMIO_i \qquad (4)$$

where ET_i and $TMIO_i$ are Execution Time, and Message-In-and-Out frequency for the ith component. Since, ET_i and $TMIO_i$ are independent on each other, OCC_i is calculated using the summation of these two factors. For simplicity, the weights of ET and TMIO in measuring total value of complexities are assumed as equal.

Lowering the Complexities of the Components

Component complexity suggests to the designer where in the system design, changes are necessary or helpful to minimize soft errors risk. These changes can be made by applying a suitable approach where he/she may change the architecture or behavioural model of the component to lower its complexity. Refactoring is a good candidate for this type of approach. The purpose of refactoring is to alter the model based on the user's requirements by keeping the functionality and other constraints of the system unaffected. In software engineering, "refactoring source code" means improving it without changing its overall results and is sometimes informally referred to as "cleaning it up" (Wikipedia, 2009). Refactoring neither fixes bugs nor adds new functionality, though it might precede either activity; rather, it improves the understandability of the code, changes its internal structure and design, and removes dead code. UML model refactoring is the equivalent of source code refactoring at the model level with the objective of preserving the model's behaviour (Hosseini & Azgomi, 2008), (Gerson, Damien, Yves Le, & Jean-Marc, 2001). It re-structures the model to improve quality factors, such as maintainability, efficiency, fault tolerance, etc., without introducing any new behaviour at the conceptual level. As the software and hardware system evolves, almost each change of requirements imposed on a system requires the introduction of small adaptations to its design model (Dobrzanski & Kuzniarz, 2006), (Boger, Sturm, & Fragemann, 2003, Revised Papers (Lecture Notes in Computer Science Vol.2591)). However, the designers face challenges to this adaptation by a single modification in the model. A possible solution to this problem can be to provide designers with a set of basic transformations so maintaining model functionality. This set of transformations is known as refactoring, which can be used gradually to improve the design (Dobrzanski & Kuzniarz, 2006). A detailed taxonomy of model transformations has been presented by (Mens & Van Gorp, 2006), (Mens, 2006). Model refactoring can be made by replacing components with ones that are more elegant, merging/splitting the states keeping the behaviour unchanged, altering code readability or understandability, formal concept analysis,

Figure 1. An example Statechart of 'user's access to server' before refactoring

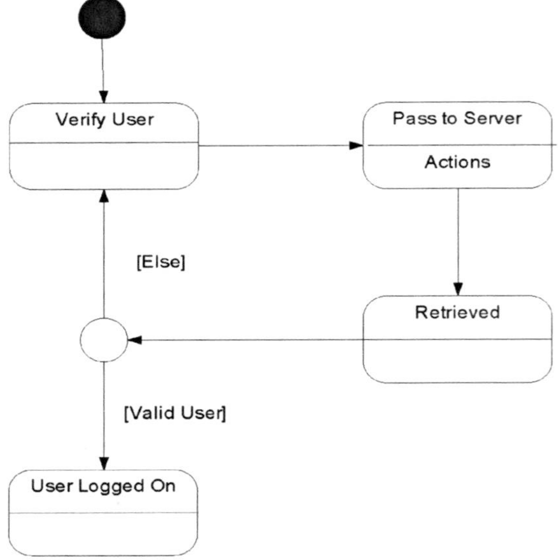

Figure 2. An example Statechart of 'user's access to server' after refactoring

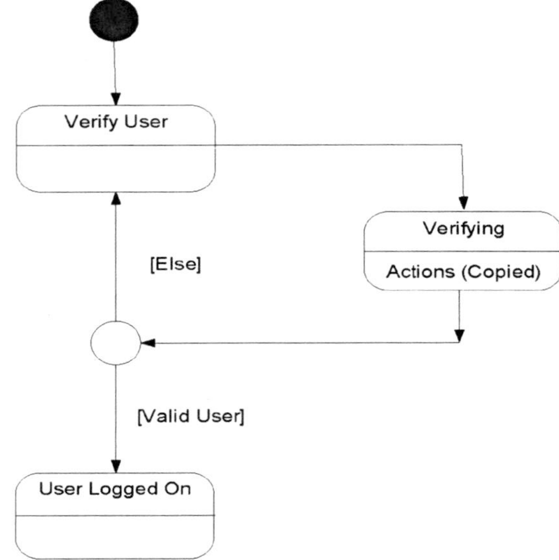

graph transformation, etc. Model refactoring can be detailed by using an example, which consists of Figure1 and Figure2. Figure1 shows an example statechart of a user's access to the server, and Figure2 shows this statechart after refactoring. Two states in Figure1, named as "Pass to Server", and "Retrieved", are merged into one state, "Verifying", in the refactored statechart (Figure 2). The actions used in "Pass to Sever" are copied into the "Verifying" state. Once the complexity ranking is returned, a model can be refactored with the goal of reducing the complexities of the components. Refactoring can be applied on the architecture or behavioural model of the component to lower the complexity, and/or severity, and/or propagation of failure of the components. The methodology of lowering the complexities of components by refactoring is shown in Figure3. As shown in Figure3, initially, the abstract model (in UML) is created from the given specifications. The model is then analysed to measure the complexities of its components. Component complexities need to be compared with a threshold value that users need to determine (for simplicity, the threshold value is ignored in this example).

The large variations among components' complexities are taken as the guideline for flagging the components as complex. If complex

Figure 3. Methodology to lower the complexities of the components by refactoring

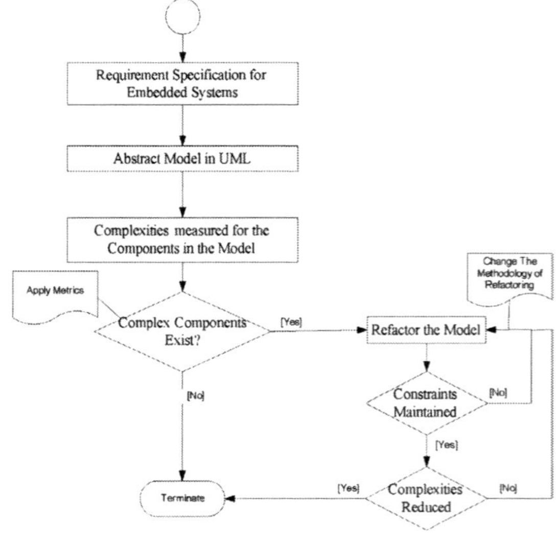

components exist in the model, then the model is analysed to be refactored to lower the components' complexities. Special attention needs to be given to the top-ranked components to lower their complexities. Other components can be examined in turn later according to their complexity ranking. Several trial and error iterations are needed to achieve the goal of lowering a component's complexity. In each trial, checks must be made to ensure the refactoring does not interfere with the functionality of the system; otherwise, the model will have to go through another refactoring method. If these constraints are maintained, then the lowering process will check whether components' complexities are sufficiently reduced or not. If the check is successful, then the process will terminate. If not, another iteration of the above steps will occur.

CASE STUDY

Two applications illustrate how the metrics can be applied to measure the complexity of the components. These are an Automated Rail Car system (ARCS), and a wireless telephony Handset System. The first is a safety critical application and the latter is not. Both must meet real-time criteria and they were chosen as they are illustrative of a broad class of systems that must have high reliability.

ARCS Model

A high-level object-model diagram for ARCS and a more detailed diagram of the composites — Terminal and Car — are shown in Figure4. ARCS assumes each pair of adjacent stations is connected by two rail tracks, one for clockwise and one for counter-clockwise travel. Several railcars are available to transport passengers between terminals. A control centre receives, processes, and sends system data to various components. In the proposed ARCS, there are four terminals and eight cars. Passengers can be in any number. A Car has four main parts: ProximitySensor, Cruiser, DestPanel, and OccupancySensor; and a terminal has six main parts: CarHandler, PlatformManager, CallCarButton, Entrance, Exit, and ExitManager. The car is to maintain maximum speed as long as it never comes within 80 meters of any other car. A stopped car will continue its travel only if the smallest distance to any other car is at least 100 meters. A car has its own destination panel. The

Figure 4. (a) High level object-model diagram for ARCS, and (b) More detailed diagrams of the components: terminal and car

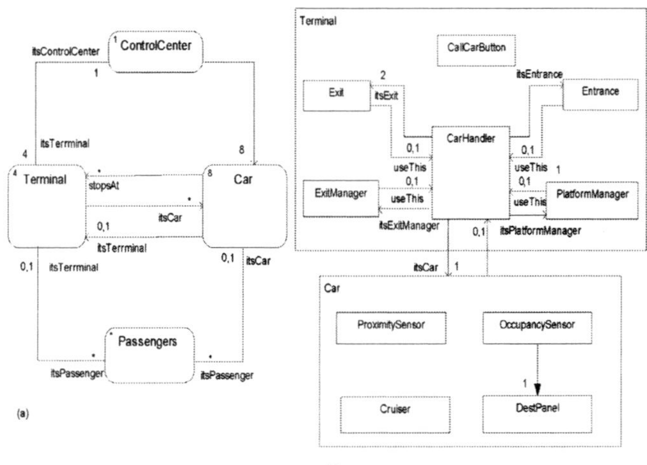

Figure 5. Statechart diagram of car

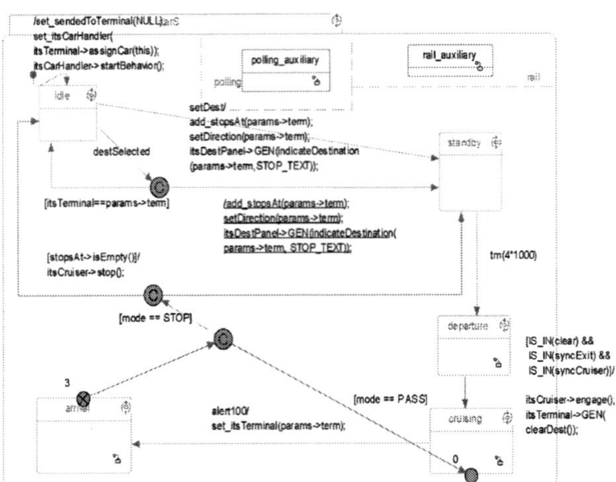

control centre communicates with various system components—receiving, processing, and providing system data. The ARCS model was created based on the analysis in (Harel & Gery, 1997).

ET Analysis of the Components in ARCS

The state changes of the Car used to measure the ET of the components in the ARCS, are shown in Figure5.

The Car stays at 'Idle' state at any terminal. If the event is generated to move the car from its source to destination then it reaches to its 'Departure' state where it continues its travel only if the smallest distance to any other car (in front) is at least 100 meters. When the car departs from its source, instantly it moves to 'Cruising' state where it continuously uses cruise-controller for maintaining speed. The cruiser can be off, engaged, or disengaged, and the car is to maintain maximum speed as long as it never comes within 80 meters of any other car. It leaves the Cruising state when it receives an event from ProximitySensor alerting the Car that it is within 100 meters from any Terminal. Reaching the Terminal is represented by its 'Arrival' state where it checks whether the current Terminal is in the set of terminals, and if it stops at or not. The Car also provides its own identity and the direction it is traveling to the system. If the Car reaches its destination, it then becomes 'Idle' again. Otherwise, it goes back to 'Cruising' state. Calculated ET for the different components to take a car from Terminal [0] to Terminal [3] is shown in Table 1. Car [0] was assumed (initially) at Terminal [0]. It was se-

Table 1. ET of the Components to Move a Car from Terminal [0] to Terminal [3]

Components	ET	Normalized Values
Car	31s 45 ms	.933
ProximitySensor	47 ms	.023
Cruiser	15 ms	.0074
DestPanel	10 ms	.005
OccupancySensor	8 ms	.004
Terminal	3 ms	.0015
CarHandler	28 ms	.014
CallCarButton	4 ms	.002
Entrance	8 ms	.004
Exit	5 ms	.0025
ExitManager	6 ms	.003
Platform Manager	15 ms	.0074
ControlCenter	1 ms	.0005

lected to move from its source (assumed as Terminal [0]) to its destination (assumed as Terminal [3]). Here, this test case was chosen randomly. The user can choose any possible test case. The system was executed to move it to 'Idle' state. Then the event to move the car to Terminal [3] (from Terminal [0]) was triggered. Since, before moving to 'Idle' state, some components change their behaviour, to calculate the ET, the time for moving to 'Idle' state was also considered with the time to move to destination from 'Idle' state. ET for each component was calculated by:

$$TR_p\ (\{\text{Automated Rail Car System}\}\ (\{\ \text{Car [0] is at Rest at Terminal [0]}\}\ \rightarrow \{\text{Car [0] is at Terminal [3]}\}) = \sum_{j=1}^{n} d_{pj} \quad (5)$$

where, the symbols are defined in (1).

MIO and TMIO Analysis in ARCS

There are two scenarios in ARCS. These are: i) CarApproachesATerminal, and ii) CarDepartsATerminal. MIO in each scenario and Total MIO (TMIO) in two scenarios for all components are calculated using Equation (2) and Equation (3). The values of MIO and TMIO for all components are shown in Table 2. In Table 2, to simplify the representation of column headings, CarApproachesATerminal Scenario, CarDepartsATerminal Scenario, and Overall Complexities of the Components are abbreviated as CAATS, CDATS, and OCC respectively. The probabilities of the two scenarios are assumed as equal since, if a car departs, there is an equal probability that it will arrive at another Terminal. The blank cells in Table 2 indicate no message from the corresponding component in the corresponding scenario. Car has the highest value of TMIO as it communicates mostly with other components. TMIO for other components are also shown in Table 2.

Overall Complexities of the Components in ARCS

The total complexities of all components are calculated using Equation (4). The last column in Table 2 shows the measured values of each component's complexity. Their values are normalized by taking the ratio between them and the total value. As shown in Table 2, Car is the most complex

Table 2. MIO, TMIO and overall complexities of all components in ARCS

Components	MIO in CAATS	MIO in CDATS	TMIO	OCC
Car	0.64	0.5	1.14	2.073
ProximitySensor	0.21	-	0.21	0.233
Cruiser	0.29	0.21	0.5	0.5074
DestPanel	-	-	-	0.005
OccupancySensor	-	-	-	0.004
Terminal	0.14	0.07	0.21	0.2115
CarHandler	0.43	0.64	1.07	1.084
CallCarButton	-	-	-	0.002
Entrance	0.14	-	0.14	0.144
Exit	-	0.14	0.14	0.1425
ExitManager	-	0.21	0.21	0.213
PlatformManager	0.14	0.07	0.21	0.2174
ControlCenter	-	-	-	0.0005

component and is followed by CarHandler, and Cruiser. The highest value of ET and largest communication dependencies (with other components) took the complexity value of Car to the highest value. In the two scenarios, not all components participated. Hence, MIO and TMIO for some components are not measured in this example. ET alone is used to measure the overall complexities of those components.

Validating the Complexities of the Components in ARCS

To validate the component's complexity measurement, trials are conducted whereby transient faults are injected into the components of the selected system. Transient faults are injected at each component, into one bit at a time. The reason is that transient faults change the value of one bit at a time and the probability of changing two bits and/or two transient faults are almost zero. The fault injection is made by changing one bit of the parameter value, or anywhere in code or in the parameter name. The probabilities of occurrences of soft errors in the components are calculated by taking the ratios between total number of soft error occurrences and total number of fault injections. This ratio can be defined as the Error/Fault injections (E/F) Ratio. In this paper, only those soft errors are counted that cause any degradation or failure in system functionality. If the soft error does not create any degradation in the system then it is not taken as a matter of concern here. Ten trials are made for transient fault injection into every component. The more trials are performed, the better the expected result. However, for this large example model, it is expected that ten trials in each component would be able to give a good idea about their probabilities of soft error proneness. Table 3 shows the E/F ratio for this example.

If these ratios are ranked in an ascending order then it is observed that Table 2 has a similar ranking to Table 3 until the Cruiser component. The next ratio is equal for ProximtySensor, PlatformManager, and ExitManager where, in Table 2, their complexity values differ a little. If that slight difference is neglected, then the complexity ranking for these components shows similar results in these tables. Other results also show a very similar complexity order as in Table 2. Hence, it can be concluded that complexity analysis is able to measure the likelihood of soft error proneness among the components of ARCS.

Table 3. E/F Ratios of the components in ARCS

Components	Number of Transient Faults Injections	Number of Soft Errors	E/F Ratio
Car	10	8	0.8
ProximitySensor		4	0.4
Cruiser		5	0.5
DestPanel		1	0.1
OccupancySensor		1	0.1
Terminal		3	0.3
CarHandler		7	0.7
CallCarButton		1	0.1
Entrance		3	0.3
Exit		3	0.3
ExitManager		4	0.4
PlatformManager		4	0.4
ControlCenter		1	0.1

Table 4. Comparison among dynamic complexity, static complexity, and E/F Ratios of the components of ARCS

Components	E/F Ratio (Normalized)	Dynamic Complexities of the Components (Normalized)	Static Complexities (Normalized)
Car	1	1	1
ProximitySensor	0.5	0.112	0.625
Cruiser	0.625	0.245	0.75
DestPanel	0.125	0.002	0.25
OccupancySensor	0.125	0.0019	0.25
Terminal	0.375	0.102	0.25
CarHandler	0.875	0.523	0.375
CallCarButton	0.125	0.001	0.25
Entrance	0.375	0.069	0.25
Exit	0.375	0.069	0.25
ExitManager	0.5	0.103	0.25
PlatformManager	0.5	0.105	0.25
ControlCenter	0.125	0.0002	0.25

Comparison with Static Complexity Analysis

This comparison shows the contribution of dynamic metrics to measure the complexities of the components over static metrics. The dynamic complexities of the components for ARCS are obtained as outlined in the section of the Methodology of Complexity Analysis. Static complexities are calculated by using McCabe's Cyclomatic complexity theorem (McCabe, 1976). The last Column in Table 4 shows the Cyclomatic Complexities of the components in ARCS.

Table 4 also allows comparison among the dynamic complexity, static complexity, and E/F ratios of the components. The values shown in Table 4 are all normalized to make the comparison possible. The normalization is done by dividing each element in each column with the highest value in the corresponding column. Since in all three columns Car has the maximum value, the normalized value for Car is obtained as '1'. The results show that both dynamic complexity and E/F ratio return a similar ranking. Static complexity, on the other hand, returned a completely different ranking and, in most cases, it failed to distinguish among the complexities of the components. Static complexity analysis, for instance, returned the same complexity value for DestPanel, OccupancySensor, Terminal, CallCarButton, Entrance, Exit, ExitManager, PlatformManager, ControlCenter. Hence, dynamic complexity is more significant than static complexity in component complexity analysis.

Lowering the Complexities of the Components in ARCS

That part of the model dealing with Car behaviour is carefully examined to determine refactoring possibilities to lower its complexity. All the states and their internal and/or external codes used in triggers, as well as actions, are checked. These areas are where refactoring could achieve the goal of reducing Car's time complexity while keeping its functionality unaffected. Two states and their internal codes of Car are merged to reduce the time complexity. Comparison among the calculated normalized ET of the components of the refactored model and existing model (to take a car from Terminal [0] to Terminal [3]) is shown in Table 5. A lower ET will result in lower complexity as well as lower complexity of the components. Table 5 shows that refactoring the model lowered the ET of Car and ProximitySensor to a measurable extent. Others, except for OccupancySensor and PlatformManager, are also lowered. The increase in complexity value of OccupancySensor and PlatformManager are not so large. For this reason, the increases in these two components can be viewed as negligible. In summary, applying refactoring is effective in lowering the complexities of the components.

A Wireless Telephony Handset System

The Handset system provides voice and data services to users by placing and receiving calls.

Table 5. Comparison among the calculated normalized ET of the components of refactored model and existing model

Components	Normalized ET of Refactored Model	Normalized ET of Existing Model
Car	0.899	.995
Proximity-Sensor	0.00051	.0015
Cruiser	.00048	.00048
DestPanel	.00016	.00032
Occupancy-Sensor	0.00035	.00026
Terminal	.00013	.000096
CarHandler	.00089	.00089
CallCarButton	.000032	.00013
Entrance	0.00022	.00026
Exit	.00016	.00016
ExitManager	.000096	.000192
Platform Manager	0.00064	.00048
ControlCenter	.000032	.000032

To deliver services, the wireless network must receive, set up, and direct incoming and outgoing call requests, track and maintain the location of users, and facilitate uninterrupted service when users move within and outside the network. When the wireless user initiates a call, the network receives the request, and validates and registers the user; once registered, the network monitors the user's location. The wireless telephone must send acceptable signal strength to the network to receive the call. When the network receives a call, it directs it to the appropriate registered user. The high-level architectural diagram (black box approach) of the Handset System is shown in Figure6.

ET Analysis of the Sub-Systems in the Handset System

The 'Call Control' Statechart diagram of CM in the Handset system was used for ET analysis and is shown in Figure7.

The statechart identifies the state-based behaviour of instances of 'Call Control' when the system receives call requests from users and connects calls. It has two main states: 'Idle' and 'Active'. Two other states: 'ConnectConfirm' and 'Connected' are nested in 'Active' state. 'Call Control' waits for an incoming call in the 'Idle' state. When an incoming call is received, it forwards the message through its 'cc_mm' port to the MM by sending a 'PlaceCallReq' event. MM, in co-operation with the DL, processes this signal and sends a call confirmation to CM. If CM does not receive a confirmation within thirty seconds then it returns to the 'Idle' state by sending a 'Disconnect' event to MM. If it receives a confirmation, the call connects, and remains connected until it receives a message to disconnect MM. DL also undergo behavioural changes during these operations. When the operation succeeds, the time of executing the 'Place Call' event at 'Idle' state, and the time when the system reached at 'Connected' state of 'Call Control' statechart

Figure 6. High level architecture of the handset system

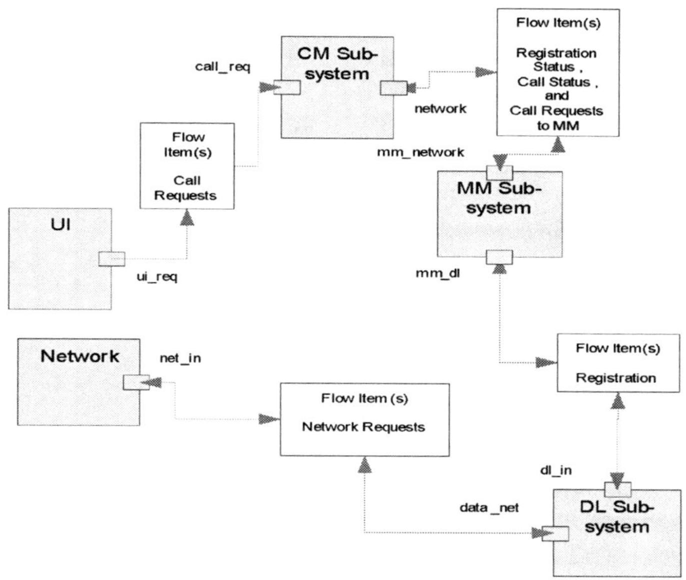

Figure 7. Call control Statechart diagram at the beginning of execution

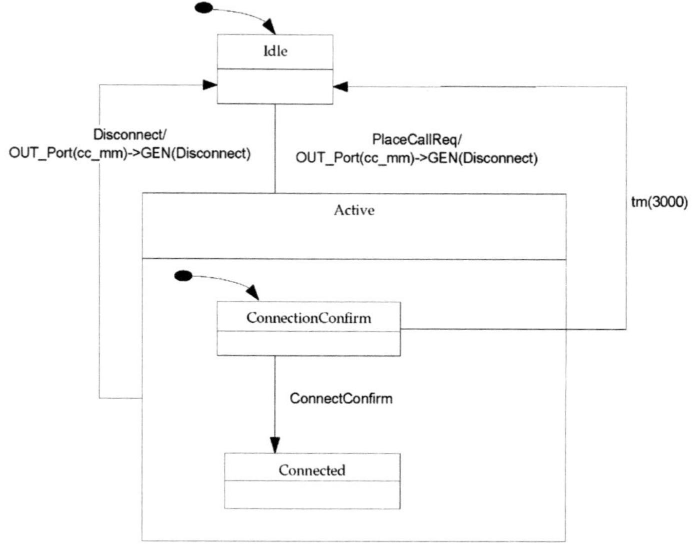

were recorded to calculate the ET of these sub-systems. ET for each sub-system was calculated by Equation (6) and this equation is derived from equation (1).

$$TR_p\ (\{ConnectionManagement\text{-}\rangle CallControl\text{-}\rangle GEN[PlaceCallReq]\}\ \{Idle\} \rightarrow \{Connected\}) = \sum_{j=1}^{n} d_{pj} \qquad (6)$$

where the symbols are defined in equation (1). The pseudo code to activate the connection in the Handset system is shown in Box 1. PlaceCallReq event's triggering status (from UI) was taken as input, and tCM (Total), tMM (Total), tDL (Total) were returned as output where they represented the total time taken by CM, MM, and DL respectively in connecting the call.

Table 6 shows ET of the sub-systems and their normalized values. As shown in the table, MM

Box 1. Pseudo code to activate the connection in the handset system

```
Input: PlaceCallReq event's triggering status
Output: tCM (Total), tMM (Total), tDL (Total)
Detail:
Start: The system is at Idle state
Step 1. Initialize tCM (Total), tMM (Total), tDL (Total)
Step 2. Input: PlaceCallReq event's triggering status
Step 3. If UI generates PlaceCallReq event in CM then
Step 4. CM sends PlaceCallReq to MM
Step 5. Update tCM (Total): tCM (Total) +=tCM (Step 3)
Step 6. CM entered at ConnetionConfirm state
Step 7. Update tCM (Total): tCM (Total) +=tCM (Step 5)
Step 8. CM sets tm (3000) at ConnetionConfirm state
Step 9. Update tCM (Total): tCM (Total) +=tCM (Step 7)
Step 10. If not MM returns Take Event PlaceCallReq to CM then CM goes to Idle
state
Exit Sub
Else
Update tMM (Total): tMM (Total) +=tMM (Step 9)
CM remains in ConnetionConfirm state
Step 11. MM checks signal strength
Step 12. Update tMM (Total): tMM (Total) +=tMM (Step 10)
Step 13. MM sends Registration Request to DL
Step 14. Update tMM (Total): tMM (Total) +=tMM (Step 12)
Step 15. DL sends Channel open confirmation to MM
Step 16. Update tDL (Total): tDL (Total) +=tDL (Step 14)
Step 17. MM updates location
Step 18. Update tMM (Total): tMM (Total) +=tMM (Step 16)
Step 19. MM sends ConnectConfirm event to CM
Step 20. Update tMM (Total): tMM (Total) +=tMM (Step 18)
Step 21. CM goes to Connected state
Step 22. Update tCM (Total): tCM (Total) +=tCM (Step 20)
End if
End if
Step 23. Output: tCM (Total), tMM (Total), tDL (Total)
End       The system is at Connected state
```

Table 6. ET of the sub-systems to activate the connection

Sub-Systems	ET	Normalized Values
CM	6	0.29
DL	1	0.05
MM	14	0.67

took the longest time in the selected operation. DL, comparatively, took negligible time, since in the selected operation; DL's interference was much lower than MM, and CM.

MIO and TMIO of the Sub-Systems in the Handset System

The probabilities of the occurrences of three scenarios in the Handset system — i) Place Call Request Successful, ii) Network Connect, and iii) Connection Management Place Call Request Success — were assumed as 0.45, 0.30, and 0.25 respectively. The assumptions were made with respect to their usage in real life scenarios.

MIO and TMIO for three different sub-systems were calculated for three different sequence diagrams using Equation (2) and Equation (3). All values of MIO and TMIO for the three sub-systems are shown in Table 7. To simplify the representation of column headings in Table 7, Place Call Request Successful Scenario, Network Connect Scenario, and Connection Management Place Call Request Success Scenario are abbreviated as PCRSS, NCS, and CMPCRSS respectively. The results shown refer to the level of communication dependency of each sub-system with other sub-systems in the Handset system. DL has the largest communication dependency among all three sub-systems followed by CM, and MM, as shown in Table 7.

Overall Complexities of the Sub-Systems in the Handset System

Overall complexities of three sub-systems were calculated using Equation (4), and the last column in Table 7 shows their overall complexities. Overall complexity is the summation of ET (during simulation), and Message-in-and-out-frequencies of the sub-systems. Though MM has the highest value of ET, and DL has the same for TMIO, considering both of the complexities, CM is the most complex sub-system in the Handset system. Overall complexities of DL and MM are almost equal.

Validating Complexities of the Sub-Systems in Handset System

To validate the component's complexity measurement, trials were conducted whereby transient faults were injected into each sub-system of the Handset system. Error/Fault injections (E/F) ratios were calculated for each sub-system. As mentioned earlier, in this paper, only those soft errors were counted that cause any degradation or failure in system functionality, and if the soft error did not create any degradation in the system then it was not taken as a matter of concern. Ten trials were made for transient fault injection into each sub-system. The more trials performed, the better the expected result. However, for this large example model, it was expected that ten trials in each sub-system would provide a good idea about

Table 7. MIO and TMIO of the sub-systems in the handset system

Sub-System Packages	MIO in PCRSS	MIO in NCS	MIO in CMPCRSS	TMIO	Overall Complexities
CM	0.7	0.33	0.83	0.62	0.91
DL	0.6	1	0.67	0.74	0.79
MM	0.2	-	0.17	0.13	0.80

Table 8. E/F ratios of the sub-systems in the handset system

Components	Number of Fault Injections	Number of Faults	Ratio
CM	10	6	0.6
MM		5	0.5
DL		3	0.3

the likelihood of soft errors. Table 8 shows the E/F ratios for this example.

If these ratios are ordered in ascending then it is observed that the order of E/F ratios shown in Table 8 is similar to the complexity order shown in Table 7. Hence, it can be concluded that complexity analysis is able to measure the likelihood of soft errors occurrences among the sub-systems of the Handset system.

Comparison with Static Complexity

This comparison shows the contribution of dynamic metrics to measuring the complexities of the components over static metrics. Static complexities were calculated using McCabe's Cyclomatic complexity theorems (McCabe, 1976). The 4th column of Table 9 shows the measured static complexities of the sub-systems in the Handset system.

Table 9 also allows comparison between the dynamic complexity, static complexity, and E/F ratios of the components. The values, shown in Table 9, were all normalized to make comparison easier. The normalization was done by dividing each element in each column with the highest value in the corresponding column. Since in all three columns CM had the maximum value, the normalized value for CM was obtained as '1'. The results show that both dynamic complexity and E/F ratios returned CM as the top ranked complex component followed by MM and DL. Static complexity on the other hand returned MM as the most complex component followed by CM and DL. Hence, dynamic complexity shows more significance than static complexity in component complexity analysis.

Lowering Complexities of the Sub-Systems in Handset System

The behaviour models of all three sub-systems were carefully examined to be refactored. All the states and their internal and/or external codes used in triggers, actions and so forth were checked to ensure refactoring could achieve the goal of reducing complexity of the sub-systems while keeping its functionality unaffected. The functionality was affected by any change made in the behavioural diagrams of CM, and DL sub-systems. The MMCallControl activity diagram and the InCall sub-activity diagram of MM sub-system could be refactored by maintaining the constraints. Two states, their internal codes, and all the forks of MMCallControl activity diagram were merged, the CheckSignal state of InCall sub-activity diagram in MM sub-system was removed, and the internal codes in CheckSignal state were merged with the VoiceData state to lower its time complexity. The calculated normalized ET of the sub-systems of

Table 9. Comparison among dynamic complexity, static complexity, and E/F ratios of the sub-systems in the handset system

Components	E/F Ratios	Dynamic Complexities of the Components	Static Complexities
CM	1	1	0.71
DL	0.5	0.87	0.57
MM	0.83	0.88	1

refactored model and existing model (to establish a handset connection) is shown in Table 10.

Lower ET will result in lower complexity of the sub-systems. Table 10 shows that refactoring the model is able to lower the ET of the CM, and MM sub-systems significantly. The ET for DL is constant. DL is the least complex sub-system in the Handset system and its complexity is so low that it does not attract any attention by designers. Hence, applied refactoring is acceptable in lowering the complexities of the sub-systems.

DISCUSSION

The case study results show the effectiveness of the proposed method in measuring the complexities of the components in two chosen examples—ARCS and the Handset system. The comparisons drawn between dynamic complexity (the approach of this research) and static complexity (McCabe's Cyclomatic complexity) indicate that, for a number of components, static complexity failed to return variations among their complexity, whereas, this chapter was able to show the variations. E/F ratios showed similar results with obtained complexity results that validate the proposed method. Static complexity, on the other hand, returned a completely different ranking to E/F ratios. Study results also showed how the application of refactoring made changes in the existing design to lower the complexities of the components to minimize the risks of soft errors. It investigated how to encourage designers to explore changes that could be made in the existing models of embedded systems to lower the dependability risks.

CONCLUSION

This chapter flags those components of a system model which are complex in architecture and in behaviour and where there is high probability of fault occurrences. Amendment in the early stages of design saves both cost and time, and it is easier for the designers to flag and defend the risk issue at the modelling level than the system is already implemented or at the later stages of design. The investigation began with the measurement of likelihood of faults in the system. These metrics are: (1) assessment of execution time during simulation, and (2) Message-In-and-Out frequency. Both of the metrics are obtained from the UML specifications that can be used in the early design phase of a system. These are dynamic metrics; that is, they work on the execution phase of the model. Developed metrics are validated by calculating the E/F ratios for the components. This chapter then developed the ways to encourage designers to explore changes that could be made in the existing model to lower the complexities of the components. Later on, the designer should take some corrective actions in those portions of the model or take some special measures like error correction code and/or duplication of hardware or software at only those portions during post design phases to reduce the risks of desired functionality degradation of SOA.

Table 10. Comparison among ET of the components of refactored model and those of existing handset model

Components	Normalized ET of Refactored Model	Normalized ET of Existing Model
CM	0.29	0.228
MM	0.05	0.0393
DL	0.67	0.67

There are open scopes to extend this paper. Some possible future directions are outlined shortly as follows.

In the current approach (for simplicity) the weights of ET and TMIO in measuring total value of complexity by Equation (4) are assumed as equal. The relative weight of different factors in measuring the complexity could be different for different application. For a specific application, depending on individual factor's influence on the whole functionality, its appropriate weight can be generated. Alternatively, weight vectors could be introduced to capture user preferences automatically based on users' selection patterns. Further extension to this paper can be made by finding the appropriate weights of ET and TMIO in measuring the complexity of each component.

Like the weight vectors, complexity threshold is a relative measure. Depending on the type of system and the type of application, the complexity of a component may vary. Every complexity pass threshold is a matter of concern for the designer. Complexity threshold should be derived or defined by the user. This paper considers that the top-ranked complex components have high probability of faults. However, there should be a threshold value of a component's complexity, which could flag whether the component is crossing the complexity boundary or not. The scope is there to measure the complexity threshold, specific to an application, to better categorize the complex components.

To lower the complexity, the current paper applies refactoring, which re-structures the model to improve fault tolerance. Alternative solutions (rather than refactoring) could be examined to achieve the best solution to lowering the complexity of the components, and that of the whole system as well.

REFERENCES

Ammar, H. H., Nikzadeh, T., & Dugan, J. B. (1997). *A methodology for risk assessment of functional specification of software systems using colored Petri nets.* Paper presented at the Fourth International Software Metrics Symposium, Los Alamitos, CA, USA.

Austin, T. M. (1999). *DIVA: A reliable substrate for deep submicron microarchitecture design.* Paper presented at the 32nd Annual International Symposium on Microarchitecture.

Boger, M., Sturm, T., & Fragemann, P. (2003). *Refactoring browser for UML.* Paper presented at the International Conference on Objects, Components, Architectures, Services, and Applications for a Networked World, Berlin, Germany. (LNCS 2591).

Bondavalli, A., Latella, D., Majzik, I., Pataricza, A., & Savoia, G. (2001). Dependability analysis in the early phases of UML based system design. *Journal of Computer Systems Science and Engineering*, *16*(5), 265–275.

Bowles, J. B. (1998). *The new SAE FMECA standard.* Paper presented at the International Symposium on Product Quality and Integrity.

Bowles, J. B. (2004). An assessment of RPN prioritization in a failure modes effects and criticality analysis. *Journal of the IEST*, *47*, 51–56.

Chen, C. L., & Hsiao, M. Y. (1984). Error-correcting codes for semiconductor memory applications: A state-of-the-art review. *IBM Journal of Research and Development*, *28*(2), 124–134. doi:10.1147/rd.282.0124

Chidamber, S. R., & Kemerer, C. F. (1994). A metrics suite for object oriented design. *IEEE Transactions on Software Engineering*, *20*(6), 476–493. doi:10.1109/32.295895

Cortellessa, V., Goseva-Popstojanova, K., Appukkutty, K., Guedem, A. R., Hassan, A., & Elnaggar, R. (2005). Model-based performance risk analysis. *IEEE Transactions on Software Engineering, 31*(1), 3–20. doi:10.1109/TSE.2005.12

Crouzet, Y., Collet, J., & Arlat, J. (2005). *Mitigating soft errors to prevent a hard threat to dependable computing.* Paper presented at the 11th IEEE International On-Line Testing Symposium, IOLTS.

Dobrzanski, L., & Kuzniarz, L. (2006). *An approach to refactoring of executable UML models.* Paper presented at the ACM Symposium on Applied Computing, New York.

Gerson, S., Damien, P., Yves Le, T., & Jean-Marc, J. (2001). Refactoring UML Models. *Proceedings of the 4th International Conference on the Unified Modeling Language: Modeling Languages, Concepts, and Tools* (pp. 134-148). Springer-Verlag.

Gold, B. T., Kim, J., Smolens, J. C., Chung, E. S., Liaskovitis, V., & Nurvitadhi, E. (2005). TRUSS: A reliable, scalable server architecture. *IEEE Micro, 25*(6), 51–59. doi:10.1109/MM.2005.122

Harel, D., & Gery, E. (1997). Executable object modeling with statecharts. *Computer, 30*(7), 31–42. doi:10.1109/2.596624

Harrison, R., Counsell, S. J., & Nithi, R. V. (1998). An evaluation of the MOOD set of object-oriented software metrics. *IEEE Transactions on Software Engineering, 24*(6), 491–496. doi:10.1109/32.689404

Hitz, M., & Montazeri, B. (1995). *Measuring product attributes of object-oriented systems.* Paper presented at the 5th European Software Engineering Conference.

Hosseini, S., & Azgomi, M. A. (2008). *UML model refactoring with emphasis on behavior preservation.* Paper presented at the 2nd IFIP/IEEE International Symposium on Theoretical Aspects of Software Engineering, Piscataway, NJ, United States.

Iyer, R. K., Nakka, N. M., Kalbarczyk, Z. T., & Mitra, S. (2005). Recent advances and new avenues in hardware-level reliability support. *IEEE Micro, 25*(6), 18–29. doi:10.1109/MM.2005.119

Jurjens, J., & Wagner, S. (2005). *Component-based development of dependable systems with UML.* (LNCS 3778), (pp. 320-344).

Khoshgoftaar, J. M. T. (1996). Software metrics for reliability assessment. In Lyu, M. (Ed.), *Handbook of software reliability engineering* (pp. 493–529).

Krishnamohan, S. (2005). *Efficient techniques for modeling and mitigation of soft errors in nanometer-scale static CMOS logic circuits.* Unpublished doctoral thesis, Michigan State University, United States-Michigan.

Lakhal, N. B., Kobayashi, T., & Yokota, H. (2006). *Dependability and flexibility centered approach for composite Web Services modeling.* Berlin, Germany.

McCabe, T. J. (1976). A complexity measure. *IEEE Transactions on Software Engineering, SE-2*(4), 308–320. doi:10.1109/TSE.1976.233837

Meaney, P. J., Swaney, S. B., Sanda, P. N., & Spainhower, L. (2005). IBM z990 soft error detection and recovery. *IEEE Transactions on Device and Materials Reliability, 5*(3), 419–427. doi:10.1109/TDMR.2005.859577

Mens, T. (2006). *On the use of graph transformations for model refactoring.* (LNCS 4143), (pp. 219-257).

Mens, T., & Van Gorp, P. (2006). A taxonomy of model transformation. *Electronic Notes in Theoretical Computer Science, 152*(1-2), 125–142. doi:10.1016/j.entcs.2005.10.021

Miskov-Zivanov, N., & Marculescu, D. (2006). *MARS-C: Modeling And Reduction of Soft errors in Combinational circuits.* Paper presented at the Proceedings of the Design Automation Conference, Piscataway, NJ, USA.

Mitra, S. M.Z., Seifert, N., Mak, T.M. & Kim, K. (2006). *Soft error resilient system design through error correction.* Paper presented at the International Conference on Very Large Scale Integration and System-on-Chip.

Mohamed, A. G., Chad, S., Vijaykumar, T. N., & Irith, P. (2003). Transient-fault recovery for chip multiprocessors. *IEEE Micro*, *23*(6), 76–83. doi:10.1109/MM.2003.1261390

Mukherjee, S. S., Emer, J., & Reinhardt, S. K. (2005). *The soft error problem: An architectural perspective.* Paper presented at the 11th International Symposium on High-Performance Computer Architecture, San Francisco, CA, USA.

Mukherjee, S. S., Kontz, M., & Reinhardt, S. K. (2002). *Detailed design and evaluation of redundant multi-threading alternatives.* Paper presented at the 29th Annual International Symposium on Computer Architecture.

Narayanan, V., & Xie, Y. (2006). Reliability concerns in embedded system designs. *Computer*, *39*(1), 118–120. doi:10.1109/MC.2006.31

Nguyen, H. T., Yagil, Y., Seifert, N., & Reitsma, M. (2005). Chip-level soft error estimation method. *IEEE Transactions on Device and Materials Reliability*, *5*(3), 365–381. doi:10.1109/TDMR.2005.858334

Oh, N., Shirvani, P. P., & McCluskey, E. J. (2002). Error detection by duplicated instructions in super-scalar processors. *IEEE Transactions on Reliability*, *51*(1), 63–75. doi:10.1109/24.994913

Oma, M., Rossi, D., & Metra, C. (2003). *Novel transient fault hardened static latch.* Paper presented at the IEEE International Test Conference (TC), Charlotte, NC, United States.

Park, J. K., & Kim, J. T. (2008). A soft error mitigation technique for constrained gate-level designs. *IEICE Electronics Express*, *5*(18), 698–704. doi:10.1587/elex.5.698

Quming, Z., & Mohanram, K. (2004). *Cost-effective radiation hardening technique for combinational logic.* Paper presented at the Proceedings of the International Conference on Computer Aided Design, Piscataway, NJ, USA.

Rashid, M. W., Tan, E. J., Huang, M. C., & Albonesi, D. H. (2005). Power-efficient error tolerance in chip multiprocessors. *IEEE Micro*, *25*(6), 60–70. doi:10.1109/MM.2005.118

Ray, J., Hoe, J. C., & Falsafi, B. (2001). *Dual use of superscalar datapath for transient-fault detection and recovery.* Paper presented at the 34th ACM/IEEE International Symposium on Microarchitecture.

Reinhardt, S. K., & Mukherjee, S. S. (2000). *Transient fault detection via simultaneous multithreading.* Paper presented at the 27th International Symposium on Computer Architecture.

Reis, G. A., Chang, J., Vachharajani, N., Rangan, R., & August, D. I. (2005). *SWIFT: SoftWare Implemented Fault Tolerance.* Paper presented at the International Symposium on Code Generation and Optimization, Los Alamitos, CA, USA.

Rockett, L. R. Jr. (1992). Simulated SEU hardened scaled CMOS SRAM cell design using gated resistors. *IEEE Transactions on Nuclear Science*, *39*(5), 1532–1541. doi:10.1109/23.173239

Rotenberg, E. (1999). *AR-SMT: A microarchitectural approach to fault tolerance in microprocessors.* Paper presented at the 29th Annual International Symposium on Fault-Tolerant Computing.

Saggese, G. P., Wang, N. J., Kalbarczyk, Z. T., Patel, S. J., & Iyer, R. K. (2005). An experimental study of soft errors in microprocessors. *IEEE Micro*, *25*(6), 30–39. doi:10.1109/MM.2005.104

Sherer. (1988). *Methodology for the assessment of software risk.* PhD Thesis, Wharton School, University of Pennsylvania.

Shye, A., Blomstedt, J., Moseley, T., Janapa Reddi, V., & Connors, D. (in press). PLR: A software approach to transient fault tolerance for multi-core architectures. *IEEE Transactions on Dependable and Secure Computing*.

Smolens, J. C., Gold, B. T., Kim, J., Falsafi, B., Hoe, J. C., & Nowatzyk, A. G. (2004). *Fingerprinting: Bounding soft-error detection latency and bandwidth.* Paper presented at the Proceedings of the 11th International Conference on Architectural Support for Programming Languages and Operating Systems, ASPLOS XI, New York, United States.

Srinivasan, J., Adve, S. V., Bose, P., & Rivers, J. A. (2004). *The case for lifetime reliability-aware microprocessors.* Paper presented at the 31st Annual International Symposium on Computer Architecture.

STMicroelectronics. (2003). New chip technology from STmicroelectronics eliminates soft error threat to electronic systems. Retrieved from http://www.st.com/stonline/press/news/year2003/t1394h.htm

Telelogic. (2009). *Homepage information*. Retrieved on January 30, 2009, from http://www.telelogic.com/

Timor, A., Mendelson, A., Birk, Y. & Suri, N. (2008). Using underutilized CPU resources to enhance its reliability. *IEEE Transactions on Dependable and Secure Computing.*

Tosun, S. (2005). *Reliability-centric system design for embedded systems.* Unpublished doctoral thesis, Syracuse University, United States-New York.

Vijaykumar, T. N., Pomeranz, I., & Cheng, K. (2002). *Transient-fault recovery using simultaneous multithreading.* Paper presented at the 29th Annual International Symposium on Computer Architecture.

Walcott, K. R., Humphreys, G., & Gurumurthi, S. (2007). *Dynamic prediction of architectural vulnerability from microarchitectural state.* Paper presented at the Proceedings of the International Symposium on Computer Architecture, New York, United States.

Wang, F. (2008). *Soft error rate determination for nanometer CMOS VLSI logic*. Paper presented at the Proceedings of the Annual Southeastern Symposium on System Theory.

Wang, L., Wong, E., & Xu, D. (2007). *A threat model driven approach for security testing.* Paper presented at the Proceedings of the Third International Workshop on Software Engineering for Secure Systems, SESS' 07, Piscataway, NJ, United States.

Wikipedia. (2009). *Home page.* Retrieved on January 30, 2009, from http://en.wikipedia.org/wiki

Wood, S. K., Akehurst, D. H., Uzenkov, O., Howells, W. G. J., & McDonald-Maier, K. D. (2008). A model-driven development approach to mapping UML state diagrams to synthesizable VHDL. *IEEE Transactions on Computers*, *57*(10), 1357–1371. doi:10.1109/TC.2008.123

Xie, Y., Li, L., Kandemir, M., Vijaykrishnan, N., & Irwin, M. J. (2004). *Reliability-aware co-synthesis for embedded systems.* Paper presented at the 15th IEEE International Conference on Application-Specific Systems, Architectures and Processors.

Yacoub, S. M., & Ammar, H. H. (2002). A methodology for architecture-level reliability risk analysis. *IEEE Transactions on Software Engineering*, *28*(6), 529–547. doi:10.1109/TSE.2002.1010058

Zhang, M. (2006). *Analysis and design of soft-error tolerant circuits.* Unpublished doctoral thesis, University of Illinois at Urbana-Champaign, United States.

Zhang, M., Mitra, S., Mak, T. M., Seifert, N., Wang, N. J., & Shi, Q. (2006). Sequential element design with built-in soft error resilience. *IEEE Transactions on Very Large Scale Integration (VLSI). Systems*, *14*(12), 1368–1378.

Chapter 15
Design and Deployment of Service Oriented Applications with Non-Functional Requirements

László Gönczy
Budapest University of Technology and Economics, Hungary

Dániel Varró
Budapest University of Technology and Economics, Hungary

ABSTRACT

As the use of SOA became a mainstream in enterprise application development, there is a growing need for designing non-functional aspects of service integration at the architectural level, instead of creating only technology specific assets (configuration descriptors). This architectural design supports flexibility and early validation of requirements. This chapter presents a model-driven method supporting the automated deployment of service configurations. This deployment technique is supported by an extensible tool chain where (i) service models are captured by a service-oriented extension of UML enabling to capture non-functional requirements, and (ii) configuration descriptors for the target deployment platform are derived by automated model transformations within the VIATRA2 framework.

INTRODUCTION

Service-Oriented Architectures (SOA) provide a flexible and dynamic platform for implementing business services. Due to the rapid increase in the number of available services, more emphasis is put on their reliability, availability, security, etc. In order to meet such non-functional requirements, a service needs to be designed for reliability by making design decisions on an architectural level.

Recently, various non-functional parameters of services have been identified by various

DOI: 10.4018/978-1-60960-493-6.ch015

XML-based web service (WS) standards such as WS-Reliability, WS-ReliableMessaging, WS-Security, etc. While these properties are attached to business-level web services, they, in fact, specify the configuration and behavior of the *service infrastructure*, i.e. services that are not part a specific application, but play a dedicated role in the underlying service middleware. A focal issue in the service infrastructure is to provide reliable messaging between services, where the reliable delivery of a message can be transparently guaranteed by the underlying platform.

Non-functional properties are captured at a low implementation-level by using dedicated XML deployment descriptors. This is unfortunate since the core business functionality of a service is typically designed using high-level visual notations like the Unified Modeling Language (UML) or the Business Process Modeling Notation (BPMN). As a consequence, service configurations cannot be designed at a high architectural level.

Up to very recently, Web services messaging standards used to capture a different subset of non-functional parameters making even closely related standards incompatible with each other. For instance, the definition of timing parameters or message ordering (e.g. InvokeInOrder parameter) was different in the WS-ReliableMessaging and WS-Reliability standards, although the underlying concepts were closely related. While recently, WS-ReliableMessaging has evolved to being the de facto standard for reliable message delivery, the standard is continuously subject to minor, non-conceptual changes, which complicates the maintenance of existing configuration files. Furthermore, each middleware typically implements the standard with middleware-specific extensions. As a consequence, the portability of service configurations is also problematic.

To tackle these problems, we propose a model-driven approach to efficiently design and deploy standards-compliant service configurations with non-functional parameters (with special focus on reliable messaging). First, we expect the service developer to create a structural diagram of the service configuration and extend it with constraints on the communication using a high-level, visual modeling notation like UML. Such constraints (implemented as contracts between communicating parties) may capture requirements on the security and reliability of the communication expressed using standard platforms like WS-Security [WS-a] and WS-Reliability [WS-b] issued by OASIS.

From such engineering models, we automatically generate service descriptors (in Web Service Description Language, WSDL), and configuration descriptors for standard platforms like Apache Axis, including the definition of non-functional requirements, and server-side deployment artifacts. These artifacts have to be extended with the Java source code of service implementations and client-side stubs of services to allow the service requester to seamlessly integrate the server-side functionality without any a priori knowledge on the service communication (including acknowledgements, encoding, etc).

Hereby, we present a model-driven method supporting the automated deployment of service configurations. This deployment technique is supported by an extensible tool chain where (i) service models are captured by a service-oriented extension of UML enabling to capture non-functional requirements, (ii) configuration descriptors for the target deployment platform are derived by automated model transformations within the VIATRA2 framework.

This chapter is structured as follows: we first present structural modeling of services on a case study with non-functional requirements. Then we present a non-functional extension in UML for modeling services which show conceptual resemblance to Service Level Agreements (SLAs) based upon existing reliability and security standards of Web service messaging. Then we present an overview of our automated model-based deployment technique including a discussion of target deployment artifacts as well as relevant metamodels and the transformation chain. Some technical details of the deployment transformations are revealed. Finally, we discuss related work and conclude our paper.

MODELING OF SERVICE CONFIGURATIONS

In order to raise the level of abstraction for service engineers when designing the configuration of the service infrastructure, we rely on high-level UML models conforming to the UML4SOA profile, which is a UML extension for modeling service-oriented applications. The UML4SOA profile (Koch et al., 2007) was developed in the SENSORIA project to capture the abstract structural, behavioral and non-functional aspects of service-oriented applications.

Motivating Example

As a running example, we use the Financial Case Study of the SENSORIA project provided by an industrial partner and described in Alessandrini and Dost (2007) in details. The Credit request scenario defines an online application which enables loan advice to bank customers. This application needs an *Authentication service* for user authentication, a *Customer transaction service* for credit requesting, an external *Balance validation service* to evaluate requests and an *Employee transaction* service to provide request review functionality. The business logic is implemented in a process orchestration language (e.g., Business Process Execution Language, BPEL).

Main steps of the credit request are the following: first the customer uploads the request, for which she must *authenticate* herself and *upload information*, containing information about guarantees and balances. Then the bank employee reviews the request, and an internal *verification of the offer* is performed before sending it to the customer and *requests for additional data* in case of high-risk credit requests. Finally, the customer accepts the offer or uploads additional data. During process execution, the request can be cancelled, which initiates compensation of successfully executed steps.

While the dynamic behavior of the loan application can be also modeled in UML4SOA Profile, here we only use the static structural diagrams and non-functional parameters of service components. On an abstract level, we define *Services* are implemented as *Components*. Each separate functionality is bound to a port, which either uses or implements an *Interface*.

The first step is to design a composite service configuration which is described by a composite structural diagram specifying components, ports and relations. Figure 1 shows the components of the Finance Case Study. As specified in the high level system description, the application consists of five components: the Credit Request Process (which will be implemented in a standard workflow language, such as BPEL), the Authentication Service (which wraps background user authentication mechanisms), the Employee Transaction System (which offers an interface to applications used by employees of credit reviewer role); the Balance Validation Service (which performs basic credit request validation), and finally, the interface for the user (the portal front-end), called Customer Transaction Service.

Non-Functional Requirements of the Case Study

Non-functional requirements of the case study include the following:

- **All services** should be available only via secure connections. This means digital signatures for the entire message and encryption of the message body. Messages sent to this service should be acknowledged.
- **Customer Transaction Service** should provide an answer to the customer about

Figure 1. Model of the financial case study

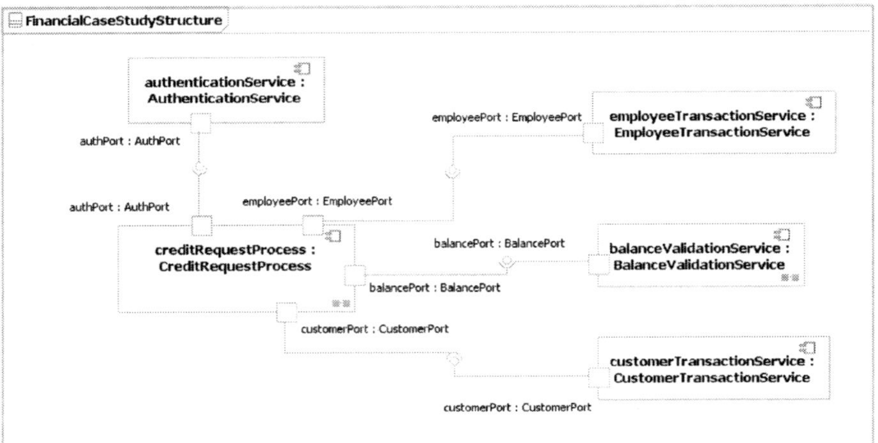

the receipt of his request soon, therefore its maximum response time should be no longer than 8 seconds.

- **Balance Validation Service** should send an acknowledgement of all incoming request. As this is a resource-intensive task, multiple instances of the same request should be identified and filtered out. Since the complete balance validation may require human interaction as well (depending on the business rules of the bank), a quick answer to all validation requests cannot be expected. However, some feedback about the initiation of the validation process should be sent back soon, with an average of 5 seconds and maximum value of 8 seconds. The throughput of this service is also of outmost importance, resulting in a requirement of 6 user requests per second. On the other hand, maximum throughput of the service is also bound due to the bank policies in 20 requests per second.
- **Authentication Service** is used by many applications, therefore its throughput can be a bottleneck in the system. To support a continuous service, a minimum throughput of 100.000 requests/hour is required. This throughput is used by multiple the applications relying on the authentication service, e.g., Credit Request Process.
- **Credit Request Process** is depending on the above services. Most of its requirements are derived from requirements of the invoked services (e.g., where and what to encrypt), but some are also implied by the customer portal interface. Such a requirement is the performance of this process and the non-repudiation of requests.

Modeling Non-Functional Parameters for SOA

In order to address non-functional requirements related to the Financial Case study, we propose non-functional extensions for modeling service oriented systems. Here we specialize the general-purpose UML4SOA profile in order to capture service configurations with reliable messaging and security requirements. After overviewing related standards in the domain of Web services, a contract-oriented approach will be elaborated which conceptually follows Service Level Agreements (SLAs) frequently used in industry.

Reliable Messaging Standards for Web Services

There are various industrial standards reflecting the emerging need for reliable Web services middleware from which we focus on reliable messaging standards in this paper. However, our approach can be adapted to support the generation of configurations of other non-functional Web services standards, such as WS-Security.

Currently, the main SOA standard in the field of reliable messaging is WS-ReliableMessaging having multiple reference implementations publicly available. This is a joint version of two previously standards: Web Service Reliable Messaging Protocol (WS-ReliableMessaging) specification of IBM, BEA, Microsoft and TIBCO, and WS-Reliability of OASIS standard. The main importance of reliable messaging standards lies in the fact that they are expected to replace the current mainstream messaging middleware (such as Message Queuing servers or JMS) which are now used together with SOAP to provide a reliable asynchronous communication service.

Reliable messaging in the fields traditional distributed systems is closely related to the guaranteed semantics of message delivery. Usual delivery classes are the following:

- *At least once delivery*. In the case of normal operation, each message is transferred at least once, with the possibility of sending multiple instances of the same message. This can only be allowed in systems where this does not have an undesired side-effect.
- *At most once delivery* guarantees that no message will be sent multiple times to the receiver, but their successful transmission is not ensured.
- *Exactly once delivery* is the strongest delivery semantics, guaranteeing both the successful message delivery (usually acknowledgements are required for each message) and the filtering of duplicate messages.

Other delivery semantics, such as "x out of y" (meaning that at least x from every y instances of the message have to be transferred) exist in the literature. For practical reasons, the maximum number of retransmission is usually also bounded by an integer.

The message delivery semantics is defined by service configurations, thus reliable messaging can be transparent to actual, business-level services. On the implementation-level, the middleware catches the outgoing and incoming SOAP messages of web services and modifies them by inserting/removing reliability specific tags in the header of the SOAP envelope.

Unfortunately, all these standards capture similar reliability attributes on a very low level of abstraction. For this purpose, we introduce a high-level modeling layer for representing and designing service configurations from which the low-level XML deployment descriptors will be generated automatically.

The following attributes are required for the configuration of reliable messaging (besides *messagingSemantics*, which selects the messaging mode as described earlier:

- *inactivityTimeout*: type: integer (seconds), after this period of time if no acknowledgment message has arrived, the connection is closed;
- *exponentialBackoff*: type: boolean, if it is set to true, time amounts between retransmissions are following an exponential distribution;
- *acknowledgementInterval*: type: integer (seconds), amount of time elapsed before sending acknowledgement message;
- *retransmissionInterval*: type: integer (seconds), after this time a request is resent by client if no acknowledgement arrived.

Security Standards

The notion of **security** covers properties related to confidentiality (no unauthorized subject can access the content of message), integrity (message content cannot be altered), non-repudability (refers to accountability of the communicating parties) and privacy (the identity and personal data of a client is not revealed to non-authorized bodies). Concepts such as authentication (checking the identity of a client) and authorization (checking whether a client might invoke a certain operation) are also of concern here.

In service-oriented systems, security should be guaranteed between service endpoints, independently from network level properties. This can be achieved using secure web services middleware. Message security is based on digital signatures and encryption of messages; here we distinguish the message header and body, however, further (application-specific) separation of message parts is also possible

The following security parameters are used as a basis for configuration generation for secure communication middleware:

- *encryptBody*, *encryptHeader*, *signBody*, *signHeader* describe whether a security method is applied on (parts of) messages between client and service, respectively,
- *signAlgorithm* and *encryptionAlgorithm* determine the security algorithms,
- *authTokenType* determines the type of the security token (e.g. username or binary),
- *useTimestamp* allows the user to specify timestamps for messages

Note that the executable set of security configurations is restricted in current middleware to certain combinations of the above parameters, therefore we will propose default values in the profile which conform to the actual deployment possibilities.

Metamodel of Non-Functional Extensions

Here, we focus on non-functional aspects and their connection to structural elements, which are most relevant for the current paper. These non-functional aspects were inspired by standard UML extensions (such as OMG, 2006). Figure2. shows the non-functional extensions and their connections to the core structural elements (in blue).

Since in real service configurations, service properties can vary for different classes of clients, we follow a contract-based approach, where non-functional properties of services are defined between two *Participant* components, namely, the service provider and the service requester. These

Figure 2. Metamodel of non-functional properties of services

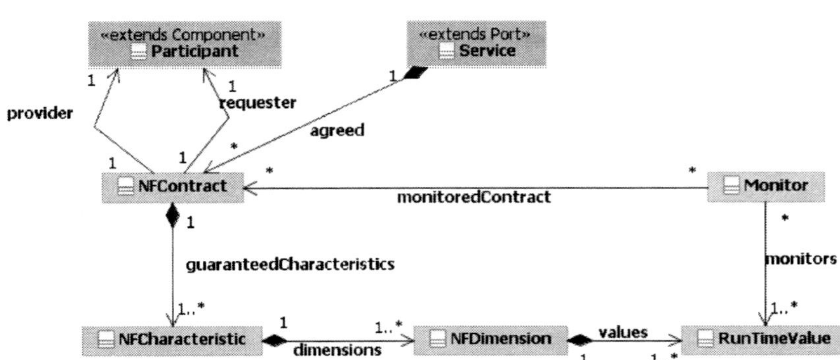

contracts are modeled by *NFContracts*. Different non-functional aspects (performance, security, etc.) are modeled in corresponding *NFCharacteristics* which group different properties in *NFDimensions* (where a *RunTimeValue* is associated to each dimension). The reason for creating separate classes for these instead of storing in properties is to correlate real SLAs where most parameters are typically bound to a range of allowed values. Moreover, concepts like average values, deviation, etc. need to be modeled in a uniform way.

During negotiation process (which is out of scope for the current paper), participants create an *agreed* contract of the *provider* and *requester*. Finally, properties of services need to be monitored runtime (modeled as *Monitor*) either by the participating parties or by involving a separate entity. A metamodel defining the concepts above is provided in Figure2.

As reliable messaging Platform Independent Model, we use the metamodel of reliable messaging in service configurations was created in Gönczy et al. (2006c) to incorporate reliable messaging attributes of these various standards.

UML Modeling of Non-Functional Properties

These extensions defined in Sec. 3.4 are used in UML modeling as defined in Table 1.

Non-Functional Properties of the Case Study

This chapter discusses how to create a model which captures the non-functional requirements of our case study for a service oriented system. Figure 3. shows the structure of an SLA template, bound to the connection between Credit Request Process and Balance Validation Service components. As derived from non-functional requirements, there will be several aspects which are described in the SLA: performance, security and reliability characteristics apply to this service connection. Here we use the previously designed non-functional extension to handle these aspects in a uniform way.

Note that here we are at the class level, which means that there could be multiple contracts for such a connection (and there could also exist multiple connections among multiple Credit Request Process and Balance Validation Service instances). The number of actual contracts is highly domain-dependent. In this case, as the functionality of the case study is likely to be included in a corporate ecosystem, most probably there will be only one instance of such a contract; however, for services which are offered to multiple clients or different client classes (e.g. normal clients and privileged clients) there can be different contract classes as well. Also in our example, the balance validation service could be invoked from other orchestrated services (e.g. consider a

Table 1. Non-functional extensions for UML4SOA

Stereotype name	Metaclass	Description	Used in
NFContract	Class	Represents a non-functional contract between a service provider and a service requester.	Class/Component diagram
NFCharacteristic	Class	Represents a non-functional aspect such as performance, security, reliable messaging, etc.	Class diagram
NFDimension	Class	Groups non-functional properties within a non-functional aspect (characteristics)	Class diagram
RunTimeValue	Attribute	An actual non-functional property.	Class diagram
Monitor	Class	An actual non-functional property	Class/Component diagram

Figure 3. Model of a service contract

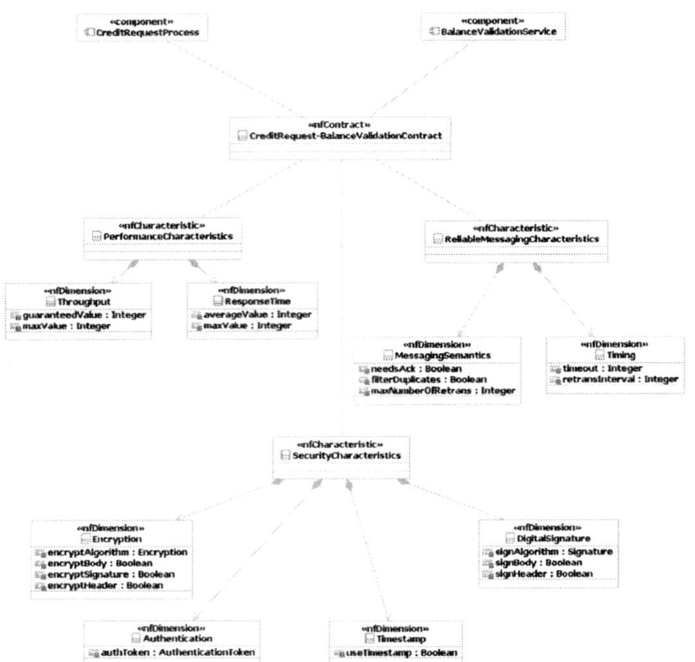

Client Evaluation Process) which result in multiple *NFContract* classes, one per each port-port connection, containing even different *NFCharacteristics*. Instances of stereotyped elements (e.g. Messaging Semantics stereotyped with <<*nfDimension*>>) are later used by model transformations for automated deployment and analysis.

In the case study model, the contact on the connection between *Credit Request Process* and *Balance Validation* service contains performance, security and reliability aspects. *Performance Characteristics* include throughput and response time, concrete values of these will be filled at the instance level (see Figure4.). *Security Characteristics* consist of the dimension of *Encryption* (specifying which part of the message should be encrypted and what kind of encryption should be used), *Authentication* (specifying the authentication token), *Timestamp* (specifying whether a timestamp is used to protect against message replay attacks) and *DigitalSignature* (describing which parts of the messages should be signed by what algorithm). *Reliable Messaging Characteristics* include two major dimensions: *MessagingSemantics* (determining the operation mode by acknowledgement creation, duplicates filtering and the maximum number of retransmission for message instances) and Timing (defining timeout for receiving acknowledgement messages and retransmission interval for message re-sending.).

In real life, not every combination of such SLAs is viable. In some technologies, for instance, if a service communicates over a secure channel, it cannot be accessed without protection. There can be some get-arounds for such problems, but we claim that such constraints usually express domain-specific requirements or best practices, therefore they should be enforced at the model level, handled by Object Constraint Language or ontology-based techniques (Gönczy et al., 2006a). SLA parameters also often contradict themselves, for instance, an engineer usually has to find a trade-off between performance and reliability. We

Figure 4. Model of a concrete service configuration

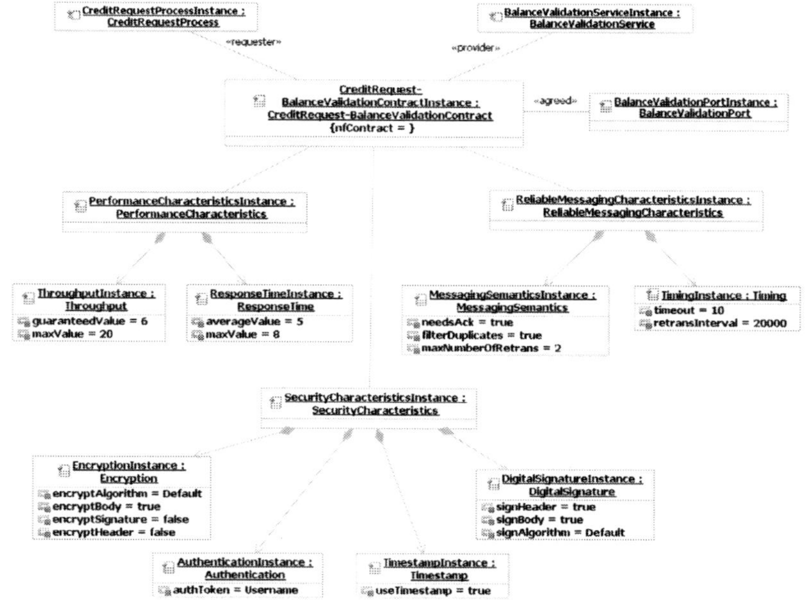

briefly present an analysis technique working on model instances in Sec.4.4.

Figure 4 shows an instance of the contract as a UML object diagram. This corresponds to a filled SLA template (where the actual template also contains additional information like concrete URLs, etc.).

The first set of these parameters directly come from the textual specification of the case study:

- **guaranteed** and **maximum** value of **Throughput**
- **average** and **maximum** values of **Response time**
- **needsAck** attribute of reliable messaging semantics
- All attributes of encryption and digital signature except the algorithm definition (**encrpytBody, encryptHeader, encrypt-Signature, signBody, signHeader**).

Another set of parameters are design decisions:

- Reliable messaging semantics is chosen to be "Exactly once", which correspond to set the middleware to **filter Duplicates**.
- **Timeout** of messaging is set to 10 seconds.
- Authentication will be based on tokens representing the user name (**authToken**).
- A **Timestamp** will be used for each message.

Finally, some parameters are set to default values.

- Lost messages will be sent again after 20000 ms (**retransInterval**).
- If a message is lost, the middle-ware will try once again to send it (**maxNumberOfRetrans**).
- **encryptAlgorithm** and **signAlgorithm** will be set to server default.

Some of these parameters are derived directly from the case study description, such as the us-age of digital signature or response time, while others (e.g., concrete signature algorithm or retransmission interval of the reliable messaging middleware).

DEPLOYMENT OF SERVICE CONFIGURATIONS

Service configuration models serve as the input for automated deployment to standards-compliant SOA platforms with support for reliable messaging carried out by model transformations. First, the general concepts of our approach is presented for by generating XML-based deployment descriptors for the business-level services themselves. Then reliable messaging parameters are set to the Apache Axis2 platform, extended with the Sandesha module also including security descriptors for the Apache Axis2 Rampart module. Our technique also helps the developer by generating client stubs and project structure for deployment of services with non-functional requirements. The current section provides only a high-level overview on main deployment artifacts, the transformation workflow, and metamodels developed. Later we give more insights into some technical details.

Deployment Artifacts

Automated deployment transformations yield the following artifacts as result:

- *Client stubs in Java* which can be deployed to any JVM (Apache specific libraries must be available). These stubs work similar to proxies generated by any well-known Web service development toolkit (or using the well-known wsdl2java tool) with the extension that security and reliable communication parameters are also handled. The application developer might use the service as defined previously in the SLA (contract on non-functional parameters) in the same way as a local Java class. Note that (following the principles of WS-Security standard) we assume that security tokens have been exchanged prior to the actual communication between service and client.
- *WSDL files of services*. These standard descriptors define interface of the services with ports, operations, messages and may also contain concrete binding information.
- Policy descriptors for Apache Axis2 server with Rampart and Sandesha modules. These descriptors can be attached to service implementations to specify non-functional requirements. Server-side project structure of the implementation. This contains Java skeletons for the service implementations, and a folder structure for the configuration files required by the Axis2.
- The service skeletons have to be extended with the implementation of business functions.

Model transformations for model-driven analysis and deployment were implemented by following a model driven approach with separated phases for model mappings and the generation of the target elements, such as XML files. Concrete deployment artifacts are created from the XML files by using Java.

Transformation Workflow

This section briefly overviews the workflow of model deployment transformations illustrated in Figure 5. The input of the transformation chain is a UML model captured using the UML4SOA Profile, containing component and object diagrams describing the services and their connections and contracts on non-functional requirements, namely, reliable message communication and security. Automated deployment is carried out in a model-driven way by first constructing platform-specific models (and metamodels) of the target deployment platforms followed by subsequent code generation steps to derive the final XML configuration files.

The actual model transformations can be realized through several steps. In a typical workflow, the following models are constructed by the chain of model transformations.

- **Platform Independent Models (PIM)**: The input of the chain is a standard UML2 model developed using EMF and serialized as XMI, which uses the UML4SOA Profile. In our actual toolchain, IBM Rational Software Architect was used as a UML modeling tool.
- **Platform Specific Models (PSM)**: After the extraction of relevant model parts, internal service models are generated within the model transformation tool (describing reliable messaging setup, security, etc.). These are then processed in order to create descriptor models which are conform to industrial standards. These can be considered as PIM2PSM mappings in the Model Driven Architecture terminology.
- **Target XML files**: These descriptor models are the basis of XML file generation. These files are directly usable as configuration descriptors on standard platforms. Besides the server configuration XML, WSDL files of the services are also created. These are PSM2CODE transformations.
- **Glue code for deployment**: For the Apache Axis platform, deployable server-side projects are also created by Java applications. These have to be extended with the implementation (source files) of the services.

Figure 5. Transformation workflow

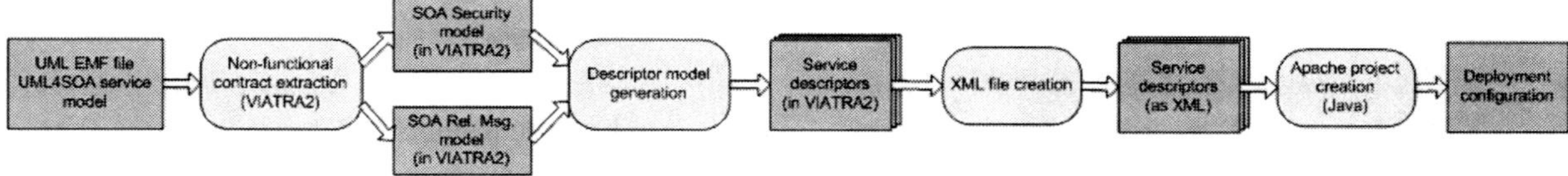

OVERVIEW OF METAMODELS

For the designated transformation chain of the deployment process, the following metamodels have been developed:

- **UML metamodel**. We used the standard EMF-based UML 2.0 metamodel as part of the Eclipse UML2 project. All of our input models correspond to the UML4SOA profile developed within the SENSORIA project.
- **SOA metamodel**. As an internal representation of service configurations, we used the SOA metamodel of Baresi et al. (2006) extended with non-functional parameters, which served as a platform-independent service model.
- **WSDL metamodel**. The WSDL metamodel is an abstraction of service interface descriptions specified in WSDL ([W3C]).
- **Security metamodel**. This metamodel describes concepts of message level security, such as encoding of the header and body of a message, type of security tokens, signature of a message part, timestamp, etc.
- **Reliable messaging metamodel**. Reliable message communication concepts and parameters are defined here (at a middleware-independent level). These include messaging semantics (at-least-once, exactly-once, etc.), timeout, ordering of messages in a sequence, etc.
- **RAMP metamodel**. The RAMP metamodel contains platform (i.e., IBM RAMP)

Figure 6. Relationship among models

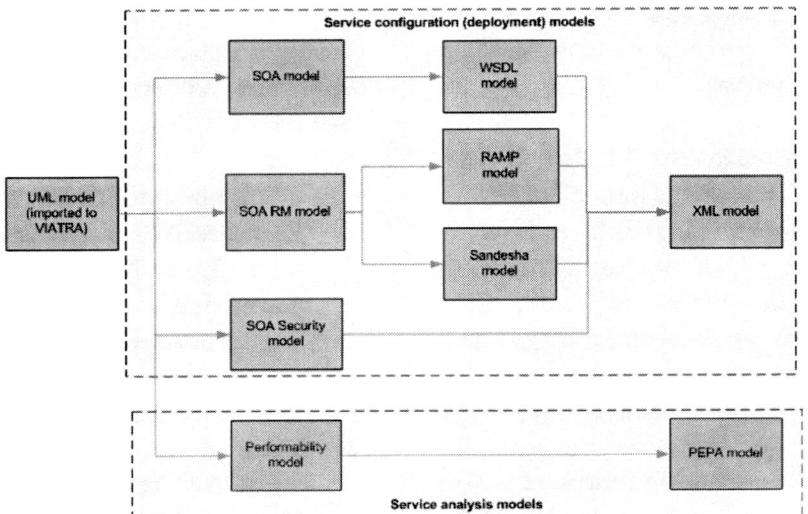

specific concepts for service configurations with reliable messaging.

- **Sandesha metamodel**. This metamodel describes the Apache-specific definition of message level security, such as encoding, use of timestamps, digital signature, etc.
- **XML metamodel**. Since our outputs are XML documents, we constructed a general XML metamodel, and the respective target metamodels were derived as a refinement.

Figure 6 shows the relations between instances of these modeling languages (depicted as boxes). Transformations (depicted as arrows) are steps which map instances of a source metamodel to elements which correspond to the target metamodel (e.g., from UML to internal SOA representation).

The main advantages of our design decisions can be summarized as follows:

- We followed a modular approach with a relatively large number of metamodels, each of which is of relatively low complexity. By having modular metamodels (i) the information related to implementation can be maintained separately and (ii) transformation development is easier as mappings are more straightforward. Moreover, the core metamodel can also be used by other transformations (e.g., for the purpose of correctness or non-functional analysis of service models)
- XML metamodel is intentionally designed to be very general. Metamodels of concrete XML languages contain elements instantiate generic XML elements (i.e. XML elements and attributes), therefore we have a reusable model-to-text transformation to print arbitrary XML documents.
- Moreover, for each model transformation, we defined a *reference metamodel* in order to support persistent traceability between the corresponding source and target languages. A reference model (i.e. an instance of a reference metamodel) captures concrete traces between a specific source model and its target equivalent.
- All model transformations were specified with a high-level yet mathematically precise formal notation using a combination of graph transformation rules (Rozenberg, 1997) and abstract state machines (Börger

and Stark, 2003) as provided by the VIATRA model transformation framework (Varró and Balogh, 2007). Some transformation details will be revealed in Sec. 5.

Non-Functional Analysis of Services

Unfortunately, service configurations are typically set up in a rather ad hoc way. While non-functional requirements are precisely captured in service-level agreements, there is no guarantee that the service configurations will actually meet these requirements. One of the reasons for this is that ``design for reliability'' is a complex task as performance and reliability requirements are contradicting: an inappropriate setup of reliability attributes may cause significant decrease in performance. As a consequence, *performability analysis* is necessitated to assess the cost of using fault-tolerant techniques in terms of performance.

From such service configuration models, automated model transformations generate formal process models for the PEPA framework (Performance Evaluation Process Algebra, (Gilmore and Tribastone, 2006)) to provide an early performability evaluation and prediction for service configurations with reliable messaging.

Then model transformations assemble the formal performability model from these elementary building blocks based upon the actual service configuration model (Performability model in Figure 6). The textual format of the model solver (PEPA tool) is then generated by a separate model-to-text transformation.

Questions which can then be evaluated by using the analysis features of the PEPA tool are related to the utilization of status of the communicating parties ("What percentage of time is spent waiting for the answer of the request?").

Note that here we do not deal with the performance analysis of services themselves, instead, we concentrate on helping the development of service configurations. Answering such questions by evaluating typical service configurations helps to find a trade-off between performance (e.g., response time) and dependability (e.g, accountability) requirements. A detailed discussion of this approach is out of scope for the current paper and can be found in Gönczy et al. (2008a).

IMPLEMENTATION OF MODEL TRANSFORMATIONS

This section provides insights into the actual deployment artifacts and model transformations used within our model-driven deployment framework. For the actual model transformations we used the VIATRA2 framework. VIATRA2 (n.d.) is a modular, open source model transformation framework built on Eclipse, which supports the efficient design of model transformations. Transformations are defined by graph transformation rules (i.e., declarative description of model patterns) and Abstract State Machines, which provide an intuitive yet precise way of capturing complex transformations.

High Level Overview of Mappings

Figure 7 shows an overview of the mapping from UML models with non-functional extensions to standards-compliant XML descriptors as used for the Apache platform. The left column shows the UML class level (e.g. that there is a connection between *NFContract* and *NFCharacteristics*, as shown in the metamodel on Figure 2). The second column shows instances of these classes (in a general representation format, independent from the case study and the concrete non-functional aspect). The "Trace model" specifies connections between models of different abstraction level, i.e., the reference metamodel to be discussed in Sec. 5.3. The XML model represents XML elements in an abstract format. Although concrete XML fragments are not shown on Figure 7, these are generated by a syntactical transformation from the XML model.

Figure 7. Mapping from UML to non-functional SOA standards

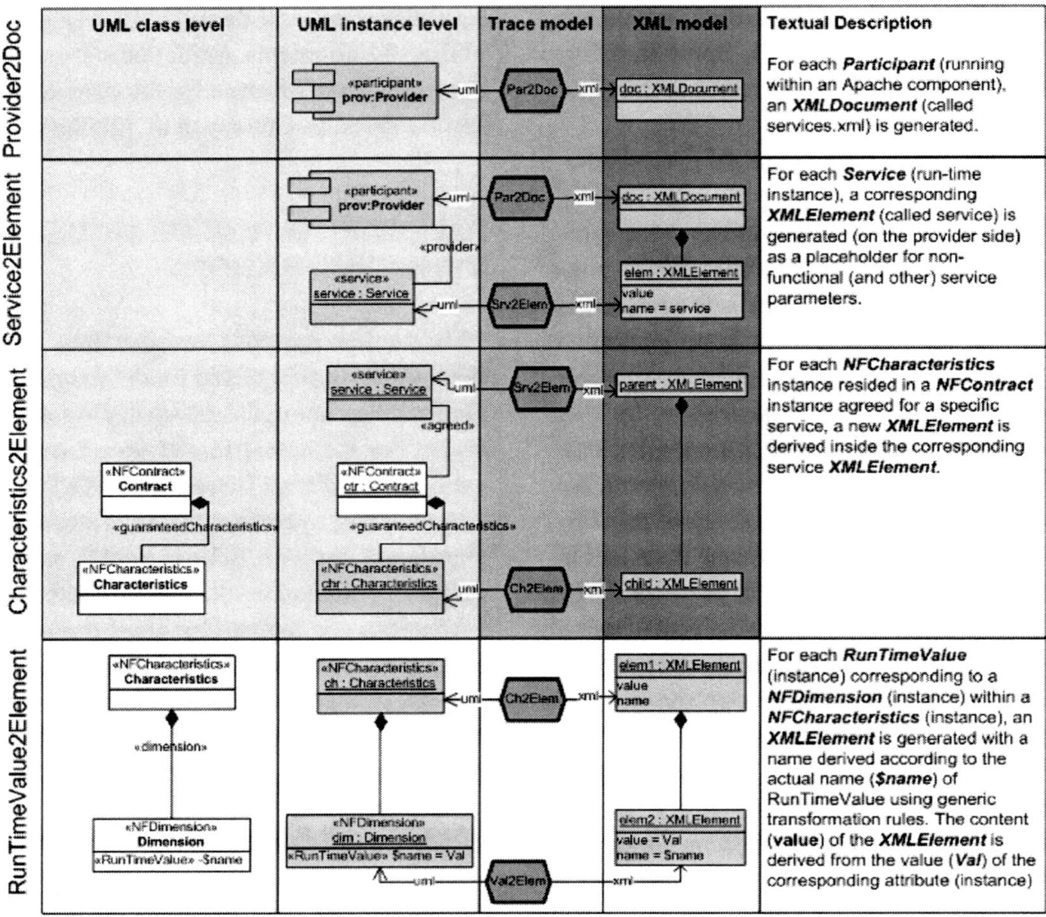

- For each «Participant» (running within an Apache component), an «XMLDocument» (called services.xml) is generated.
- For each «NFCharacteristics» instance resided in a «NFContract» instance related to a (service provider) «Participant», an «XMLElement» is derived with corresponding name.
- For each «RunTimeValue»(instance) corresponding to a «NFDimension» (instance) within a «NFCharacteristics» (instance), an «XMLElement» is generated with a name derived according to the actual name («$name») of «RunTimeValue» using generic transformation rules. The content (value) of the «XMLElement» is derived from the value («Val») of the corresponding attribute (instance).

This transformation scheme is uniformly applicable to different «NFCharacteristics» (with minor adjustments to handle names of elements in case of «$name»). Note that Figure 7 provides an end-to-end specification of the transformation. In the actual VIATRA2 implementation, multiple trace models are used to bridge all intermediate transformation steps (from UML models to PIM models, from PIM models to PSM models, or from PSM models to XML models).

Realization of Metamodels in VIATRA

Designing metamodels. In the VIATRA framework, metamodels and models are described as directed graphs using the VIATRA Textual Modeling Language (abbreviated as VTML). Alternatively, metamodels captured in common metamodeling frameworks (like EMF) can also be imported to VIATRA. The following code fragment shows a part of the Sandesha metamodel.

```
entity(Sandesha) {
     entity(SandeshaSpecification);
     subtypeOf(SandeshaSpecification,
RelMsgSpecification);
     relation(acknowledgementInterva
l, SandeshaSpecification, datatypes.
Integer);
     relation(retransmissionInterv
al, SandeshaSpecification, datatypes.
Integer);
subtypeOf(SandeshaSpecification.re-
transmissionInterval, RelMsgSpecifi-
cation.timeout);
relation(maximumRetransmissionCou
nt, SandeshaSpecification, datatypes.
Integer);
subtypeOf(SandeshaSpecification.maxi-
mumRetransmissionCount,
RelMsgSpecification.maxNumberOfRe-
trans);
relation(exponentialBackoff, Sande-
shaSpecification, datatypes.Boolean);
relation(inactivityTimeout, Sandesha-
Specification, datatypes.Integer);
relation(sequenceRemovalTimeout, San-
deshaSpecification, datatypes.Inte-
ger);
relation(invokeInOrder, Sandesha-
Specification, datatypes.Boolean);
}
```

Metamodel of Sandesha

Here Sandesha serves as top-level class in the generalization hierarchy (defined as a VIATRA entity). Then entity SandeshaSpecification represents a specification derived as a subtype of RelMsgSpecification using the subtypeOf (generalization) construct. As shown by the example of retransmission interval, parameters of a Sandesha specification are also derived from the general reliable messaging specification. The line relation(invokeInOrder, SandeshaSpecification, Boolean) defines a new attribute to class SandeshaSpec of type Boolean. Internally, this is represented as a relation (or graph edge) leading from entity (node) SandeshaSpec to (built-in) entity Boolean, which will store whether the ordering of the messages will be preserved.

Note that this latter attribute is specific to the WS-Reliability standard, so the transformation generating the Platform Specific Model (the Sandesha model) should handle this parameter either by adding a default value of by deriving it from other requirements.

Parts of this metamodel are illustrated on Figure 8 (we neglected some of the subtypeOf relations to keep the diagram simple).

Reference metamodel. A general purpose reference metamodel was also designed to store mappings between arbitrary source and target modeling languages as models. When executing a model transformation, a reference model is built up in addition to generating the target model.

```
General reference metamodel
entity(ReferenceMetamodel) {
     entity(SourceElement);
     entity(TargetElement);
     entity(RefModelElement);
     relation(from, RefElement, Sour-
ceElement);
     relation(to, RefElement, Targe-
tElement);
}
```

Figure 8. Metamodel of Sandesha

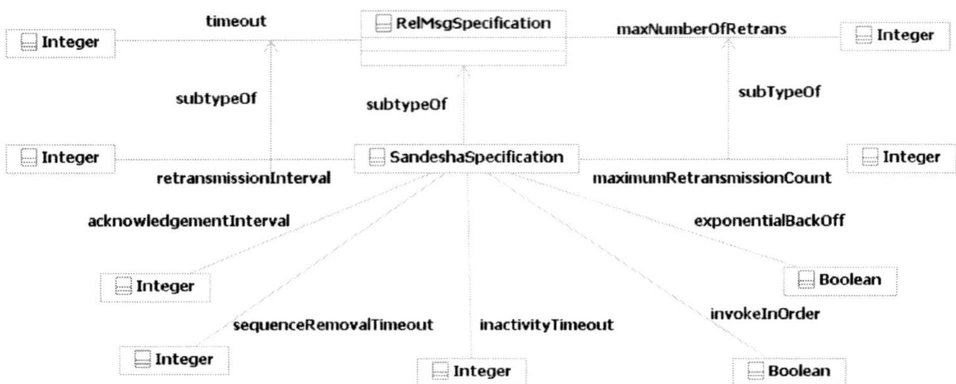

The above textual VIATRA2 code correspond to entites and relations as shown in Figure 9.

Realization of Model Transformations

Model transformations are also captured in a textual way by using a combination of (i) graph patterns for querying models, (ii) graph transformation rules for elementary model manipulations, and (iii) abstract state machines for assembling complex transformations from simple rules.

Graph patterns. Graph patterns define structural constraints and conditions on models. They are the atomic units of transformations. In the following example, we define the *timeoutPattern* pattern which specifies when a UML Property is interpreted as an *inactivityTimeout* attribute. The pattern is seeking for a Class (*NFTiming*) stereotyped as <<NFDimension>>, which has a Property (*TO*) called *inactivityTimeout.* Then it searches for an instance specification of this class *NFTimingInst* (i.e. a dimension within a concrete contract), and takes the value (*TOValue*) of the corresponding slot (*TOValue*), which will be interpreted as a numeric parameter.

```
Graph pattern example.
pattern timeoutPattern(NFTimingInst,
TOInst, TOValue) = {
 // Find a class with stereotype
<<NFDimension>>
     uml2.Class(NFTiming);
     uml2.Element.
appliedStereotype(S1, NFTiming,
NFDimStereotype);
     uml2.Stereotype(NFDimStereotype)
;
     uml2.NamedElement.
name(S1,NFDimStereotype, NM1);
```

Figure 9. Concepts of a reference metamodel

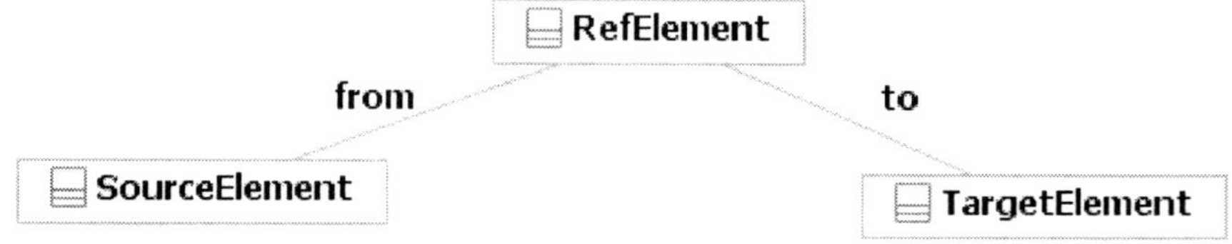

```
 uml2.String(NM1);
 check(value(NM1) == "NFDimension");
     // Seek for a property called
inactivityTimeout
     uml2.Element.ownedElement(OE1,
NFTiming, TO);
     uml2.Property(TO);
     check(name(TO)=="inactivityTime
out");
// Find an instance of this class
 uml2.InstanceSpecification(NFTiming
Inst);
 uml2.InstanceSpecification.
classifier(CF1, NFTimingInst, NFTim-
ing);
     uml2.Slot(TOInst);
     uml2.Slot.
definingFeature(DF1,TOInst, TO);
     uml2.Slot.value (DV, TO, TOVal-
ue);
     uml2.String(TOValue);
}
```

Figure 10 shows the above graph pattern as an object diagram. Nodes of the graphs are objects while (typed) relations are represented as associations.

Graph transformation rules. Basic model manipulations can be specified in a declarative style using graph transformation rules. Graph transformation provides a rule and pattern-based paradigm for the precise manipulation of graph models. Traditionally, a graph transformation rules consist of a left-hand side (LHS) graph and a right-hand side (RHS) graph. The application of a GT rule on a given instance model replaces a match of its left-hand side (LHS) pattern with an image of its right-hand side (RHS) pattern.

In a graph transformation rule in VIATRA, the precondition corresponds to the LHS graph using an arbitrary graph pattern, while the postcondition pattern generalizes the RHS graph. Additional (imperative) actions can be triggered after rule execution using abstract state machine rules.

A sample graph transformation rule is described below, which generates a new *timeout* value (*RMValue*) for an existing *RelMsgSpec* (passed as input) in the intermediate platform-independent SOA model for each UML Property called *inactivityTimeout* (which was specified previously by pattern *timeoutPattern*). Furthermore, a corresponding reference structure (*Ref(R)*) is also generated to interconnect the timeout property (*TO*) with the newly generated *RMValue.*

```
Graph transformation rule: UML2SOARM.
gtrule createTimeout(in TimingInst,
out TOInst, in RMSpec, in UML2SOA) =
{
          // Left Hand Side
```

Figure 10. Graph pattern

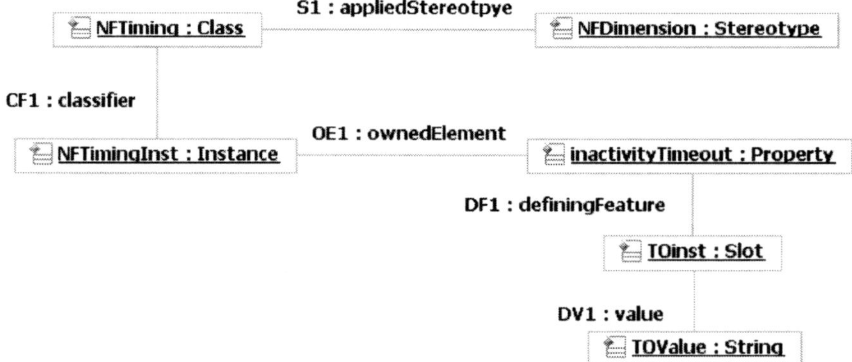

```
          precondition find
timeoutPattern(TimingInst, TOInst,
TOValue);
          // Right Hand Side
          postcondition pattern
rhs(TimingInst, TOInst, RMValue, RM-
Spec) = {
           // RMSpec is obtained as
input parameter, thus not created
           RM.RelMsgSpec(RMSpec);
        // Creating target model ele-
ments
           RM.RelMsgSpec.timeout (T,
RMSpec, RMValue);
           datatypes.
Integer(RMValue);
           // Creating references
           Ref(R) in UML2SOA;
           Ref.from(R1, R, TOInst);
           Ref.to(R2, R, RMValue);
}
action {
          // Initializing RMValue
          setValue(RMValue,
toInteger(value(TOValue)));
          }
}
```

This transformation rule is illustrated by Figure 11. Note that entire Left Hand Side is covered by the previously discussed **timeoutPattern.** Newly created elements (i.e., the Right Hand Side) are colored and tagged as <<new>>. There is one part of this rule which is VIATRA-specific: the action which now copies the value of TOValue String to RMValue integer (assuming that this does not break datatype constraints, i.e., such a conversion can be performed).

In a subsequent step, this platform-independent *RelMsgSpec* element is refined to *Sandesha-Specification* as illustrated by the following transformation rule. In this step, the *timeout* parameter of the *RelMsgSpec* element is transformed to a *retransmissionInterval* attribute. Furthermore, the transformation initializes the *inactivityTimeout* parameter with appropriate default values. As an alternate solution, the developer could be prompted to specify the exact values for such middleware specific attributes. Our transformations check if such a value is specified by the configuration engineer, and takes default values only when no such a value is found.

```
Graph transformation rule: SOARM2San-
desha.
gtrule timeout2retransmissionInterva
l(out TO, out RetInt, in RMSpec, in
UML2SOA) = {
          // Left Hand Side
          precondition pattern lhs
(RMSpec, SandSpec, RMValue) = {
           // RelMsgSpec is already
transformed
           RM.RelMsgSpec(RMSpec);
```

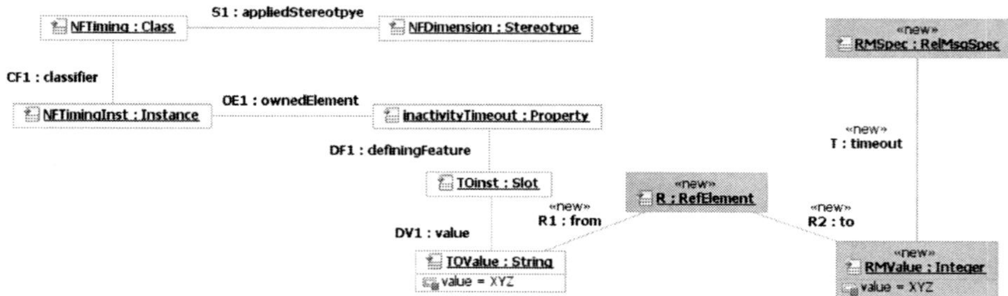

Figure 11. Illustration of a graph transformation rule

```
           Sandesha.SandeshaSpecific
ation(SandSpec);
           Ref(Spec2Spec);
           Ref.
from(R1,Spec2Spec,RMSpec);
           Ref.
to(R2,Spec2Spec,SandSpec);
           RM.RelMsgSpec.
timeout(T,RMSpec,TOValue);
           datatypes.
Integer(RMValue);
  }
          // Right Hand Side
          postcondition pattern
rhs(SandSpec, SandValue, SOA2Sande-
sha) = {
           // SandSpec is obtained as
input parameter from LHS
           Sandesha.SandeshaSpecifica
tion(SandSpec);
           // retransmissionInterval
attribute is derived
           Sandesha.SandeshaSpecifi-
cation.retransmissionInterval(IV1,San
dSpec,SandValue);
           datatypes.
Integer(SandValue);
}
action {
          // Initializing RMValue
          setValue(SandValue,
toInteger(value(RMValue)));
          }
}
```

Assembling complex transformations. Finally, complex transformations are assembled by abstract state machines. Below, we define parts of the *uml2soa* transformation taking a UML Model as input parameter. This input model will be supplied by the UML2 importer of the VIATRA framework. The transformation will generate a SOA model as output extended with non-functional attributes for reliable messaging. Furthermore, a reference model is also derived to store the mapping between the source and the target model.

```
Complex transformation.
machine uml2soa {
     rule main(in UMLModel, out UML-
2SOAModel, out SOAModel) = seq {
         ...
         // Generate all inactivity-
Timeout attributes
         forall Timing below UML-
Model with
         apply createRelMsgSpec(Timi
ng,RMSpec,SOAModel,UML2SOAModel) do
              forall TO below UML-
Model with
                   apply createTimeo
ut(Timing,TO,RMSpec,SOAModel, UML2SO-
AModel) do
                   print("Rule make-
Timeout applied");
              }
}
```

In the transformation extract above, first we generate a *RelMsgSpec* element for each appropriate UML substructure (by applying rule *createRelMsgSpec*). Then for each of such corresponding pairs, we apply rule *createTimeout* using again the *forall* construct to initiate the matching of the graph pattern for all occurrences in a given model.

Creating XML documents. Once the model instances of XML documents (e.g. Sandesha configurations) are ready, a textual output will be generated. This model-to-code transformation does not depend on the actual XML dialect, as it follows to general XML document patterns. Of course, model of a document which conforms to a Web service standard (e.g. model of a Sandesha document which conforms to WS-ReliableMessaging) should be "linked" to an actual XML structure. Therefore, Sandesha metamodel can be extended with **subTpyeof** relations which describe how the model elements will be implemented in XML. Parts of the Sandesha XML file will be specific to this standard (e.g. the namespace); these are passed as parameters.

Note that all model transformations have been designed to allow for an incremental execution. This means that when the source UML model is changed by the designer, these changes are propagated incrementally to the target deployment descriptors. In other terms, target models and XML documents are generated on-demand. The VIATRA2 model transformation framework is able to trace all existing matches of patterns in an efficient and scalable way (Bergman et al., 2008) and update only those parts of the model that are touched during propagating the changes.

Deployment Results of the Case Study

The resulted XML descriptor showing the non-functional configuration of the *Customer Transaction Service* is discussed below.

First, the functional specification of each service instance is described including its name, URI and the available operations.

```
<?xml version='1.0'?>
<!--Generated document: BalanceVali-
dationServiceAxisXML-->
<serviceInstance
uri='http://192.168.0.198'
    name='BalanceValidationService'>
    <operations>
        <operation
name='requestAdditionalData'></opera-
tion>
        <operation
name='applyForCredit'></operation>
        <operation name='updateAddi
tionalInformation'></operation>
        <operation
name='acceptOffer'></operation>
        <operation
name='whichDataShouldChanged'></op-
eration>
        <operation
name='updateApplication'></operation>
        <operation
name='uploadBalance'></operation>
        <operation
name='requestBalance'></operation>
    </operations>
...
</serviceInstance>
```

Then, security-related parameter are attached to the service instance describing that (i) user names are used as authentication type, (ii) the body of a message should be encrypted in case of service invocation (but its signature and header should not) using the default encryption algorithm (set at the server level) (iii) the header and the body of the message should be signed using the default sign algorithm (set at the server level), (iv) timestamps shall be attached to each message.

```
    <SecurityParams>
        <AuthTokenType>username</
AuthTokenType>
        <EncryptBody>true</Encrypt-
Body>
        <EncryptSignature>false</
EncryptSignature>
        <EncryptAlgorithm>default</
EncryptAlgorithm>
        <SignBody>true</SignBody>
        <EncryptHeader>false</En-
cryptHeader>
        <UseTimeStamp>true</Use-
TimeStamp>
        <SignHeader>true</Sign-
Header>
        <SignAlgorithm>default</
SignAlgorithm>
    </SecurityParams>
```

Reliable messaging parameters should also be set for the service instance. Reliability messaging parameters are also set for the communication. The specification expresses that in case of message loss (due to lack of acknowledgement within 100 ms), the message will be retransmitted after 10 seconds at most two times.

```
<reliabityParams>
          <InactivityTimeout>10</In-
activityTimeout>
          <MaximumRetransmission-
Count>2</MaximumRetransmissionCount>
          <ExponentialBackoff>false</
ExponentialBackoff>
          <AcknowledgementInter-
val>100</AcknowledgementInterval>
          <RetransmissionInter-
val>20000</RetransmissionInterval>
          <SequenceRemovalTime-
out>60</SequenceRemovalTimeout>
          <InvokeInOrder>true</In-
vokeInOrder>
     </reliabityParams>
```

According to the standard, similar reliable messaging and security parameters should be set for the connections of the service instance, which is not discussed here in more details.

The communication between server and client also need some client stubs which hide the details of Web services parameters (e.g, retransmission interval, etc.). These correspond to ports which are connected to required interfaces (e.g. balancePort of Credit Request Process component). Such classes are generated from the xml files, using Ant scripting. For instance, for the connection between Credit Request Process and the Balance Validation Service, 2 classes will be created:

- Balance Validation Service will be skeleton which wraps with the above functionality. This should be extended to pointers to the method implementations (e.g. Java function calls).
- A Balance Validation Client class will be created, which performs similar functional invocations as any proxy generated from a WSDL file, with the extension that it handles the apache sandesha and rampart specific parameters as well. Note that this also implies that the business workflow must use this proxy instead of built-in service invocation (for instance, this class should be called as a web service from a BPEL process instead of the remote Balance Validation service, as BPEL cannot handle non-functional parameters).

RELATED WORK

A framework for automated WSDL generation from UML models is described in Vara et al. (2005), using the UML extensions of MIDAS (Caceres et al., 2003). In Gronmo et al. (2004), Web service descriptions are mapped to UML models, and (after using visual modeling techniques) a composite service can be created for which the descriptor is automatically generated. However, none of these works considers non-functional properties of Web services.

Non-functional aspects of e-business applications are discussed among others in Balogh et al. (2005), having some description of deployment optimization for J2EE applications, but without discussing details of model-based deployment.

General Service Oriented Architecture elements were considered as typed graphs with graph transformation rules visually describing their behavior in Baresi et al. (2006) where a similar core metamodel was used.

Alwagait and Ghandeharizadeh (2004) aims to develop a dependable web services framework, which relies on extended proxies. However, this needs a modification at the client side in order to handle exceptions and find new service instances.

Moreover, the reconfiguration of client side proxies uses non-standard WSDL extensions while we concentrated on standards-compliant solutions.

Integration of non-functional aspects in the development by model transformations is also investigated in Cortellessa et al. (2006)) and Jonkers et al. (2005), focusing on parts of the engineering process.

In a service-oriented environment, PEPA has already been used to analyze (application-specific) high-level UML models or workflow-like descriptions of services with attached Service Level Agreements (Wirsing et al., 2006). In this approach, the authors investigate performance parameters (compared to performability in our case). However, the main essential difference is the (performance-related) behavior of services needs to be modeled explicitly on the UML-level. In contrast, our technique relies only on architectural level UML models, and the core building blocks of (business-independent) performability-related behavior are instantiated in accordance with the UML model of service configurations, which allows better reusability.

In general, our work is complementary to security engineering research as security is one aspect which can be included in an SLA. Moreover, we created transformations which enable the integration of novel techniques as well, assuming that contract-based security can be interpreted in the technical environment.

Modeling of security aspects in UML has been considered in several works. Jürjens introduced the UMLSec profile (Jürjens, 2002), which can be used for system level security specification and analysis. Our work is more specific to services as it concentrates on messaging standards in service oriented systems. UMLSec profile could be used together with our non-functional extensions as the messaging-oriented specifications can be converted to Service Level Objectives, i.e., parts of the SLA.

Security requirements of services are can be modeled at a high level in SI-*, enabling the goal-oriented design of business processes (Massacci et al., 2007). Such requirements can be considered as input from the business level for our non-functional UML models. Security-by-contract is also discussed in several technical environments (e.g..NET platform, (Desmet et al., 2008). These technical platforms could be incorporated at the level of Platform Specific Models in our transformations as well.

Another interesting complementary research direction is that of access control and policies. Security policies in SOA environment are discussed in Wolter et al. (2008) and in Alam et al. (2008). These works will be considered when implementing further developments to this approach, as they help to evaluate the security SLAs of different partners. They also implement access control policies using the eXtensible Access Control Markup Language (XACML) which is currently not included in our transformations. However, our approach can be extended easily with new aspects (NFCharacteristics) and settings (NFDimensions) which could be used to cover access control as well.

Basin et al. (2006) discusses how model-driven security engineering can help the development of J2EE and.NET applications. This is also a complementary work, as it focuses rather on Role based Access Control Policies, which may be an input for our method which aims at modeling SLAs, where the security parameters of messaging between two parties are modeled. We have not considered here how and on what basis partners decide to guarantee access to each other's business functionalities, we rather concentrated on services which can be access point to systems they implemented.

A discussion forum on model-driven security is available at modeldrivensecurity.org.

Concerning previous work of the same authors, verification of the behavior of the system (i.e., checking the conformance to requirements on reliable messaging) was performed in Gönczy et al. (2006c), thus giving a formal semantics which can be checked by using verification techniques and tools. The same metamodels were also the basis of test generation for reliable message brokers (Gönczy et al., 2007).

A high-level initial overview of a service development framework was introduced in Gönczy et al. (2006a); however, the current paper contains significantly more details and standards integrated. Gönczy et al. (2006b) shares some conceptually similar ideas in order to carry out a model-based performance evaluation to analyze BPEL processes with SLA requirements.

An overview on how non-functional properties were managed within the SENSORIA project is available in Gilmore et al. (2010) while more detailed of our performability analysis method and related transformations are described in Gönczy et al. (2008a, 2008b).

CONCLUSION AND FUTURE WORK

We presented a methodology for high-level modeling of standards-compliant service configurations with nonfunctional requirements followed by an model-based deployment process automated by model transformations. We used a Finance Case Study developed by industrial partners of the SENSORIA project to illustrate the deployment process.

The main innovation of our current work primarily lies in that (i) non-functional contracts of services can be captured using a standard modeling notation like UML in a flexible and extensible way. Moreover, (ii) their deployment for industrial platforms like Apache Axis is automated by a systematically designed transformation chain including the automated configuration of non-functional parameters (such as reliable and secure message communication). Finally, (iii) actual transformations are captured using intuitive formal notations and explicit trace models as requested in many business-critical applications. Thanks to underlying VIATRA2 model transformation framework, the actual transformations can be executed in an incremental way to react to changes in the high-level service models, thus only parts of changed artifacts are required to be re-generated upon model changes.

It is worth pointing out that in previous work (Gönczy et al., 2008a), we also developed an analysis method to estimate the "cost of reliability" in terms of message delay, which precedes the deployment phase to assure that the target configuration fulfills performability requirements.

Currently, we are working on a mapping from UML4SOA models to Service Component Architecture models, which facilitate the development of complex Web applications.

ACKNOWLEDGMENT

This work has been supported by the EU FET-GC2 IP project SENSORIA (IST-2005-016004).

REFERENCES

W3C. (2008). *Web Services Description Language* (WSDL) 1.1. Retrieved from http://www.w3.org/TR/wsdl

Alam, M., Hafner, M., & Breu, R. (2008). Constraint based role based access control in the SECTET-framework: A model-driven approach. *Journal of Computer Security*, *16*(2).

Alessandrini, M., & Dost, D. (2007). *D8.3.a: Requirements modelling and analysis of selected scenarios-finance case study*. Retrieved from http://www.sensoria-ist.eu/

Alwagait, E., & Ghandeharizadeh, S. (2004). Dew: A dependable Web Services framework. *Research Ideas in Data Engineering*, *1*, 111–118.

Balogh, A., Varró, D., & Pataricza, A. (2005). *Model-based optimization of enterprise application and service deployment* (pp. 84–98). ISAS.

Baresi, L., Heckel, R., Thöne, S., & Varró, D. (2006). Style-based modeling and refinement of Service-Oriented Architectures. *Software and Systems Modeling*, *5*(2), 187–207. doi:10.1007/s10270-006-0001-4

Basin, D., Doser, J., & Lodderstedt, T. (2006). Model driven security: From UML models to access control infrastructures. In *ACM Transactions on Software Engineering and Methodology*, 2006.

Bergmann, G., Horváth, Á., Ráth, I., & Varró, D. (2008). A benchmark evaluation of incremental pattern matching in graph transformation. *Proceedings of International Conference on Graph Transformations* (ICGT), (LNCS 5214). Springer-Verlag.

Börger, E., & Stark, R. (2003). *Abstract state machines. A method for high-level system design and analysis*. Springer-Verlag.

Caceres, P., Marcos, E., & Vera, B. (2003). A MDA-based approach for Web Information System development. Workshop in Software Model Engineering (WiSME@UML2003).

Cortellessa, V., Marco, A. D., & Inverardi, P. (2006). Software performance model-driven architecture. In *Proceedings of the 2006 ACM Symposium on Applied Computing*. (pp. 1218–1223). New York: ACM Press.

Desmet, L., Joosen, W., Massacci, F., Philippaerts, P., Piessensa, F., Siahaan, I., et al. (2008). *Security-by-contract on the.NET platform*. (Information Security Technical Report).

Gilmore, S., Gönczy, L., Koch, N., Mayer, P. & Varró, D. (2010). Non-functional properties in the model-driven development of service-oriented systems. *Journal of Software and Systems Modeling.*

Gilmore, S., & Tribastone, M. (2006). *Evaluating the scalability of a Web Service-based distributed e-learning and course management system*. Workshop on Web Services and Formal Methods (WS-FM 2006). Springer-Verlag.

Gnesi, S., ter Beek, M., Baumeister, H., Hoelzl, M., Moiso, C., Koch, N., et al. (2006). *D8.0: Case studies scenario description*. Retrieved from http://www.sensoria-ist.eu/

Gönczy, L., Ávéd, J., & Varró, D. (2006a). Model-based deployment of Web Services to standards-compliant middleware. In P. Isaias & M.B. Nunes (Eds.), *Proceedings of the Iadis International Conference on WWW/Internet 2006*(ICWI2006). Iadis Press.

Gönczy, L., Chiaradonna, S., Giandomenico, F. D., Pataricza, A., Bondavalli, A., & Bartha, T. (2006b). Dependability evaluation of Web Service-based processes. In M. Telek (Ed.), *Proceedings of European Performance Engineering Workshop* (EPEW 2006), (LNCS), (pp. 166–180). Budapest: Springer.

Gönczy, L., Déri, Z., & Varró, D. (2008a). Model driven performability analysis of service configurations with reliable messaging. In *Proceedings of the Workshop on Model Driven Web Engineering* (MDWE2008).

Gönczy, L., Déri, Z., & Varró, D. (2009). *Model transformations for performability analysis of service configurations*. Models in Software Engineering: Workshops and Symposia at MODELS 2008, Toulouse, France, September 28 - October 3, 2008. (pp. 153-166). Berlin, Heidelberg: Springer-Verlag.

Gönczy, L., Heckel, R., & Varró, D. (2007a). Model-based testing of service infrastructure components. In Petrenko, et al. (Eds.), *Proceedings of TESTCOM/FATES 2007*. (LNCS 4581). Tallinn, Estiona: Springer.

Gönczy, L., Kovács, M., & Varró, D. (2006c). Modeling and verification of reliable messaging by graph transformation systems. In *Proceedings of the Workshop on Graph Transformation for Verification and Concurrency* (ICGT2006). Elsevier.

Gronmo, R., Skogan, D., Solheim, I., & Oldevik, J. (2004). Model-driven Web Services development. In *Proceedings of the IEEE International Conference on e-technology, e-commerce and e-service* (EEE'04), (pp. 42–45). Los Alamitos, CA: IEEE Computer Society.

IBM. (2009). Reliable asynchronous message profile (RAMP) toolkit. Retrieved from http://www.alphaworks.ibm.com/tech/ramptk

Jonkers, H., Iacob, M.-E., Lankhorst, M. M., & Strating, P. (2005). *Integration and analysis of functional and non-functional aspects in model-driven e-service development* (pp. 229–238). In EDOC.

Jürjen, J. (2002). UMLsec: Extending UML for secure systems development. In *Proceedings of 5th International Conference on The Unified Modeling Language*, (LNCS Vol.2460), Springer.

Koch, N., & Brendl, D. (2007). *D8.2.a: Requirements modelling and analysis of selected scenarios-automotive case study*. Retrieved from http://www.sensoria-ist.eu/

Koch, N., Mayer, P., Heckel, R., Gönczy, L. & Montangero, C. (2007). *D1.4.a: UML for service-oriented systems*. Koch, N. & Brendl, D. (2007).

Massacci, F., Mylopoulos, J., & Zannone, N. (2007). *Computer-aided support for secure tropos*. Automated Software Engineering Journal.

Object Management Group. (2006). *UML profile for QoS and fault tolerance*. Retrieved from http://www.omg.org

Röttger, S., & Zschaler, S. (2004). *Model-driven development for non-functional properties: Refinement through model transformation. (LNCS 3273)* (pp. 275–289). Springer.

Rozenberg, G. (Ed.). (1997). *Handbook of graph grammars and computing by graph transformations: Foundations*. Retrieved from http://sensoria-ist.eu

Somodi, T. (2008). *Model-driven development of Web Services with non-functional requirements*. Master's thesis, Budapest University of Technology and Economics.

Vara, J. M., de Castro, V., & Marcos, E. (2005). WSDL automatic generation from UML models in a MDA framework. In *Proceedings of the International Conference on Next Generation Web Services Practices*, (p. 319). IEEE Computer Society.

Varró, D., & Balogh, A. (2007). The model transformation language of the VIATRA2 framework. *Science of Computer Programming, 68*(3), 214–234. doi:10.1016/j.scico.2007.05.004

VIATRA2. (2008). *VIATRA2 framework at Eclipse GMT*. Retrieved from http://www.eclipse.org/gmt/

Wirsing, M., Clark, A., Gilmore, S., Hölzl, M., Knapp, A., & Koch, N. (2006). *Semantic-based development of service-oriented systems. (LNCS 4229)* (pp. 24–45). Springer-Verlag.

Wolter,, C., Menzel, M., Schaad.A., Miseldine, P. & Meinel, C. (2008). Model-driven business process security requirement specification. *Journal of System Architecture*.

Chapter 16
Dependability Assessment of Service-Oriented Architectures Using Fault Injection

Nik Looker
Durham University, UK

Malcolm Munro
Durham University, UK

ABSTRACT

Dependability assessment is an important aspect of any software system and shows the degree of trust and quality of service that is delivered by a system. Validation and verification techniques commonly employed to ensure that systems are fit for use attempt to remove all faults so that error conditions cannot occur but since it is not feasible to verify all states a system can achieve, it is not possible to completely test a system. Conversely, dependability assumes that failures may occur in a system and that mechanisms exist to mitigate any failures and thus provide a trustworthy system. This chapter discusses the different issues associated with dependability. The different techniques that can be used to assess dependability are discussed and are related to Service Orientated Architectures. A number of cases studies are used to show the practicality of the techniques used.

INTRODUCTION

Dependability (Avizienis, Laprie, Randell & Landwehr, 2004) is a discipline that provides an assessment of how much trust can be placed on a system to deliver a Quality of Service (QoS). Systems need not be fault free but should deliver their functionality when required. This is because it is virtually impossible to engineer a system that can be guaranteed to be fault free; so dependability assumes that faults exist in a system but mechanisms exist to either eliminate them or tolerate their presence. In either case a dependable system will perform its intended function. Validation and

DOI: 10.4018/978-1-60960-493-6.ch016

verification techniques, on the other hand, attempt to determine that a system contains no faults. This is an important discipline and increases the overall reliability of a system but is difficult to achieve with current techniques. Dependability is a more realistic approach since it measures the reliance that can be placed upon a system rather than validating it against its specification and includes methods that increase this.

This paper provides a review of dependability and some useful fault injection based assessment techniques that can be applied to web services that implemented a Service-Oriented Architecture (SOA). We present a number of case studies, based on some of our previous work, to demonstrate how these assessment techniques can be applied.

BACKGROUND

Service Oriented Architectures

A service in economics and marketing terminology is defined by Boone and Kurtz (1988) as "... intangible tasks that satisfy both business and consumer needs". This definition originated to describe activities in the service industry such as hotels, garages, barbers, etc. In general terms a service is not owned by the customer but is something that is utilized to complete a task. The advantage of utilizing a service to do this is that the customer does not have to design, maintain or run the service. This definition can readily be adapted to software services.

A service in software terms is an entity that communicates with other entities via messages (Cabrera, Kurt & Box, 2004). This definition does not specify that the services be networked or the method in which messages should be exchanged. Further it does not specify that the entities must perform tasks or satisfy a specified requirement but this is usually taken as implied.

Software services can be characterized as that they:

- Must communicate over a network.
- Must provide an interface that can be utilized by external systems to access functionality.
- Should be discoverable in someway so that external systems can utilize them.
- Should be loosely coupled which allows composed systems to be adaptable.

Services are often used to implement client/server architectures (Cabrera, Kurt, & Box, 2004), which are systems that are composed of a client that utilizes a service provided by a server. The client accesses the service on the server to perform some task. A service may also implement its functionality by making us of other services in the same way as a client.

At an abstract level all that is required to implement a set of services and the exchange of messages between them is a remote invocation method and an interface definition language that defines the interface. Unfortunately most distributed systems rarely run on identical hardware and are frequently required to communicate with legacy systems and other organizations hardware/software. To overcome this problem and allow service-based systems to be constructed middleware is used. Middleware (Vinoski, 2002) is connectivity software that consists of a set of enabling services that allow multiple processes running on one or more machines to communicate across a network. Middleware eliminates differences between machines in a heterogeneous environment by marshalling data and includes an agreed set of useful functions.

Distributed services must be organized into a system to be useful and a common architectural model used to accomplish this is a Service Oriented Architecture. A SOA is an architecture that represents software functionality as discoverable services on a network. Channabasavaiah, Holley, and Tuggle (2004) define a SOA as "an application architecture within which all functions are defined as independent services with well-defined invokable interfaces, which can be called in defined sequences to form business processes"

The main principles are not new, for instance CORBA provides functionality by offering functions as components (Pritchard, 1999), but SOAs provide a number of advantages such as loose coupling and late binding. However, these advantages come with potential problems not least in the area of dependability.

Loose coupling (Bennett et al., 2003) is the capability of services to be composed and utilized on demand, possibly using different system technologies, to create a working system. This can be accomplished using a combination of Dynamic composition, which is the composing of systems from existing services that are discovered at runtime, and by late binding. Loose coupling implies that a service is referentially transparent from any data or other services that it requires. From a dependability point of view this makes it difficult to assess a complete system since each time the system is composed it may be composed of different services. It can also have an impact on the integrity of the system since the integrity of the services used may be in question, for instance it may bind to a malicious service.

Late Binding (Bennett & Xu, 2003) is the property of a system that allows a system to bind to a service at runtime, rather than at compile time. A provider of a new service can make it available at runtime and an existing system can utilize the new implementation without modification of its own code. This implies that the system is written in such a way as to accommodate the new services in some way rather than just dynamically composing itself from already known service definitions. Whilst late binding is a very useful facility and essential for the construction of loosely coupled systems it means that new services can potentially be deployed which have not been assessed with the combination of services being used by an SOA. Thus the integrity of the service could be called into question.

Dependability is a key factor for SOAs. Many traditional distributed systems performing business-to-business (B2B) operations, for instance those in the banking domain, perform computations that require very little execution time but the impact of incorrect results can have far reaching financial consequences. Conversely, scientific Grid applications often perform tasks that require many days to complete so any failures during this time can have a considerable impact in terms of time and hence indirectly to costs thorough man hours lost.

The cost and difficulty of containing and recovering from faults in service-based applications may be higher than that for normal applications because of the third-party nature of the environment. Whilst the heterogeneous nature of services within an SOA means that many service-based applications will be functioning in environments where interaction faults are more likely to occur. Dependability means are therefore an advantage in these situations since they can be used to mitigate faults without the need to remove them.

Dependability

Quality of Service

When assessing the reliability of a system it is useful to have some agreed measurement to determine the quality of a system. A commonly used measurement is Quality of Service (QoS), which Haas and Brown (2004) have defined as "...an obligation accepted and advertised by a provider entity to service consumers," where an obligation is defined as "...a kind of policy that prescribes actions and/or states of an agent and/or resource."

The factors that go to make up the obligation cover a wide range of factors that are combined to define the QoS offered by a system. The following factors are commonly used for the quality aspect (Mani & Nagarajan, 2002):

- **Availability:** whether a Service is present and ready for use.
- **Accessibility:** the degree the Service is capable of serving a request and a specific point in time.
- **Integrity:** maintaining the correctness of any interaction. If a transaction fails data should remain in a consistent state.
- **Performance:** the throughput of a Service and the latency. Throughput is defined as the number of requests serviced in a given period and the latency is the time taken to service a request.
- **Reliability:** the capability of maintaining the Service and service quality.
- **Regulatory:** corresponds to rules, laws, standards and specifications. This can have an affect on areas such as availability, performance, and reliability through Service Level Agreements (SLA).
- **Security:** defines confidentiality for parties using a service.

Some attributes can be quantitatively measured and others remain harder to quantify. For example Reliability can be measured by failures over time but the effectives of Regulatory cannot be measured by any simple metrics.

Dependability

Quality of Service attempts to give a measurement of the overall quality of a service and utilizes some of the same attributes present in Dependability, whilst Dependability is concerned not only with measuring the dependability of a system but also with the means to improve the dependability of the System (Birman, K. 2005).

The IFIP Working Group on Dependable Computing and Fault Tolerance defines dependability as:

"The notion of dependability, defined as the trustworthiness of a computing system which allows reliance to be justifiably placed on the service it delivers, enables these various concerns to be subsumed within a single conceptual framework."

Dependability can be assessed and improved by the use of the following:

- **Attributes:** A way to assess the Dependability of a system
- **Threats:** An understanding of what can affect the Dependability of a system
- **Means:** Ways to increase the Dependability of a system

Attributes are measurements that can be applied to a system to determine its overall dependability. A generally agreed list of attributes is:

- **Availability:** The probability that a service is present and ready for use
- **Reliability:** The capability of maintaining the service and service quality
- **Safety:** The absence of catastrophic consequences
- **Confidentiality:** That information is accessible only to those authorized to use it
- **Integrity:** The absence of improper system alterations
- **Maintainability:** The capacity to undergo modifications and repairs (Avizienis, Laprie, Randell, & Landwehr, 2004)

As with QoS some attributes are quantifiable by direct measurements whilst others are more subjective. For instance Confidentiality cannot be measured directly via metrics but is a subjective assessment that requires judgmental information to be applied to give a level of confidence, whereas Reliability can be quantified by physical metrics.

Security is sometimes classed as an attribute but the current view is to aggregate it together with dependability and treat it as a composite term called Dependability and Security (Avizienis, Laprie, Randell, & Landwehr, 2004). The reasoning behind this is that a dependable system must also be secure since otherwise its Integrity and Confidentiality could not be guaranteed. Here the term Dependability will be assumed to be the composite definition of Dependability and Security even if not explicitly stated.

Threats can affect a system and cause a drop in Dependability. There are three main terms that must be clearly understood:

- **Fault:** A fault (which is usually referred to as a bug for historic reasons) is a defect in a system. The presence of a fault in a system may or may not lead to a failure, for instance although a system may contain a fault its input and state conditions may never cause this fault to be executed so that an error occurs and thus never exhibits as a failure.
- **Error:** An error is a discrepancy between the intended behavior of a system and its actual behavior inside the system boundary. Errors occur at runtime when some part of the system enters an unexpected state due to the activation of a fault.
- **Failure:** A failure is an instance in time when a system displays behavior that is contrary to its specification. An error may not necessarily cause a failure, for instance an exception may be thrown by a system but this may be caught and handled using fault tolerance techniques so the overall operation of the system will conform to the specification.

Faults, Errors and Failures operate according to a mechanism is known as a Fault-Error-Failure chain (Avizienis, Magnus, Laprie & Randell, 2000). As a general rule a fault, when activated, can lead to an error (an invalid state) this may lead to another error or a failure (which is an observable deviation from the specified behavior at the system boundary).

Once a fault is activated an error is created. An error may act in the same way as a fault in that it can create further error conditions, therefore an error may propagate multiple times within a system boundary without causing an observable failure. If an error propagates outside the system boundary a failure is said to occur. A failure is basically the point at which it can be said that a Service is failing to meet its specification. Since the output data from one service may feed into another, a failure in one service may propagate into another Service as a fault so a chain can be formed.

Means are ways to increase Dependability by breaking the Fault-Error-Failure chain. There are four means of improving the dependability of a system:

1. Fault Prevention deals with preventing faults being incorporated into a system and result from use of development methodologies, and good implementation techniques.
2. Fault Removal during development requires verification so that faults can be detected and removed before a system is put into production. Once systems have been put into production a system is needed to record failures and remove them via a maintenance cycle
3. Fault Forecasting predicts likely faults so that they can be removed or their effects can be circumvented
4. Fault Tolerance deals with putting mechanisms in place that will allow a system to function in the presence of faults but still deliver the required service, although that service may be at a degraded level

The first three means are directly related to assessment results and thus the assessment can influence the developmental workflow of an SOA. Fault tolerance is linked to the assessment in so far as fault tolerance design patterns can be assessed and their function can be validated.

Dependability means are intended to reduce the number of failures presented to the user of a system. A detailed review of dependability means is given in Avizienis, Laprie, Randell, and Landwehr (2004).

Assessment Methods

The focus here is on Dependability Analysis (Avizienis, Laprie, Randell & Landwehr, 2004) rather than more traditional validation testing and can be assessed using either model-based or measurement-based techniques (Marsden, Fabre, & Arlat, 2002).

Model-based techniques can be used in the design stage to predict potential errors and faults in algorithms. Measurement can be applied to existing systems to provide metrics on dependability. Modeling can only make predictions of the dependability of a system since it is derived from system design, specification and code documents. Once a system has been implemented actual measurement techniques can be used to obtain specific metrics and allow data on dependability to be derived from them.

Measurement based techniques are useful because they can be applied to existing systems, and may not require access to source code or design documentation. There are two main measurement techniques:

1. Observation
2. Fault Injection

Observation (Kalyanakrishnam, Kalbarczyk, & Iyer, 1999) measurements can be performed by the examination of errors and failures in a large set of deployed systems. This technique uses existing logs, either logs maintained by the system administrator or logs generated automatically by the system. Analysis of the data can obtain information on the frequency of faults and the activity that was in progress when they occurred. Since failures and errors may occur infrequently data must be collected over a long period of time and from a large number of systems. Even with this it is unlikely that this technique will catch rarely seen errors (Hecht & Hecht, 1996).

Fault Injection (Voas & McGraw, 1998) is a group of techniques that attempt to induce faults into a running system to assess, not only its tolerance to faults but it can also be used to exercise seldom used control pathways within the system which would otherwise go unused for long periods of time (Carreira & Silva, 1998). Fault injection can be used to simulate unusual input conditions and exercise the boundaries between software components that would otherwise rely on being exercised by calls generated by other components in response to user input. Since this input will go through a number of intermediate steps it is extremely unlikely that this would be able to exercise all conditions of the component using traditional testing techniques (Whittaker, 2001).

Compile-Time Injection (also know as code mutation) is an injection technique where source code is modified to add simulated faults into a system. This technique has the advantage that it can be used to simulate both hardware and software faults. It has been shown to induce faults into a system that are very close in nature to those produced by programming faults (Daran & Thevenod-Fosse, 1996). The main drawbacks of this technique are:

1. It requires that the source code must be available to the test team, which will most likely not be the case for third-party service based systems.
2. There is the chance that unintended faults will be introduced during the code modification, especially if the faults are being injected by hand.
3. Since the source code is being altered this technique cannot be used as part of a certification processes since the system under test will be a different system to that which was shipped.

Runtime Injection techniques use a software trigger to inject a fault into a running software system. Faults can be injected in a number of ways:

- **Time based triggers:** These triggers can be based on either hardware or software timers. When the timer reaches a specified time an interrupt is generated and the interrupt handler associated with the timer can inject the fault.
- **Interrupt based triggers:** Hardware exceptions and software trap mechanisms are used to generate an interrupt at a specific place in the system code or on a particular event within the system, for instance access to a specific memory location. This method of trigger implementation is capable of injecting a fault on a specific event.
- **Code based triggers:** This technique involves inserting code into the target system source just before an event is to occur. This code performs the fault injection and then the original statement can execute with the fault present. This method differs from compile-time injection in that it injects its faults at runtime rather than at compile time and rather than corrupt existing code it adds code to perform the fault injection. Its main disadvantage is that it requires the system source code to be modified but it has the advantage that the fault injector can be compiled into the system as a library and run as part of the system and does not require explicit hardware triggering.

Fault Injection for SOA

There are a number of places a fault can be injected into a system, for example at the memory interface by corruption, at the kernel interfaces by intercepting operating systems calls, and at the network interface by intercepting network packets. This text is concerned with network level fault injection because it more suited to a service based environment that is dependent on message passing.

This technique is concerned with the corruption, loss or reordering of network packets at the network interface. The fault should be injected at the application level. Faults are then processed normally by the protocol stacks at both ends and can be relayed to the application layer. The faults injected are based on corrupting packet header information and injecting random byte errors.

Looker, Munro and Xu (2005) demonstrate a novel fault injection mechanism that allows network level fault injection to be used to simulate Code Insertion fault injection whilst circumventing the need for modifications to the service source code. This is accomplished by intercepting middleware messages rather than network level messages within the protocol stack, decoding the middleware message in real-time and injecting appropriate faults.

Standard network level fault injection is achieved by operating on network packets at the network interface. Since the fault injection is done at this interface changes to these packets tend to be reflected at the middleware level as random corruption of data. Even reordering and dropping of packets may only result in corruption of a data stream because a middleware level message may span more than one physical network packet. Reordered or dropped packets may be subject to error correction such as retransmission and thus faults injected may not reach the middleware layer. Packets corrupted at this level may be rejected by the network protocol stack by mechanisms such as checksums. It is thus difficult to target a particular element of a middleware message with any level of certainty. Therefore network level fault injection has traditionally been used for assessing network protocol stacks not service based systems.

The Looker et al. method takes the basic concept described above and moves the fault injection point away from the network interface to the actual middleware transport layer. Since middleware messages are then intercepted as complete entities, it is possible to corrupt, reorder or drop complete messages, rather than just part of a network packet. Messages can thus be modified and passed on to the rest of the protocol stack. In this way faults can be injected but not be filtered out by the protocol stack.

If messages are intercepted before they are signed or encrypted (or after they are decrypted and the signature checked in the case of incoming messages), individual elements can be corrupted within a message without that message being rejected by the middleware. It is thus possible to produce meaningful perturbations of such items as input parameters.

CASE STUDIES

These case studies examine the use of fault injection as an assessment method for SOA, specifically examining its application to Web Services. A Web Service is a software service defined by a number of standards that can be used to provide interoperable data exchange and processing between dissimilar machines and architectures. For the purposes of this paper it is concerned with Web Services defined by the W3C that are described by WSDL (Christensen, Curbera, Meredith, & Weerawarana, 2001) and implemented using SOAP (Box, Ehnebuske, Kakivava, Layman, Mendelsohn, Nielsen, Thatte & Winer, 2000) and the RPC model.

The first case study uses fault injection to determine adherence to web services standards. The issues discovered touch on most dependability attributes but in particular impact reliability and availability since interoperability with other middleware implementations cannot be guaranteed. The second case study examines two different fault injection techniques and examines the tradeoffs that can be made in selecting a technique. The last case study applies a fault injection technique to a dependability mean to show its affect on the overall dependability of the system.

Protocol Assessment through Fault Injection

This case study demonstrates how network level fault injection can be applied to assess the dependability of a protocol stack. This has traditionally been a major use of network level fault injection since one of the primary functions of a network protocol stack is to detect and correct errors in transmitted data, which is essentially what is done when network level fault injection is performed.

The Axis SOAP stack is examined in terms of corruption of SOAP messages and compliance with the W3C specifications (Box et al., 2000). It is performed using a tool called FIT (Looker & Xu, 2007), which is a middleware level fault injection tool, thus allowing injected faults to be targeted at the middleware message protocol rather than the network protocol used to transport it.

In this case study the effects of fault injection on a representative sample of types defined by the XML schema (XSD) was examined. To do this a simple service was written which included a method for each *xsd* type. Each routine received a specific *xsd* type and echoed it back unchanged as the return value. A test program was written which called each service method in turn with a valid instance of the type and compared the return result with the original data sent. In each case the value returned should be identical with that sent. The combination of the service and the test program provide a simple test bed to test *xsd* types.

Baseline Experiment

A baseline experiment was undertaken to determine the normal operating conditions of the test bed. Table 1 shows the results of this experiment, described by two criteria for each *xsd* type assessed: 1) comparison of the returned value with the sent value; and 2) any exception thrown.

In general the protocol stack operated as expected and no exceptions were generated but an unexpected outcome of this experiment was the

Table 1. baseline experiment results

xsd:type	Returned value equals sent value	Exception Generated
Map to built-in Java type	TRUE	None
Map to Standard Java Library Class	TRUE	None
Date	FALSE	None
DateTime	FALSE	None
Map to Apache Axis Class	TRUE	None

Date and DateTime returned values did not match the original values sent. These types are implemented using the Java Standard Library Date class. Equality between two Date instances is obtained only if they match to the millisecond. Examination of the SOAP messages exchanged and the W3C specifications show that the ASCII format of Date passed within the SOAP message does not specify Date to the millisecond, so when they are passed into the Java Date class a slight discrepancy is introduced, hence the returned instance will not match the one originally sent.

The *xsd* types defined in Table 1 can be grouped into three groupings: 1) *xsd* types mapped to built-in Java types (dark grey in table) which comprise *double*, *int*, *boolean*, *byte*, *float*, *long* and *short*; 2) *xsd* types mapped to Java Standard Library classes (light grey in table) which comprise *String*, *Date*, *DateTime*, *Decimal*, *QName* and *AnySimpleType*; and 3) *xsd* types that require specially written classes within Apache Axis (white in table) which comprise *AnyURI, Duration, GDay, GMonth, GMonthDay, GYear, GYearMonth, Language, Name, NCName, NegativeInteger, NMTOKENS, NonNegativeInteger, NonPositiveInteger, NMToken, NormalizedString, NOTATION, PositiveInteger, Time, Token, UnsignedInt, UnsignedByte, UnsignedLong* and *UnsignedShort*.

Protocol Invalidation

This experiment attempts to invalidate the protocol whilst retaining syntactically correct XML to determine if the implementation follows the SOAP protocol specification.

Thompson, Beech, Maloney, and Mendelsohn (2004) specify that "An element may be valid without content if it has the attribute xsi:nil with the value true. An element so labeled must be empty, but can carry attributes if permitted by the corresponding complex type". Since the test program generates SOAP messages that contain data within the elements, if xsi:nil="true" is added as an attribute to the *part* it should fail the scheme validation. By this definition, a SOAP message exchanging a non-null parameter should not contain the xsi:nil attribute. A fault was therefore created to add xsi:nil="true" to an element and was applied to each request message (see Box 1).

Table 2 shows the results from this experiment. The results show that only certain types generated an exception, and these did not seem to be descriptive of the schema validation. Of the types that returned a value, the value returned was null. It can therefore be concluded that setting xsi:nil, rather than causing an XML schema violation, is implemented by the middleware to infer that the element is empty and any contents should be silently discarded. This causes a null object to be passed to the service and this null object is passed back in the normal way.

The exceptions generated can be explained by the *xsd* type implementations in Java being classified into two distinct groupings: 1) mapping to built-in types; and 2) implemented through Java classes, either standard Java classes or specifically written.

Box 1. Modified SOAP message


```
<?xml version="1.0" encoding="UTF-8"?>
<soapenv:Envelope
 xmlns:xsi="http://www.w3.org/2001/XMLSchema-instance"
 xmlns:soapenv="http://schemas.xmlsoap.org/soap/envelope/"
 xmlns:xsd="http://www.w3.org/2001/XMLSchema">
 <soapenv:Body>
  <ns1:fooDouble
   xmlns:ns1="http://www.nik.looker.name/TestService/"
   soapenv:encodingStyle="http://schemas.xmlsoap.org/soap/encoding/">
   <fooDoubleRequest href="#id0"></fooDoubleRequest>
  </ns1:fooDouble>
  <multiRef
   xmlns:soapenc="http://schemas.xmlsoap.org/soap/encoding/"
   xsi:type="xsd:double"
   xsi:nil="true"
   soapenv:encodingStyle="http://schemas.xmlsoap.org/soap/encoding/"
   soapenc:root="0"
   id="id0">
    0.0
  </multiRef>
 </soapenv:Body>
</soapenv:Envelope>
```


The groups that do not generate any exceptions are groups of *xsd* types that map to Java classes, and therefore the null parameter can be passed as a valid parameter. This indicates that no schema validation is explicitly performed. The group that generates exceptions (the dark grey shaded group in Table 2) map to built-in types. These types cannot assume a null value in Java, so the implementation is mapping the null value to a generic Java *Object* and attempting to match to *method(Object)* which does not exist in the service; consequently the misleading exception is thrown. It can therefore be concluded that the exception is being thrown as a consequence of executing an unexpected control pathway, rather than a deliberately implemented piece of guard code in the middleware.

Table 2. Protocol invalidation results

xsd:type	Returned value equals sent value	Exception Generated
Map to built-in Java type	No result returned	No such operation
Map to Standard Java Library Class	FALSE	None
Map to Apache Axis Class	FALSE	None

Injecting Bad Data

This experiment examines two *xsd* types when invalid data is injected. It examines whether ASCII characters, which invalidate the schema for the xsd types, are detected by the middleware and rejected.

Box 2: Language message after injection

```
<?xml version="1.0" encoding="UTF-8"?>
 <soapenv:Envelope
  xmlns:xsi="http://www.w3.org/2001/XMLSchema-instance"
  xmlns:soapenv="http://schemas.xmlsoap.org/soap/envelope/"
  xmlns:xsd="http://www.w3.org/2001/XMLSchema">
  <soapenv:Body>
   <ns1:fooLanguage
    xmlns:ns1="http://www.nik.looker.name/TestService/"
    soapenv:encodingStyle="http://schemas.xmlsoap.org/soap/encoding/">
    <fooLanguageRequest
     xsi:type="xsd:language">
      some bad data
   </fooLanguageRequest>
  </ns1:fooLanguage>
 </soapenv:Body>
</soapenv:Envelope>
```

The first type is an *xsd language* type. A valid *language* type has strict rules about the data that can be encoded with in it. The encoding follows a schema that defines the types and positions of ASCII characters that can be included in this element. Box 2 shows the message after the fault is injected. The new element contents are invalid since both the characters contained and the placement of the characters are invalid.

The unmarshaling of this invalid data did not generate any exceptions (see Table 3). The only consequence of this injection was that the returned value was not equal to the original value. Since this type is built upon a string type, it is reasonable to assume that the unmarshaling process assumes that the input data is valid and inserts it directly into the class instance without validating it. Conversely a check of the Apache Axis class that implements this type in Java shows that validation is done when the normal constructors are used.

Table 3. Invalid data results

Xsd:type	Returned value equals sent value	Exception Generated
Language	FALSE	None
PositiveInteger	No result returned	Number Format Exception

The second *xsd* type assessed was *PositiveInteger*. When bad data was injected into this message exchange a *Number Format Exception* was generated. Whilst this would appear to be a valid exception closer inspection of the code revealed that this exception was generated as part of the standard Java string to number parsing mechanism, not as part of an explicit validation mechanism. This exception can therefore be considered an interaction fault.

Invalid by Omission Faults

This experiment injected syntactically correct data into the elements containing xsd types, but in one case the data invalidated the type's schema by omission (it should have started with a minus sign). This test gave an appropriate exception but, as above, this was generated by the Java class parsing the value, rather than a direct validation against the schema.

Table 4. Invalid by omission results

xsd:type	Returned value equals sent value	Exception Generated
NonNegativeInteger	FALSE	None
NonPositiveInteger	No result returned	NumberFormatException

The nonNegativeInteger was also injected as a control and since the value 128 was a correct value for this type the only consequence of this injection was that the returned value did not match the originally sent value.

SUMMARY

This case study has demonstrated how fault injection can be used to perform a dependability assessment of a middleware protocol. The dependability of network and middleware protocols is key to the operation of SOAs since it forms the foundation that SOAs are built upon. Whilst the failures encountered here were relatively minor the potential does exist to exploit them since the validation mechanism used by this middleware resides in the Java classes used to implement both client and server. This would allow an attacker to inject faults directly by sending either hand crafted SOAP messages or modifying existing SOAP stack code.

Comparison of Network Level Fault Injection with Code Insertion

This case study compares network level fault injection to Code Insertion fault injection and demonstrates that it can achieve comparable results. Code Insertion fault injection can create targeted faults which are useful in assessing specific elements of a system but are relatively invasive since they require modifications to the source code.

A test bed system was used based on a simulation of a self-regulating heating system (see Figure 1). As in the previous case study the FIT tool was used to perform middleware level fault injection.

The system was composed of three services and a client:

1. Heater coil
2. Thermocouple
3. Controller

The test bed assumes that the elements of the system are implemented as networked services. The system was designed with three non-functional requirements:

1. The heater coil service was designed to allow only small stepped changes to the power.
2. The heater coil had an upper limit to its temperature output of 100°C, if set above this limit the coil would burn out.

Figure 1. SOA with fault injection instrumentation

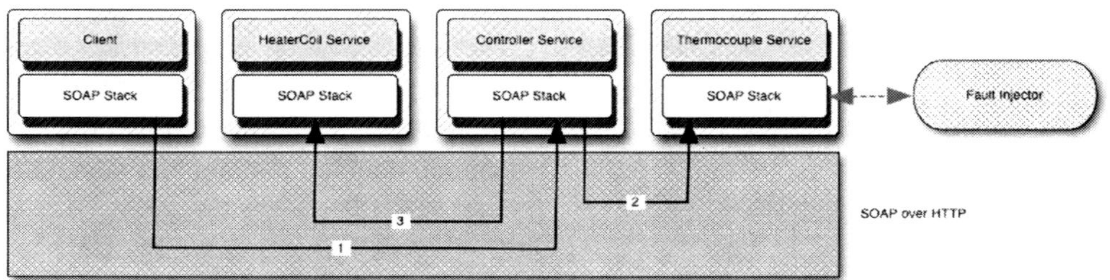

3. The heater coil is calibrated in terms of power, not temperature so gauging the temperature is reliant on the thermocouple.

Each service is hosted on a physically separate server. The *Controller* increments or decrements the temperature of the *Heater Coil* (3) based upon the temperature returned by the *Thermocouple* (2). To affect the system we therefore inject faults on the server hosting the *Thermocouple*.

The controller is hosted on a third server (1). It allows a required temperature to be set. The *Controller* service runs a continuous polling loop that periodically polls the *Thermocouple* service to check that the actual temperature is equivalent to the required temperature. If it is not the *Controller* increments or decrements the power supplied by the *HeaterCoil*, thereby increasing or decreasing the temperature.

In the simulated system the *Thermocouple* requests the currently set power from the *HeaterCoil* and calculates the temperature based on this. In the real system this information would come from the thermocouple hardware.

A simple state machine is implemented by the controller to first increase the temperature to 10˚C, then decrease the temperature to 5˚C and finally increase and hold the temperature at 7˚C.

The test case is performed using two different configurations:

1. A middleware level fault injection system
2. A system using standard Code Insertion.

By comparing the results from these two configurations it can be demonstrate that middleware level fault injection can be used to produce compatible results to Code Insertion whilst being less invasive.

Middleware Level Fault Injection Experiment

The fault injection tool required a slightly modified protocol stack to installed on any server on which faults are to be injected. By strategically positioning this stack on certain machines faults can be propagated to other unmodified machines, this allowing the possibility that it could be used as part of a certification process for individual components of a system. For example if the instrumented SOAP stack is positioned on the server running the *HeaterCoil* service it could be used to certification test the *Thermocouple* or *Controller* since no changes are made to these servers.

Our system is set up to certification test the *HeaterCoil* service so we have chosen to position the instrumented SOAP stack on the machine running the *Thermocouple* service (see Figure 1). In this way we can monitor the output of the *Thermocouple* driver and inject faults into the messages received from the *HeaterCoil* (without modifying the *HeaterCoil* code or environment).

The fault injector was configured to monitor temperature response messages between the *Thermocouple* and the *Controller*. A trigger was created to inject a fault into the getPower responses received by the *Thermocouple* from the *HeaterCoil* after the temperature had reached a certain limit. By modifying this response to give a constantly low value we will attempt to force the controller to continually increase the power emitted by the heater coil, thus causing the heater coil to exceed its maximum power.

Code Insertion Experiment

This configuration demonstrates that Code Insertion can produce similar results to those of middleware level fault injection system. The original code for the services was taken and perturbation functions were inserted at appropriate points to perturb parameters in a similar way to those given above.

Two points were identified for Code Insertion in this scenario but in practice with a complex SOA many more insertion points would potentially be needed, for instance where RPC calls are called from multiple places in the code. One example is given in Box 3 with inserted code marked in grey. This example shows the perturbation required to corrupt the simulated temperature calculation in the *Thermocouple* service by reading back the power setting from the *Heater Coil* service. The perturbation function simply 'wraps' the returned result so that the extra logic is called.

Box 3. Instrumented thermocouple routine

```
private int inject1(int power) {
  int injectPower;
  if (power > 5) {
    injectPower = 5;
  } else {
    injectPower = power;
  }
  System.out.println(power + "," +
    injectPower);
  return injectPower;
}
public int getTemp(int ctx)
  throws java.rmi.RemoteException {
  HeaterCoilServiceLocator locator =
    new HeaterCoilServiceLocator();
  try {
    HeaterCoil service =
      locator.getHeaterCoil(new URL(
        getHeaterContext(ctx).
        getUrl()));
    return inject1(service.getPower(
      getHeaterContext(ctx).
      getCtx())) *
        POWER_TO_TEMP;
} catch (MalformedURLException e) {
    e.printStackTrace();
    throw new RemoteException(
      e.getMessage());
  } catch (ServiceException e) {
    e.printStackTrace();
    throw new RemoteException(
      e.getMessage());
  }
}
```

Results

Three series of data were collected:

1. The Control experiment (Figure 2)
2. Fault injection using middleware level fault injection (Figure 3 and Figure 4)
3. Fault injection using Code Insertion (Figure 3 and Figure 4).

In each case both returned and actual temperature were recorded. The data from the control experiment indicates that the system functions according to its state machine (see Figure 2). The fault injection experiments produced identical data (see Figure 3 & Figure 4). This data demonstrates a problem with the design of the SOA. Once a trigger condition has been met the fault injection modifies the power sent to the *Thermocouple* to a power that indicates a temperature of 1°C and holds at this temperature. The controller is written in a simple fashion. According to its criteria the temperature is too low so it keeps ramping the power to increase the temperature. The heater coil soon exceeds its maximum operating temperature and in a real system would malfunction.

SUMMARY

This case study has demonstrates that middleware level fault injection and Code Insertion fault injection are comparable producing similar results when experiments are preformed. The

Figure 2. Control experiment

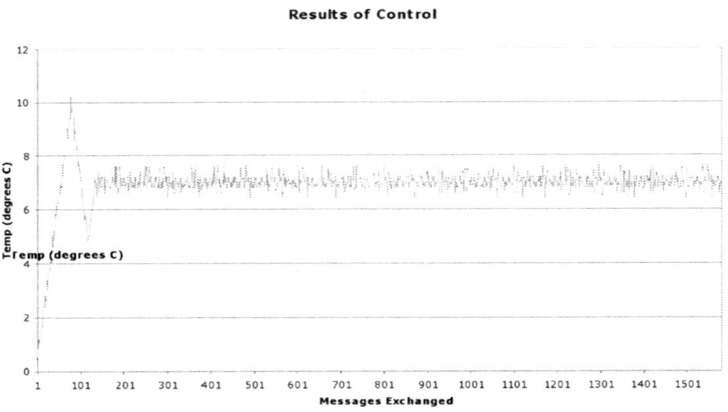

Figure 3. Temperature returned after fault injection

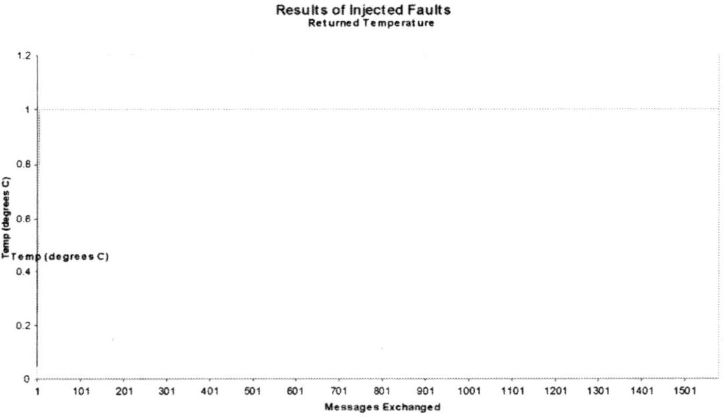

Figure 4. Actual temperature during fault injection

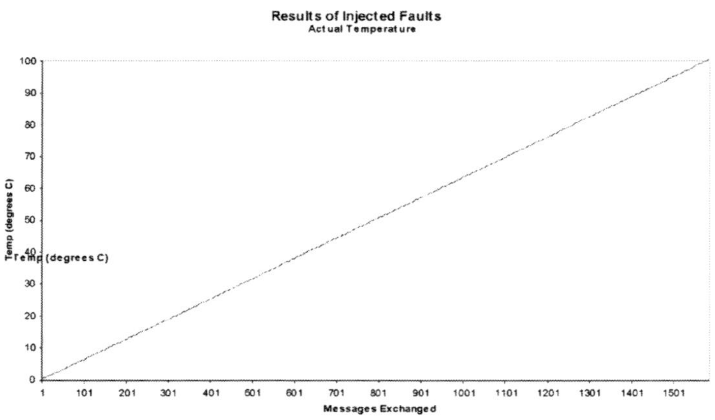

comparison of middleware level fault injection with Code Insertion has indicated that it is less intrusive, requiring just one set of modifications to the network stack on one machine as opposed to many potential modifications for Code Insertion.

Middleware level fault injection also allows specific components within a SOA to be certification tested, provided that strategic decisions on instrumented SOAP stacks are taken based upon which components will be certification tested.

Finally Code Insertion requires access to the service source code to allow placement of extra code where as middleware level fault injection can be based entirely on the WSDL specification since it requires no modifications to the service code.

Fault Tolerance

Whilst the first two case studies have concentrated on assessing dependability through the use of fault injection it must not be forgotten that dependability also includes the concept of dependability Means. This case study demonstrates how dependability means can be used to increase the dependability of a web service system and also how fault injection can be used to assess any improvement introduced.

Redundancy has many attractions for providing fault tolerance and once it has been introduced into a system it can also be used to protect against Byzantine faults through the use of the n-Version model (Pease, Shostak, & Lamport, 1980). The n-Version model is a well-proven mechanism for providing protection against physical failure (Lyu, 1995) under certain conditions. This case study applies this technique to the domain of Web Services to achieve increases in system dependability (Littlewood, Popov, & Strigini, 2000).

The n-Version model uses *n* independently implemented versions of a software component run in parallel. By running the components in parallel with the same input data a set of results is obtained. By using a voting mechanism on these results individual failures in a component can be eliminated and the integrity of the final result is increased. The voter guarantees, to some agreed level of integrity, to return a correct result or flag an error.

Test Scenario

To provide a test bed to demonstrate this fault tolerance technique an SOA was constructed that simulated a typical stock market trading system (See Figure 5). The system was composed of a number of Web Services: 1) A Stock Service to supply real-time stock quotes; 2) A Trade Service to automatically trade shares; and 3) A Bank Service. The Trade Service implemented a simple automatic buying and selling mechanism. Upper and lower limits were set which trigger trading of shares. Shares were sold when the high limit was exceeded and purchased when the quoted price was less than the lower limit.

Two configurations of the test bed system were used. The first was a system implemented without any fault tolerance (See Figure 5). This was used to collect a baseline set of measurements so that comparisons could be made. The second was the same system but with the Stock Service replicated and called through a voter algorithm (See Figure 6).

Figure 5. Simple stock trading system

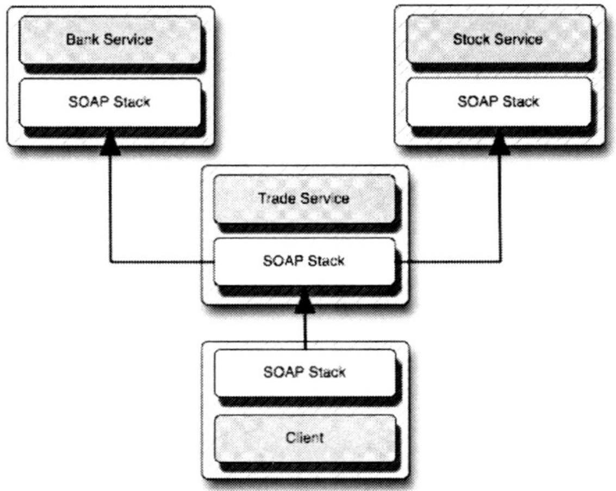

Figure 6. Trading system with replication

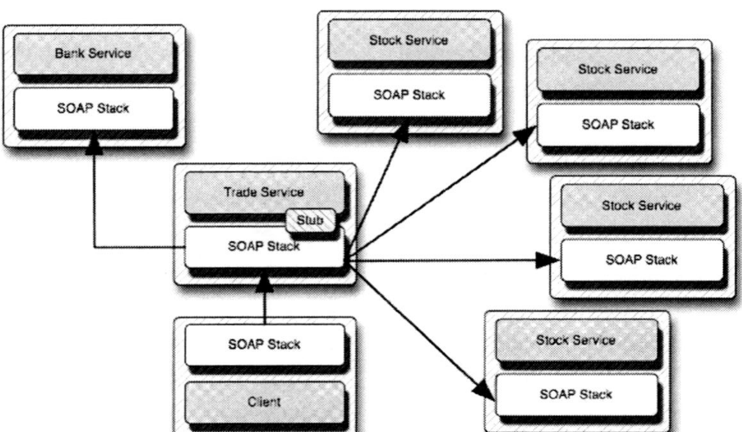

Corrupted Results

To determine whether an n-Voter algorithm increases the reliability of a system, faults were injected into the Web Services returning stock quotes to the trading system. This was done using code insertion with a perturbation function being manually inserted into each Stock service so that each quote returned had a one in five chance of returning a corrupt result. A random number generator controlled the fault injection automatically so that over time the same distribution of faults would be injected into all Stock services. Code insertion fault injection was used since we had access to the source code to undertake the experiment and it is less complex to implement. These factors should be traded off when selecting a technique to use.

Four different system configurations were used. The first two use no replication and the second two use replications to increase reliability. The results are given in Table 5. Each configuration was executed for a period of approximately 24 hours.

The first column describes the operation of the system with no replication and no injected faults. It is included as a baseline. As can be seen under normal conditions the system functions with no incorrect quotes being returned and no race condition mismatches. Incorrect results and No-Consensus calculations are taken as an average of all quotes whilst mismatches are taken as an average of trigger quotes since a mismatch can only occur on a trigger.

When faults are introduced into the unreplicated system there is a 20% increase in incorrect results which is expected because there

Table 5. Corrupted results

	No Replicas	No Replicas	4 Replicas	7 Replicas
	No Faults	Injected Faults	Injected Faults	Injected Faults
Incorrect Results (%)	0.0	20.8	2.8	0.5
Quote Mismatch (%)	0.0	47.0	12.6	2.5
No-Consensus (%)	N/A	N/A	15.9	14.1
Sample Size	2337	2451	2551	2265

is no mechanism in place to prevent them being processed. The 47% mismatches are caused by incorrect quotes being returned as either the trigger or buy/sell price.

The system was then tested using an n-Voter algorithm using 4 replicas (which should compensate for 1 corrupted service) and then 7 replicas (which should compensate for 2 corrupted services). The results showed a marked improvement in reliability with incorrect results dropping to below 3% when 4 replicas were used. The results also show that a percentage of the attempted requests are rejected since a consensus cannot be reached. This is preferable to returning an incorrect result.

SUMMARY

This case study has demonstrated the n-Voter algorithm and its application to Web Services. It can be easily applied to systems with a minimum of change and gives tangible benefits in terms of data integrity and system reliability.

CONCLUSION

This paper has described how Dependability techniques can be applied to SOA to assess and increase certain non-functional requirements. It examines Dependability as a mechanism that measures the dependability of a system through a number of attributes and presents means that can be applied to a system to increase its dependability by breaking fault-error-failure chains. This paper also showed how Dependability techniques can be applied to service based systems to assess and increase Dependability.

The first case study examined how fault injection can be applied to SOA middleware to assess its Dependability attributes. This case study used middleware level fault injection to inject faults into middleware messages rather than network packets, and thus demonstrated how the middleware protocol can be assessed. This showed clear faults within the middleware assessed.

The second case study compared middleware level fault injection with another commonly used form of fault injection, Code Insertion, and showed the two to be comparable. The major benefit of middleware level fault injection over Code Insertion is that middleware level can be used without access to service source code.

The final case study examined the application of a Dependability means, fault tolerance, to an SOA. This demonstrated that in a service based environment a well proven algorithm such as the n-Voter algorithm can be easily applied and provide a substantial increase in Dependability since, in concept, it requires replicated services called through a voter service.

REFERENCES

Avizienis, A., Laprie, J., Randell, B., & Landwehr, C. (2004). Basic concepts and taxonomy of dependable and secure computing. *IEEE Transactions on Dependable and Secure Computing*, *1*(1), 11–33. doi:10.1109/TDSC.2004.2

Avizienis, A., Magnus, U. V., Laprie, J. C., & Randell, B. (2000). Fundamental concepts of dependability. In [Cambridge, MA: IEEE.]. *Proceedings of, ISW-2000*, 7–12.

Bennett, K., Gold, N., Layzell, P., Zhu, F., Brereton, O., Budgen, D., et al. (2003). *A broker architecture for integrating data using a Web Services Environment.* Service-Oriented Computing - ICSOC 2003. Retrieved from http://www.springerlink.com/content/eyckw7ymgd19ytdu

Bennett, K., & Xu, J. (2003). Software services and software maintenance. In *Proceedings of the Seventh European Conference on Software Maintenance and Reengineering,* (pp. 3-12).

Birman, K. (2005). *Distributed systems: Technologies, Web Services, and applications*. Springer.

Birman, K. (2006). The untrustworthy Web Services revolution. *Computer, 39*(2), 98–100. doi:10.1109/MC.2006.73

Boone, L., & Kurtz, D. (1988). *Contemporary business* (5th ed.). Dryden Press.

Box, D., Ehnebuske, D., Kakivaya, G., Layman, A., Mendelsohn, N., Nielsen, H. F., et al. (2000). *Simple Object Access Protocol* (SOAP) 1.1. Retrieved from http://www.w3.org/TR/2000/NOTE-SOAP-20000508

Cabrera, L. F., Kurt, C., & Box, D. (2004). *An introduction to the Web Services Architecture and its specifications*. MSDN White Paper. Retrieved from http://msdn.microsoft.com/en-us/library/ms996441.aspx

Carreira, J., & Silva, J. G. (1998). Why do some (weird) people inject faults? *Software Engineering Notes, 23*(1), 42–43. doi:10.1145/272263.272273

Channabasavaiah, K., Holley, K., & Tuggle, E., Jr. (2008). *Migrating to a Service-Oriented Architecture, part 1*. Retrieved September 10, 2008, from http://www.ibm.com/developerworks/webservices/library/ws-migratesoa/

Christensen, E., Curbera, F., Meredith, G., & Weerawarana, S. (2001). *Web Services Description Language* (WSDL). Retrieved from http://www.w3.org/TR/2001/NOTE-wsdl-20010315

Daran, M., & Thevenod-Fosse, P. (1996). Software error analysis: A real case study involving real faults and mutations. *Software Engineering Notes, 21*(3), 158–171. doi:10.1145/226295.226313

Haas, H., & Brown, A. (2004). *Web Services glossary*. W3C. Retrieved September 10, 2008, from http://www.w3.org/TR/ws-gloss/

Hecht, H., & Hecht, M. (1996). Qualitative interpretation of software test data. In Min, Y., & Tang, D. (Eds.), *Computer-aided design, test, and evaluation for dependability* (pp. 175–181). Beijing: International Academic Publishers.

Kalyanakrishnam, M., Kalbarczyk, Z., & Iyer, R. (1999). *Failure data analysis of a LAN of Windows NT based computers. Reliable Distributed Systems* (pp. 178–189). Lausanne, Switzerland: IEEE Computer Society.

Littlewood, B., Popov, P., & Strigini, L. (2000). *Choosing between fault-tolerance and increased V&V for improving reliability. DSN* (pp. B42–B43). New York: IEEE.

Looker, N., Munro, M., & Xu, J. (2005). A comparison of network level fault injection with code insertion. In *Proceedings of the 29th Annual International Computer Software and Applications Conference (COMPSAC 2005),* (pp. 479-484). Edinburgh, UK.

Looker, N., & Xu, J. (2007). Dependability assessment of Grid middleware. In *Proceedings of 37th Annual IEEE/IFIP International Conference on Dependable Systems and Networks (DSN '07),* (pp. 125-130). Edinburgh, UK.

Lyu, M. R. (1995). *Software fault tolerance* (pp. 315–333). Chichester, New York: John Wiley.

Mani, A., & Nagarajan, A. (2002). *Understanding Quality of Service for Web Services*. Retrieved March 1, 2008, from http://www.ibm.com/developerworks/java/library/ws-quality.html

Marsden, E., Fabre, J., & Arlat, J. (2002). *Dependability of CORBA systems: Service characterization by fault injection*. Symposium on Reliable Distributed Systems, (pp. 276-285). Osaka, Japan: IEEE Computer Society.

Pease, M., Shostak, R., & Lamport, L. (1980). Reaching agreement in the presence of faults. *Journal of the Association of Computing Machinery, 27*(2), 228–234.

Pritchard, J. (1999). *COM and CORBA side by side: Architectures, strategies, and implementations,* (pp. xix, 430). Reading, MA: Addison-Wesley.

Thompson, H. S., Beech, D., Maloney, M., & Mendelsohn, N. (2004). *XML schema part 1: Structures*, (2nd ed.). Retrieved from http://www.w3.org/TR/xmlschema-1/

Vinoski, S. (2002). Where is middleware? *IEEE Internet Computing*, 83–85. doi:10.1109/4236.991448

Voas, J., & McGraw, G. (1998). *Software fault injection: Inoculating programs against errors*. John Wiley & Sons.

Whittaker, J. A. (2001). Software's invisible users. *IEEE Software*, *18*(3), 84–88. doi:10.1109/52.922730

Compilation of References

Aagedal, J. O. (2001). *Quality of Service support in development of distributed systems*. PhD Thesis, University of Oslo, Norway.

Aagedal, J., & Milosevic, Z. (1998). Enterprise modeling and QoS for command and control systems. *The Second International Enterprise Distributed Object Computing Workshop*, IEEE, November 3-5, 1998, (pp. 88-101).

Aalst, W. M. P. V. D. (2001). Exterminating the dynamic change bug: A concrete approach to support workflow change. *Information Systems Frontiers*, *3*(3), 297–317. doi:10.1023/A:1011409408711

Abadi, M. & Lamport, L. (2009). Composing specifications. *ACM Transactions of Programming Language Systems, 15*(1).

Adopted Specification, O. M. G. (2004). *UML profile for modeling Quality of Service and fault tolerance characteristics and mechanisms*. Retrieved from http:// www. omg.org

Agarwal, V., Chafle, G., Dasgupta, K., Kamik, N., Kumar, A., & Mittal, S. (2005). Synthy: A system for end to end composition of Web Services. *Journal of Web Semantics*, *3*, 311–339. doi:10.1016/j.websem.2005.09.002

Aggarwal, R., Verma, K., Miller, J., & Milnor, W. (2004). Constraint driven Web Service composition in METEOR-S. Proceedings of IEEE International Conference on Services Computing. New York, NY.

Alam, M., Hafner, M., & Breu, R. (2008). Constraint based role based access control in the SECTET-framework: A model-driven approach. *Journal of Computer Security*, *16*(2).

Alessandrini, M., & Dost, D. (2007). *D8.3.a: Requirements modelling and analysis of selected scenarios-finance case study*. Retrieved from http://www.sensoria-ist.eu/

Al-Masri, E., & Mahmoud, Q. (2008a). Discovering Web Services in search engines. *IEEE Internet Computing*, *12*(3), 74–77. doi:10.1109/MIC.2008.53

Al-Masri, E., & Mahmoud, Q. (2008b). *Investigating Web Services on the World Wide Web* (pp. 795–804). WWW.

Al-Masri, E., & Mahmoud, Q. H. (2007b). *QoS-based discovery and ranking of Web Services* (pp. 529–534). ICCCN.

Al-Masri, E., & Mahmoud, Q. (2007c). QoS-based discovery and ranking of Web Services. In *Computer Communications and Networks,* 529–534.

Al-Masri, E., & Mahmoud, Q. H. (2007a). Discovering the best Web Service. In *WWW '07: Proceedings of The 16th International Conference on World Wide Web,* (pp. 1257–1258). New York: ACM.

Alonso, G., Casati, F., Kuno, H., & Machiraju, V. (2004). *Web Services: Concepts, architectures and applications*. Springer-Verlag.

Alwagait, E., & Ghandeharizadeh, S. (2004). Dew: A dependable Web Services framework. *Research Ideas in Data Engineering*, *1*, 111–118.

Amazon, E. C-2 Support Team. (2007). Amazon EC-2 outage report. Retrieved from http://developer.amazon webservices.com/ connect/message. jspa?message ID = 56849#56849

Ammar, H. H., Nikzadeh, T., & Dugan, J. B. (1997). *A methodology for risk assessment of functional specification of software systems using colored Petri nets.* Paper presented at the Fourth International Software Metrics Symposium, Los Alamitos, CA, USA.

Andrieux, A., Czajkowski, K., Dan, A., Keahey, K., Ludwig, H., Nakata, T., et al. (2007). *Web Services agreement specification (WS-agreement)*. OGF proposed recommendation (GFD.107). Retrieved from http://www.ogf.org/documents/GFD.107.pdf

Angelov, S., & Grefen, P. (2001). B2B e-contract handling-a survey of projects, papers and standards. (Technical Report TR-CTIT-01-21), University of Twente.

Angelov, S., & Grefen, P. (2004). The business case for B2B e-contracting. In *Proceedings of the 6th International Conference on Electronic Commerce, (ICEC'04)*, Delft (The Netherlands). Battre', D., Hovestadt, M., Kao, O., Keller, A. & Voss, K. (2007). Planning-based scheduling for SLA-awareness and Grid integration. In *Proceedings of The 26th Workshop of the UK Planning and Scheduling Special Interest Group (PlanSIG2007)*, Prague (Czech Republic).

Antkiewicz, M., & Czarnecki, K. (2004). FeaturePlugin: Feature modeling plug-in for Eclipse. In *Proceedings of the 2004 OOPSLA workshop on Eclipse technology eXchange (Eclipse '04 at OOPSLA '04)*, (pp. 67–72). Vancouver, Canada.

Arcelli, F., Raibulet, C., & Tisato, F. (2004). Modeling QoS through architectural reflection. In *Proceedings of the 2005 International Conference on Software Engineering Research and Practice,* (pp. 347-363), Las Vegas, Nevada, USA.

Arnold, A., Vincent, A., & Walukiewicz, I. (2003). Games for synthesis of controllers with partial observation. *Theoretical Computer Science, 303*(1), 7–34. doi:10.1016/S0304-3975(02)00442-5

ART DECO. (2010). *Adaptative infrastructures for decentralised organizations*. Retrieved from http://artdeco.elet.polimi.it/

Au, T. C., & Nau, D. (2007). Reactive query policies: A formalism for planning with volatile external information. In *Proceedings of the IEEE Symposium on Computational Intelligence and Data Management (CIDM),* (pp. 243–250).

Au, T. C., Kuter, U., & Nau, D. S. (2005). Web Service composition with volatile information. In *Proceedings of the International Semantic Web Conference (ISWC),* (pp. 52-66).

Au, T. C., Nau, D. S., & Subrahmanian, V. S. (2004). Utilizing volatile external information during planning. In *Proceedings of the European Conference on Artificial Intelligence (ECAI),* (pp. 647-651).

Austin, T. M. (1999). *DIVA: A reliable substrate for deep submicron microarchitecture design.* Paper presented at the 32nd Annual International Symposium on Microarchitecture.

AUTOSAR. (2006a). *Requirements on operating system (version 2.0.1). Technical report.* Automotive Open System Architecture GbR.

AUTOSAR. (2006b). *Specification of operating system (version 2.0.1). Technical report.* Automotive Open System Architecture GbR.

Avizienis, A., Laprie, J.-C., Randell, B., & Landwehr, C. (2004). Basic concepts and taxonomy of dependable and secure computing. *IEEE Transactions on Dependable and Secure Computing, 1*(1), 11–33. doi:10.1109/TDSC.2004.2

Avizienis, A., Magnus, U. V., Laprie, J. C., & Randell, B. (2000). Fundamental concepts of dependability. In [Cambridge, MA: IEEE.]. *Proceedings of, ISW-2000*, 7–12.

Bachelechner, D., Siorpaes, K., Lausen, H., & Fensel, D. (2006). Web Service discovery-a reality check. In *Demos and Posters of the 3rd European Semantic Web Conference.*

Bachmann, F., Bass, L., Buhman, C., Comella-Dorda, S., Long, F., Robert, J., et al. (2000). *Volume II: Technical concepts of component-based software engineering.* (Technical Report, CMU/SEI-2000-TR-008, 2000).

Balbiani, P., Cheikh, F., & Feuillade, G. (2007). Considérations relatives à la décidabilité et à la complexité du problème de la composition de services. In *Journées Francophones modèle formels de l'interaction,* 261–268. Annales du LAMSADE.

Balbiani, P., Cheikh, F., & Feuillade, G. (2008). Composition of interactive Web Services based on controller synthesis. In *Proceedings of the 2nd International Workshop on Web Service Composition and Adaptation*. Honolulu, USA: IEEE.

Balbiani, P., Cheikh, F., & Feuillade, G. (2008). Composition of Web Services: Algorithms and complexity. In *Proceedings of The 1st Interaction and Concurrency Experience*. Reykjavik, Iceland: ENTCS.

Balogh, A., Varró, D., & Pataricza, A. (2005). *Model-based optimization of enterprise application and service deployment* (pp. 84–98). ISAS.

Bansal, S., & Vidal, J. M. (2003). Matchmaking of Web Services-based on the DAML-S service model. In *Proceedings of the II International Joint Conference on Autonomous Agents and Multiagent Systems,* (pp. 926–927).

Baresi, L., Heckel, R., Thöne, S., & Varró, D. (2006). Style-based modeling and refinement of Service-Oriented Architectures. *Software and Systems Modeling, 5*(2), 187–207. doi:10.1007/s10270-006-0001-4

Baresi, L., Ghezzi, C., & Guinea, S. (2004). Smart monitors for composed services. *ICSOC '04: Proceedings of the 2nd international conference on Service oriented computing,* (pp. 193-202). ACM Press.

Barreiro, D., Licchelli, O., Albers, P., & de Araújo, R.-J. (2008). *Personalized reliable Web Service compositions*. WONTO.

Basin, D., Doser, J., & Lodderstedt, T. (2006). Model driven security: From UML models to access control infrastructures. In *ACM Transactions on Software Engineering and Methodology*, 2006.

Bass, L. (2006). Principles for designing software architecture to achieve quality attribute requirements. In *SERA '06: Proceedings of the Fourth International Conference on Software Engineering Research, Management and Applications*, (p. 2), Washington, DC, USA. IEEE Computer Society.

Batory, D. S. (2005). Feature models, grammars, and propositional formulas. In *Proceedings of the 9th Software Product Line Conference (SPLC '05)*, (pp. 7–20).

Beco, S., Cantalupo, B., & Matskanis, N. L. G. & Surridge, M. (2005). OWL-WS: A workflow ontology for dynamic Grid Service composition. In *Proceedings of the First International Conference on e-Science and Grid Computing.*

Beeri, C., Eyal, A., Kamenkovich, S., & Milo, T. (2006). Querying business processes. Proceedings of the 32nd International Conference on Very Large Data Bases. Korea.

Benavides, D., Segura, S., Trinidad, P., & Ruiz-Cortés, A. (2006). A first step towards a framework for the automated analysis of feature models. In *Managing Variability for Software Product Lines*. Working With Variability Mechanisms.

Benavides, D., Ruiz-Cortés, A., & Trinidad, P. (2005). Automated reasoning on feature models. *Proceedings of Advanced Information Systems Engineering: 17th International Conference, CAiSE 2005*, (LNCS 3520), (491–503).

Benavides, D., Segura, S., Trinidad, P., & Ruiz-Cortés, A. (2007). FAMA: Tooling a framework for the automated analysis of feature models. In *Proceeding of the First International Workshop on Variability Modeling of Software-Intensive Systems (VAMOS).*

Bennett, K., & Xu, J. (2003). Software services and software maintenance. In *Proceedings of the Seventh European Conference on Software Maintenance and Reengineering,* (pp. 3-12).

Bennett, K., Gold, N., Layzell, P., Zhu, F., Brereton, O., Budgen, D., et al. (2003). *A broker architecture for integrating data using a Web Services Environment.* Service-Oriented Computing - ICSOC 2003. Retrieved from http://www.springerlink.com/content/eyckw7ymgd19ytdu

Berardi, D., Cheikh, F., Giacomo, G. D., & Patrizi, F. (2008). Automatic service composition via simulation. *International Journal of Foundations of Computer Science, 19*(2), 429–451. doi:10.1142/S0129054108005759

Berardi, D., Giacomo, G. D., Mecella, M., & Calvanese, D. (2006). *Composing Web Services with nondeterministic behavior* (pp. 909–912). ICWS.

Berardi, D., Calvanese, D., De Giacomo, G., Hull, R., & Mecella, M. (2005). Automatic composition of transition-based Semantic Web Services with messaging. In *Proceedings of the 31st International Conference on Very Large Data Bases,* (pp.613–624). Trondheim, Norway: ACM.

Berardi, D., Calvanese, D., De Giacomo, G., & Mecella, M. (2006). Composing Web Services with nondeterministic behavior. *In Proceedings of the IEEE International Conference on Web Services,* (pp. 909-912). Chicago: IEEE Computer Society.

Bergmann, G., Horváth, Á., Ráth, I., & Varró, D. (2008). A benchmark evaluation of incremental pattern matching in graph transformation. *Proceedings of International Conference on Graph Transformations* (ICGT), (LNCS 5214). Springer-Verlag.

Bertoli, P., Pistore, M., & Traverso, P. (2006). Automated Web Service composition by on-the-fly belief space search. In *Proceedings of the Sixteenth International Conference on Automated Planning and Scheduling,* (pp. 358–361). Cumbria, UK: AAAI.

Beuche, D. (2003). *Variant management with pure variants*. Technical report, pure-systems GmbH. http://www.pure-systems.com/.

Beuche, D., Guerrouat, A., Papajewski, H., Schröder-Preikschat, W., Spinczyk, O., & Spinczyk, U. (1999). On the development of object-oriented operating systems for deeply embedded systems-the PURE project. In *Object-Oriented Technology: ECOOP '99 Workshop Reader*, Lisbon, Portugal. (LNCS 1743), (pp. 27–31). Springer-Verlag.

Birman, K. (2005). *Distributed systems: Technologies, Web Services, and applications*. Springer.

Birman, K. (2006). The untrustworthy Web Services revolution. *Computer*, *39*(2), 98–100. doi:10.1109/MC.2006.73

Birman, K. P., Renesse, R. v., & Vogels, W. (2004). Adding high availability and autonomic behavior to Web Services. *Proceedings of the 26th International Conference on Software Engineering (ICSE 2004),* (pp. 17-26). Edinburgh: IEEE Computer Society.

BITKOM Consortium. (2007). Betriebssichere Rechnenzentren. Retrieved from http://www.bitkom.org

Blanco, E., Cardinale, Y., Vidal, M.-E., & Graterol, J. (2008). Techniques to produce optimal Web Service compositions. In *Proceedings of 2008 IEEE Congress on Services 2008 - Part I (SERVICES-1 2008),* (pp. 553–558). Honolulu, HI: IEEE Computer Society.

Boger, M., Sturm, T., & Fragemann, P. (2003). *Refactoring browser for UML.* Paper presented at the International Conference on Objects, Components, Architectures, Services, and Applications for a Networked World, Berlin, Germany. (LNCS 2591).

Bondavalli, A., Latella, D., Majzik, I., Pataricza, A., & Savoia, G. (2001). Dependability analysis in the early phases of UML based system design. *Journal of Computer Systems Science and Engineering*, *16*(5), 265–275.

Bonet, B., Haslum, P., Hickmott, S., & Thiébaux, S. (2008). *Directed unfolding of petri nets* (pp. 172–198).

Boone, L., & Kurtz, D. (1988). *Contemporary business* (5th ed.). Dryden Press.

Börger, E., & Stark, R. (2003). *Abstract state machines. A method for high-level system design and analysis*. Springer-Verlag.

Borgida, A., & Murata, T. (1999). Tolerating exceptions in workflows: A unified framework for data and processes. In *Proceedings of the International Conference on Work Activities Coordination and Collaboration (WACC),* (pp. 59–68).

Bormann, F., et al. (2005). Towards context-aware service discovery: A case study for a new advice of charge service. Proceedings of the 14th IST Mobile and Wireless Communications Summit. Dresden.

Bowles, J. B. (2004). An assessment of RPN prioritization in a failure modes effects and criticality analysis. *Journal of the IEST*, *47*, 51–56.

Bowles, J. B. (1998). *The new SAE FMECA standard.* Paper presented at the International Symposium on Product Quality and Integrity.

Box, D., Ehnebuske, D., Kakivaya, G., Layman, A., Mendelsohn, N., Nielsen, H. F., et al. (2000). *Simple Object Access Protocol* (SOAP) 1.1. Retrieved from http://www.w3.org/TR/2000/NOTE-SOAP-20000508

BPEL4WS. (2007). Specifications. Retrieved from http://www128.ibm.com/developerworks/ library/specification/ws-bpel/

Brambilla, M., Ceri, S., Comai, S., & Tziviskou, C. (2005). Exception handling in workflow-driven Web applications. In *Proceedings of the World Wide Web conference (WWW)*, (pp. 170–179). New York: ACM.

Brickley, D., & Guha, R. V. (2000). *Resource Description Framework (RDF) schemas.* W3C. Retrieved from http://www.w3.org/TR/2000/CR-rdf-schema-20000327/

Broens, T., et al. (2004). Context-aware, ontology-based, service discovery. Ambient Intelligence, (LNCS 3295), (pp.72-83).

Brogi, A., Corfini, S., & Popescu, R. (2008). Semantics-based composition oriented discovery of Web Services. *ACM Transactions on Internet Technology*, *8*(4), 1–39. doi:10.1145/1391949.1391953

BuDDy Developers. (2009). *BuDDy project.* Retrieved from http://sourceforge.net/projects/buddy

Bulka, D. (1992). Fault tree models for reliability analysis of an FDDI token ring network. *Proceedings of the 30th Annual Southeast Regional Conference.*

Burbeck, S. (2000). *The Tao of e-business services. Emerging Technologies.* IBM Software Group.

Buskens, R., & Gonzalez, O. (2007). *Model-centric development of highly available software systems.* Springer-Verlag.

Buyya, R., Yeo, C. S., & Venugopal, S. (2008). Market-oriented Cloud Computing: Vision, hype, and reality for delivering IT services as computing utilities, Keynote Paper. In *Proceedings of 10th IEEE International Conference on High Performance Computing and Communications (HPCC 2008)*, Dalian, (China).

Cabrera, L. F., Kurt, C., & Box, D. (2004). *An introduction to the Web Services Architecture and its specifications.* MSDN White Paper. Retrieved from http://msdn.microsoft.com/en-us/library/ms996441.aspx

Caceres, P., Marcos, E., & Vera, B. (2003). A MDA-based approach for Web Information System development. Workshop in Software Model Engineering (WiSME@UML2003).

Canfora, G., Di Penta, M., Esposito, R., Perfetto, F., & Villani, M. L. (2006). Service composition (re)binding driven by application-specific QoS. Proceedings of the 4th International Conference on Service Oriented Computing. Chicago, USA.

Cardellini, V., Casalicchio, E., Grassi, V., & Presti, F. L. (2007). Flow-based service selection for Web Service composition supporting multiple QoS classes. In *Proceedings of IEEE 2007 International Conference on Web Services.*

Cardoso, J., & Sheth, A. (2003). Semantic e-workflow composition. *Journal of Intelligent Information Systems*, *21*(3), 191–225. doi:10.1023/A:1025542915514

Cardoso, J., Sheth, A., Miller, J., Arnold, J., & Kochut, K. (2004). Quality of service for workflows and Web Service processes. *Journal of Web Semantics*, *1*(3), 281–308. doi:10.1016/j.websem.2004.03.001

Carreira, J., & Silva, J. G. (1998). Why do some (weird) people inject faults? *Software Engineering Notes*, *23*(1), 42–43. doi:10.1145/272263.272273

Casati, F., Ilnicki, S., Jin, L.-J., & Shan, M.-C. (2000). An open, flexible, and configurable system for service composition. In *Proceedings of the 2nd International Workshop on Advanced Issues of E-Commerce and Web-Based Information Systems,* (pp. 125 – 132).

Casola, V., Fasolino, A. R., Mazzocca, N., & Tramontana, P. (2007). A policy-based evaluation framework for quality and security in Service Oriented Architectures. In *Proceedings of IEEE International Conference on Web Services,* (pp. 1181-1190).

Cerami, E. (2002). *Web services essentials.* O'Reilly.

Chafle, G., Dasgupta, K., Kumar, A., Mittal, S., & Srivastava, B. (2006). Adaptation in Web Service composition and execution. In *IEEE International Conference on Web Services (ICWS),* (pp. 549-557).

Chafle, G., Doshi, P., Harney, J., Mital, S., & Srivastava, B. (2007). Improved adaptation of Web Service compositions using value of changed information. In *Proceedings of the IEEE International conference on Web Services (ICWS)* (pp. 784-791).

Chan, P. W., Lyu, M. R., & Malek, M. (2007). *Reliable Web Services: Methodology, experiment and modeling.* IEEE International Conference on Web Services.

Channabasavaiah, K., Holley, K., & Tuggle, E., Jr. (2008). *Migrating to a Service-Oriented Architecture, part 1.* Retrieved September 10, 2008, from http://www.ibm.com/developerworks/webservices/library/ws-migratesoa/

Charfi, A., & Mezini, M. (2004). Aspect oriented Web Service composition with AO4BPEL. *Proceedings of The European Conference on Web Services.*

Charfi, A., & Mezini, M. (2005). An aspect based process container for BPEL. *Proceedings of The First Workshop on Aspect-Oriented Middleware Developement.* Genoble, France.

Cheikh, F. (2009). Problème de la composition: Modèle et complexité. PhD thesis, Université de Toulouse.

Cheikh, F., De Giacomo, D., & Mecella, M. (2006). Automatic Web Services composition in trustaware communities. In *Proceedings of the 3rd ACM Workshop On Secure Web Services,* (pp. 43-52). Alexandria, VA: ACM.

Chen, S., & Hwang, C. (1991). *Fuzzy multiple attribute decision making: Method and applications. (LNEMS 375).* New York: Springer-Verlag.

Chen, C. L., & Hsiao, M. Y. (1984). Error-correcting codes for semiconductor memory applications: A state-of-the-art review. *IBM Journal of Research and Development, 28*(2), 124–134. doi:10.1147/rd.282.0124

Chen, G., & Kotz, D. (2000). *A survey of context-aware mobile computing research.* In (Technical Report TR2000-381), Darthmouth Computer Science. Hanover, USA.

Chen, H., Yu, T., & Lin, K. (2003). QCWS: An implementation of QoS-capable multimedia Web services. In *Proceedings of the Fifth International Symposium on Multimedia Software Engineering,* (pp. 38-45).

Chen, L., Shadbolt, N. R., Goble, C. A., Tao, F., Cox, S. J., Puleston, C., et al. (2003). Towards a knowledge-based approach to semantic service composition. In *2nd International Semantic Web Conference (ISWC),* (pp. 319-334).

Cheng, B.H.C., de Lemos, R., Giese, H., Inverardi, P. & Magee, J. (2009). Software engineering for self-adaptive systems. (LNCS 5525).

Chia, L. T., Zhou, C., & Lee, B. S. (2004). DAML-QoS ontology for Web Services. *The International Conference on Web Services ICWS,* (p. 472-479). San Diego: IEEE Computer Society.

Chidamber, S. R., & Kemerer, C. F. (1994). A metrics suite for object oriented design. *IEEE Transactions on Software Engineering, 20*(6), 476–493. doi:10.1109/32.295895

Chiu, D. K. W., Li, Q., & Karlapalem, K. (1999). A meta modeling approach to workflow management systems supporting exception handling. *Information Systems, 24*(2), 159–184. doi:10.1016/S0306-4379(99)00010-1

Choonhwa, L., & Helal, S. (2003). Context attributes: An approach to enable context-awareness for service discovery. Proceedings of Symposium on Applications & the Internet. Orlando, USA.

Chorfi, H., & Jemni, M. (2004). PERSO: Towards an adaptive e-learning system. *Journal of Interactive Learning, 15*(4), 433–447.

Christensen, E., Curbera, F., Meredith, G., Weerawarana, S. & W3C. (2001). *Web Services Description Language (WSDL) 1.1.*

Christensen, E., Curbera, F., Meredith, G., & Weerawarana, S. (2001). *Web Services Description Language* (WSDL). Retrieved from http://www.w3.org/TR/2001/NOTE-wsdl-20010315

Clarke, E. M., Long, D. E., & McMillan, K. L. (1989). *Compositional model checking.* In Proceedings of the 4th Symposium on Logic in Computer Science, (pp. 353-362).

Claro, D. B., Albers, P., & Hao, J.-K. (2006). Web Services composition. In *Semantic Web Services* (pp. 195–225). Processes and Applications.

Coady, Y., & Kiczales, G. (2003). Back to the future: A retroactive study of aspect evolution in operating system code. In M. Akşit (Ed.), *Proceedings of the 2nd International Conference on Aspect-Oriented Software Development (AOSD '03),* (pp. 50–59). Boston:ACM Press.

Coady, Y., Kiczales, G., Feeley, M., & Smolyn, G. (2001). Using AspectC to improve the modularity of path-specific customization in operating system code. In *Proceedings of the 3rd Joint European Software Engineering Conference and ACM Symposium on the Foundations of Software Engineering (ESEC/FSE '01).*

CoDAMoS. (2008). Ontology. Retrieved from www.cs.kuleuven.ac.be/cwis/research/distrinet/ projects/CoDAMoS/ontology/

Combs, V. T., Hillman, R. G., Muccio, M. T., & McKeel, R. W. (2005). Joint Battlespace Infosphere: Information management within a C2 enterprise. *Proceedings of the 10th International Command and Control Research and Technology Symposium.*

Commuzi, M., & Pernici, B. (2005). An architecture for flexible Web Service QoS negotiation. Proceedings of the 9th IEEE Enterprise Computing Conference. The Netherlands.

Constantinescu, I., Faltings, B., & Binder, W. (2004). *Large scale, type-compatible service composition* (pp. 506–513). ICWS.

Contreras, J. L., & Sourrouille, J. L. (2001). A framework for QoS management. In *Proceedings of the 39th International Conference and Exhibition on Technology of Object-Oriented Languages and Systems,* (pp. 183-193).

Cortellessa, V., Goseva-Popstojanova, K., Appukkutty, K., Guedem, A. R., Hassan, A., & Elnaggar, R. (2005). Model-based performance risk analysis. *IEEE Transactions on Software Engineering, 31*(1), 3–20. doi:10.1109/TSE.2005.12

Cortellessa, V., Marco, A. D., & Inverardi, P. (2006). Software performance model-driven architecture. In *Proceedings of the 2006 ACM Symposium on Applied Computing.* (pp. 1218– 1223). New York: ACM Press.

Cotroneo, D., Di Flora, C. & Russo, S. (2003). *An enhanced Service Oriented Architecture for developing Web-based applications. Journal of Web Engineering.*

Cover, R. (2008). *Universal description, discovery, and integration.* Technical Report. Retrieved from http://xml.coverpages.org/uddi.html

Crnkovic, I., Larsson, M., & Preiss, O. (2005). *Concerning predictability in dependable component-based systems: Classification of quality attributes.* In de Lemos et al. (Eds.), *Architecting dependable systems III,* (LNCS 3549), (pp. 257 -278).

Crnkovic, I., Schmidt, H., Stafford, J., & Wallnau, K. (2001). *Proceedings of the 4th ICSE Workshop on Component-Based Software Engineering: Component Certification and System Predication,* 2001

Crouzet, Y., Collet, J., & Arlat, J. (2005). *Mitigating soft errors to prevent a hard threat to dependable computing.* Paper presented at the 11th IEEE International On-Line Testing Symposium, IOLTS.

Cuddy, S., Katchabaw, M., & Lutfiyya, H. (2005). Context-aware service selection based on dynamic and static service attributes. Proceedings of IEEE International Conference on Wireless and Mobile Computing, Networking and Communication. Montreal, Canada.

Cysneiros, L. M., & do Prado Leite, J. C. S. (2004). Non-functional requirements: From elicitation to conceptual models. *IEEE Transactions on Software Engineering, 30*(5), 328–350. doi:10.1109/TSE.2004.10

Cysneiros, L., & Leite, J. (2004). Nonfunctional requirements: From elicitation to conceptual models. *IEEE Transactions on Software Engineering, 30,* 328–350. doi:10.1109/TSE.2004.10

Czarnecki, K., & Eisenecker, U. W. (2000). *Generative programming. Methods, tools and applications.* Addison-Wesley.

Czarnecki, K., Helsen, S., & Eisenecker, U. W. (2005a). Formalizing cardinality-based feature models and their specialization. *Software Process Improvement and Practice, 10*(1), 7–29. doi:10.1002/spip.213

Czarnecki, K., Helsen, S., & Eisenecker, U. W. (2005b). Staged configuration through specialization and multi-level configuration of feature models. *Software Process Improvement and Practice, 10*(2), 143–169. doi:10.1002/spip.225

Czarnecki, K., & Wasowski, A. (2007). Feature diagrams and logics: There and back again. In *Proceedings of the 11th Software Product Line Conference (SPLC '07),* (pp. 23–34).

Dahlin, M., Baddepudi, B., Chandra, V., Gao, L., & Nayate, A. (2003). End-to-end WAN service availability. *IEEE/ACM Transactions on Networking, 11*(2). doi:10.1109/TNET.2003.810312

Dal Lago, U., Pistore, M., & Traverso, P. (2002). Planning with a language for extended goals. In *Proceedings of the 18th National Conference on Artificial Intelligence and 14th Conference on Innovative Applications of Artificial Intelligence,* (447–454). Alberta, Canada: AAAI Press.

Damiano, G., Giallonardo, E., & Zimeo, E. (2007). OnQoS-QL: A query language for service selection and ranking. *Proceedings of ICSOC '07 Workshop on Non Functional Properties and Service Level Agreements.* Vienna, Austria.

Dantas, A., & Borba, P. (2003). Adaptability aspects: An architectural pattern for structuring adaptive applications with aspects. In *Proceedings of the 3rd Latin American Conference on Pattern languages of Programming,* (pp. 12-15).

Daran, M., & Thevenod-Fosse, P. (1996). Software error analysis: A real case study involving real faults and mutations. *Software Engineering Notes, 21*(3), 158–171. doi:10.1145/226295.226313

Darwiche, A. (1995). Model-based diagnosis using causal networks. In *Proceedings of International Joint Conference on Artificial Intelligence (IJCAI-95),* (pp. 211-219).

De Bruijn, J., Lausen, H., Krummenacher, R., Polleres, A., Predoiu, L., Kifer, M., et al. (2005). *The Web Service Modeling Language WSML.* Retrieved from http://www.wsmo.org/TR/d16/d16.1/v0.21/

Dean, M., & Schreiber, G. (2004). *OWL Web ontology language reference.* W3C recommendation. Retrieved from http://www.w3.org: http://www.w3.org/TR/owl-ref/

Debusmann, M., & Keller, A. (2003). SLA-driven management of distributed systems using the common information model. Proceedings of the 8th IFIP/IEEE International Symposium on Integrated Network Management. USA, March.

Desai, N., Chopra, A. K., & Singh, M. P. (2006a). Business process adaptations via protocols. In *IEEE Conference on Services-Centered Computing (SCC),* (pp. 601-608).

Desai, N., Mallya, A. U., Chopra, A. K., & Singh, M. P. (2006b). Owl-p: A methodology for business process modeling and enactment. In *Proceedings of Agent-Oriented Information Systems-iii,* (LNCS 3529), (pp. 79-94).

Desmet, L., Joosen, W., Massacci, F., Philippaerts, P., Piessensa, F., Siahaan, I., et al. (2008). *Security-by-contract on the.NET platform.* (Information Security Technical Report).

Deubler, M., Meisinger, M., & Kruger, I. (2005). Modelling crosscutting services with UML sequence diagrams. Proceedings of ACM/IEEE 8th International Conference on Model Driven Engineering Languages and Systems, Jamaica.

Di Modica, G., Tomarchio, O., & Vita, L. (2009). Dynamic SLAs management in service oriented environments. *Journal of Systems and Software, 82*(5), 759–771. doi:10.1016/j.jss.2008.11.010

Dialani, V., Miles, S., Moreau, L., Roure, D. D., & Luck, M. (2002). Transparent fault tolerance for Web Services based architectures. *Proceedings of the Eighth International Europar Conference (EURO-PAR '02).* Padeborn, Germany: Springer-Verlag.

Dobrzanski, L., & Kuzniarz, L. (2006). *An approach to refactoring of executable UML models.* Paper presented at the ACM Symposium on Applied Computing, New York.

Dolbec, J., & Shepard, T. (1995). *A component based software reliability model.* Ontario: Department of Electrical and Computer Engineering, Royal Military College of Canada.

Doshi, P., Goodwin, R., Akkiraju, R. & Verma, K. (2005). Dynamic workflow composition using Markov decision processes. *Journal of Web Services research (JWSR), 2*(1), 1–17.

Doulkeridis, C., Loutas, N., & Vazirgiannis, M. (2006). A system architecture for context-aware service discovery. *Electronic Notes in Theoretical Computer Science, 146*(1), 101–116. doi:10.1016/j.entcs.2005.11.010

Dubois, D., & Prade, H. (1984). Criteria aggregation and ranking of alternatives in the framework of fuzzy set theory. *Studies in the Management Sciences, 20,* 209–240.

Duftler, M.J., Mukhi, N.K., Slominski, A. & Sanc. (2009). *Web Services Invocation Framework (WSIF).*

Duschka, O., & Levy, A. (1997). Recursive plans for information gathering. In *Proceedings IJCAI-97.*

Dustdar, S., & Schreiner, W. (2005). A survey on Web Services composition. *International Journal of Web and Grid Services*, *1*(1), 1–30. doi:10.1504/IJWGS.2005.007545

ECDB. (2007). An open source approach to configuration management. Retrieved from http://www.cmdb.info

Eclipse Foundation. (2008a). Rich client platform. Retrieved from http://www.eclipse.org/ home/ categories/ rcp.php

Eclipse Foundation. (2008b). Eclipse modeling framework. Retrieved from http://www.eclipse.org/ modeling/ emf/ ?project = emf

Eclipse Foundation. (2008c). Graphical modeling framework. Retrieved from http://www.eclipse.org/ modeling/ gmf/

Eclipse Foundation. (2008d). M2M project. Retrieved from http://www.eclipse.org/m2m/

Engel, M., & Freisleben, B. (2006). TOSKANA: A toolkit for operating system kernel aspects. In Rashid, A., & Aksit, M. (Eds.), *Transactions on AOSD II, (LNCS 4242)* (pp. 182–226). Springer-Verlag.

Engel, M., & Freisleben, B. (2005). Supporting autonomic computing functionality via dynamic operating system kernel aspects. In P. Tarr (Ed.), *Proceedings of the 4th International Conference on Aspect-Oriented Software Development (AOSD '05)*, (pp. 51–62). Chicago: ACM Press.

Erl, T. (2005). *Service-Oriented Architecture: Concepts, technology and design*. USA: Prentice Hall PTR.

Erradi, A., & Maheshwari, P. (2005). *AdaptiveBPEL: A policy-driven middleware for flexible Web Services composition*. Enschede, The Netherlands: Proceedings of Middleware for Web Services.

Erradi, A., & Maheshwari, P. (2005). WSBus: QoS-aware middleware for relaible Web Services interaction. *Proceedings of the IEEE International Conference on e-Technology, e-Commerce and e-Service.* Hong Kong, China.

Erradi, A., Maheshwari, P., & Padmanabhuni, S. (2005). Towards a policy driven framework for adaptive Web Services composition. *Proceedings of International Conference on Next Generation Web Services Practices.*

Erradi, A., Maheshwari, P., & Tosic, V. (2006). A policy-based middleware for enhancing Web Services reliability using recovery policies. *Proceedings of the 2006 IEEE International Conference on Web Services.* Chicago, USA.

Esparza, J., Romer, S., & Vogler, W. (1996). An improvement of McMillan's unfolding algorithm. In *Tools and algorithms for construction and analysis of systems*, (p. 87- 106).

Etxeberria, L., & Sagardui, G. (2008). Variability driven quality evaluation in software product lines. *Proceedings of the Software Product Line Conference, 2008. SPLC '08. 12th International*, (pp 243–252).

Ezenwoye, O., & Sadjadi, S. M. (2005). *Composing aggregate Web Services in BPEL.* Miami: School of Computing and Information Science, Florida International University.

Ezenwoye, O., & Sadjadi, S. M. (2007). TRAP/BPEL: A framework for dynamic adaptation of composite services. *Proceedings of the International Conference on Web Information Systems and Technologies (WEBIST 2007).* Barcelona, Spain.

Ezenwoye, O., Sadjadi, S. M., Carey, A., & Robinson, M. (2007). Grid Service composition in BPEL for scientific applications. *Proceedings of the International Conference on Grid computing, high-performAnce and Distributed Applications (GADA '07).* Vilamoura, Algarve, Portugal.

Farrell, J., & Lausen, H. (2007). *Semantic annotations for WSDL and XML schema.* W3C recommendation. Retrieved from http://www.w3.org/TR/sawsdl/

Ferguson, D., Storey, T., Lovering, B. & Shewchuk, J. (2003). *Secure, reliable, transacted Web Services.*

Fernández, A., & Ossowski, S. (2007). Semantic service composition in service-oriented multiagent systems-a filtering approach. In Huang, J. (Eds.), *Service-oriented computing: Agents, semantics, and engineering* (pp. 78–91). Springer. doi:10.1007/978-3-540-72619-7_6

Florescu, D., Levy, A., Manolescu, I., & Suciu, D. (1999). Query optimization in the presence of limited access patterns. In *Proceedings of ACM SIGMOD Conference on Management of Data,* (pp. 311–322).

Foster, I., Kesselman, C., Nick, J. M., & Tuecke, S. (2002). Grid Services for distributed system integration. *Computer*, *35*(6), 37–46. doi:10.1109/MC.2002.1009167

Foster, H., Uchitel, S., Magee, J., & Kramer, J. (2007). WS-Engineer: A model-based approach to engineering Web Service compositions and choreography. In *Test and analysis of Web Services*, (pp. 87–119). Springer.

Foster, I., Kesselman, C. & Tuecke, S. (2001). *The anatomy of the Grid: Enabling scalable virtual organizations*. (LNCS 2150).

Franch, X. (1998). Systematic formulation of non-functional characteristics of software. In *Proceedings of the Third International Conference on Requirements Engineering*, (pp. 174-181).

Frankova, G., Malfatti, D., & Aiello, M. (2006). Semantics and extensions of WS-agreement. *Journal of Software*, *1*(1), 23–31. doi:10.4304/jsw.1.1.23-31

Friedman, M., & Weld, D. (1997). Efficiently executing information-gathering plans. In *Proceedings of IJCAI-97*.

Fujitsu. (2007). Fujitsu inter-stage business process manager. Retrieved from http://www.fujitsu.com /global/ services/ software/interstage/ bpm/index.html

Fussell, J. (1975). How to calculate system reliability and safety characteristics. *IEEE Transactions on Reliability*, *24*(3). doi:10.1109/TR.1975.5215142

Gamma, E., Helm, R., Johnson, R., & Vlissides, J. (1995). *Design patterns: Elements of reusable object-oriented software*. New York: Addison-Wesley Publishing Company.

Gardner, T. (2004). UML modelling of automated business processes with a mapping to BPEL4WS. Proceedings of the 2nd European Workshop on OO and Web Services. Oslo, Norway.

Garey, M. R., & Johnson, D. S. (1979). *Computers and intractability: A guide to the theory of NP-completeness*. New York: Freeman and Company.

Garlan, D., Cheng, S. W., Huang, A.-C., Schmerl, B., & Steenkiste, P. (2004). Rainbow: Architecture-based self-adaptation with reusable infrastructure. In *IEEE Computer, 37*(10), 46-54.

Garofalakis, J., Panagys, Y., Sakkopoulos, E., & Tsakalidis, A. (2006). Contemporary Web Service discovery mechanisms. *Journal of Web Engineering*, *5*(3), 265–290.

Georgalas, N., & Azmoodeh, M. (2004a). Using MDA in technology-independent specifications of NGOSS architectures. *Proceedings of the 1st European Workshop on MDA (MDA-IA 2004)*, Enschede, Netherlands.

Georgalas, N., Azmoodeh, M., Clark, T., Evans, A., Sammut, P., & Willans, J. (2004b). MDA-driven development of standard-compliant OSS components: The OSS/J inventory case study. *Proceedings of the 2nd European Workshop on Model Driven Architecture with emphasis on Methodologies and Transformations (EWMDA 2004)*, Canterbury, UK, 7-8 September 2004.

Gerson, S., Damien, P., Yves Le, T., & Jean-Marc, J. (2001). Refactoring UML Models. *Proceedings of the 4th International Conference on the Unified Modeling Language: Modeling Languages, Concepts, and Tools* (pp. 134-148). Springer-Verlag.

Giallonardo, E., & Zimeo, E. (2007). More semantics in QoS matching. *IEEE International Conference on Service-Oriented Computing and Applications, SOCA '07,* (p. 163-171). Newport Beach, CA: IEEE Computer Society.

Gilani, W., Sincero, J., & Spinczyk, O. (2007). Aspectizing a Web server for adaptation. In *Proceedings of the Twelfth IEEE Symposium on Computers and Communications (ISCC'07)*, Aveiro, Portugal. IEEE Computer Society Press.

Gilman, L., & Schreiber, R. (1996). *Distributed computing with IBM MQSeries*. Wiley.

Gilmore, S., & Tribastone, M. (2006). *Evaluating the scalability of a Web Service-based distributed e-learning and course management system*. Workshop on Web Services and Formal Methods (WS-FM 2006). Springer-Verlag.

Gilmore, S., Gönczy, L., Koch, N., Mayer, P. & Varró, D. (2010). Non-functional properties in the model-driven development of service-oriented systems. *Journal of Software and Systems Modeling*.

Gimpel, H., Ludwig, H., Dan, A., & Kearney, R. (2003). PANDA: Specifying policies for automated negotiations of service contracts. Proceedings of the 1st International Conference on Service Oriented Computing, Trento, Italy.

Glen, A. G., Leemis, L., & Drew, J. H. (2004). Computing the distribution of the product of two continuous random variables. *CSDA*, *44*(3), 451–464.

GLOBE, Global Link Over Business Environment. (2010). *Homepage information*. Retrieved from ttp://plone.rcost.unisannio.it:443/globe/

Gnesi, S., ter Beek, M., Baumeister, H., Hoelzl, M., Moiso, C., Koch, N., et al. (2006). *D8.0: Case studies scenario description*. Retrieved from http://www.sensoria-ist.eu/

Goel, S., Sharda, H., & Taniar, D. (2003). Message-oriented-middleware in a distributed environment. *Third International Workshop on Innovative Internet Community Systems*, (pp. 93-103).

Gokhale, S., & Trivedi, K. S. (1997). Structure-based software reliability prediction. In *Proceedings of Fifth International Conference on Advanced Computing*, Chennai, India, December 1997.

Gokhale, S., Wong, W. E., Trivedi, K. S., & Horgan, J. R. (1998). *An analytical approach to architecture-based software reliability prediction*, (p. 13). IEEE International Computer Performance and Dependability Symposium (IPDS'98), 1998.

Gold, B. T., Kim, J., Smolens, J. C., Chung, E. S., Liaskovitis, V., & Nurvitadhi, E. (2005). TRUSS: A reliable, scalable server architecture. *IEEE Micro*, *25*(6), 51–59. doi:10.1109/MM.2005.122

Gomadam, K., Ranabahu, A., Ramaswamy, L., Sheth, A. P., & Verma, K. (2007). A semantic framework for identifying events in a Service Oriented Architecture. In *Proceedings of the IEEE International Conference on Web Services (ICWS,)* (pp. 545-552).

Gönczy, L., Ávéd, J., & Varró, D. (2006a). Model-based deployment of Web Services to standards-compliant middleware. In P. Isaias & M.B. Nunes (Eds.), *Proceedings of the Iadis International Conference on WWW/Internet 2006*(ICWI2006). Iadis Press.

Gönczy, L., Chiaradonna, S., Giandomenico, F. D., Pataricza, A., Bondavalli, A., & Bartha, T. (2006b). Dependability evaluation of Web Service-based processes. In M. Telek (Ed.), *Proceedings of European Performance Engineering Workshop* (EPEW 2006), (LNCS), (pp. 166–180). Budapest: Springer.

Gönczy, L., Déri, Z., & Varró, D. (2008a). Model driven performability analysis of service configurations with reliable messaging. In *Proceedings of the Workshop on Model Driven Web Engineering* (MDWE2008).

Gönczy, L., Déri, Z., & Varró, D. (2009). *Model transformations for performability analysis of service configurations*. Models in Software Engineering: Workshops and Symposia at MODELS 2008, Toulouse, France, September 28 - October 3, 2008. (pp. 153-166). Berlin, Heidelberg: Springer-Verlag.

Gönczy, L., Heckel, R., & Varró, D. (2007a). Model-based testing of service infrastructure components. In Petrenko, et al. (Eds.), *Proceedings of TESTCOM/FATES 2007*. (LNCS 4581). Tallinn, Estiona: Springer.

Gönczy, L., Kovács, M., & Varró, D. (2006c). Modeling and verification of reliable messaging by graph transformation systems. In *Proceedings of the Workshop on Graph Transformation for Verification and Concurrency* (ICGT2006). Elsevier.

Gotz, D., & Mayer-Patel, K. (2004). A general framework for multidimensional adaption. In *Proceedings of the International Conference on Multimedia and Expo (ICME),* (pp. 612-619).

Gramm, A., Naumowicz, T., Ritter, H., Schiller, J., & Tian, M. (2003). A concept for QoS integration in Web. *Proceedings of the First Web Services Quality Workshop*. Rome: IEEE Computer Society.

Grassi, V. (2005). Architecture-based dependability prediction for service-oriented Computing. ACM SIGSOFT Software Engineering Notes, 30*(4)*.

Grassi, V. & Patella, S. (2006). *Reliability prediction for service oriented computing environments*. Internet Computing, 2006.

Grirori, D., Corrales, J. C., & Bouzeghoub, M. (2006). Behavioral matching for service retrieval. Proceedings of the International Conference on Web Services. USA.

Gronmo, R., Skogan, D., Solheim, I., & Oldevik, J. (2004). Model-driven Web Services development. In *Proceedings of the IEEE International Conference on e-technology, e-commerce and e-service* (EEE'04), (pp. 42–45). Los Alamitos, CA: IEEE Computer Society.

Grottke, M., Sun, H., Fricks, R. M., & Trivedi, K. S. (2008). Ten fallacies of availability and reliability analysis. *Proceedings of the 5th International Service Availability Symposium.*

GSTool. (2009). Home index. http://www.bsi.de/ gstool/ index.htm

Gurguis, S., & Zeid, A. (2005). Towards autonomic Web Services: Achieving self-healing using Web Services. *Proceedings of DEAS'05*. Missouri, USA.

Haas, H., & Brown, A. (2004). *Web Services glossary*. W3C. Retrieved September 10, 2008, from http://www.w3.org/TR/ws-gloss/

Haas, L., Kossmann, D., Wimmers, E., & Yang, J. (1997). Optimizing queries across diverse data sources. In *Proceedings of VLDB Conference.*

Haas, P., & Swami, A. (1992). Sequential sampling procedures for query estimation. In *Proceedings of VLDB Conference.*

Hagel, J. III, & Brown, J. S. (2002). *Out of the box strategies for achieving profits today and growth tomorrow through Web Services*. Boston: Harvard Business School Press.

Hall, R. J., & Zisman, A. (2004). Behavioral Models as Service Descriptions. International Conference on Service Oriented Computing. New York, USA.

Han, A. S. Y., & Bussler, C. (1998). A taxonomy of adaptive workflow management. In *Proceedings of the CSCW-98 Workshop, Towards Adaptive Workflow Systems.*

Hapner, M., Burridge, R., & Sharma, R. (1999). *Java message service specification*. Sun Microsystems.

Harel, D., & Gery, E. (1997). Executable object modeling with statecharts. *Computer*, *30*(7), 31–42. doi:10.1109/2.596624

Harney, J., & Doshi, P. (2009a). Selective querying for adapting Web Service compositions using the value of changed information. *IEEE Transactions on Services Computing*, *1*(3), 169–185. doi:10.1109/TSC.2008.11

Harney, J., & Doshi, P. (2009b). Selective querying for adapting hierarchical Web Service compositions using aggregated volatility. In *Proceedings of the IEEE International Conference on Web Services (ICWS),* (pp. 43-50). IEEE©.

Harrison, R., Counsell, S. J., & Nithi, R. V. (1998). An evaluation of the MOOD set of object-oriented software metrics. *IEEE Transactions on Software Engineering*, *24*(6), 491–496. doi:10.1109/32.689404

Hausmann, J. R., Heckel, R., & Lohman, M. (2004). Model-based discovery of Web Services. Proceedings of the International Conference on Web Services. USA.

He, H. (2003). *What is Service-Oriented Architecture?* O'Reilly Press.

Hecht, H., & Hecht, M. (1996). Qualitative interpretation of software test data. In Min, Y., & Tang, D. (Eds.), *Computer-aided design, test, and evaluation for dependability* (pp. 175–181). Beijing: International Academic Publishers.

Hitz, M., & Montazeri, B. (1995). *Measuring product attributes of object-oriented systems*. Paper presented at the 5th European Software Engineering Conference.

Hoare, C. (1978). Communicating sequential processes. *Communications of the ACM*, *21*(8), 666–677. doi:10.1145/359576.359585

Hoare, C. A. (1985). *Communicating sequential processes*. New Jersey: Prentice-Hall.

Hoffmann, J., Weber, I., Kaczmarek, T., & Ankolekar, A. (2008). *Combining scalability and expressivity in the automatic composition of Semantic Web Services* (pp. 98–107). ICWE.

Horrocks, I., Patel-Schneider, P. F., & van Harmelen, F. (2003). From SHIQ and RDF to OWL: The making of a Web ontology language. *Journal of Web Semantics*, *1*(1), 7–26. doi:10.1016/j.websem.2003.07.001

Hoschek, W. (2002). The Web Service discovery architecture. Proceedings of the IEEE/ACM Supercomputing Conference. Baltimore, USA.

Hosseini, S., & Azgomi, M. A. (2008). *UML model refactoring with emphasis on behavior preservation.* Paper presented at the 2nd IFIP/IEEE International Symposium on Theoretical Aspects of Software Engineering, Piscataway, NJ, United States.

Hou, W., Ossoyoglu, G. & Doglu. (1991). Error-constrained count query evaluation in relational databases. In *Proceedings of SIGMOD.*

HP. (2007). Mercury business technology optimization enterprise. Retrieved from http://www.mercury.com / us/products/

HP. (2009). An insider's view to the HP universal CMDB. A technical white paper, HP. Retrieved from http://www. rubik solutions.com/ Admin/Public/ DWSDownload. aspx? File = %2FFiles% 2FFiler%2FPDF +UCMDB% 2FUcmdb_white paper.pdf

Huang, L., & Boehm, B. (2006). How much software quality investment is enough: A value-based approach. *IEEE Software*, (September/October): 2006.

Hull, R., & Su, J. (2005). Tools for composite Web Services: A short overview. *SIGMOD Record, 34*(2), 86–95. doi:10.1145/1083784.1083807

Hütel, H., & Shukla, S. (1996). *On the complexity of deciding behavioural equivalences and preorders, a survey. Basic Reasearch in Computer Science (RS-96-39).* Aahrus, Denmark: University of Aarhus, Department of Computer Science.

IBM. (2005). *Business process execution language for Web Services version 1.1.* Retrieved from http://www-128. ibm.com/developerworks/library/specification/ws-bpel/

IBM. (2007). IBM Tivoli availability process manager. Retrieved from http://www-306. ibm.com/ software/tivoli/ products/ availability- process-mgr/

IBM. (2009). Reliable asynchronous message profile (RAMP) toolkit. Retrieved from http://www.alphaworks. ibm.com/tech/ramptk

IEEE Computer Society. (1990). *IEEE standard glossary of software engineering terminology.* (IEEE Std 610.12-1990). The Institute of Electronical and Electronics Engineers, Inc, 1990.

Immonen, A., & Niemela, E. (2008). *Survey of reliability and availability prediction methods from the viewpoint of software architecture.* Software and System Modeling.

International Telecommunications Union. (2008). Final draft of revised recommendation. *E (Norwalk, Conn.), 800,* Retrieved from http://www.itu.int/ md/T05-SG02-080506 -TD-WP2-0121/en.

ISO/IEC JTC1/SC21. (1997). Working draft for open distributed processing-reference model-Quality of Service.

ISO/IEC. (1998). International Standard 13236: Information Technology-Quality of Service: framework, 1st ed.

ISO/IEC. (1999). Technical Report 13243: Information Technology-Quality of Service: Guide to methods and mechanisms, 1st ed.

IsoGraph. (2008). *Reliability workbench technical specification.* Retrieved from http://www.isograph- software. com/ _techspecs/ wk32tech spec.pdf

IT Governance Institute. (2007). CobiT 4.1. Retrieved from http://www.itgi.org/cobit

IT Infrastructure Library. (2007). *Official site.* Retrieved from http://www.itil-officialsite.com

Iyer, R. K., Nakka, N. M., Kalbarczyk, Z. T., & Mitra, S. (2005). Recent advances and new avenues in hardware-level reliability support. *IEEE Micro, 25*(6), 18–29. doi:10.1109/MM.2005.119

Janota, M., & Kiniry, J. (2007). Reasoning about feature models in higher-order logic. In *Proceedings of the 11th Software Product Line Conference (SPLC '07)*, (pp. 13–22).

Jategaonkar, L., & Meyer, A. R. (1996). Deciding true concurrency equivalences on safe, finite nets. *Theoretical Computer Science, 154*(1), 107–143. doi:10.1016/0304-3975(95)00132-8

JENA. (2010). *A Semantic Web framework for Java.* Retrieved from http://jena.sourceforge.net/

Jiang, W., & Schulzrinne, H. (2003). Assessment of VoIP service availability in the current Internet. *Proceedings of the Passive and Active Measurement Workshop.*

Jin, J. & Nahrstedt, K. (2002). Classification and comparison of QoS specification languages for distributed multimedia applications. UIUC CS Tech Report, 2002.

Jin, J., Machiraju, V., & Sahai, A. (2002). *Analysis on service level agreements of Web Services*. (Technical Report HPL-2002-180), HP Laboratories Palo Alto.

Jingjun, Z., Furong, L., Yang, Z., & Liguo, W. (2007). Non-functional attributes modeling in software architecture. In *Proceedings of the 8th ACIS International Conference on Software Engineering, Artificial Intelligence, Networking and Parallel/Distributed Computing,* (pp. 149-153).

Joita, L., Rana, O. F., Chacn, P., Chao, I., & Ardaiz, O. (2005). Application deployment using Catallactic Grid middleware. In *Proceedings of the 3rd International Workshop on Middleware for Grid Computing (MGC05)*, Grenoble (France).

Jones, S., Kozlenkov, A., Mahbub, K., Maiden, M., Spanoudakis, G., Zachos, K., et al. (2005). Service discovery for service centric systems. eChallenges. Slovenia.

Jonkers, H., Iacob, M., Lankhorst, M., & Straiting, P. (2005). Integration and analysis of functional and non-functional Aspects in model-driven e-service development. *Proceedings of IEEE International Enterprise Distributed Object Computing (EDOC) Conference*, Enschede, Netherlands, September 19-23, 2005.

Jürjen, J. (2002). UMLsec: Extending UML for secure systems development. In *Proceedings of 5th International Conference on The Unified Modeling Language*, (LNCS Vol.2460), Springer.

Jurjens, J., & Wagner, S. (2005). *Component-based development of dependable systems with UML*. (LNCS 3778), (pp. 320-344).

Kalayci, S., Ezenwoye, O., Viswanathan, B., Dasgupta, G., Sadjadi, S. M., & Fong, L. (2008). Design and implementation of a fault tolerant job flow manager using job flow patterns and recovery policies. *Proceedings of the 6th International Conference on Service Oriented Computing (ICSOC'08).* Sydney, Australia.

Kalyanakrishnam, M., Kalbarczyk, Z., & Iyer, R. (1999). *Failure data analysis of a LAN of Windows NT based computers. Reliable Distributed Systems* (pp. 178–189). Lausanne, Switzerland: IEEE Computer Society.

Keller, A. & Ludwig, H. (2003). The WSLA framework: Specifying and monitoring service level agreements for Web Services. *Journal of Network and Systems Management, Special Issue on e-Business Management, 11*(1).

Keller, A., & Ludwig, H. (2002). Defining and monitoring service level agreements for dynamic e-business. Proceedings of the 16th System Administration Conference, USA.

Keller, U., Lara, R., Lausen, H., Polleres, A., & Fensel, D. (2005). Automatic location of services. Proceedings of the European Semantic Web Conference. Crete, Greece.

Kephart, J. O., & Chess, D. M. (2003). The vision of autonomic computing. *IEEE Computer*, *36*(1), 41–50.

Khedr, M., & Karmouch, A. (2002). *Enhancing service discovery with context information*. Spain: Intelligent Tutoring Systems.

Khomenko, V., Koutny, M., & Vogler, W. (2002). Canonical prefixes of petri net unfoldings. In *CAV '02: Proceedings of the 14th International Conference on Computer Aided Verification,* (pp. 582–595). London: Springer-Verlag.

Khoshgoftaar, J. M. T. (1996). Software metrics for reliability assessment. In Lyu, M. (Ed.), *Handbook of software reliability engineering* (pp. 493–529).

Kiczales, G., Lamping, J., Mendhekar, A., Maeda, C., Lopes, C. V., Loingtier, J. M., et al. (1997). Aspect-oriented programming. *Proceedings of the European Conference on Object-Oriented Programming (ECOOP).* (LNCS 1241). Springer-Verlag.

Kirwan, B. (1994). *A guide to practical human reliability assessment*. London: Taylor and Francis Ltd.

Kleiman, S., & Eykholt, J. (1995). Interrupts as threads. *ACM SIGOPS Operating Systems Review*, *29*(2), 21–26. doi:10.1145/202213.202217

Klein, M., & Bernstein, A. (2004). Toward high-precision service retrieval. *IEEE Internet Computing*, 30–36. doi:10.1109/MIC.2004.1260701

Klein, M., & Kazman, R. (1999). *Attribute-based architectural styles*. (Technical Report CMU/SEI-99-TR-022), Software Engineering Institute, Carnegie Mellon University, Pittsburgh, PA, 1999.

Klensin, J. (2001). *Simple mail transfer protocol.* (RFC 2821).

Klusch, M., Fries, B., & Sycara, K. (2006). Automated Semantic Web service discovery with OWLS-MX. Proceedings of the International Conference on Autonomous Agents and Multiagent Systems. Japan.

Ko, J. M., Kim, C. O., & Kwon, I.-H. (2008). Quality-of-Service oriented Web Service composition algorithm and planning architecture. *Journal of Systems and Software, 81*(11), 2079–2090. doi:10.1016/j.jss.2008.04.044

Koch, N., & Brendl, D. (2007). *D8.2.a: Requirements modelling and analysis of selected scenarios-automotive case study.* Retrieved from http://www.sensoria-ist.eu/

Koch, N., Mayer, P., Heckel, R., Gönczy, L. & Montangero, C. (2007). *D1.4.a: UML for service-oriented systems.* Koch, N. & Brendl, D. (2007).

Kokash, N., van den Heuvel, W. J., & D'Andrea, V. (2006). Leveraging Web Services discovery with customizable hybrid matching. Proceedings of the International Conference on Web Services. USA.

Kozlenkov, A., Spanoudakis, G., Zisman, A., Fasoulas, V., & Sanchez, F. (2007). Architecture-driven service discovery for service centric systems. *International Journal of Web Services Research, 4*(2). doi:10.4018/jwsr.2007040104

Kozlenkov, A., & Zisman, A. (2004). Discovering, recording, and handling inconsistencies in software specifications. *International Journal of Computer and Information Science, 5*(2), 89–108.

Kozlenkov, A., Fasoulas, V., Sanchez, F., Spanoudakis, G., & Zisman, A. (2006). A framework for architecture-driven service discovery. Proceedings of the International Workshop on Service Oriented Software Engineering. China.

Krafzig, D., Banke, K., & Slama, D. (2004). *Enterprise SOA: Service-Oriented Architecture best practices.* Prentice Hall PTR.

Kramler, G., Kapsammer, E., Kappel, G., & Retschitzegger, W. (2005). Towards using UML 2 for modelling Web Service collaboration protocols. Proceedings of the 1st Conference on Interoperability of Enterprise Software and Applications. Geneva, Switzerland.

Kreger, H. & IBM Software Group. (2001). *Web Services Conceptual Architecture (WSCA 1.0).*

Krishnamohan, S. (2005). *Efficient techniques for modeling and mitigation of soft errors in nanometer-scale static CMOS logic circuits.* Unpublished doctoral thesis, Michigan State University, United States-Michigan.

Krishnamurthy, S., & Mathur, A. P. (1997). On the estimation of reliability of a software system using reliabilities of its components. *Proceedings ISSRE '97,* November 02-05, 1997.

Krishnamurthy, Y., Kachroo, V., Karr, D., Rodrigues, C., Loyall, J., Schantz, R., et al. (2001). Integration of QoS-enabled distributed object computing middleware for developing next-generation distributed applications. *ACM SIGPLAN Notices, 36*(8).

Kritikos, K., & Plexousakis, D. (2007). Semantic QoS-based Web Service discovery algorithms. *Proceedings of the Fifth European Conference on Web Services in ECOWS'07,* (p. 181-190). Halle, Germany: IEEE Computer Society.

Kruchter, P. (1995). The 4+1 view model of architecture. *IEEE Software, 6*(12), 42–50. doi:10.1109/52.469759

Krueger, C. W. (2007a). The 3-tiered methodology: Pragmatic insights from new generation software product lines. In *Proceedings of the 11th Software Product Line Conference (SPLC '07)*, (pp. 97–106).

Krueger, C. W. (2007b). BigLever software gears and the 3-tiered SPL methodology. In *OOPSLA '07: Companion to the 22nd ACM SIGPLAN conference on object-oriented programming systems and applications*, (pp. 844–845). New York: ACM.

Kuter, U., Sirin, E., Nau, D. S., Parsia, B., & Hendler, J. A. (2004). Information gathering during planning for Web Service composition. In *Proceedings of the International Semantic Web Conference (ISWC),* (p. 335-349).

Lakhal, N. B., Kobayashi, T., & Yokota, H. (2006). *Dependability and flexibility centered approach for composite Web Services modeling.* Berlin, Germany.

Laprie, J.-C. (1995). Dependable computing and fault tolerance: Concepts and terminology. *25th International Symposium on Fault-Tolerant Computing (FCTS-25), 3.* Pasadena, California.

Lauer, H. C., & Needham, R. M. (1979). On the duality of operating system structures. *ACM SIGOPS Operating Systems Review*, *13*(2), 3–19. doi:10.1145/850657.850658

Levy, A., Rajaraman, A., & Ordille, J. (1996). Querying heterogeneous information sources using source descriptions. In *Proceedings of the VLDB Conference.*

Lewis, L., & Ray, P. (1999). Service level management definition, architecture, and research challenges. *Proceedings of the Global Telecommunication Conference 1999 (Globecom'99)*, (pp. 1974-1978).

Leymann, F. (2006). Choreography for the Grid: Towards fitting BPEL to the resource framework: Research articles. *Concurrent Computing: Practical Experience*, *18*(10), 1201–1217. doi:10.1002/cpe.996

Leymann, F. & Karastoyanova, D. (2008). Service Oriented Architecture–overview of technologies and Standards. *Information Technology, 50.*

Li, B., & Nahrstedt, K. (2000). QualProbes: Middleware QoS profiling services for configuring adaptive applications. J. Sventek and G. Coulson (Eds.), *Middleware 2000*, (LNCS 1795), (pp. 256-272). Springer-Verlag.

Li, L., & Horrock, I. (2003). A software framework for matchmaking based on Semantic Web technology. WWW Conference Workshop on e-Services and the Semantic Web. Budapest, Hungary.

Liedtke, J. (1995). On μ-kernel construction. In *Proceedings of the 15th ACM Symposium on Operating Systems Principles (SOSP '95)*, ACM SIGOPS Operating Systems Review. ACM Press.

Lin, M., Xie, J., & Guo, H. (2005). Solving Qos-driven Web Service dynamic composition as fuzzy constraint satisfaction. *Proceedings of the 2005 IEEE Conference.*

LINA & INRIA Atlas Group. (2006). ATL: Atlas Transformation Language user manual. Retrieved from http://www.eclipse.org/ m2m/atl/doc/ATL User Manual[v0.7].pdf

Ling, Y., & Sun, W. (1992). A supplement to Sampling-based methods for query size estimation in a database system. *SIGMOD Record*, *21*(4), 12–15. doi:10.1145/141818.141820

Lipton, R., & Naughton, J. (1990). Query size estimation by adaptive sampling (Extended Abstract). In *PODS '90: Proceedings of the 9th ACM SIGACT-SIGMOD-SIGART Symposium on Principles of Database Systems,* (pp. 40–46).

Lipton, R., Naughton, J., & Schneider, D. (1990). Practical selectivity estimation through adaptive sampling. In *Proceedings of SIGMOD,* (pp. 1–11).

Littlewood, B., Popov, P., & Strigini, L. (2000). *Choosing between fault-tolerance and increased V& V for improving reliability. DSN* (pp. B42–B43). New York: IEEE.

Liu, X., & Yen, J. (1996). An analytic framework for specifying and analyzing imprecise requirements. *Proceedings of the 18th IEEE International Conference on Software Engineering (ICSE-1996)*, (pp. 60-69). Berlin.

Liu, Y., Ngu, A. H., & Zeng, L. Z. (2004). Qos computation and policing in dynamic Web service selection. In *WWW Alt. '04: Proceedings of the 13th international World Wide Web conference on Alternate track papers & posters*, (pp. 66–73), New York: ACM.

LOCOSP. (2009). *LOCOSP*. Retrieved from http://plone.rcost.unisannio.it/locosp

Loesch, F., & Ploedereder, E. (2007). Optimization of variability in software product lines. In *Proceedings of the 11th Software Product Line Conference (SPLC '07)*, (pp. 151–162).

Lohmann, D., Spinczyk, O., & Schröder-Preikschat, W. (2005). On the configuration of non-functional properties in operating system product lines. In *Proceedings of the 4th AOSD Workshop on Aspects, Components, and Patterns for Infrastructure Software (AOSD-ACP4IS '05)*, (pp 19–25). Chicago, IL, USA. Northeastern University, Boston (NU-CCIS-05-03).

Lohmann, D., Streicher, J., Hofer, W., Spinczyk, O., & Schröder-Preikschat, W. (2007a). Configurable memory protection by aspects. In *Proceedings of the 4th Workshop on Programming Languages and Operating Systems (PLOS '07)*, (pp. 1–5). New York: ACM Press.

Lohmann, D., Streicher, J., Spinczyk, O., & Schröder-Preikschat, W. (2007b). Interrupt synchronization in the CiAO operating system. In *Proceedings of the 6th AOSD Workshop on Aspects, Components, and Patterns for Infrastructure Software (AOSD-ACP4IS '07)*, New York: ACM Press.

Looker, N., & Xu, J. (2007). Dependability assessment of Grid middleware. In *Proceedings of 37th Annual IEEE/IFIP International Conference on Dependable Systems and Networks (DSN '07),* (pp. 125-130). Edinburgh, UK.

Looker, N., Munro, M., & Xu, J. (2005). A comparison of network level fault injection with code insertion. In *Proceedings of the 29th Annual International Computer Software and Applications Conference (COMPSAC 2005),* (pp. 479-484). Edinburgh, UK.

Ludwig, H., Keller, A., Dan, A., King, R. P., & Franck, R. (2003). *Web Service Level Agreement (WSLA) language specification.* IBM.

Ludwig, H., Dan, A., & Kearney, R. (2004). CREMONA: An architecture and library for creation and monitoring of WS-agreements. In *Proceedings of the Second International Conference on Service-Oriented Computing*, New York City.

Lumpe, M., Achermann, F., & Nierstrasz, O. (2000). A formal language for composition. In Leavens, G., & Sitaraman, M. (Eds.), *Foundations of component based systems* (pp. 69–90). Cambridge University Press.

Lumpe, M., Schneider, J. G., Nierstrasz, O., & Achermann, F. (1997). *Towards a formal composition language. Proceedings of ESEC '97 Workshop on Foundations of Component-Based Systems*, September 1997, (pp. 178-187).

Luo, Z., Sheth, A. P., Kochut, K., & Miller, J. A. (2000). Exception handling in workflow systems. *Applied Intelligence, 13*(2), 125–147. doi:10.1023/A:1008388412284

Lycett, M. & Paul, R.J. (1998). *Component-based development: Dealing with non-functional aspects of architecture*. ECOOP, 1998.

Lyu, M. R. (1995). *Software fault tolerance* (pp. 315–333). Chichester, New York: John Wiley.

Maamar, Z., Narendra, N. C., Benslimane, D., & Sattanathan, S. (2007). Policies for context-driven transactional Web Services. In *Proceedings of the International Conference on Advanced Information Systems Engineering (CAiSE),* (pp. 249-263).

MacKensie, C. M., Laskey, K., McCabe, F., Brown, P. F., Metz, R., & Hamilton, B. A. (2006). *Reference model for Service Oriented Architecture 1.0.* OASIS Committee Specification.

Mahbub, K., & Spanoudakis, G. (2007). Monitoring WS-Agreements: An event calculus based approach. In Baresi, L., & diNitto, E. (Eds.), *Springer monograph on test and analysis of Web Services*. Springer Verlang. doi:10.1007/978-3-540-72912-9_10

Mahrenholz, D., Spinczyk, O., Gal, A., & Schröder-Preikschat, W. (2002). An aspect-oriented implementation of interrupt synchronization in the PURE operating system family. In *Proceedings of the 5th ECOOP Workshop on Object Orientation and Operating Systems (ECOOP-OOOS '02)*, (pp. 49–54). Malaga, Spain.

Majithia, S., Walker, D. W., & Gray, W. A. (2004). Automated composition of Semantic Grid services. In *Proceedings of AHM.*

Majzik, I., Domokos, P., & Magyar, M. (2007). *Tool-supported dependability evaluation of redundant architectures in computer based control systems*. Formal Methods for Automation and Safety in Railway and Automotive Systems.

Malek, M., Hoffmann, G., Milanovic, N., Bruening, S., Meyer, R., & Milic, B. (2007). Methods and tools for availability assessment (Methoden und Werkzeuge zur Verfuegbarkeitsermittlung). Retrieved from http://edoc.hu-berlin.de/ series/ informatik -berichte/ 219/PDF/219.pdf

Mani, A., & Nagarajan, A. (2002). *Understanding Quality of Service for Web Services*. IBM Developer Works.

Mani, A., & Nagarajan, A. (2002). *Understanding Quality of Service for Web Services*. Retrieved March 1, 2008, from http://www.ibm.com/developerworks/java/library/ws-quality.html

Margolis, B. (2007). *SOA for the business developer: Concepts, BPEL, and SCA*. Mc Press.

Marsden, E., Fabre, J., & Arlat, J. (2002). *Dependability of CORBA systems: Service characterization by fault injection*. Symposium on Reliable Distributed Systems, (pp. 276-285). Osaka, Japan: IEEE Computer Society.

Martinez, E., & Lesperance, Y. (2004). Web Service composition as a planning task: Experiments using knowledge-based planning. In *ICAPS-P4WGS*.

Massacci, F., Mylopoulos, J., & Zannone, N. (2007). *Computer-aided support for secure tropos*. Automated Software Engineering Journal.

Massarelli, M., Raibulet, C., Cammareri, D., & Perino, N. (2009). Ensuring Quality of Services at runtime–a case study. In *Proceedings of the IEEE International Conference on Services Computing,* (pp. 540-543)

Maximilien, E. M., & Singh, M. (2004). A framework and ontology for dynamic Web service selection. *IEEE Internet Computing*, *8*(5), 84–93. doi:10.1109/MIC.2004.27

McCabe, T. J. (1976). A complexity measure. *IEEE Transactions on Software Engineering*, *SE-2*(4), 308–320. doi:10.1109/TSE.1976.233837

McKinley, P.K., Sadjadi, S.M., Kasten, E.P. & Cheng, B.H. (2004). Composing adaptive software. *IEEE Computer*, 56-64.

Meaney, P. J., Swaney, S. B., Sanda, P. N., & Spainhower, L. (2005). IBM z990 soft error detection and recovery. *IEEE Transactions on Device and Materials Reliability*, *5*(3), 419–427. doi:10.1109/TDMR.2005.859577

Mecella, M., Ouzzani, M., Paci, F., & Bertino, E. (2006). Access control enforcement for conversation-based Web Services. In *Proceedings of the 15th International World Wide Web Conference,* (257-266). Edinburgh: ACM.

Mens, T., & Van Gorp, P. (2006). A taxonomy of model transformation. *Electronic Notes in Theoretical Computer Science*, *152*(1-2), 125–142. doi:10.1016/j.entcs.2005.10.021

Mens, T. (2006). *On the use of graph transformations for model refactoring*. (LNCS 4143), (pp. 219-257).

Merriam Webster Online. (2008). *Dictionary service*. Retrieved from http://www.merriam- webster.com/ dictionary/ service

Meyer, A., & Stockmeyer, L. (1972). The equivalence problem for regular expressions with squaring requires exponential space. In *Proceedings of the 13th Annual Symposium on Switching and Automata Theory,* (125–129). Maryland, USA: IEEE.

Meyer, H., & Weske, M. (2006). *Automated service composition using heuristic search*. (LNCS 4102), (pp. 81-96).

Michelson, B.M. (2005). *Service oriented world cheat sheet: A guide to key concepts, technology, and more*.

Mikhaiel, R., & Stroulia, E. (2006). Interface- and usage-aware service discovery. 4th International Conference on Service Oriented Computing. Chicago, USA.

Milanovic, N. (2006). *Contract-based Web Service composition*. Berlin: Humboldt University.

Milanovic, N., & Malek, M. (2005). *Architectural support for automatic service composition-services computing*. IEEE International Conference on Service Computing, 2, (pp. 133-140).

Milner, R. (1989). *Communication and concurrency*. New Jersey: Prentice-Hall.

Miskov-Zivanov, N., & Marculescu, D. (2006). *MARS-C: Modeling And Reduction of Soft errors in Combinational circuits*. Paper presented at the Proceedings of the Design Automation Conference, Piscataway, NJ, USA.

Misra, K. B. (1992). *Reliability analysis and prediction*. Elsevier.

Mitra, S. M.Z., Seifert, N., Mak, T.M. & Kim, K. (2006). *Soft error resilient system design through error correction*. Paper presented at the International Conference on Very Large Scale Integration and System-on-Chip.

Mitra, S., Kumar, R., & Basu, S. (2007). Automated choreographer synthesis for Web Services composition using I/O automata. In *proceedings of IEEE International Conference on Web Services,* (pp. 364–371). Utah, USA: IEEE Computer Society.

Mohamed, A. G., Chad, S., Vijaykumar, T. N., & Irith, P. (2003). Transient-fault recovery for chip multiprocessors. *IEEE Micro*, *23*(6), 76–83. doi:10.1109/MM.2003.1261390

Morato, J., Marzal, M. A., Llorens, J., & Moreiro, J. (2004). WordNet application. Proceedings of The Second Global Wordnet Conference. Brno, Czech Republic.

Mukherjee, S. S., Emer, J., & Reinhardt, S. K. (2005). *The soft error problem: An architectural perspective.* Paper presented at the 11th International Symposium on High-Performance Computer Architecture, San Francisco, CA, USA.

Mukherjee, S. S., Kontz, M., & Reinhardt, S. K. (2002). *Detailed design and evaluation of redundant multithreading alternatives.* Paper presented at the 29th Annual International Symposium on Computer Architecture.

Muller, R., Greiner, U., & Rahm, E. (2004). Agentwork: A workflow system supporting rule-based workflow adaptation. *Journal of Data and Knowledge Engineering, 51*(2), 223–256. doi:10.1016/j.datak.2004.03.010

Muppala, J., Ciardo, G., & Trivedi, K. (1994). *Stochastic reward nets for reliability prediction.* Communications in Reliability. *Maintainability and Serviceability, 1*(2), 9–20.

Muscholl, A., & Walukiewicz, I. (2008). *A lower bound on Web Services composition.* Computing Reasearch Repository.

Mylopoulos, J., Chung, L., & Nixon, B. (1992). Representing and using non-functional requirements: A process-oriented approach. *IEEE Transactions on Software Engineering, 18*, 483–497. doi:10.1109/32.142871

Nagarajan, M., Verma, K., Sheth, A. P., Miller, J. A., & Lathem, J. (2006). Semantic interoperability of Web Services–challenges and experiences. In *Proceedings of the 4th IEEE International Conference on Web Services,* (pp. 373-382).

Nahrstedt, K., & Smith, J. (1995) The QoS broker. In *IEEE Multimedia Magazine, 2*(1), 53-67.

Narayanan, V., & Xie, Y. (2006). Reliability concerns in embedded system designs. *Computer, 39*(1), 118–120. doi:10.1109/MC.2006.31

Narendra, N. C., & Gundugola, S. (2006). Automated context-aware adaptation of Web Service executions. In *Proceedings of the ACS/IEEE International Conference on Computer Systems and Applications (AICCSA),* (pp. 179–187).

Narendra, N. C., Ponnalagu, K., Krishnamurthy, J., & Ramkumar, R. (2007). Run-time adaptation of non-functional properties of composite Web Services using aspect-oriented programming. In *Proceedings of the International Conference on Services-Oriented Computing (ICSOC),* (pp. 546-557).

Nelson, V. P. (1990). Fault-tolerant computing: Fundamental concepts. *IEEE Computer, 23*(7), 19–25.

Newcomer, E., & Lomow, G. (2005). *Understanding SOA with Web Services. (Independent Technology Guides).* Addison-Wesley Professional.

Nguyen, H. T., Yagil, Y., Seifert, N., & Reitsma, M. (2005). Chip-level soft error estimation method. *IEEE Transactions on Device and Materials Reliability, 5*(3), 365–381. doi:10.1109/TDMR.2005.858334

Nguyen, X. T., Kowalczyk, R., & Han, J. (2006). Using dynamic asynchronous aggregate search for quality guarantees of multiple Web Services compositions. Proceedings of the 4th International Conference on Service Oriented Computing. Chicago, USA.

Nickull, D. (2005). *Service Oriented Architecture.* White Paper.

Oasis Open. (2007). *OASIS Web Services business process execution language.* Retrieved from http://www.oasis-open.org/committees/tc_home.php?wg_abbrev=wsbpel

Object Management Group. (2004). Meta Object Facility (MOF) 2.0 core specification. Retrieved from http://www.omg.org/ cgi-bin/ apps/ doc?ptc/ 03-10-04.pdf

Object Management Group. (2008). Business process modeling notation specification. Retrieved from http://www.bpmn.org/ Documents/OMG Final Adopted BPMN 1-0 Spec 06-02-01.pdf

Object Management Group. (2006). *UML profile for QoS and fault tolerance.* Retrieved from http://www.omg.org

Oh, N., Shirvani, P. P., & McCluskey, E. J. (2002). Error detection by duplicated instructions in super-scalar processors. *IEEE Transactions on Reliability, 51*(1), 63–75. doi:10.1109/24.994913

Oinn, T., Addis, K., Ferris, J., Marvin, D., Senger, M., & Greenwood, M. (2004). Taverna: A tool for the composition and enactment of bioinformatics workflows. *Bioinformatics (Oxford, England)*, *20*(17). doi:10.1093/bioinformatics/bth361

Oma, M., Rossi, D., & Metra, C. (2003). *Novel transient fault hardened static latch*. Paper presented at the IEEE International Test Conference (TC), Charlotte, NC, United States.

OMG. (2003). UML profile for modeling Quality of Service and fault-tolerance characteristics and mechanisms, revised submission. Retrieved on May 4, 2003, from http://www.omg.org/

OMG. (2004). Data distribution service for real-time systems, formal. Retrieved December 2004, from http://www.omg.org/

Ortiz, G., & Hernändez, J. (2006). Toward UML profiles for Web Services and their extra-functional properties. *Proceedings of the 2006 IEEE International Conference on Web Services*, September 2006.

OSEK/VDX Group. (2005). *Operating system specification 2.2.3*. OSEK/VDX Group. Retrieved from http://www.osek-vdx.org/

Ouzzani, M., & Bouguettaya, A. (2004). Query processing and optimization on the Web. *Distributed and Parallel Databases*, *15*(3), 187–218. doi:10.1023/B:DAPD.0000018574.71588.06

Ouzzani, M., & Bouguettaya, A. (2004). Efficient access to Web Services. *IEEE Internet Computing*, *8*(2), 34–44. doi:10.1109/MIC.2004.1273484

Overton, C. (2002). On the theory and practice of Internet SLAs. *Journal of Computer Resource Measurement*, *106*, 32–45.

OWL-S. (2007). OWL-S version 1.0. Retrieved from www.daml.org/services/owl-s/1.0

Paech, B., & Kerkow, D. (2004). Non-functional requirements engineering-quality is essential. *Proceedings of REFSQ'04*.

Pantazoglou, M., Tsalgatidou, A., & Athanasopoulos, G. (2006). Discovering Web Services in JXTA peer-to-peer services in a unified manner. Proceedings of the 4th International Conference on Service Oriented Computing. Chicago, USA.

Pantazoglou, M., Tsalgatidou, A., & Spanoudakis, G. (2007). Behavior-aware, unified service discovery. In Proceedings of the Service-Oriented Computing: A look at the inside Workshop. Austria. De Paoli, F., Lulli, G. & Maurino, A. (2006). Design of quality-based composite Web Services. Proceedings of the 4th International Conference on Service Oriented Computing. Chicago, USA.

Paolucci, M., Kawamura, T., Payne, T. R., & Sycara, K. P. (2002). Semantic matching of Web Services capabilities. In *Proceedings of the International Semantic Web Conference,* (p. 333-347).

Papadimitriou, C., & Steiglitz, K. (1982). *Combinatorial optimisation: Algorithms and complexity*. Prentice-Hall Inc.

Papadimitriou, C. H. (1994). *Computational complexity*. Addison-Wesley.

Papakonstantinou, Y., Gupta, A., & Haas, L. (1996). Capabilities-based query rewriting in mediator systems. In *Conference on Parallel and Distributed Information Systems.*

Papazoglou, M. P., & van den Heuvel, W.-J. (2007). Service Oriented Architectures: Approaches, technologies and research issues. *The VLDB Journal*, *16*(3), 389–415. doi:10.1007/s00778-007-0044-3

Papazoglou, M., & Georgakopoulos, D. (2003). Service-oriented computing. *Communications of the ACM*, 25–28.

Papazoglou, M. P. (2003). Service-oriented computing: Concepts, characteristics and directions. In *Proceedings of 4th International Conference on Web Information Systems Engineering (WISE 2003)*, (pp. 3–12), Rome (Italy). IEEE Computer Society.

Papazoglou, M., Aiello, M., Pistore, M., & Yang, J. (2008). XSRL: A request language for Web Services. Retrieved from rom http://citeseer.ist.psu.edu/575968.html

Paques, H., Liu, L. & Pu, C. (2004). Adaptation space: A design framework for adaptive Web Services. *Journal of Web Services research (JWSR), 1*(3), 1-24.

Park, J. K., & Kim, J. T. (2008). A soft error mitigation technique for constrained gate-level designs. *IEICE Electronics Express*, *5*(18), 698–704. doi:10.1587/elex.5.698

Park, D. (1981). Concurrency and automata on infinite sequences. In *proceedings of the 5th GI Conference,* (pp. 167-183). Karlsruhe, Germany: Springer.

Pataricza, A., Majzik, I., Huszerl, G., & Varnai, G. (2003). *UML-based design and formal analysis of a safety-critical railway control software module*. Formal Methods for Railway Operation and Control Systems.

Pathak, J., Basu, S., Lutz, R., & Honavar, V. (2006). Parallel Web Service composition in MOSCOE: A choreography-based approach. In *proceedings of the Fourth IEEE European Conference on Web Services,* (pp. 3-12). Zürich, Switzerland: IEEE Computer Society.

Patterson, D. (2002). A simple way to estimate the cost of downtime. *Proceedings of the 16th System Administrator Conference-LISA '02.* Retrieved from http://roc.cs. berkeley.edu/ papers/Cost_ Downtime_ LISA.pdf

Pawar, P., & Tokmakoff, A. (2006). Ontology-based context-aware service discovery for pervasive environments. Proceedings of the IEEE International Workshop On Service Integration in Pervasive Environment. Lyon, France.

Pease, M., Shostak, R., & Lamport, L. (1980). Reaching agreement in the presence of faults. *Journal of the Association of Computing Machinery*, *27*(2), 228–234.

Pistore, M., Marconi, A., Bertoli, P., & Traverso, P. (2005). Automated composition of Web Services by planning at the knowledge level. In *the proceedings of the Nineteenth International Joint Conference on Artificial Intelligence,* (pp. 1252-1259). Scotland: Professional Book Center.

Pistore, M., Traverso, P., & Bertoli, P. (2005). Automated composition of Web Services by planning in asynchronous domains. *In the proceedings of the Fifteenth International Conference on Automated Planning and Scheduling,* (pp. 2–11). California: AAAI.

Plakosh, D., Smith, D., & Wallnau, K. (1999). *Builder's guide for WaterBeans components*. (Technical Report CMU/SEI-99-TR-024), Software Engineering Institute, Carnegie Mellon University, Pittsburgh, PA, 1999.

Poernomo, I., Jayaputera, J., & Schmidt, H. (2005). Timed probabilistic constraints over the distributed management taskforce common information model. *Proceedings of IEEE International Enterprise Distributed Object Computing (EDOC) conference*, Enschede, Netherlands, September 19-23, 2005.

Polze, A., Milanovic, N., & Schoebel, M. (2006). *Fundamentals of service-oriented engineering*. HPI, University of Potsdam.

Pritchard, J. (1999). *COM and CORBA side by side: Architectures, strategies, and implementations,* (pp. xix, 430). Reading, MA: Addison-Wesley.

Protégé. (2000). *The Protege project*. Retrieved from http://protege.stanford.edu

Provan, G., & Chen, Y.-L. (1999). Model-based diagnosis and control reconfiguration for discrete event systems: An integrated approach. In *Proceedings of 38th IEEE Conference on Decision and Control*, (pp. 1762-1768).

Prud'hommeaux, E., & Seaborne, A. (2008). *SPARQL query language for RDF.* W3C recommendation. Retrieved from http://www.w3.org/TR/rdf-sparql-query/

Puterman, M. L. (1994). *Markov decision processes*. NY: John Wiley & Sons.

Quming, Z., & Mohanram, K. (2004). *Cost-effective radiation hardening technique for combinational logic.* Paper presented at the Proceedings of the International Conference on Computer Aided Design, Piscataway, NJ, USA.

Rahmani, H., GhasemSani, G. & Abolhassani, H. (2008). Automatic Web Service composition considering user non-functional preferences. *Next Generation Web Services Practices*, *0*, 33–38. doi:10.1109/NWeSP.2008.27

Raibulet, C. (2008). Facets of adaptivity. In *Proceedings of the 2nd European Conference on Software Architecture*, (LNCS 5292), (pp. 342-345).

Raibulet, C., & Demartini, C. (2004). Toward service oriented distributed architectures. In Y. Manolopoulos (Ed.), *Proceedings in Informatics 19, Distributed Data & Structures, 5,* 31-43. Canada: Carleton Scientific.

Raibulet, C., & Masciadri, L. (2009). Evaluation of dynamic adaptivity through metrics: An achievable target? In *Proceedings of the Joint IEEE/IFIP Conference on Software Architecture 2009 & European Conference on Software Architecture 2009,* (pp. 341-344).

Raibulet, C., & Massarelli, M. (2008). Managing non-functional aspects in SOA through SLA. In *Proceedings of the First IEEE International Workshop on Engineering Non-Functional INformation for Emerging Systems,* (pp. 701-705).

Raibulet, C., Arcelli, F., & Mussino, S. (2006). Exploiting reflection to design and manage services for an adaptive resource management system. In *Proceedings of the IEEE International Conference on Service Systems and Service Management,* (pp. 1363-1368). Troyes, France.

Raibulet, C., Ubezio, L., & Gobbo, W. (2008). Leveraging on strategies to achieve adaptivity in a distributed architecture. In *Proceedings of the 7th Workshop on Adaptive and Reflective Middleware,* (pp. 53-54). Leuven, Belgium.

Rainer, A. (2006). Web Service composition using answer set programming. In *PuK.*

Rao, J., Küngas, P., & Matskin, M. (2004). Logic-based Web Services composition: From service description to process model. In *proceedings of the IEEE International Conference on Web Services*, (pp. 446-453). California, USA: IEEE Computer Society.

Rashid, M. W., Tan, E. J., Huang, M. C., & Albonesi, D. H. (2005). Power-efficient error tolerance in chip multiprocessors. *IEEE Micro, 25*(6), 60–70. doi:10.1109/MM.2005.118

Ray, J., Hoe, J. C., & Falsafi, B. (2001). *Dual use of superscalar datapath for transient-fault detection and recovery.* Paper presented at the 34th ACM/IEEE International Symposium on Microarchitecture.

Reddy, K. K., Maralla, K., Kumar, R., & Thirumaran, M. (2009). A greedy approach with criteria factors for QoS-based Web Service discovery. In *COMPUTE '09: Proceedings of the 2nd Bangalore Annual Compute Conference,* (pp. 1–5).

Reichert, M., & Dadam, P. (1998). Adeptflex-supporting dynamic changes of workflows without losing control. *Journal of Intelligent Information Systems, 10*(2), 93–17. doi:10.1023/A:1008604709862

Reinecke, P., van Moorsel, A. P. A., & Wolter, K. (2006). The fast and the fair: A fault-injection-driven comparison of restart oracles for reliable Web Services. *Proceedings of the 3rd International Conference on the Quantitative Evaluation of Systems.*

Reinhardt, S. K., & Mukherjee, S. S. (2000). *Transient fault detection via simultaneous multithreading.* Paper presented at the 27th International Symposium on Computer Architecture.

Reis, G. A., Chang, J., Vachharajani, N., Rangan, R., & August, D. I. (2005). *SWIFT: SoftWare Implemented Fault Tolerance.* Paper presented at the International Symposium on Code Generation and Optimization, Los Alamitos, CA, USA.

Rockett, L. R. Jr. (1992). Simulated SEU hardened scaled CMOS SRAM cell design using gated resistors. *IEEE Transactions on Nuclear Science, 39*(5), 1532–1541. doi:10.1109/23.173239

Rosenmüller, M., Siegmund, N., Schirmeier, H., Sincero, J., Apel, S., Leich, T., et al. (2008). FAME-DBMS: Tailor-made data management solutions for embedded systems. In *Proceedings of the Workshop on Software Engineering for Tailor-Made Data Management (SETMDM).*

Roshandel, R., & Medvidovic, N. (2004). Toward architecture-based reliability estimation. In *Proceedings of the Twin Workshops on Architecting Dependable Systems, International Conference on Software Engineering* (ICSE 2004), Edinburgh, UK, May 2004, and *The International Conference on Dependable Systems and Networks* (DSN-2004), Florence, Italy, June 2004

Rotenberg, E. (1999). *AR-SMT: A microarchitectural approach to fault tolerance in microprocessors.* Paper presented at the 29th Annual International Symposium on Fault-Tolerant Computing.

Röttger, S., & Zschaler, S. (2004). *Model-driven development for non-functional properties: Refinement through model transformation. (LNCS 3273)* (pp. 275–289). Springer.

Rozenberg, G. (Ed.). (1997). *Handbook of graph grammars and computing by graph transformations: Foundations*. Retrieved from http://sensoria-ist.eu

Ruckhaus, E., Ruiz, E., & Vidal, M.-E. (2008). Query evaluation and optimization in the Semantic Web. *TPLP*, *8*(3), 393–409.

Russell, S., & Norvig, P. (2003). *Artificial Intelligence: A modern approach* (2nd ed.). Prentice Hall.

Sadjadi, S. M., McKinley, P. K., & Cheng, B. H. (2005). Transparent shaping of existing software to support pervasive and autonomic computing. *Proceedings of the 1st Workshop on the Design and Evolution of Autonomic Application Software 2005.* St. Louis, Missouri.

Saggese, G. P., Wang, N. J., Kalbarczyk, Z. T., Patel, S. J., & Iyer, R. K. (2005). An experimental study of soft errors in microprocessors. *IEEE Micro*, *25*(6), 30–39. doi:10.1109/MM.2005.104

Sahner, R. A., Trivedi, K. S., & Puliafito, A. (2002). *Performance and reliability analysis of computer systems*. Kluwer Academic Publishers.

Sakellariou, R., & Yarmolenko, V. (2005). On the flexibility of WS-agreement for job submission. In *Proceedings of the 3rd International Workshop on Middleware for Grid Computing (MGC05)*, Grenoble (France).

Sanders, W. (2007). *Moebius manual*. University of Illinois.

Sato, N. &. Trivedi, K.S (2007). *Accurate and efficient stochastic reliability analysis of composite services using their compact Markov reward model representations*. Services Computing, 2007.

Scallan, T. (2000). Monitoring and diagnostics of CORBA systems. *Java Developers Journal,* 138-144.

Scheer, G. W., & Dolezilek, D. J. (2004). *Comparing the reliability of ethernet network topologies in substation control and monitoring networks*. (Schweitzer Engineering Laboratories Technical Report 6103).

Schirmeier, H., & Spinczyk, O. (2007). Tailoring infrastructure software product lines by static application analysis. In *Proceedings of the 11th Software Product Line Conference (SPLC '07)*, (pp. 255–260). IEEE Computer Society Press.

SECSE A2.D12. (2008). Platform for architecture-time service discovery V3.0.

SECSE A2.D8. (2006). Platform for architecture service discovery V2.0: specification.

Service Availability Forum. (2008). *General information*. Retrieved from http://www.saforum.org/

Shen, Z., & Su, J. (2005). Web Service discovery based on behaviour signatures. Proceedings of the IEEE International Conference on Service Computing. USA.

Sherer. (1988). *Methodology for the assessment of software risk.* PhD Thesis, Wharton School, University of Pennsylvania.

Sheth, A., Cardoso, J., Miller, J., & Kochut, K. (2002). Qos for service-oriented middleware. In *Proceedings of the World Multiconference on Systemics, Cybernetics and Informatics (SCI),* (pp. 528-534).

Shooman, M. L. (1991). A micro software reliability model for prediction and test apportionment. *Proceedings 1991 International, Symposium on Software Engineering* (Austin, Texas), (pp. 52-59). May 1991.

Shye, A., Blomstedt, J., Moseley, T., Janapa Reddi, V., & Connors, D. (in press). PLR: A software approach to transient fault tolerance for multi-core architectures. *IEEE Transactions on Dependable and Secure Computing*.

Siegmund, N., Kuhlemann, M., Rosenmüller, M., Kästner, C., & Saake, G. (2008). Integrated product line model for semi-automated product derivation using non-functional properties. In *Proceedings of the International Workshop on Variability Modelling of Software-Intensive Systems (VAMOS)*, (pp. 25–23).

Siewiorek, D., & Swarz, R. (1982). *The theory and practice of reliable system design*. Digital Press.

Singh, M., & Huhns, M. (2005). *Service-oriented computing. Semantics, process, agents*. Wiley.

Sirin, E. (2004). *OWL-S API.*

Smolens, J. C., Gold, B. T., Kim, J., Falsafi, B., Hoe, J. C., & Nowatzyk, A. G. (2004). *Fingerprinting: Bounding soft-error detection latency and bandwidth.* Paper presented at the Proceedings of the 11th International Conference on Architectural Support for Programming Languages and Operating Systems, ASPLOS XI, New York, United States.

SNMP. (2009). An architecture for describing Simple Network Management Protocol (SNMP) management frameworks–RFC 3411. Retrieved from http://www.ietf.org/rfc/rfc3411.txt

Sommerville, I. (2006). *Software engineering* (8th ed.). Addison-Wesley.

Somodi, T. (2008). *Model-driven development of Web Services with non-functional requirements*. Master's thesis, Budapest University of Technology and Economics.

Spanoudakis, G., & Constantopoulos, P. (1996). Elaborating analogies from conceptual models. *International Journal of Intelligent Systems, 11*(11), 917–974. doi:10.1002/(SICI)1098-111X(199611)11:11<917::AID-INT4>3.3.CO;2-V

Spanoudakis, G. & Zisman, A. (In press). Discovering services during hybrid service-based system design.

Spanoudakis, G., & Zisman, A. (2006). UML-based service discovery tool. Proceedings of the 21st IEEE International Conference on Automated Software Engineering Conference. Japan.

Spanoudakis, G., Zisman, A., & Kozlenkov, A. (2005). A service discovery framework for service centric systems. Proceedings of the IEEE International Conference on Service Computing. USA.

Spinczyk, O., & Lohmann, D. (2007). The design and implementation of AspectC++. *Knowledge-Based Systems. Special Issue on Techniques to Produce Intelligent Secure Software, 20*(7), 636–651.

Spinczyk, O., & Lohmann, D. (2004). Using AOP to develop architecture-neutral operating system components. In *Proceedings of the 11th ACM SIGOPS European Workshop*, (pp.188–192). New York: ACM Press.

Srinivasan, J., Adve, S. V., Bose, P., & Rivers, J. A. (2004). *The case for lifetime reliability-aware microprocessors.* Paper presented at the 31st Annual International Symposium on Computer Architecture.

Srivastava, U., Munagala, K., Widom, J., & Motwani, R. (2006). Query optimization over Web Services. In *VLDB'2006: Proceedings of the 32nd International Conference on Very Large Data Bases,* (pp. 355–366). VLDB Endowment.

Stafford, J., & McGregor, J. D. (2002). Issues in predicting the reliability of composed components. *Proceedings of the 5th ICSE CBSE Workshop*, Orlando, Florida, May 2002.

Stahl, T., & Voelter, M. (2006). *Model-driven software development: Technology, engineering, management*. Wiley.

Sterling, L., & Juan, T. (2005). The software engineering of agent-based intelligent adaptive systems. In *Proceedings of the International Conference on Software Engineering,* (pp. 704-705). St. Louis, Missouri.

STMicroelectronics. (2003). New chip technology from STmicroelectronics eliminates soft error threat to electronic systems. Retrieved from http://www.st.com/stonline/press/news/year2003/t1394h.htm

Stohr, E., & Zhao, J. (1997). A technology adaptation model for business process automation. In *Proceedings of the Hawaii International Conference on System Sciences (HICSS),* (pp. 405).

Strong, D. M., & Miller, S. M. (1995). Exceptions and exception handling in computerized information processes. *ACM Transactions on Information Systems, 13*(2), 206–233. doi:10.1145/201040.201049

Sturm, R., Morris, W., & Jander, M. (2000). *Foundations of service level management.* SAMS Publishing.

Sycara, K., et al. (2009). *OWL-S 1.2 release.* Retrieved from http://www.ai.sri.com/daml/services/owl-s/1.2/overview/

Taher, L., Basha, R., & El Khatib, H. (2005). QoS information & computation framework for QoS-based discovery for Web Services. *UPGRADE. The European Journal for the Informatics Professional, 6*(4).

Tai, S., Mikalsen, T., Wohlstadter, E., Desai, N., & Rouvellou, I. (2004). Transaction policies for service-oriented computing. *Data & Knowledge Engineering, 51*(1), 59–79. doi:10.1016/j.datak.2003.03.001

Tai, S., Mikalsen, T., & Rouvellou, I. (2003). Using message-oriented middleware for reliable Web Services messaging. *Proceedings of Second International Workshop of Web Services, E-Business, and the Semantic Web*, (pp. 89-104).

Taylor, R. N., Medvidović, N., & Dashofy, E. M. (2009). *Software architecture: Foundations, theory, and practice*. John Wiley & Sons, Inc.

Taylor, I., Shields, M., Wang, I., & Harrison, A. (2007). The Triana workflow environment: Architecture and applications. In I. Taylor, E. Deelman, D. Gannon, and M. Shields, (Eds.), *Workflows for e-science*. (pp. 320-339). New York, Secaucus, NJ: Springer.

Telelogic. (2009). *Homepage information*. Retrieved on January 30, 2009, from http://www.telelogic.com/

Telemanagement Forum. (2004c). *TMF eTOM process framework*. Retrieved from www.tmforum.org

TeleManagement Forum. (2004a). *New generation operations systems and software*. Retrieved from http://www.tmforum.org/browse.asp?catID=1911

TeleManagement Forum. (2004b). *NGOSS architecture technology neutral specification: Contract description: Business and system views*.

TeleManagement Forum. (2005). *NGOSS contract examples: Examples of the NGOSS lifecycle and methodology for NGOSS contract definition*.

Thain, D., Tannenbaum, T., & Livny, M. (2003). *Grid computing: Making the global infrastructure a reality*. John Wiley and Sons.

Tham, C., Jiang, Y., & Ko, C. (2000a). Monitoring QoS distribution in multimedia networks. *International Journal of Network Management*, *10*, 75–90. doi:10.1002/(SICI)1099-1190(200003/04)10:2<75::AID-NEM355>3.0.CO;2-#

Tham, C., Jiang, Y., & Ko, C. (2000b). Challenges and approaches in providing QoS monitoring. *International Journal of Network Management*, *10*, 323–334. doi:10.1002/1099-1190(200011/12)10:6<323::AID-NEM382>3.0.CO;2-K

Thompson, H. S., Beech, D., Maloney, M., & Mendelsohn, N. (2004). *XML schema part 1: Structures*, (2nd ed.). Retrieved from http://www.w3.org/TR/xmlschema-1/

Tian, M., Gramm, M., Ritter, H., & Schiller, J. (2004). Efficient selection and monitoring of QoS-aware Web Services with the WS-QoS framework. In *Proceedings of the IEEE/WIC/ACM International Conference on Web Intelligence*, (pp. 152-158). Washington, DC, USA.

Timor, A., Mendelson, A., Birk, Y. & Suri, N. (2008). Using underutilized CPU resources to enhance its reliability. *IEEE Transactions on Dependable and Secure Computing*.

Tomasic, A., Raschid, L. & Valduriez, P. (1998). Scaling access to distributed heterogeneous data sources with Disco. *IEEE Transactions On Knowledge and Data Engineering*.

Tosic, V., Pagurek, B., Esf, B., Patel, K., & Ma, W. (2002). Web Service Offerings Language (WSOL) and Web Service composition management. In *Proceedings of of the Object-Oriented Web Services Workshop at OOPSLA 2002*.

Tosun, S. (2005). *Reliability-centric system design for embedded systems*. Unpublished doctoral thesis, Syracuse University, United States-New York.

Tran, V. X., Tsuji, H., & Masuda, R. (2009). *A new QoS ontology and its QoS-based ranking algorithm for Web Services. Simulation modelling practice and theory*. Elsevier.

Traverso, P., & Pistore, M. (2004). Automatic composition of Semantic Web Services into executable processes. In *Proceedings of the International Semantic Web Conference (ISWC)*.

Trivedi, K. S. (1999). *SHARPE 2000 GUI manual*. Duke University.

Trivedi, K., Malhotra, M., & Fricks, R. (1994). *Markov reward approach to performability and reliability analysis*. In the 2nd International Workshop on Modeling, Analysis, and Simulation of Computer and Telecommunication Systems, 1994.

Tsai, W. T., Jin, Z., Wang, P., & Wu, B. (2007). Requirement engineering in service-oriented system engineering. *Proceedings of the 2007 IEEE International Conference on e-Business Engineering*, (pp. 661-668). Hong Kong, China, October 2007.

Turner, W. P., Seader, J., & Brill, K. (2005). *Industry standard tier classification define site infrastructure performance*. White paper, The Uptime Institute.

van der Aalst, W. M. P., & Jablonski, S. (2000). Dealing with workflow change: Identification of issues and solutions. *International Journal of Computer Systems Science and Engineering*, *15*(5), 267–276.

Van der Aalst, M. P. W., ter Hofstede, A. H. M., & Weske, M. (2003). Business process management: A survey. *In Proceedings of the Business Process Management: International Conference BPM'03*. WSMO working group. (2004). *WSMO homepage*. Retrieved from http://www.wsmo.org/f

van Moorsel, A. P. A., & Wolter, K. (2006). Analysis of restart mechanisms in software systems. *IEEE Transactions on Software Engineering*, *32*(8). doi:10.1109/TSE.2006.73

Vara, J. M., de Castro, V., & Marcos, E. (2005). WSDL automatic generation from UML models in a MDA framework. In *Proceedings of the International Conference on Next Generation Web Services Practices*, (p. 319). IEEE Computer Society.

Varró, D., & Balogh, A. (2007). The model transformation language of the VIATRA2 framework. *Science of Computer Programming*, *68*(3), 214–234. doi:10.1016/j.scico.2007.05.004

Verma, K., Doshi, P., Gomadam, K., Miller, J., & Sheth, A. (2006). Optimal adaptation in Web processes with coordination constraints. In *Proceedings of IEEE International Conference on Web Services (ICWS)*, (pp. 257-264).

VIATRA2. (2008). *VIATRA2 framework at Eclipse GMT*. Retrieved from http://www.eclipse.org/gmt/

Vijaykumar, T. N., Pomeranz, I., & Cheng, K. (2002). *Transient-fault recovery using simultaneous multithreading*. Paper presented at the 29th Annual International Symposium on Computer Architecture.

Vinoski, S. (2002). Where is middleware? *IEEE Internet Computing*, 83–85. doi:10.1109/4236.991448

Voas, J., & McGraw, G. (1998). *Software fault injection: Inoculating programs against errors*. John Wiley & Sons.

Vogels, W. (2003). Web Services are not distributed objects: Common misconceptions about the fundamentals of Web Service technology. *IEEE Internet Computing*, *7*(6).

W3 Consortium. (2004). *Web Services glossary*. Retrieved from www.w3.org/ TR/2004/ NOTE-ws-gloss-20040211

W3C Simple Object Access Protocol. (2007). *SOAP information*. Retrieved from http://www.w3.org/TR/soap/

W3C Web Service Definition Language. (2001). *Homepage information*. http://www.w3.org/TR/wsdl

W3C Working Group. (2004). *Web Services Architecture*. Retrieved from http://www.w3.org/TR/ws-arch/

W3C. (2003). Web Services reliability (WS-reliability version 1.0). Retrieved from http://sunonedev.sun.com/platform/technologies/ws-reliability.v1.0.pdf

W3C. (2008). *Web Services Description Language* (WSDL) 1.1. Retrieved from http://www.w3.org/TR/wsdl

Wada, H., Champrasert, P., Suzuki, J., & Oba, K. (2008). Multiobjective optimization of SLA-aware service composition. In *Proceedings of IEEE Congress on Services, Workshop on Methodologies for Non-functional Properties in Services Computing.*

Wada, H., Suzuki, J., & Oba, K. (2006). Modelling non-functional aspects in Service Oriented Architecture. In *Proceedings of the IEEE International Conference on Services Computing,* (pp. 222-229). Washington, DC, USA.

Wada, H., Suzuki, J., & Oba, K. (2007). A feature modeling support for non-functional constraints in Service Oriented Architecture. *Proceedings of the 4th IEEE International Conference on Services Computing (SCC)*, Salt Lake City, UT, July 2007.

Waeldrich, O., & Ziegler, W. (2006). *A WS-agreement based negotiation protocol*. Technical report, Fraunhofer Institute SCAI. VIOLA - Vertically Integrated Optical Testbed for Large Application in DFN. Retrieved from http://www.fz-juelich.de/zam/grid/VIOLA/

Walcott, K. R., Humphreys, G., & Gurumurthi, S. (2007). *Dynamic prediction of architectural vulnerability from microarchitectural state.* Paper presented at the Proceedings of the International Symposium on Computer Architecture, New York, United States.

Wallnau, K. (2003). *Volume III: A technology for predictable assembly from certifiable components.* (Technical Report, CMU/SEI-2003-TR-009), 2003.

Walter, M. (2007). OpenSESAME-simple but extensive structured availability modeling environment. Retrieved from http://www.lrr.in.tum.de/ ~walterm/ opensesame/

Wang, Z. (2001). *Internet QoS: Architectures & mechanisms for Quality of Service.* Morgan Kaufmann Publishers.

Wang, D., & Trivedi, K. S. (2005). Modeling user-perceived service availability. *Revised selected papers from the Second International Service Availability Symposium.*

Wang, F. (2008). *Soft error rate determination for nanometer CMOS VLSI logic.* Paper presented at the Proceedings of the Annual Southeastern Symposium on System Theory.

Wang, G., Chen, A., Wang, C., Fung, C., & Uczekaj, S. (2004). Integrated Quality of Service (QoS) management in service-oriented enterprise architectures. *Proceedings of the 8th IEEE International Enterprise Distributed Object Computing Conference*, IEEE CS Press, Monterey, CA, September 2004, (pp. 21-32).

Wang, G., Wang, C., Chen, A., Wang, H., Fung, C., Uczekaj, S., et al. (2005). Service level management using QoS monitoring, diagnostics, and adaptation for networked enterprise systems. *Proceedings of the 9th IEEE International Enterprise Distributed Object Computing Conference*, IEEE CS Press, Enschede, the Netherlands, September 2005, (pp. 239-248).

Wang, L., Wong, E., & Xu, D. (2007). *A threat model driven approach for security testing.* Paper presented at the Proceedings of the Third International Workshop on Software Engineering for Secure Systems, SESS' 07, Piscataway, NJ, United States.

Wang, W. L., Wu, Y., & Chen, M. H. (1999). *An architecture-based software reliability model.* IEEE Pacific Rim International Symposium on Dependable Computing, Hong Kong, 1999.

Wang, X., Vitvar, T., Kerrigan, T., & Toma, I. (2006). A QoS-aware selection model for Semantic Web Services. Proceedings of the 4th International Conference on Service Oriented Computing. USA.

Wang, Y., & Stroulia, E. (2003). Semantic structure matching for assessing Web-Service similarity. Proceedings of the International Conference on Service Oriented Computing. Italy.

Web Service Reliable Messaging Protocol. (2008). WSRMP. Retrieved from http://download. boulder. ibm. com/ ibmdl/pub/ software/dw/ specs/ws-rm/ ws-reliable messaging 200502.pdf.

Web Services Description Language (WSDL) 1.1. (2001). *TR.* Retrieved from http://www.w3.org/TR/wsdl

Weske, M. (2007). *Business process management: Concepts, languages, architectures.* Springer-Verlag.

Whittaker, J. A. (2001). Software's invisible users. *IEEE Software, 18*(3), 84–88. doi:10.1109/52.922730

Wikipedia. (2009). *Home page.* Retrieved on January 30, 2009, from http://en.wikipedia.org/wiki

Wirsing, M., Clark, A., Gilmore, S., Hölzl, M., Knapp, A., & Koch, N. (2006). *Semantic-based development of service-oriented systems. (LNCS 4229)* (pp. 24–45). Springer-Verlag.

Woit, D., & Mason, D. (1998). Software system reliability from component reliability. *Proceedings of 1998 Workshop on Software Reliability Engineering* (SRE `98), July, 1998.

Wolstencroft, P. A., Hull, D., Wroe, C., Lord, P., Stevens, R., & Goble, C. (2007). The myGrid ontology: Bioinformatics service discovery. *International Journal of Bioinformatics Research and Applications, 3*(3), 303–325. doi:10.1504/IJBRA.2007.015005

Wolter,, C., Menzel, M., Schaad.A., Miseldine, P. & Meinel, C. (2008). Model-driven business process security requirement specification. *Journal of System Architecture.*

Wood, S. K., Akehurst, D. H., Uzenkov, O., Howells, W. G. J., & McDonald-Maier, K. D. (2008). A model-driven development approach to mapping UML state diagrams to synthesizable VHDL. *IEEE Transactions on Computers, 57*(10), 1357–1371. doi:10.1109/TC.2008.123

WS-Agreement. (2007). Web Services agreement specification. Retrieved from http://force.gridforum.org/sf/ projects/graap-ws

WSDL. (2009). TR. Retrieved from http://www.w3.org/TR/wsdl

WSML. (2009). Syntax. Retrieved from http://www.wsmo.org/wsml/wsml-syntax

WSMO. (2010). Submission. Retrieved from http://www.w3.org/Submission/2005/SUBM-WSMO-20050603.

Wu, D., Parsia, B., Sirin, E., Hendler, J., & Nau, D. (2003). Automating daml-s Web Services composition using shop2. In *Proceedings of the International Semantic Web Conference (ISWC),* (pp. 195-210).

Wu, J., & Wu, Z. (2005). Similarity-based Web Service matchmaking. Proceedings of the IEEE International Conference on Services Computing. USA.

Wu, Y., & Doshi, P. (2007). Regret-based decentralized adaptation ofWeb processes with coordination constraints. In *Proceedings of IEEE Services-Centered Computing (SCC),* (pp. 262-269).

Xiang, J., Liu, L., Qiao, W., & Yang, J. (2007). SREM: A Service Requirements Elicitation Mechanism based on ontology. *Proceedings of the 2007 IEEE International Conference on Computer Software and Applications*, (pp. 196-203). Beijing, China, July, 2007.

Xie, Y., Li, L., Kandemir, M., Vijaykrishnan, N., & Irwin, M. J. (2004). *Reliability-aware co-synthesis for embedded systems.* Paper presented at the 15th IEEE International Conference on Application-Specific Systems, Architectures and Processors.

Yacoub, S. M., & Ammar, H. H. (2002). A methodology for architecture-level reliability risk analysis. *IEEE Transactions on Software Engineering*, *28*(6), 529–547. doi:10.1109/TSE.2002.1010058

Yankee Group. (2008). Global server operating system reliability survey 2007-2008. Retrieved from http://www.yankeegroup.com/ Research Document. do?id = 16063

Yu, J., & Buyya, R. (2005). A taxonomy of workflow management systems for Grid computing. *Journal of Grid Computing*, *3*(3-4), 171–200. doi:10.1007/s10723-005-9010-8

Yu, H.Q. & Rei -Marganiec, S. (2008). Non-functional property-based service selection: A survey and classification of approaches. In *Proceedings of the Non-Functional Properties and Service Level Agreements in Service Oriented Computing Workshop co-located with The 6th IEEE European Conference on Web Services.*

Yunyao, L. Y., Yanh, H., & Jagadish, H. (2005). *NaLIX: An interactive natural language interface for querying XML*. Baltimore, USA: SIGMOD.

Zadorozhny, V., Bright, L., Raschid, L., Urhan, T., & Vidal, M.-E. (2000). *Web query optimizer.* International Conference on Data Engineering, (p. 661).

Zadorozhny, V., Raschid, L., Vidal, M., Urhan, T., & Bright, L. (2002). Efficient evaluation of queries in a mediator for WebSources. In *Proceedings of the ACM SIGMOD Conference on the Management of Data.*

Zeng, L., Benatallah, B., Ngu, A. H. H., Dumas, M., Kalagnanam, J., & Chang, H. (2004). QoS-aware middleware for Web Services composition. *IEEE Transactions on Software Engineering*, *30*(5).

Zeng, L., Benatallah, B., Ngu, A. H. H., Dumas, M., & Kalagnanam, J. (2003). Quality driven Web Services composition. *Proceedings of the 12th International Conference World Wide Web*, 2003.

Zhang, M., Mitra, S., Mak, T. M., Seifert, N., Wang, N. J., & Shi, Q. (2006). Sequential element design with built-in soft error resilience. *IEEE Transactions on Very Large Scale Integration (VLSI). Systems*, *14*(12), 1368–1378.

Zhang, M. (2006). *Analysis and design of soft-error tolerant circuits.* Unpublished doctoral thesis, University of Illinois at Urbana-Champaign, United States.

Zhao, H., & Doshi, P. (2007). Haley: A hierarchical framework for logical composition ofWeb Services. In *Proceedings of IEEE International Conference on Web Services (ICWS),* (pp. 312-319).

Ziegler, W., Waldrich, O., Wieder, P., Nakata, T., & Parkin, M. (2008). Considerations for negotiation and monitoring of service level agreements. (Technical Report TR-0167, CoreGRID).

Zimmermann, H. (1991). *Fuzzy set theory and its applications*. Boston: Kluwer Academic.

Zisman, A., & Spanoudakis, G. (2006). UML-based service discovery framework. Proceedings of the 4th International Conference on Service Oriented Computing. Chicago, USA

Zisman, A., Spanoudakis, G., & Dooley, J. (2008). A framework for dynamic service discovery. Proceedings of the IEEE International Conference on Automated Software Engineering. Italy.

Zisman, A., Spanoudakis, G. & Dooley, J. (In press). SerDiQueL: A Service Discovery Query Language.

About the Contributors

Nikola Milanovic is co-founder and CEO of Model Labs. The Berlin-based company offers innovative model-based software product family for system integration and service availability assessment. Previously, he was senior researcher at Berlin University of Technology (TU Berlin) and Hasso-Plattner Institute (HPI) in Potsdam. Milanovic received his PhD in computer science from the Humboldt University in Berlin.

* * *

Eduardo Blanco has been Assistant Professor in Computer Science Department at Universidad Simón Bolívar since 2003. He graduated in Computer Engineering in 1998 at Universidad Simón Bolívar, Venezuela. He received his M.Sc degree Computer Science from the Universidad Simón Bolívar, Venezuela, in 2002 and he is currently finishing his PhD studies at the same University. His research interests include distributed object processing, operating systems, high performance on Grid platforms, Web Services composition, Web Service discovery, including Web and Grid semantic. He is a member of the Parallel and Distributed Systems Group. He has written a range of publications in areas such as Grid computing, sequential and parallel profiling for Java applications, collaborative frameworks, and Semantic Web. His home page is http://www.ldc.usb.ve/~eduardo.

Daniele Cammareri is a former student of the Università degli Studi di Milano-Bicocca in Italy, where he received his Master degree in Computer Science in December 2009. His main academic interests concern software engineering, and in particular, object-oriented development, agile methodologies, and project management. He is the co-author of three previously published papers related to the adaptivity aspects in software systems.

Yudith Cardinale has been a Full Professor in Computer Science Department at Universidad Simón Bolívar since 1996. She graduated with honors in Computer Engineering in 1990 at Universidad Centro-Occidental Lisandro Alvarado, Venezuela. She received her M.Sc degree and PhD in Computer Science from the Universidad Simón Bolívar, Venezuela, in 1993 and 2004. Her research interests include parallel processing, distributed object processing, operating systems, high performance on Grid platforms, Web Services composition, including Web and Grid semantic. She is a member of the Parallel and Distributed Systems Group. She has written a range of publications in areas such as parallel computing, Grid computing, parallel checkpointing, collaborative frameworks, and Semantic Web. Her home page is http://www.ldc.usb.ve/~yudith.

Fahima Cheikh is contractual teacher and researcher attached to the Computer and Science department at Toulouse Capitole University, since September 2008. She got her Ph.D. in Computer Science from Paul Sabatier University (UPS) in June 2009. She did her thesis under the direction of Philippe Balbiani, in Logic Interaction Language and Computation team (LILaC) of The Institute of Computer Science in Toulouse (IRIT). Her research interests concern: controller synthesis, service composition, and access control. Dr. Cheikh got her post graduate degree (1 year) following her Master in Artificial Intelligence at Paul Sabatier University, in June 2005. She got her engineering degree in Operational Research at Science and Technology University of Houari Boumedienne (USTHB) Algiers, in September 2002.

Giuseppe Di Modica is currently an assistant professor at Engineering Faculty of University of Catania (Italy). He received his Degree in Computer Engineering in 2000 from the Engineering Faculty of University of Catania (Italy). Since then, he has been engaged in research on distributed systems with the Department of Computer and Telecommunications Engineering of Catania University. In 2005 he received the Ph.D. in Computer Science and Telecommunication Engineering from University of Catania. The Ph.D. thesis discussed was entitled "A user-centric analysis of the interworking between heterogeneous wireless systems." His research interests include mobile agents, ad-hoc networks, wireless networking, mobile P2P computing, and Grid and service oriented architectures. He is currently a research assistant at Engineering Faculty of University of Catania (Italy).

Prashant Doshi is an assistant professor of computer science at the University of Georgia and directs the THINC lab. His research interests lie in both services-oriented computing (SOC), specifically in dynamic service compositions, and in artificial intelligence (AI), specifically in decision-making under uncertainty. He has carried out research in Web Service modeling, Web Service composition and constraint-aware adaptations of Web Service compositions. He has also had short stints at the IBM T. J. Watson Research Center where he worked in the e-Business Group. He has published extensively in journals, conferences, and other forums in both the fields of SOC and AI. His research has led to publications in Journal of Web Services Research, IEEE Transactions on Services Computing, Journal of Services-Oriented Computing, WWW, ICWS, SCC, ICSOC, as well as Journal of AI Research, and National Conference on AI (AAAI). He has served on the program committees of several conferences and workshops in the fields of SOC and AI.

Onyeka Ezenwoye is an Assistant Professor at South Dakota State University. His research interests include adaptive service composition, fault tolerant distributed systems and software engineering. He holds Doctorate and Master's degrees in Computer Science from Florida International University in Miami, Florida. He has a Bachelor's degree in Software Engineering from The University of Manchester in Manchester, England. He is a member of IEEE, and ACM.

Nektarios Georgalas is a Principal Researcher at British Telecom, in BT Innovate and Design, BT's R&D arm. During his career with BT, since 1998, he has been actively involved in and has managed numerous collaborative and internal research projects in areas such as active networks, market-driven data management systems, policy-based management, distributed information systems, and SOA/Web Services. He currently focuses on Product Lifecycle Management and Rapid Service Assembly for the Communication Service Provider 2.0. Nektarios has led numerous international collaborations on the application of Model Driven Architecture and the NGOSS standards in telecoms OSS environments and has been very active leading and contributing in key programmes within the TeleManagement Forum.

Ester Giallonardo is a post Ph.D. researcher at University of Sannio, where she received the Master and the Ph.D. degrees in Computer Engineering. She defended a Ph.D. thesis on "Quality of Service and semantics in service level agreements." Her research interests are in service oriented computing, Web Service, business process management, and Semantic Web.

László Gönczy completed his PhD studies at Budapest University of Technology and Economics (BUTE) where he is now working as a research associate. He is also the Director of Services and Education at the OptXware Research and Development Ltd. He holds an MSc in Software Engineering from BUTE and an MSc in Engineer-Economics from Corvinus University of Budapest. His professional interest includes model-driven development of Service-Oriented Architectures and dependability analysis based on high level system models. He has been involved in several research and industrial R+D projects and published articles in these fields. He has recently been working on SENSORIA EU FP6 and CoMiFin and e-Freight FP7 projects.

John Harney is currently a PhD candidate in the Dept. of Computer Science at the University of Georgia. His research interests lie in understanding volatility and its effect on service compositions, and intelligently adapting service compositions in response to revised information. He has published and presented papers in many conferences including WWW, ICWS, and ICSOC and is the lead author of an article in the IEEE Transactions on Services Computing.

Wanja Hofer is pursuing his PhD in Computer Science at Friedrich-Alexander University Erlangen-Nuremberg, Germany. His research focus is in embedded operating systems, especially in making embedded kernels configurable and tailorable. He investigates adaptability of operating system kernels both in direction of the application (e.g., the CiAO project) and in direction of the underlying hardware abstractions (e.g., the Sloth project). Wanja can be reached at wanja@cs.fau.de.

Jingwen Jin received her BS and MS in Physics and Computer Science, respectively, from the Federal University of Pernambuco in Brazil, and her PhD in Computer Science from the University of Illinois Urbana-Champaign in 2005. She worked at Intel as a Research Scientist from 2006 to 2008, and is now an Advanced Computing Technologist at Boeing Research and Technology. Jingwen has served on the program committee of IEEE ICCCN, WEBIST, and COQODS-II, and has been a reviewer for conferences and journals including IEEE JSAC, TPDS, RTAS, ICDCS, ACM SIGMETRICS, and Middleware. Her research focuses are in middleware, distributed systems, and networking.

Xiaoqing (Frank) Liu is currently a professor and a director of the McDonnel Douglass Foundation software engineering laboratory in the Missouri University of Science and Technology, Rolla, Missouri, US. He has been working on requirements engineering, software quality management, knowledge based software engineering, and collaborative systems since 1992. He has published more than 70 papers in peer-reviewed journals and conferences in the above areas and several other software engineering application areas. He participates in more than 20 sponsored research projects as a principal investigator or co-principal investigator sponsored by the National Science Foundation, Sandia National Laboratory, U.S. Air Force, University of Missouri Research Board, Boeing Co., and Toshiba Co.

Daniel Lohmann is assistant professor at the Distributed Systems and Operating Systems group at Friedrich-Alexander University Erlangen-Nuremberg. He has been conducting research in the domain of (embedded) operating systems, software-product lines, and aspect-oriented software development since 2003. Daniel holds a doctoral degree from Friedrich-Alexander University. His current research activities are focused on applying AOP ideas for the fine-grained configuration of nonfunctional properties in system software and the new challenges of the manycore area. Before joining the PhD programme at Friedrich-Alexander University he worked as a software developer, consultant and IT trainer. Daniel is a member of the ACM, GI, and EUROSYS.

Nik Looker is a Software Engineer in the Centre for Advanced Instrumentation at Durham University writing control software for Optical Astronomy Instruments and has worked for over 20 years in the fields of distributed systems, operating systems and embedded applications. After receiving his BSc in Computing from Oxford Brookes University in 1993, he pursued a successful career in industry focusing mainly on small footprint embedded mobile telecommunications systems and test equipment as well as RTOS kernel design and implementation. In 2002, he moved to Durham University to undertake research in middleware dependability assessment and has been involved in may research projects including eDemand, AliC, NECTISE and received his PhD in Computer Science from Durham University in 2006. He has published many conference and journal papers on dependability and has served on numerous program committees for IEEE conferences and workshops.

Marco Massarelli is a former student of the Università degli Studi di Milano-Bicocca in Italy, where he received his master degree in Computer Science in April 2010. His academic career covered various software engineering areas such as software architectures, software development, object-oriented methodologies, software test and analysis, software evolution and reverse engineering and project management. As a personal interest he constantly studies Web design and Web-related technologies and trends. He is an avid reader of everything related to the technology, including science-fiction.

Bratislav Milic is a senior researcher at Humboldt University in Berlin where he is involved in several industrial projects in areas of dependable computing and wireless multi-hop networks. He finished his undergraduate studies at School of Electrical Engineering at Belgrade University, Serbia. He was PhD student at Institute for Informatics at Humboldt University in Berlin between 2004 and 2009.

Malcolm Munro is Emeritus Professor of Software Engineering at the School of Engineering and Computer Science at Durham University, United Kingdom. His research area is software engineering with a focus on how systems change and evolve over time, and how to develop and maintain systems using Service Oriented Architectures. He has been actively involved with the IEEE International Conference on Software Maintenance and the International Workshop on Program Comprehension. He has led a number of UK EPSRC funded projects including GUSTT (Guided Slicing and Targeted Transformation), and Jigsaw (distributed and dynamic visualisation generation), and been involved with the e-Demand project (a demand-led service-based architecture for dependable e-science applications).

Douglas G. Myers has been awarded the degrees of BA in English (Hons), Masters in Engineering Science and PhD, all from the University of Western Australia. He is currently the program leader for Computer Systems Engineering at Curtin University in Western Australia. He has written a book on digital signal processing and a number of chapters of books covering image processing with applications to remote sensing and agriculture. He has also written a number of papers in these fields, and in embedded systems design. His current research interests are in systems level design of embedded systems and concurrent computing.

Cesar Ortega-Sanchez received the B.Eng. degree in electronic engineering from the Metropolitan Autonomous University, Mexico City in 1990, the M.Sc. in Digital Systems from Brunel University, UK in 1992, and PhD degree in electronics from University of York, UK in 2000. He is currently Senior Lecturer at the Department of Electrical and Computer Engineering, Curtin University, Perth, Australia. He teaches and supervises undergraduate and postgraduate theses in topics related to digital electronics, FPGAs, microcontrollers and embedded systems. His research interests are in embedded systems using FPGAs, bio-inspired architectures, and evolvable systems. He has published over 50 papers in his area of expertise and participates in technical committees of several international conferences. Dr Ortega-Sanchez is the current Chair of the IEEE Computational Intelligence Society, Western Australia Chapter. He has been a member of the IEEE since 2000.

Nicolò Perino has been a Ph.D. student in Computer Science at the University of Lugano since 2009 under the supervision of Prof. Mauro Pezzè. He is interested in software engineering and in particular in autonomic and self-healing systems area. His research is focused on detecting and healing techniques for functional failures in Web and desktop applications. He received his Bachelor and Master degree in Computer Science from Università degli Studi di Milano-Bicocca in 2007 and 2009 where he took an internship at STMicroelectionics about the interoperability issues among UML tools. During his Master and Doctoral studies, he taught as assistant for several courses in various computer science disciplines.

Claudia Raibulet is an Assistant Professor at the Universitá degli Studi di Milano-Bicocca in Italy. She received her Master degree in Computer Science from POLITEHNICA University of Bucarest, Romania in 1997 and her PhD degree from Politecnico di Torino, Italy in 2002. She is involved in software engineering and reverse engineering courses. Her research interests concern various software engineering areas including software architectures, object-oriented methodologies, development of adaptive systems, mobile systems, distributed systems, software architecture reconstruction, and design pattern detection. Claudia Raibulet co-authored more than fifty research papers published in international journals, conferences, and workshops. She is involved in referee activities for various international journals, as well as in organizing and program committees for international conferences and workshops.

Muhammad Sheikh Sadi received B.Sc. Eng. in Electrical and Electronic Engineering from Khulna University of Engineering and Technology, Bangladesh in 2000, M.Sc. Eng. in Computer Science and Engineering from Bangladesh University of Engineering and Technology, Dhaka, Bangladesh in 2004, and completed PhD in Electrical and Computer Engineering, from Curtin University of Technology, Australia in 2010. He is currently Assistant Professor at the Department of Computer Science and Engineering, Khulna University of Engineering and Technology, Bangladesh. He teaches and supervises undergraduate and postgraduate theses in topics related to embedded systems, digital system design, soft errors tolerance, et cetera. He has published over 15 papers in his area of expertise. Muhammad Sheikh Sadi is a member of the IEEE since 2004.

Masoud Sadjadi received his B.S. in Hardware Engineering in 1995, M.S. in Software Engineering in 1999, and Ph.D. in Computer Science from Michigan State University in 2004. He has been an Assistant Professor of Computer Science in FIU since 2004. Dr. Sadjadi is a co-founder of the Autonomic Computing Research Laboratory at FIU, is a founding faculty member and a steering committee member of the Latin American Grid (LA Grid) Initiative. Dr. Sadjadi is currently the Principle Investigator of a $2.3 million grant from the highly competitive NSF PIRE program, conducting research in cyberinfrastructure enablement and facilitating on-site student and faculty research within top research institutions world-wide. Dr. Sadjadi's research has been supported by NSF, IBM, Kaseya, TeraGrid, Amazon, and FIU for a total of over $4.7 million as PI or Co-PI. He has published 68 publications and served in different roles for numerous international conferences and journals.

Rodolfo Santiago is an Advanced Computing Technologist at Boeing. His research interests include distributed real time systems and networking technologies. Prior to joining Boeing, Rodolfo was a Principal Engineer for startups Terago and Mathstar. He also worked as a Lead Software Engineer at Motorola and was a Member of the Technical Staff at Teledyne Controls. He holds an MS degree in Computer Science from the George Washington University and a BS degree in Electronics and Communications Engineering from De La Salle University.

Wolfgang Schröder-Preikschat studied computer science at the Technical University of Berlin, Germany, where he also received his Ph.D. and venia legendi. After spending about ten years as a research associate and director of the system software department at the German National Research Center of Computer Science (GMD), Research Institute for Computer Architecture and Software Technique (FIRST), Berlin, Dr. Schröder-Preikschat became a full professor for computer science (computer networks and operating systems) at the University of Potsdam, Germany, in 1995. From 1997 to 2002, he was a full professor for computer science (operating systems and distributed systems) at the University of Magdeburg, Germany. Since 2002, he has held the professorship on distributed systems and operating systems at the Friedrich-Alexander University of Erlangen-Nuremberg, Germany. The main research interests of Dr. Schröder-Preikschat are in the domain of real-time embedded distributed/parallel operating systems. Dr. Schröder-Preikschat is member of ACM, EuroSys, GI, IEEE, and USENIX.

David Shaw is an Advanced Computing Technologist at Boeing Research & Technology. Prior to joining Boeing, he held a Senior Software Engineer position at Intel Corporation until 2006. His research interests include computer architecture, software engineering, distributed systems and networking technologies. He received both his BS and MS in Computer Science from the University of Washington.

Julio Sincero was born in Maringá, Brasil, in 1981. He received the B. Sc. degree in Computer Science from Universidade Federal de Santa Catarina, Florianopolis, Brasil, and the M. Sc. degree in Computational Engineering from the Friedrich-Alexander University Erlangen-Nuremberg, Erlangen, Germany in 2004 and 2006, respectively. He is currently pursuing the Ph.D. degree in Computer Science at Friedrich-Alexander University Erlangen-Nuremberg. His research interests include software product lines, variability management and system software.

Adel Taweel is an academic at the University of King's College London (University of London). He has received his Ph.D. in Software Engineering from the University of Keele (UK), and worked as a research assistant and then as a lecturer at the same university (2001). Dr. Taweel has worked as a Senior Research Fellow at the University of Manchester (2003) and then at the University of Birmingham (2006), before recently taking his current position. Dr. Taweel is a reviewer for several national and international journals and conferences, a member of a number of professional institutions (IET, IEEE), a member of the Software Engineering Association (SEA) and serves as a consultant for the UK Department of Health, and a member of several national and international committees.

Orazio Tomarchio received his Degree in Computer Engineering from the Engineering Faculty of University of Catania (Italy) in 1995. Since then, he has been engaged in research on distributed systems with the Department of Computer and Telecommunications Engineering of Catania University. In 1999, he received the PhD in Computer Science from University of Palermo. The PhD thesis discussed was entitled "Design and implementation of a mobile agent platform and its application for distributed systems management." The scientific activity of Dr. Tomarchio has been focused on studying distributed systems, particularly with regard to programming and management techniques. His main research interests include mobile agents, network and QoS management techniques, mobile P2P computing, middleware for MANETs, and Grid and Service Oriented Architectures.

Dániel Varró is an associate professor at the Budapest University of Technology and Economics. His main research interest is model-driven systems and software engineering with special focus on model transformations. He regularly serves in the programme committee of various international conferences in the field. He is the founder of the VIATRA2 model transformation framework, and the principal investigator at his university of the SENSORIA, DIANA and SecureChange European Projects. Previously, he was a visiting researcher at SRI International, at the University of Paderborn and TU Berlin. He is a three time recipient of the IBM Faculty Award.

María-Esther Vidal received her Bachelor's in Computer Engineering in 1987, Masters in Computer Science in 1991, and PhD in Computer Science in 2000 from the University Simón Bolívar, Caracas Venezuela. She is a Full Professor of the Computer Science department at the University Simón Bolívar and has been Assistant Researcher at the Institute of Advanced Computer Studies in the University of Maryland (UMIACS) (1995-1999), and Visitor Professor at UMIACS (2000-2009) and in Universidad Politecnica de Catalunya (2003). She has published on her research in AAAI, IJCAI, SIGMOD, CoopIs, WIDM, WebDB, ICDE, DILS, DEXA, ALPWS, ACM SAC, CAISE, OTM, EDBT, SIGMOD RECORDS, and TPLP Journal. Her current research interests are query rewriting and optimization in emerging infrastructures. Prof. Vidal is a member of SIGMOD. Her home page is http://www.ldc.usb.ve/~mvidal.

Guijun Wang is a Technical Fellow of the Boeing Company. His current research interests include Service Oriented Architecture for system of systems, quality of service management, enterprise distributed computing, and systems and software engineering. In addition to research, Guijun has extensive experiences in architecting and engineering large scale distributed systems. He is a Boeing certified Software Architect. Guijun has over 35 publications in international journals, conferences, and book chapters. He served on the steering committee of the IEEE international Enterprise Distributed Object Computing (EDOC) conferences, 2002-2009. He was the Program Co-Chair, General Chair, and Panel Chair for EDOC 2000, 2001, and 2002, respectively. He was a panelist to IEEE EDOC 2008 panel - Industrial Standards for Web Services: Achieved Results and Challenges for the Future. He co-chaired

IEEE EDOC Advances in Quality of Service Management workshops, 2006-2009. Guijun received his Ph.D. in Computer Science from the University of Kansas.

Changzhou Wang, an Associate Technical Fellow of the Boeing Company, received his Ph.D. in Information Technology from George Mason University, Fairfax, Virginia. He has over ten years of research and development experience as a key contributor, a task leader and the Principal Investigator (of government contracts). Changzhou has over 20 technical publications in international peer-reviewed journals, conferences and books, two US patents and eight US patents pending. He has served the program committee of multiple IEEE international Enterprise Distributed Object Computing (EDOC) conferences. His current research interests include data mining, service oriented software architecture, quality of service management, and information management.

Haiqin Wang is an Advanced Computing Technologist in Boeing Research & Technology. Her research areas include decision-support systems for airplane diagnosis, information management quality of service diagnostics and prognostics, system health knowledge discovery, and cyber situational awareness. She received her PhD in Intelligent Systems Program from University of Pittsburgh and served in Artificial Intelligence conference committees including AAAI, FLAIRS. Dr. Wang invented various methods for automatically generating Bayesian belief networks from domain knowledge such as airplane maintenance manuals, sequential patterns, and monitoring databases for diagnosis and prognosis. She also has US patents pending on cyber security events prediction, complex process analysis and management.

Eugenio Zimeo graduated in Electronic Engineering at the University of Salerno, Italy, and received the PhD degree in Computer Science from the University of Naples, Italy, in 1999. Currently, he is an Assistant Professor at the University of Sannio in Benevento, Italy. His primary research interests are in the areas of software architectures and frameworks for distributed systems, high performance middleware, and service oriented and Grid computing. He has published about 70 scientific papers in journals and conferences of the field and leads many large research projects.

Andrea Zisman holds PhD, MSc, and BSc degrees in Computer Science. She is a Reader in the Department of Computing, City University London. Andrea has been research active in the areas of software and service engineering where she has published extensively. Her research interests are in service discovery, service adaptation, service composition, verification of multi-stakeholders distributed systems, consistency management and traceability of software artefacts, secure software engineering, and interoperability of distributed heterogeneous database systems. Her research has contributed to the development of a number of research prototypes and industrial tools. Andrea has given tutorials in many international conferences and has served in the organising and program committees of various international conferences and workshops, has acted as a reviewer for many international journals, and has co-edited special issues of journals. Andrea has been principal and co-investigator in several European, EPSRC, and industry funded research projects. For more information see: http://www.soi.city.ac.uk/~zisman.

Index

T

U

V

W

Breinigsville, PA USA
20 March 2011

257762BV00004B/4/P

9 781609 604936